JNANESHWAR'S GITA

BLESSING

To write a commentary on the Bhagavad Gita, *the inspired song of the Lord Himself, is not a task for just anyone. It is therefore our supreme good fortune that a great saint, a being who has realized the Lord, expounded its divine teachings. Jnaneshwar Maharaj, as my Guru Swami Muktananda used to say so lovingly, was not just a great being in a human body. He made his human body a vehicle for exalted service to all of mankind as well as to God.*

There are thousands of commentaries on the Bhagavad Gita. *Whoever studies it wants to put its wisdom into action and feels the need to express his own understanding about its teachings. However, as you read* Jnaneshwari *you come to realize that Jnaneshwar Maharaj did not have to struggle to follow the injunctions of the* Gita, *nor did he need to let everyone know what he understood. Jnaneshwar is like a radiant sun bursting with joy and inspiration, who wants only to create still more suns. As a result, no one can escape the vision of God.*

Jnaneshwar Maharaj is the embodiment of perfect love. Though in his life he had to undergo trials and tribulations imposed upon him by society, nothing could impede the power of his true nature, or what he had to offer the world.

Jnaneshwari *overflows with nectar. Reading it again and again we continuously taste its elixir. May everyone who touches* Jnaneshwari, *or even casts a glance upon it, be totally suffused with the loving compassion of God. May everyone who reads* Jnaneshwari *perceive the Truth in its fullness.*

Your,

Swami Chidvilasananda
South Fallsburg, New York
September 11, 1988

JNANESHWAR'S GITA

A RENDERING OF THE *JNANESHWARI*

BY SWAMI KRIPANANDA

FOREWORD BY IAN M.P. RAESIDE

INTRODUCTION BY

SHANKAR GOPAL TULPULE

State University of New York Press

ACKNOWLEDGMENTS

I wish to express my gratitude to Margaret Parkinson and Karen Sorensen, who helped prepare the manuscript; to Uma Berliner, who did the copyediting; to Shane Conroy, who designed the cover; and to Leesa Stanion, who compiled the index.
Swami Kripananda

Published by
State University of New York Press, Albany

Printed in the United States of America

For information, address State University of New York Press, State University Plaza, Albany, N.Y., 12246

PB/ISBN 0-7914-0047-6
HC/ISBN 0-7914-0046-8

DEDICATION

"Now, on the pedestal of my heart, I will place the feet of my Guru. If the Lord wishes to save a hungry man, even sand boiled in water will turn into the sweetest rice. In the same way, when the Guru accepts a person as his own, this earthly existence becomes a life of liberation. How can I describe the glory of the Guru?"

—Jnaneshwar Maharaj

This book is lovingly offered to Gurumayi Chidvilasananda, who brings the grace and glory of the Siddha tradition into the present day.

PREFACE

Jnaneshwari is a commentary on the *Bhagavad Gita* completed in 1290 C.E. by the Poet-Saint Jnaneshwar. There is in print a scholarly English-language edition of *Jnaneshwari* first published by Allen & Unwin in 1948, and now published by SUNY Press. The translation was done by Vitthal G. Pradhan and edited by Hester M. Lambert.

The English of that edition is dated. Shri Pradhan died in 1950 and his English was for another era. Swami Kripananda has simply put the *Jnaneshwari* into the contemporary idiom in rather the same way that Robert Bly put Tagore's translation of Kabir into contemporary language. The rendering of the *Bhagavad Gita* incorporated in this book is based on Winthrop Sargeant's translation published by SUNY Press.

Once the great modern-day Master Swami Muktananda was asked why he loved Jnaneshwar so much. He said,

Jnaneshwar wrote his commentary not simply through the intellect but in the complete freedom of divine inspiration. Jnaneshwar's words seem to be the very words of the Lord. He has depicted the very heart of the Lord.

Maharashtra has produced a large number of saints, both men and women, one more powerful than another, and these saints have come from all possible sections of society, from all classes. Though Jnaneshwar was the youngest of them all, yet he was the greatest. The oldest among them accept Jnaneshwar as the king of knowledge. They all accepted his supremacy, and they sang his praises. Jnaneshwar's works are extremely fine.

At another time Swami Muktananda said,

During the period of my sadhana I was quite an avid reader. I had read so many works, and in none of them did I come across a satisfying description of the different stages of sadhana, the different spiritual experiences and visions that come to a seeker. It was only in the works of Jnaneshwar that I came across the perfect explanation of what had happened to me, a perfect description of all the different visions. That was why I was so fascinated by him.

CONTENTS

FOREWORD

Jnāneśwarī, so called from its author Jnāneśwar or Jnānadev but which calls itself *Bhāvārthadīpikā*—the lamp of simple explanation—is by any account the most seminal work of Marathi literature. Composed according to tradition in 1290 by a young brahman of the Nath sect, on the instruction and to the glory of his guru Nivṛttināth, it is a huge verse expansion of the *Bhagavad Gītā* in the simple *ovī* metre in which so much of later Marathi literature was written. Taking each verse of the *Gītā* it expounds its meaning with a series of brilliantly vivid and down-to-earth examples and images, thus making this crucial work of Indian philosophy accessible to the common man and woman in the common tongue of the region.

The status of *Jnāneśwarī* is such that—for almost all educated Marathi speakers, whatever their sect or creed, whether they are devout or skeptical, orthodox or modernizing—it is the work that first comes to mind in answer to the question, "What is the greatest creation of Marathi literature?" Yet it can hardly be called popular. Its language, though undoubtedly modernized since the 13th century, is still Old Marathi, and in places hard to understand. Those for whom it is pious duty to read, recite, or ponder on a section of it daily are usually devout and educated brahmans. Its overall message may well be that *bhakti*, the way of devotion, is the most effective pathway to God for the ordinary man, but it is not essential reading for the *bhaktas* and it expounds many other paths with skill and some complaisancy. Its comprehensiveness is such that, like the *Gītā* itself, it can be interpreted in many ways.

One assertion that can be made with confidence about *Jnāneśwarī* is that it is incontrovertibly monist. Whatever path the human soul chooses it must be clear that the phenomenal world is an illusory manifestation of unchanging *brahman*, that action must be performed without desire for its fruit, and that one should cultivate rigorous detachment, being indifferent to pleasure or pain, praise or blame. In *Jnāneśwarī* we have a marvellous text, a tremendous sustained sermon on life with a sweep and gusto, a piling on of imagery, and a development of simile that is almost numbing in its power. And the whole of this great work consists of philosophical exposition. After the first *adhyāya* which, as in the *Gītā*, sets the scene, there is scarcely any narrative.

The language—tense, vivid, and really quite simple if you happen to have been brought up speaking Old Marathi but with plenty of Sanskrit words mixed in—is extraordinarily difficult to translate into readable English or, I should imagine, readable anything else. Subedar produced a version in 1932, but this was based on a shortened and partly modernized Marathi text and is written in great slabs of prose without reference to verse numbers. In 1941 Edwards, in his *Dnyaneshwar the Out-caste Brahmin*, published the eighteenth *adhyāya* from a conflation of unpublished translations left by Justin Abbott and Pandit Godbole. This is based on the orthodox (non-Rajvade) edition of *Jnāneśwarī*. It is accurate enough but suffused with a kind of 1930-ish schoolmasterly tone. Taking almost at random verses 1530-31 of XVIII (1540-41 in Edwards) we find:

> O Pandav, just tell Me if all the propositions of the *Gītā*
> Shastra have made their full impression on your heart?
> We delivered these propositions to your ears, but did
> your ears in the same manner deliver them to your heart?
> I hope they were not useless on account of inattention or
> negligence on your part.

This is a perfect example of the chatty but plonking tone of the missionary teacher.

In 1953 Bhagwat produced a translation based on Bhide's edition, which my old teacher Hester Lambert described as in a style that was "somewhat too free to accompany the standard version of the Marathi work." The main objection to Bhagwat is that his Indian English produces some very odd words, some too grand, and some too colloquial. He rather punctiliously indicates additions and alternative translations in brackets while running verses together and providing their numbers only sporadically. The verses quoted above appear as:

> Now tell me, Oh Son of Pandu, if you have heard with concentrated attention all theories and established truths of the *(Gītā)* Scripture (1540). Has the knowledge that we (I) poured into your ears been impressed on your mind with the (same) effectiveness, or has any portion of it been spilt out (and wasted) or been ignored and discarded through negligence?

The Pradhan-Lambert version of this starts: "Now, O Pandava, tell me whether with full attention thou hast understood the principles of this great teaching—" unexceptionable except for the "thous" and the "hasts." It is a great shame that Miss Lambert never edited these out, but she was an ex-missionary and the biblical tone probably sounded more familiar to her ear.

This revised version takes the Pradhan-Lambert text and puts it into a form that could well sound more gratefully on the ear of a modern reader and so be delivered to the heart or impressed on the mind more effectively. But those who would fully appreciate the drive and bite of *Jnāneśwarī* would still do well to hear a little bit of it at least in the original Marathi:

> tari sāngha pāṃ pānḍavā, ha śāstrasiddhāntu āghavā,
> tuja ekacitteṃ phāvā, gelā ahe?
>
> āmhiṃ jaiseṃ heṃ jiyā riti, ugāṇileṃ kānācāṃ hātiṃ,
> ihiṃ taiseṃ tūjhāṃ cittiṃ, paiṭheṃ keleṃ kiṃ?

Ian M.P. Raeside
School of Oriental and African Studies, University of London

INTRODUCTION

The Jnanadevi *is a great work.*
Realize at least one of its verses.
Saint Namadeva[1]

My Jnanoba is the maya-bapa *(mother and father in one) of* Sadhakas, *of seekers.*
Saint Ekanatha[2]

Jnaneshwara is not far removed even in time from the "last of the Romans," the greatest Vedantic commentators, and his interpretation (of the Bhagavad Gita*) is absolutely mystical and in a way super-Vedantic. Jnaneshwara was not merely one of the greatest saints of Maharashtra but also certainly one of the greatest interpreters of the* Bhagavad Gita *that has ever lived.*
R.D. Ranade[3]

A work like the *Jnaneshwari* requires no introduction. It introduces itself to the reader. For it is the outcome of the deep mystical experience of its author that is ineffable and which can be shared only by one who has it. Namadeva aptly calls it '*brahmananda-lahari*,' a ripple of the bliss of the *Brahman*. Jnanadeva was not only a great mystic but also a poet par excellence who could confidently say: "In words I will give form to the formless and cause the senses to experience what is beyond their power to know" (*Jna.* 6.36). At the same time he was conscious of the fact that in the *adhyatma-sastra,* or the Science of the Spirit, it is personal experience that counts and nothing else. But he had the rare capacity to please his audience and uplift them by his verbal skill; hence the production of this monumental work called the *Jnaneshwari,* which speaks for itself. Here we can only try to look at it from different angles.

Not much is known, unfortunately, that can be called authentic about the life of Jnanadeva. All that we know about him for certain is that he and his two brothers, Nivrtti and Sopana, and his sister, Mukta, were the progeny of an ascetic-turned-householder; that consequently they became social outcasts and had to go to Paithan, the then center of learning, to obtain a testimonial of purity from the *pandits;* that on securing it they all went to Nevase where Jnanadeva wrote his exposition of the *Bhagavad Gita* which became known as the *Jnaneshwari;* that he entered into a spiritual comradeship with Namadeva, the great *Bhagavata* of Pandharpur; that together they walked as pilgrims to the holy places of the North; and finally, that on their return from the pilgrimage, Jnanadeva passed away in the state of meditation, or entered eternal *samadhi,* at Alandi, near Poona, in A.D. 1296. Although the time and place of the birth of Jnanadeva are controversial, the fact remains certain that the *Jnaneshwari* was written in A.D. 1290, and that was the central fact of his life. Whether he was fifteen (taking the birth year to be A.D. 1275) or nineteen (presuming the birth year to be A.D. 1271) when he produced this unique literary work is a futile query. For neither of these is a sufficiently mature age for the production of a highly philosophical work like the *Jnaneshwari* unless, of course, it can be explained on the basis of the 'brought-over' from the previous birth or births—an explanation that was indirectly supported by Jnanadeva himself *(Jna.* 6.451). But these details are of little importance to a super-mystic like Jnanadeva whose life's mission was to attain God for himself as well as for others.

Two currents of thought contributed to the spiritual life of Jnanadeva; *Yoga* of the Nathas, and *Bhakti* of the Bhagavatas. Jnanadeva synthesized these, creating the *advaita-bhakti,* or monistic devotion, which he expounded in each of his four works: the *Jnaneshwari,* the *Amrtanubhava,* the *Cangadeva-pasasti,* and the *Gatha*—the last of which is a collection of his *abhangas,* or devotional poems. However, it is the *Jnaneshwari,* his expositional commentary on the *Bhagavad Gita,* that can be called his *magnum opus.* Its unique combination of philosophy, poetry, and mysticism has been aptly expressed by Ranade, and we can do no better than to refer to his chapter on Jnanadeva's interpretation of the *Bhagavad Gita* (see note 3). The *Jnaneshwari* contains about nine-thousand verses in the popular *ovi* meter, which the poet handles with unsurpassed skill. The *Jnaneshwari* is not a commentary in the strict Sanskritic sense of the term, but rather a popular interpretation of the *Bhagavad Gita* explaining its teaching in an extremely poetical manner. The author knows where to expatiate and where to summarize the original thought of the *Bhagavad Gita;* it is this selectiveness behind the literary form that gives rise to the beauty his work eventually attained. Single terms like *ahimsa* (non-violence), or *acaryopasanam* (service of the teacher) from the *Bhagavad Gita* (13.7), for example, have inspired him to compose more than a hundred verses, each by way of exposition. Similarly, his commentary of the last chapter of the *Bhagavad Gita* has run into more than eighteen hundred verses based on the meager seventy-eight of the original. It owes its length to his ovations in praise of his favorite ideals such as his *guru,* Nivrttinatha, the *Bhagavad Gita* itself, the Marathi language which is his tool of expression, and finally, his audience. These and similar digressions make the *Jnaneshwari* one of the classics of Marathi literature. To give another instance of the poetic brilliance and the mystic grandeur of Jnanadeva, one may read, at the beginning of the eleventh chapter, his exposition of the *cit-surya,* or the Sun of Reality, which surpasses a similar metaphor by Plato where he speaks of the Idea of the Good as the Sun of the world of Ideas. The dialogue between Krisna and Arjuna towards the end of the same chapter, depicting the latter's reaction to the Cosmic vision he had experienced through the grace of Krisna, is another proof of the highly poetical mind of Jnanadeva.

At the same time, Jnanadeva is very original in his approach to the *Bhagavad Gita.* Although he generally follows Sankara, he does not simply render the Sanskrit commentary into Marathi. Sankara's is a *padabhasya* that explains every word in the *Bhagavad Gita.* Jnanadeva's is a total critique that brings out the essence of the original in a very lucid manner. One is a Vedantin full of dialectic, the other is a saint made of pure love—love for every creature. One argues, the other persuades. Sankara's motive was to explain and interpret the *Bhagavad Gita* and he stops there. Jnanadeva, on the other hand, has used the *Bhagavad Gita* as a means to a higher end, namely, to lead the world Godward. Describing the miseries of the world, he asks the question: "Shouldn't one escape when surrounded on all sides by a forest fire? So why shouldn't a person worship God when born into this world?" (*Jna.* 9.488). But Jnanadeva does not merely pose the question; he answers it positively and shows the way out: "Leave it [the world] at once and follow the path of devotion, by which you will reach My perfect abode" (*Jna.* 9.511). It is the path of devotion, the Pathway to God, that the *Jnaneshwari* exhorts. The *Vedas* preached the way of action (in the form of sacrifices) and the *Upanisads* presented the way of knowledge. But, apart from the question of their efficacy, both were beyond the reach of the common man. The *Bhagavad Gita* had given an assurance that those who take refuge in God, though they are lowly born, also attain to the highest goal (*Jna.* 9.32). But a Jnanadeva was necessary to appear on the scene and declare to the world that there is a way to sing the glory of the Name of God that is eternal and open to everyone.

If the *Jnaneshwari* teaches anything, it teaches the way of *Bhakti.* It is an easy, but long, long way. In fact, it is endless. The aspiring mystic goes on continuously approaching God, and instead of reaching a final and perfect identity between the two, the devotee meets God at infinity. There is only a little difference left between them, which disappears upon the mystic's giving up the ghost. The reason for this asymptotic approximation to Reality, as Ranade calls it, is the physical, mental and other limitations of the seeker. As long as he has a body and a mind and has to live in the world, he must fall short of total divine attainment. As Jnanadeva says, "Even though the devotee may reach union with god, yet he remains a devotee" (*Jna.* 7.113). The saint remains a saint as long as he has to discharge his bodily functions. This doctrine of asymptotism as propounded in the *Jnaneshwari* can be said to be a veritable landmark in the history of the philosophy of mysticism.

It is surprising to find parallel thought in the writings of the Chinese philosopher, Confucius, who lived in the fifth century B.C. To the question "How can the finite man attain the infinte *Cheng*?" Confucius answers:

> Cheng *is actually to be reached only by the sage, but it is the business of the ordinary man...to seek and strive with all his faculties to approach it. It is true that the path of this approach, though convergent, is endless—asymptotic, like the mathematical straight-line that draws ever nearer to a curve yet never meets it. There is no need for dismay on that account, however, for the path is rich in compensation and promise."*[4]

It is exactly in the same strain when Ranade says that "God-realization is a continuous process, and not an event." As Jnanadeva himself tells us:

> *Granted that one completely renounces the world, meets the proper guru, gets initiated into the right way—granted all this, granted that the seed that is sown is the best of its kind and is sown in the best of the land, yet it is only in course of time that a rich harvest can be reaped. (Jna. 18.995-997)*

The utterances of these three great mystics belonging to different times are peculiarly identical for the simple reason that, in the words of Heracleitos, "those that are awake have one common world." Saint Jnanadeva is such a wakeful person. So he too tells us, after Confucius, that not only the goal, but also, the Pathway to it, is full of bliss: "Wherever the pilgrim sets his foot, a store-house of eternal bliss opens before him" (*Jna.* 16.158). The *Jnaneshwari* leads us on this blissful Pathway, the pathway upon which even Siva is still a pilgrim, so that we can reach the "endless end."

It was more than fifty years ago, actually in 1933, that Ranade wrote: "The World will await the day when the whole of the *Jnaneshwari* may be translated into English, and thus be made available to the world of scholars."[5] That day has arrived with the publication of the present modernized English rendering of the *Jnaneshwari.*

NOTES AND REFERENCES

1. This praise of the *Jnaneshwari* comes from Saint Namadeva, the contemporary biographer of Jnanadeva. He calls his work *Jnanadevi.* (*Sakalasanta-Gatha,* vol. II, Poona 1983, p. 193, No. 699)
2. This is a tribute paid to Jnanadeva by Saint Ekanath (A.D. 1533-1599) who was responsible for researching and establishing the text of the *Jnaneshwari* in the year A.D. 1584. According to him, Saint Jnanadeva is the affectionate guide for the pilgrims on the Pathway to God. (*Sakalasanta-Gatha,* vol. III, Poona 1983, p. 663, No. 3519)
3. R.D. Ranade, The *Bhagavad Gita* as a Philosophy of God-realization, Nagpur 1959, p. 55.
4. Edward Herbert, *A Confucian Note-book,* John Murrary, London, 1950, p. 20. *'Cheng'* is the state akin to *samadhi,* or unison with the Divine.
5. R.D. Ranade, *Mysticism in Maharashtra,* Poona 1933, p. 178.

BIBLIOGRAPHY

Ranade, R.D. *Mysticism in Maharashtra,* Poona 1933.
Ranade, R.D. *The* Bhagvadgita *as a Philosophy of God-realization* (Ch. V), Poona 1959.
Tulpule, S.G. *The Classical Marathi Literature,* Wisebaden 1979.
Sardar, G.B. *The Saint-Poets of Maharashtra,* Bombay 1969.
Vaudeville, Charlotte. *Línvocation: le Haripath de Dnyandev,* Paris 1969.
Dandekar, S.V. (Ed.). *Sartha Jnanesvari,* 8th edition, Poona 1986.

S.G. Tulpule
Indian Institute of Advanced Study
Shimla (India)
18th August, 1988

JNANESHWAR'S GITA

1

THE DEPRESSION OF ARJUNA

SALUTATIONS to Shri Ganesh!

1 OM! Salutations to the Supreme Being, described in the Vedas! Victory to that self-existent One, of the pure nature of the Self!

2 O Lord! You are Ganesh, the illuminer of all intelligence. Nivritti's servant says, Listen to my story.

3 The Vedas in their perfection are like the god's beautiful form. Their flawless words are his resplendent body.

4 The Smritis are his limbs, the marking of the verses shows their structure, and a treasure house of beauty lies in their meaning.

5 The eighteen Puranas are his rich ornaments, the theories expounded in them are the gems, and the rhythmic style provides the settings for those gems.

6 The metrical form is his colorful garment, and the composition is its fine, shining texture.

7 The epic poems and their dramas, read with delight, are like jingling bells giving out the music of meaning.

8 The principles expounded in them and the appropriateness of the words expressing them are precious jewels set in the bells.

9 The wisdom of Vyasa and the other sages is his waistcloth, its tasseled end gleaming with purity.

10 The six systems of philosophy are his six arms, and the different theories expounded in them are the six weapons held in his hands.

11 The art of reasoning is the hatchet, logic is the goad, and the philosophy of Vedanta is the delicious sweet held in his hand.

12 In one hand he holds a broken tooth, symbolizing the rejection of Buddha's teachings, refuted by the Vedantic commentaries.

13 The teaching of the universal Self is his lotus-like hand held in the varada mudra, and the establishment of dharma is his other hand held in the abhaya mudra.

14 Pure discrimination is his straight trunk, in which supreme bliss dwells.

15 Impartial discussion is his pure white tusk. Ganesh is the small-eyed elephant god, the remover of obstacles, who represents the subtle eye of wisdom.

16 Action and knowledge are his two ears, and the bees hovering over his temples are sages who taste the nectar of these teachings.

17 Duality and nonduality unite like lustrous corals on his temples.

18 The ten principal Upanishads, containing the honey of knowledge, are the fragrant flowers adorning the crown of his head.

19 The A of AUM is his legs, the U is his big belly, and the M is his great circular head.

20 When these three come together, they form the sacred syllable AUM, the primal cause of all being.

21 Now I salute Sharada, the lover of wisdom, sense, and skill, who delights in speech, the enchantress of the world.

22 My Guru dwells in my heart. By his grace I have been rescued from the ocean of worldly existence and have become devoted to the path of discrimination.

23 Just as when a person applies a magic ointment to his eyes, his vision improves and he can find his way to a great storehouse of treasure,

24 Or when he has found a wish-fulfilling gem, all his wishes are fulfilled, Jnanadeva says that all his desires have been satisfied through the grace of Shri Nivritti.

25 Similarly, those wise people who serve their

Gurus thereby attain the goal of their lives, just as when the roots of a tree are watered the branches begin to sprout.

26 Just as bathing in the sea confers the same benefits as bathing in the holy places of all three worlds, and just as all essences may be experienced in the taste of nectar,

27 So I have saluted my Guru again and again, for he fulfills all my wishes.

28 Now listen to the great mystic story, the source of all wonderful stories, which is like a beautiful garden full of the trees of discrimination.

29 It is the origin of all bliss, the great storehouse of truth, and the ocean of nectar of the nine feelings.

30 It is the place of beatitude, the primal abode of learning, and the everlasting seat of all the sciences.

31 It is the home of all religion, the heart of all good people, and the treasure house of the beauty of Sharada.

32 Through Vyasa's intellect, the goddess Saraswati has revealed herself throughout the three worlds in the different episodes in this work.

33 Therefore, this poem is the king of all epics and the storehouse of the greatness of all writings. All the feelings derive their beauty from it.

34 Hear also another of its merits: the wealth of language has been related to science, and the tenderness of the highest knowledge has increased.

35 Through this story wisdom itself has become wise, love is added to delight, and the blessedness of joy has increased.

36 Through it sweetness is added to the quality of sweetness, beauty is added to love, and dignity is imparted to all that is good.

37 Because of this story there is artistry in art, and righteousness is powerful. By means of it, all of Janmejaya's sins were miraculously annulled.

38 If we reflect for a moment, we understand that all color derives its beauty from this story, and goodness acquires its essence from it.

39 Just as when the sun shines the whole world becomes illumined, similarly, through Vyasa's intellect the entire universe has derived its spiritual light from this work.

40 Just as seeds planted in good soil multiply freely, all meaning has found its fullest expression in the Mahabharata.

41 Just as a person becomes civilized from living in a city, so everything reflects the light of Vyasa's speech.

42 Just as the charm of beauty reaches its perfection in a woman in the prime of her youth;

43 As when spring appears in a garden, a wealth of beauty is brought forth, even greater than before;

44 Or as gold nuggets appear dull, but the gold assumes a special glory when made into ornaments;

45 Similarly, Vyasa's words impart charm to every episode, and they are reflected throughout all history.

46 The Puranas, feeling that they would thus be raised to eminence, have turned with humility to the Mahabharata for inspiration in all forms of stories and episodes.

47 Thus it is said that what is not found in the Mahabharata does not exist in any of the three worlds, and that everything else is just a remnant of Vyasa's work.

48 The sage told this story to King Janmejaya. It is the sweetest narration in the world and the source of the highest truths.

49 So, listen to this story which is unequalled, matchless, most pure, and the source of all auspiciousness.

50 The Mahabharata is like a lotus, and the episode called the Gita, in which Shri Krishna converses with Arjuna, is like its pollen.

51 The Gita is the divine butter churned by Vyasa from the ocean of the Vedas with the churning rod of his intellect.

52 When the butter was heated in the fire of wisdom and boiled to perfection by discrimination, it became the delicious ghee of the Gita.

53 The dispassionate seek it, and saints desire to experience it. Those who have realized their oneness with the Divine take delight in it.

54 Devotees long to listen to it. It is the most worthy of worship in all the three worlds. It is expounded in the section called Bhishma Parva.

55 It is called the Song of the Lord. The creator, Brahma, praised it, as did Lord Shiva. Sanaka and other great sages treated it with great reverence.

56 Just as the chakora bird picks up the tender and luscious drops of nectar falling from the moon in the sharada season,

57 In the same way, listeners should enjoy this story with dispassionate and gentle minds.

58 It should be pondered silently and enjoyed apart from any action of the senses. In this way, the inner Self may grasp its truths.

59 Just as a bee may carry away pollen without the lotus being aware of it, this is the way to understand this work.

60 Just as the lotus, remaining in its place, embraces the rising moon and experiences the joy of it,

61 Similarly, only one who approaches it with seriousness and a tranquil heart can understand this work.

62 Those of you who, like Arjuna, are qualified to listen to this work, I beseech you sages to listen now to my words.

63 I say this lovingly and, touching your feet, I implore you; for I know you feel reverence in your hearts.

64 Just as it is the nature of parents to be pleased when their child lisps out his words,

65 So have you good people accepted me as your own. Why should I beseech you when I know you will overlook my shortcomings?

66 But there is another fault: I claim to understand the Gita, and I have asked you to listen to me.

67 In my eagerness, I have thoughtlessly undertaken this work. Would a firefly show its light in the presence of the sun?

68 Just as the titibha bird tries to sound the depth of the ocean with its tiny beak, similarly, with little knowledge I am setting out on this task.

69 Listen! In order to encompass the sky, one must be greater than it is; so, truly, it is beyond my capacity to expound the Gita.

70 Its meaning is so deep that even Lord Shambhu explained it to Bhavani when she questioned him about it with wonder.

71 Then Hara said, O Beloved, just as your nature is incomprehensible, so is the meaning of the Gita difficult to understand, since it is always new.

72 It was given forth by the Supreme Being Himself, from whose voice, in sleep, emanated the ocean of the Vedas.

73 Therefore, how can I, who am dull of intellect, hope to understand such a work? It is unfathomable, and even the Vedas were bewildered by it.

74 Who can grasp the infinite, or illumine the great light? How could an insect hold the firmament in its grasp?

75 But in this matter there is one source of strength, through which I may speak with confidence, and that is my gracious Guru. So says Jnanadeva.

76 Without this, I would be a fool. Though I have been thoughtless, the light of the grace of the saints enlightens me.

77 It is the property of the philosopher's stone to turn iron into gold. Also, the dead return to life through the power of nectar.

78 If Saraswati herself were to appear to a mute person, he would obtain the gift of speech.

79 Can anything be impossible for the child of Kamadhenu? For this reason, I have set out to expound this work.

80 Therefore, I ask you to add whatever may be lacking and to reject whatever is superfluous.

81 Now, I beg you, pay attention to me. I will say what you inspire in me, just as a puppet dances when moved by a string.

82 Blessed by your grace, I am obedient to the saints. Make of me whatever you please.

83 Then the Guru says, Enough of this. There is no need to say all this. Now give your mind to this work.

84 Nivritti's disciple, rejoicing at these words, said, Listen carefully.

धृतराष्ट्र उवाच । *dhrtarāstra uvāca*

धर्मक्षेत्रे कुरुक्षेत्रे समवेता युयुत्सवः ।
मामकाः पाण्डवाश्चैव किम् अकुर्वत संजय ॥
dharmakṣetre kurukṣetre
samavetā yuyutsavaḥ
māmakāḥ pāṇḍavāś cāiva
kim akurvata samjayāca

Dhritarashtra spoke:

1. When they were in the field of virtue, in the field of the Kurus, assembled together, desiring to fight, what did my army and that of the sons of Pandu do, Sanjaya?

85 Dhritarashtra, moved by affection for his sons, said, O Sanjaya, tell me what happened on the battlefield of the Kurus.

86 On that field which is called the abode of righteousness, my sons and the Pandavas have arrayed themselves, intent on fighting.

87 Tell me what they have been doing there so long, facing one another.

संजय उवाच । *sañjaya uvāca*

दृष्ट्वा तु पाण्डवानीकं व्यूढं दुर्योधनस् तदा ।
आचार्यमुपसंगम्य राजा वचनमब्रवीत् ॥
dṛṣṭvā tu pāṇḍavānīkaṁ
vyūḍhaṁ duryodhanas tadā
ācāryamupasaṁgamya
rājā vacanam abravīt

Sanjaya spoke:
2. Seeing indeed the army of the sons of Pandu arrayed, King Duryodhana, approaching his Master (Drona), spoke these words:

पश्यैतां पाण्डुपुत्राणाम् आचार्य महतीं चमूम् ।
व्यूढां द्रुपदपुत्रेण तव शिष्येण धीमता ॥
paśyāitāṁ pāṇḍuputrāṇām
ācārya mahatīṁ camūm
vyūḍhāṁ drupadaputreṇa
tava śiṣyeṇa dhīmatā

3. Behold O Master, this great army of the sons of Pandu arrayed by the son of Drupada, wise by your instruction.

88 Then Sanjaya said, The army of the Pandavas rose up like the jaws of death spread out at the time of the universal dissolution,
89 Just like the gathering of a dense mass of clouds. It was like the Kalakuta poison seething everywhere. Who could control it?
90 It seemed like the fire at the bottom of the ocean which, fanned by the wind of the universal dissolution, rises up in flames to the heavens, having dried up the ocean's waters.
91 Similarly, this invincible army, arranged in various positions was a terrifying sight.
92 But Duryodhana regarded it with contempt, just as a lion would despise a herd of elephants.
93 Then he approached Drona and said to him, Do you see this huge army of the Pandavas,
94 Skillfully arrayed for battle like a moving fortress by the intelligent son of Drupada?
95 See how Drupada's son, to whom you taught the art of war and made him an expert in it, has spread out his army like the sea!

अत्र शूरा महेष्वासा भीमार्जुनसमा युधि ।
युयुधानो विराटश्च द्रुपदश्च महारथः ॥
atra śūrā maheṣvāsā
bhīmārjunasamā yudhi
yuyudhāno virāṭaś ca
drupadaś ca mahārathaḥ

4. Here are heroes, mighty archers, equal in battle to Bhima and Arjuna, Yuyudhana and Virata, and Drupada, the great warrior;

96 There are also incomparable warriors, skilled in the use of weapons and missiles, well versed in the art of war.
97 In strength and courage they are equal to Bhima and Arjuna. I will tell you their names.
98 There is the great warrior Yuyudhana, the King Virata, and Drupada, the great chariot fighter.

धृष्टकेतुश्चेकितानः काशिराजश्च वीर्यवान् ।
पुरुजित् कुन्तिभोजश्च शैब्यश्च नरपुङ्गवः ॥
dhṛṣṭaketuś cekitānaḥ
kāśirājaś ca vīryavān
purujit kuntibhojaś ca
śāibyaś ca narapuṅgavaḥ

5. Dhrishtaketu, Chekitana, and the valorous King of Kashi, Purojit and Kuntibhoja and Shaibya, bull among men,

99 Look at Chekitana, Dhrishtaketu, and the valiant King of Kashi, Uttamauju, the best of kings, and Shaibya.
100 Kuntibhoja and Yudhamanyu have come and all the other kings, including Purojit.

युधामन्युश्च विक्रान्त उत्तमौजश्च वीर्यवान् ।
सौभद्रो द्रौपदेयाश्च सर्व एव महारथाः ॥
yudhāmanyuś ca vikrānta
uttamāujaś ca vīryavān
sāubhadro drāupadesyāś ca
sarva eva mahārathāḥ

6. And mighty Yudhamanyu and valorous Uttamaujas; the son of Subhadra and the sons of Draupadi, all indeed great warriors.

101 There is the joy of Subhadra's heart, the youthful Abhimanyu. Duryodhana said, Look, O Drona.
102 There are many more, such as the sons of Draupadi, all of them great chariot warriors, too numerous to mention, all gathered.

अस्माकं तु विशिष्टा ये तान् निबोध द्विजोत्तम ।
नायका मम सैन्यस्य संज्ञार्थं तान् ब्रवीमि ते ॥
asmākaṁ tu viśiṣṭā ye
tān nibodha dvijottama
nāyakā mama sāinyasya
saṁjñārthaṁ tān bravīmi te

7. Those of ours who are indeed distinguished, know them! O Highest of the Twiceborn, the leaders of my army I name for you by proper names:

103 Now listen, and I will tell you, the names of the famous warriors on our side, the leaders of our armies.

104 To give you some idea, I will mention just a few. In the first place, you yourself are the chief.

भवान् भीष्मश् च कर्णश् च कृपश्च समितिंजयः ।
अश्वत्थामा विकर्णश्च सौमदत्तिस्तथैव च ॥
bhavān bhīsmaś ca karṇaś ca
kṛpaś ca samitiṁjayaḥ
aśvatthāmā vikarṇaś ca
sāumadattis tathāiva ca

8. Your Lordship and Bhishma and Karna and Kripa, always victorious in battle, Ashvatthama and Vikarna and the son of Somadatta also;

105 Here is Bhishma, the son of Ganga, adorned with courage and as resplendent as the sun; Karna, the lion among these elephants in the form of his enemies,

106 Who even by his thought would be able to destroy the whole universe singlehandedly. And isn't Kripacharya enough, even by himself?

107 There is Vikarna the brave, and a little farther away you can see Ashwatthama, who is feared even by the god of death.

108 There are Samitinjaya, Saumadatta, and many more, whose courage even the creator cannot measure.

अन्ये च बहवः शूरा मदर्थे त्यक्तजीविताः
नानाशस्त्रप्रहरणा. सर्वे युद्धविशारदाः ॥
anye ca bahavaḥ śūrā
madarthe tyaktajīvitāḥ
nānāśastrapraharaṇāḥ
sarve yuddhaviśāradāḥ

9. And many other heroes whose lives are risked for my sake, attacking with various weapons, all skilled in battle.

109 These men are expert at using weapons with the power of mantras. They have taught the use of all kinds of missiles.

110 All of them are incomparable warriors in this world and full of valor. Nevertheless, they have followed me with all their heart and soul.

111 Just as a chaste wife in her heart loves only her husband, I am everything to these warriors.

112 In the interest of my cause, they consider their lives as valueless. They are pure and selfless in their loyalty to their master.

113 They are familiar with the art of war, and they have conquered even fame. In short, they are models of warriorship.

114 Thus our army is made up of soldiers of every kind, and it would be impossible to count them.

अपर्याप्तं तद् अस्माकं बलं भीष्माभिरक्षितम् ।
पर्याप्तं त्विदम् एतेषां बलं भीमाभिरक्षितम् ॥
aparyāptam tad asmākaṁ
balaṁ bhīṣmābhirakṣitaṁ
paryāptaṁ tu idam eteṣām
balaṁ bhīmabhirakṣitam

10. Sufficient is that force of ours guarded by Bhishma; insufficient though is the force guarded by Bhima.

115 Moreover, Bhishma, the best of all the warriors and the most courageous fighter in battle, has been placed in command of our army.

116 Under his direction this army is organized like a fortress. Compared with it, even the three worlds are insignificant.

117 The ocean itself is impassable, but what if the great sea fire were added to it?

118 Just as the great wind and the fire of destruction combine to bring about the end of the universe, so is our army with its general, Ganga's son.

119 Who will fight against him? The army of the Pandavas seems insignificant compared with ours.

120 The mighty Bhimasena is its general. Then he stopped speaking.

अयनेषु च सर्वेषु यथाभागम् अवस्थिता
भीष्मम् एवाभिरक्षन्तु भवन्तः सर्व एव हि ॥
ayaneṣu ca sarveṣu
yathābhāgam avasthitāḥ
bhīṣmam evābhirakṣantu
bhavantaḥ sarva eva hi

11. And in all movements, stationed each in his respective place, all of you, indeed, protect Bhishma!

121 Then Duryodhana told all the troops, Arrange yourselves in your respective detachments.

122 The command should be given to those great chariot fighters who direct the various sections of the battlefield.

123 They should each command their own troops and obey Bhishma. He told Drona, You watch over everything.

124 Especially protect Bhishma. You must consider him my own self, for our whole army depends entirely on him.

तस्य संजनयन् हर्षं कुरुवृद्धः पितामहः ।
सिंहनादं विनद्योच्चैः शङ्खं दध्मौ प्रतापवान् ।।

tasya saṁjanayan harṣaṁ
kuruvṛddhaḥ pitāmahaḥ
siṁhanādaṁ vinadyoccāiḥ
śaṅkhaṁ dadhmāu pratāpavān

12. Making him (Duryodhana) happy, the aged Kuru, his grandsire, roaring like a lion, blew his conch horn powerfully.

125 Hearing the king's words, the commander rejoiced and roared like a lion.
126 That marvelous sound was heard throughout the three worlds and resounded on all sides.
127 In harmony with the reverberating echoes, the godlike Bhishma blew his divine conch with all his might.
128 The two sounds together deafened the three worlds, as if the heavens were crashing down.
129 The skies were shattered by the thunder, the ocean heaved, and the whole creation trembled.
130 The valleys were filled with the din. Then all the warriors beat their war drums.

ततः शङ्खाश्च भेर्यश्च पणवानकगोमुखाः ।
सहसैवाभ्यहन्यन्त स शब्दस् तुमुलो ऽभवत् ।।

tataḥ śaṅkhāś ca bheryaś ca
paṇavānakagomukhāḥ
sahasāivābhyahanyanta
sa śabdas tumulo 'bhavat

13. And thereupon the conch horns and the kettledrums, the cymbals, drums and trumpets all at once were sounded. The uproar was tremendous.

131 Then there was heard the terrific roar of countless battle instruments, and it appeared that the end of the world had come.
132 What was the state of the faint-hearted? The timid were blown away like dry leaves. Even the god of death was terrified.
133 There were drums, horns, conches, and bugles, with the terrible cries of the warriors.
134 Some beat their weapons violently, shouting with fury, so the elephants could not be restrained.
135 Some even died right where they stood, brave men's teeth chattered, and incomparable fighters also shook with fear.
136 The terrible, deafening sound of all those instruments of war reverberated so that even the creator was afraid. The gods exclaimed, "The day of universal destruction will certainly come!"

ततः श्वेतैर् हयैर् युक्ते महति स्यन्दने स्थितौ ।
माधवः पाण्डवश्चैव दिव्यौ शङ्खौ प्रदध्मतुः ।।

tataḥ śvetāir hayāir yukte
mahati syandane sthitāu
mādhavaḥ pāṇḍavaścāiva
divyāu śaṅkhāu pradadhmatuḥ

14. Then, standing in the great chariot yoked with white horses, Krishna and Arjuna sounded forth their divine conch horns.

137 While this commotion was heard even in the abode of the gods, listen to what occurred in the army of the Pandavas.
138 Behold that chariot which was the essence of victory and the treasure house of light, to which there were yoked four horses as swift as Garuda.
139 It was as resplendent as a winged Meru. Its brilliance shone in all the four quarters of the earth.
140 And the Lord of Vaikuntha Himself was its charioteer! Who could accurately describe it!
141 At the head of the chariot sat an image of the monkey god, the incarnation of Shri Shankara, and the holder of the Sharnga bow was the charioteer along with Arjuna.
142 Behold this wondrous act of the Lord! What great love He had for His disciple, that He served Arjuna as his charioteer!

पाञ्चजन्यं हृषीकेशो देवदत्तं धनंजयः ।
पौण्ड्रं दध्मौ महाशङ्खं भीमकर्मा वृकोदरः ।।

pāñcajanyaṁ hṛṣīkeśo
devadattaṁ dhanaṁjayaḥ
pāuṇḍraṁ dadhmāu mahāśaṅkhaṁ
bhīmakarmā vṛkodaraḥ

15. Krishna blew his Panchajanya; Arjuna blew Devadatta, while Bhima, terrible in action, blew the great conch horn Paundra.

143 Seated in front with His disciple behind Him, He joyfully blew His conch called Panchajanya.
144 While the deep sound was reverberating, just as all the stars fade when the sun rises,
145 All the warlike sounds of the Kuru army were silenced, and it was impossible to tell when they faded away.
146 Similarly, Arjuna blew loudly on his conch

named Devadatta, with a deep, resounding tone.

147 These two terrible sounds united, and the whole universe seemed to be shattered to pieces.

148 At that moment Bhimasena grew furious, as if the god of destruction were enraged, and he blew on his great conch called Paundra.

अनन्तविजयं राजा कुन्तीपुत्रो युधिष्ठिरः ।
नकुलः सहदेवश्च सुघोषमणिपुष्पकौ ॥

anantavijayam rājā
kuntīputro yudhiṣṭhiraḥ
nakulaḥ sahadevaś cā
sughoṣamaṇipuṣpakāu

16. King Yudhishthira, son of Kunti, blew Anantavijaya; Nakula and Sahadeva blew Sughosa and Manipushpaka.

149 The sound of the conches was like thunderclaps on the day of destruction. Yudhishthira also blew his Anantavijaya.

150 Then Nakula blew his conch Sughosa, and Sahadev his Manipushpaka. Hearing these sounds, even the god of death trembled with fear.

काश्यश्च परमेष्वासः शिखण्डी च महारथः ।
धृष्टद्युम्नो विराटश्च सात्यकिश्चापराजितः ॥

kāśyaś ca parameṣvāsaḥ
śikhaṇḍī ca mahārathaḥ
dhṛṣṭadyumno virāṭaś ca
sātyakiścāparājitaḥ

17. And the King of Kashi, supreme archer, and Shikhandi, that great warrior, Dhrishtadyumna and Virata and Satyaki, the invincible;

151 On the field there were many kings, such as Drupada and the sons of Draupadi, the King of Kashi,

द्रुपदो द्रौपदेयाश्च सर्वशः पृथिवीपते ।
सौभद्रश्च महाबाहुः शङ्खान् दध्मुः पृथक् पृथक् ॥

drupado drāupadeyāś ca
sarvaśaḥ pṛthivīpate
sāubhadraś ca mahābāhuḥ
śaṅkhān dadhmuḥ pṛthak pṛthak

18. Drupada and the sons of Draupadi all together, O Lord of the Earth, and the strong armed son of Subhadra blew their conch horns, each his own.

152 Satyaki, the unconquerable, the son of Arjuna, Dhristadyumna, the best of kings, Shikhandi,

153 The others like Virata, all leading warriors, continuously blew their conches.

स घोषो धार्तराष्ट्राणां हृदयानि व्यदारयत् ।
नभश्च पृथिवीं चैव तुमुलो व्यनुनादयन् ॥

sa ghoṣo dhārtarāṣṭrāṇāṁ
hṛdayāni vyadārayat
nabhaś ca pṛthivīṁ cāiva
tumulo vyanunādayan

19. The noise burst asunder the hearts of the sons of Dhritarashtra, and the tumult caused the sky and the earth to resound.

154 Terrified by the vibrations of these sounds, Shesha and Kurma were confused and tried to throw off the burden of the earth.

155 The foundations of the three worlds were shaken, the mountains Meru and Mandara began to rock, and the ocean heaved up to the skies.

156 The earth was about to turn upside down, the sky was terrified, and the stars were about to fall.

157 A cry arose in the highest heaven that the universe had been destroyed, and the gods were helpless.

158 The sun did not shine, the cries of lamentation echoed throughout all the three worlds, as if the great light of the final dissolution had vanished.

159 Even the Supreme Being was astonished and exclaimed, "Is this the end of all things?" Then suddenly this chaos ceased.

160 The universe was saved when Lord Krishna and the others blew their great conches. Otherwise, the end of the age might have occurred.

161 Although the deep sounds had ceased, their echoes continued to reverberate, so that the army of the Kauravas was destroyed.

162 Just as a lion may kill a herd of elephants, so the sound struck terror into the Kauravas' hearts.

163 As they heard the thunder, they lost heart and cried out to one another, "Beware! Beware!"

अथ व्यवस्थितान् दृष्ट्वा धार्तराष्ट्रान् कपिध्वजः ।
प्रवृत्ते शस्त्रसंपाते धनुर् उद्यम्य पाण्डवः ॥

atha vyavasthitān dṛṣṭvā
dhārtarāṣṭrān kapidhvajaḥ
pravṛtte śastrasaṁpāte
dhanur udyamya pāṇḍavaḥ

20. Then, Arjuna, having seen the sons of

Dhritarashtra drawn up in battle array, raised his bow as the clash of weapons began.

164 Then those great and fearless warriors, full of courage, began to assemble the army.

165 At that point the army rushed forward with redoubled vigor, so that the three worlds trembled.

166 Those brave archers shot forth a stream of arrows, like the downpour from the clouds on the day of final destruction.

167 At the sight of it, Arjuna inwardly rejoiced and hastily turned to look at the two armies.

168 When he saw the Kaurava warriors arrayed for battle, Arjuna gracefully picked up his bow.

हृषीकेशं तदा वाक्यम् इदम् आह महीपते ।
सेनयोर् उभयोर् मध्ये रथं स्थापय मे ऽच्युत ॥

hṛsīkeśam tadā vākyam
idam āha mahīpate
senayor ubhayor madhye
rathaṁ sthāpaya me 'cyuta

21. Arjuna then spoke these words to Krishna: O Lord of the earth, cause my chariot to stand in the middle between the two armies, imperishable one,

169 Then Arjuna spoke these words to the Lord, Now quickly place my chariot between the two armies,

यावद् एतान् निरीक्षे ऽहं योद्धुकामान् अवस्थितान् ।
कैर् मया सह योद्धव्यम् अस्मिन् रणसमुद्यमे ॥

yāvad etān nirīkṣe 'haṁ
yoddhukāmān avasthitān
kāir mayā saha yoddhavyam
asmin raṇasamudyame

22. Until I behold these warriors, battle-hungry and arrayed. With whom must I fight in undertaking this battle?

170 While I look for a moment at all these warriors gathered here for battle.

171 They have all come together here, and I wish to see those with whom I will have to fight on the battlefield.

योत्स्यमानान् अवेक्षे ऽहं य एते ऽत्र समागताः ।
धार्तराष्ट्रस्य दुर्बुद्धेर् युद्धे प्रियचिकीर्षवः ॥

yotsyamānān avekṣe 'haṁ
ya ete 'tra samāgatāḥ
dhārtarāṣṭrasya durbuddher
yuddhe priyacikīrṣavaḥ

23. I behold those who are about to give battle, having come together here, wishing to do service in warfare for the evil-minded son of Dhritarashtra (Duryodhana).

172 These evil-minded and impatient Kauravas pretend that they love to fight, although they lack the spirit for it.

173 They make believe that they are eager to fight, but they have no courage in battle. Having narrated all this to the king, Sanjaya said,

एवम् उक्तो हृषीकेशो गुडाकेशेन भारत ।
सेनयोर् उभयोर् मध्ये स्थापयित्वा रथोत्तमम् ॥

evam ukto hṛsīkeśo
guḍākeśena bhārata
senayor ubhayor madhye
sthāpayitvā rathottamam

24. Thus Krishna was addressed by Arjuna, O Dhritarashtra, having caused the chief chariot to stand in the middle between the two armies.

174 When Arjuna said this, Lord Krishna drove his chariot and placed it between the two armies.

भीष्मद्रोणप्रमुखतःसर्वेषां च महीक्षिताम् ।
उवाच पार्थ पश्यैतान् समवेतान् कुरून् इति ॥

bhīṣmadroṇapramukhataḥ
sarveṣāṁ ca mahīkṣitām
uvāca pārtha paśyāitān
samavetān kurūn iti

25. Before the eyes of Bhishma and Drona and all these rulers of the earth, Arjuna said: Behold these Kurus assembled.

175 There before him he saw Bhishma, Drona, other relatives, and many kings.

176 When his chariot was driven in front of them, Arjuna eagerly looked at them all.

177 Then he exclaimed, Look, O Lord! All these are our family members and relatives, our elders and teachers. Shri Krishna was astonished for a moment at this remark.

178 He said to Himself, What does this mean? What does he have in his mind?

179 Then He looked into the future and immediately knew what was in Arjuna's mind, but He remained silent.

तत्रापश्यत् स्थितान् पार्थः पितॄन् अथ पितामहान् ।
आचार्यान् मातुलान् भ्रातॄन् पुत्रान् पौत्रान् सखींस् तथा ॥

tatrāpaśyat sthitān pārthaḥ
pitṝn atha pitāmahān
ācāryān mātulān bhrātṝn
putrān pāutrān sakhīṅs tathā

26. Arjuna saw standing there fathers, then grandfathers, teachers, maternal uncles, brothers, sons, grandsons, friends as well;

180 There on the battlefield Arjuna could see all his elders, grandparents, uncles, other relative, and teachers.

181 He saw his friends, sons, and brothers-in-law among them.

श्वशुरान् सुहृदश्चैव सेनयोर् उभयोर् अपि।
तान् समीक्ष्य स कौन्तेयः सर्वान् बन्धून् अवस्थितान्॥

śvaśurān suhṛdaścāiva
senayor ubhayor api
tān samīkṣya sa kāunteyaḥ
sarvān bandhūn avasthitān

27. Arjuna saw fathers-in-law, companions, in the two armies, and contemplated all his kinsmen, arrayed.

182 Arjuna saw there his dear ones, his young grandsons, fathers-in-law, and his other relatives.

183 There were both old and young, those who were under obligation to him, and those whom he had protected in distress.

184 Thus Arjuna could see all his relatives in both armies, standing ready to fight at that moment.

कृपया परयाविष्टो विषीदन्न् इदम् अब्रवीत्।
दृष्ट्वेमं स्वजनं कृष्ण युयुत्सुं समुपस्थितम्॥

kṛpayā parayāviṣṭo
viṣīdann idam abravīt
dṛṣṭvemaṁ svajanaṁ kṛṣṇa
yuyutsuṁ samupasthitam

28. Filled with infinite pity, despondent, he said this: Having seen my own people, Krishna, desiring to fight, approaching,

185 At this his heart was bewildered, and he naturally felt pity. Unable to bear such humiliation, he lost courage.

186 Just as highborn women, virtuous and beautiful, cannot tolerate another woman with superior qualities;

187 Just as a lustful man, enchanted by another woman, forgets his own wife and recklessly follows his passion;

188 Or as a man, practicing austerities, attains spiritual powers, becomes confused, and forgets his goal;

189 It was the same with Arjuna. He was overcome by pity, and manliness left him.

190 Just as a person who recites mantras may become mad and appear to be possessed by an evil spirit, similarly, Arjuna was overcome by infatuation.

191 When his heart melted with compassion, his manliness deserted him, just as a moonstone melts when it is touched by moonlight.

192 In this way Arjuna was overcome by pity. Full of sadness, he addressed Lord Krishna,

193 Listen to me, O Lord! When I look at this army of warriors, everywhere I see my own family members.

194 All these warriors are standing here, ready to fight, but how can this be right for me?

195 The very thought of it bewilders and unnerves me. My mind has almost lost its stability.

सीदन्ति मम गात्राणि मुखं च परिशुष्यति।
वेपथुश्च शरीरे मे रोमहर्षश्च जायते॥

sīdanti mama gātrāṇi
mukhaṁ ca pariśuṣyati
vepathuś ca śarīre me
romaharṣaś ca jāyate

29. My limbs sink down, my mouth dries up, my body trembles, and my hair stands on end;

गाण्डीवं स्रंसते हस्तात् त्वक् चैव परिदह्यते।
न च शक्नोम्य् अवस्थातुं भ्रमतीव च मे मनः॥

gāṇḍīvaṁ sraṁsate hastāt
tvak cāiva paridahyate
na ca śaknomy avasthātuṁ
bhramatīva ca me manaḥ

30. Gandiva (Arjuna's bow) falls from (my) hand, my skin burns, I am unable to remain as I am, and my mind seems to ramble.

196 See how my body trembles, my mouth is parched, and my limbs are weak.

197 My hair stands on end, I am feverish, and because of this distress I cannot hold my Gandiva bow.

198 I cannot hold onto it; it slips from my hand without my knowledge. My heart is weighed down with foolishness.

199 Although my heart is harder than a diamond, bold and courageous, this madness is even stronger.

200 Arjuna, who had conquered Shankar and had overcome the god of death, was immediately overwhelmed with confusion,

201 Just as a bee can easily pierce the hardest wood but may be caught in a tender bud;

202 There it may lose its life, for it does not

know how to tear apart the petals. Pity is like this, so soft and yet so hard.

203 Sanjaya said, Listen, O King! Affection is the illusion of the Supreme Being, and not even the creator himself can control it. This is the reason for Arjuna's confusion.

204 Listen, O King! When Arjuna saw all his friends and relatives, he forgot about the honor of battle.

205 I do not understand how such pity has arisen in Arjuna's heart. Then Arjuna said, O Krishna! It is not right for me to remain here.

206 My mind is completely bewildered, and my speech is confused at the thought of killing all these relatives of mine.

निमित्तानि च पश्यामि विपरीतानि केशव ।
न च श्रेयो ऽनुपश्यामि हत्वा स्वजनम् आहवे ।।
nimittāni ca paśyāmi
viparītāni keśava
na ca śreyo 'nupaśyāmi
hatvā svajanam āhave

31. I perceive inauspicious omens, O Krishna, and I foresee misfortune in destroying my own people in battle.

207 If the Kauravas must be killed, then why not kill Yudhishthira and those others? All of them are equally my relatives.

208 This war is shameful! I do not like it at all. What is the use of this evil?

209 O Lord, from every standpoint this battle is evil, so it would be an excellent thing to avoid it.

न काङ्क्षेविजयं कृष्ण न च राज्यं सुखानि च ।
किं नो राज्येन गोविन्द किं भोगैर् जीवितेन वा ।।
na kāṅkṣe vijayam kṛṣṇa
na ca rājyaṁ sukhāni ca
kiṁ no rājyena govinda
kiṁ bhogāir jīvitena vā

32. I do not desire victory, Krishna, nor kingship nor pleasures. What is kingship to us, Krishna? What are enjoyments, even life?

210 The desire for victory is nothing to me. What good would it do me to become a king?

येषाम् अर्थे काङ्क्षितं नो राज्यं भोगाः सुखानि च ।
त इमे ऽवस्थिता युद्धे प्राणांस् त्यक्त्वा धनानि च ।।
yeṣām arthe kāṅkṣitaṁ no
rājyaṁ bhogāḥ sukhāni ca
ta ime 'vasthitā yuddhe
prāṇāṅs tyaktvā dhanāni ca

33. Those for whose sake we desire kingship, enjoyments, and pleasures, they are arrayed here in battle, abandoning their lives and riches.

211 Take these pleasures, which can only be enjoyed by slaying these people. Arjuna spoke in this way.

212 I can bear anything except this kind of pleasure. I am even prepared to die.

213 My mind cannot entertain the thought, even in a dream, that we should kill these men and then enjoy the pleasures of a kingdom.

214 What good would it do us to have been born? For whom should we wish to live if our minds were to think evil of our elders?

215 Every family desires a son. Is destroying our families to be the fruit of it?

216 How can we hold such a thought in our minds, or speak with words as hard as diamonds? We should always seek their good.

217 These men should enjoy whatever we acquire in this world. Our lives should be spent in their interest.

218 We should overcome all the kings in the world to satisfy our families,

219 And here they stand before us. What strange turn of fate is this? They are standing here ready to fight with us.

220 They have left behind their wives, their children, and all their treasures, and have submitted their lives to weapons of destruction.

221 How can I kill them? With what weapons can I attack them? How can I strike at my own heart?

आचार्याः पितरः पुत्रास् तथैव च पितामहाः ।
मातुलाः श्वशुराः पौत्राः श्यालाः संबन्धिनस् तथा ।।
ācāryāḥ pitaraḥ putrās
tathāiva ca pitāmahāḥ
mātulāḥ śvaśurāḥ pāutrāḥ
śyālāḥ saṁbandhinas tathā

34. Teachers, fathers, sons, and also grandfathers, maternal uncles, fathers-in-law, grandsons, brothers-in-law, and other kinsmen.

222 Don't You know who they are? Over there are Bhishma and Drona, who have been so good to us,

223 Our brothers-in-law, fathers-in-law, uncles, sons, grandsons, and other relatives who are so dear to us.

224 Listen! These are all our close relatives. It is a sin even to speak of killing them.

एतान् न हन्तुम् इच्छामि घ्नतो ऽपि मधुसूदन ।
अपि त्रैलोक्यराज्यस्य हेतोः किं नु महीकृते ।।

etān na hantum icchāmi
ghnato 'pi madhusūdana
api trāilokyarājyasya
hetoḥ kiṁ nu mahīkṛte

35. I do not desire to kill them who are bent on killing, Krishna, even for the sovereignty of the three worlds. How much less then for the earth!

225 It would be better for them to perform any unworthy action and to kill us, than for me to think of killing them.
226 Even if I could attain undisputed sovereignty over all the three worlds, I could never commit such an evil action.

निहत्य धार्तराष्ट्रान् नः का प्रीतिः स्याज् जनार्दन ।
पापम् एवाश्रयेद् अस्मान् हत्वैतान् आततायिनः ।।

nihatya dhārtarāṣṭrān naḥ
kā prītiḥ syāj janārdana
pāpam evāśrayed asmān
hatvāitān ātatāyinaḥ

36. What joy would it be for us to strike down the sons of Dhritarashtra, O Krishna! Evil thus would cling to us, having killed these aggressors.

227 O Krishna, if I were to do this, who would have respect for me? And how could I look You in the face?
228 If I were to kill my relatives, I would become the abode of all sin. I would lose You, who have become so dear to me.
229 If I became burdened with the sins of destroying my family, how could I look at You?
230 Just as the cuckoo does not remain in a garden when it sees a fierce fire spreading there;
231 And when the chakora bird sees a lake full of mud, it abandons it and leaves;
232 Similarly, O Lord, if my righteousness were destroyed, Your love for me would vanish and You would desert me.

तस्मान् नार्हा वयं हन्तुं धार्तराष्ट्रान् स्वबान्धवान् ।
स्वजनं हि कथं हत्वा सुखिनः स्याम माधव ।।

tasmān nārhā vayaṁ hantuṁ
dhārtarāṣṭrān svabāndhavān
svajanam hi kathaṁ hatvā
sukhinaḥ syāma mādhava

37. Therefore we are not justified in killing the sons of Dhritarashtra, our own kinsmen. How, having killed our own people, could we be happy, Krishna!

233 Therefore, I will not do this, nor will I take a weapon in my hand in this battle, for it seems utterly contemptible to me.
234 If we were to lose You, what would become of us? Without You my heart would be broken with grief.
235 Arjuna said, It would be impossible for us to enjoy the reward if we destroyed these Kauravas.

यद्यप्येते न पश्यन्ति लोभोपहतचेतसः ।
कुलक्षयकृतं दोषं मित्रद्रोहे च पातकम् ।।

yadyapyete na paśyanti
lobhopahatacetasaḥ
kulakṣayakṛtaṁ doṣaṁ
mitradrohe ca pātakam

38. Even if those whose thoughts are overpowered by greed do not perceive the wrong caused by the destruction of the family, and the crime of treachery to friends,

कथं न ज्ञेयम् अस्माभिः पापाद् अस्मान् निवर्तितुम् ।
कुलक्षयकृतं दोषं प्रपश्यद्भिर् जनार्दन ।।

kathaṁ na jñeyam asmābhiḥ
pāpād asmān nivartitum
kulakṣayakṛtaṁ doṣaṁ
prapaśyadbhir janārdana

39. Why should we not know enough to turn back from this evil, through discernment of the wrong caused by the destruction of the family, O Krishna!

236 Even if these men, deluded by pride, have come to fight, we should recognize what is good for us.
237 If a lion suddenly appeared in our path, we would save our lives by avoiding it.
238 How can we do this and kill our relatives at the same time? Would we knowingly swallow deadly poison?
239 What do we gain, O Lord, if we abandon the light which we have and choose a pit of darkness?
240 If we found ourselves near a fire and made no effort to avoid it, we could be burned to death in an instant.
241 So knowing that we are approaching the very incarnation of sin, should we go forward into it?

कुलक्षये प्रणश्यन्ति कुलधर्माः सनातनाः ।
धर्मे नष्टे कुलं कृत्स्नम् अधर्मो ऽभिभवत्युत ।।

kulakṣaye praṇaśyanti
kuladharmāḥ sanātanāḥ
dharme naṣṭe kulaṁ kṛtsnam
adharmo 'bhibhavatyuta

40. In the destruction of the family, the ancient family laws vanish; when the law has perished, lawlessness overpowers the entire family also.

242 Just as when two pieces of wood are rubbed against each other fire is produced, and all the wood in the world can be burned up by it,
243 Similarly, if the members of a family kill one another out of spite, from that sin the whole family will perish.
244 Through this sin, all the dharma of the family is destroyed, and unrighteousness enters the family.

अधर्माभिभवात् कृष्ण प्रदुष्यन्ति कुलस्त्रियः ।
स्त्रीषु दुष्टासु वार्ष्णेय जायते वर्णसंकरः ॥
adharmābhibhavāt kṛṣṇa
praduṣyanti kulastriyaḥ
strīṣu duṣṭāsu vārṣṇeya
jāyate varṇasaṁkaraḥ

41. Because of the ascendancy of lawlessness, Krishna, the family women are corrupted; when women are corrupted, O Krishna, the intermixture of caste is born.

245 Then all considerations of right and wrong, the proper performance of duties, and all standards of conduct are ignored.
246 When a person's lamp is extinguished and he walks in the darkness, he is in danger of falling even though he may walk straight.
247 In the same way, if a family is destroyed, its dharma will be lost and nothing will remain.
248 When self-control is lacking, the senses run wild and the women of the family commit adultery.

संकरो नरकायैव कुलघ्नानां कुलस्य च ।
पतन्ति पितरो ह्येषां लुप्तपिण्डोदकक्रियाः ॥
saṁkaro narakāyāiva
kulaghnānāṁ kulasya ca
patanti pitaro hyeṣāṁ
luptapiṇḍodakakriyāḥ

42. Intermixture brings to hell the family destroyers and the family, too; the ancestors of these indeed fall, deprived of offerings of rice and water.

249 The noblest mix with the most vulgar, the castes mingle, and all the family traditions are destroyed.
250 If an offering of rice is thrown out on a public road, crows will fall on it from every side. Similarly, great sin enters into such a family.
251 Then the entire family and those who have destroyed it must descend into hell.
252 In this way the family will be degraded, and its ancestors in heaven will be drawn into hell.
253 When the daily and periodical duties are no longer performed, who is left to carry out the rites of the dead?
254 Then how is it possible for the ancestors to live in the heaven world? They will also have to enter hell along with the family.
255 When the tip of a person's finger is bitten by a serpent, his whole body soon becomes affected by the poison. Similarly, such a sin will overwhelm the whole family, even up to its origins in Brahma.

दोषैर् एतैः कुलघ्नानां वर्णसंकरकारकैः ।
उत्साद्यन्ते जातिधर्माः कुलधर्माश्च शाश्वताः ॥
doṣāir etāiḥ kulaghnānāṁ
varṇasaṁkarakārakāiḥ
utsādyante jātidharmāḥ
kuladharmāś ca śāśvatāḥ

43. By these wrongs of the family destroyers, producing intermixture of caste, caste duties are abolished, and eternal family laws also.

उत्सन्नकुलधर्माणां मनुष्याणां जनार्दन ।
नरके ऽनियतं वासो भवतीत्यनुशुश्रुम ॥
utsannakuladharmāṇāṁ
manuṣyāṇāṁ janārdana
narake 'niyataṁ vāso
bhavatītyanuśuśruma

44. Men whose family laws have been obliterated, O Krishna, dwell indefinitely in hell, thus we have heard repeatedly,

अहो बत महत् पापं कर्तुं व्यवसिता वयम् ।
यद् राज्यसुखलोभेन हन्तुं स्वजनम् उद्यताः ॥
aho bata mahat pāpaṁ
kartuṁ vyavasitā vayam
yad rājyasukhalobhena
hantuṁ svajanam udyatāḥ

45. Ah! Alas! We are resolved to do a great evil, which is to be intent on killing our own people, through greed for royal pleasures.

256 O Lord, listen to me. This great sin would be

contagious and corrupt all people.

257 If a fire should break out in one's house, others would also soon be enveloped in flames, and everything in the home would be burned.

258 Similarly, all others who come in contact with this family are attacked by troubles.

259 Arjuna said, Because of manifold sins the family will experience the deepest horrors of hell.

260 So abysmal is the ruin of the family, that once they fall into hell, they cannot escape from it, even at the end of a great age.

261 O Lord, one hears about this in various ways. Shouldn't it trouble us now? Please listen! Why are our hearts so hard?

262 Shouldn't we avoid this sin, realizing that the kingship we desire is only momentary?

263 Tell me, is it so small a sin to look at our elders with the idea of killing them?

यदि माम् अप्रतीकारम् अशस्त्रं शस्त्रपाणयः ।
धार्तराष्ट्रा रणे हन्युस् तन् मे क्षेमतरं भवेत् ॥

yadi mām apratīkāram
aśastraṁ śastrapāṇayaḥ
dhārtarāṣṭrā raṇe hanyus
tan me kṣemataraṁ bhavet

46. If the armed sons of Dhritarashtra should kill me in battle while I was unresisting and unarmed, this would be a greater happiness for me.

264 It would be far better for me to put down my weapon and be struck by their arrows than to live in this way.

265 Death itself would be more welcome. I cannot commit such a sin.

एवम् उक्त्वा ऽर्जुन संख्ये रथोपस्थ उपाविशत् ।
विसृज्य सशरं चापं शोकसंविग्नमानसः ॥

evam uktvā 'rjuna saṁkhye
rathopastha upāviśat
visṛjya saśaraṁ cāpaṁ
śokasaṁvignamānasaḥ

47. Thus having spoken on the battlefield, Arjuna sat down upon the seat of the chariot, throwing down both arrow and bow, with a heart overcome by sorrow.

266 Sanjaya said to Dhritarashtra, Arjuna spoke like this on the battlefield. Listen!

267 Arjuna was greatly dejected. He was choked with uncontrollable grief and jumped down from his chariot.

268 Just as a prince is distressed when he is deprived of his throne, or as the sun is bereft of its splendor when eclipsed by Rahu,

269 Or just as an ascetic, overcome by fascination with psychic powers, becomes helpless and dominated by desire,

270 In the same way, Arjuna was unnerved by grief when he abandoned his chariot.

271 Flinging away his bow and arrow, he wept in spite of himself. This is what happened, O King, said Sanjaya.

272 Now Lord Krishna, seeing Arjuna so dejected, explained to him the great truth.

273 Jnanadeva, the disciple of Nivritti, will tell this most interesting story in detail.

2

THE YOGA OF KNOWLEDGE

संजय उवाच । *sañjaya uvāca*

तं तथा कृपयाविष्टम् अश्रुपूर्णाकुलेक्षणम् ।
विषीदन्तम् इदं वाक्यम् उवाच मधुसूदनः ॥

taṁ tathā kṛpayāviṣṭam
aśrupūrṇākulekṣaṇam
viṣīdantam idaṁ vākyam
uvāca madhusūdanaḥ

Sanjaya spoke:
1. To him thus overcome by pity, despairing, whose eyes were filled with tears and downcast, Krishna spoke these words:

THEN Sanjaya said to the king, Listen, O King! Arjuna, overcome with grief, began to weep.
2 Seeing all his kinsmen before him, Arjuna was filled with deep affection, and his heart melted with pity. To what can it be compared?
3 His heart, though valiant, became tender, like salt dissolving in water or clouds driven by the wind.
4 Overcome by compassion, he seemed to wither like a swan caught in the mud.
5 Seeing Arjuna overcome with deep emotion, Lord Krishna said:

श्रीभगवान् उवाच । *śrībhagavān uvāca*

कुतस्त्वा कश्मलम् इदं विषमे समुपस्थितम् ।
अनार्यजुष्टम् अस्वर्ग्यम् अकीर्तिकरम् अर्जुन ॥

kutastvā kaśmalam idaṁ
viṣame samupasthitam
anāryajuṣṭam asvargyam
akīrtikaram arjuna

The Blessed Lord spoke:
2. Whence has this timidity of yours come to you in time of danger? It is not acceptable in you, does not lead to heaven, and causes disgrace, Arjuna.

6 O Arjuna, first consider if your behavior is proper in this place. Who are you? What are you doing?
7 What is the matter with you? What prevents you from acting? Why this grief?
8 Do not allow unworthy thoughts to enter your mind. Do not lose courage, for at the mention of your name, defeat would flee to the four quarters.
9 You are the incarnation of heroism, a prince among warriors. The fame of your might echoes throughout the three worlds.
10 Didn't you overcome Hara in battle? Didn't you slay the demons Nivatakavacha? Haven't you made the heavenly poets sing of your brave deeds?
11 When compared to you, the three worlds are insignificant, O Arjuna; so great is your valor.
12 In spite of this, today you weep, your head droops, and you abandon all your courage.
13 Consider this, O Arjuna. You are weakened by pity. Tell me, is the sun ever swallowed up by darkness?
14 Does the wind stand in terror of a cloud? Can nectar ever die? Is fire ever consumed by fuel?
15 Will salt ever dissolve water? Will the Kalakuta poison die from being touched? Will a small frog ever swallow a large serpent?
16 Has such a wonder ever happened that a jackal should fight against a lion? But your actions seem to indicate that these things

might really happen.

17 Therefore, O Arjuna, pay no attention to these unworthy thoughts. Wake up and take courage.

18 Rid yourself of this foolishness. Arise and take up your bow. Of what use is pity on the battlefield?

19 O Arjuna, you have wisdom. Why don't you reflect now? Is pity appropriate at the time of battle?

20 Lord Krishna said, This will mar your present fame and prevent you from entering heaven.

क्लैब्यं मा स्म गमः पार्थ नैतत् त्वय्युपपद्यते ।
क्षुद्रं हृदयदौर्बल्यं त्यक्त्वोत्तिष्ठ परंतप ॥

klāibyaṁ mā sma gamaḥ pārtha
nāitat tvayyupapadyate
kṣudraṁ hṛdayadāurbalyaṁ
tyaktvottiṣṭha paraṁtapa

3. Do not become a coward, Arjuna. This is not suitable to you. Abandoning base faintheartedness, stand up, Arjuna!

21 So, do not grieve, O Arjuna. Be full of courage and shake off this dejection.

22 This does not befit you. By this, all that you have acquired will be lost. Consider this.

23 At the hour of battle, pity is of no value. Have these men only now become your kinsmen?

24 Haven't you already known them as such? Haven't you recognized them as kinsmen? This excess of feeling is out of place.

25 Is today's battle a new thing in your life? In your race there is always some occasion for strife.

26 Then what has come over you today? Why has pity come to you? I do not know, O Arjuna, but you have acted wrongly.

27 If you hold onto this illusion, the reputation that you have will vanish, and then for you both heaven and earth will be lost.

28 Faintheartedness is never a sign of goodness; moreover, for a warrior it is the same as defeat in battle.

29 Thus, in various ways the most merciful Lord taught him. Hearing this, Arjuna spoke:

अर्जुन उवाच *arjuna uvāca*

कथं भीष्मम् अहं संख्ये द्रोणं च मधुसूदन ।
इषुभिः प्रतियोत्स्यामि पूजार्हावरिसूदन ॥

kathaṁ bhīṣmam ahaṁ saṁkhye
droṇaṁ ca madhusūdana
iṣubhiḥ pratiyotsyāmi
pūjārhāvarisūdana

Arjuna spoke:

4. How can I kill in battle Bhishma and Drona, O Krishna? How can I fight with arrows against these two venerable men, O Krishna?

30 O Lord! There is no need to say anymore. Listen! First consider this fight Yourself.

31 It is wrong to think of this as war; instead, it seems that a great crime is being committed. It has fallen to us to destroy our elders.

32 Look! Reverence is due to our parents, and our actions should please them. How can we slay them with our own hands?

33 O Lord! The saints and sages are worthy of our salutations. Whenever possible, we should worship them. How can we abuse them with our speech?

34 Likewise, we should show proper reverence to our family teachers. I am greatly indebted to Bhishma and Drona.

35 How can we slay them now, O Lord, when even in our dreams we have never harbored any spite against them?

36 What a wretched life! What fate has befallen all these people? Should we display our warriors' training by killing them?

37 I, Arjuna, was taught by Drona. It was he who instructed me in the science of archery. Shall I repay him by taking his life?

38 Am I the demon Bhasmasura, that I should betray one from whom I have received such kindness?

39 We are told that the sea is calm, and on the surface it appears to be so. And it seems that Drona's heart is never disturbed.

40 The sky appears to be boundless. Can it be measured? In the same way, Drona's heart is deep and unfathomable.

41 Nectar perhaps might be spoiled, and the force of time might break the thunderbolt, but nothing could ever shake his purpose.

42 There is no greater love than a mother's, but Drona is kindness incarnate.

43 Drona is the source of all compassion, the storehouse of all virtue, the boundless ocean of learning.

44 Therefore, we regard him as a great saint, and he is full of compassion for us. How then can we think of destroying him?

गुरून् अहत्वा हि महानुभावान् ।
श्रेयो भोक्तुं भैक्ष्यमपीह लोके
हत्वार्थकामांस् तु गुरूनिहैव
भुञ्जीय भोगान् रुधिरप्रदिग्धान् ॥

gurūn ahatvā hi mahānubhāvān
śreyo bhoktuṁ bhāikṣyamapīha loke
hatvārthakāmāṅs tu gurūn ihāiva
bhuñjīya bhogān rudhirapradigdhān

5. Indeed, instead of slaying these noble gurus it would be preferable to live on alms here on earth; having slain the gurus, with desire for worldly gain, I would enjoy here on earth delights smeared with blood.

45 I cannot find it in my heart to slay such men in battle and then enjoy a kingdom.
46 It would be far better to go begging for alms than to enjoy even more unattainable things than this.
47 I will not take up a weapon against them. It would be better to leave my country or to retire into solitude in the mountains.
48 Shall we drown in blood by shooting sharp arrows into their hearts to win the pleasure of kingship?
49 Having won it, what should we do then? How could we enjoy such tainted pleasures? I cannot accept this proposal.

न चैतद् विद्मः कतरन् नो गरीयो
यद् वा जयेम यदि वा नो जयेयुः ।
यान् एव हत्वा न जिजीविषामस्
तेऽवस्थिताः प्रमुखे धार्तराष्ट्राः

na cāitad vidmaḥ kataran no garīyo
yad vā jayema yadi vā no jayeyuḥ
yān eva hatvā na jijīviṣāmas
te 'vasthitāḥ pramukhe dhārtarāṣṭrāḥ

6. And this we do not know: which for us is preferable, whether we should conquer them or they should conquer us. The sons of Dhritarashtra, having killed whom we would not wish to live, are standing before us.

50 Arjuna said, O Krishna, listen! But hearing Arjuna's words, Krishna was not pleased.
51 Realizing this, Arjuna was afraid. Again he said, O Lord, why do You not listen to my words?
52 I have expressed what is in my mind, but You know best what is right.
53 These men are arrayed here for battle. If we engage in conflict with them, we must be ready to die.
54 Should we slay them or immediately abandon the battlefield? We don't know which course of action is better.

कार्पण्यदोषोपहतस्वभावः
पृच्छामि त्वां धर्मसंमूढचेताः ।
यच्छ्रेयः स्यान् निश्चितं ब्रूहि तन् मे
शिष्यस् तेऽहं शाधि मां त्वां प्रपन्नम् ॥

kārpaṇyadoṣopahataṣvabhāvaḥ
pṛcchāmi tvāṁ dharmasaṁmūḍhacetāḥ
yacchreyaḥ syān niścitaṁ brūhi tan me
śiṣyas te 'haṁ śādhi māṁ tvāṁ prapannam

7. My own being is overcome by pity and weakness. My mind is confused as to my duty. I ask you which is preferable, for certain? Tell that to me, your pupil. Correct me, I beg of you.

55 I feel confused when I wonder what is proper for us, and my mind is distracted because of this confusion.
56 When darkness pervades all space, one's vision is dimmed, and then even things which are near are invisible.
57 O Lord! I am in a predicament, for a mind overcome with confusion cannot understand where its own good lies.
58 Therefore, O Krishna, You know everything and should tell us what is right, for You are our friend and are everything to us.
59 You are truly our teacher, brother, and father. You are our chosen deity. You alone are our protector in time of difficulty.
60 The Guru never forsakes his disciples. The sea never refuses the water of a river.
61 How could a child live, having been abandoned by its mother? O Krishna, listen!
62 O Lord, You are everything to us. We have no one but You. If what I have already said displeases You,

न हि प्रपश्यामि ममापनुद्याद्
यच्छोकम् उच्छोषणम् इन्द्रियाणाम् ।
अवाप्य भूमावसपत्नमृद्ध
राज्यं सुराणाम् अपि चाधिपत्यम् ॥

na hi prapaśyāmi mamāpanudyād
yacchokam ucchoṣaṇam indriyāṇām
avāpya bhūmāvasapatnaṁ ṛddhaṁ
rājyaṁ surāṇām api cādhipatyam

8. Indeed, I do not see what will dispel this sorrow of mine which dries up my senses, even if I should obtain on earth unrivaled and prosperous royal power, or even the sovereignty of the gods.

63 Tell us quickly what is appropriate for us, O

Krishna, and how we may not fail to perform our duty.

64 The grief that has arisen in my heart at the sight of my kinsmen cannot be removed except by Your words.

65 Even if I should obtain the whole earth and gain the sovereignty of Indra, the doubt in my mind could not be resolved.

66 Just as seeds which have been roasted can never germinate, even though they may be sown in the richest soil and plentifully watered;

67 Or just as when a person's days are numbered, no medicine can have any effect, for only the purest nectar would be of any use;

68 Similarly, none of the pleasures of a kingdom can entice me at all. O Krishna, Your compassion alone is my support.

69 Arjuna spoke in this way, and for a short time his confusion disappeared, but then a fresh wave of distraction overwhelmed him.

70 It seemed to me that there was really no wave; it was something else. He was swallowed up by the great serpent of infatuation,

71 Which, at the most intense moment of his pity, attacked his innermost heart. Thus, the waves of grief would not subside.

72 Realizing the force of this, Lord Krishna, who with a mere glance can destroy poison, hastened towards him like a snake charmer.

73 Krishna was near Arjuna when he was suffering in this way, and by the power of His grace He would protect him.

74 With this in mind, I said that Arjuna was attacked by the serpent of infatuation.

75 Here was Arjuna overcome by infatuation, just as the sun is at times overshadowed by a mass of clouds.

76 Like a mountain consumed by fire in summer, Arjuna was afflicted with grief.

77 Then Lord Krishna turned towards him, like a cloud of deep blue, moist with the nectar of kindness, and spoke to him.

78 The brilliance of His glance was like flashing lightning, and His deep speech was like the roar of thunder.

79 That generous cloud will now send down such a shower of rain that Arjuna, like a mountain, will cool down and the green shoots of knowledge will begin to burst forth.

80 Jnanadeva, the disciple of Nivritti, says: Listen with full attention to this story.

संजय उवाच । *sañjaya uvāca*

एवम् उक्त्वा हृषीकेशं गुडाकेशः परंतप ।
न योत्स्य इति गोविन्दम् उक्त्वा तूष्णीं बभूव ह ॥

evam uktvā hṛṣīkeśaṁ
guḍākeśaḥ paraṁtapa
na yotsya iti govindam
uktvā tūṣṇīṁ babhūva ha

Sanjaya spoke:
9. Thus having addressed Krishna, Arjuna said, "I shall not fight," and having spoken, he became silent.

81 While narrating this, Sanjaya said, O King, what did Arjuna, again overcome with grief, say?

82 Listen. He sorrowfully said to Lord Krishna, "I will not fight. Do not try to persuade me."

83 With these words, he suddenly fell silent. Lord Krishna was astonished to see him in such a condition.

तम् उवाच हृषीकेशः प्रहसन्न् इव भारत ।
सेनयोर् उभयोर् मध्ये विषीदन्तम् इदं वचः ॥
tam uvāca hṛṣīkeśaḥ
prahasann iva bhārata
senayor ubhayor madhye
viṣīdantam idaṁ vacaḥ

10. To him, the dejected Arjuna, Krishna, beginning to laugh, O Dhritarashtra, in the middle between the two armies, spoke these words:

84 He said to Himself, What is he thinking of? Arjuna is quite ignorant. What can be done?

85 How can he be brought back to his senses? How can he be made to take heart? Just as an exorcist considers how to cast out an evil spirit,

86 Or just as a physician who finds someone suffering from a dangerous illness, as the crisis approaches, instantly prescribes a magic remedy like nectar,

87 Similarly, between the two armies, Krishna reflected on how Arjuna could cast off his infatuation.

88 Having decided what to do, He began to speak in an angry tone, just as a mother's love is often concealed in her anger.

89 The potency of nectar is hidden in the bitter taste of medicine. Even though it is not outwardly visible, it is revealed by the effectiveness of the medicine.

90 In the same way, Krishna spoke to Arjuna

with words which, though seemingly bitter, were actually very sweet.

श्रीभगवान् उवाच । *śrībhagavān uvāca*

अशोच्यान् अन्वशोचस् त्वं प्रज्ञावादांश्च भाषसे ।
गतासून् अगतासूंश्च नानुशोचन्ति पण्डिताः ।।

aśocyān anvaśocas tvaṁ
prajñāvādāṅś ca bhāṣase
gatāsūn agatāsūṅś ca
nānuśocanti paṇḍitāḥ

The Blessed Lord spoke:
11. You have mourned those that should not be mourned, and yet you speak words as if with wisdom; the wise do not mourn for the dead or for the living.

91 Then He said to Arjuna, I am astonished at what you have said in the midst of all this.
92 You pretend to be wise, and yet you do not give up your ignorance. You wish to be taught, and yet you talk too much.
93 Your wisdom is like that of a man who, having been born blind, afterwards loses his reason and wanders here and there.
94 You are utterly ignorant of yourself, and yet you are ready to grieve for these Kauravas. This constantly surprises Me.
95 O Arjuna, tell Me if you believe that the three worlds owe their existence to you. Isn't it true that the universe is without beginning?
96 Is it wrong to say that there is only one Supreme Being from whom all creatures emanate?
97 Do you think that you have created this life? Is it true that you destroy all who die?
98 Through the blindness of egoism, are you saying that these men are immortal because you have not thought of killing them?
99 You are allowing confusion to enter your mind when you think that you are the one who destroys and that those men are the ones who perish.
100 All this has existed from beginningless time. It is born and it dies according to its own nature. Tell me then why you should grieve.
101 It is ignorance that causes you to believe in this way. You shouldn't have this wrong kind of understanding; yet you speak to Me of morality!
102 The wise grieve neither for the living nor the dead, whether they live or pass away.

न त्वेवाहं जातु नासं न त्वं नेमे जनाधिपाः ।
न चैव न भविष्यामः सर्वे वयम् अतः परम् ।।

na tvevāhaṁ jātu nāsaṁ
na tvaṁ neme janādhipāḥ
na cāiva na bhaviṣyāmaḥ
sarve vayam ataḥ param

12. Truly there was never a time when I was not, nor you, nor these lords of men; and neither will there be a time when we shall cease to be from this time onward.

103 O Arjuna, listen to what I tell you. Here are you and I and these kings and all others.
104 Such ideas, that we remain forever or that we perish, cannot remain when examined without confusion.
105 The idea that things can be born or die is only an illusion. In reality, matter is indestructible.
106 When the surface of water is agitated by the wind, waves appear on it; yet who can say what it is that is born and from where?
107 Similarly, when the wind ceases to blow and the surface of the water once more becomes calm, consider this: what is it that has died?

देहिनो ऽस्मिन् यथा देहे कौमारं यौवनं जरा ।
तथा देहान्तरप्राप्तिर् धीरस् तत्र न मुह्यति ।।

dehino 'smin yathā dehe
kāumāraṁ yāuvanaṁ jarā
tathā dehāntaraprāptir
dhīras tatra na muhyati

13. Just as in the body childhood, adulthood, and old age happen to an embodied being, so also he (the embodied being) acquires another body. The wise one is not deluded about this.

108 Moreover, there is only one body that passes through all the different stages of life. Surely this is evident.
109 You experience childhood, then in adolescence it vanishes. Yet the body does not perish with each stage.
110 However, physical bodies eventually die. One who knows this is not disturbed by any grief arising from mental confusion.

मात्रास्पर्शास् तु कौन्तेय शीतोष्णसुखदुःखदाः ।
आगमापायिनो ऽनित्यास् तांस् तितिक्षस्व भारत ।।

mātrāsparśās tu kāunteya
śītoṣṇasukhaduḥkhadāḥ
āgamāpāyino 'nityās
tāṅs titikṣasva bhārata

14. Physical sensations, truly, Arjuna, causing cold, heat, pleasure, or pain, come and go and are impermanent. So manage to endure them, Arjuna.

111 A person fails to understand this because of the domination of the senses. The heart is in their power, and so it is confused.
112 Objects are enjoyed through the senses, and from the senses joy and grief arise. Because of this contact the mind is plunged into confusion.
113 The effects of sense objects are not uniform; sometimes pain is the result, sometimes pleasure.
114 Listen! Both praise and blame are associated with the realm of words. When they are heard, they give rise to love or hate.
115 Softness and hardness are both qualities experienced by touch. When the body feels them, they cause pleasure or pain.
116 Form may be ugly or beautiful, and through the eye they produce dislike or delight.
117 Fragrance and stench are different odors, and through the sense of smell they arouse satisfaction or disgust.
118 Likewise, taste is manifold and produces likes and dislikes. The contact with sense objects is, therefore, the cause of corruption.
119 If one gives in to the desires of the senses, one feels heat and cold and is caught up in pleasure and pain.
120 It is the nature of the senses to find nothing more attractive than sense objects.
121 But what is the true nature of these objects? They are like the water of a mirage, or like an elephant seen in a dream.
122 Like these, they are ephemeral, so reject them, O Arjuna. Don't let yourself be affected by contact with them.

यं हि न व्यथयन्त्येते पुरुषं पुरुषर्षभ ।
समदुःखसुखं धीरं सो ऽमृतत्वाय कल्पते ॥

yaṁ hi na vyathayantyete
puruṣaṁ puruṣarṣabha
samaduḥkhasukhaṁ dhīraṁ
so 'mṛtatvāya kalpate

15. Indeed, the man whom these (i.e the sensations) do not afflict, O Arjuna, the wise one, to whom happiness and unhappiness are the same, is ready for immortality.

123 The person who is not bound by these objects is not affected by pleasure or pain, and for him there is no need for rebirth.
124 O Arjuna! You should understand that a person who does not fall into their power is truly immortal.

नासतो विद्यते भावो नाभावो विद्यते सतः ।
उभयोर् अपि दृष्टो ऽन्तस् त्वनयोस्तत्त्वदर्शिभिः ॥

nāsato vidyate bhāvo
nābhāvo vidyate sataḥ
ubhayor api dṛṣṭo 'ntas
tvanayor tattvadarśibhiḥ

16. It is found that the unreal has no being; it is found that there is no non-being of the real. The certainty of both these propositions is indeed surely seen by the perceivers of truth.

125 Now listen, Arjuna. I will tell you something else. Wise men understand this:
126 Within this body dwells the same Consciousness which pervades all things. Philosophers accept this.
127 When milk is mixed with water it becomes one with it; still, it can be separated by the royal swans.
128 Through fire the alloy mixed with gold is burned out, and those who have the knowledge can extract the pure gold.
129 When milk is churned by those who know how, butter finally appears.
130 When grain and chaff are winnowed together, the husks are blown away and the heavy grain is left.
131 Similarly, when this is properly understood, the outer visible world vanishes, and for the wise only God remains.
132 They do not consider that impermanent things are real, for they have realized the Truth.

अविनाशि तु तद् विद्धि येन सर्वम् इदं ततम् ।
विनाशम् अव्ययस्यास्य न कश्चित् कर्तुम् अर्हति ॥

avināśi tu tad viddhi
yena sarvam idaṁ tatam
vināśam avyayasyāsya
na kaścit kartum arhati

17. Know that that by which all this universe is pervaded is indeed indestructible; no one is able to accomplish the destruction of the imperishable.

133 Considering the real and the unreal, you will see that the unreal is illusory while the real is eternal.
134 That which has manifested the three worlds

has neither name, color, form, nor sign.
135 It is eternal, all-pervasive, and beyond the reach of birth and death. No one can ever destroy It, no matter how much he may try.

अन्तवन्त इमे देहा नित्यस्योक्ताः शरीरिणः ।
अनाशिनोऽप्रमेयस्य तस्माद् युध्यस्व भारत ॥
antavanta ime dehā
nityasyoktāḥ śarīriṇaḥ
anāśino 'prameyasya
tasmād yudhyasva bhārata

18. These bodies inhabited by the eternal, the indestructible, the immeasurable embodied Self, are said to come to an end. Therefore fight, Arjuna!

136 All bodies are destructible by nature. Therefore, fight, O Arjuna.

य एनं वेत्ति हन्तारं यश्चैनं मन्यते हतम् ।
उभौ तौ न विजानीतो नायं हन्ति न हन्यते ॥
ya enaṁ vetti hantāraṁ
yaścāinaṁ manyate hatam
ubhāu tāu na vijānīto
nāyaṁ hanti na hanyate

19. He who imagines this (the embodied Self) the slayer and he who imagines this (the embodied Self) the slain, neither of them understands this (the embodied Self) does not slay, nor is it slain.

137 With pride in your form, having thought only of your body, you say, "I am the killer, and these are the ones who die."
138 But you don't understand, O Arjuna. If you think in terms of reality, you are not the slayer, nor can these be slain.

न जायते म्रियते वा कदाचिन्
नायं भूत्वा भविता वा न भूयः ।
अजो नित्यः शाश्वतोऽयं पुराणो
न हन्यते हन्यमाने शरीरे ॥
na jāyate mriyate vā kadācin
nāyaṁ bhūtvā bhavitā vā na bhūyaḥ
ajo nityaḥ śāśvato 'yaṁ purāṇo
na hanyate hanyamāne śarīre

20. Neither is this (the embodied Self) born nor does it die at any time, nor, having been, will it again come not to be. Birthless, eternal, perpetual, primeval, it is not slain when the body is slain.

139 Whatever is seen in a dream appears to be real at the time, but when remembered on waking it has no reality.
140 Similarly, know that this is an illusion, and your confusion, therefore, is vain. A shadow cut with a weapon is not wounded.
141 When a pot of water is turned upside down, the surface can no longer reflect the sun. Nevertheless, the sun is not destroyed with the reflection.
142 The air inside a house seems to have the shape of the house, but if the house is torn down, the air resumes its natural form.

वेदाविनाशिनं नित्यं य एनम् अजम् अव्ययम् ।
कथं स पुरुषः पार्थ कं घातयति हन्ति कम् ॥
vedāvināśinaṁ nityaṁ
ya enam ajam avyayam
kathaṁ sa puruṣaḥ pārtha
kaṁ ghātayati hanti kam

21. He who knows this, the indestructible, the eternal, the birthless, the imperishable, in what way does this man cause to be slain, Arjuna? Whom does he slay?

143 Similarly, though the body may die, the Self does not. Therefore, O Beloved, do not cling to this delusion.

वासांसि जीर्णानि यथा विहाय
नवानि गृह्णाति नरोऽपराणि ।
तथा शरीराणि विहाय जीर्णान्य्
अन्यानि संयाति नवानि देही ॥
vāsāṁsi jīrṇāni yathā vihāya
navāni gṛhṇāti naro 'parāṇi
tathā śarīrāṇi vihāya jīrṇāny
anyāni saṁyāti navāni dehī

22. As, after casting away worn out garments, a man later takes new ones, so, after casting away worn out bodies, the embodied Self encounters other, new ones.

144 Just as a person puts on a new garment, in the same way, the Self takes on a new body.

नैनं छिन्दन्ति शस्त्राणि नैनं दहति पावकः ।
न चैनं क्लेदयन्त्यापो न शोषयति मारुतः ॥
nāinaṁ chindanti śastrāṇi
nāinaṁ dahati pāvakaḥ
na cāinaṁ kledayantyāpo
na śoṣayati mārutaḥ

23. Weapons do not pierce this (the embodied Self), fire does not burn this, water does not wet this, nor does the wind cause it to wither.

अच्छेद्योऽयम् अदाह्योऽयम् अक्लेद्योऽशोष्य एव च ।
नित्यः सर्वगतः स्थाणुर् अचलोऽयं सनातनः ॥
acchedyo 'yam adāhyo 'yam
akledyo 'śoṣya eva ca

nityaḥ sarvagataḥ sthāṇur
acalo 'yaṁ sanātanaḥ

24. This cannot be pierced, burned, wetted or withered; this is eternal, all pervading, fixed; this is unmoving and primeval.

145 It is eternal, pure, without beginning or limitation. It cannot be cut by any weapon.
146 It cannot be submerged by the final deluge, fire can never consume it, and even the strongest winds cannot wither it.
147 O Arjuna, this is not visible to the eye of reason, but meditation eagerly reaches out for it.

अव्यक्तो ऽयम् अचिन्त्यो ऽयम् अविकार्यो ऽयम् उच्यते ।
तस्माद् एवं विदित्वैनं नानुशोचितुम् अर्हसि ॥
avyakto 'yam acintyo 'yam
avikāryo 'yam ucyate
tasmād evaṁ viditvāinaṁ
nānuśocitum arhasi

25. It is said that this is unmanifest, unthinkable, and unchanging. Therefore, having understood in this way, you should not mourn.

148 He is ever inaccessible to the mind, and He is not attainable by any special practices. O Arjuna, this Supreme Being is immeasurable.
149 O Arjuna, He is everlasting, immovable, all-pervasive, and eternally perfect.
150 He transcends the three qualities, is beyond form, without source or change, and all-pervasive.
151 O Arjuna, know Him in this way and see Him as the Self of all. Then all your grief will pass away.

अथ चैनं नित्यजातं नित्यं वा मन्यसे मृतम् ।
तथापि त्वं महाबाहो नैनं शोचितुमर्हसि ॥
atha cāinaṁ nityajātaṁ
nityaṁ vā manyase mṛtam
tathāpi tvaṁ mahābāho
nāinaṁ śocitumarhasi

26. And moreover even if you think this to be eternally born or eternally dead, even then you should not mourn for this, Arjuna.

152 Even if you don't believe this and think that the Self is subject to death, still you should not grieve, O Arjuna.
153 For birth, life, and dissolution follow one another in eternal progression, like the ceaseless flow of the river Ganges.
154 At its source it never fails, it is always flowing into the ocean, and in the middle of its course it also flows continuously.
155 It passes through these three stages in succession, and no creature can ever arrest its flow.
156 Therefore, you should not grieve for these warriors, for these conditions have been the same throughout all time.
157 If you don't agree, O Arjuna, seeing that people are subject to birth and death,
158 Even then there is no cause for you to grieve, for birth and death are inevitable.

जातस्य हि ध्रुवो मृत्युर् ध्रुवं जन्म मृतस्य च ।
तस्मादपरिहार्ये ऽर्थे न त्वं शोचितुमर्हसि ॥
jātasya hi dhruvo mṛtyur
dhruvaṁ janma mṛtasya ca
tasmādaparihārye 'rthe
na tvaṁ śocitumarhasi

27. For the born, death is certain; for the dead there is certainly birth. Therefore, for this, inevitable in consequence, you should not mourn.

159 What is born dies, and what dies is born again. Like the wheels of a water clock, this cycle continues.
160 Just as sunrise and sunset follow each other, in this world birth and death are certain.
161 At the time of the great dissolution, even the three worlds perish, so birth and death are inevitable.
162 If you believe this, then why do you grieve, O Arjuna? Knowing this, why should you profess ignorance?

अव्यक्तादीनि भूतानि व्यक्तमध्यानि भारत ।
अव्यक्तनिधानान्येव तत्र का परिदेवना ॥
avyaktādīni bhūtāni
vyaktamadhyāni bhārata
avyaktanidhanānyeva
tatra kā paridevanā

28. Beings are such that their beginnings are unmanifest, their middles are manifest, and their ends are unmanifest again. What complaint can there be over this?

163 Moreover, O Arjuna, there is absolutely no reason for grief.
164 All these beings are formless before birth. When born, they take on individual form.
165 After the dissolution of their bodies, they do not exist separately but revert to their original state.

166 The life in between is like a dream to a sleeping person. Likewise, the appearance of form in the Self is due to the power of cosmic illusion.
167 When water is agitated by the wind, it appears in the form of ripples. Gold is fashioned in the shape of ornaments according to a person's desire.
168 Similarly, all that has form is the result of illusion, like the clouds which appear in the sky. You should realize this.
169 Why then do you grieve for something that is not subject to birth? Consider instead the Self which never fades away.

आश्चर्यवत् पश्यति कश्चिदेनम्
आश्चर्यवद् वदति तथैव चान्यः।
आश्चर्यवच्चैनम् अन्यः शृणोति
श्रुत्वाप्येनं वेद न चैव कश्चित्॥

āścaryavat paśyati kaścidenam
āścaryavad vadati tathāiva cānyaḥ
āścaryavaccāinam anyaḥ śṛṇoti
śrutvāpyenaṁ veda na cāiva kaścit

29. Someone perceives this as a wonder, another declares this as a wonder, still another hears of this as a wonder; but even having heard of this, no one knows it.

170 When the saints experience longing for the Self, they renounce all desire, become dispassionate, and retire into the wilderness.
171 When the great sages saw It, they observed vows of celibacy and practiced austerities.
172 Some, while singing Its praises with detached minds, become wholly absorbed in It.
173 Others, with a steadfast heart, at the sight of It forget all worldly activities.
174 Some, hearing of It, lose all consciousness of their bodies. Others attain union with It through direct experience.
175 Just as the currents of all rivers reach the ocean and never flow back again,
176 In the same way, the minds of the masters of yoga, once turned towards the Self become merged in It. Through the power of thought, they do not experience rebirth.

देही नित्यं अवध्यो ऽयं देहे सर्वस्य भारत।
तस्मात् सर्वाणि भूतानि न त्वं शोचितुमर्हसि॥

dehī nityaṁ avadhyo 'yaṁ
dehe sarvasya bhārata
tasmāt sarvāṇi bhūtāni
na tvaṁ śocitumarhasi

30. This, the embodied Self, is eternally indestructible in the body of all, Arjuna. Therefore you should not mourn for any being.

177 Listen! That which is everywhere and in everyone is the one life infusing the whole universe. Though it may be threatened, it cannot be killed.
178 Because of the nature of this, everything is born and dies. Then what can cause you to grieve?
179 O Arjuna, I cannot understand why you cannot accept this. Moreover, grief does not suit you.

स्वधर्मम् अपि चावेक्ष्य न विकम्पितुम् अर्हसि।
धर्म्याद् धि युद्धाच्छ्रेयो ऽन्यत् क्षत्रियस्य न विद्यते॥

svadharmam api cāvekṣya
na vikampitum arhasi
dharmyād dhi yuddhācchreyo 'nyat
ksatriyasya na vidyate

31. And, perceiving your own caste duty, you should not tremble. Indeed, anything superior to righteous battle does not exist for the kshatriya (man of warrior caste).

180 Why don't you consider this? What are you thinking? You have forgotten your duty which is your path to salvation.
181 If any calamity were to befall the Kauravas, if any mishap were to overtake you, or if the great age were to come to an end now,
182 Even then you must never abandon your own sacred duty. Can you save yourself by compassion?
183 O Arjuna! Your heart has melted with pity, but this is out of place on the battlefield.
184 Cow's milk must not be given to a person who has a fever, or it will act as a poison.
185 In the same way, if action is not suitable to the occasion, it is harmful to a person's welfare. So arouse yourself.
186 Why do you grieve without reason? Attend to your duty. If you follow it, no evil will ever befall you.
187 If a person stays on the road, he remains safe. If he carries a lamp, he doesn't stumble
188 So, O Arjuna, when a person observes his duty, all his desires are easily fulfilled.
189 You should know, then, that nothing is more worthy of a warrior than fighting.
190 Free your mind of deception and fight blow for blow. Why should I speak you you about what is obvious?

यदृच्छया चोपपन्नं स्वर्गद्वारम् अपावृतम् ।
सुखिनः क्षत्रियाः पार्थ लभन्ते युद्धम् ईदृशम् ॥

yadṛcchayā copapannaṁ
svargadvāram apāvṛtam
sukhinaḥ kṣatriyāḥ pārtha
labhante yuddham īdṛśam

32. And if by good fortune they gain the open gate of heaven, happy are the kshatriyas, Arjuna, when they encounter such a fight.

191 O Arjuna, consider this war; it is truly fortunate for you. Perhaps it reveals the calling of your entire life.
192 Should it be called a battle? Or has heaven become manifest in this form, revealed by your valor?
193 Or has fame herself, attracted by your qualities and filled with passion, come to choose you as her lord?
194 A warrior who has acquired great merit, and who has such an opportunity for battle, is like a person who has found a wish-fulfilling gem in his path.
195 You are confronted with this battle, like a yawning man into whose mouth nectar unexpectedly drops.

अथ चेत् त्वम् इमं धर्म्यं संग्रामं न करिष्यसि ।
ततः स्वधर्मं कीर्तिं च हित्वा पापम् अवाप्स्यसि ॥

atha cet tvam imaṁ dharmyaṁ
saṁgrāmaṁ na kariṣyasi
tataḥ svadharmaṁ kīrtiṁca
hitvā pāpam avāpsyasi

33. Now, if you will not undertake this righteous war, thereupon, having avoided your own duty and glory, you shall incur evil.

196 If you avoid this war and grieve unnecessarily, you will only harm yourself.
197 If you throw away your weapon in this battle today, you will certainly lose all that your forefathers have gained.
198 Then your present fame will be lost, the world will curse you, and great sins will find you.
199 Just as a woman without a husband is scorned everywhere, so is the state of a person who has abandoned his duty.
200 Just as a corpse thrown out on waste land is attacked on all sides by vultures, a person who fails to perform his duty will be surrounded by great sin.
201 Therefore, if you abandon your duty you will incur guilt, and you will be dishonored until the end of the age.

अकीर्तिं चापि भूतानि कथयिष्यन्ति तेऽव्ययाम् ।
संभावितस्य चाकीर्तिर् मरणाद् अतिरिच्यते ॥

akīrtiṁ cāpi bhūtāni
kathayiṣyanti te 'vyayām
saṁbhāvitasya cākīrtir
maraṇād atiricyate

34. And also people will relate your undying infamy; and, for one who has been honored, disgrace is worse than dying.

202 A wise man should wish to live as long as he is not stained by dishonor. How then can you escape from here?
203 Being free from malice and full of compassion, you may perhaps turn back, but others will not approve of your action.
204 They will attack you on every side and will shoot arrows at you. You will not escape because of your compassion.
205 Even if you are able to escape such dangers to your life, existence will be worse than death for you.

भयाद् रणाद् उपरतं मंस्यन्ते त्वां महारथाः
येषां च त्वं वहुमतो भूत्वा यास्यसि लाघवम् ॥

bhayād raṇād uparataṁ
maṅsyante tvāṁ mahārathāḥ
yeṣāṁ ca tvaṁ bahumato
bhūtvā yāsyasi lāghavam

35. The great warriors will think that you have abstained from the battle through fear, and among those by whom you have been held in high esteem you shall come to be held lightly.

206 There is one other matter which you have not considered. You have come here eager to fight, and if through compassion you should return,
207 Tell me, is it likely that your enemies will understand this?
208 They will say, "Arjuna has gone! He is afraid of us!" Would such slander please you?
209 Men make great efforts and even sacrifice their lives, O Arjuna, and they increase their good name.
210 Your fame has been easily won. It is unbroken and as incomparable as the heavens.
211 Your fame is without limit or equal, and your merit is the finest in all three worlds.
212 The princes of all countries are the poets

who chant your praises. At this, even the heart of the god of death trembles with fear.

213 Your renown, which is as clear as the waters of the Ganges, is so great that the sight of it has astonished the foremost warriors of the earth.

214 Hearing of your marvelous valor, they have come here in despair of their lives.

215 Just as the roar of a lion seems as terrible as death to a raging elephant, so are you a terror to the Kauraṿas.

216 Just as mountains fear the thunderbolt, and as serpents dread the eagle, so do all of these regard you, O Arjuna.

217 If you should now turn back without fighting, you will lose all your greatness and will become worthless.

अवाच्यवादांश्च बहून् वदिष्यन्ति तवाहिताः ।
निन्दन्तस् तव सामर्थ्यं ततो दुःखतरं तु किम् ॥
avācyavādāṅśca bahūn
vadiṣyanti tavāhitāḥ
nindantas tava sāmarthyaṁ
tato duḥkhataraṁ tu kim

36. And your enemies will speak many words of you that should not be spoken, deriding your capacity. What greater hardship is there than that?

218 Your enemies will prevent you from fleeing; they will surround and hold you. Despising you, they will utter abuse for you yourself to hear.

219 Then your heart will break. Why shouldn't you fight bravely now? If you conquer your opponents, you will enjoy the whole earth.

हतो वा प्राप्स्यसि स्वर्गं जित्वा वा भोक्ष्यसे महीम् ।
तस्माद् उत्तिष्ठ कौन्तेय युद्धाय कृतनिश्चयः ॥
hato vā prāpsyasi svargaṁ
jitvā vā bhokṣyase mahīm
tasmād uttiṣṭha kāunteya
yuddhāya kṛtaniścayaḥ

37. Either, having been slain, you shall attain heaven, or, having conquered, you shall enjoy the earth. Therefore stand up, Arjuna, resolved to fight.

220 If you fight in the battle and lose your life, you will enjoy heavenly bliss.

221 Therefore, O Arjuna, pay no attention to these thoughts. Stand up and seize your bow, ready to fight.

222 Look! By fulfilling your duty, you destroy sin. What is this confusion in your mind about sin?

223 Does a person drown in a boat, or stumble on the highway? Calamity may befall one who doesn't know how to walk.

224 A person can even die from drinking nectar if he takes poison with it. Similarly, sin can arise from performing one's duty with the wrong motive.

225 Therefore, O Arjuna, there is no sin against your duty as a warrior in fighting without a selfish motive.

सुखदुःखे समे कृत्वा लाभालाभौ जयाजयौ ।
ततो युद्धाय युज्यस्व नैवं पापम् अवाप्स्यसि ॥
sukhaduḥkhe same kṛtvā
lābhālābhāu jayājayāu
tato yuddhāya yujyasva
nāivaṁ pāpam avāpsyasi

38. Holding pleasure and pain to be alike, likewise gain and loss, victory and defeat, then engage in battle! Thus you shall not incur evil.

226 Do not delight in happiness, do not be downcast in pain, and do not be concerned with gain or loss.

227 You should not consider thoughts of the future, such as whether you will win a victory or lose your life.

228 A person should perform his own proper duty, and whatever may come, he should endure it with a steady mind.

229 When the mind is in this state, naturally no sin is incurred. Therefore, fight with confidence.

एषा ते ऽभिहिता सांख्ये बुद्धिर् योगे त्विमां शृणु ।
बुद्ध्या युक्तो यया पार्थ कर्मबन्धं प्रहास्यसि ॥
eṣā te 'bhihitā sāṁkhye
buddhir yoge tvimāṁ śṛṇu
buddhyā yukto yayā pārtha
karmabandhaṁ prahāsyasi

39. This (insight) is wisdom, as declared in the theory of Sankhya; now hear it as applied in arduous practice; yoked with this determination, Arjuna, you shall rid yourself of the bondage of karma.

230 This path of wisdom has been briefly explained to you. Now listen to the explanation of the path of union through reason.

231 O Arjuna, a person who is utterly detached while performing actions cannot be troubled by the bonds of action.

नेहाभिक्रमनाशो ऽस्ति प्रत्यवायो न विद्यते ।
स्वल्पम् अप्य् अस्य धर्मस्य त्रायते महतो भयात् ।।
nehābhikramanāśo 'sti
pratyavāyo na vidyate
svalpam apy asya dharmasya
trāyate mahato bhayāt

40. Here (in the yoga doctrine of practice) no effort is lost, nor is any loss of progress found. Even a little of this discipline protects one from great danger.

232 Similarly, when a person is wearing impenetrable armor, he can endure the attack of any weapon and remain unharmed and victorious.

233 He doesn't lose his life in this world and still attains liberation when he faithfully follows this path.

234 Continue all prescribed actions, but don't desire their fruit. Just as an exorcist cannot be harmed by an evil spirit,

235 Similarly, when a person has attained full enlightenment, the limitation of matter cannot bind him.

236 That wisdom which is subtle and steady, in which sin has no place, and which contact with the three qualities cannot contaminate,

237 O Arjuna, if your heart, through merit, should be illumined even a little by such wisdom, then every fear of life in this world would be removed.

व्यवसायात्मिका बुद्धिर् एकेह कुरुनन्दन ।
बहुशाखा ह्यनन्ताश्च बुद्धयो ऽव्यवसायिनाम् ।।
vyavasāyātmikā buddhir
ekeha kurunandana
bahuśākhā hyanantāś ca
buddhayo 'vyavasāyinām

41. Here there is a single resolute understanding, Arjuna. The thoughts of the irresolute have many branches and are, indeed, endless.

238 Just as the flame of a lamp, however small, sheds great light, so this wisdom should not be despised.

239 O Arjuna, the true desire for this wisdom is rare in this world, but many learned men seek it.

240 Just as the touchstone is rarely found, in comparison with other objects, and just as it is only through good fortune that one finds even a drop of nectar,

241 Similarly, it is difficult to attain wisdom. Just as the ocean is forever the goal of the Ganges, the goal of this wisdom is the highest Self.

242 Look, O Arjuna! There is only one wisdom in the world, and it dwells only in the Supreme.

243 All other forms of enlightenment are evil. They are for the most part full of passion, and only the thoughtless indulge in them.

244 They experience existence, heaven, and hell, O Arjuna. They never find the bliss of Self-realization.

याम् इमां पुष्पितां वाचं प्रवदन्त्यविपश्चितः ।
वेदवादरताः पार्थ नान्यद् अस्तीति वादिनः ।।
yām imāṁ puṣpitāṁ vācaṁ
pravadantyavipaścitaḥ
vedavādaratāḥ pārtha
nānyad astīti vādinaḥ

42. The ignorant ones proclaim this flowery discourse, Arjuna, delighting in the letter of the Veda and saying, "There is nothing else."

245 They speak with the authority of the Vedas, teaching only action, and with desire for the fruit of action.

246 They say, "We must be born in this world and perform sacrificial rites in order to enjoy heavenly pleasures."

247 O Arjuna, such people of faulty logic say, "Beyond desire there is no happiness in the universe."

कामात्मानः स्वर्गपरा जन्मकर्मफलप्रदाम् ।
क्रियाविशेषबहुलां भोगैश्वर्यगतिं प्रति ।।
kāmātmānaḥ svargaparā
janmakarmaphalapradām
kriyāviśeṣabahulāṁ
bhogāiśvaryagatiṁ prati

43. Full of desires, intent on heaven, they offer rebirth as the fruit of action, and are addicted to many specific rites aimed at the goal of enjoyment and power.

भोगैश्वर्यप्रसक्तानां तयापहृतचेतसाम् ।
व्यवसायात्मिका बुद्धिःसमाधौ न विधीयते ।।
bhogāiśvaryaprasaktānāṁ
tayāpahṛtacetasām
vyavasāyātmikā buddhiḥ
samādhāu na vidhīyate

44. To those (the ignorant ones) attached to enjoyment and power, whose thought is stolen away by this kind of talk, resolute

insight in meditation is not granted.

248 Such people, overcome by desire, perform action with their hearts set only on the enjoyment of pleasure.

249 They perform many ceremonies, omitting no rites, and carry out their religious duties with great care.

250 They are at fault in one thing only: they set their hearts on the desire for heaven, and so lose sight of the Lord of sacrifices, the true enjoyer.

251 It is as though camphor were heaped up and set on fire, or rich dishes were mixed with poison;

252 Or as though a vessel full of nectar, found by good luck, were kicked over. In the same way, these people destroy any merit they may gain by their desire for the fruit of action.

253 People should strive for merit with great effort. Why should they long for earthly existence? But if they lack wisdom and do not know this, what can help them?

254 Just as a cook might prepare choice dishes and then sell them for money, similarly, the unenlightened throw away merit for the sake of enjoyment.

255 Understand, O Arjuna, that evil tendencies fill the minds of those who indulge in controversies about the Vedas.

त्रैगुण्यविषया वेदा निस्त्रैगुण्यो भवार्जुन ।
निर्द्वन्द्वो नित्यसत्त्वस्थो निर्योगक्षेम आत्मवान् ॥

trāiguṇyaviṣayā vedā
nistrāiguṇyo bhavārjuna
nirdvandvo nityasattvastho
niryogakṣema ātmavān

45. The Vedas are such that their scope is confined to the three qualities; be free from those three qualities, Arjuna, indifferent toward the pairs of opposites, eternally fixed in truth, free from thoughts of acquisition and comfort, and possessed of the Self.

256 Know for certain that the Vedas are pervaded by the three qualities. The Upanishads are pure;

257 Everything else which describes the performance of action and which teaches that heaven is the only goal, is enveloped in passion and ignorance.

258 Understand that this leads only to pleasure and pain; do not set your heart on it.

259 Reject all thought of the three qualities, do not speak in terms of "me" and "mine," and hold only the bliss of the Self in your heart.

यावानर्थ उदपाने सर्वतः संप्लुतोदके ।
तावान्सर्वेषु वेदेषु ब्राह्मणस्य विजानतः ॥

yāvān artha udapāne
sarvataḥ saṁplutodake
tāvān sarveṣu vedeṣu
brāhmaṇasya vijānataḥ

46. As much value as there is in a well when water is flooding on every side, so much is the value in all the Vedas for a brahman who knows.

260 Though much is said in the Vedas and various distinctions are suggested, still we should only accept what is for our good.

261 When the sun has risen all paths become visible. Yet, tell me, is it possible to travel by all of them?

262 Even if the earth's surface is flooded with water, we drink only enough to quench our thirst.

263 Similarly, the wise examine the meaning of the Vedas and accept only what has to do with the eternal.

कर्मण्येवाधिकारस्ते मा फलेषु कदाचन ।
मा कर्मफलहेतुर् भूर् मा ते सङ्गो ऽस्त्व् अकर्मणि ॥

karmaṇyevādhikāraste
mā phaleṣu kadācana
mā karmaphalahetur bhūr
mā te saṅgo 'stv akarmaṇi

47. Your right is to action alone; never to its fruits at any time. Never should the fruits of action be your motive; never let there be attachment to inaction in you.

264 Listen, O Arjuna. When you understand things in this way, it is best for you to perform your own duty.

265 When we have taken all things into consideration, we realize that we should never neglect our appointed duty.

266 But do not desire the fruit of action, and avoid action which is prohibited. Perform right action with no thought for the result.

योगस्थः कुरु कर्माणि सङ्गं त्यक्त्वा धनंजय ।
सिद्ध्यसिद्ध्योः समो भूत्वा समत्वं योग उच्यते ॥

yogasthaḥ kuru karmāṇi
saṅgaṁ tyaktvā dhanaṁjaya
siddhyasiddhyoḥ samo bhūtvā
samatvaṁ yoga ucyate

48. Fixed in yoga, perform actions, having abandoned attachment, Arjuna, and having become indifferent to success or failure. It is said that evenness of mind is yoga.

267 Perform all your actions with an attentive mind, O Arjuna, steadfast in yoga and renouncing attachment to the fruit of action.
268 Do not rejoice unduly if by good fortune you successfully accomplish something.
269 And if for any reason you are prevented from completing an action, you should not be disappointed.
270 If it meets with success, well and good. If it cannot be completed, even so regard it as good.
271 If you offer to God every action that you undertake, know that it will surely be accomplished.
272 Such even-mindedness in action whether right or wrong is the state of yoga, which is highly esteemed by the best of people.

दूरेण ह्यवरं कर्म बुद्धियोगाद् धनंजय ।
बुद्धौ शरणम् अन्विच्छ कृपणाः फलहेतवः ॥
dūreṇa hyavaraṁ karma
buddhiyogād dhanaṁjaya
buddhāu śaraṇam anviccha
kṛpaṇāḥ phalahetavaḥ

49. Action is inferior by far to the yoga of wisdom, Arjuna. Seek refuge in wisdom! Despicable are those whose motives are based on the fruit of action.

बुद्धियुक्तो जहातीह उभे सुकृतदुष्कृते ।
तस्माद् योगाय युज्यस्व योगः कर्मसु कौशलम् ॥
buddhiyukto jahātīha
ubhe sukṛtaduṣkṛte
tasmād yogāya yujyasva
yogaḥ karmasu kāuśalam

50. He whose wisdom is established casts off, here in the world, both good and evil actions; therefore devote yourself to yoga! Yoga is skill in action.

273 O Arjuna, an evenly balanced mind is the essence of yoga, in which the mind and pure intelligence are united.
274 When we consider this yoga of pure intelligence, the yoga of action with attachment seems to be inferior, O Arjuna.
275 But this yoga of pure intelligence can be attained only when the yoga of action is practiced, for action that is performed after the desire for its fruit is renounced naturally leads to evenness of mind.
276 Therefore, the yoga of pure intelligence is steady, O Arjuna. Concentrate on it, and relinquish any desire for the fruit of action.
277 Those who have practiced this yoga have reached the other shore and have freed themselves from the bondage of sin and merit.

कर्मजं बुद्धियुक्ता हि फलं त्यक्त्वा मनीषिणः ।
जन्मबन्धविनिर्मुक्ताः पदं गच्छन्त्य् अनामयम् ॥
karmajaṁ buddhiyuktā hi
phalaṁ tyaktvā manīṣiṇaḥ
janmabandhavinirmuktāḥ
padam gacchanty anāmayam

51. Those who are established in wisdom, the wise ones, who have abandoned the fruit born of action, and are freed from the bondage of rebirth, go to the place that is free from pain.

278 They perform action, but they are not bound by it. In this way, O Arjuna, they are freed from the cycle of birth and death.
279 Then, those who are united with pure Consciousness reach the unshakable state of perfection.

यदा ते मोहकलिलं बुद्धिर् व्यतितरिष्यति ।
तदा गन्तासि निर्वेदं श्रोतव्यस्य श्रुतस्य च ॥
yadā te mohakalilaṁ
buddhir vyatitariṣyati
tadā gantāsi nirvedaṁ
śrotavyasya śrutasya ca

52. When your intellect crosses beyond the thicket of delusion, then you shall become disgusted with that which is yet to be heard and with that which has been heard (in the Veda).

280 When you have thrown off this delusion, you will become like them and non-attachment will pervade your mind.
281 Having acquired a profound and perfect knowledge of the Self, your mind will easily become detached.
282 Then, O Arjuna, all need to know anything else or to recall any past knowledge will disappear.

श्रुतिविप्रतिपन्ना ते यदा स्थास्यति निश्चला ।
समाधावचलाबुद्धिस् तदा योगम् अवाप्स्यसि ॥
śrutivipratipannā te
yadā sthāsyati niścalā
samādhāvacalābuddhis
tadā yogam avāpsyasi

53. When your intellect stands fixed in deep

meditation, unmoving, disregarding Vedic doctrine, then you shall attain Self-realization.

283 Your mind, which was previously distracted by the activity of the senses, will stand as it was before, firmly established in the Self.
284 When the mind has become steady in the joy of contemplation, then you will attain the state of complete union.

अर्जुन उवाच । *arjuna uvāca*

स्थितप्रज्ञस्य का भाषा समाधिस्थस्य केशव ।
स्थितधीः किं प्रभाषेत किम् आसीत व्रजेत किम् ॥
sthitaprajñasya kā bhāṣā
samādhisthasya keśava
sthitadhīḥ kiṁ prabhāṣeta
kim āsīta vrajeta kim

Arjuna spoke:
54. How does one describe him who is of steady wisdom, who is steadfast in deep meditation, Krishna? How does he who is steady in wisdom speak? How does he sit? How does he move?

285 Arjuna said, O Lord, please explain to me the meaning of all this.
286 Krishna replied, O Arjuna, ask me with an open heart whatever you wish.
287 Then Arjuna said to Lord Krishna, Tell me who is a person with a stable mind and how he can be recognized?
288 Who is called even-minded? What are the characteristics of one who enjoys the bliss of contemplation?
289 In what state does he live? What does he look like? O Krishna, tell me all this.

श्रीभगवान् उवाच । *śrībhagavān uvāca*

प्रजहाति यदा कामान् सर्वान् पार्थ मनोगतान् ।
आत्मन्येवात्मना तुष्टः स्थितप्रज्ञस्तदोच्यते ॥
prajahāti yadā kāmān
sarvān pārtha manogatān
ātmanyevātmanā tuṣṭaḥ
sthitaprajñastadocyate

The Blessed Lord spoke:
55. When he leaves behind all desires emerging from the mind, Arjuna, and is contented in the Self by the Self, then he is said to be one whose wisdom is steady.

290 Then what did Lord Krishna, the incarnation of the highest Self and the abode of the six qualities, say?
291 He said, Listen, O Arjuna! All the strong desires of the heart are obstacles to the experience of the highest bliss.
292 He whose heart is always satisfied in the Self, who has renounced all desire,
293 And whose mind rests in the joy of the Self, know that such a person is even–minded.

दुःखेष्वनुद्विग्नमनाः सुखेषु विगतस्पृहः ।
वीतरागभयक्रोधः स्थितधीर् मुनिर् उच्यते ॥
duḥkheṣvanudvignamanāḥ
sukheṣu vigataspṛhaḥ
vītarāgabhayakrodhaḥ
sthitadhīr munir ucyate

56. He whose mind is not agitated in misfortune, whose desire for pleasures has disappeared, whose passion, fear, and anger have departed, and whose meditation is steady, is said to be a sage.

294 A person whose mind is not disturbed though he may suffer pain, who is not troubled by the desire for pleasure,
295 Into whose mind desire and anger do not enter, and who knows no fear, is perfect, O Arjuna.
296 The sage who is beyond limitation and without earthly bondage or a sense of difference should be known as one of steady wisdom.

यः सर्वत्रानभिस्नेहस् तत्तत् प्राप्य शुभाशुभम् ।
नाभिनन्दति न द्वेष्टि तस्य प्रज्ञा प्रतिष्ठिता ॥
yaḥ sarvatrānabhisnehas
tattat prāpya śubhāśubham
nābhinandati na dveṣṭi
tasya prajñā pratiṣṭhitā

57. He who is without attachment on all sides, encountering this or that, pleasant or unpleasant, neither rejoicing nor disliking; his wisdom stands firm.

297 He is always the same everywhere, just as when the moon sheds her light she does not say, "This is good," or "That is bad."
298 Similarly, his even-mindedness is unbroken, he has compassion for all creatures, and his mind is never subject to change.
299 A person who is not overjoyed when he receives something good and is not distressed when evil comes to him,
300 Know that he is even-minded, free from joy and sorrow, and filled with the enlightenment of the Self, O Arjuna.

यदा संहरते चायं कूर्मो ऽङ्गानीव सर्वशः ।
इन्द्रियाणीन्द्रियार्थेभ्यस् तस्य प्रज्ञा प्रतिष्ठिता ॥
yadā saṁharate cāyaṁ

kūrmo 'ṅgānīva sarvaśaḥ
indriyāṇīndriyārthebhyas
tasya prajñā pratiṣṭhitā

58. And when he withdraws completely the senses from the objects of the senses, as a tortoise withdraws its limbs into its shell, his wisdom stands firm.

301 Listen, Arjuna, there is one more thing I will tell you. There are some seekers who resolutely give up the pleasure of the senses.
302 Just as a tortoise may extend its limbs or withdraw them at will,

विषया विनिवर्तन्ते निराहारस्य देहिनः ।
रसवर्जं रसो ऽप्यस्य परं दृष्ट्वा निवर्तते ॥
viṣayā vinivartante
nirāhārasya dehinaḥ
rasavarjaṁ raso 'pyasya
paraṁ dṛṣṭvā nivartate

59. Sense objects turn away from the abstinent man, but the taste for them remains; but the taste also turns away from him who has seen the Supreme.

303 So is the understanding of the even-minded person, whose senses are under his control and act according to his bidding.
304 Those who subdue their hearing and their other senses, yet do not control the taste for them, are consequently bound by them in a thousand ways.
305 If the upper leaves of a tree are plucked off and yet the tree is watered at the roots, how can it be destroyed?
306 Just as the tree branches out luxuriantly due to the power of the water, in the same way, attachment to sense objects is nourished in the mind through a taste for them.
307 The other senses can be separated from their objects, but taste cannot easily be controlled, for no living thing can exist without it.
308 However, O Arjuna, when a person experiences the state of union with the Supreme, he is easily able to control these desires.
309 When a person realizes that he and the Supreme are one, the awareness of bodily feelings ceases, and the senses forget their objects.

यततो ह्यपि कौन्तेय पुरुषस्य विपश्चितः ।
इन्द्रियाणि प्रमाथीनि हरन्ति प्रसभं मनः ॥
yatato hyapi kāunteya
puruṣasya vipaścitaḥ
indriyāṇi pramāthīni
haranti prasabhaṁ manaḥ

60. The turbulent senses carry away forcibly the mind, Arjuna, even of the striving man of wisdom.

310 Moreover, O Arjuna, even those who ceaselessly strive to curb their senses are not always successful.
311 Those who dwell where yoga is practiced, who build walls of mental control around themselves, and who keep a firm grip on their minds,
312 Even they are tormented. So great is the power of the senses that even a knower of incantations may be deceived by an evil spirit.
313 It is like this with sense objects which are disguised as psychic powers. In contact with the senses they ensnare the mind.
314 When this happens the mind goes astray, and the practice of control is crippled. Such is the strength of the senses.

तानि सर्वाणि संयम्य युक्त आसीत मत्परः ।
वशे हि यस्येन्द्रियाणि तस्य प्रज्ञा प्रतिष्ठिता ॥
tāni sarvāṇi saṁyamya
yukta āsīta matparaḥ
vaśe hi yasyendriyāṇi
tasya prajñā pratiṣṭhitā

61. Restraining all these senses, disciplined, he should sit, intent on Me; he whose senses are controlled, his wisdom stands firm.

315 Listen, O Arjuna! Whoever abandons attachment to all sense pleasures and destroys their power,
316 Is known to be steadfast in yoga. His mind is not deluded by pleasure,
317 He is always full of the knowledge of the Self, and he never forgets Me in his heart.
318 On the other hand, earthly existence never comes to an end for a person who outwardly gives up sense objects but dwells upon them in his heart.
319 Just as when a person takes a drop of poison, its effect increases and inevitably destroys his life,
320 Similarly, if even a doubt about sense objects remains in the mind, it may destroy all understanding.

ध्यायतो विषयान् पुंसः सङ्गस् तेषूपजायते ।
सङ्गात् संजायते कामः कामात् क्रोधो ऽभिजायते ॥
dhyāyato viṣayān puṁsaḥ
saṅgas teṣūpajāyate

saṅgāt saṁjāyate kāmaḥ
kāmāt krodho 'bhijāyate

62. For a man dwelling on the objects of the senses, an attachment to them is born; from attachment, desire is born; from desire, anger is born;

क्रोधाद् भवति संमोहः संमोहात् स्मृतिविभ्रमः ।
स्मृतिभ्रंशाद् बुद्धिनाशो बुद्धिनाशात् प्रणश्यति ॥
krodhād bhavati saṁmohaḥ
saṁmohāt smṛtivibhramaḥ
smṛtibhraṁśād buddhināśo
buddhināśāt praṇaśyati

63. From anger arises delusion; from delusion, loss of the memory; from loss of the memory, destruction of discrimination; from destruction of discrimination one is lost.

321 If a person dwells on sense objects in his mind, then attachment will arise within detachment. In attachment there is the image of desire.
322 Where there is desire, anger has first been present, and in anger there has been delusion.
323 When delusion appears, memory will be lost, just as a flame is extinguished by a gust of wind.
324 Then, blinded by ignorance, a person loses everything and the pure reason in his mind is confused.
325 Just as at sunset the night envelops the light of the sun, so is a person's condition when his memory fails.
326 When a blind man has to run, he rushes pitifully here and there. In the same way, pure wisdom becomes bewildered, O Arjuna.
327 When memory is confused, reason is entirely defeated and all knowledge is destroyed.
328 Just as the body is reduced to a wretched condition when consciousness fails, so is the state of a person who loses his reason.
329 Listen, O Arjuna! Just as a spark set to fuel bursts into flame and could set fire to the three worlds,
330 Similarly, thinking about sense objects, even unwittingly, leads to great loss.

रागद्वेषवियुक्तस्तु विषयान् इन्द्रियैश्चरन् ।
आत्मवश्यैर् विधेयात्मा प्रसादम् अधिगच्छति ॥
rāgadveṣaviyuktas tu
viṣayān indriyāiścaran
ātmavaśyāir vidheyātmā
prasādam adhigacchati

64. With the elimination of desire and hatred, even though moving among the objects of the senses, he who is controlled by the Self, by self-restraint, attains tranquility.

331 If all sense objects are entirely driven from the mind, attachment and aversion will automatically perish.
332 O Arjuna, there is one more thing. If attachment and aversion die out, no harm can follow even when the senses are interested in sense objects.
333 Just as the sun in the sky is not contaminated by the earth which it touches with its rays,
334 So is one who is indifferent to sense pleasures, free from desire and anger, and filled with the bliss of the Self.
335 When he sees only himself in the universe, how can sense pleasures disturb him?
336 If water could be drowned in water, or fire burned by fire, then the perfect man might be affected by contact with sense objects.
337 He steadily becomes one with everything, so his understanding is well balanced. Believe that this is true.

प्रसादे सर्वदुःखानां हानिर् अस्योपजायते ।
प्रसन्नचेतसो ह्याशु बुद्धिः पर्यवतिष्ठते ॥
prasāde sarvaduḥkhānāṁ
hānir asyopajāyate
prasannacetaso hyāśu
buddhiḥ paryavatiṣṭhate

65. In tranquility the cessation of all sorrows is born for him. Indeed, for the tranquil-minded the intellect at once becomes steady.

338 When the heart is always at peace, the miseries of worldly existence cannot enter it.
339 If a person contains with himself a fountain of nectar, he is not troubled by hunger or thirst.
340 Similarly, if the heart is peaceful, where can a place be found for pain? The mind naturally dwells in the highest Self.
341 Just as a flame in a windless place will not flicker, similarly, the even-minded person remains united with the Self.

नास्ति बुद्धिर् अयुक्तस्य न चायुक्तस्य भावना ।
न चाभावयतः शान्तिर् अशान्तस्य कुतः सुखम् ॥
nāsti buddhir ayuktasya

na cāyuktasya bhāvanā
na cābhāvayataḥ śāntir
aśāntasya kutaḥ sukham

66. There is no wisdom in him who is uncontrolled, and there is likewise no concentration in him who is uncontrolled, and in him who does not concentrate, there is no peace. How can there be happiness for him who is not peaceful?

342 He who does not reflect on this union in his heart is bound by sense objects and their qualities.

343 For him, O Arjuna, steady wisdom is impossible, and even a longing for it never arises in him.

344 If there is no stability in the mind, O Arjuna, how can it be at peace?

345 Where there is no center of peace, bliss can never enter even unintentionally. Salvation is not for the sinner.

346 If seeds could germinate after being thrown into the fire, then happiness might come to a person without peace.

347 The unharmonized state of the heart is the cause of all pain, so it is essential to control the senses.

इद्रियाणां हि चरतां यन् मनो ऽनुविधीयते ।
तदस्य हरति प्रज्ञां वायुर् नावम् इवाम्भसि ॥
indriyāṇāṁ hi caratāṁ
yan mano 'nuvidhīyate
tadasya harati prajñāṁ
vāyur nāvam ivāmbhasi

67. When the mind runs after the wandering senses, then it carries away one's understanding, as the wind carries away a ship on the waters.

348 Those people whose actions follow the bidding of the senses do not cross over the ocean of worldly life, though they may seem to do so.

349 When a boat has arrived at the shore, a storm may still arise and destroy it.

350 Similarly, even if a person who has attained this state indulges in sense pleasures, he is overcome by the pain of worldly life.

तस्माद् यस्य महाबाहो निगृहीतानि सर्वशः ।
इन्द्रियाणीन्द्रियार्थेभ्यस् तस्य प्रज्ञा प्रतिष्ठिता ॥
tasmād yasya mahābāho
nigṛhītāni sarvaśaḥ
indriyāṇīndriyārthebhyas
tasya prajñā pratiṣṭhitā

68. Therefore, O Arjuna, the wisdom of him whose senses are withdrawn from the objects of the senses; that wisdom stands firm.

351 Therefore, O Arjuna, what greater goal is there than keeping the senses under control?

352 A person whose senses are obedient to his command has reached a state of wisdom.

353 Now, O Arjuna, there is still one more subtle characteristic of the perfect man, which I will tell you. Listen!

या निशा सर्वभूतानां तस्यां जागर्ति संयमी ।
यस्यां जाग्रति भूतानि सा निशा पश्यतो मुनेः ॥
yā niśā sarvabhūtānāṁ
tasyāṁ jāgarti saṁyamī
yasyāṁ jāgrati bhūtāni
sā niśā paśyato muneḥ

69. The man of restraint is awake in that which is night for all beings; the time in which all beings are awake is night for the sage who sees.

354 A person who remains conscious when all other beings are asleep, and is apparently asleep when others are awake,

355 He alone is beyond limitation, well balanced, and a lord among sages.

आपूर्यमाणम् अचलप्रतिष्ठं
समुद्रम् आपः प्रविशन्ति यद्वत् ।
तद्वत् कामा यं प्रविशन्ति सर्वे
स शान्तिम् आप्नोति न कामकामी ॥
āpūryamaṇam acalapratiṣṭhaṁ
samudram āpaḥ praviśanti yadvat
tadvat kāmā yaṁ praviśanti sarve
sa śāntim āpnoti na kāmakāmī

70. Like the ocean, which becomes filled yet remains unmoved and stands still as the waters enter it, he whom all desires enter and who remains unmoved attains peace; not so the man who is full of desire.

356 O Arjuna, he may be recognized by one further characteristic. Listen to it. Just as the ocean is continuously calm,

357 Even though all rivers flow into it, filling it to the full, it neither increases nor does it pass beyond its boundaries.

358 In the summer, O Arjuna, if all the rivers were to dry up, even then the ocean would not decrease.

359 Similarly, even if the perfect man should acquire psychic powers, he would not be

disturbed by them, nor would he be discouraged if he did not gain them.

360 Tell me, is any light needed in the house of the sun? Would it be enveloped in darkness if no lamp were placed there?

361 Similarly, whether or not he acquires psychic powers, he is unaware of them, for he is absorbed in the highest bliss.

362 How can a person who considers Indra's heaven to be poor enjoy living in a hut in the forest?

363 One who finds fault with nectar will not drink porridge. In the same way, one who has experienced the bliss of the Self takes no interest in psychic powers.

364 How surprising this is, O Arjuna! When even the bliss of heaven is considered to be of little value, are psychic powers of any significance?

विहाय कामान् यः सर्वान् पुमांश्चरति निःस्पृहः ।
निर्ममो निरहंकारः स शान्तिम् अधिगच्छति ।।

vihāya kāmān yaḥ sarvān
pumāṅścarati niḥspṛhaḥ
nirmamo nirahaṁkāraḥ
sa śāntim adhigacchati

71. The man who abandons all desires acts free from longing. Indifferent to possessions, free from egotism, he attains peace.

365 You may know that a person who takes delight in the bliss of the Self and who feeds on the highest joy is well balanced in his understanding.

366 Overcoming all egoism, abandoning all desires, he moves through the universe, for he himself has become the universe.

एषा ब्राह्मी स्थितिः पार्थ नैनां प्राप्य विमुह्यति ।
स्थित्वा ऽस्याम् अन्तकाले ऽपि ब्रह्मनिर्वाणम् ऋच्छति ।।

eṣā brāhmī sthitiḥ pārtha
nāināṁ prāpya vimuhyati
sthivā 'syām antakāle 'pi
brahmanirvāṇam ṛcchati

72. This is the divine state, Arjuna. Having attained this, he is not deluded; fixed in it, even at the hour of death, he reaches the bliss of God.

367 This is the limitless, divine state enjoyed by those whose desires are dead. They easily reach union with the highest Self.

368 The pain of death has no power to disturb the mind of such an enlightened being when he reaches the state of union with divine wisdom.

369 This is the state about which Krishna told Arjuna, said Sanjaya.

370 Hearing these words of Krishna, Arjuna thought, "This teaching which I have heard is good.

371 The Lord has forbidden all action, so I am forbidden to fight."

372 Arjuna was inwardly delighted with these words of Lord Krishna. Still in doubt, he will now ask further questions.

373 Such an occasion should be highly esteemed, for it is the storehouse of all duty, the boundless ocean of the nectar of pure wisdom.

374 Krishna, Lord of the enlightened, will Himself explain all this. Jnanadeva, disciple of Nivritti, will comment on it.

3

THE YOGA OF ACTION

अर्जुन उवाच। *arjuna uvāca*

ज्यायसी चेत् कर्मणस् ते मता बुद्धिर्जनार्दन।
तत्किं कर्मणि घोरे मां नियोजयसि केशव॥

jyāyasī cet karmaṇas te
matā buddhirjanārdana
tatkiṁ karmaṇi ghore māṁ
niyojayasi keśava

Arjuna spoke:
1. If it is Your conviction that knowledge is better than action, O Krishna, then why do You urge me to engage in this terrible action?

ARJUNA said, O Lord! I have listened to Your words attentively.

2 O Krishna, it appears from them that action and agent no longer exist. If this is Your definite opinion,

3 Then why, O Lord, do You call on me to fight? Aren't You ashamed to incite me to carry out this terrible action?

4 You condemn all action, and then do You urge me to cause this destruction?

5 O Krishna, consider this: You approve of the cessation of action and yet, at the same time, You command me to kill.

व्यामिश्रेणेव वाक्येन बुद्धिं मोहयसीव मे।
तद् एकं वद निश्चित्य येन श्रेयो ऽहम् आप्नुयाम्॥

vyāmiśreṇeva vākyena
buddhiṁ mohayasīva me
tad ekaṁ vada niścitya
yena śreyo 'ham āpnuyām

2. With speech that seems equivocal, You confuse my intelligence. Tell me surely this one thing: how should I attain the highest good?

6 O Lord! Even if You should advise us in this way, what should we ignorant people do? Would this be the end of all discrimination?

7 If this is really Your teaching, what can false teaching be like? Now all our eagerness for knowledge of the divine is truly finished.

8 If a physician were to prescribe a healing diet and then himself give poison, tell me, how could the patient live?

9 This advice which You have given us is like setting a blind man on the wrong road, or giving an intoxicating drink to a monkey.

10 In the first place I am ignorant, and then I am completely confused. O Krishna, that is why I have asked for Your guidance.

11 How strange are Your ways! There is confusion in Your teaching. Should You behave like this towards a disciple?

12 With my body, mind, and soul, I ought to place confidence in Your words; but if You behave like this, then everything is finished.

13 If You're giving me advice like this, then You'll really be uplifting me! How is there any hope of gaining knowledge?

14 Not only is there nothing new to learn, but still greater harm has been done. My mind, which was steady, has become disturbed.

15 Besides, O Krishna, I cannot understand Your ways. Do You want to test my mind under this pretext?

16 Are You deceiving me, or does Your teaching have a hidden implication? When I consider it, I truly cannot understand.

17 So listen, O Lord. Do not speak of such deep meaning. Tell me those things in Marathi.

18 My understanding is truly very dull, but I will listen well, O Krishna. Speak with certainty.

19 If a disease is to be cured, medicine must be

given, but it should be sweet and palatable.
20 These truths, which are so full of meaning, should be properly told, but in a way that will enlighten my mind.
21 O Lord! You are my own teacher! Then why shouldn't You grant my desire? Why should I stand in awe of anyone? You are our mother!
22 If through good fortune someone were to obtain the milk of the cow who satisfies all desires, why should he hesitate to ask for what he wants?
23 If the wish-fulfilling gem were to fall into his hand, why shouldn't he express his wishes? Why shouldn't he ask for what pleases him?
24 If a person were to reach the ocean of nectar and then suffer from thirst, why should he have taken the trouble to reach it?
25 Similarly, O Krishna, if having worshiped You for many lifetimes it is now my good fortune to have found You,
26 Then, O highest Lord, why shouldn't I ask You for what I want? What a rich harvest there is now for my mind!
27 Today my desires have been fulfilled, my merit has borne fruit, and all my longings have been crowned with success.
28 You who are the abode of all auspiciousness, the Lord of all the gods, have now become mine.
29 Just as there is no time when a child may not nurse at its mother's breast,
30 So, O Lord, I will ask You whatever I wish, if it pleases You.
31 Tell me clearly what I should do, and what will be beneficial to me later.

श्रीभगवान् उवाच। *śrībhagavān uvāca*

लोके ऽस्मिन् द्विविधा निष्ठा पुरा प्रोक्ता मया ऽनघ।
ज्ञानयोगेन सांख्यानां कर्मयोगेन योगिनाम्॥

loke 'smin dvividhā niṣṭhā
purā proktā mayā 'nagha
jñānayogena sāṁkhyānāṁ
karmayogena yoginām

The Blessed Lord spoke:
3. In this world there is a two-fold basis (of devotion) taught since ancient times by Me, O Arjuna: that of knowledge—the yoga of the followers of Samkhya and that of action—the yoga of the yogins.

32 Surprised at these words, Lord Krishna said, O Arjuna, listen to the deeper meaning of what I have said.
33 While explaining the yoga of discrimination, at the same time I have expounded the Sankhya philosophy.
34 You have not understood My purpose, so you have been needlessly confused. You should realize that I have spoken about both of these things.
35 Listen! O best of warriors, I have revealed these two paths in this world, and they have existed eternally.
36 One is called the path of knowledge and is followed by the sages. Those who tread it attain Self-realization.
37 The other is known as the path of action. Seekers who become proficient in it eventually reach final liberation from worldly life.
38 Though these paths are two, ultimately they become one, just as food whether prepared or unprepared gives the same satisfaction.
39 Just as two rivers which flow east and west seem separate, but eventually both merge in the same ocean,
40 Similarly, both these teachings have the same goal, but the practice of them depends on a person's ability.
41 A bird can seize a fruit even when it is flying, but can a person do this so swiftly?
42 Climbing from one bough to another, he will eventually reach the fruit.
43 Like the bird, wise men who follow the path of knowledge may quickly attain liberation,
44 But yogis also attain perfection in due course of time by resorting to the path of action and performing their duties.

न कर्मणाम् अनारम्भान् नैष्कर्म्यं पुरुषो ऽश्नुते।
न च संन्यसनादेव सिद्धिं समधिगच्छति॥

na karmaṇām anārambhān
nāiṣkarmyaṁ puruṣo 'śnute
na ca saṁnyasanādeva
siddhiṁ samadhigacchati

4. Not by abstention from actions does a man attain the state beyond karma, and not by renunciation alone does he approach perfection.

45 By failing to carry out his duties, a person cannot become free from the obligation of performing actions, as in the case of the perfected sage.
46 O Arjuna, it is both useless and foolish to say that a person can become free from his

duty merely by not doing it.
47 When it is necessary to cross a river, can it be done by abandoning the boat?
48 If a person is to satisfy his hunger, he either must cook food himself or accept what has already been prepared.
49 As long as a person is not free of desire, he must perform action. When he attains contentment, then his activity naturally ceases.
50 Listen, O Arjuna! Performing right action is unavoidable for a person whose heart is set on liberation.
51 Moreover, is action something that can be performed or abandoned at will?
52 To say such a thing would be ridiculous. You must carefully think this out. Remember that, beyond all doubt, a person does not renounce action merely by avoiding it.

न हि कश्चित् क्षणमपि जातु तिष्ठत्यकर्मकृत् ।
कार्यते ह्यवशः कर्म सर्वः प्रकृतिजैर् गुणैः ॥

na hi kaścit kṣaṇamapi
jātu tiṣṭhatyakarmakṛt
kāryate hyavaśaḥ karma
sarvaḥ prakṛtijāir guṇāiḥ

5. *Indeed, no one, even in the twinkling of an eye, ever exists without performing action; everyone is forced to perform action, even action which is against his will, by the qualities which originate in material nature.*

53 As long as a person is born of nature, it is ignorant to say that he can either perform or avoid action. Action depends on the qualities inherent in matter.
54 Even if a person gave up every required action, would the tendencies of his sense organs cease?
55 Would his ears stop hearing? Would the light of his eyes fail? Would his nostrils close up and stop smelling?
56 Would the rhythm of his breath cease, or his mind be unable to function? Would his sensations of hunger and thirst come to an end?
57 Would his waking and sleeping stop? Would his feet forget how to walk? Would birth and death cease?
58 If all these do not stop, then has anything been given up? Therefore, it is impossible for those who are in a physical body to avoid action.
59 Action is born of the qualities of nature and is dependent on them, so it is useless to say that a person can choose whether or not to act.
60 If a person gets in a car and remains motionless within it, he still moves as he travels along inside the car.
61 Just as a dry leaf, lifted by the wind, circles in the air although it doesn't move of itself,
62 In the same way, even a person who is detached from action is always active due to the force of nature and the tendencies of the organs of action.
63 Therefore, it is impossible to stop performing action as long as there is any connection with matter. Those who say, in spite of all this, that they can stop acting are simply being stubborn.

कर्मेन्द्रियाणि संयम्य य आस्ते मनसा स्मरन् ।
इन्द्रियार्थान् विमूढात्मा मिथ्याचारः स उच्यते ॥

karmendriyāṇi saṁyaṁya
ya āste manasā smaran
indriyārthān vimūḍhātmā
mithyācāraḥ sa ucyate

6. *He who sits, restraining his organs of action, while in his mind brooding over the objects of the senses, with a deluded mind, is said to be a hypocrite.*

64 Those who give up right action and seek to become free from action merely by controlling the tendencies of their sense organs,
65 Have not really given up action, for the thought of the action still remains in their minds. Such an outer show is contemptible.
66 O Arjuna, there is no doubt at all that such people are completely attached to sense objects.
67 Listen to Me, O Arjuna, and I will explain to you the characteristics of those who are detached from the senses.

यस् त्विन्द्रियाणि मनसा नियम्यारभते ऽर्जुन ।
कर्मेन्द्रियैः कर्मयोगम् असक्तः स विशिष्यते ॥

yas tvindriyāṇi manasā
niyamyārabhate 'rjuna
karmendriyāiḥ karmayogam
asaktaḥ sa viśiṣyate

7. *But he who undertakes the control of the senses by the mind, Arjuna, and, without attachment, engages the organs of action in the yoga of action, is superior.*

68 A person whose mind is firm, who is absorbed in the Self, yet is outwardly active like other people,

69 Who doesn't act under the impulse of his senses, who is not afraid of contact with sense objects, who doesn't avoid any proper action,

70 Who isn't carried away by the waves of sensory stimulation although he uses the senses to perform his actions,

71 Such a person is not bound by desire, nor is he contaminated by the darkness of delusion, just as a lotus leaf remains untainted by the water on which it floats.

72 In this earthly life, such a person appears to be like everyone else, in the same way that the reflection of the sun in water seems to be part of it.

73 Although such a person seems to be quite ordinary, if one observes him more closely one cannot know his true disposition.

74 Recognizing him by these signs, you will know that he is liberated and free from the bonds of desire.

75 O Arjuna, he is a yogi, highly regarded in this world. I tell you, try to be like him.

76 Control your mind, be steady of heart, and then your senses may freely perform actions.

नियतं कुरु कर्म त्वं कर्म ज्यायो ह्यकर्मणः ।
शरीरयात्रापि च ते तैर् दत्तान् अप्रदायैभ्यो

niyataṁ kuru karma tvaṁ
karma jyāyo hyakarmaṇaḥ
śarīrayātrāpi ca te
na prasiddhyed akarmaṇaḥ

8. Perform your duty, for action is indeed better than non-action, and even the mere maintenance of your body could not be accomplished without action.

77 You say that you would be free from action, but that is not possible in this world. Consider how a person can disobey the law.

78 Therefore, perform whatever action is right and proper, according to the occasion and without a selfish motive.

79 O Arjuna, there is one more thing which you don't know, and that is how a person may easily attain freedom from action.

80 He who performs duties which are proper to his station in life certainly attains liberation by that very practice.

यज्ञार्थात् कर्मणो ऽन्यत्र लोको ऽयं कर्मबन्धनः ।
तदर्थं कर्म कौन्तेय मुक्तसङ्गः समाचर ॥

yajñārthāt karmaṇo 'nyatra
loko 'yaṁ karmabandhanaḥ
tadarthaṁ karma kāunteya
muktasañgaḥ samācara

9. Aside from action for the purpose of sacrifice, this world is bound by action. Perform action for the purpose of sacrifice, Arjuna, free from attachment.

81 O Beloved! Know that a person's duty is his daily sacrifice, and he can incur no sin by performing it.

82 When a person gives up his duty and develops a liking for wrongful action, then bondage to earthly life follows.

83 Therefore, the performance of one's own duty is ceaseless sacrifice. He who does his duty creates no bonds for himself.

84 This world is bound by action. He who is swayed by the senses is deprived of performing his daily sacrifice.

85 O Arjuna, now I will tell you a story about this.

सहयज्ञाः प्रजाः सृष्ट्वा पुरोवाच प्रजापतिः ।
अनेन प्रसविष्यध्वम् एष वो ऽस्त्विष्टकामधुक्

sahayajñāḥ prajāḥ sṛṣṭvā
purovāca prajāpatiḥ
anena prasaviṣyadhvam
eṣa vo 'stviṣṭakāmadhuk

10. Having created mankind along with sacrifice, Prajapati, (the Lord of Creatures) anciently said, "By this (i.e. sacrifice), may you bring forth; may this be your wish-fulfilling cow."

86 When Brahma created nature, he created all beings along with perpetual sacrifice; but because the meaning of the sacrifice was very subtle, they did not understand it.

87 His creatures prayed to him saying, O God, what is our refuge here? Then Brahma, born of the lotus, said to them,

88 Your duties have been prescribed for you according to your castes. Follow them, and your desires will naturally be fulfilled.

89 You don't need to observe any vow or rule, nor do you have to mortify your body, nor do you have to visit any remote place of pilgrimage.

90 You don't have to do any yogic practices, special devotions, charms, or incantations.

91 Worship no other deity. Perform without striving the sacrifices that are ordained for you, without doing any of these other things.

92 Perform them with a disinterested mind, just as a chaste woman is devoted to her husband.

93 The sacrifice ordained for you is the only one you need to perform, said the Lord of the highest heaven.

94 So if you perform your own duty, it will be like the wish-fulfilling cow for you. O my people, it will never forsake you.

देवान् भावयतानेन ते देवा भावयन्तु वः।
परस्परं भावयन्तः श्रेयः परम् अवाप्स्यथ ।।

devān bhāvayatānena
te devā bhāvayantu vaḥ
parasparaṁ bhāvayantaḥ
śreyaḥ param avāpsyatha

11. "By this (i.e. sacrifice) may you nourish the gods and may the gods nourish you; by nourishing each other, you shall attain the "highest welfare."

95 In this way, all the gods will be propitiated and will fulfill all your desires.

96 If you worship the gods by performing your duty, they will assure your welfare and security.

97 If you worship the gods, they will be pleased with you, and affection will spring up between you.

98 As a result, you will easily accomplish whatever you want to do, and all the desires of your heart will be fulfilled.

99 All that you say will turn out to be true, you will be able to command others, and psychic powers will be at your service,

100 Just as the wealth of the forest always waits at the door of spring, the lord of seasons, gracefully bearing an abundance of fruit.

इष्टान् भोगान् हि वो देवा दास्यन्ते यज्ञभाविता:।
यो भुङ्क्ते स्तेन एव सः ।। न प्रसिद्ध्येद् अकर्मणः ।।

iṣṭān bhogān hi vo devā
dāsyante yajñabhāvitāḥ
tāir dattān apradāyāibhyo
yo bhuṅkte stena eva saḥ

12. "The gods, nourished by the sacrifice, will indeed give you desired enjoyments; he who enjoys these gifts while not offering to them in return, is a thief."

101 In this way, fortune will seek you with all its delights.

102 O Beloved, if you will only act in this way, devoted solely to your duty, you will be rich in all happiness and free from desire.

103 If a person who has gained all wealth becomes carried away by the senses and longs for sense objects;

104 Or if he does not worship the Supreme Lord, according to his position in life, with the wealth given him by the gods who are pleased by his sacrifice;

105 If he does not make sacrifices to the fire, worship the gods, or give food to the brahmins;

106 If he loses his devotion to his Guru, if he does not offer hospitality to guests or satisfy his fellow men;

107 If he fails to perform his duty and becomes conceited in his prosperity, and if he becomes engrossed in enjoying sense pleasures;

108 Great harm will come to him, he will lose all that he possesses, and he will no longer be able to enjoy even his current pleasures.

109 Just as consciousness departs from the body of a dead person, or as the goddess of wealth leaves the house of an unfortunate person,

110 Similarly, if a person neglects his duty, then his happiness will be cut off from its source. Just as when a lamp is extinguished the light disappears,

111 If a person departs from his own nature, then he is no longer free. Lord Krishna said clearly, This is true. Listen, O My people.

112 Death will punish the person who abandons his duty. It will call him a thief and take everything away from him.

113 Then, just as ghosts surround a graveyard at night, all kinds of sin will encompass him.

114 All the afflictions of the three worlds and every kind of sin and misery will be with him.

115 O My creatures! When a person goes mad and is reduced to a miserable state, weeping will not set him free, even at the end of the world.

116 So don't abandon your duty or let your senses go astray. This is what Lord Krishna teaches all people.

117 Just as water animals will soon die if they leave the water, so you shouldn't forget your duties.

118 Therefore, I tell you all again and again that you should be zealous in performing your duty.

यज्ञशिष्टाशिनः सन्तो मुच्यन्ते सर्वकिल्बिषैः ।
भुञ्जते ते त्वघं पापा ये पचन्त्यात्मकारणात् ।।

yajñaśiṣṭāśinaḥ santo
mucyante sarvakilbiṣaiḥ
bhuñjate te tvaghaṁ pāpā
ye pacantyātmakāraṇāt

13. The good, who eat the remainder of the sacrifice, are released from all evils; but the wicked, who cook only for their own sake, eat their own impurity.

119 Look! He who uses what wealth he possesses to carry out his duty with no desire for the fruit;

120 Who worships his teachers, his relatives, and the fire; who pays respect to brahmins and gives offerings for the sake of his ancestors,

121 Throwing into the fire whatever remains of the offerings;

122 And who eats all this happily in his own home with his family—his sins are thereby destroyed.

123 Because he enjoys the remains of the sacrifice, he is freed from all his sins, just as a leper is healed by nectar.

124 He whose mind is firmly fixed on what is real cannot be deceived by illusion, and he who eats of the remains of the sacrifice is free from sin.

125 Therefore, whatever a person gains from performing his duty should be used to carry out that duty, and whatever remains, he should enjoy contentedly.

126 O Arjuna, you should act only in this way. Thus Lord Krishna told him the ancient story.

127 Those who consider the body to be the Self, and who think that they should enjoy sense pleasures, see nothing except this.

128 Ignorant of any act of sacrifice, they seek only the selfish enjoyment of pleasure.

129 Preparing dishes to satisfy their senses, these sinful people nourish themselves on evil.

130 You should regard all worldly wealth as material for offerings, and dutifully pour it out as an oblation to the Supreme.

131 See how foolish people, instead of acting in this way, prepare all kinds of food for their own satisfaction!

132 The food with which a sacrifice is performed and which is pleasing to the Highest is not ordinary food.

133 Don't think of it as ordinary food, but rather as a form of God, for it is the means of life for all creation.

अन्नाद् भवन्ति भूतानि पर्जन्याद् अन्नसंभवः ।
यज्ञाद् भवति पर्जन्यो यज्ञः कर्मसमुद्भवः ।।

annād bhavanti bhūtāni
parjanyād annasaṁbhavaḥ
yajñād bhavati parjanyo
yajñaḥ karmasamudbhavaḥ

14. Beings exist from food, food is brought into being by rain, rain from sacrifice, and sacrifice is brought into being by action.

कर्म ब्रह्मोद्भवं विद्धि ब्रह्माक्षरसमुद्भवम् ।
तस्मात् सर्वगतं ब्रह्म नित्यं यज्ञे प्रतिष्ठितम् ।।

karma brahmodbhavaṁ viddhi
brahmākṣarasamudbhavam
tasmāt sarvagataṁ brahma
nityaṁ yajñe pratiṣṭhitam

15. Know that ritual action originates in Brahman (the Vedas) and Brahman arises from the Imperishable; therefore the all-pervading Brahman is eternally established in sacrifice.

134 All creatures grow from the food they eat, and the rain produces this food.

135 Rain is born in the sacrifice, and the cycle of actions gives rise to sacrifice. Brahman, in the form of the Vedas, is the source of all action.

136 The Imperishable, higher than the highest, sends forth the Vedas. Therefore, this whole creation, movable and immovable, rests in Brahma.

137 Listen, O Arjuna! The Vedas have their permanent dwelling in the sacrifice, which is the embodiment of action.

एवं प्रवर्तितं चक्रं नानुवर्तयतीह यः ।
अघायुरिन्द्रियारामो मोघं पार्थ स जीवति ।।

evaṁ pravartitaṁ cakraṁ
nānuvartayatīha yaḥ
aghāyurindriyārāmo
moghaṁ pārtha sa jīvati

16. He who does, here on earth, turn the wheel thus set in motion, lives, Arjuna, maliciously, full of sense delights, and in vain.

138 O Arjuna! In this way I have briefly recounted to you the origin and the tradition of the sacrifice.

139 Sacrifice takes the form of your own proper duty. He who is full of conceit never performs it in this world.

140 Know that he who does evil and only gratifies his senses is a storehouse of sin and a burden to the earth.
141 O Arjuna, his life and actions are as fruitless as a mass of clouds which produce no rain.
142 And the life of a person who fails to perform his duty is as useless as the false teat hanging from the neck of a goat.
143 Listen, O Arjuna! No one should abandon his duty, but rather he should follow it with his whole heart.
144 Moreover, where there is life in the body, duty accompanies it as a matter of course. Why should a person give up what is right?

यस्त्वात्मरतिरेव स्याद् आत्मतृप्तश्च मानवः।
आत्मन्येव च संतुष्टस् तस्य कार्यं न विद्यते ॥

yastvātmaratireva syād
ātmatṛptaśca mānavaḥ
ātmanyeva ca saṁtuṣṭas
tasya kāryaṁ na vidyate

17. He whose delight is only in the Self, whose satisfaction is in the Self, and who is content only in the Self; for him the need to act does not exist.

नैव तस्य कृतेनार्थो नाकृतेनेह कश्चन।
न चास्य सर्वभूतेषु कश्चिद् अर्थव्यपाश्रयः॥

nāiva tasya kṛtenārtho
nākṛteneha kaścana
na cāsya sarvabhūteṣu
kaścid arthavyapāśrayaḥ

18. He has no purpose at all in action, or in non-action, and he has no need of any being for any purpose whatsoever.

145 Only a person who always takes delight in the Self, even while his body continues to function, is unaffected by action.
146 For he is content in the light of the Self, and as his work is accomplished, he is naturally not touched by the action.
147 When the senses are gratified, after the means of gratification passes away, there is satisfaction in the Self, and there is no need for action.
148 O Arjuna, as long as a person's mind has not reached enlightenment, he must find some means to attain it.

तस्माद् असक्तः सततं कार्यं कर्म समाचर।
असक्तो ह्याचरन्कर्म परम् आप्नोति पूरुषः॥

tasmād asaktaḥ satataṁ
kāryaṁ karma samācara
asakto hyācarankarma
param āpnoti pūruṣaḥ

19. Therefore, constantly unattached, perform that action which is your duty. Indeed, by performing action while unattached, man attains the Supreme.

149 Therefore, perform your own appointed duty with restraint and without attachment.
150 O Arjuna, those who attain the state of non-attachment to the fruits of their actions by performing their duty, reach the highest bliss even in this world.

कर्मणैव हि संसिद्धिम् आस्थिता जनकादयः।
लोकसंग्रहमेवापि संपश्यन् कर्तुमर्हसि॥

karmaṇāiva hi saṁsiddhim
āsthitā janakādayaḥ
lokasaṁgrahamevāpi
saṁpaśyan kartum arhasi

20. Perfection was attained by kings like Janaka with action alone. For the mere maintenance of the world, you should act.

151 King Janaka and others attained the bliss of liberation without giving up any action.
152 Therefore, O Arjuna, carefully observe your duty. There is another good thing which results from this.
153 If we ourselves perform action, others will follow our example, and in time they will avoid calamity.
154 Even those people who have achieved their desires and have attained non-attachment must perform action for the sake of the people.
155 Just as a man who can see will lead the way for a blind man, in the same way those who know the path should point it out to those who don't know it.
156 If we didn't do this, how could the ignorant understand? How could they know the path?

यद्यद् आचरति श्रेष्ठस् तत्तद् एवेतरो जनः।
स यत् प्रमाणं कुरुते लोकस्तदनुवर्तते॥

yadyad ācarati śreṣṭhas
tattad evetaro janaḥ
sa yat pramāṇaṁ kurute
lokastadanuvartate

21. Whatever the greatest man does, thus do the rest; whatever standard he sets, the world follows that.

157 In this world, whatever the older people do, others usually regard it as a duty and try to do the same.

158 So, naturally, work should never be abandoned. Above all, good men should perform work.

न मे पार्थास्ति कर्तव्यं त्रिषु लोकेषु किंचन ।
नानवाप्तमवाप्तव्यं वर्त एव च कर्मणि ।।

na me pārthāsti kartavyaṁ
trisu lokeṣu kiṁcana
nānavāptamavāptavyaṁ
varta eva ca karmaṇi

22. For Me, O Arjuna, there is nothing whatever to be done in the three worlds, nor is there anything not attained to be attained. Nevertheless I engage in action.

यदि ह्यहं न वर्तेयं जातु कर्मण्यतन्द्रितः ।
मम वर्त्मानुवर्तन्ते मनुष्याः पार्थ सर्वशः ।।

yadi hyahaṁ na varteyaṁ
jātu karmaṇyatandritaḥ
mama vartmānuvartante
manuṣyāḥ pārtha sarvaśaḥ

23. Indeed, if I, unwearied, should not engage in action at all, mankind would follow My path everywhere, O Arjuna.

उत्सीदेयुर् इमे लोका न कुर्यां कर्म चेदहम् ।
संकरस्य च कर्ता स्याम् उपहन्याम् इमाः प्रजाः ।।

utsīdeyur ime lokā
na kuryāṁ karma cedaham
saṁkarasya ca kartā syām
upahanyām imāḥ prajāḥ

24. If I did not perform action, these worlds would perish and I would be the cause of confusion; I would destroy these creatures.

159 O Arjuna! Why should I speak to you of others? Look, I Myself act in the same way.
160 One cannot say that I perform My duty because I am in some difficulty or because I need someone.
161 You know that I possess powers unequaled by anyone else in the world.
162 How then do I perform My duty? I do it as if I desired the fruit of it. I have only one motive.
163 All creatures are dependent on Me, and they must not be led astray.
164 If I were to remain content in the Self with all My desires satisfied, how could people attain salvation?
165 If they saw My ways they would follow My ways, and the stability of all the worlds would collapse.

सक्ताः कर्मण्यविद्वांसो यथा कुर्वन्ति भारत ।
कुर्याद् विद्वांस् तथासक्तश् चिकीर्षुर् लोकसंग्रहम् ।।

saktāḥ karmaṇyavidvāṁso
yathā kurvanti bhārata
kuryād vidvāṅs tathāsaktaś
cikīrṣur lokasaṁgraham

25. While those who are unwise act from attachment to action, O Arjuna, so the wise should act without attachment, intending to maintain the welfare of the world.

166 Therefore, especially a person who is powerful and who has great knowledge should never stop working.
167 The disinterested person should work with his whole heart, in the same way that a foolish person works who hopes for the fruit of his actions.
168 O Arjuna, the stability of the worlds must be maintained.
169 Therefore, we should follow the path of duty and show the way to the people, and we shouldn't consider ourselves to be different from them.

न बुद्धिभेदं जनयेद् अज्ञानां कर्मसङ्गिनां
जोषयेत् सर्वकर्माणि । विद्वान् युक्तः समाचरन् ।।

na buddhibhedaṁ janayed
ajñānāṁ karmasaṅgināṁ
joṣayet sarvakarmāṇi
vidvān yuktaḥ samācaran

26. One should not unsettle the minds of the ignorant who are attached to action; the wise one should cause them to enjoy all actions, while himself performing actions in a disciplined manner.

170 How can a child who is nursing at its mother's breast eat spicy food? O Arjuna, a child should not be given that kind of food.
171 Similarly, non-attachment to the fruit of work should not be indiscriminately taught to those who are unworthy.
172 They should be encouraged to perform the right actions. Such action alone should be praised, and those who are disinterested should show it by their conduct.
173 When action is performed in this way for the welfare of the world, it can have no power to bind.

प्रकृतेः क्रियमाणानि गुणैः कर्माणि सर्वशः ।
अहंकारविमूढात्मा कर्ताहम् इति मन्यते ।।

prakrteḥ kriyamāṇāni
guṇāiḥ karmāṇi sarvaśaḥ
ahaṁkāravimūḍhātmā
kartāham iti manyate

27. Actions in all cases are performed by the qualities of material nature; he whose mind is confused by egoism imagines, "I am the doer."

174 O Arjuna, if we carry another person's burden on our head, won't it weigh us down?
175 Similarly, although both good and evil actions are performed by the qualities of nature, a deluded fool imagines that he is the doer.
176 Therefore, it is not right to reveal this sublime truth to an ignorant person who is deluded by egoism.

तत्त्ववित् तु महाबाहो गुणकर्मविभागयोः ।
गुणा गुणेषु वर्तन्त इति मत्वा न सज्जते ।।
tattvavit tu mahābāho
guṇakarmavibhāgayoḥ
guṇā guṇeṣu vartanta
iti matvā na sajjate

28. But he who knows the truth, O Arjuna, about the two roles of the qualities and action, thinking, "The qualities work among the qualities," is not attached.

177 This sense of egoism, from which all actions arise, is not found in people who know the truth.
178 They live in the body as a witness, free from the egoism of the body, and controlling its qualities and functions.
179 Therefore, although they live in the body, they are not bound by the chains of action any more than the sun is affected by the actions of the creatures on whom it shines.

प्रकृतेर् गुणसंमूढाः सज्जन्ते गुणकर्मसु ।
तान् अकृत्स्नविदो मन्दान् कृत्स्नविन् न विचालयेत् ।।
prakṛter guṇasaṁmūḍhāḥ
sajjante guṇakarmasu
tān akṛtsnavido mandān
kṛtsnavin na vicālayet

29. Those deluded by the qualities of material nature are attached to the actions of the qualities. The perfect knower should not disturb the foolish men of incomplete knowledge .

180 Action affects only that person who is deluded by the qualities and who lives controlled by nature.
181 The senses carry on their activities prompted by the qualities. A person who takes responsibility for those actions is bound by them.
182 Arjuna, now listen carefully while I tell you what is good for you.

मयि सर्वाणि कर्माणि संन्यस्याध्यात्मचेतसा ।
निराशीर् निर्ममो भूत्वा युध्यस्व विगतज्वरः ।।
mayi sarvāṇi karmāṇi
saṁnyasyādhyātmacetasā
nirāśīr nirmamo bhūtvā
yudhyasva vigatajvaraḥ

30. Deferring all actions in Me, meditating on the supreme Spirit, having become free from desire and selfishness,with your fever departed, fight!

183 When you perform all your appointed actions, surrender them to Me, but concentrate all the thoughts of your heart on the Self.
184 Don't allow pride to enter your mind, thinking, "This is action," "I am the doer," or "I will do it."
185 Don't be attached to your body, and give up all desire. Then you may enjoy all pleasures at the appropriate time.
186 Now, pick up your bow, get into this chariot, and with a calm mind embrace the duties of a warrior.
187 Let your fame spread throughout the world, lend dignity to the performance of duty, and release the earth from this burden.
188 Now, O Arjuna, set aside all doubt and do nothing else but concentrate on fighting.

ये मे मतम् इदं नित्यम् अनुतिष्ठन्ति मानवाः ।
श्रद्धावन्तो ऽनसूयन्तो मुच्यन्ते ते ऽपि कर्मभिः ।।
ye me matam idaṁ nityam
anutiṣṭhanti mānavāḥ
śraddhāvanto 'nasūyanto
mucyante te 'pi karmabhiḥ

31. Men who constantly practice this teaching of Mine, believing, not sneering, are also released from the bondage of actions.

189 O Arjuna, this is My definite opinion: those who eagerly accept this teaching and practice it with faith,
190 Are freed from the bondage of actions even while they perform them. Therefore, action should certainly be performed.

ये त्वेतद् अभ्यसूयन्तो नानुतिष्ठन्ति मे मतम् ।
सर्वज्ञानविमूढांस् तान् विद्धि नष्टान् अचेतसः ।।
ye tvetad abhyasūyanto
nānutiṣṭhanti me matam
sarvajñānavimūḍhāṅs tān
viddhi naṣṭān acetasaḥ

32. But those who, sneering at this, do not practice My teaching, confusing all wisdom, know them to be lost and mindless.

191 On the other hand, those who are attached to nature, who indulge their senses and disregard My teaching,

192 Who regard it as being of little importance, and who despise it or chatter about it,

193 Know that those people are intoxicated with the wine of infatuation, poisoned by sense pleasures, and sunk in the mire of ignorance.

194 Just as a corpse has no use for a jewel placed in its hand, just as dawn has no meaning for a blind man,

195 Or just as a crow is not concerned with the rising of the moon, similarly, a fool does not value discrimination.

196 Not only do they disregard our words; they even scorn them. Can a moth bear the light?

197 So, Arjuna, do not argue with those who turn away from this sublime teaching.

सदृशं चेष्टते स्वस्याः प्रकृतेर् ज्ञानवान् अपि ।
प्रकृतिं यान्ति भूतानि निग्रहः किं करिष्यति ॥

sadṛśam ceṣṭate svasyāḥ
prakṛter jñānavān api
prakṛtiṁ yānti bhūtāni
nigrahaḥ kim kariṣyati

33. One acts according to one's own material nature. Even the wise man does so. Beings follow their own material nature; what will restraint accomplish?

198 In the first place, a wise person shouldn't indulge his senses for the sake of pleasure.

199 Should a person play with a serpent? Would it be good for him to stay around a tiger? If he were to swallow poison, could he digest it?

200 Even if he is playing and lights a fire, it leaps up in flames and cannot be controlled. So it is not good to encourage the activity of the senses.

इन्द्रियस्येन्द्रियस्यार्थे रागद्वेषौ व्यवस्थितौ ।
तयोर् न वशम् आगच्छेत् तौ ह्यस्य परिपन्थिनौ ॥

indriyasyendriyasyārthe
rāgadveṣāu vyavasthitāu
tayor na vaśam āgacchet
tāu hyasya paripanthināu

34. Passion and hatred are seated in the senses in relation to their objects. One should not come under the power of these two; they are indeed one's enemies.

201 Furthermore, O Arjuna, why should a person give pleasure to his body, which is subject to nature?

202 Why should we pamper our bodies day and night regardless of the expense?

203 This body is composed of the five elements and at death returns to them again.

204 Indulging the body is obviously disastrous. Don't set your heart on it.

205 It is true that the enjoyment of sense objects gratifies the mind.

206 It is like the accomplice of a thief who poses as an honest man and remains quiet for a while, until he has passed beyond the city limits.

207 O Beloved, sense pleasures are sweet. Don't let the longing for them arise in your mind. Don't enjoy them without considering the consequences.

208 Desire, which resides in the senses, arouses a harmful yearning for pleasures, just as the bait on a hook attracts the fish.

209 Just as the fish cannot see the concealed hook, which can deprive it of its life,

210 Similarly, a person who is allured by passion and seeks pleasure from sense objects is cast into the flames of anger.

211 Just as a hunter lures his prey to the place of its death to kill it,

212 It is the same with sensual desires. Therefore, avoid them, O Arjuna. Understand also that both desire and anger are destructive.

213 Don't have anything to do with them, and don't let your mind even remember them. Don't let anything destroy your devotion to the Self.

श्रेयान् स्वधर्मो विगुणः परधर्मात् स्वनुष्ठितात् ।
स्वधर्मे निधनं श्रेयः परधर्मो भयावहः ॥

śreyān svadharmo viguṇaḥ
paradharmāt svanuṣṭhitāt
svadharme nidhanam śreyaḥ
paradharmo bhayāvahaḥ

35. Better one's own duty though deficient than the duty of another well performed. Better is death in one's own duty; the duty of another invites danger.

214 O Beloved! It is best to perform our own duty, no matter how difficult it may be.

215 Another person's duty may appeal to us more; nevertheless, we should carry out our own.

216 How could a brahmin, however poor, eat food in the house of an outcaste, even though it might be delicious.
217 Why should anyone perform an improper action or want what is undesirable? Just think, does a person get what he desires?
218 Is it wise for a person to destroy his thatched hut because he sees the beautiful mansions of others?
219 Just as a person appreciates his own wife, however unattractive she may be, when he lives with her,
220 In the same way our own duty, however arduous and difficult it may be, will lead us to the happiness of heaven.
221 Sugar and milk are both known for their sweetness, but if they are harmful to a person suffering from worms, should he eat them?
222 O Arjuna, if he does eat them, they may satisfy him temporarily, but ultimately he will not be able to digest them.
223 Therefore, if we seek our own welfare, we shouldn't do what is proper for another person but not for ourselves.
224 If we spend our life performing our own duty, it will go well for us both here and hereafter.

अर्जुन उवाच। *arjuna uvāca*

अथ केन प्रयुक्तो ऽयं पापं चरति पूरुषः।
अनिच्छन्नपि वार्ष्णेय बलाद् इव नियोजितः॥

atha kena prayukto 'yaṁ
pāpaṁ carati pūruṣaḥ
anicchannapi vārṣṇeya
balād iva niyojitaḥ

Arjuna spoke:
36. Then impelled, by what does a man commit this evil, unwillingly even, O Krishna, as if urged by force?

225 When Krishna had spoken, Arjuna said, O Lord, I have a request to make.
226 I have listened to everything You have told me, and I will now ask You what I want to know.
227 O Lord, how is it that we see the equanimity of even wise men disturbed and they leave the right path to go astray?
228 Wise people know which methods to use and which to avoid. What influences them to take on the duties of others?
229 A blind person cannot distinguish the seed from the husk. Why is it that sometimes a person with good vision makes the same mistake?
230 The same people who gave up their original attachments are not satisfied now with new ones. Even those who take up the life of a hermit return to worldly life.
231 They go into seclusion and escape from evil, but they are forcibly dragged back into it.
232 The fiend which seizes this life grabs hold of them, and when they try to escape, it seeks them out.
233 This is a kind of tyranny. What is this power? Tell me this.

श्रीभगवान् उवाच। *śrībhagavān uvāca*

काम एष क्रोध एष रजोगुणसमुद्भवः।
महाशनो महापाप्मा विद्ध्येनम् इह वैरिणम्॥

kāma eṣa krodha eṣa
rajoguṇasamudbhavaḥ
mahaśano mahāpāpmā
viddhyenam iha vāiriṇam

The Blessed Lord spoke:
37. This force is desire, this force is anger; its source is the rajas guna. Voracious and greatly injurious, know this to be the enemy.

234 Then the highest of all beings said, Listen I will tell you.
235 Know that they are desire and anger, which are both without compassion and are regarded as death itself.
236 They are serpents in the storehouse of knowledge, tigers in the desert of sense objects, and violent men on the path of devotion.
237 They are rocks endangering the fortress of the body, like a wall surrounding the village of the senses. Like mental confusion and other similar states, they create turmoil throughout the whole world.
238 This is the influence of passion on the mind, born of demoniacal forces and nurtured by ignorance.
239 They are passionate, but favored by the quality of darkness, which also infuses them with its power of error.
240 In the house of death they are regarded as friends, for they are the enemies of life.
241 When they are hungry, even the entire universe would not be a morsel large enough to satisfy them. They spread their greed towards the various activities of mankind.

242 Delusion is the younger sister of hope. The fourteen worlds are merely a trifle for her to hold in her grasp.

243 Lust, for whom the three worlds are a small mouthful eaten with great pleasure, thrives through the power of her service.

244 Illusion and selfishness, which make the world dance in delight, trade with them.

245 Don't you know that, through these, hypocrisy has spread throughout the world? Truth has been robbed of its possessions and filled with the straw of wrong conduct.

246 They have ravished the chaste figure of peace. Having adorned delusion with ornaments, they have corrupted numerous sages.

247 They have devastated the place of discrimination, stripped dispassion naked, and twisted the neck of tranquility.

248 They have ravaged the forest of contentment, demolished the fortress of courage, and uprooted the plant of joy.

249 They have plucked the tender shoots of understanding, wiped out the name of happiness, and kindled the fire of affliction in the heart.

250 They were formed with the body and are attached to life, but when they are looked for, neither Brahma nor anyone else can find them.

251 They are the neighbors of consciousness and are seated next to wisdom. They are always ready to fight and cannot be driven away.

252 They can drown a person without water, burn him without fire, and silently hold fast all creatures.

253 They kill without weapons, bind without ropes, and strike down a wise person for a wager.

254 They bury a person without earth, ensnare him without a noose, and are unequaled in strength.

धूमेनाव्रियते वह्निर् यथा ऽदर्शो मलेन च ।
यथोल्बेनावृतो गर्भस् तथा तेनेदम् आवृतम् ॥
dhūmenāvriyate vahnir
yathā 'darśo malena ca
yatholbenāvṛto garbhas
tathā tenedam āvṛtam

38. As fire is obscured by smoke, and a mirror by dust, as the embryo is enveloped by the membrane, so the intellect is obscured by passion.

255 Just as serpents encircle the roots of a sandalwood tree, and as the womb surrounds the embryo,

256 Just as there can be no sun without light, no smoke without fire, and no mirror without dust,

257 Similarly, we have never known knowledge to exist without these.

आवृतं ज्ञानम् एतेन ज्ञानिनो नित्यवैरिणा ।
कामरूपेण कौन्तेय दुष्पूरेणानलेन च ॥
āvṛtaṁ jñānam etena
jñānino nityavāiriṇā
kāmarūpeṇa kāunteya
duṣpūreṇānalena ca

39. O Arjuna, the knowledge even of the wise ones is obscured by this eternal enemy, having the form of desire, which is as insatiable fire.

258 Just as a seed grows covered by a husk, in the same way wisdom, however pure it may be, is surrounded by these. In this way, it is difficult to reach.

259 First overcome these, and then obtain wisdom. Until then you cannot conquer attraction and aversion.

260 All the strength a person uses to control them is just like the fuel which feeds a fire.

इन्द्रियाणि मनो बुद्धिर् अस्याधिष्ठानमुच्यते ।
एतैर् विमोहयत्येष ज्ञानम् आवृत्य देहिनम् ॥
indriyāṇi mano buddhir
asyādhiṣṭhānam ucyate
etāir vimohayatyeṣa
jñānam āvṛtya dehinam

40. The senses, the mind and the intellect are said to be its (i.e. the eternal enemy's) abode; with these, it confuses the embodied one, obscuring his knowledge.

तस्मात् त्वम् इन्द्रियाण्यादौ नियम्य भरतर्षभ ।
पाप्मानं प्रजहि ह्येनं ज्ञानविज्ञाननाशनम् ॥
tasmāt tvam indriyāṇyādāu
niyamya bharatarṣabha
pāpmānaṁ prajahi hyenaṁ
jñānavijñānanāśanam

41. Therefore, restraining the senses first, O Arjuna, kill this evil demon which destroys knowledge and discrimination.

इन्द्रियाणि पराण्याहुर् इन्द्रियेभ्यः परं मनः ।
मनसस् तु परा बुद्धिर् यो बुद्धेः परतस् तु सः ॥
indriyāṇi parāṇyāhur
indriyebhyaḥ paraṁ manaḥ
manasas tu parā buddhir
yo buddheḥ paratas tu saḥ

42. They say that the senses are superior. The mind is superior to the senses; moreover, the intellect is superior to the mind; that which is superior to the intellect is the Self.

261 Whatever means a person may use to try to conquer them only strengthens them. For this reason, those who practice hatha yoga have been overcome by them.
262 In such difficulties, there is only one effective method. I will explain it to you if you will accept it.
263 The senses are their principal stronghold; nature gives birth to activity. First, destroy them completely.
264 Then the activity of the mind will be slowed, the reason will be set free, and the home of these sinful actions will be demolished.

एवं बुद्धेः परं बुद्ध्वा संस्तभ्यात्मानम् आत्मना ।
जहि शत्रु महाबाहो कामरूपं दुरासदम् ॥
evaṁ buddheḥ paraṁ buddhvā
saṁstabhyātmānam ātmanā
jahi śatruṁ mahābāho
kāmarūpaṁ durāsadam

43. Thus having known that which is higher than the intellect, sustaining the self by the Self, kill the enemy, O Arjuna, which has the form of desire and is difficult to conquer.

265 If these are driven from the heart, they will undoubtedly be destroyed, just as a mirage fades away without the sun.
266 Similarly, if attraction and aversion disappear, the kingdom of God will be established. Then everyone may enjoy his own bliss.
267 This is the true relationship of the Guru and the disciple, just like that of the body and the soul. Stand firmly in it and never leave it.
268 In this way spoke the Master of all perfected beings, the Lord of the gods.
269 Now Krishna will return to the matter about which Arjuna questions Him.
270 With what words can we tell it? Who can describe its sweetness? The listeners will be contented with the happiness of hearing this.
271 Jnanadeva, the disciple of Nivritti, says, My friends, let your understanding be awakened so you can enjoy the dialogue between Lord Krishna and Arjuna.

4

THE YOGA OF WISDOM

THE day of good fortune for the ear has come, for it has heard the treasure of the *Gita*, as though its dream had come true.
2 The subject of this chapter is discrimination. It is being explained by Krishna, the Lord of the world; and Arjuna, the best of devotees, is listening.
3 It is as if a sweet sound were mingled with fragrance, or fragrance with fine taste, so great is the beauty of this story.
4 What great good fortune! For here we find the Ganges of nectar. Or it may be that the austerities of the listeners have borne fruit.
5 Now let all the other senses enter the dwelling of the ear for the joy of hearing this dialogue called the *Gita*.
6 Enough of this digression. Let us turn to the dialogue between Krishna and Arjuna.
7 At that time Sanjaya told the king that Arjuna had been visited by good fortune, for Lord Narayana had spoken to him with great affection.
8 Even the divine Lakshmi, so close to Him, had not experienced the joy of this love. The blossoming of Krishna's love for Arjuna brought this to him.
9 Although the hopes of Sanaka and others greatly increased, they were not fulfilled in this way.
10 The Lord's affection for Arjuna seems incomparable. What great merit has he earned?
11 I am very moved by the intimate affection between Krishna and Arjuna. Out of His love for Arjuna, the immortal Krishna took on a human form.
12 On the other hand, He cannot be reached by yogis, He is incomprehensible to the Vedas, and He remains invisible to the eyes of meditation.
13 What impulse could have moved Him to such compassion, He who is one with the Self, who is unchanging and eternal?
14 See how He who is beyond form, who is the folds of the garment of the three worlds, has been overcome by His love for Arjuna!

श्रीभगवान् उवाच । *śrībhagavān uvāca*

इमं विवस्वते योगं प्रोक्तवान् अहम् अव्ययम् ।
विवस्वान् मनवे प्राह मनुर् इक्ष्वाकवे ऽब्रवीत् ॥

imaṁ vivasvate yogaṁ
proktavān aham avyayam
vivasvān manave prāha
manur ikṣvākave 'bravīt

The Blessed Lord spoke:

1. I proclaimed this imperishable yoga to Vivasvat; Vivasvat communicated it to Manu, and Manu imparted it to Ikshvaku.

15 Then Krishna told Arjuna, We explained this yoga to Vivasvat, but many ages have passed since then.
16 Then Vivasvat taught the knowledge of yoga to Manu.
17 Manu practiced it himself and taught it to his son Ikshvaku. In this way, it has been handed down from age to age.

एवं परम्पराप्राप्तम् इमं राजर्षयो विदुः ।
स कालेनेह महता योगो नष्टः परंतप ॥

evaṁ paramparāprāptam
imaṁ rājarṣayo viduḥ
sa kāleneha mahatā
yogo naṣṭaḥ paraṁtapa

2. Thus received by succession, the royal seers knew this; after a long time here on earth, this yoga has been lost, Arjuna.

18 Thereafter, many royal sages knew this yoga, but since then it has remained unknown.

19 Creatures are addicted to sense pleasures and are attached to their bodies. For this reason, they have forgotten the knowledge of the Self.

20 The longing for Self-knowledge has wandered away from them, and sense pleasures are the goal of their lives. Existence and the limitations of the body have become dear to them.

21 What would be the use of expensive clothes in a village of naked ascetics? Of what use is the sun to a blind person?

22 In a gathering of the deaf, who could appreciate singing? How can jackals appreciate the moonlight?

23 How can crows, whose eyes are then blind, recognize the moon as it rises?

24 Similarly, if foolish people have not even come to the edge of dispassion and are unfamiliar with the language of discrimination, how can they reach God?

25 No one knows how this infatuation developed, but because of it time has passed and yoga has disappeared from the world.

स एवायं मया ते ऽद्य योगः प्रोक्तः पुरातनः ।
भक्तो ऽसि मे सखा चेति रहस्यं ह्येतद् उत्तमम् ।।

sa evāyaṁ mayā te 'dya
yogaḥ proktaḥ purātanaḥ
bhakto 'si me sakhā ceti
rahasyaṁ hyetad uttamam

3. This ancient yoga is today declared by Me to you, since you are My devotee and friend. This secret is supreme indeed.

26 O Arjuna, today I have truly taught you that same yoga. Have no doubt about it.

27 It is My deep secret, but how can I hide it from you, who are so dear to Me?

28 O Arjuna, you are the embodiment of love, the heart of devotion, and friendship itself.

29 Because you are the home of intimacy, how can I deceive you now?

30 Although we are ready to fight, still for a while we must be patient and not confused. First, your ignorance must be cleared away.

अर्जुन उवाच । *arjuna uvāca*

अपरं भवतो जन्म परं जन्म विवस्वतः ।
कथम् एतद् विजानीयां त्वम् आदौ प्रोक्तवान् इति ।।

aparaṁ bhavato janma
paraṁ janma vivasvataḥ
katham etad vijānīyāṁ
tvam ādāu proktavān iti

Arjuna spoke:
4. Your birth was later, the birth of Vivasvat earlier; how should I understand this, that You declared it in the beginning?

31 Arjuna said, O Krishna, storehouse of all mercy, listen to me. It is any wonder that a mother loves her child?

32 You are a shelter to all those afflicted by worldly life, a mother to the helpless. Truly, it is Your kindness that has given birth to us.

33 O Lord, if a child is born crippled, this burden has to be borne throughout its life. Why should I speak of this to You?

34 Pay attention to what I ask You. Don't be angry with me for questioning You.

35 O Krishna, You have spoken to me of ancient things, but for now I do not understand.

36 Even our ancestors did not know who Vivasvat was. How then did You teach him?

37 We are told that he belonged to the remote past. O Krishna, You are of the present time, so this is inconsistent.

38 We know nothing about Your life. How could we ever say that You told a lie?

39 Therefore, tell me the whole story of how You taught this yoga to the sun, so I may clearly understand it.

40 Then Krishna said, O Arjuna, if there is any doubt in your mind that I existed when Vivasvat lived,

41 Don't you know that you and I have had many births? Yet you have no memory of your own.

42 O Arjuna, I remember every incarnation I have ever had.

श्रीभगवान् उवाच । *śrībhagavān uvāca*

बहूनि मे व्यतीतानि जन्मानि तव चार्जुन ।
तान्यहं वेद सर्वाणि न त्वं वेत्थ परंतप ।।

bahūni me vyatītāni
janmāni tava cārjuna
tānyahaṁ veda sarvāṇi
na tvaṁ vettha paraṁtapa

The Blessed Lord spoke:
5. Many of My births have passed away, and also yours, Arjuna. I know them all; you do not know them, Arjuna.

अजो ऽपि सन्न् अव्ययात्मा भूतानाम् ईश्वरो ऽपि सन् ।
प्रकृतिं स्वाम् अधिष्ठाय संभवाम्यात्ममायया ।।

ajo 'pi sann avyayātmā
bhūtānām īśvaro 'pi san

prakṛtiṁ svām adhiṣṭhāya
saṁbhavāmyātmamāyayā

6. Although I am birthless and My nature is imperishable, although I am the Lord of all beings, yet, by controlling My own material nature, I come into being by My own power.

43 I remember everything in the past. Although I always remain unborn, I become incarnate through the power of illusion.

44 Even so, this does not affect My eternal nature at all. Birth and death, which I appear to undergo, are expressions of the power of illusion working through Me.

45 My freedom is not affected by this, although I still seem to be bound by action. In reality, this is only delusion caused by distorted reasoning.

46 In a mirror, one object may seem to be two, but are there really two objects?

47 O Arjuna, I am really formless, but when I function in the world of nature for a special purpose, I act as though I were incarnate.

यदा यदा हि धर्मस्य ग्लानिर् भवति भारत ।
अभ्युत्थानम् अधर्मस्य तदा ऽत्मानं सृजाम्यहम् ॥

yadā yadā hi dharmasya
glānir bhavati bhārata
abhyutthānam adharmasya
tadā 'tmānaṁ sṛjāmyaham

7. Whenever a decrease of righteousness exists, Arjuna, and there is a rising up of unrighteousness, then I manifest Myself.

48 In the natural course of the world from the beginning, I have watched over the performance of all duties and rites from age to age.

49 When unrighteousness overpowers righteousness, I set aside My formlessness and become incarnate.

50 Then, for the sake of My devotees, I assume a form and drive out the darkness of ignorance.

परित्राणाय साधूनां विनाशाय च दुष्कृताम् ।
धर्मसंस्थापनार्थाय संभवामि युगे युगे ॥

paritrāṇāya sādhūnāṁ
vināśāya ca duṣkṛtām
dharmasaṁsthāpanārthāya
saṁbhavāmi yuge yuge

8. For the protection of the good and the destruction of evil doers, for the sake of establishing righteousness, I am born in every age.

51 Then I break the bonds of unrighteousness, tear up all evidence of sin, and raise the banner of happiness through righteous people.

52 I destroy the families of demons, increase the honor of saints and sages, and unite morality with religion.

53 Removing the soot of confusion, I light the lamp of discrimination. Then yogis enjoy a perpetual feast of light.

54 The universe becomes filled with the joy of the Self, righteousness dwells on earth, and My devotees feast on virtue.

55 O Arjuna, when I manifest in a physical body, the mountain of sin is shattered and the day of righteousness dawns.

56 For this purpose, I take birth age after age. He who knows this is truly wise in this world.

जन्म कर्म च मे दिव्यम् एवं यो वेत्ति तत्त्वतः ।
त्यक्त्वा देहं पुनर्जन्म नैति माम् एति सो ऽर्जुन ॥

janma karma ca me divyam
evaṁ yo vetti tattvataḥ
tyaktvā dehaṁ punarjanma
nāiti mām eti so 'rjuna

9. He who knows in truth My divine birth and action, having left his body, he is not reborn; he comes to Me, Arjuna.

57 A person who understands My birth although I am unborn, who understands My action, although I am above all action, and who knows that I am unchanging, may be called liberated.

58 In the company of active people, he remains still; living in the body, he is not bound by it; and at the hour of death, he attains My true nature.

वीतरागभयक्रोधा मन्मया माम् उपाश्रिताः ।
बहवो ज्ञानतपसा पूता मद्भावम् आगताः ॥

vītarāgabhayakrodhā
manmayā mām upāśritāḥ
bahavo jñānatapasā
pūtā madbhāvam āgatāḥ

10. Thinking solely of Me, resorting to Me, many whose greed, fear, and anger have departed, purified by the austerity of knowledge, have attained My state of being.

59 Furthermore, those who grieve neither for themselves nor for others, who are free from desire, who never tread the path of anger,

60 Who always dwell in Me, who live only to serve Me, who are content in the realization of the Self, who are free from all attachment,

61 Who are filled with the fire of penance, who are the dwelling place of wisdom, and who add holiness to sacred places of pilgrimage,

62 Such people easily attain My nature and become one with Me, for there is no separation between them and Me.

63 If the alloy of brass were completely removed from gold, would it be necessary to add anything in its place?

64 Similarly, those who are purified by penance, wisdom, and restraint of the senses have merged into My being. What doubt is there of this?

ये यथा मां प्रपद्यन्ते तांस् तथैव भजाम्यहम् ।
मम वर्त्मानुवर्तन्ते मनुष्याः पार्थ सर्वशः ।।
ye yathā māṁ prapadyante
tāṁs tathāiva bhajāmyaham
mama vartmānuvartante
manuṣyāḥ pārtha sarvaśaḥ

11. In whatever way, men take refuge in Me, I reward them. Men everywhere, Arjuna, follow My path.

65 Know this also: in whatever way people are devoted to Me, that is how I serve them.

66 All people are by nature solely devoted to Me and live only in Me.

काङ्क्षन्तः कर्मणां सिद्धिं यजन्त इह देवताः ।
क्षिप्रं हि मानुषे लोके सिद्धिर् भवति कर्मजा ।।
kāñksantaḥ karmaṇāṁ siddhiṁ
yajanta iha devatāḥ
kṣipraṁ hi mānuṣe loke
siddhir bhavati karmajā

12. Desiring the success of ritual acts, men sacrifice here on earth to the Vedic gods. Quickly indeed in the world of men ritual acts bring success.

67 Lacking wisdom, they have gone astray and have come to believe in duality. As a result, they see diversity in Me, the One.

68 They see diversity in oneness, give names to the nameless, and speak of the inexpressible One as a god or a goddess.

69 Deluded by their minds, they divide the indivisible into higher and lower.

70 Then, with various goals in mind and with appropriate ceremonies, they worship those whom they believe to be their gods.

71 They achieve whatever they desire, but you should recognize that this is undoubtedly the fruit of action.

72 Know that, besides action, there is nothing that gives or takes. It is true that action alone bears fruit in the world of men.

73 Only what is sown in a field can grow there. Only what is reflected in a mirror can be seen in it.

74 O Arjuna, by a natural law, when we stand at the foot of a hill, we hear the sound of our own voices returning to us as an echo.

75 Similarly, O Arjuna, I am the witness of all forms of worship, and each person obtains the fruits according to his faith.

चातुर्वर्ण्यं मया सृष्टं गुणकर्मविभागशः ।
तस्य कर्तारम् अपि मां विद्ध्यकर्तारम् अव्ययम् ।।
cāturvarṇyaṁ mayā sṛṣṭaṁ
guṇakarmavibhāgaśaḥ
tasya kartāram api māṁ
viddhyakartāram avyayam

13. The system of four castes was created by Me, according to the distribution of the qualities and their acts. Although I am the creator of this (the system), know Me to be the eternal non-doer.

76 In the same way, I have created the four castes according to the distribution of different qualities and actions.

न मां कर्माणि लिम्पन्ति न मे कर्मफले स्पृहा ।
इति मां यो ऽभिजानाति कर्मभिर न स बध्यते ।।
na māṁ karmāṇi limpanti
na me karmaphale spṛhā
iti māṁ yo 'bhijānāti
karmabhir na sa badhyate

14. Actions do not taint Me; I have no desire for the fruit of action; thus he who comprehends Me is not bound by actions.

77 This system has come about because of Me, but I did not establish it. He who realizes this is liberated.

एवं ज्ञात्वा कृतं कर्म पूर्वैर् अपि मुमुक्षुभिः ।
कुरु कर्मैव तस्मात् त्वं पूर्वैः पूर्वतरं कृतम् ।।
evaṁ jñātvā kṛtaṁ karma
pūrvāir api mumukṣubhiḥ
kuru karmāiva tasmāt tvaṁ
pūrvaiḥ pūrvataraṁ kṛtam

15. Having known this, the ancients, seeking release, also performed action. Therefore perform action as it was earlier performed by the ancients.

78 Each one has been assigned his functions according to the mixture of the qualities present in him.

79 O Arjuna, though all are one, the four castes were formed by the distribution of qualities and actions.
80 From this standpoint, I did not really create this system.
81 Knowing Me to be this way, those who sought liberation in former times carried out their work, O Arjuna.
82 Just as seeds which have been fried can never germinate even if they are sown in the ground, similarly, the actions of those people proved to be the cause of their liberation.
83 One other thing, O Arjuna. Wise people should never try to determine by their own judgment what is action and what is inaction.

किं कर्म किम् अकर्मेति कवयो ऽप्य् अत्र मोहिताः ।
तत् ते कर्म प्रवक्ष्यामि यज् ज्ञात्वा मोक्ष्यसे ऽशुभात् ॥
kiṁ karma kim akarmeti
kavayo 'py atra mohitāḥ
tat te karma pravakṣyāmi
yaj jñātvā mokṣyase 'śubhāt

16. "What is action? What is inaction?" Thus, even the wise are confused in this matter. This action I shall explain to you, having known which, you shall be released from evil.

84 What is action, and what characterizes inaction? Even wise people are bewildered by this problem.
85 When we look at a counterfeit coin, we doubt what our eye sees because the coin resembles a genuine coin.
86 Similarly, under the delusion of non-attachment to action, even those who are able to create another world by the power of their thought become involved in actions.
87 Then what about foolish people? Even the wise who have subtle vision are confused. Therefore, listen to Me and I will explain this to you.

कर्मणो ह्यपि बोद्धव्यं बोद्धव्यं च विकर्मणः ।
अकर्मणश्च बोद्धव्यं गहना कर्मणो गतिः ॥
karmaṇo hyapi boddhavyaṁ
boddhavyaṁ ca vikarmaṇaḥ
akarmaṇaśca boddhavyaṁ
gahanā karmaṇo gatiḥ

17. One must know the nature of action, the nature of wrong action, and also the nature of inaction. The way of action is profound.

88 Action is that natural activity which makes possible the manifestation of the universe. First understand this thoroughly.
89 Then fully understand the action which is prescribed for the various castes and stages of life with their particular practices.
90 Understand also the nature of unlawful action which is prohibited, so that you don't become entangled in it.
91 The world is dependent on action; it is universal. Now listen to the characteristics of those beings who have attained their goal.

कर्मण्यकर्म यः पश्येद् अकर्मणि च कर्म यः ।
स बुद्धिमान् मनुष्येषु स युक्तः कृत्स्नकर्मकृत् ॥
karmaṇyakarma yaḥ paśyed
akarmaṇi ca karma yaḥ
sa buddhimān manuṣyeṣu
sa yuktaḥ kṛtsnakarmakṛt

18. He who perceives inaction in action, and action in inaction, is wise among men; he is a yogi and performs all actions.

92 He who carries out his duties with detachment, who has no desire for the fruits of his action,
93 And to whom nothing in the world matters more than his duty, has truly understood freedom from action.
94 Yet he performs well all religious rites. By these signs, he is known to be wise.
95 Just as a person standing near water sees his own reflection in it, and yet knows that he is different from the reflection,
96 Or just as a person on a boat sees the trees on the shore passing rapidly by him, and yet knows that they are actually not moving,
97 Similarly, while in the midst of action, he clearly knows that it is illusory and that he is detached from it.
98 Also, when the sun rises and sets, it seems to move although it is actually motionless. In the same way, realize that freedom from action lies in action.
99 Such a person seems like other people, but he is not affected by human nature, like the sun which cannot be drowned in water.
100 He sees the world without seeing it, does everything without doing it, and enjoys all pleasures without being involved in them.
101 Though he is seated in one place, he travels everywhere, for even while in the body he has become the universe.

यस्य सर्वे समारम्भाः कामसंकल्पवर्जिताः ।
ज्ञानाग्निदग्धकर्माणं तम् आहुः पण्डितं बुधाः ॥

yasya sarve samārambhāḥ
kāmasaṁkalpavarjitāḥ
jñānāgnidagdhakarmāṇaṁ
tam āhuḥ paṇḍitaṁ budhāḥ

19. He who has excluded desire and motive from all his enterprises, and has consumed his karma in the fire of knowledge, him the wise men call a sage.

102 One who does not tire of action, yet who has no desire for its fruit,
103 Whose mind is not tainted by such thoughts as, "I will perform this action," and "I will finish what I have begun,"
104 Who has burned up all actions in the flames of the fire of knowledge, know that such a person is God in human form.

त्यक्त्वा कर्मफलासङ्गं नित्यतृप्तो निराश्रयः ।
कर्मण्य् अभिप्रवृत्तो ऽपि नैव किंचित् करोति सः ॥
tyaktvā karmaphalāsaṅgaṁ
nityatṛpto nirāśrayaḥ
karmaṇy abhipravṛtto 'pi
nāiva kiṁcit karoti saḥ

20. He who has abandoned all attachment to the fruits of action, always content, not dependent, even when performing action, does, in effect, nothing at all.

निराशीर् यतचित्तात्मा त्यक्तसर्वपरिग्रहः ।
शारीरं केवलं कर्म कुर्वन् नाप्नोति किल्बिषम् ॥
nirāśīr yatacittātmā
tyaktasarvaparigrahaḥ
śārīraṁ kevalaṁ karma
kurvan nāpnoti kilbiṣam

21. Performing action with the body alone, without wish, restrained in thought and self, with all motives of acquisition abandoned, he incurs no evil.

यदृच्छालाभसंतुष्टो द्वन्द्वातीतो विमत्सरः ।
समः सिद्धाव् असिद्धौ च कृत्वा ऽपि न निबध्यते ॥
yadṛcchālābhasaṁtuṣṭo
dvandvātīto vimatsaraḥ
samaḥ siddhāv asiddhāu ca
kṛtvā 'pi na nibadhyate

22. Content with whatever comes to him, transcending the dualities (i.e. pleasure, pain, etc.), free from envy, constant in mind whether in success or in failure, even though he acts, he is not bound.

105 A person who is indifferent to his body and without desire for the fruit of action is full of joy.
106 O Arjuna, he is the sanctuary of contentment and is never satiated while feasting on his own inner light.
107 Having rejected all desire and selfishness, he increasingly enjoys the delights of heavenly bliss.
108 He who is content with whatever he obtains, for whom there is no thought of either "mine" or "not mine,"
109 Becomes whatever he sees with his eyes or hears with his ears.
110 The walking of his feet, the speaking of his mouth, and all his other actions are the Supreme moving through him.
111 Furthermore, he sees the whole universe as not different from himself. Then how can action affect him?
112 Nothing is left in him of the duality from which jealousy springs, so he is without jealousy. Is there any need to say more?
113 He is free in every way and, even though he acts, he is free from action. Though he possesses attributes, he is beyond all attributes. There is no doubt about this.

गतसङ्गस्य मुक्तस्य ज्ञानावस्थितचेतसः ।
यज्ञायाचरतः कर्म समग्रं प्रविलीयते ॥
gatasaṅgasya muktasya
jñānāvasthitacetasaḥ
yajñāyācarataḥ karma
samagraṁ pravilīyate

23. The work of one who is free from attachment, who is liberated, whose thought is established in knowledge, who does work only as a sacrifice, is wholly dissolved.

114 Though he inhabits a body, he appears as the Self. Tested by God's touchstone, he is utterly pure.
115 Since this is so, even if he performs any actions out of interest, they are completely absorbed into him.
116 Just as untimely clouds, which appear in the sky but yield no rain, suddenly disappear and become as they were before,
117 Similarly, although such a person performs all actions according to the prescribed rites, by his state of harmony he attains union with all.

ब्रह्मार्पणं ब्रह्म हविर् ब्रह्माग्नौ ब्रह्मणा हुतम् ।
ब्रह्मैव तेन गन्तव्यं ब्रह्मकर्मसमाधिना ॥

brahmārpaṇaṁ brahma havir
brahmāgnāu brahmaṇā hutam
brahmāiva tena gantavyaṁ
brahmakarmasamādhinā

24. Brahman is the offering, Brahman is the oblation poured out by Brahman into the fire of Brahman, Brahman is to be attained by him who always sees Brahman in action.

118 In his mind there exists no such differences as, "This is an oblation," "I am the sacrificer," or "This is the one who partakes of the sacrifice."

119 The sage performing the sacrifice regards the ritual, the offerings, and the chanting as the eternal Self.

120 O Arjuna, one who understands that all action is God is free from the bonds of action, even though he performs actions.

दैवम् एवापरे यज्ञं योगिनः पर्युपासते ।
ब्रह्माग्नाव् अपरे यज्ञ यज्ञेनैवोपजुह्वति ॥

dāivam evāpare yajñaṁ
yoginaḥ paryupāsate
brahmāgnāv apare yajnaṁ
yajñenāivopajuhvati

25. Some yogins perform sacrifice to the gods; others offer sacrifice, by sacrifice itself, in the fire of Brahman.

121 Those who have left behind the youth of indiscrimination, who have committed themselves to non-attachment, and who perform the worship of the fire of yoga,

122 Who perform sacrifices night and day, who burn the ignorance of their minds in the fire of their Guru's words,

123 Make offerings to the fire of yoga, which is called the divine sacrifice. In this way, O Arjuna, they strive for the joy of the Self.

124 Listen, I will tell you more. There are those who maintain the sacrificial fire in the form of God and who offer the sacrifice itself as an oblation to that fire.

श्रोत्रादीनीन्द्रियाण्य् अन्ये संयमाग्निषु जुह्वति ।
शब्दादीन् विषयान् अन्य इन्द्रियाग्निषु जुह्वति ॥

śrotrādīnīndriyāṇy anye
saṁyamāgniṣu juhvati
śabdādīn viṣayān anya
indriyāgniṣu juhvati

26. Others offer senses like hearing in the fire of restraint; still others offer sound and other objects of the senses in the fire of the senses.

125 Some perform the sacrifice in the form of restraint. They make the pure offering of the senses the oblation, with prayers proceeding from the three lower chakras.

126 Others, when the sun of dispassion breaks forth, then prepare the sacrificial hearth of restraint and uncover the fire of the senses.

127 Then, when the flames of dispassion arise, the fuel of the passions is burned up, and the smoke of desire disappears from the vessel of the five senses.

128 Then, carefully following the injunctions of the Vedas, they constantly offer oblations of sense objects into the cauldron of the fire of the senses.

सर्वाणीन्द्रियकर्माणि प्राणकर्माणि चापरे ।
आत्मसंयमयोगाग्नौ जुह्वति ज्ञानदीपिते ॥

sarvānīṇdriyakarmāṇi
prāṇakarmāṇi cāpare
ātmasaṁyamayogāgnāu
juhvati jñānadīpite

27. Others offer all actions of the senses and actions of the vital breath in the fire of the yoga of self-restraint, which is kindled by knowledge.

129 O Arjuna, some entirely wash away all evil tendencies, while others churn the power of discrimination, using the heart as the churning rod.

130 They hold it firmly with tranquility, press it down with fortitude, and churn it vigorously with the words of the Guru.

131 When they churn like this with concentrated minds, their action quickly bears fruit and the fire of wisdom is kindled.

132 When the smoke of the attraction of psychic powers disperses, then a subtle flash appears;

133 And the passions of the mind, made powerless by means of self-control, are thrown into it.

134 The fire blazes up with these passions as fuel, and they are burned up with all the desires of the heart.

135 Such sacrificers, chanting "I am That," throw offerings of the activities of the senses into the kindled fire of wisdom.

136 Having completed the offering, and using the inhalation and the exhalation as a ladle, they perform ablutions in the waters of union with God.

137 Then the bliss of Self-realization, which is all that remains of the offerings poured into the fire of self-control, is the rice cake which they eat.

138 By this kind of sacrifice, some have freed themselves from the bondage of the three

worlds. Although there are many such sacrifices, there is only one goal to be attained.

द्रव्ययज्ञास् तपोयज्ञा योगयज्ञास् तथापरे ।
स्वाध्यायज्ञानयज्ञाश्च यतयः संशितव्रताः ॥
dravyayajñās tapoyajñā
yogayajñās tathāpare
svādhyāyajñānayajñāśca
yatayaḥ saṁśitavratāḥ

28. Some offer as sacrifice their material possessions or their austerities and practice of yoga, while ascetics of severe vows offer study of the scriptures and knowledge as sacrifice.

139 One of these is called the sacrifice of wealth, another arises from the practice of austerity, and still others are called the sacrifices of yoga.

140 In some people, words are poured out in sacrifice. This is called the sacrifice of speech. The sacrifice in which knowledge is imparted is called the sacrifice of wisdom.

141 O Arjuna, all these sacrifices are difficult to perform, but they are possible for a self-controlled person through his merit.

142 The sacrificers are proficient, and they possess the wealth of yoga. They sacrifice their personal selves on the altar of the Self.

अपाने जुह्वति प्राणं प्राणे ऽपानं तथापरे ।
प्राणापानगती रुद्ध्वा प्राणायामपरायणाः ॥
apāne juhvati prāṇaṁ
prāṇe 'pānaṁ tathāpare
prāṇāpānagatī ruddhvā
prāṇāyāmaparāyaṇāḥ

29. Some offer inhalation into exhalation, and others exhalation into inhalation, restraining the path of inhalation and exhalation, intent on control of the vital breath.

143 Some people offer as a sacrifice their vital force through regular practice.

144 Some of them sacrifice the inhalation in the fire of the exhalation, while others control both. O Arjuna, these are called practitioners of *pranayama*.

अपरे नियताहाराः प्राणान् प्राणेषु जुह्वति ।
सर्वे ऽप्येते यज्ञविदो यज्ञक्षपितकल्मषाः ॥
apare niyatāhārāḥ
prāṇān prāṇeṣu juhvati
sarve 'pyete yajñavido
yajñakṣapitakalmaṣāḥ

30. Others who have restricted their foods offer the life breath into the life breath; all these are knowers of sacrifice, and their evils have been destroyed through sacrifice.

145 There are still others who regulate their food intake by using the posture of vajrasana. They sacrifice their vital force by pouring it out into life.

146 These are all seekers of liberation who wash away their mental impurities by means of such sacrifices.

यज्ञशिष्टामृतभुजो यान्ति ब्रह्म सनातनम् ।
नायं लोको ऽस्त्य् अयज्ञस्य कुतो ऽन्यः कुरुसत्तम ॥
yajñaśiṣṭāmṛtabhujo
yānti brahma sanātanam
nāyaṁ loko 'sty ayajñasya
kuto 'nyaḥ kurusattama

31. The enjoyers of the nectar of the sacrificial remnants go to primeval Brahman. Not even this world is for the non-sacrificing; how then the other, Arjuna?

147 There are those whose ignorance has been removed. There remains only the essential Self in which there is no longer any difference between the fire and the sacrificer.

148 When the sacrificer obtains his desire, the sacrifice ends and nothing else remains to be done.

149 This is the state which thought does not enter, where desire has no place, and which is not contaminated by any contact with the evil of duality.

150 That pure and eternally perfect knowledge, which is the result of the sacrifice, is experienced by those who are established in the Self, as they chant, "I am God."

151 As they are satisfied with the nectar which remains from the sacrifice, and as they attain the state of immortality, they are easily united with God.

152 However, for those embodied souls who allow no room in themselves for dispassion, who do not worship the fire of self-control, and who never perform the sacrifice of yoga,

153 Their worldly welfare comes to nothing. So why consider their heavenly state? Think about this, O Arjuna.

एवं बहुविधा यज्ञा वितता ब्रह्मणो मुखे ।
कर्मजान् विद्धि तान् सर्वान् एवं ज्ञात्वा विमोक्ष्यसे ॥
evaṁ bahuvidhā yajñā
vitatā brahmaṇo mukhe
karmajān viddhi tān sarvān
evaṁ jñātvā vimokṣyase

32. Thus sacrifices are of many kinds, spread out before Brahman. Know them all to be born of action. Thus knowing, you shall be released.

154 All these various sacrifices I have described are fully explained in the Vedas.

155 But what need is there for this description? Understand that they result from action, and then the bonds of action will not easily be formed.

श्रेयान् द्रव्यमयाद् यज्ञाज् ज्ञानयज्ञः परंतप ।
सर्वं कर्माखिलं पार्थ ज्ञाने परिसमाप्यते ॥

śreyān dravyamayād yajñāj
jñānayajñaḥ paraṁtapa
sarvaṁ karmākhilaṁ pārtha
jñāne parisamāpyate

33. Better than the sacrifice of material possessions is the wisdom sacrifice, Arjuna; all action without exception, Arjuna, is fully comprehended in wisdom.

156 O Arjuna, all lesser actions, which have their origin in the Vedas, and which have as their highest reward happiness in heaven,

157 Are material sacrifices; but these are inferior to knowledge as a sacrifice, just as the light of the stars fades when the sun rises.

158 Look! This is the treasure of supreme joy. To attain it, yogis darken their eyes with the color of understanding.

159 This is the goal of all action for seekers, a storehouse of understanding for those who have reached detachment, and the means of satisfaction for the hungry.

160 When a person attains this, his mental activity is stilled, his reason loses its insight, and his senses forget their contact with their sense objects.

161 The mind can no longer function, and words lose their power of expression. When a person reaches this state, he finds what he wants to know.

162 At this point, the longing of dispassion is fulfilled, the quest for discrimination is satisfied, and Self-realization is attained without further striving.

163 O Arjuna, this knowledge is supreme. If a person wishes to find it, he should serve the sages with all his heart.

तद् विद्धि प्रणिपातेन परिप्रश्नेन सेवया ।
उपदेक्ष्यन्ति ते ज्ञानं ज्ञानिनस् तत्त्वदर्शिनः ॥

tad viddhi praṇipātena
paripraśnena sevayā
upadekṣyanti te jñānaṁ
jñāninas tattvadarśinaḥ

34. Know this! Through humble submission, through enquiry, through service (on your own part), the knowing ones, the perceivers of truth, will be led to teach you knowledge.

164 They are the dwelling place of all knowledge, and service to them is the threshold by which you can enter. Take hold of it, O Arjuna.

165 Therefore, prostrate yourself at their feet with your body, mind, and soul, and serve them in all humility.

166 Then, whatever you ask, they will explain it to you. Your heart will be enlightened, and all your desires will vanish.

यज् ज्ञात्वा न पुनर् मोहम् एवं यास्यसि पाण्डव ।
येन भूतान्य् अशेषेण द्रक्ष्यस्य् आत्मन्य् अथो मयि ॥

yaj jñātvā na punar moham
evaṁ yāsyasi pāṇḍava
yena bhūtāny aśeṣeṇa
drakṣyasy ātmany atho mayi

35. Knowing that, you shall not again fall into delusion, Arjuna; and by that knowledge you shall see all beings in yourself, and also in Me.

167 With the light of their teaching, your mind will lose its fear, and you will become as free from doubt as the Lord Himself.

168 Then you will see yourself, along with all other creatures, as being absorbed forever in My eternal form.

169 O Arjuna, through the Guru's mercy, the morning of wisdom will dawn, and the darkness of confusion will be dispelled.

अपि चेद् असि पापेभ्यः सर्वेभ्यः पापकृत्तमः ।
सर्वं ज्ञानप्लवेनैव वृजिनं संतरिष्यसि ॥

api ced asi pāpebhyaḥ
sarvebhyaḥ pāpakṛttamaḥ
sarvaṁ jñānaplavenāiva
vṛjinaṁ saṁtariṣyasi

36. Even if you were the most evil of all evildoers, you would cross over all wickedness by the boat of knowledge.

यथैधांसि समिद्धो ऽग्निर् भस्मसात्कुरुते ऽर्जुन ।
ज्ञानाग्निः सर्वकर्माणि भस्मसात् कुरुते तथा ॥

yathāidhāṁsi samiddho 'gnir
bhasmasāt kurute 'rjuna
jñānāgniḥ sarvakarmāṇi

bhasmasāt kurute tathā

37. As the kindled fire reduces firewood to ashes, Arjuna, so the fire of knowledge reduces all actions to ashes.

170 Even if you are a storehouse of sins, an ocean of confusion, and a mountain of infatuation,
171 All this will be insignificant before the pure power of wisdom; it is that great.
172 Just look! This illusory universe, which is the shadow of the formless, cannot equal its light.
173 What are mental impurities before it? Even to mention them would be an insult. Nothing in this world can be compared to its magnitude.
174 Could clouds withstand the hurricane at the time of the great dissolution, which scatters into space the ashes of the three worlds?
175 Could grass suppress the fire of this destruction which, with the fury of the wind, can even be kindled by water?

न हि ज्ञानेन सदृशं पवित्रम् इह विद्यते ।
तत् स्वयं योगसंसिद्धः कालेनात्मनि विन्दति ॥
na hi jñānena sadṛśaṁ
pavitram iha vidyate
tat svayaṁ yogasaṁsiddhaḥ
kālenātmani vindati

38. No purifier equal to knowledge is found here in the world; he who is himself perfected in yoga in time finds that knowledge in the Self.

176 This could never happen. It would be silly even to consider it. Nothing is as sacred as wisdom.
177 Wisdom is the highest thing. What can equal it? Just as spirit is one without a second, so is wisdom.
178 Is there any reflection as brilliant as the sun? Could anyone hold the sky in his grasp?
179 O Arjuna, if one could find a match for the earth, then wisdom might find its equal.
180 From whatever point of view you may consider it, the sacredness of wisdom will be found only in wisdom itself.
181 Just as the taste of nectar can only be described as nectarean, so can wisdom only be compared to itself.
182 It would be a waste of time to say more than this. Then Arjuna said, What You say is true.
183 But when Arjuna was about to ask how this wisdom might be known, the Lord was aware of his thought.
184 He said, O Arjuna, listen carefully to what I say. I will tell you how you can obtain this wisdom.

श्रद्धावाँल् लभते ज्ञानं तत्परः संयतेन्द्रियः ।
ज्ञानं लब्ध्वा परां शान्तिम् अचिरेणाधिगच्छति ॥
śraddhāvāṅl labhate jñānaṁ
tatparaḥ saṁyatendriyaḥ
jñānaṁ labdhvā parāṁ śāntim
acireṇādhigacchati

39. He who possesses faith attains knowledge; devoted to that (knowledge), restraining his senses, having attained knowledge, he quickly attains supreme peace.

185 A person who rejects all sense objects for the sake of the bliss of the Self, who never thinks about the senses,
186 Whose mind harbors no desire, who has no interest in the material world, and who takes delight in faith,
187 Such a person is sought out by wisdom, in which perfect peace is found.
188 When that wisdom is established in the heart and the tender shoots of peace break through, then at once the light of the Self shines forth.
189 Then, wherever he looks, he will see only limitless peace.
190 It would be impossible to describe how the seeds of wisdom are spread far and wide. Enough of this.

अज्ञश्चाश्रद्दधानश्च सशयात्मा विनश्यति ।
नायं लोको ऽस्ति न परो न सुख सशयात्मनः ॥
ajñaścāśraddadhānaśca
samśayātmā vinaśyati
nāyaṁ loko 'sti na paro
na sukhaṁ saṁśayātmanaḥ

40. The man who is ignorant, and does not have faith, who is of a doubting nature, is destroyed. Neither this world nor that beyond, nor happiness, is for him who doubts.

191 Listen! How can I describe the life of a person who has no desire for this wisdom? Death would be preferable to such a life.
192 Like an empty house or a body without consciousness, life without wisdom would be a mere illusion.
193 But if a person who lacks wisdom has a strong desire to obtain it, there is some hope of his gaining it.
194 Without such a desire, it is out of the question. If this eagerness does not exist in a person's mind, know that he has fallen into the fire of doubt.

195 When a person feels a distaste for nectar, he clearly realizes that death is near.

196 The person who takes delight in sense pleasures and who has no regard for wisdom is obviously entangled in doubt.

197 Then, if he falls into doubt, he is utterly destroyed and loses all hope of happiness in this world and the next.

198 Just as a person suffering from fever cannot feel heat or cold and perceives fire and moonlight as the same,

199 Similarly, the doubting person cannot distinguish between truth and falsehood, right and wrong, or what is beneficial and what is harmful.

200 Just as a blind person does not recognize night and day, similarly, one who doubts cannot understand the truth.

201 There is no sin more terrible than doubt. It is a dangerous trap for all creatures.

202 Therefore, cast away your doubt and overcome that state which arises from lack of wisdom.

203 When the darkness of ignorance clouds the mind, it increases in strength and blocks the path of faith.

204 It also envelops the reason, and all the three worlds are pervaded by doubt.

योगसंन्यस्तकर्माणं ज्ञानसंछिन्नसंशयम् ।
आत्मवन्तं न कर्माणि निबध्नन्ति धनंजय ।।
yogasaṁnyastakarmāṇaṁ
jñānasaṁchinnasaṁśayam
ātmavantaṁ na karmāṇi
nibadhnanti dhanaṁjaya

41. Action does not bind him who has renounced action through yoga, whose doubt is cut away by knowledge, and who is possessed of the Self, Arjuna.

तस्माद् अज्ञानसंभूतं हृत्स्थं ज्ञानासिना ऽत्मनः ।
छित्त्वैनं संशयं योगम् आतिष्ठोत्तिष्ठ भारत ।।
tasmād ajñānasaṁbhūtaṁ
hṛtsthaṁ jñānāsinā 'tmanaḥ
chittvāinaṁ saṁśayaṁ yogam
ātiṣṭhottiṣṭha bhārata

42. Therefore, having cut away, with your own sword of knowledge, this doubt that proceeds from ignorance and abides in your heart, resort to yoga! Stand up, Arjuna.

205 Though this ignorance may increase in strength, there is one way to overcome it—by holding the sword of wisdom in your hand.

206 When ignorance is utterly destroyed by the sharp sword of wisdom, then all impurity vanishes from the mind.

207 Therefore, O Arjuna, arise at once and strike the doubt which resides in your heart.

208 Sanjaya said, Hear, O King, how Krishna, the father of omniscience and the light of wisdom, spoke with compassion,

209 And how Arjuna, pondering what He said, now and then asked questions.

210 The excellence of this story should be honored by the nine kinds of feelings. It is the refuge in this world for the minds of all good people.

211 In this way, tranquility will again be established. Listen, therefore, to this Marathi dialogue, full of meaning and deeper than the ocean.

212 Just as the sun appears to be no larger than the palm of your hand, yet even the three worlds are too small to contain its light, it is the same with the meaning of these words. You should now experience this.

213 Just as the wish-fulfilling tree grants all desires, in the same way these words are most significant. Pay attention to them.

214 So be it. What more needs to be said? Although wise people already know this, still I ask them to pay close attention to it.

215 This poem has poetic power and tranquility, just as a young wife who is beautiful and virtuous should have devotion to her husband.

216 It is natural to like sugar. If medicine is added to it, why shouldn't it be taken cheerfully now and then?

217 The breeze from the Malaya mountains is gentle and fragrant. If, by good fortune, it is laden with the taste of nectar and is mingled with the sound of music,

218 Then its touch will soothe the body, its flavor will delight the tongue, and the ears will greet it joyfully.

219 Listening to this story is the same: it will be a feast for the ear and will easily remove all the sorrows of life.

220 If an enemy can be killed by a spell, what need is there to use a weapon? If a disease can be cured by milk and rice, why drink the bitter juice of neem leaves?

221 In this way, liberation may be attained by means of the ears without harming the mind or mortifying the senses.

222 Therefore, the words of the *Gita* are excellent to console all minds. Jnanadeva, the disciple of Nivritti, says, Listen!

5

THE YOGA OF RENUNCIATION OF ACTION

अर्जुन उवाच । *arjuna uvāca*

संन्यासं कर्मणां कृष्ण पुनर् योगं च शंससि ।
यच्छ्रेय एतयोर् एकं तन् मे ब्रूहि सुनिश्चितम् ॥

saṁnyāsaṁ karmaṇāṁ kṛṣṇa
punar yogaṁ ca śaṁsasi
yacchreya etayor ekaṁ
tan me brūhi suniścitam

Arjuna spoke:
1. You praise renunciation of actions, and again You praise yoga, Krishna. Which one is the better of these two? Tell this to me definitely.

THEN Arjuna said to Lord Krishna, What are You saying? If Your words were consistent, my mind might consider them.

2 Previously You explained the renunciation of action, so now how can You encourage the yoga of action?

3 It seems that You speak with a double meaning. Our ignorant minds cannot understand it as You would like us to, O Krishna.

4 Listen. If You teach only one truth, tell us plainly what it is. Is there any need for others to tell You this?

5 For this reason I ask You, who are like a mother, not to explain this truth in an ambiguous way.

6 O Lord, let's forget the past. Now tell us definitely which of these two paths is the better one.

7 The path that You show must have a certain end, it must bear certain fruit, and be straight and easy to follow,

8 Just as it is easy to travel in a comfortable vehicle which moves fast and in which a person's sleep is not disturbed.

9 The Lord was pleased with Arjuna's words and said, It will be as you say. Now, listen!

10 A person who is fortunate enough to have the cow of plenty as his mother, could even have the moon to play with.

11 Think of the compassion of Lord Shiva. Didn't He give the ocean of milk to satisfy Upamanyu's desire for rice and milk?

12 So if Lord Krishna, the storehouse of generosity, gives Himself to the great warrior, why shouldn't Arjuna be filled with bliss?

13 Is this any wonder? With the consort of Lakshmi as his Master, shouldn't he ask for everything he wishes?

14 So the Lord gladly gave what Arjuna asked for. Now I will tell you what Krishna said.

श्रीभगवान् उवाच । *śrībhagavān uvāca*

संन्यास: कर्मयोगश्च नि:श्रेयसकराव् उभौ ।
तयोस् तु कर्मसंन्यासात् कर्मयोगो विशिष्यते ॥

saṁnyāsaḥ karmayogaśca
niḥśreyasakarāv ubhāu
tayos tu karmasaṁnyāsāt
karmayogo viśiṣyate

The Blessed Lord spoke:
2. Both renunciation and the yoga of action lead to incomparable bliss; of the two, however, the yoga of action is superior to the renunciation of action.

15 He said, O Arjuna, truly, renunciation and yoga, when properly understood, are both means to attain liberation.

16 Yet for everyone, both the wise and the ignorant, the yoga of action is very easy to practice, just as it is safer for women and children to cross over water in a boat.

17 So the easier of the two is the yoga of action, by which a person effortlessly attains the fruit of renunciation.

ज्ञेय: स नित्यसंन्यासी यो न द्वेष्टि न काङ्क्षति।
निर्द्वन्द्वो हि महाबाहो सुखं बन्धात् प्रमुच्यते।।

jñeyaḥ sa nityasaṁnyāsī
yo na dveṣṭi na kāṅkṣati
nirdvandvo hi mahābāho
sukhaṁ bandhāt pramucyate

3. He is to be known as the eternal sannyasi who neither hates nor desires, who is indifferent to the pairs of opposites, O Arjuna. He is easily liberated from bondage.

18 I will describe to you the characteristics of the *sannyasi.* Then you will realize that these two paths are not different.

19 A person who does not grieve if he loses something, who doesn't care if he doesn't get anything, whose mind is as stable as Mount Meru,

20 Whose heart has forgotten the sense of "I" and "mine," such a person is an eternal ascetic, O Arjuna.

21 He who attains such a state of mind is freed from the bondage of desire and finds unending joy in the heart of all bliss.

22 There is no need for him to give up his home for anything else, for the mind which is subject to desire has become free from its influence.

23 Just as when a fire has been extinguished, it is possible to put cotton on the ashes,

24 Similarly, in the midst of worldly life, an ascetic whose mind is free from attachment is not aware of the bonds of action.

25 When a person gives up desire, he attains renunciation. Then renunciation of action and the yoga of action are joined.

सांख्ययोगौ पृथग्बाला: प्रवदन्ति न पण्डिता:।
एकम् अप्य् आस्थित: सम्यग् उभयोर् विन्दते फलम्।।

sāṁkhyayogāu pṛthagbālāh
pravadanti na paṇḍitāḥ
ekam apy āsthitaḥ saṁyag
ubhayor vindate phalam

4. "Sankhya and yoga are different," the childish declare; not the wise. Even with one of them, practiced correctly, one finds the fruit of both.

26 Furthermore, O Arjuna, how can the ignorant understand the systems of Sankhya and yoga?

27 Naturally, the ignorant regard these two as different, but is the light in every lamp different?

28 Those who have had a direct experience of the truth consider both to be one.

यत् सांख्यै: प्राप्यते स्थानं तद् योगैर् अपि गम्यते।
एकं सांख्यं च योगं च य: पश्यति स पश्यति।।

yat sāṁkhyāiḥ prāpyate sthānaṁ
tad yogāir api gamyate
ekaṁ sāṁkhyaṁ ca yogaṁ ca
yaḥ paśyati sa paśyati

5. The place that is attained by the followers of Sankhya is also attained by the followers of yoga. Sankhya and yoga are one. He who perceives this, truly perceives.

29 Whatever is attained by Sankhya is also reached through yoga. They are essentially one.

30 Just as the sky and the heavens are not different, similarly, for a person who recognizes that Sankhya and yoga are one,

31 Day has dawned in the world. Only a person who realizes that Sankhya and yoga are not different has seen the Self.

संन्यासस् तु महाबाहो दु:खम् आप्तुम् अयोगत:।
योगयुक्तो मुनिर् ब्रह्म नचिरेणाधिगच्छति।।

samnyāsas tu mahābāho
duḥkham āptum ayogataḥ
yogayukto munir brahma
nacireṇādhigacchati

6. Renunciation indeed, O Arjuna, is difficult to attain without yoga; the sage who is disciplined in yoga quickly attains Brahman.

32 O Arjuna, he who climbs the mountain of liberation by the path of yoga quickly reaches the summit of the highest bliss.

33 If a person abandons this yoga, his hopes are in vain, for he will not attain renunciation.

योगयुक्तो विशुद्धात्मा विजितात्मा जितेन्द्रिय:।
सर्वभूतात्मभूतात्मा कुर्वन्न् अपि न लिप्यते।।

yogayukto viśuddhātmā
vijitātmā jitendriyaḥ
sarvabhūtātmabhūtātmā
kurvann api na lipyate

7. He who is devoted to yoga, whose self is purified, whose self is subdued, whose senses are conquered, whose self has become the self of all beings, is not tainted even when acting.

34 If a person has freed his mind from doubt, purified it by the Guru's words, and then becomes absorbed in the Self—

35 Just as salt is in small, separate grains, but when thrown into the sea it quickly becomes one with it—

36 He whose mind is free from desire becomes one with the Self. Though he appears to be limited by space, he pervades the three worlds.

37 Then such ideas as "doer," "act," or "should" cease to exist for him. Even though he performs actions, he is not the doer of them.

नैव किञ्चित् करोमीति युक्तो मन्यते तत्त्ववित्
पश्यञ्शृण्वन् स्पृशञ्जिघ्रन्न् अश्नन् गच्छन् स्वपञ्श्वसन्

nāiva kiñcit karomīti
yukto manyate tattvavit
paśyañśṛṇvan spṛśañjighrann
aśnan gacchan svapañśvasan

8. "I do not do anything," thus, steadfast in yoga, the knower of truth should think, whether seeing, hearing, touching, smelling, eating, walking, sleeping, breathing,

प्रलपन् विसृजन् गृह्णन्न् उन्मिषन् निमिषन्न् अपि ।
इन्द्रियाणीन्द्रियार्थेषु वर्तन्त इति धारयन् ॥

pralapan visṛjan gṛhṇann
unmiṣan nimiṣann api
indriyāṇīndriyārtheṣu
vartanta iti dhārayan

9. Talking, excreting, grasping, opening the eyes and shutting the eyes, believing "The senses abide in the objects of the senses."

38 For there remains no thought of egoism in him, O Arjuna. Then how can any thought remain in his mind that he is the doer of his actions?

39 Even though he has not given up his body, he possesses every characteristic of a being who is not in a body.

40 Yet he has a body like other people, and outwardly he appears to participate fully in worldly activities.

41 Consider this! He sees with his eyes and hears with his ears, though he himself is not involved in these actions.

42 He experiences touch, he enjoys fragrance, and he also speaks when it is appropriate.

43 He takes food, gets rid of what should be eliminated, and at the proper time he is ready to sleep.

44 He goes wherever he wants, and in this way performs all actions.

ब्रह्मण्य् आधाय कर्माणि सङ्गं त्यक्त्वा करोति यः ।
लिप्यते न स पापेन पद्मपत्त्रम् इवाम्भसा ॥

brahmaṇy ādhāya karmāṇi
saṅgaṁ tyaktvā karoti yaḥ
lipyate na sa pāpena
padmapattram ivāmbhasā

10. Offering his actions to Brahman, having abandoned attachment, he who acts is not tainted by evil any more than a lotus leaf by water.

45 What need is there to mention every action? He does everything—breathes in and out, opens and closes his eyes, and all the rest.

46 O Arjuna, he seems to perform all actions but, because of the power of Self-realization, he is not the doer.

47 As long as he was asleep on the bed of delusion, he was deluded by the pleasure of his dreams; then he awoke in the dawn of wisdom. This is the reason.

कायेन मनसा बुद्ध्या केवलैर् इन्द्रियैर् अपि ।
योगिनः कर्म कुर्वन्ति सङ्गं त्यक्त्वाऽत्मशुद्धये ॥

kāyena manasā buddhyā
kevalāir indriyāir api
yoginaḥ karma kurvanti
saṅgaṁ tyaktvā 'tmaśuddhaye

11. With the body, with the mind, with the intellect, even merely with the senses, the yogins perform action toward self-purification, having abandoned attachment.

48 The tendencies of the senses are attracted to their sense objects, activated by spiritual energy.

49 Just as a person can carry out all household activities by the light of a lamp, in the same way a yogi's body performs all actions.

50 Though he performs actions, he is not bound by them, just as a lotus leaf is not touched by water.

51 Bodily action is that in which reason plays no part and which does not spring up as an idea in the mind.

52 Speaking in simple terms, yogis perform actions with their bodies, just like the movements of children.

53 When the body, composed of the five elements, is asleep, the mind alone functions as in a dream.

54 O Arjuna, how strange is the working of desire! It does not allow the body to wake, and yet makes it experience pain and pleasure.

55 The actions which occur without the aware-

ness of the senses belong only to the mind.

56 Yogis also perform these, but since they have given up egoism, they are beyond action.

57 When the mind has succumbed to confusion and resembles the mind of a ghost, these activities become disorderly.

58 Such a person sees form, hears when called, and speaks with his mouth, but he has no understanding.

59 In short, any action that is performed without a motive is purely action of the senses.

60 But be sure that whatever is universally known is the pure work of reason. Lord Krishna said this to Arjuna.

61 With reason as their guide, they carefully perform actions, but they are free from the bondage of action.

62 They have no trace of egoism either in their reason or in their body, so they remain pure even while performing actions.

63 O Beloved! The only truly selfless action is that which is performed with no thought for the fruit. Yogis know this well, having learned this principle from their Gurus.

64 Nivritti said, Now you have uttered words which surpass all speech and in which the spirit of tranquility overflows its borders.

65 Only those who have completely freed themselves from the crippling senses are worthy to listen.

66 Let us end this digression so the thread of the story will not be lost and the sequence of the verses will not be broken.

67 Fortunately, you have easily been able to explain that which is too difficult for the mind to grasp, and which is unattainable by reason.

68 If you have already said that which is beyond words, why digress? Let's proceed with the story.

69 Knowing the eagerness of his listeners, Jnaneshwar, the disciple of Nivritti, said, Now listen further to the conversation of these two.

70 Then Krishna said to Arjuna, I will now clearly explain to you the characteristics of a perfected being.

युक्तः कर्मफलं त्यक्त्वा शान्तिमाप्नोति नैष्ठिकीम् ।
अयुक्तः कामकारेण फले सक्तो निबध्यते ॥

yuktaḥ karmaphalaṁ tyaktvā
śāntimāpnoti nāiṣṭhikīm
ayuktaḥ kāmakāreṇa
phale sakto nibadhyate

12. He who is disciplined in yoga, having abandoned the fruit of action, attains steady peace; the undisciplined one, attached to fruit, is bound by actions prompted by desire.

सर्वकर्माणि मनसा संन्यस्यास्ते सुखं वशी ।
नवद्वारे पुरे देही नैव कुर्वन् न कारयन् ॥

sarvakarmāṇi manasā
saṁnyasyāste sukhaṁ vaśī
navadvāre pure dehī
nāiva kurvan na kārayan

13. Renouncing all actions with the mind, the embodied one sits happily, as the ruler within the city of nine gates, not acting at all, nor causing action.

71 Eternal peace takes home to itself the person who has attained union with the Self through yoga, and who has become detached from the fruit of action.

72 Because of the bondage of action, O Arjuna, others are tied with the knot of desire to the stake of the enjoyment of the fruit.

73 A perfected being performs all actions, just as a person would who desires their fruit, but then he renounces them as though he had not performed them.

74 Wherever he looks he will see a world of joy, and he finds great enlightenment.

75 He seems to live in the body of nine gates, and yet he is not there. Renouncing all fruit, he engages in action, yet he does not act.

न कर्तृत्वं न कर्माणि लोकस्य सृजति प्रभुः ।
न कर्मफलसंयोगं स्वभावस् तु प्रवर्तते ॥

na kartṛtvaṁ na karmāṇi
lokasya sṛjati prabhuḥ
na karmaphalasaṁyogaṁ
svabhāvas tu pravartate

14. The Lord does not create either the agency (the means of action) or the actions of people, or the union of action with its fruit. Nature, on the other hand, proceeds (in all this).

76 The Lord of all, who is free from actions, commands the whole expanse of the three worlds.

77 Even if it is said that He is the doer, He is still unaffected by any action. His indifference is untainted by it.

78 The absence of doership does not disturb the Lord's great sleep, nor does it distress

Him. Nevertheless, He generates the whole array of the five elements.

79 Although He pervades the life of the world, He Himself belongs to none. He is quite unaware of the creation or dissolution of this world.

नादत्ते कस्यचित् पापं न चैव सुकृतं विभुः ।
अज्ञानेनावृतं ज्ञानं तेन मुह्यन्ति जन्तवः ।।
nādatte kasyacit pāpaṁ
na cāiva sukṛtaṁ vibhuḥ
ajñānenāvṛtaṁ jñānaṁ
tena muhyanti jantavaḥ

15. The Lord does not receive either the evil or the good deeds of anyone. Knowledge is enveloped by ignorance. By it (ignorance) people are deluded.

80 Although merit and sin are very close to Him, He does not see them. Why say anymore?

81 Assuming bodily form, He sports with mortals, but this does not corrupt His formlessness.

82 People say that He creates, maintains, and destroys; but listen, Arjuna, this is ignorance.

ज्ञानेन तु तद् अज्ञानं येषां नाशितम् आत्मनः ।
तेषाम् आदित्यवज् ज्ञानं प्रकाशयति तत् परम् ।।
jñānena tu tad ajñānaṁ
yesāṁ nāśitam ātmanaḥ
teṣām ādityavaj jñānaṁ
prakāśayati tat param

16. But for those in whom this ignorance of the Self is destroyed by knowledge, that knowledge of theirs causes the Supreme to shine like the sun.

83 When ignorance is utterly destroyed and its darkness is dispelled, a person realizes that the Lord does not perform actions.

84 When he understands that the Lord is not the doer and that from the very beginning he has always been essentially one with the Supreme,

85 When this idea arises in his mind through discrimination, how can any trace of duality remain in him? From his own experience, he recognizes that the whole world is in a state of liberation,

86 Just as when the sun rises radiant in its mansion in the east, darkness vanishes at once from the four quarters of the earth.

87 How can I adequately describe the feeling of harmony in the hearts of those who are filled with this all-embracing wisdom?

तद्बुद्धयस् तदात्मानस् तन्निष्ठास् तत्परायणाः ।
गच्छन्त्यपुनरावृत्तिं ज्ञाननिर्धूतकल्मषाः ।।
tadbuddhayas tadātmānas
tanniṣṭhās tatparāyaṇāḥ
gacchantyapunarāvṛttim
jñānanirdhūtakalmaṣāḥ

17. They whose minds are absorbed in that (i.e. the Supreme), whose selves are fixed on that, whose basis is that, who hold that as the highest object, whose evils have been shaken off by knowledge, go to the end of rebirth.

88 Is it strange to say that they regard not only themselves but the whole universe as God?

89 Just as good fortune never looks at misery even out of curiosity, as true discrimination doesn't know delusion,

90 Just as the sun sees no trace of darkness even in a dream, as nectar hears no tale of death,

91 And just as the moon has no memory of heat, similarly, such wise beings can perceive no difference between creatures.

विद्याविनयसंपन्ने ब्राह्मणे गवि हस्तिनि ।
शुनि चैव श्वपाके च पण्डिताः समदर्शिनः ।।
vidyāvinayasaṁpanne
brāhmaṇe gavi hastini
śuni cāiva śvapāke ca
paṇḍitāḥ samadarśinaḥ

18. The wise see the same (atman) in a brahman endowed with wisdom and cultivation, in a cow, in an elephant, and even in a dog or in an outcaste.

92 How can any concept remain, such as this creature is a fly, that one is an elephant, this man is an outcaste, that one is a brahmin, this is my son, and that is someone else's?

93 Or that this is a cow, that is a dog, this is a noble man, and that is an ordinary one—how can anyone dream of such things?

94 How can such differences exist? When egoism has been utterly destroyed, what is left that can produce any sense of separateness?

95 Then you can understand that God is everywhere, eternal and unchanging, and that you yourself are God. Know that this is the secret of an evenly balanced mind.

इहैव तैर् जितः सर्गो येषां साम्ये स्थितं मनः ।

निर्दोषं हि समं ब्रह्म तस्माद् ब्रह्मणि ते स्थिताः ॥

ihāiva tāir jitaḥ sargo
yeṣāṁ sāmye sthitaṁ manaḥ
nirdoṣaṁ hi samaṁ brahma
tasmād brahmaṇi te sthitāḥ

19. Even here on earth, rebirth is conquered by those whose mind is established in impartiality. Brahman is spotless and impartial; therefore they are established in Brahman.

96 Such a person may not have given up contact with sense objects nor mortified his senses; yet, being free from desire, he experiences detachment.

97 Like others he follows worldly pursuits, yet at the same time he has freed himself from the lack of awareness of ordinary people.

98 Though he is in the body, other people do not recognize him, like a ghost which is in the world and yet invisible to human beings,

99 Or just as water plays upon water when agitated by the wind, making people think that the wave is different from the water.

100 This is how a person is who has reached harmony in all things. He is truly God Himself.

न प्रहृष्येत् प्रियं प्राप्य नोद्विजेत् प्राप्य चाप्रियम् ।
स्थिरबुद्धिर् असंमूढो ब्रह्मविद् ब्रह्मणि स्थितः ॥

na prahṛṣyet priyaṁ prāpya
nodvijet prāpya cāpriyam
sthirabuddhir asammūḍho
brahmavid brahmaṇi sthitaḥ

20. One should not rejoice upon attaining what is pleasant, nor should one shudder upon encountering what is unpleasant; with firm intellect, undeluded, knowing Brahman, one is established in Brahman.

101 O Arjuna, a person who has reached this state of even-mindedness has one other characteristic, about which I will tell you briefly, said Krishna.

102 Just as a mountain cannot be washed away by a mirage, similarly, a person who is not affected by joy or grief,

103 Is truly established in even-mindedness. Krishna said, He is truly God, O Arjuna.

बाह्यस्पर्शेष्वसक्तात्मा विन्दत्यात्मनि यत् सुखम् ।
स ब्रह्मयोगयुक्तात्मा सुखम् अक्षयम् अश्नुते ॥

bāhyasparśeṣvasaktātmā
vindatyātmani yat sukham
sa brahmayogayuktātmā
sukham akṣayam aśnute

21. He whose self is unattached to external sensations, who finds happiness in the Self, whose Self is united with Brahman through yoga, reaches imperishable happiness.

104 Is it any wonder that a person who does not wish to give up the bliss of the Self in order to return to the slavery of the senses finds no pleasure in sense objects?

105 He fully enjoys the bliss of the Self, and once his heart is established in it, he will never leave it.

106 Once the chakora bird has fed on clear moonbeams among beds of lotus flowers, will it want to lick the sand?

107 Similarly, need it be said that a person who has attained the bliss of the Self and has attained Self-realization naturally gives up all contacts with sense objects?

ये हि संस्पर्शजा भोगा दुःखयोनय एव ते ।
आद्यन्तवन्तः कौन्तेय न तेषु रमते बुधः ॥

ye hi saṁsparśajā bhogā
duḥkhayonaya eva te
ādyantavantaḥ kāunteya
na teṣu ramate budhaḥ

22. Pleasures born of contact, indeed, are wombs (i.e. sources) of pain, since they have a beginning and an end (i.e. are not eternal), Arjuna. The wise man is not content with them.

108 Now your curiosity will certainly make you wonder about those who are deluded by sense pleasures.

109 People who don't know themselves indulge in sense pleasures, just as a hungry person will even eat husks,

110 Or just as a thirsty deer will rush to a mirage in the desert.

111 Similarly, those who haven't seen the Self and who haven't tasted its bliss desire sense objects and relish them.

112 Otherwise, it is absurd to say that there is happiness in sense objects. Why isn't it possible to use lightning to illumine the world?

113 Tell me, if the shadow of clouds could afford protection against wind, rain, and heat, why should people build three-story houses?

114 It is as futile to talk ignorantly of sense pleasures as it is to call a poisonous root sweet.

115 Just as Mars might be called auspicious or a mirage might be called water, in the same way there is no sense in talking about the

pleasures derived from sense objects.

116 Enough of all this talking. Would the shade of a serpent's hood be cooling for a mouse?

117 O Arjuna, just as a piece of bait on a hook is good only as long as it is not eaten by a fish, it is the same with the contact with sense objects. Understand this clearly.

118 When sense objects are seen with a dispassionate eye, they are as appealing as the fat of a jaundiced body, O Arjuna.

119 Therefore, understand that the happiness gained from enjoying sense objects is actually painful. But what can fools do? They cannot live without it.

120 These poor people have no understanding of inner happiness, so they have to indulge their senses. Do maggots ever feel disgusted by sores?

121 To such unfortunate people, pain appears to be the heart of pleasure. They are like frogs immersed in the mire of sense objects. How can fish give up water?

122 If all creatures became indifferent to sense pleasures, the worldly births which are the source of suffering would serve no purpose.

123 Who would suffer the pangs of life in the womb or the pain of life and death?

124 If the people who are addicted to sense pleasures gave them up, what place would there be for sin? Wouldn't the term "worldly existence" lose its meaning?

125 Those who regard the pain of the senses as pleasure confuse the falseness of ignorance with truth.

126 For this reason, O Arjuna, when sense objects are rightly viewed, they are seen as evil. Be careful that you don't forget and walk on that path.

127 Dispassionate people renounce them as if they were poison. The pleasure of the senses which manifests as pain does not appeal to the dispassionate.

शक्नोतीहैव यः सोढुं प्राक् शरीरविमोक्षणात् ।
कामक्रोधोद्भवं वेगं स युक्तः स सुखी नरः ॥
śaknotīhāiva yaḥ soḍhuṁ
prāk śarīravimokṣaṇāt
kāmakrodhodbhavaṁ vegaṁ
sa yuktaḥ sa sukhī naraḥ

23. He who is able to endure here on earth, before liberation from the body, the agitation that arises from desire and anger, is disciplined; he is a happy man.

128 There is no trace of this in the hearts of the wise, for they have learned to control the physical tendencies of their bodies.

129 They are completely unaware of outer affairs; there is only the experience of bliss in their hearts.

130 Even so, they enjoy it in a different way, not like a bird pecking at fruit. They are unaware of any distinction between the enjoyer and the object enjoyed.

131 The enjoyer becomes one with the object of enjoyment, the mountain of egoism is removed, and they cling firmly to their inner joy.

132 They are united in that embrace, just as when water is mixed with water there is no sign of any separation.

133 Their separateness vanishes, just like the wind is lost in the sky. In such a union there remains only the bliss of the Self.

134 When all trace of duality disappears, could a person say that he alone remains? Who would there be to bear witness to it?

135 Let's stop all this now. Should we try to express the inexpressible? Those who enjoy inner happiness know the secret.

136 Those who enjoy this bliss to the fullest, who are absorbed in the Self, are truly molded in the bliss of the Self.

137 They are the image of bliss, the green shoots of the tree of joy, a palace built by great wisdom.

138 They are the abode of discrimination, the very essence of God, and the ornamented limbs of Self-knowledge.

139 They are the essence of truth and are forms of the spirit. Isn't this enough praise for them?

140 When you take delight in praising the saints, you forget the subject of your talk, although you speak extremely well on other subjects.

141 Now control your enthusiasm, light the lamp of the meaning of the *Gita*, and bring the auspicious dawn into the temple of the hearts of the righteous.

142 Jnaneshwar heard these quiet words of his Guru and said, Listen to what Krishna says.

यो ऽन्तःसुखो ऽन्तरारामस् तथान्तर्ज्योतिर् एव यः ।
स योगी ब्रह्मनिर्वाणं ब्रह्मभूतो ऽधिगच्छति ॥
yo 'ntaḥsukho 'ntārāramas
tathāntarjyotir eva yaḥ
sa yogī brahmanirvāṇam

brahmabhūto, 'dhigacchati

24. He who finds his happiness within, his delight within, and his light within, this yogin attains the bliss of Brahman, becoming Brahman.

लभन्ते ब्रह्मनिर्वाणम् ऋषय: क्षीणकल्मषा: ।
छिन्नद्वैधा यतात्मान: सर्वभूतहिते रता: ॥
labhante brahmanirvāṇam
ṛṣayaḥ kṣīṇakalmaṣāḥ
chinnadvāidhā yatātmānaḥ
sarvabhūtahite ratāḥ

25. The seers, whose evils have been destroyed, whose doubts have been cut away, whose selves are restrained, who delight in the welfare of all beings, attain the bliss of Brahman.

143 O Arjuna, those who plunge into the depths of infinite bliss, become established in it and become one with That.

144 A person who sees his oneness with the universe through the light of the Self can be considered the highest Self while he is still in the body.

145 The Self is supreme, unchanging, and infinite, and the dispassionate are worthy to attain it.

146 It flourishes in the great sages and is shared by those who are free of desire. Those who are free of doubt enjoy this rich harvest.

कामक्रोधवियुक्तानां यतीनां यतचेतसाम् ।
अभितो ब्रह्मनिर्वाणं वर्तते विदितात्मनाम् ॥
kāmakrodhaviyuktānāṁ
yatīnāṁ yatacetasām
abhito brahmanirvāṇaṁ
vartate viditātmanām

26. To those ascetics who have cast aside desire and anger, whose thought is controlled, who are knowers of the Self, the bliss of Brahman exists everywhere.

147 Those who have become liberated from sense pleasures and have controlled their minds, sleep in the Self and do not awake again.

148 That is the peace of the Eternal, the goal of all who have attained enlightenment. O Arjuna, they are the Self.

149 If you want to know how they become like this, how they attain the state of the Eternal while still in the body, I will briefly explain.

स्पर्शान् कृत्वा बहिर् बाह्यांश् चक्षुश्चैवान्तरे भ्रुवो: ।
प्राणापानौ समौ कृत्वा नासाभ्यन्तरचारिणौ ॥
sparśan kṛtvā bahir bāhyāṁś
cakṣuścāivāntare bhruvoḥ
prāṇāpānāu samāu kṛtvā
nāsābhyantaracāriṇāu

27. Expelling outside contacts and fixing the gaze between the two eyebrows, equalizing the inhalation and exhalation, moving within the nostrils,

यतेन्द्रियमनोबुद्धिर् मुनिर् मोक्षपरायण: ।
विगतेच्छाभयक्रोधो य: सदा मुक्त एव स: ॥
yatendriyamanobuddhir
munir mokṣaparāyaṇaḥ
vigatecchābhayakrodho
yah sadā mukta eva saḥ

28. The sage whose highest aim is release; whose senses, mind and intellect are controlled; from whom desire, fear and anger have departed, is forever liberated.

भोक्तारं यज्ञतपसां सर्वलोकमहेश्वरम् ।
सुहृदं सर्वभूतानां ज्ञात्वा मां शान्तिमृच्छति ॥
bhoktāraṁ yajñatapasāṁ
sarvalokamaheśvaram
suhṛdaṁ sarvabhūtānāṁ
jñātvā māṁ śāntimṛcchati

29. Having known Me, the enjoyer of sacrifices and austerities, the mighty Lord of all the world, the friend of all creatures, he (the sage) attains peace.

150 When they have eliminated all sense desires by means of dispassion, they concentrate the mind within the body.

151 With the gaze turned inwards and fixed on the space between the eyebrows where the three nadis—*ida, pingala*, and *sushumna*—meet;

152 Stopping the breath moving through the right and left nostrils, and equalizing the outgoing and incoming breaths, they make the mind steady in the *sahasrara* at the crown of the head.

153 Just as when the Ganges reaches the ocean, carrying with it the water from the streets, the different streams cannot be distinguished,

154 Similarly, O Arjuna, all distinctions between various desires cease when the mind becomes stilled in the inner space by controlling the breath.

155 Then, look! The mental canvas with the painting of worldly existence is torn apart, just as reflections disappear when a lake

dries up.

156 When the mind has stopped functioning, where is there any place for egoism or passion? Therefore, a person who has realized the Self becomes God while still in the body.

157 I have spoken earlier of those who have attained the Self while in the body. They have reached this state by following this path.

158 Climbing the mountains of restraint and crossing the ocean of constant practice, they have attained their goal.

159 Having purified themselves and accomplished their earthly tasks, they have become one with the essential truth.

160 When Krishna explained the purpose of yoga in this way, Arjuna was filled with wonder.

161 Krishna, realizing this, smiled and asked Arjuna, Have these words brought you peace of mind?

162 Arjuna replied, O Lord, You are a master at understanding others' minds, and You have understood very well the tendency of my own mind.

163 You have already understood what I wanted You to explain further. Show me again clearly what You have already told me.

164 But listen to me. The path You have pointed out is like a bridge; a person can use it to cross a river more easily than by swimming.

165 Similarly, the path of yoga is easier than the path of knowledge for people as weak as we are, but it still takes time to learn it. We will be patient, though.

166 Will You now test our understanding? Let your explanation be complete, even if it is lengthy.

167 Then Krishna said, If you find this path a good one, what can I lose by explaining it to you again? I will gladly speak of it.

168 O Arjuna, if you will listen and then put it into practice, will it be a waste of time to explain it?

169 Krishna's heart was already compassionate, and He had a special affection for Arjuna. Who can understand the wonder of His love?

170 It was like a shower of the waters of compassion or the birth of a new love. It would be difficult to describe that compassionate look of Krishna's.

171 It was as if it were molded out of nectar, an intoxication of love. It was captured in Arjuna's fascination and could not be withdrawn.

172 The more we digress about this, the longer our story will be, but the nature of His love defies all description.

173 Is there any reason for wonder? Who could possibly fathom the Lord, who is even unaware of Himself?

174 However, judging from those last words of His, it seems that He was bewitched. He said forcefully to Arjuna,

175 Listen, O Beloved! I will happily explain all this in a way that you will understand.

176 What this yoga represents, what its purpose is, who is qualified to practice it,

177 I will now explain everything that has been said about these things.

178 Listen carefully to Me. With these words, Krishna will begin to speak about the subject of the next chapter.

6

THE YOGA OF MEDITATION

THEN Sanjaya said to the king, O great King! Listen to the teaching of yoga which Lord Krishna will now explain to Arjuna.
2 It was as though Krishna had prepared for Arjuna a great feast of the essence of God; and we, the guests, had arrived at the right time.
3 I cannot express how great our good fortune is. It is as though a thirsty man, when drinking water, discovered that it was nectar.
4 It is the same with you and me, for without effort on our part we have been given this truth. Then Dhritarashtra said, I do not ask this of you.
5 From these words of the king, Sanjaya understood what was in the king's heart, possessed by his affection for his sons.
6 Perceiving this, he smiled and said to himself, the old king has been blinded by his love for his children; otherwise, my words were relevant at this time.
7 But how can he understand that? How can a blind person see the light of day? But Sanjaya didn't want to say this, for fear that the king would be offended.
8 However, inwardly he was delighted that he had the opportunity to hear the discussion between Lord Krishna and Arjuna.
9 In the fullness of joy and with steady purpose, he will now begin to speak respectfully to the king.
10 This is the sixth discourse of the *Gita*, Sanjaya's story.
11 Just as the nectar arose from the ocean of milk, we are given here the essence of the meaning of the *Gita*, the other shore of the ocean of discrimination, the treasure of the wealth of yoga,
12 The resting place of primordial matter, which cannot be expressed by the Vedas, and from which springs the root of the vine of the *Gita*.
13 This sixth discourse will be explained in beautiful language, so listen to it carefully.
14 My language is Marathi, but I will compose this work with such beautiful words and style that it will easily surpass nectar.
15 Even a lovely melody cannot equal its sweet delicacy, and its charm will exceed the power of fragrance.
16 Furthermore, overcome by its sweetness, tongues will spring up in the ears, and hearing it, the various sense organs will begin to quarrel among themselves.
17 Although listening to speech is the function of the ears, the sense of taste will say, "This joy is mine. My words will be the fragrance enjoyed by the sense of smell."
18 Marveling at the flowing style, the eyes will be filled with satisfaction and exclaim, "What a wonder! The treasure house of beauty has been opened for us here!"
19 When the sentences have been arranged, the mind will rush forward with outstretched arms to embrace the words.
20 In this way the senses will compete with each other, but each one will understand the meaning in its own way, just as the sun illumines the whole world.
21 Such a wide range of meaning is rarely found, and he who understands these words will find in them all the qualities of the wish-fulfilling gem.
22 I respectfully offer to those who are dispassionate full dishes of food in the form of these words, served with the essence of eternal bliss.
23 Only those who have lighted the lamps of

the radiance of the Self can partake of this food without the awareness of the senses.

24 While doing so, the listeners must ignore the craving of the ears, for the mind alone should enjoy it.

25 With his individuality merged in God, and the veil withdrawn from the inner meaning of the words, a person should freely enjoy the supreme bliss of the Self.

26 If such pleasure is the result, then this explanation will serve a good purpose. Otherwise, it will be nothing but a story told to the deaf and the dumb.

27 Enough of this! There is no need to arouse the listeners further. Dispassionate people naturally have the right to hear it.

28 Only those who, out of their love for Self-realization, have given up all thought of heaven and earth can appreciate its sweetness.

29 Just as crows cannot recognize the moon, ordinary people will never be able to understand this work.

30 Just as the chakora bird feeds on moonbeams, similarly, this writing is meant only for the wise. Since the ignorant cannot comprehend it, there is no need to go into it further.

31 I have spoken of all this in my digression, and you good people must forgive me. Now I will speak of Krishna's teaching.

32 It is difficult for the mind to grasp, and it can hardly be expressed in words, but with the light of Nivritti's grace I will be able to understand it.

33 That which a person cannot see with his eyes he may perceive without their aid if he has acquired the subtle power of wisdom.

34 The alchemist can find gold in iron if, by good fortune, he can discover the touchstone.

35 What can't we do if we have the Guru's grace? Jnanadeva says, I have this in abundance.

36 In the strength of that grace I will speak. In words I will give form to the formless and cause the senses to experience what is beyond their power to know.

37 The Lord in whom the six qualities dwell—success, wealth, benevolence, knowledge, dispassion, and sovereignty—

38 Who is therefore called blessed, said to Arjuna, Now pay attention to Me.

श्रीभगवान् उवाच । *śrībhagavān uvāca*

अनाश्रितः कर्मफलं कार्यं कर्म करोति यः ।
स संन्यासी च योगी च न निरग्निर् न चाक्रियः ॥

anāśritaḥ karmaphalaṁ
kāryaṁ karma karoti yaḥ
sa saṁnyāsī ca yogī ca
na niragnir na cākriyaḥ

The Blessed Lord spoke:
1. He who performs that action which is his duty, while renouncing the fruit of action, is a renunciant and a yogin; not he who is without a consecrated fire, and who fails to perform sacred rites.

39 Listen! The yogi and the *sannyasi* cannot be regarded as different. When correctly understood, the two are one.

40 Apart from the apparent difference of name, even yoga itself is *sannyasa*. When seen in the light of the Self, there is no difference between them.

41 Just as the same person may be given different names, as two roads lead to the same place,

42 And just as different vessels may be filled with the same kind of water, we should regard the apparent difference between yoga and *sannyasa* in the same way.

43 Listen, Arjuna. Everyone considers a person to be a true yogi if he performs actions, yet does not desire their fruit.

44 Just as the earth naturally produces vegetation without any awareness of itself, and doesn't look forward to the grain that grows,

45 Similarly, the yogi performs actions whenever the occasion demands, according to his circumstances and the duties of his caste and stage of life.

46 He does what is right without any egoism, and he doesn't set his heart on the fruit of his actions.

47 Such a person is a true yogi. Listen, Arjuna! He is truly a master of yoga.

48 If there is some duty to be performed but a person says, "I will give up this work, for it leads to bondage," and then he immediately begins another task,

49 His work is useless, like that of a stubborn servant who washes off one liniment and then persists in applying another.

50 According to his destiny he already carries on his shoulders the burden of a house-

holder's duties. The practice of *sannyasa* only adds to it.

51 So a person shouldn't refrain from worshiping the fire or fail to carry out his appointed duties. This bliss of yoga is within one's own Self.

यं संन्यासम् इति प्राहुर् योगं तं विद्धि पाण्डव ।
न ह्य् असंन्यस्तसंकल्पो योगी भवति कश्चन ।।

yaṁ saṁnyāsam iti prāhur
yogaṁ taṁ viddhi pāṇḍava
na hy asaṁnyastasaṁkalpo
yogī bhavati kaścana

2. That which they call renunciation, know that to be yoga, Arjuna. Without renouncing selfish purpose, no one becomes a yogin.

52 Know that a *sannyasi* is the same as a yogi. This truth has been universally proclaimed in various scriptures.

53 When the will is finally renounced, then the essence of yoga is discovered through the poise gained from experience.

आरुरुक्षोर् मुनेर् योगं कर्म कारणम् उच्यते ।
योगारूढस्य तस्यैव शमः कारणम् उच्यते ।।

āruruksọr muner yogaṁ
karma kāraṇam ucyate
yogārūḍhasya tasyāiva
śamaḥ kāraṇam ucyate

3. For the sage desirous of attaining yoga, action is said to be the means; for him who has already attained yoga, tranquility is said to be the means.

54 Now, Arjuna, if you wish to climb to the summit of the mountain of yoga, don't fail to do so by the path of action.

55 By the path of yogic postures, you may rise from the lower levels of sense-restraint and climb upwards by the steep ascent of *pranayama*.

56 Then you can reach the cliff of *pratyahara*, which is slippery even for the feet of reason and from which hatha yogis, in spite of their boasting, are hurled down.

57 Even though they are helpless on the cliff of *pratyahara*, with the strength derived from discipline they cling to it with the claws of dispassion.

58 In this way, aided by the power of the *prana*, they come to the broad road of mental concentration and continue until they pass the peak of meditation.

59 Then they will reach the end of the path, all desire for further progress will be satisfied, and those who seek the goal will attain it in the joy of the Self.

60 *Samadhi* comes at the highest level, where no path remains and where all memories of the past vanish.

61 Now I will tell you the characteristics of a person who has attained yoga by these means and who reaches limitless perfection.

यदा हि नेन्द्रियार्थेषु न कर्मस्व् अनुसज्जते ।
सर्वसंकल्पसंन्यासी योगारूढस् तदोच्यते ।।

yadā hi nendriyārtheṣu
na karmasv anusajjate
sarvasaṁkalpasaṁnyāsī
yogārūḍhas tadocyate

4. When he is attached neither to the objects of the senses nor to actions, and has renounced all purpose, he is then said to have attained yoga.

62 For a person who sleeps in the chamber of Self-awareness, sense objects don't often visit the house of his senses.

63 His mind is not disturbed when either pleasure or pain touches his body, and when sense objects present themselves before him he remains unconcerned.

64 His senses are engaged in their appropriate functions, yet his heart entertains no desire for the fruit.

65 While his body is fully awake, he is like a person who has fallen asleep. Know that such a person is perfectly established in yoga.

66 At this point Arjuna said, O Krishna! All this fills me with wonder. Tell me who has granted him such merit.

उद्धरेद् आत्मना ऽत्मानं नात्मानम् अवसादयेत् ।
आत्मैव ह्यात्मनो बन्धुर् आत्मैव रिपुर् आत्मनः ।।

uddhared ātmanā 'tmānaṁ
nātmānam avasādayet
ātmāiva hyātmano bandhur
ātmāiva ripur ātmanaḥ

5. One should uplift oneself by the Self; one should not degrade oneself; for the Self alone can be a friend to oneself, and the Self alone can be an enemy of oneself.

67 Then Lord Krishna smiled and said, Isn't your question a strange one? In this state of union, who will give what, and to whom?

68 When a person in a state of deep ignorance falls asleep on the bed of delusion, he experiences the painful dream of life and death.

69 Afterwards, when he suddenly awakes, he realizes that all this was an illusion, and the realization of his own Self also arises from within.

70 O Arjuna, such a person brings about his own downfall by indulging in self-conceit.

बन्धुर् आत्मा ऽत्मनस् तस्य येनात्मैवात्मना जितः ।
अनात्मनस् तु शत्रुत्वे वर्तेतात्मैव शत्रुवत् ॥

bandhur ātmā 'tmanas tasya
yenātmāivātmanā jitaḥ
anātmanas tu śatrutve
vartetātmāiva śatruvat

6. For him who has conquered himself by the Self, the Self is a friend; but for him who has not conquered himself, the Self remains hostile, like an enemy.

71 A person should give up egoism. Then he will become what he really is, and he will have assured his own welfare.

72 Otherwise, like a chrysalis in its cocoon, the Self will be its own enemy by imposing on the body the concept of selfhood.

73 How strange it would be if some unfortunate person should wish to be blind at the moment when he discovers a treasure, or if he should close his eyes;

74 Or if a person out of sheer madness should entertain some false idea in his heart, such as, "I am not myself; I am lost."

75 He is himself, yet what can be done if he doesn't think so? Can death result from a wound received in a dream?

76 The unenlightened person is like a parrot which, perplexed by the fact that the rod is spinning beneath its feet because of the weight of its body, clings to the rod and cannot fly away when it should do so.

77 In vain it twists its neck and contracts its chest in order to clasp the rod more and more firmly with its claws.

78 It imagines that it is really bound and, caught in this illusion, it grasps the rod even more firmly, although its feet are actually free.

79 Can it be said that it is caught, when it is really not held at all? Even if it were dragged away by force, it would not loosen its hold.

80 Therefore, the person who is filled with conceit is his own enemy. The enlightened being does not hold onto such illusions, said Lord Krishna.

जितात्मनः प्रशान्तस्य परमात्मा समाहितः ।
शीतोष्णसुखदुःखेषु तथा मानापमानयोः ॥

jītātmanaḥ praśāntasya
paramātmā samāhitaḥ
śītoṣṇasukhaduḥkheṣu
tathā mānāpamānayoḥ

7. The highest Self of him who has conquered himself and is peaceful, is steadfast in cold, heat, pleasure, and pain; thus also in honor and dishonor.

81 The higher Self is not far from a person who has conquered his senses and whose desires have been subdued.

82 Just as pure gold remains when all impurities have been separated from it, similarly, the individual soul becomes God when the will has ceased to function.

83 When the shape of a pot no longer exists, the space inside it merges into the space outside. It doesn't have to move to another place.

84 In the same way, a person whose false individuality is destroyed becomes the highest Self.

85 Then heat and cold, the turmoil of pleasure and pain, and the concepts of honor and dishonor no longer exist for him.

86 Wherever the sun travels in its path, the universe becomes light. Similarly, whatever such a person acquires truly becomes himself.

87 Just as showers of rain falling from the clouds do not pierce the ocean, in the same way the master of yoga is indifferent to good and evil.

ज्ञानविज्ञानतृप्तात्मा कूटस्थो विजितेन्द्रियः ।
युक्त इत्युच्यते योगी समलोष्टाश्मकाञ्चनः ॥

jñānavijñānatṛptātmā
kūṭastho vijitendriyaḥ
yukta ityucyate yogī
samaloṣṭāśmakāñcanaḥ

8. The yogin who is satisfied with knowledge and discrimination, who is unchanging, with conquered senses, to whom a clod, a stone, and gold are the same, is said to have attained samadhi.

88 When he considers worldly knowledge, he sees that it is false. When he sees rightly, he knows that he himself is wisdom.

89 Since no sense of duality remains in him, there is no longer any need to consider such ideas as "partial" or "all-pervasive."

90 In this way, a person who has conquered his senses while still in the body experiences

the bliss of the highest Self.

91 Being self-controlled and harmonized, for him there is never such a thing as "small" or "great."

92 He regards a heap of gold as large as Mount Meru and a clod of earth as the same.

93 He considers even a jewel which is so precious that in comparison the whole earth is of little worth, as no more valuable than a stone.

सुहृन्मित्रार्युदासीन मध्यस्थद्वेष्यबन्धुषु ।
साधुष्व् अपि च पापेषु समबुद्धिर् विशिष्यते ।।

suhṛnmitrāryudāsīna-
madhyasthadveṣyabāndhuṣu
sādhuṣv api ca pāpeṣu
samabuddhir viśiṣyate

9. He who is equal-minded toward friend, companion, and enemy, who is neutral among enemies and kinsmen, and who is impartial among the righteous and also among the evil, is to be distinguished among men.

94 How can he imagine such strange differences as a friend or an enemy, an indifferent person or a well-wisher?

95 Who is a relative and who is hateful for a person who has realized his oneness with the whole universe?

96 Furthermore, O Arjuna, in his sight there can be neither high nor low. When gold is tested by the touchstone, is it assigned different values?

97 Just as by means of the touchstone only the purest possible gold is obtained, similarly, such a person regards all living and nonliving beings with complete impartiality.

98 Even though all created things may vary in form, they are nevertheless made of the same gold, the eternal Absolute.

99 He has attained this supreme wisdom in its fullness, so he is not deceived by the outer appearances of all these forms.

100 When we look at the piece of cloth, we find thread throughout the whole fabric. In fact, there is nothing but thread.

101 A person who experiences this direct perception has unchanging evenness of mind.

102 He is worthy of being called the holiest of the holy. The mere sight of him commands respect, and in his company even a deluded person becomes absorbed in God.

103 Religion lives through his words, the sight of him produces the highest psychic powers, and he takes constant pleasure in heavenly bliss.

104 When we remember him, his greatness is imparted to us. Let it be so. And to praise him will be to our advantage.

योगी युञ्जीत सततम् आत्मानं रहसि स्थितः ।
एकाकी यतचित्तात्मा निराशीर् अपरिग्रहः ।।

yogī yuñjīta satatam
ātmānaṁ rahasi sthitaḥ
ekākī yatacittātmā
nirāśīr aparigrahaḥ

10. The yogin should concentrate constantly on the Self, remaining in solitude, alone, with controlled mind and body, having no desires and destitute of possessions.

105 A person for whom the day of nonduality dawns and never sets remains in the unceasing bliss of the Eternal.

106 O Arjuna, he who possesses this kind of discrimination is unique, for in all the three worlds he is the only one who has no household possessions.

107 These are the characteristics of a perfected being, said Lord Krishna out of the fullness of His knowledge.

108 He is the father of all wise men, light to the eyes of those who see, and the one whose thought created the universe.

109 The rich garment of the Vedas, fashioned in the workshop of the sacred syllable, is inadequate to encompass his glory.

110 From the great luster of his body, the sun and moon derive their greatness and give forth their light. Can the world exist without that luster?

111 How can you comprehend the qualities of a being whose name alone cannot be contained by the whole of space?

112 Enough of this praise. Under this pretext, I cannot tell whose qualities he has actually described and why.

113 Furthermore, if I were to reveal the whole secret of the Eternal, which casts out all thought of duality, then the joy of My affection for Arjuna would be destroyed.

114 Therefore, Krishna did not tell Arjuna everything, but drew a thin veil over it. He allowed Arjuna to retain the notion that his mind was separate, so Arjuna could enjoy the experience.

115 Oneness with God is an obstacle to this

enjoyment. Those who seek it are impoverished, and the sight of them may affect his love for Me.

116 If his egoism vanished and he became one with Me, what could I do alone without his love?

117 Who could soothe Me with the sight of him, speak to Me when My heart is full, or embrace Me in the warm clasp of love?

118 If he reached this state of union with Me, with whom could I speak of the precious secret that cannot be contained in the heart?

119 With this compassionate thought, Krishna reached out with His mind to draw to Himself Arjuna's mind in conversation, under the pretext of this explanation.

120 If this seems difficult to understand when you hear it, remember that Arjuna is just an image molded out of Krishna's bliss.

121 Just as a childless woman who bears a child in her old age dances in deep ecstasy,

122 So it was with Krishna. I wouldn't have said this if I hadn't seen His great love for Arjuna.

123 See how strange this is! On the one hand there is this teaching, and on the other hand there is the battle! Krishna danced with the delight of Arjuna's love.

124 How could love feel shame, or passion become weary? How could there be madness without delusion?

125 The meaning of this is that Arjuna was the refuge of Krishna's affection. He was like a mirror reflecting Krishna's heart, overjoyed with love.

126 Being so pure and holy, his heart was the most fertile field in which to plant the seed of devotion. Therefore, he was most worthy of Lord Krishna's grace.

127 It was as though Arjuna were the deity presiding over universal brotherhood, which is the step to the attainment of self-surrender.

128 Arjuna was so dear to Krishna that the Master wasn't praised, while His servant's virtues were recited.

129 Consider how a wife is lovingly devoted to her husband, and he has great respect for her. Isn't such a virtuous woman more worthy of praise than her husband?

130 Similarly, it has delighted me to praise Arjuna more than Krishna, who has become the abode of the good fortune of the three worlds.

131 Through love of him, the formless One has taken form, and in spite of His perfection, has felt a longing for him.

132 Then the listeners exclaimed, Oh what good fortune! What beautiful language! Doesn't its excellence surpass even that of the Vedas?

133 There is nothing strange about this. When I speak in my mother-tongue, Marathi, literary excellence will appear in it like the different colors in the sky.

134 How clearly the moonlight of divine knowledge shines, with the cool rays of its meaning! In the same way the meaning of the verses, like lotus flowers, naturally comes into bloom.

135 See how desire has been awakened in the desireless listeners. This desire arises also in the great, and they sway with it, their hearts being enlightened.

136 Realizing this, Nivritti's disciple said, Pay attention and understand that in the coming of Lord Krishna, a great day has dawned for the Pandavas.

137 Born of Devaki and raised with great care by Yashoda, now He has come to the aid of the Pandavas.

138 The fortunate Arjuna didn't have to serve Him for many years or to wait for opportunities to seek His favor.

139 Enough of this digression! Continue the story without delay. Then Arjuna said in a friendly manner, O Lord, these signs of saintliness are not found in me.

140 Moreover, if I were judged by such a standard, I would undoubtedly fall far short of it. But by hearing Your teaching, I may become great.

141 If it is Your will, I will become the Absolute. Shouldn't I practice what You teach?

142 I don't understand what You say, but hearing it, I revere it in my heart. What sublime qualities does a person need to attain this?

143 May they be also in me! Will You, in Your great saintliness, make me Yours? Then Lord Krishna smiled and said, Why shouldn't I? I will do it.

144 Listen! As long as a person hasn't attained contentment, he has great difficulty being happy. However once he has attained it, what can he lack?

145 A devotee of the Supreme may become the Absolute without any difficulty. See how Krishna bends under the weight of the har-

vest of Arjuna's good fortune!

146 He who has been so difficult to attain, even for Indra and all the other gods who have spent thousands of lifetimes striving for Him, has become Arjuna's servant. This cannot be described in words.

147 Now listen to me. When Arjuna asked the Lord to make him one with the Absolute, the Lord listened to him attentively.

148 He realized the great longing in Arjuna's heart and knew that the seed of dispassion had entered the womb of reason.

149 Although the days of fulfillment had not yet been completed, still with the fullness of the spring of dispassion, the flower of union with God was ready to burst forth.

150 It wouldn't be long before he would realize the fruit of union with God, for he had developed dispassion. Lord Krishna was sure of this.

151 He knew that whatever practices Arjuna might follow would bear fruit even from the beginning, and that if he were taught the method of yoga, it would have good results.

152 With such thoughts in His mind, Krishna then said to Arjuna, Listen while I tell you about this royal path.

153 You can already see the abundant fruit of liberation lying at the foot of the tree of earthly existence. Even Shiva is still a pilgrim on this path.

154 Multitudes of yogis have set out by various ways to find God, and the footprints of their experience have made an easy path.

155 They have traveled steadily by the straight path of Self-realization, avoiding the side roads of ignorance.

156 All the sages have traveled this path, seekers have attained perfection in this way, and those who know the Self have reached exalted positions.

157 Once this path is perceived, hunger and thirst are forgotten. Traveling on it, there is no awareness of night or day.

158 Wherever the pilgrim sets his foot, a storehouse of eternal bliss opens before him. Even if he goes astray, he ultimately attains heavenly bliss.

159 Like the sun, this path proceeds from the east towards the west, and one has to walk along it steadily, O Arjuna.

160 He who travels along this road becomes identified with his destination. Why should I say this? You will easily understand.

161 Then Arjuna exclaimed, O Lord, when will this be? Why don't You rescue me from the ocean of desire in which I am plunged?

162 Then Lord Krishna said, Why are you so impatient? I am explaining it all to you. Besides, you have asked me to do so.

शुचौ देशे प्रतिष्ठाप्य स्थिरम् श्रासनम् श्रात्मनः ।
नात्युच्छ्रितं नातिनीचं चैलाजिनकुशोत्तरम् ॥

śucāu deśe pratiṣṭhāpya
sthiram āsanam ātmanaḥ
nātyucchritaṁ nātinīcaṁ
cāilājinakuśottaram

11. Establishing a firm seat for himself in a clean place, not too high, not too low, covered with a cloth, an antelope skin, and kusha grass,

163 Now I shall describe it in detail, but it can only be useful through experience. First, a suitable place must be found.

164 It should be a place where a person can sit comfortably without wanting to get up, and such that when he sees it, his tendency toward dispassion will increase.

165 The place should be one which is frequented by saints, which will induce a feeling of contentment and fill the mind with courage.

166 The place should be very beautiful so that a person will want to practice yoga there and his heart will experience Self-realization.

167 If a heretic should enter the place unawares, even he would feel a strong inclination to practice penance.

168 If some pleasure-loving person happened to pass that way and unexpectedly found it, he wouldn't think of returning to a life of worldly desire.

169 A person who was reluctant to stay there would be forced to remain, the deluded would be persuaded to sit there, and dispassion would be awakened with a tap on the shoulder.

170 When a sensual person beheld it, he would experience such delight that he would even be willing to sacrifice a kingdom for the sake of resting there.

171 It must be as clean as it is beautiful, a place where the highest bliss is revealed.

172 There is one more condition: it should be frequented by seekers of yoga and not disturbed by the footsteps of passers-by.

173 It should be surrounded by a grove of shady trees which have roots as sweet as nectar and which are always bearing fruit.
174 There should be streams here and there which are clear even in the rainy season, and springs nearby.
175 The air should be cool rather than hot, and gentle breezes should blow softly over it.
176 Silence should reign there. It should not be frequented by animals, nor should there be parrots or bees near it.
177 However, swans may float on the water, there may be a few cranes nearby, and an occasional cuckoo.
178 There would be no harm if a peacock were present now and then, but not all the time.
179 O Arjuna, it would be good if there were a secluded hermitage near the spot, or a temple of Shiva,
180 Either of these, according to one's preference. The yogi should for the most part sit in solitude.
181 He should look for such a place and, if he feels it is suitable, set up his meditation seat there.
182 He should place a pure deerskin on carefully laid young blades of kusha grass and, on that, a clean folded cloth.
183 He should place the tender grass with care so that it remains well bound together.
184 If the seat were too high, the body might sway; if it were too low, it would be affected by contact with the earth.
185 It should be neither too high nor too low, and it should be evenly balanced. Enough has been said.

तत्रैकाग्रं मनः कृत्वा यतचित्तेन्द्रियक्रियः ।
उपविश्यासने युञ्ज्याद् योगमात्मविशुद्धये ॥

tatrāikāgraṁ manaḥ kṛtvā
yatacittendriyakriyaḥ
upaviśyāsane yuñjād
yogamātmaviśuddhaye

12. There, having directed his mind to a single object, with his thought and the activity of the senses controlled, seating himself on the seat, he should practice yoga for the purpose of self-purification.

186 Then, with his mind concentrated, the seeker should remember the presence of his Guru.
187 He remains in this way until the remembrance of his Guru causes a sense of purity to pervade his heart and the hardness of egoism to melt away.
188 All objects are forgotten, the restlessness of the senses is stopped, and the mind becomes quiet within the heart.
189 The yogi should continue this until he reaches a sense of union, and he should remain seated with this awareness.
190 The body will maintain its balance, the breathing will keep its own rhythm, and the perception will be heightened.
191 The outgoing tendencies of the mind are withdrawn, and a sense of repose is felt within. The exercise begins the moment this posture is adopted.

समं कायशिरोग्रीवं धारयन्न् अचलं स्थिरः ।
संप्रेक्ष्य नासिकाग्रं स्वं दिशश्चानवलोकयन् ॥

samaṁ kāyaśirogrīvaṁ
dhārayann acalaṁ sthiraḥ
saṁprekṣya nāsikāgraṁ svaṁ
diśaścānavalokayan

13. Holding the body, head and neck erect, motionless and steady, gazing at the tip of his own nose and not looking in any direction,

192 Now listen. I will tell you about the perfection of the yogic posture. You should fix the calves against the thighs,
193 And cross the soles of the feet firmly at the base of the spine, where the muladhara chakra is,
194 So that the right one is below, pressing against the perineum, and the left one is resting on it freely.
195 There are four inches between the anus and the generative organ. Leaving a space of one-and-a-half inches on each side,
196 Press the heel into the remaining space of one inch, keeping the body well balanced on it.
197 Now raise the buttocks very slightly and take hold of the two ankles.
198 Then, O Arjuna, the whole body will be supported on the top of the heel.
199 Know that this is what is called the *mulabandha* posture, otherwise known as *vajrasana*.
200 In this way you establish the proper position, close the lower passages of the body, and restrain the breath within the body.
201 Rest the cupped palms of both hands on the left foot. The shoulders will appear to be raised.

202 Hold the head firm between the shoulders, and begin to close the eyes.
203 The upper eyelids drop and the lower ones are extended. In this way the eyes remain half open.
204 The vision remains within and doesn't wander outside. It continues to be focused on the tip of the nose.
205 In this way the vision remains firmly inside and doesn't tend outward again. Its downward focus remains steady.
206 Then any interest in looking around or noticing outer forms stops completely.
207 Compress the neck and throat, and force the chin into the cavity between the collarbones and down onto the chest.
208 The larynx is hidden in this position. O Arjuna, this posture is called *jalandhara.*
209 The navel rises upward, the stomach is compressed, and the heart cavity expands.
210 O Arjuna, the yogic posture formed by drawing the navel and the penis toward each other is called *uddiyana.*

प्रशान्तात्मा विगतभीर् ब्रह्मचारिव्रते स्थितः ।
मनः संयम्य मच्चित्तो युक्त आसीत मत्परः ।।
praśāntātmā vigatabhīr
brahmacārivrate sthitaḥ
manaḥ saṁyamya maccitto
yukta āsīta matparaḥ

14. With quieted mind, banishing fear, established in the brahmacharin vow of celibacy, controlling the mind, with thoughts fixed on Me, he should sit, concentrated, devoted to Me.

211 Then the signs of yogic experience appear outwardly in the body, and inwardly the mind stops functioning.
212 Thought subsides, mental energy dies down, and the body and mind find rest.
213 Hunger is forgotten and sleep disappears. Even the memory of them is lost; no trace is left.
214 The downward moving vital force confined in the body turns back. Becoming compressed, it begins to expand.
215 As it becomes more and more agitated, in the free space above, it rumbles and struggles against the solar plexus.
216 When the struggle ceases, the whole body trembles to its very core. In this way the impurities of childhood are expelled.
217 Instead of turning downward, it moves in the interior of the body and expels the bodily secretions.
218 It releases the ocean of the bodily fluids, reduces the fat, and even draws the marrow out of the bones.
219 It clears out the arteries and loosens the limbs. The seeker should not allow himself to be frightened by these things.
220 It reveals and removes diseases, and it stirs up the elements of earth and water.
221 O Arjuna, the heat produced by the practice of this posture awakens the force called Kundalini.
222 Just as the brood of a female serpent bathed in turmeric lies curled up in sleep,
223 So lies Kundalini, very small and coiled three-and-a-half times, like a female serpent with her head turned downwards.
224 It is like a ring of lightning, folds of flaming fire, or a bar of pure gold.
225 Bound fast by threads, it is confined between two folds; but when it is compressed by the *vajra* posture, it is awakened.
226 Then, like a star shooting through space, like the sun falling from its place in the sky, or like a point of light bursting forth like a sprouting seed,
227 It breaks its bonds, grips the body, and appears in the region of the navel.
228 For long years it has hungered for this awakening and, once this occurs, it extends its mouth upwards with great eagerness.
229 Then, O Arjuna, it holds firmly in its grasp the air which fills the cavity below the heart.
230 The fire arising from it spreads upward and downward and begins to consume the flesh.
231 Not only does it do this, but it also consumes the fleshy tissue of the heart.
232 It attacks the palms of the hands and the soles of the feet, penetrates the upper parts of the body, and passing through them, it searches out the joints of the limbs.
233 While not leaving its place in the lower body, it draws the vitality from the nails and, cleansing the skin, causes it to cleave to the bones.
234 It cleanses the hollow of the bones, scours the inner recesses of the heart, and withers the hair of the body.
235 It drains the ocean of the seven bodily fluids, parches the whole body, and produces a state of intense heat.
236 The air which passes twelve inches out of

the two nostrils is inhaled once again.
237 Then the exhaled breath is drawn upward and the inhaled breath downward. They are prevented from meeting by the petals of the *chakras*.
238 Otherwise, the two would intermingle. This would displease Kundalini, who would say, "Go back! What are you doing here?"
239 Listen, Arjuna! The element of earth is entirely consumed, and the element of water is dried up.
240 When these two elements have been consumed, Kundalini is fully satisfied and, pacified, remains close to the *sushumna*.
241 The venom, which in its satisfaction it sends forth from its mouth, is the nectar which sustains vitality.
242 This fire arises from within, but when it begins to cool down, both internally and externally the limbs regain the strength which they had lost.
243 The *nadis* are closed off, the nine types of *prana* disappear, and the bodily functions cease.
244 The *ida* and *pingala nadis* merge into the *sushumna*, the three knots are loosened, and the six petals of the *svadhishthana chakra* open out.
245 Then the two *pranas* within the sun or *pingala nadi*, and the moon or *ida nadi*, cannot even cause the flame of a lamp to flicker.
246 The energy of mental activity subsides, and the sense of smell associated with the nose enters the *sushumna* and joins Kundalini.
247 Slowly from above, the lake of moon-nectar turns downward on one side and pours into the mouth of Kundalini.
248 This nectar fills the *nadis*, circulates throughout the whole body, and is absorbed into it along with the *prana*.
249 Just as when molten metal is poured into a heated mold, the melted wax pours out and only the metal remains, taking the form of the mold,
250 Similarly, beauty incarnates in the form of the body, covered by a veil of skin.
251 The sun remains concealed under a veil of clouds, but when they pass its light is boundless.
252 Similarly, the dried surface of the skin flakes off, just as husks are shed from grain.
253 The beauty of the limbs looks like natural marble or the sprouting of seed jewels,
254 As if the lovely hues of the evening sky were transferred to the body, or as if an image were fashioned from an inner radiance of the spirit,
255 Which, when it is seen, is like the richness of turmeric molded from the essence of nectar. It seems to be the very incarnation of peace,
256 As if it were made of the colors in a picture of joy, the very form of heavenly bliss, or growing saplings of the wish-fulfilling tree.
257 It is like a bud of the golden champaka tree, an image of nectar, or a ripe harvest of tenderness,
258 The sphere of the moon saturated with the moisture of the *sharada* season, or splendor itself incarnate seated in a yogic posture.
259 This is how the yogi's body appears when Kundalini has drunk of the nectar. Even the god of death is afraid to look at it.
260 Old age vanishes, the knot of youth is loosened, and the lost bloom of childhood reappears.
261 Whatever his age, the term youth should be interpreted as strength. Such is his incomparable fortitude.
262 Just as ever-new jewel buds open on the boughs of a tree of gold, fine new fingernails grow.
263 New teeth appear, very small, set like rows of diamonds on each side.
264 Over the whole body, tiny new hairs spring forth like small splinters of rubies.
265 The palms of the hands and the soles of the feet are like red lotus flowers, and in the eyes there shines an indescribable luster.
266 Just as the shell of an oyster no longer holds the pearl when it is fully developed, and it bursts open at the joint with the force of its growth,
267 Similarly, the vision, which strives to pass outwards, when it cannot be held within the eyelids, embraces the heavens, even with half-opened eyes.
268 Listen! Although the body has the appearance of gold, it has the lightness of air, for no particles of earth or water remain in it.
269 The yogi can then see beyond all oceans, hear the thoughts of the heavens, and read the mind of the ant.
270 He rides the horses of the winds and walks on the surface of water, though his feet do not touch it. In such a way he acquires

many superhuman powers.

271 Listen to this. Grasping the *prana* by the hand, ascending the stairway of the ether, Kundalini enters the heart by the steps of the *sushumna nadi.*

272 She is the Mother of the worlds, the glory of the empire of the soul, who gives shelter to the tender sprouts of the seed of the universe,

273 The *lingam* of the formless Absolute, the vessel of Shiva, the supreme Self, and the true source of the *prana.*

274 When the young Kundalini enters the heart, the *chakra* there is awakened and sounds are heard.

275 They are faintly heard by the consciousness of pure reason, which is connected with the power of Kundalini.

276 In the volume of that sound, the four levels of speech lie pictured in the form of the sacred syllable.

277 A person must experience this to understand it. How can he imagine it? We cannot know what the source of this sound is.

278 O Arjuna, I have forgotten to tell you one thing: as long as air exists, the sound arises in the etheric space and vibrates there.

279 As the etheric space reverberates with the thunder of this sound, the windows of the *sahasrara,* the crown center, suddenly burst open.

280 Listen! There exists here another great space in the form of a lotus, where Consciousness appears.

281 In the innermost cavity of the heart, the divine Kundalini lays out before Consciousness the feast of Her own luster.

282 She offers a morsel of food, dressed with the vegetable of reason, in which no trace of duality is visible.

283 Her brilliance then vanishes and is transformed into the *prana.* How can I describe its appearance?

284 It is like an image formed out of air, when the golden cloth in which it was wrapped has been removed.

285 It is like a flame which comes in contact with a gust of wind and flickers out, or like a streak of lightning which flashes across the sky and instantly disappears.

286 It resembles a necklace of gold or a fountain of brilliant light, as far as the lotus-like heart *chakra.*

287 Upon entering the cave of the heart, it loses its separateness and is merged into the power dwelling within it.

288 Then, although it is called power, it should be known as the *prana. Nada, bindu, kala, jyoti* become imperceptible.

289 Control of the mind, restraint of the breath, and inclination towards meditation are now of little importance.

290 The idea of accepting or rejecting a particular thought is now irrelevant. The subtle elements are clearly destroyed.

291 "One body devours another." This is the secret teaching of the Natha sect, but now Lord Vishnu has revealed it.

292 Imagining my listeners to be customers, I have untied the bundle of that secret and opened out before them the folded sheet of the inner meaning of these wares.

युञ्जन्न् एवं सदा ऽत्मानं योगी नियतमानसः ।
शान्तिं निर्वाणपरमां मत्संस्थाम् अधिगच्छति ॥

yuñjann evaṁ sadā 'tmānaṁ
yogī niyatamānasaḥ
śāntiṁ nirvāṇaparamāṁ
matsaṁsthām adhigacchati

15. Thus, continually disciplining himself, the yogin whose mind is subdued goes to nirvana, to supreme peace, to union with Me.

293 Listen! When Kundalini loses its luster, the gross form of the body disappears and is no longer visible to physical sight.

294 In reality it has the same limbs, yet it looks as if it were molded out of air,

295 Like the inner stalk of a plantain tree divested of its sheath or like limbs fashioned from ether.

296 When this is the condition of his body, the yogi seems to be a spirit. When this happens, it seems like a miracle to those who are still in the body.

297 Look! As the adept walks, he leaves psychic powers in the train of his footsteps, but we are not concerned with these.

298 O Arjuna, bear in mind that the three grosser elements of the body have disappeared along with the body itself.

299 Water dissolves earth, fire absorbs water, and in the heart *chakra* the vital air consumes fire.

300 The vital air alone remains, and it continues in the form of the body. After a time, even it

merges into etheric space.
301 Then the name Kundalini loses its significance, and its appropriate name is Maruti, although the force remains until it is absorbed into Shiva.
302 Now it leaves the heart *chakra*, breaks through the end of the *sushumna nadi*, and enters the space in the roof of the mouth.
303 Then, climbing onto the back of the sacred syllable, it passes beyond the *pashyanti* level of speech.
304 Then, just as a river flows into the ocean, it enters the space between the eyebrows, symbolized by the final M of the sacred syllable OM.
305 After settling into the center of the Absolute, it reaches out with the arms of its awareness of oneness with the Self and embraces the Supreme.
306 At that moment the veil of the five elements is torn apart, and the individual soul is united with the supreme Self. Then everything, including etheric space, is absorbed in that union.
307 Just as water from the ocean is drawn up into the clouds and pours down again into itself as rain,
308 In the same way the Self, having lived in bodily form, enters the supreme Self. Such is this union, O Arjuna.
309 There remains no thought about whether it is separate or whether it is truly one with the supreme Self.
310 Just as space merges into space, the yogi experiences this state of union and remains in it.
311 It would be impossible for words to describe this state or discuss it in conversation.
312 O Arjuna, when this is the case, anyone, even *vaikhari*, who is ambitious enough to express an opinion on it, is far from this state.
313 The M of the sacred syllable cannot enter the space between the eyebrows, for the *prana* moving alone fails to reach that etheric space.
314 As soon as it appears there, the power of speech vanishes and the etheric space is destroyed.
315 How can speech plumb the depths of the great void of the Supreme, where there is no place even for ether?
316 Therefore, it is true that this can neither be expressed in words nor heard by the ear.
317 If by good fortune Self-realization can be attained through experience, then one should strive to remain in it.
318 Beyond this, there is no more to know. So then, O Arjuna, let this be enough. There is no point in saying more.
319 In this state language withdraws, imagination dies away, and not even the wind of thought can enter.
320 This is the highest principle, without beginning and beyond measure, the beauty of the state beyond the mind, and the dawning of the experience of the soul's oneness with God,
321 The end of all form, the goal of the search for liberation, that in which beginning and end merge into one.
322 It is the root of the universe, the fruit of the tree of yoga, and the very essence of bliss.
323 It is the seed of the subtle elements and the light from which the sun emanates. O Arjuna, it is My own nature.
324 This four-armed Being has become manifest in great splendor, seeing that the godless have persecuted the multitudes of My devotees.
325 Those who persevere unswervingly towards the goal enjoy the indescribable bliss of being one with the Self.
326 Those who follow the method I prescribe, having purified themselves, reach a state comparable to Mine, even while in the body.
327 It seems as if the liquid of the supreme Self has been poured into the mold of their bodies.
328 If this realization were to shine from the inner Self, it would overwhelm the whole universe. Then Arjuna said, Truly this is so.
329 O Lord, the method which You describe, being the way to attainment, surely leads to the goal.
330 Those who steadfastly tread this path unfailingly attain union with God. I have understood this from Your teaching.
331 O Lord, even hearing this teaching brings enlightenment to the mind. How then could the realization of it not lead to union with the Self?
332 There is no fault in this. But I beg You to listen for a moment to what I say, O Krishna.
333 I appreciate the yoga that You have taught, O Krishna, but because of my unworthiness

I cannot practice it.
334 I will do these practices willingly if, with my whole heart, I can gladly follow this path successfully.
335 Otherwise, if I am unable to do as the Lord commands me, I ask You what I can do with such unworthiness.
336 Impelled by such a desire, I must question You further. Therefore, O Lord, please listen attentively to my words.
337 I have listened patiently to the method which You have described. If a person who wishes practices this, can he succeed in it?
338 Or can he gain nothing without worthiness? Then Lord Krishna said, O Arjuna, what are you asking?
339 This question relates to the Ultimate, yet even in the case of ordinary tasks is it possible to succeed without adequate ability?
340 Whether a person is fit or not can only be known by his success, but whatever a worthy person does bears fruit right from the beginning.
341 Here nothing can be obtained without effort. Besides, is there any great storehouse from which worthiness can be easily drawn?
342 Wouldn't a person who is inclined to dispassion and who restrains his bodily needs be considered worthy for this?
343 In this way you may also become worthy. Thus the Lord answered the question in Arjuna's mind at this time.
344 Again, He said, O Arjuna, the essence of this teaching is that an undisciplined person is entirely unfit for this work.
345 A person who is a slave of his palate or who spends his life sleeping is not fit for the practice of yoga.
346 Or if he restricts too rigidly his hunger and thirst and rejects all food,
347 Or if a person refuses to sleep and plays the role of obstinacy incarnate, his body will not be his own. How can he possibly practice yoga?
348 Therefore a person should avoid excessive enjoyment of sense pleasures and complete abstention from them.

नात्यश्नतस् तु योगो ऽस्ति न चैकान्तम् अनश्नतः ।
न चातिस्वप्नशीलस्य जाग्रतो नैव चार्जुन ॥

nātyaśnatas tu yogo 'sti
na cāikāntam anaśnataḥ
na cātisvapnaśīlasya
jāgrato nāiva cārjuna

16. Yoga is not eating too much, nor is it not eating at all, and not the habit of sleeping too much, and not keeping awake either, Arjuna.

युक्ताहारविहारस्य युक्तचेष्टस्य कर्मसु ।
युक्तस्वप्नावबोधस्य योगो भवति दुःखहा ॥

yuktāhāravihārasya
yuktaceṣṭasya karmasu
yuktasvapnāvabodhasya
yogo bhavati duḥkhahā

17. For him who is moderate in food and diversion, whose actions are disciplined, who is moderate in sleep and waking, yoga destroys all sorrow.

349 A person should eat enough food but with proper restraint, and he should perform all actions in the same way.
350 Speech should be moderate, walking should be steady, and the need for regular sleep should be respected.
351 A person should be quiet in the waking state, so the bodily fluids will be balanced and calm.
352 When the sense organs are satisfied in this way with moderation and regularity, the mind becomes happy.

यदा विनियतं चित्तम् आत्मन्य् एवावतिष्ठते ।
निःस्पृहः सर्वकामेभ्यो युक्त इत्य् उच्यते तदा ॥

yadā viniyataṁ cittam
ātmany evāvatiṣṭhate
niḥspṛhaḥ sarvakāmebbyo
yukta ity ucyate tadā

18. When he is absorbed in the Self alone, with controlled mind, free from longing, from all desires, then he is said to be a saint.

353 The more outer discipline is established, the greater the inner happiness. Then yoga can be protected without much effort.
354 Just as when a person's good fortune is increasing, diligence is unimportant and all kinds of prosperity come to him unsought,
355 Similarly, a disciplined person can easily turn to yogic practice, and his experience will ripen into Self-realization.
356 Therefore, O Arjuna, that fortunate person who is disciplined wears the royal adornment of the final beatitude.
357 A person in whom there exists the sacred union of moderation and yogic practice, and whose mind is resolved to remain forever in

this holy place, is said to be harmonized in yoga.

यथा दीपो निवातस्थो नेङ्गते सोपमा स्मृता ।
योगिनो यतचित्तस्य युञ्जतो योगम् आत्मनः ॥

yathā dīpo nivātastho
neñgate sopamā smṛtā
yogino yatacittasya
yuñjato yogam ātmanaḥ

19. As a lamp in a windless place does not flicker, to such is compared the yogin of controlled mind, performing the yoga of the Self.

358 Furthermore, one characteristic of such a person is that his mind is like a lamp set in a windless place.
359 Knowing your desire, I will now tell you something else. Listen carefully.
360 You are eager to know yoga, yet you don't want to practice it. Are you afraid it is difficult?
361 O Arjuna, don't let your mind be troubled like this. The wicked senses try in vain to frighten people.
362 Doesn't the tongue consider medicine an enemy when, in reality, it steadies a person's life which is coming to an end?

यत्रोपरमते चित्तं निरुद्धं योगसेवया ।
यत्र चैवात्मना ऽत्मानं पश्यन्न् आत्मनि तुष्यति ॥

yatroparamate cittaṁ
niruddhaṁ yogasevayā
yatra cāivātmanā 'tmānaṁ
paśyann ātmani tuṣyati

20. When the mind comes to rest, restrained by the practice of yoga, and when beholding the Self, by the self, he is content in the Self,

सुखम् आत्यन्तिकं यत् तद् बुद्धिग्राह्यम् अतीन्द्रियम् ।
वेत्ति यत्र न चैवायं स्थितश्चलति तत्त्वतः ॥

sukham ātyantikaṁ yat tad
buddhigrāhyam atīndriyam
vetti yatra na cāivāyaṁ
sthitaścalati tattvataḥ

21. He knows that infinite happiness which is grasped by the intellect and transcends the senses, and, established there, does not deviate from the truth.

363 Similarly, that which is really conducive to our welfare is painful. Apart from this, is there anything as easy as yoga?
364 The senses can be controlled by the resolute practice of the yogic posture which I have explained to you.
365 Moreover, when the senses have been restrained in this manner, the mind reaches out to meet the Self.
366 It turns away from sense objects and begins to look within. It immediately recognizes its own true nature, saying, "I am the Self."
367 When this recognition takes place, the mind is seated on the throne of supreme bliss and becomes absorbed in this union.

यं लब्ध्वा चापरं लाभं मन्यते नाधिकं ततः ।
यस्मिन् स्थितो न दुःखेन गुरुणापि विचाल्यते ॥

yaṁ labdhvā cāparaṁ lābhaṁ
manyate nādhikaṁ tataḥ
yasmin sthito na duḥkhena
guruṇāpi vicālyate

22. Having attained this, no greater gain can he imagine; established in this, he is not moved even by profound sorrow.

368 Then even if mountains of difficulties greater than Mount Meru should oppress such a person, his mind will in no way be crushed by their weight.
369 Or if he is struck by weapons or burned by fire, his mind, absorbed in the bliss of the Self, is not disturbed at all.
370 Having entered the Self, he is unaware of his body. He even forgets it in the fullness of his joy.

तं विद्याद् दुःखसंयोग वियोगं योगसंज्ञितम् ।
स निश्चयेन योक्तव्यो योगो ऽनिर्विण्णचेतसा ॥

taṁ vidyād duḥkhasaṁyoga
viyogaṁ yogasaṁjñitam
sa niścayena yoktavyo
yogo 'nirviṇṇacetasā

23. Let this, the dissolution of union with pain, be known as yoga; this yoga is to be practiced with determination and with an undismayed mind.

371 Because of the sweetness of this joy, the mind which was held in the bondage of worldly life gives up all desire.
372 The beauty of this yoga, this kingdom of contentment for which wisdom is essential,
373 Must be clearly seen by the mind through the practice of yoga. Seeing it, the seer becomes transformed into it.

संकल्पप्रभवान् कामांस् त्यक्त्वा सर्वान् अशेषतः ।
मनसैवेन्द्रियग्रामं विनियम्य समन्ततः ॥

saṁkalpaprabhavān kāmāṅs
tyaktvā sarvān aśeṣataḥ

manasāivendriyagrāmam
viniyamya samantataḥ

24. Abandoning those desires whose origins lie in one's intention, all of them, without exception, and completely restraining the multitude of senses with the mind,

374 O Beloved, in one sense this yoga is easy to practice. If desire experiences sorrow at the death of her children,
375 When she learns that the power of sense objects has been destroyed and sees that the senses have been subdued, she dies of a broken heart.
376 Strive for this dispassion. Then the pilgrimage of desire is finished, and pure reason dwells joyfully in the mansion of courage.

शनैः शनैर् उपरमेद् बुद्ध्या धृतिगृहीतया ।
आत्मसंस्थं मनः कृत्वा न किंचिद् अपि चिन्तयेत् ।।
śanāiḥ śanāir uparamed
buddhyā dhṛtigṛhītayā
ātmasaṁsthaṁ manaḥ kṛtvā
na kiṁcid api cintayet

25. Little by little, he should come to rest, with the intellect firmly held. His mind having been established in the Self, he should not think of anything.

यतो यतो निश्चरति मनश्चञ्चलम् अस्थिरम् ।
ततस्ततो नियम्यैतद् आत्मन्य् एव वशं नयेत् ।।
yato yato niścarati
manaścañcalam asthiram
tatastato niyamyāitad
ātmany eva vaśaṁ nayet

26. Whenever the unsteady mind, moving to and fro, wanders away, he should restrain it and control it in the Self.

377 If reason, supported by steadfastness, slowly leads the mind by the path of Self-realization to the temple of the Self and installs it there,
378 This is one way to attain the Self. Consider this, but if you find it impractical, there is another easy method. Listen.
379 A person should take a vow to stick to a resolute decision and not depart from it.
380 If the mind can be steadied in this way, then the work will be easy. If not, it may be allowed to move freely.
381 Then, wherever it goes, the resolution will bring it back and steadiness will be restored.

प्रशान्तमनसं ह्येनं योगिनं सुखम् उत्तमम् ।
उपैति शान्तरजसं ब्रह्मभूतम् अकल्मषम् ।।
praśantamanasaṁ hyenaṁ
yoginaṁ sukham uttamam
upāiti śantarajasaṁ
brahmabhūtam akalmaṣam

27. The yogin whose mind is peaceful, whose passions are calmed, who is free of evil and has become one with Brahman, attains the highest bliss.

382 Thus, in the course of time, the mind will acquire steadiness and will easily approach the Eternal.
383 When it beholds That, it will become one with it, duality will be lost in nonduality, and the universe will become illumined by the splendor of unity.
384 Just as the sky alone fills the universe when the clouds, which seemed separate from it, have melted away,
385 Similarly, when the mind has become absorbed in Consciousness, that alone is the all-pervasive essence. This result can easily be obtained in this way.
386 Many have attained this yogic state simply by being utterly indifferent to the wealth of the imagination.

युञ्जन्न् एवं सदा ऽत्मानं योगी विगतकल्मषः ।
सुखेन ब्रह्मसंस्पर्शम् अत्यन्त सुखम् अश्नुते ।।
yuñjann evaṁ sadā 'tmānaṁ
yogī vigatakalmaṣaḥ
sukhena brahmasaṁsparśam
atyantaṁ sukham aśnute

28. Thus constantly disciplining himself, the yogin, freed from evil, easily encountering Brahman, attains happiness beyond end.

387 With joy, they have easily entered the Eternal. Just as salt cannot be separated from water,
388 In the same way, they attain union. Then, in the palace of oneness with the Eternal, the world sees the festival of supreme bliss.
389 However, this is as difficult as if a person had to walk with his legs on his back. If you cannot attain this, listen to another way, O Arjuna.

सर्वभूतस्थम् आत्मानं सर्वभूतानि चात्मनि ।
ईक्षते योगयुक्तात्मा सर्वत्र समदर्शनः ।।
sarvabhūtastham ātmānaṁ
sarvabhūtāni cātmani
īkṣate yogayuktātmā
sarvatra samadarśanaḥ

29. He who is disciplined by yoga sees the Self present in all beings, and all beings present in the Self. He sees the same (Self) at all times.

390 There is no doubt that I exist in all forms and that everything abides in Me.
391 Everything has been created in this way, and spirit and matter are intermingled. You should understand this.

यो मां पश्यति सर्वत्र सर्वं च मयि पश्यति
तस्याहं न प्रणश्यामि स च मे न प्रणश्यति ।।

yo māṁ paśyati sarvatra
sarvaṁ ca mayi paśyati
tasyāhaṁ na praṇaśyāmi
sa ca me na praṇaśyati

30. He who sees Me everywhere, and sees all things in Me; I am not lost to him, and he is not lost to Me.

392 O Arjuna, whoever worships Me as the One existing in all beings through his realization of unity,
393 Who knows that despite the multiplicity of beings there is no duality in their hearts, and who knows that My essence pervades everything everywhere,
394 It is irrelevant to say that he and I are one. Don't speak like that, O Arjuna, for I am truly he.
395 Just as a lamp and its light are one, so is he in Me and I in him.
396 Just as wetness is essentially one with water, and space and ether exist within the same boundaries, similarly, a person's body is infused with My form.

सर्वभूतस्थितं यो मां भजत्य् एकत्वम् आस्थितः ।
सर्वथा वर्तमानो ऽपि स योगी मयि वर्तते ।।

sarvabhūtasthaṁ yo māṁ
bhajaty ekatvam āsthitaḥ
sarvathā vartamāno 'pi
sa yogī mayi vartate

31. The yogin who, established in oneness, honors Me as abiding in all beings, in whatever way he otherwise acts, dwells in Me.

397 O Arjuna, just as woven thread is one with the cloth, in the same way he sees Me everywhere as one and the same.
398 Ornaments are fashioned in many shapes, yet there are not different kinds of gold. It is the same with a person who has attained the stability of union.
399 The person for whom the night of delusion has been followed by the dawn of unity is like a tree which has many leaves although they were not planted individually.
400 Even though he may be imprisoned in a body composed of the five elements, he is My equal through his experience of Self-realization. What power can bind him?
401 Because of this experience he is embraced by My all-pervasiveness, although he should not be called all-pervasive.
402 Though he has a body, he is not of the body. Can a person express what is beyond the power of speech?

आत्मौपम्येन सर्वत्र समं पश्यति यो ऽर्जुन ।
सुखं वा यदि वा दुःखं स योगी परमो मतः ।।

ātmāupamyena sarvatra
samaṁ paśyati yo 'rjuna
sukhaṁ vā yadi vā duḥkhaṁ
sa yogī paramo mataḥ

32. He who sees equality in everything in the image of his own Self, Arjuna, whether in pleasure or in pain, is thought to be a supreme yogin.

403 Let's leave this now. A person who regards the entire creation as being like himself,
404 Whose mind is no longer aware of feelings of pleasure and pain or of good and evil deeds,
405 He sees all kinds of distinctions and strange things as merely the limbs of his own body.
406 But what need is there to be specific? A person who has realized that he is one with everything in the universe,
407 Although he has a body and the world may consider him happy or unhappy, yet I am certain that he is truly the Eternal.
408 Therefore, O Arjuna, strive to realize this oneness, to see the universe in yourself and yourself in the universe.
409 For this reason, I repeatedly tell you that there is no higher realization than the awareness of unity.

अर्जुन उवाच । *arjuna uvāca*

यो ऽयं योगस् त्वया प्रोक्तः साम्येन मधुसूदन ।
एतस्याहं न पश्यामि चञ्चलत्वात् स्थितिं स्थिराम् ।।

yo 'yaṁ yogas tvayā proktaḥ
sāmyena madhusūdana
etasyāhaṁ na paśyāmi
cañcalatvāt sthitiṁ sthirām

Arjuna spoke:
33. This yoga which is declared by You as evenness of mind, Krishna, I do not per-

ceive the steady continuance of this because of (the mind's) instability.

410 Then Arjuna said, O Lord, it is true that, prompted by Your kindness towards me, You have explained this; but it isn't enough because of the nature of the mind.

411 It is impossible to know the nature and extent of the mind. The three worlds are too small for its activities.

चञ्चलं हि मनः कृष्ण प्रमाथि बलवद् दृढम् ।
तस्याहं निग्रहं मन्ये वायोर् इव सुदुष्करम् ॥

cañcalaṁ hi manaḥ kṛṣṇa
pramāthi balavad dṛḍham
tasyāhaṁ nigrahaṁ manye
vāyor iva suduṣkaram

34. The mind, indeed, is unstable, Krishna, turbulent, powerful and obstinate; I think it is as difficult to control as the wind.

412 Could a monkey ever practice meditation? Will the wind stop blowing when told to do so?

413 Will the mind which harasses reason, shakes resolution, and plays games with courage;

414 Which deludes discrimination, disturbs contentment, and compels us, though we want to be still, to wander in every direction;

415 Which becomes agitated when it is curbed, and is even made bold by the attempt to control the senses—can the mind give up its own nature?

416 Such a mind will never remain stable and allow the Self to acquire equanimity.

श्रीभगवान् उवाच । *śrībhagavān uvāca*

असंशयं महाबाहो मनो दुर्निग्रहं चलम् ।
अभ्यासेन तु कौन्तेय वैराग्येण च गृह्यते ॥

asaṁśayaṁ mahābāho
mano durnigrahaṁ calam
abhyāsena tu kāunteya
vāirāgyeṇa ca gṛhyate

The Blessed Lord spoke:
35. Without doubt, O Arjuna, the mind is unsteady and difficult to restrain; but by practice, Arjuna, and by indifference to worldly objects, it is restrained.

417 Then Lord Krishna said, What you say is true. The mind is truly fickle.

418 But if it can be led into constant practice, in due course of time it will become stable.

419 In this one respect it is good: it frequents places familiar to it. Therefore show it often the delight of the experience of the Self.

असंयतात्मना योगो दुष्प्राप इति मे मतिः ।
वश्यात्मना तु यतता शक्यो ऽवाप्तुम् उपायतः ॥

asaṁyatātmanā yogo
duṣprāpa iti me matiḥ
vaśyātmanā tu yatatā
śakyo 'vāptum upāyataḥ

36. I agree that yoga is difficult to attain by him whose self is uncontrolled; but by him whose self is controlled, by striving, it is possible to attain through proper means.

420 On the other hand, one has to admit that the mind is hard to control for those who are not dispassionate and who do not observe discipline.

421 If a person never practices self-restraint, if there is no thought of dispassion in his mind, and if he is submerged in the waters of sense objects,

422 If during his life he has never been supported by the practice of yoga, tell me, can his mind ever become stable?

423 So begin to restrain the mind by this method. Then how can you fail to achieve that resolution?

424 Is all yogic practice useless? Instead, confess that you are unable to practice it.

425 If you possess the strength of yoga, how can your mind be restless? Can't even all the primordial elements be under your control?

अर्जुन उवाच । *arjuna uvāca*

अयतिः श्रद्धयोपेतो योगाच्चलितमानसः ।
अप्राप्य योगसंसिद्धिं कां गतिं कृष्ण गच्छति ॥

ayatiḥ śraddhayopeto
yogāccalitamānasaḥ
aprāpya yogasaṁsiddhiṁ
kāṁ gatiṁ kṛṣṇa gacchati

Arjuna spoke:
37. One who is uncontrolled though he has faith, whose mind has fallen away from yoga, who does not attain perfection in yoga, which way, Krishna, does he go?

कच्चिन् नोभयविभ्राष्टश् छिन्नाभ्रम् इव नश्यति ।
अप्रतिष्ठो महाबाहो विमूढो ब्रह्मणः पथि ॥

kaccin nobhayavibhraṣṭaś
chinnābhram iva naśyati
apratiṣṭho mahābāho
vimūḍho brahmaṇaḥ pathi

38. Is he not lost like a disappearing cloud, having fallen from both worlds, having no solid ground, O Krishna, confused on the path of Brahman?

एतन् मे संशयं कृष्ण छेत्तुम् अर्हस्य् अशेषतः ।
त्वदन्यः संशयस्यास्य छेत्ता न ह्य् उपपद्यते ॥
etan me saṁśayaṁ kṛṣṇa
chettum arhasy aśeṣataḥ
tvadanyaḥ saṁśayasyāsya
chettā na hy upapadyate

39. You are able, Krishna, to dispel the totality of this doubt of mine; other than You, no one comes forth to help me erase this doubt.

426 At this point Arjuna said, What You say, O Lord, is true. The strength of the mind cannot be compared with the power of yoga.
427 But what is that yoga? How can I know it? I still don't have an idea of it. Therefore, O Lord, I said that the mind is uncontrollable.
428 O Krishna, for the first time in my life, I have heard of this yoga through Your grace.
429 I have one other doubt, O Lord, and only You can resolve it.
430 Tell me this, O Krishna. A person may strive to attain Self-realization through faith, but without any yogic practice.
431 He leaves the village of the senses and sets out on the road of earnestness, intending to reach the city of the attainment of the Self.
432 But he does not reach Self-realization, neither can he retrace his steps. At this point, the sun of his life sets.
433 Just as untimely clouds, thin as a veil, neither remain in the sky nor turn to rain,
434 So both ways are lost to such a person: his goal is far away but also, because of his faith, he loses his former state of not seeking for it.
435 If a person, though full of faith, delays and fails to reach his goal, is he entirely lost? What is his fate?

श्रीभगवान् उवाच *śrībhagavān uvāca*

पार्थ नैवेह नामुत्र विनाशस् तस्य विद्यते ।
न हि कल्याणकृत् कश्चिद् दुर्गतिं तात गच्छति ॥
pārtha nāiveha nāmutra
vinaśas tasya vidyate
na hi kalyāṇakṛt kaścid
durgatiṁ tāta gacchati

The Blessed Lord spoke:
40. Arjuna, neither here on earth nor in heaven above is there found to be destruction of him; no one who does good goes to misfortune, My Son.

436 Then Lord Krishna said, O Arjuna, is any goal other than liberation possible for a person who is striving for deliverance?
437 It may happen that for a time he may have to rest from his efforts, but during that delay he may still enjoy happiness which even the gods cannot attain.
438 However, if he had made greater progress in the practice of yoga, he would certainly have reached the awareness of his oneness with the Eternal before the end of his life.
439 Because he didn't progress rapidly enough, naturally he had to wait. But there is no doubt that he will eventually attain liberation.

प्राप्य पुण्यकृतां लोकान् उषित्वा शाश्वतीः समाः ।
शुचीनां श्रीमतां गेहे योगभ्रष्टो ऽभिजायते ॥
prāpya puṇyakṛtāṁ lokān
uṣitvā śāśvatīḥ samāḥ
śucīnāṁ śrīmatāṁ gehe
yogabhraṣṭo 'bhijāyate

41. Attaining the worlds of the meritorious, having dwelt there for endless years, he who has fallen from yoga is born again in the dwelling of the radiant and the illustrious.

440 Hear how wonderful this is! Such a person easily finds the blessedness which is difficult even for Indra to attain with a hundred sacrifices.
441 He enjoys the wonderful but unprofitable pleasures of that world, and his mind becomes satiated with them.
442 Consequently, he is reborn in the world of mortals, but in a family which is the mother of all righteousness, and he will grow like a shoot in a prosperous field.
443 He is reborn in a family which follows the path of righteousness, speaks the truth, and considers whatever must be done in the light of the scriptures,
444 In which the Vedas are a living deity, whose only concern is the performance of its own proper duty, and for whom the discrimination between good and evil is the only counsellor,

445 In a family whose welfare is looked after by the consort of Vishnu, and prosperity is the presiding goddess.

446 A person who falls from yoga is reborn in a family possessing great merit and the harvest of all happiness.

अथवा योगिनाम् एव कुले भवति धीमताम् ।
एतद् धि दुर्लभतरं लोके जन्म यद् ईदृशम् ॥
athavā yoginām eva
kule bhavati dhīmatām
etad dhi durlabhataram
loke janma yad īdṛśam

42. Or he may be born in the family of wise yogins; such a birth as this is very difficult to attain in the world.

तत्र तं बुद्धिसंयोगं लभते पौर्वदेहिकम् ।
यतते च ततो भूयः संसिद्धौ कुरुनन्दन ॥
tatra taṁ buddhisaṁyogaṁ
labhate pāurvadehikam
yatate ca tato bhūyaḥ
saṁsiddhāu kurunandana

43. There he regains the knowledge derived from a former body, and he strives onward once more toward perfection, Arjuna.

447 Or he is born into a family which burns the sacrificial fire of wisdom, is versed in the knowledge of the Eternal, and is heir to the land of the highest bliss;

448 Who, seated on the throne of the highest truth, rule over the three worlds, and who are like birds singing in the garden of contentment;

449 Who sit in the chief place in the city of discrimination, enjoying the fruit of the Eternal. He may be born in the family of such yogis.

450 Although his outer form may appear small, the dawning of Self-knowledge appears in him, just as light precedes the rising of the sun.

451 Without waiting till maturity to attain this state, in his youth he comes to possess all knowledge.

452 As he acquires such a perfected intellect, his mind gives forth learning and his lips reveal all the branches of knowledge.

453 He enters a birth that the gods in heaven crave, constantly performing sacrifices and repeating prayers,

454 And for which the immortal ones become poets and sing the praises of this mortal world. O Arjuna, in this way such a person is reborn.

पूर्वाभ्यासेन तेनैव ह्रियते ह्य् अवशो ऽपि सः ।
जिज्ञासुर् अपि योगस्य शब्दब्रह्मातिवर्तते ॥
pūrvābhyāsena tenāiva
hriyate hy avaśo 'pi saḥ
jijñāsur api yogasya
śabdabrahmātivartate

44. He is carried on, even against his will, by prior practice; he who even wishes to know of yoga transcends Brahman in the form of sound (i.e. Vedic recitation).

455 The pure knowledge which was his when he left his former life, he attains anew in full measure in this life.

456 Just as a fortunate person who is born feet first can easily see, with an application of magic ointment, the treasures of the lower worlds,

457 Similarly, the intellect of such a person effortlessly grasps the most abstruse problems, knowledge which ordinarily can be gained only with the help of the Guru.

458 The powerful senses are under the control of his mind, the mind becomes one with the *prana*, and the *prana* begins to mingle with the ether.

459 We don't know how this happens, but because of his past practice, meditation seeks out the house of his mind.

460 Know that such a person is the presiding deity of yoga, the glory of the beginning of yogic practice, and the incarnation of perfection in yoga.

461 He is the standard by which worldly happiness is measured, the lamp which reveals all yoga. Just as if fragrance had assumed the form of a sandalwood tree,

462 In the same way he appears to be the embodiment of contentment, or a person drawn out of the great store of those who have reached perfection. The seeker of yoga has risen to this condition.

प्रयत्नाद् यतमानस् तु योगी संशुद्धकिल्बिषः ।
अनेकजन्मसंसिद्धस् ततो याति परां गतिं ॥
prayatnād yatamānas tu
yogī saṁśuddhakilbiṣaḥ
anekajanmasaṁsiddhas
tato yāti parām gatiṁ

45. Through persevering effort and controlled mind, the yogin, completely cleansed

of evil, and perfected through many births, then goes to the supreme goal.

463 After millions of years and thousands of births, he arrives at the shore of Self-realization.
464 Thus all means to this end come naturally to him, and he sits on the throne of discrimination.
465 Then with the speed of thought itself, he leaves behind even discrimination and becomes one with that which is beyond thought.
466 The cloud of the mind vanishes, the air loses its very nature, and is absorbed into itself.
467 He enjoys such indescribable bliss that the sacred syllable lowers its head, and language retreats before him.
468 Thus he becomes the embodiment of the state of the Absolute, which is the source of all activity, and is truly the very form of the Formless.
469 During many past lives he has swept away the mass of confusion, and the moment of his birth is the final moment of his marriage to God.
470 Entering nonduality, he becomes wedded to the Eternal, just as clouds merge into the sky.
471 While still in the body, he becomes one with the Eternal, from which the universe proceeds and into which it will again be absorbed.

तपस्विभ्यो ऽधिको योगी ज्ञानिभ्यो ऽपि मतो ऽधिकः ।
कर्मिभ्यश् चाधिको योगी तस्माद् योगी भवार्जुन ॥

tapasvibhyo 'dhiko yogī
jñānibhyo 'pi mato 'dhikaḥ
karmibhyaś cādhiko yogī
tasmād yogī bhavārjuna

46. The yogin is superior to the ascetics, he is also thought to be superior to the learned, and the yogin is superior to those who perform ritual works. Therefore, be a yogin, Arjuna.

472 People of devotion, supported by the arm of fortitude, plunge into action in the hope of attaining this union,
473 For which the wise wearing the armor of knowledge, fight with worldly existence on the battlefield of life.
474 Longing earnestly for this union, ascetics cling fast, unsupported, to the steep precipice of the fortress of penance.
475 This union is the object of worship for all worshipers and the sacrificial objects of those who perform sacrifices. In short, it is that which should always be venerated by everyone,
476 The final goal, the highest truth which can be attained by all seekers, the Eternal, which the yogi himself becomes.
477 Therefore, he is respected by all men of action, worthy to be known by the wise, and the highest master among ascetics.
478 He whose entire concentration is directed towards the union of the lower self with the higher Self, like the confluence of two rivers, rises to greatness while still in the body.
479 Therefore, O Arjuna, I always say to you, be a yogi with all your heart.

योगिनाम् अपि सर्वेषां मद्गतेनान्तरात्मना ।
श्रद्धावान् भजते यो मां स मे युक्ततमो मतः ॥

yoginām api sarveṣāṁ
madgatenāntarātmanā
śraddhāvān bhajate yo māṁ
sa me yuktatamo mataḥ

47. Of all these yogins, he who has merged his inner Self in Me, honors Me, full of faith, is thought to be the most devoted to Me.

480 O Beloved, know that the person who is called a yogi is the god of gods, My greatest joy, My very life.
481 To such a person, worship, the worshiper, and the object of worship are always Me, through the experience of union.
482 O Arjuna, then it is certain that the love existing between him and Me cannot be described in words.
483 Sanjaya said, Thus spoke Krishna, who is to His devotees as the moon is to the chakora bird, the only Lord of the three worlds, the ocean of all virtues.
484 Then Krishna realized that Arjuna's eagerness to hear more on this subject had become twice as strong as before.
485 His mind was happier, for His words had found a mirror of response. Therefore, He will now joyfully explain everything.
486 This subject will be covered in the following chapter, in which the feeling of tranquility will be explained and in which the seeds of this knowledge will be sown so the shoots can come forth.

487 The soil of the spiritual ground has been prepared in the minds of the wise with showers of purity.
488 It has been prepared by the listeners' attentiveness, as precious as gold, and now Nivritti's disciple is eager to sow the seed.
489 Jnanadeva says, Truly my Guru has fulfilled my wish, for he has laid his hand on my head and has sown the seeds of knowledge.
490 Whatever my lips speak will be acceptable to the hearts of the good. But let that be; I must now tell what Krishna has taught.
491 It must be heard with the ear of the mind, and the words must be seen with the eye of the intellect. In this way there will be mutual profit.
492 These words must be embraced in the heart with the arms of attentiveness; then they will delight the minds of the good.
493 These words will bring peace of mind, revive the sense of purpose, and bring immeasurable joy to the soul.
494 Now Krishna will joyfully speak with Arjuna. I will now tell of it in the *ovi* meter.

7

THE YOGA OF WISDOM AND REALIZATION

श्रीभगवान् उवाच । *śrībhagavān uvāca*

मय्य् आसक्तमनाः पार्थ योगं युञ्जन् मदाश्रयः ।
असंशयं समग्रं मां यथा ज्ञास्यसि तच्छृणु ॥

mayy āsaktamanāḥ pārtha
yogaṁ yuñjan madāśrayaḥ
asaṁśayaṁ samagraṁ māṁ
yathā jñāsyasi tac chṛṇui

The Blessed Lord spoke:

1. With mind absorbed in Me, Arjuna, practicing yoga, dependent on Me, you shall know Me completely, without doubt; hear that!

ज्ञानं ते ऽहं सविज्ञानम् इदं वक्ष्याम्य् अशेषतः ।
यज् ज्ञात्वा नेह भूयो ऽन्यज् ज्ञातव्यम् अवशिष्यते ॥

jñānaṁ te 'haṁ savijñānam
idaṁ vakṣyāmy aśeṣataḥ
yaj jñātvā neha bhūyo 'nyaj
jñātavyam avaśiṣyate

2. To you I shall explain in full this knowledge, along with realization, which, having been understood, nothing further remains to be known here in the world.

LISTEN! Then Lord Krishna said to Arjuna, Truly you have now become perfected in yoga.

2 Now I will impart to you knowledge and direct experience, so you will know Me fully, like a jewel that is lying on the palm of your hand.

3 If you should ask what is the use of worldly knowledge here, I will tell you that you must first acquire it.

4 Then, when you attain true wisdom, Consciousness closes its eyes, just as a boat moored to the shore does not move.

5 Where personal awareness cannot enter, thought withdraws and logical reasoning becomes ineffective.

6 There is wisdom, O Arjuna. Knowledge of worldly affairs is practical knowledge, although the apparent sense of reality in it is actually ignorance. Distinguish between these three things.

7 I will now reveal the secret of how ignorance can be dispelled, worldly knowledge burned up, and true wisdom made manifest.

8 When a person understands that secret even a little, many longings of his mind are satisfied.

9 As a result of this, the speaker's voice falls silent, the listener's longing vanishes, and there remain no distinctions such as great or small.

मनुष्याणां सहस्रेषु कश्चिद् यतति सिद्धये ।
यतताम् अपि सिद्धानां कश्चिन् मां वेत्ति तत्त्वतः ॥

manuṣyāṇāṁ sahasreṣu
kaścid yatati siddhaye
yatatām api siddhānāṁ
kaścin māṁ vetti tattvataḥ

3. Of thousands of men, scarcely anyone strives for perfection; even of the striving and the perfected, scarcely anyone knows Me in truth.

10 O Beloved, among thousands of people, rarely is there one who has an earnest desire for this; and among these, hardly one attains knowledge of it.

11 O Arjuna, just as in the world an army of thousands is formed of chosen warriors,

12 And when the weapons strike them down in battle, one warrior alone among them all is seated on the throne of victory;

13 Similarly, thousands enter the great waters

of the search for God, but scarcely one is able to reach the further shore of attainment.

14 Therefore, O Beloved, this is no ordinary matter; it is of great importance. I will explain it in due course of time. Now let's return to the present subject.

भूमिर् आपो ऽनलो वायुः खं मनो बुद्धिर् एव च ।
अहंकार इतीयं मे भिन्ना प्रकृतिर् अष्टधा ॥
bhūmir āpo 'nalo vāyuḥ
khaṁ mano buddhir eva ca
ahaṁkāra itīyaṁ me
bhinnā prakrtiṛ aṣṭadhā

4. Earth, water, fire, air, ether, mind, intellect—and egoism—this, My material nature, is divided into eight parts.

15 O Arjuna, listen! Just as reflections are like shadows of our own bodies, similarly, divine intelligence and the primary elements are shadows of Me.

16 This is called My nature. It has eight parts, and the three worlds emanate from it.

17 If you want to know what these eight divisions are, listen to this explanation:

18 Earth, water, fire, air, ether, mind, intellect, and ego are its eight parts.

अपरेयम् इतस् त्व् अन्यां प्रकृतिं विद्धि मे पराम् ।
जीवभूतां महाबाहो ययेदं धार्यते जगत् ॥
apareyam itas tv anyāṁ
prakṛtiṁ viddhi me parām
jīvabhūtāṁ mahābāho
yayedaṁ dhāryate jagat

5. Such is My inferior nature, but know it as different from My highest nature, the Self, O Arjuna, by which this universe is sustained.

19 O Arjuna, the equilibrium of this eightfold matter rests in My higher nature, which is called the life element.

20 It is this which quickens dead matter, awakens consciousness, and causes the mind to experience sorrow and delusion.

21 By association with awareness, the intellect acquires discrimination and the world is upheld by the skill of the ego.

एतद्योनीनि भूतानि सर्वाणीत्य् उपधारय ।
अहं कृत्स्नस्य जगतः प्रभवः प्रलयस् तथा ॥
etadyonīni bhūtāni
sarvāṇīty upadhāraya
ahaṁ kṛtsnasya jagataḥ
prabhavaḥ pralayas tathā

6. All creatures have their birth in this, My highest nature. Understand this! I am the origin and also the dissolution of the entire universe.

22 When the higher nature by its own innate tendency intermingles with the lower, beings are created.

23 The fourfold division of form begins spontaneously. Although their value is the same, the classes vary.

24 Millions of species are formed with innumerable subdivisions so that the storehouse of space can hardly contain them. The womb of the original void is filled with these various types, like coins in a treasury.

25 Many coins of the same kind are minted from the five elements, and the divine nature alone can keep track of their number.

26 The coins which are produced are multiplied and then melted down. When they are circulated, they are involved in the business of good and evil deeds.

27 Let us leave that metaphor; I will explain it to you clearly. It is nature who creates the multitude of names and forms.

28 And this divine nature is reflected in Me alone. Therefore, I am the beginning and the end of the universe.

मत्तः परतरं नान्यत् किंचिद् अस्ति धनंजय ।
मयि सर्वम् इदं प्रोतं सूत्रे मणिगणा इव ॥
mattaḥ parataraṁ nānyat
kiṁcid asti dhanaṁjaya
mayi sarvam idaṁ protaṁ
sūtre maṇigaṇā iva

7. Nothing higher than Me exists, O Arjuna. On Me all this universe is strung like pearls on a thread.

29 The universe is like a mirage: when you observe it more closely, you find that it is caused by the sun and not by its rays.

30 Similarly, O Arjuna, when the created world, emanating from this higher nature vanishes, I am the only reality.

31 Whatever is born, exists, and disappears, rests wholly in Me. I hold the universe together just as gems are threaded on a string.

रसो ऽहम् अप्सु कौन्तेय प्रभास्मि शशिसूर्ययोः ।
प्रणवः सर्ववेदेषु शब्दः खे पौरुषं नृषु ॥
raso 'ham apsu kāunteya,
prabhāsmi śaśisūryayoḥ
praṇavaḥ sarvavedeṣu

śabdaḥ khe pāuruṣaṁ nṛṣu

8. I am the liquidity in the waters, Arjuna, I am the radiance in the moon and sun, the sacred syllable (Om) in all the Vedas, the sound in the air, and the manhood in men.

पुण्यो गन्धः पृथिव्यां च तेजश्चास्मि विभावसौ ।
जीवनं सर्वभूतेषु तपश्चास्मि तपस्विषु ॥

puṇyo gandhaḥ pṛthivyāṁ ca
tejaścāsmi vibhāvasāu
jīvanaṁ sarvabhūteṣu
tapaścāsmi tapasviṣu

9. I am the pure fragrance in the earth, and the brilliance in the fire, the life in all beings, and the austerity in ascetics.

32 Know that I am the moisture in water, the touch of the wind, and the radiance in the sun and moon.
33 I am also the natural pure fragrance of the earth, the sound in the heavens, and the sacred syllable of the Vedas.
34 Think of Me as the humanity in men, the principle of individuality, and the essence of all human activity. I tell you this truth.
35 The word fire is the outer covering of the inner light. When this covering is removed, the light is Me.
36 All creatures of the various species born in the three worlds are sustained by the food which they need.
37 Some live on air, others on green herbs, and still others on different kinds of food or on water.
38 These various forms of nourishment, which differ according to the nature of each creature, are all permeated with My undivided life.

बीजं मां सर्वभूतानां विद्धि पार्थ सनातनम्
बुद्धिर् बुद्धिमताम् अस्मि तेजस् तेजस्विनाम् अहम् ॥

bījaṁ māṁ sarvabhūtānāṁ
viddhi pārtha sanātanam
buddhir buddhimatām asmi
tejas tejasvinām aham

10. Know Me to be the primeval seed of all creatures, Arjuna; I am the intelligence of the intelligent; the splendor of the splendid, am I.

बलं बलवतां चाहं कामरागविवर्जितम् ।
धर्माविरुद्धो भूतेषु कामो ऽस्मि भरतर्षभ ॥

balaṁ balavatāṁ cāham
kāmarāgavivarjitam
dharmāviruddho bhūteṣu
kāmo 'smi bharatarṣabha

11. And the might of the mighty I am, which is freed from lust and passion, and I am that desire in beings which is according to law, Arjuna.

39 The principle which, at the beginning of time, diffuses itself through germination and which, at the end, engulfs the letters of the sacred syllable;
40 Which, as long as creation continues, seems to exist in the form of the universe, but which at its dissolution becomes formless;
41 I am that principle, existing eternally, the seed of the universe. I now reveal this to you.
42 When it becomes clear to you and when you make it your own through discrimination, you will understand its highest purpose.
43 Leaving this digression, I am the austerity of the ascetic.
44 I am the enduring strength of the strong and the intellect of those who are endowed with intelligence.
45 Krishna said, In all creatures I am that desire through which dharma becomes their highest aspiration.
46 This desire, through the channel of feeling, generally follows the path of the senses, but is not allowed to work against dharma.
47 Leaving the wrong road of forbidden actions, it follows the path of prescribed duties and travels with the help of the torch of discipline.
48 When desire follows the proper direction, a person fulfills his duty and participates in worldly life with the freedom he gains at the holy place of liberation.
49 This desire causes the vine of the entire creation to grow on the arbor of the greatness of the Vedas, until it sends forth new foliage with the fruits of action and reaches the Absolute.
50 The Father of yogis said, I am this restrained desire, the source of all created objects.
51 It is not possible to describe this in detail. You should know that all created objects evolve from Me.

ये चैव सात्त्विका भावा राजसास् तामसाश्च ये ।
मत्त एवेति तान् विद्धि न त्व् अहं तेषु ते मयि ॥

ye cāiva sāttvikā bhāvā
rājasās tāmasāśca ye

matta eveti tān viddhi
na tv ahaṁ teṣu te mayi

12. And those states of being which are sattvic, and those which are rajasic and tamasic, know that they proceed from Me. But I am not in them; they are in Me.

52 Every condition of the mind, whether pure, active, or lazy, is born of My nature. You should realize this.

53 Though they evolve from My nature, I am not in them any more than waking consciousness is present in deep sleep.

54 A seed is solid with condensed sap, and through its shoots it will become wood.

55 Yet can you say that there is any quality of the seed in the wood? Similarly, I am not in these various states, though I may appear to be subject to modification.

56 Although clouds form in the sky, the sky is not in the clouds. Or we can say that there is water in the clouds, yet the clouds are not in the water.

57 Lightning, which flashes brilliantly, is born of the agitation of water; but is there any water in that flash of lightning?

58 Smoke emerges from the fire, but there is no fire in the smoke. Similarly, all creatures have emanated from Me, yet I am not in them.

त्रिभिर् गुणमयैर् भावैर् एभिः सर्वम् इदं जगत् ।
मोहितं नाभिजानाति माम् एभ्यः परम् अव्ययम् ॥

tribhir guṇamayāir bhāvāir
ebhiḥ sarvam idaṁ jagat
mohitaṁ nābhijānāti
mām ebhyaḥ param avyayam

13. All this universe is deluded by these three states of being, composed of the qualities. It does not recognize Me, who am higher than these, and eternal.

59 Water is covered by the weeds growing in it, and the sky is veiled by masses of clouds.

60 Although we may say that a dream is false, during sleep it appears to be a reality. At that time, are we aware that it is a dream?

61 Isn't the eye deprived of its sight when it is veiled by a cataract?

62 Similarly, all of this is a reflection of Me. The shadow of the three *gunas* has spread over Me like a screen.

63 Because of this, My creatures do not know Me. Although they are Mine, they are not one with Me, just as pearls born of water do not melt in it.

64 If a pot is made out of earth and is immediately broken up again, it becomes one with the earth. If it is baked in the fire, however, it remains separate from it.

65 In the same way, all creatures are part of Me, but because of the great illusion, they have acquired the state of individuality.

दैवी ह्य् एषा गुणमयी मम माया दुरत्यया ।
माम् एव ये प्रपद्यन्ते मायाम् एतां तरन्ति ते ॥

dāivī hy eṣā guṇamayī
mama māyā duratyayā
mām eva ye prapadyante
māyām etāṁ taranti te

14. Divine indeed is this illusion of Mine made up of the three qualities, and difficult to penetrate; only those who resort to Me transcend this illusion.

66 O Arjuna, how is it possible for a person to become one with Me, having crossed over the great river of illusion?

67 First, there gushes out of the rocky side of the mountain of the Absolute a stream in the form of desire, and from that the great elements emerge in small bubbles.

68 Then it flows on in the manifestation of the created world, and gathering speed with time, it overflows the high banks of activity and cessation from activity.

69 With showers of rain from the clouds in the form of the three qualities, the great flood of delusion swells the stream, and it sweeps away the cities of restraint and self-control.

70 The whirlpools of hate and the cross-currents of envy swirl on its surface, and the great fish of error and sin flash within it.

71 In its course, too, are eddies of worldly affairs and the rapids of action and wrong action, on which the weeds of pleasure and pain are swept along.

72 The billows of lust dash against the island of sexual love, and masses of souls in the form of foam are cast upon it.

73 In the stream of egoism, spouts of infatuation with learning, wealth, and power gush out, and waves of sense objects leap forth.

74 The rise and fall of the flood of day and night causes the great depths of birth and death, in which the bubbles of the five elements come and go in the form of bodies.

75 The fish of infatuation and delusion swallow the bait of courage, and swirling eddies

of ignorance are formed.

76 In the turbid water of perplexity, they sink in the mire of the expectation of happiness, and heaven resounds with the gurgling of passion.

77 The streams of darkness are powerful, and the stillness of the waters of purity is deep. This river of illusion is difficult to cross.

78 With the constant gushing of the waves of birth and death, even the bastions of the highest heaven collapse, and the rocks of the universe crash under the blows.

79 This terrible deluge of illusion has not yet subsided. Who can cross over it?

80 Those who have plunged into this river and have tried to swim across it with the arms of their own intellect have been lost. Some have been sucked into the deep pool of knowledge by their own pride.

81 Others, who embarked on the raft of the Vedas with stones of egoism fastened to them, were swallowed up by the fish of infatuation.

82 Still others clothed themselves with the vigor of youth, and seeking the support of the god of love, have been devoured by the crocodile of sensual pleasure.

83 Then, caught in the net of confusion on the waves of old age, and bound fast on every side,

84 They were dashed against the rocks of grief. Whirling around in the eddies of anger, whenever they rose to the surface, they were attacked by the vultures of misfortune.

85 Sunk in the mud of sorrow, they were drawn into the sands of death. So their reliance on the help of desire was in vain.

86 Some, fastening to their waist a bundle of sacrificial rites, were trapped in the cave of heavenly pleasure.

87 Others, placing their faith in action, became entangled in the whirlpool of prescribed duties and forbidden actions in the hope of reaching the other shore and liberation.

88 It is almost impossible to cross this river, where the boat of dispassion cannot land and the rope of discrimination cannot reach the other side.

89 If we were to say that a person can cross over this river of illusion by his own efforts, I will tell you what that kind of talk is like:

90 If disease did not attack a person addicted to immoderate eating, if a good man could understand the evil thoughts of the wicked, if a sensuous person would refuse to accept prosperity,

91 If thieves could meet together in an assembly, if a fish could safely swallow the hook of a fisherman, if a coward could chase away a ghost,

92 If a young deer could gnaw away a net, or if an ant could climb to the top of Mount Meru, then perhaps a living creature might see the other shore of the river of Maya.

93 O Arjuna, just as a lustful man cannot resist a woman, similarly, an individual soul cannot cross over this river of illusion.

94 Only those who have served Me with devotion have succeeded in crossing it. For them the waters of Maya have vanished, even while they are on this shore.

95 Casting off the burden of egoism, avoiding the winds of desire, searching the waters of earthly love to find a shallow inlet,

96 If a person has found the food of pure reason, at the descent of union he leaps across to the further shore of freedom.

97 If he finds the boat of self-inquiry and places his whole trust in the experience of the Self, with a good Guru as his boatman,

98 Then, if he strikes through the water with the arms of detachment and is supported by the strength of oneness with the Self, he easily reaches the shore of the cessation of all activity.

99 Those who have served Me like this have crossed over My river of Maya, but devotees such as these are very few.

न मां दुष्कृतिनो मूढाः प्रपद्यन्ते नराधमाः ।
माययापहृतज्ञाना आसुरं भावम् आश्रिताः ॥

na māṁ duṣkṛtino mūḍhāḥ
prapadyante narādhamāḥ
māyayāpahṛtajñānā
āsuraṁ bhāvam āśritāḥ

15. Evil doers, lowest of men, deprived of knowledge by illusion, do not seek Me, attached as they are to a demoniacal existence.

चतुर्विधा भजन्ते मां जनाः सुकृतिनोऽर्जुन ।
आर्तो जिज्ञासुर् अर्थार्थी ज्ञानी च भरतर्षभ ॥

caturvidhā bhajante māṁ
janāḥ sukṛtino 'rjuna
ārto, jijñāsur arthārthī
jñānī ca bharatarṣabha

16. Among benevolent men, four kinds

worship Me, Arjuna: the distressed, those who desire wealth, those who desire knowledge, and the man of wisdom, Arjuna.

100 Besides these, there are many others who have forgotten their true Self, having become possessed by the evil spirit of egoism.
101 They have forgotten the clothing of a well-disciplined life, have lost all sense of shame about their future state of degeneration, and perform actions prohibited by the Vedas.
102 Look, O Arjuna, they abandon the very purpose for which they have taken birth.
103 In the streets they gather together with various emotions in order to satisfy their craving for vain egotistical chatter.
104 Needless to say, having been swallowed up by Maya, they are unable to remember the wounds of sorrow and affliction.
105 Therefore, they fail to find Me. Now hear the four ways in which men worship Me, seeking to increase their own spiritual welfare.
106 The first are those who suffer, the second are the seekers of knowledge, the third are those who crave wealth, and the fourth are the wise.
107 Of all these, the sorrowful ones worship Me because of their sorrow, the seekers of knowledge for the sake of knowledge, and the third desiring to obtain wealth.
108 The fourth, however, are not impelled by such motives, so know that the wise are true worshipers of Me.

तेषां ज्ञानी नित्ययुक्त एकभक्तिर् विशिष्यते।
प्रियो हि ज्ञानिनो ऽत्यर्थम् अहं स च मम प्रियः॥
teṣām jñānī nityayukta
ekabhaktir viśiṣyate
priyo hi jñānino 'tyartham
ahaṁ sa ca mama priyaḥ

17. Of them the man of wisdom, eternally steadfast, devoted to the One alone, is preeminent. I am indeed exceedingly fond of the man of wisdom, and he is fond of Me.

109 By the light of his wisdom the darkness of separateness is removed, and then he becomes fully united with Me. Nevertheless, he still remains My devotee.
110 The strange thing is that just as a crystal may appear to be water, so the wise man seems to be separate from Me.
111 Just as when the wind ceases to blow, it no longer appears to be separate from the sky, similarly, that devotee is united with Me, though his individuality as a devotee remains the same.
112 When the wind blows, it seems to be different from the sky, and yet the sky remains as it was.
113 In the same way, while acting in the body he appears to be worshiping Me, but having attained Self-realization, he is one with Me.
114 Through the dawn of wisdom, he knows I am his own Self. I, too, joyfully consider him My Self.
115 Having reached the state that is beyond individuality, is a person who performs actions in the world different from Me, just because he is in a separate body?

उदाराः सर्व एवैते ज्ञानी त्व् आत्मैव मे मतम्।
आस्थितः स हि युक्तात्मा माम् एवानुत्तमां गतिम्॥
udārāḥ sarva evāite
jñānī tv ātmāiva me matam
āsthitaḥ sa hi yuktātmā
mām evānuttamāṁ gatim

18. All these are indeed noble, but the man of wisdom is thought to be My very Self. He, indeed, whose mind is steadfast, abides in Me, the supreme goal.

116 All devotees cling to Me, some having self-interest as their motive, but I love only the wise.
117 In order to milk a cow, a person ties her with a rope, but her affection for her calf is so strong that she gives it milk without being tied.
118 The calf knows none but its mother. Seeing her it says, "This is my mother."
119 In this way the calf is solely dependent on its mother, and the cow is devoted to her calf. The Lord has spoken truly.
120 Again the Lord said, These devotees whom I have already described are very dear to Me,
121 For when they learn to know Me, they never look back, just as a river flowing towards the ocean never turns back from it.
122 Similarly, a person in whom Self-realization flows like a river from the depths of his heart and unites with Me, truly becomes Me.
123 The wise man is the soul of my soul. I shouldn't have said this, but how could I avoid it?

बहूनां जन्मनाम् अन्ते ज्ञानवान् मां प्रपद्यते।
वासुदेवः सर्वम् इति स महात्मा सुदुर्लभः॥

bahūnāṁ janmanām ante
jñānavān māṁ prapadyate
vāsudevaḥ sarvam iti
sa mahātmā sudurlabhaḥ

19. At the end of many births, the man of wisdom resorts to Me, thinking "Vasudeva (Krishna) is all." Such a great soul is hard to find.

124 Avoiding the dangers of desire and anger in the forest of sense objects, he reaches the ascent of good desire.

125 Then, O Arjuna, in the company of good people, he follows the straight road of right action, avoiding the obscure path of unrighteousness.

126 He proceeds on his journey through countless births, discarding the sandals of attachment. Can he care about the fruit of desire?

127 Traveling on along through the night of union with the body, he sees the end of action and the dawn appears.

128 Then the morning rays of the Guru's grace and the sunshine of wisdom fall on him, and the glory of equanimity is revealed to his sight.

129 Then, wherever he turns his gaze, I am there before him. Even when he is alone, I am present there.

130 In short, there is none but Me everywhere, just as a pot immersed in water has water both inside and outside.

131 So he is in Me, and I am both within him and without. This experience cannot be expressed in words.

132 In this way, he sees the storehouse of wisdom and lives knowing that he and the universe are one.

133 He is the best of devotees. He alone is wise, for he has attained the awareness that the Lord pervades everything.

134 O Arjuna, such a being is truly rare. The whole of creation is contained in the treasure house of his Self-realization.

कामैस् तैस्तैर् हृतज्ञानाः प्रपद्यन्ते ऽन्यदेवताः ।
तंतं नियमम् आस्थाय प्रकृत्या नियताः स्वया ॥
kāmāis tāistāir hṛtajñānāḥ
prapadyante 'nyadevatāḥ
taṁtaṁ niyamam āsthāya
prakṛtyā niyayāḥ svayā

20. Men whose knowledge has been carried away by these and those desires, resort to other gods, having recourse to this and that religious rite, constrained by their own material natures.

135 O Arjuna, in addition to him, many worship Me; but they offer their worship for their own satisfaction, for they are blinded by the darkness of desire.

136 Desire has entered their hearts through greed for the fruit of their action, and this desire extinguishes the lamp of their wisdom.

137 Thus, they sink into inner and outer darkness. Though I am so near, they lose sight of Me and worship other gods.

138 Being already slaves of material life, they are impoverished by their enjoyment of pleasures. See how eagerly they worship these gods!

139 They take certain vows, perform many rites, and offer all manner of oblations.

यो यो यां यां तनुं भक्तः श्रद्धयार्चितुम् इच्छति ।
तस्य तस्याचलां श्रद्धां ताम् एव विदधाम्य् अहम् ॥
yo yo yāṁ yāṁ tanuṁ bhaktaḥ
śraddhayārcituṁ icchati
tasya tasyācalāṁ śraddhāṁ
tām eva vidadhāmy aham

21. Whoever desires to honor with belief whatever worshiped form, on him I bestow immovable faith.

140 With whatever desires a person may worship other deities, truly it is I who fulfill them.

141 Thus, they worship those deities in whom they have placed their trust, performing the proper rites until they obtain the fruit of their devotion.

स तया श्रद्धया युक्तस् तस्याराधनम् ईहते ।
लभते च ततः कामान् मयैव विहितान् हि तान् ॥
sa tayā śraddhayā yuktas
tasyārādhanam īhate
labhate ca tataḥ kāmān
mayāiva vihitān hi tān

22. He, who, endowed with this faith, desires to propitiate that form, receives from it his desires because those desires are decreed by Me.

142 Serving the gods in this way, a person reaps the fruit of his service. Nevertheless, it proceeds from Me.

अन्तवत् तु फलं तेषां तद् भवत्य् अल्पमेधसाम् ।
देवान् देवयजो यान्ति मद्भक्ता यान्ति माम् अपि ॥

antavat tu phalaṁ teṣāṁ
tad bhavaty alpamedhasām
devān devayajo yānti
madbhaktā yānti mām api

23. But temporary is the fruit for those of small understanding. To the gods the god-worshipers go; My worshipers come surely to Me.

143 These worshipers do not know Me, for they can never rise above desire. The satisfaction that they gain is passing and imaginary.
144 Truly speaking, such worship only serves worshipers in this worldly life, for the enjoyment of its fruit is as momentary as a dream.
145 But let's leave this matter. Whatever deity he may choose, the person who worships other gods acquires their nature.
146 Those who follow the path of devotion to Me with their body, mind, and soul, attain Me at the end of their lives.

अव्यक्तं व्यक्तिम् आपन्नं मन्यन्ते माम अबुद्धयः ।
परं भावम् अजानन्तो ममाव्ययम् अनुत्तमम् ॥
avyaktaṁ vyaktim āpannaṁ
manyante mām abuddhayaḥ
paraṁ bhāvam ajānanto
mamāvyayam anuttamam

24. Though I am unmanifest, the unintelligent think of Me as having manifestation, not knowing My higher being which is imperishable and unsurpassed.

147 But people don't do this; instead, they destroy their own good. It is as if they were trying to swim in water held in the palm of their hand.
148 Why should a person immersed in an ocean of nectar keep his mouth closed and meditate on a pool of water?
149 Why should he die when he's bathing in nectar? Since he is in it, why shouldn't he become one with it?
150 Similarly, O Arjuna, why shouldn't a person escape from the snare of the fruit of action and soar high on the wings of Self-realization to become its master?
151 Then, courageously rising upwards, he reaches those higher realms and can wander there at his pleasure.
152 Why try to measure the immeasurable? Why consider Me, the unmanifest, as manifest? When I am present here, why do people exhaust themselves striving to reach Me?
153 Even if they really consider all this, O Arjuna, it seems that creatures cannot comprehend Me.

नाहं प्रकाशः सर्वस्य योगमायासमावृतः ।
मूढो ऽयं नाभिजानाति लोको माम् अजम् अव्ययम् ॥
nāhaṁ prakāśaḥ sarvasya
yogamāyāsamāvṛtaḥ
mūḍho 'yaṁ nābhijānāti
loko mām ajam avyayam

25. I am not manifest to all, being enveloped in yoga maya; this deluded world does not recognize Me, the birthless and imperishable.

154 These creatures have become blinded by the veil of illusion, so they fail to perceive Me even in the full light of day.
155 Can it be said that there is anything in which I don't exist? Can there be water without wetness?
156 What isn't touched by the wind? Is there anything that isn't contained in space? Truly, I am the One alone who pervades the whole universe.

वेदाहं समतीतानि वर्तमानानि चार्जुन ।
भविष्याणि च भूतानि मां तु वेद न कश्चन ॥
vedāhaṁ samatītāni
vartamānāni cārjuna
bhaviṣyāṇi ca bhūtāni
māṁ tu veda na kaścana

26. I know the departed beings and the living, Arjuna, and those who are yet to be; but no one knows Me.

157 All creatures who have existed have become Me, and I am also in those who exist now.
158 Those who are born in the future will also be in Me. But these are mere words, for nothing is ever born, nor can anything ever die.
159 Thus, O Arjuna, I am eternally present. The entire creation has come about in another way.

इच्छाद्वेषसमुत्थेन द्वन्द्वमोहेन भारत ।
सर्वभूतानि संमोहं सर्गे यान्ति परंतप ॥
icchādveṣasamutthena
dvandvamohena bhārata
sarvabhūtāni saṁmohaṁ
sarge yānti paraṁtapa

27. Because of the arising of desire and hatred, because of the deluding (power) of the opposites, Arjuna, all beings fall into delusion at birth.

160 Listen while I explain all this briefly to you. When egoism and the body were attracted to each other,
161 A daughter called desire was born to them. When she reached maturity in love, she was married to hate.
162 They had a son called veil of duality, and the child was brought up by his grandfather egoism.
163 He was always opposed to resolution, refused all discipline, and grew fat on the juice of craving.
164 Intoxicated with the wine of dissatisfaction, he amused himself with passion in the arena of the sense objects, O Arjuna.
165 He scattered thorns of doubt on the path of devotion and opened up by-ways of wrong action.
166 In this way creatures are deluded and becoming involved in the complexity of worldly life, are beaten with clubs of sorrow.

येषां त्व् अन्तगतं पापं जनानां पुण्यकर्मणाम्।
ते द्वन्द्वमोहनिर्मुक्ता भजन्ते मां दृढव्रताः॥

yeṣāṁ tv antagataṁ pāpaṁ
janānāṁ puṇyakarmaṇām
te dvandvamohanirmuktā
bhajante mām dṛḍhavratāḥ

28. But those in whom evil has come to an end, those men whose actions are pure; they, liberated from the deluding power of the opposites, worship Me with firm vows.

167 However, those who see the sharp thorns of illusion and don't allow themselves to be distracted by them,
168 Trample under foot these sharp thorns in the path of steadfast devotion and cross over the forest of sin.
169 Moreover, they run toward Me on the swift course of righteousness and are saved from the attack of thieves.

जरामरणमोक्षाय माम् आश्रित्य यतन्ति ये।
ते ब्रह्म तद् विदुः कृत्स्नम् अध्यात्मं कर्म चाखिलम्॥

jarāmaraṇamokṣāya
mām āśritya yatanti ye
te brahma tad viduḥ kṛtsnam
adhyātmaṁ karma cākhilạm

29. Those who strive toward release from old age and death, depending on Me, know Brahman thoroughly, as well as the Self and all action.

170 O Arjuna, for those who are earnest in their efforts to achieve liberation from birth and death,
171 Their struggles one day will blossom into the fruit of supreme Consciousness; when this ripens, it will abundantly yield the juice of perfection.
172 At that time they will reach the supreme goal of life, they will fully experience the glory of Self-knowledge, their life of action will be fulfilled, and their mental activity will cease.
173 This is the reward of Self-knowledge reaped by the person who has invested his wealth in me.
174 Then he truly draws the interest of an evenly balanced mind, his commerce in union prospers, and he no longer knows the calamity of separateness.

साधिभूताधिदैवं मां साधियज्ञं च ये विदुः।
प्रयाणकाले ऽपि च मां ते विदुर् युक्तचेतसः॥

sādhibhūtādhidāivaṁ māṁ
sādhiyajñaṁ ca ye viduḥ
prayāṇakāle 'pi ca māṁ
te vidur yuktacetasaḥ

30. They who know Me as the Adhibhuta and the Adhidaiva, as well as the chief of sacrifice, they truly know Me with steadfast thought even at the hour of death.

175 Those who have understood Me in My earthly form and have reached the highest deity,
176 And who with the power of Self-knowledge see Me in the sacrifice, do not grieve at the time of death.
177 Otherwise, when the thread of life is cut, the spirit is plunged into confusion. What wonder is it that a person who is alive feels as though the day of final destruction is near?
178 But who knows how to tell this? Those who are attached to Me do not fall away from Me at this time.
179 Know that such perfected yogis are wholeheartedly attached to Me.
180 Arjuna had not caught in the cupped hands of his attention the nectar of the words which Lord Krishna had poured out for him because he had fallen behind for a moment.
181 At that time, the fruit of the words of the Absolute, succulent with the juice of deep

meaning and fragrant with the perfume of devotion,
182 Fell suddenly into Arjuna's ears from the tree of Lord Krishna, shaken by the wind of His great compassion.
183 This fruit was created from the great truths dipped in the water of the essence of God, and covered with the sweetness of the highest bliss.
184 Because of its purity and excellence, Arjuna began to feel a longing for this higher wisdom and to drink deeply of the nectar of wonder.
185 He scorned heaven and its pleasures, and his innermost heart vibrated with ecstasy.
186 Fascinated by the beauty of that fruit, he felt an ardent desire to taste it and his delight increased.
187 With the hand of inference, he took this fruit in the form of the spoken word and placed it in the mouth of Self-experience.
188 But the tongue of thought could not soften it, and the teeth of reason could not bite through it. Realizing this, Arjuna did not eat it.
189 He become perplexed and thought, Aren't these like stars reflected in water? I've been deceived by the simplicity of these words.
190 They are folds in the garment of the heavens, and our intellects are utterly unable to fathom their meaning.
191 Then, wondering in his heart how these things could be explained, he looked again at Lord Krishna.
192 The great warrior implored Him saying, O Lord, it is strange that I haven't heard these words before.
193 Usually, with attentive listeners, it is possible to explain quickly the meaning of various principles.
194 But here, O Lord, it isn't so. One hears these words, and even wonder itself experiences wonder.
195 As soon as the rays of Your words entered my ears, wonder caught my attention.
196 O Lord, I am eager to know their meaning, so please explain it. I cannot bear even the slightest delay.
197 Reflecting on what the Lord had already said and on what was yet to come, he managed to restrain his eagerness.
198 Notice how cleverly Arjuna has asked for this wisdom. He has touched Lord Krishna's heart without overstepping the bounds of reverence and is ready to embrace the Lord's heart.
199 Whatever we need to learn from our teachers, we should ask them in this way. Arjuna knew this well.
200 See with what delight Sanjaya tells of Arjuna's questions and the way in which the omniscient Lord replies!
201 Listen to the story, which will be told in Marathi. The eye will perceive the meaning before the ears hear it,
202 And the senses will be revived by the beauty of the words, even before the tongue of reason has tasted the inner meaning.
203 The nose enjoys the fragrance of malati buds, but doesn't their beauty also please the eye?
204 Similarly, after the senses have enjoyed the beauty of the Marathi language, they will be ready to approach the deeper truths.
205 Jnanadeva, the disciple of Nivritti, says, Listen, for I am going to utter words that will surpass all other speech.

8

THE YOGA OF THE IMPERISHABLE ABSOLUTE

अर्जुन उवाच । *arjuna uvāca*

किं तद् ब्रह्म किम् अध्यात्मं किं कर्म पुरुषोत्तम ।
अधिभूतं च किं प्रोक्तम् अधिदैवं किम् उच्यते ॥

kim tad brahma kim adhyātmam
kim karma purusottama
adhibhūtam ca kim proktam
adhidāivam kim ucyate

Arjuna spoke:
1. What is this Brahman? What is the Adhyatma? What is action, O highest among Spirits? And the Adhibhuta, what is it declared to be? And the Adhidaiva, what is it said to be?

THEN Arjuna said, Have you heard me, O Lord? Please answer my questions.
2 Will You tell me what the Absolute is? And what is action, and who is the supreme Spirit? I am listening; tell me clearly.
3 What is the Supreme Being, and what is the highest Deity?

अधियज्ञः कथं कोऽत्र देहेऽस्मिन् मधुसूदन ।
प्रयाणकाले च कथं ज्ञेयोऽसि नियतात्मभिः ॥

adhiyajñaḥ kathaṁ ko 'tra
dehe 'smin madhusūdana
prayāṇakāle ca kathaṁ
jñeyo 'si niyatātmabhiḥ

2. In what manner, and what, is the Adhiyajna here in this body, O Krishna? And how at the hour of death are You to be known by those who are self-controlled?

4 O Lord, what is present in all sacrifice, and how can it be recognized in this body? It cannot be understood by logical reasoning.
5 Also, O Krishna, show me in what way a disciplined person can know You at the time of his death.
6 If a fortunate man were asleep in a house built of wish-fulfilling stones, his words would not be meaningless even if they were spoken in a dream.
7 As soon as Lord Krishna heard what Arjuna said, He replied, O Arjuna, listen while I answer your question.
8 Arjuna was like the young calf of the wishing cow, resting in a grove of trees which grant desires. It is no wonder that his longing was satisfied.
9 Even one whom Lord Krishna kills in anger attains the realization of the Eternal. Why then shouldn't one whom He teaches out of kindness attain it?
10 Because Arjuna alone had such boundless love for Him, his desires were always fulfilled.
11 Aware that Arjuna was about to ask Him a question, He prepared to serve him with the answer as if it were a dish of food.
12 A mother's love for her baby is so great that even when it has left the breast, she knows when it is hungry. She doesn't nurse the baby only when it tells her.
13 Therefore, it is not surprising that the Guru is filled with love for his disciple. Listen to what the Lord said.

श्रीभगवान् उवाच । *śrībhagavān uvāca*

अक्षरं ब्रह्म परमं स्वभावोऽध्यात्मम् उच्यते ।
भूतभावोद्भवकरो विसर्गः कर्मसंज्ञितः ॥

akṣaraṁ brahma paramaṁ
svabhāvo 'dhyātmam ucyate
bhūtabhāvodbhavakaro
visargaḥ karmasaṁjñitaḥ

The Blessed Lord spoke:
3. Brahman is the supreme imperishable; the Adhyatma is said to be the inherent

nature of the individual, which originates the being of creatures; action is known as the creative power (of the individual, which causes him to be reborn in this or that condition of being).

14 Then said the Lord of all: That which pervades this perishable body never leaves it.

15 In its subtlety it resembles the void, but not in its nature. It is as subtle as though it had been strained through a cloth of ether.

16 It is so subtle that it would pass through a bag of worldly knowledge, yet even when shaken it doesn't pass out of the body. That is the Eternal.

17 It brings forms to birth, yet it doesn't experience birth. When they pass away, it doesn't know death.

18 This is the very essence of the eternal existence of the Supreme. This is what is called *adhyatma*, O Arjuna.

19 Just as a bank of clouds of different colors suddenly appears in a clear sky, and no one knows how,

20 In the same way the various subtle elements arise in that pure and formless Eternal, appearing in the form of worlds.

21 The primal thought shoots forth from the soil of the changeless Eternal, producing all the differentiated forms of the Absolute.

22 If we examine each of these closely, we will find that they are infused with the life force of God, and countless lives appear and disappear in them.

23 The individual lives that make up the worlds give rise to countless desires, and in this way the universe expands.

24 God, the One without a second, pervades the whole and pours forth a flood of varieties.

25 It isn't possible to know how this unity and diversity arose. All movable and immovable beings come into existence for apparently no purpose, and countless species are born.

26 The number of these lives is as limitless as the leaves of a tree. When we consider how all this takes birth, we find the source is the great void of non-being.

27 In short, there is no visible creator, no origin, nor in the end is there any cause; there is only the spontaneous process of generation.

28 The process by which forms become manifest in the unmanifest, without a creator, is called activity.

अधिभूतं क्षरो भावः पुरुषश्चाधिदैवतम्।
अधियज्ञोऽहम् एवात्र देहे देहभृतां वर॥

adhibhūtaṁ kṣaro bhāvaḥ
puruṣaścādhidāivatam
adhiyajño 'ham evātra
dehe dehabhṛtāṁ vara

4. The Adhibhuta is the perishable nature of being (or the sphere of the supreme Spirit in acting on the individual, i.e. nature). The Adhidaivata is the supreme divine Agent itself (the purusha). The Adhiyajna (Lord of Sacrifice) is Myself, here in this body, O Arjuna.

29 Now I will explain briefly to you what is called *adhibhuta*. In the same way that a cloud appears and then vanishes,

30 This has no real existence in itself and will inevitably disappear—whatever derives its form from the five elements,

31 Whatever is manifested by the combination of these elements, and the names and forms which melt into nothingness when they dissolve.

32 That is *adhibhuta*. Now we must consider *adhidaiva*, who partakes of what is created by matter.

33 It is the eye of consciousness, the ruler of the senses, the tree on which the bird of desire rests at the time of death.

34 He is a reflection of the supreme Self, but is wrapped in the slumber of egoism, and is alternately pleased and displeased with the dreamlike concerns of the world.

35 He is called the individual soul and dwells in the house of the body.

36 O Arjuna, he who subdues the power of the senses while still in the body is *adhiyajna*, and I Myself am that.

37 In fact, I am both *adhidaiva* and *adhiyajna*. When gold is mixed with an alloy, doesn't it become impure gold?

38 Still, the quality of the gold itself is not spoiled, nor does it really become one with the alloy. However, as long as it is mixed, it is considered to be alloyed gold.

39 In the same way, as long as *adhibhuta* and the others are concealed by the veil of ignorance, they appear to be different.

40 When this covering is withdrawn and the boundaries of separateness are removed, can

it be said that they have become one? But were they ever two?

41 If some hairs were placed under a crystal, the stone would appear to be split into pieces.

42 When the hairs are removed, can you tell where the division was? Were the pieces cemented together? Was the split in the stone?

43 It is a whole, as it always was, but the hairs made it appear to be divided. When the hairs are removed, the stone appears as it was before.

44 Similarly, when egoism disappears, the original unity is revealed. In the same way, I am that *adhiyajna* through which this unity is always present.

45 This is the sacrifice which I meant when I said that all sacrifice is action.

46 It is the refuge of all creatures, the storehouse of disinterested happiness. O Arjuna, I am now revealing it to you.

47 First, oblations of the sense objects are offered in the blazing fire of the senses, burning with the fuel of dispassion.

48 With the *vajrasana* posture as the ground and assuming the proper *mudras*, a person should build an altar on his lap.

49 Then he should pour oblations of the senses into the cauldron of the fire of restraint, while reciting many hymns in the form of yoga.

50 The mind, the breath, and self-control—an abundant supply of offerings—feed the smokeless fire of wisdom.

51 All these are offered in the sacrifice of wisdom. Then wisdom loses itself in the object of wisdom, until the pure object of wisdom is all that remains.

52 This, O Beloved, is called *adhiyajna*. When the omniscient Krishna spoke in this way, Arjuna understood.

53 Knowing this, Krishna said, You have listened well, O Arjuna. Arjuna was very happy at Krishna's pleasure.

54 A mother can be pleased only when her child is satisfied, and a good teacher can rejoice only when his disciple attains something.

55 Krishna's heart could not contain His pure joy, but He mentally restrained it before Arjuna could be affected by it.

56 He spoke gentle and kind words, like the fragrance of ripened joy or billows of cool nectar, and said,

अन्तकाले च माम् एव स्मरन् मुक्त्वा कलेवरम् ।
यः प्रयाति स मद्भावं याति नास्त्य् अत्र संशयः ॥

antakāle ca mām eva
smaran muktvā kalevaram
yaḥ prayāti sa madbhāvaṁ
yāti nāsty atra saṁśayaḥ

5. *And at the hour of death, he who dies remembering Me, having relinquished the body, goes to My state of being. In this matter there is no doubt.*

57 Listen, O Arjuna! When illusion is burned out, then the wisdom which consumed it is burned up also.

58 *Adhiyajna*, about which I have just told you, means that those who know I am that in the beginning also know it at the time of death.

59 They regard the body as just a sack and attain the Self, their true nature. Just as the space enclosed in a house is still space,

60 They sleep in the room of determination in the home of Self-realization, and they have no memory of the external world.

61 Achieving complete union, they become Me, and the outer sheaths of the five elements fall away from them without their knowing it.

62 When a person has no awareness of the body, although it may still be alive, how can he be distressed when it falls away? Therefore, at the end of his life there can be no suffering for a Self-realized being.

63 His consciousness is molded from unity and poured into the heart of eternity. It is never corrupted, as though it had been washed in the ocean of union with the Supreme.

64 If a pot is submerged in water, there is water both inside and outside it. Then, if the pot should accidentally be broken, would the water also be broken?

65 If a serpent sheds its skin, or if a person removes his clothes because of the heat, is there any change in the limbs of his body?

66 Likewise, although this outer form perishes, the Self continues to exist without it. When the mind grasps this knowledge, how can it be disturbed?

67 Those who know Me at the hour of death give up their bodies and become one with Me.

यं यं वापि स्मरन् भावं त्यजत्य् अन्ते कलेवरम् ।
तं तं एवैति कौन्तेय सदा तद्भावभावितः ॥

yaṁ yaṁ vāpi smaran bhāvaṁ

tyajaty ante kalevaram
taṁ taṁ evāiti kāunteya
sadā tadbhāvabhāvitaḥ

6. Moreover, whatever state of being he remembers when he gives up the body at the end, he goes respectively to that state of being, Arjuna, transformed into that state of being.

68 Usually, when death strikes, a person becomes that which his heart remembers at the final moment.
69 If some unfortunate person, running at full speed, accidentally falls into a well,
70 There is no one to help him avoid it. He simply has to fall in.
71 Similarly, whatever comes before his mind at the moment of death, he cannot avoid becoming one with it.
72 In the same way, whatever desires a person has while he is awake, he sees in his dreams as soon as he closes his eyes.
73 The longings that a person has while alive, which remain fixed in his heart, come to his mind at the moment of death.

तस्मात् सर्वेषु कालेषु माम् अनुस्मर युद्य च ।
मय्य् अर्पितमनोबुद्धिर् माम् एवैष्यस्य् असंशयम् ॥
tasmāt sarveṣu kāleṣu
mām anusmara yudhya ca
mayy arpitamanobuddhir
mām evāiṣyasy asaṁśayam

7. Therefore, at all times meditate on Me, with your mind and intellect fixed on Me. In this way, you shall surely come to Me.

74 Whatever a person remembers at the time of death, he will attain that state. So remember Me at all times.
75 Whatever you see with your eyes, hear with your ears, think with your mind, or speak,
76 Both within and without, you should know that it is all Me. At all times I am present in everything.
77 O Arjuna, if this union takes place, a person doesn't die even though his body may die. How can there be any fear for you in fighting?
78 If you will completely surrender your mind and intellect to My being, then I give you My word that you will come to Me.

अभ्यासयोगयुक्तेन चेतसा नान्यगामिना ।
परमं पुरुषं दिव्यं याति पार्थानुचिन्तयन् ॥
abhyāsayogayuktena
cetasā nānyagāminā
paramaṁ puruṣaṁ divyaṁ
yāti pārthānucintayan

8. With a mind disciplined by the practice of yoga, which does not turn to anything else, to the divine supreme Spirit he goes, Arjuna, meditating on Him.

79 If any doubt arises in your mind about how this may be, just practice it. If it doesn't happen as I have told you, then you can be angry with Me.
80 O Beloved, harmonize your mind with this practice, for even a lame man can climb a mountain if he makes the effort.
81 Similarly, through practice keep the highest Being constantly before your mind. Then let the body live or die!
82 When the mind, having wandered after countless objects, finally chooses the Self, who will even remember whether the body exists or not?
83 When rivers rush to meet the sea, do they turn back to see what is happening behind them?
84 No, they remain merged in the ocean. Similarly, when the mind is united with the Self, birth and death cease. This is supreme bliss.

कविं पुराणम् अनुशासितारम्
अणोर् अणीयांसम् अनुस्मरेद् यः ।
सर्वस्य धातारम् अचिन्त्यरूपम्
आदित्यवर्णं तमसः परस्तात् ॥
kaviṁ purāṇam anuśāsitāram
aṇor aṇīyāṁsam anusmared yaḥ
sarvasya dhātāram acintyarūpam
ādityavarṇaṁ tamasaḥ parastāt

9. He who meditates on the ancient seer, the ruler, smaller than the atom, who is the supporter of all, whose form is unthinkable, and who is effulgent like the sun, beyond darkness;

85 He is older than the heavens and smaller than the smallest particle. His power activates the universe.
86 This witness is formless being, in Him there is neither birth nor death, and He sees everything there is.
87 The entire creation was born from Him, and everything lives through Him. Reason dreads Him, and He is beyond the power of imagination to conceive.

88 Look! A moth cannot consume fire, nor can darkness enter the light. Similarly, in full daylight He appears as darkness to the human eye.
89 But to the enlightened He is perpetual dawn, as brilliant as the rays of the sun which never sets.
90 If a person who knows that pure Supreme Being remembers Him with a steady mind when the hour of death has struck,

प्रयाणकाले मनसाचलेन
भक्त्या युक्तो योगबलेन चैव ।
भ्रुवोर् मध्ये प्राणम् आवेश्य सम्यक्
स तं परं पुरुषम् उपैति दिव्यम् ।।
prayāṇakāle manasācalena
bhaktyā yukto yogabalena cāiva
bhruvor madhye prāṇam āveśya samyak
sa taṁ paraṁ puruṣam upāiti divyam

10. At the hour of death, with unmoving mind, endowed with devotion and with the power of yoga, having made the vital breath enter between the two eyebrows, he reaches this divine supreme Spirit.

91 Sitting in the lotus posture, facing north and holding in his heart the joy of the yoga of action,
92 With a concentrated mind filled with love for Self-realization, and eagerly reaching out to attain it,
93 With his practice of yoga completed, his life force rises from the *muladhara chakra* at the base of the spine through the *sushumna nadi* towards the *sahasrara* at the crown of the head.
94 Though outwardly it appears that the *prana* has become one with the mind, in fact it then enters the head.
95 When it enters the space between the eyebrows it destroys both active and lifeless matter, just as the sound dies away inside a bell.
96 O Arjuna, the dying man may leave his body like a lamp that has been covered so that no one can tell when and how it was extinguished.
97 Such a man is the pure supreme Self. He is called the highest, and he reaches My eternal abode.

यद् अक्षरं वेदविदो वदन्ति
विशन्ति यद् यतयो वीतरागाः ।
यद् इच्छन्तो ब्रह्मचर्यं चरन्ति
तत् ते पदं संग्रहेण प्रवक्ष्ये ।।
yad akṣaraṁ vedavido vadanti
viśanti yad yatayo vītarāgāḥ
yad icchanto brahmacaryaṁ caranti
tat te padaṁ saṁgraheṇa pravakṣye

11. That which those who know the Vedas call the imperishable, which the ascetics, free from passion, enter, desiring which they follow a life of chastity, that path I shall explain to you briefly.

98 This is called the indestructible by those wise men who are the storehouse of that wisdom which is the aid of all knowledge.
99 Even a whirlwind could not break up the true ethereal space. How could clouds remain in existence without it?
100 Similarly, whatever knowledge can grasp is bounded by its limits. What is beyond those limits is called the indestructible.
101 Therefore, what the knowers of the Vedas describe as indestructible is higher than matter. It is the essence of the highest Spirit.
102 Overcoming the evil of sense objects, subduing their senses, and seated at the foot of the tree of the body,
103 Such dispassionate beings wait for this unceasingly. Those who are detached love it deeply.
104 Yearning for it, seekers consider the difficulties of celibacy unimportant and mercilessly restrain their senses.
105 That place which is inaccessible and unfathomable, on the edge of which even the Vedas sink exhausted,
106 Those who leave their bodies in this manner go there. Once again, I will speak to you of this state, O Arjuna.
107 Then Arjuna said, O Lord, I was about to speak to You of this very matter. But You Yourself have shown me this favor. Do tell me.
108 But I beg You to explain it simply. Lord Krishna, the light of the three worlds, replied, Don't I know you? I will be brief.

सर्वद्वाराणि संयम्य मनो हृदि निरुध्य च।
मूर्ध्न्य् आधायात्मनः प्राणम् आस्थितो योगधारणाम् ।।
sarvadvārāṇi saṁyamya
mano hṛdi nirudhya ca
mūrdhny ādhāyātmanaḥ prāṇam
āsthito yogadhāraṇām

12. Closing all the gates of the body, and confining the mind in the heart, having placed the vital breath in the head, established in yoga concentration,

109 Fix your mind in the innermost cave of your heart, and curb its tendency to run after outer objects.

110 This is possible only when the gateways of the senses are firmly closed by the doors of restraint.

111 Then the mind is easily confined and remains silent in the heart, just as a person with his arms and legs broken cannot leave his house.

112 O Arjuna, when the attention is fixed in this way, the life force should be transmuted into the sacred syllable and brought up through the *sushumna* to the space between the eyebrows.

113 As soon as it reaches this center, it should be held there with firm resolution, until the three components of the sacred syllable, merge together in the crown center.

ओम् इत्य् एकाक्षरं ब्रह्म व्याहरन् माम् अनुस्मरन् ।
यः प्रयाति त्यजन् देहं स याति परमां गतिम् ॥
om ity ekākṣaraṁ brahma
vyāharan mām anusmaran
yaḥ prayāti tyajan dehaṁ
sa yāti paramāṁ gatim

13. Uttering the single-syllable "Om"—Brahman—meditating on Me, he who goes forth, renouncing the body, goes to the supreme goal.

114 Until then the life force should be held still in the space between the eyebrows. After its union with the sacred syllable, it begins to rejoice in the half syllable at the end.

115 Then all memory ceases, and with it the life force is lost. Beyond that only the Eternal remains.

116 Therefore, he who remembers the one name, the sacred syllable of the Absolute which is My highest form,

117 And who leaves his body in this way, most certainly comes to Me. There is no higher goal than this.

अनन्यचेताः सततं यो मां स्मरति नित्यशः ।
तस्याहं सुलभः पार्थ नित्ययुक्तस्य योगिनः ॥
ananyacetāḥ satataṁ
yo māṁ smarati nityaśaḥ
tasyāhaṁ sulabhaḥ pārtha
nityayuktasya yoginaḥ

14. He who thinks of Me constantly, whose mind does not ever go elsewhere, for him, the yogin who is constantly devoted, I am easy to reach, Arjuna.

118 O Arjuna, perhaps you are still doubtful about how a person may remember Me at the moment of death.

119 At this time, when the senses have lost their power and the joys of life have departed, and when all the inner and outer signs of death are present,

120 Who is then able to sit up, restrain all activity, and in his heart remember the sacred syllable?

121 You may have such doubts in your mind. But the person who has served Me during his life, I serve at the hour of his death.

122 Those who have given up all sense objects, who have controlled their desires, and who have installed Me in their heart, enjoy eternal bliss.

123 If after having experienced Me they feel dissatisfied, and hunger and thirst don't affect them, what can their sight and other senses do?

124 Those who have experienced union with Me and who have clung to Me in their hearts, worship Me and become one with Me.

125 If it were necessary for such people to remember Me at the moment of their death and for Me to come to them, what would be the value of their devotion to Me?

126 If a poor man in his distress were to call pitifully to Me to come to his aid, wouldn't I hasten to relieve him in his difficulty?

127 If My devotees were in this same position, who would feel any longing for devotion? So you shouldn't have this doubt at all.

128 O Arjuna, I couldn't bear the thought that I should remember to go to them whenever they turn to Me.

129 Knowing My debt to them, I repay it by being the servant of My devotees at the hour of their death.

130 So that My beloved devotees won't feel that wind of the weakening of the body, I enclose them in a case of Self-realization.

131 Moreover, I cover this case with the cool shadow of remembrance of Me, and in this way I bring them steadfastness of mind.

132 Therefore, the distress of death never affects My people, and I bring them joyfully to Myself.

133 When my devotees give up their bodies and

shake off the dust of egoism, I make them one with Me by arousing in them a pure feeling for Me.

134 My devotees feel no attachment to their bodies, so when they leave them they do not experience any separation.

135 They don't expect Me to come to them at death and take them to Myself, for they have already become one with Me.

136 The bodily form exists only as a shadow reflected in water. After all, moonlight is in the moon itself.

137 For those who are always devoted to Me, I am easily attained, and they are certainly united with Me at death.

माम् उपेत्य पुनर्जन्म दुःखालयम् अशाश्वतम् ।
नाप्नुवन्ति महात्मानः संसिद्धिं परमां गताः ॥

mām upetya punarjanma
duḥkhālayam aśāśvatam
nāpnuvanti mahātmānaḥ
saṁsiddhiṁ paramāṁ gatāḥ

15. Approaching Me, those whose souls are great, who have gone to supreme perfection, do not incur rebirth, that impermanent home of misfortune.

138 A plantation of trees of distress, the hearth of the fire of calamity, an oblation to the crow of death,

139 The nourisher of poverty, which makes fear increase and is the storehouse of all the pains of life,

140 The root of evil tendencies, the fruit of evil conduct, the essence of delusion,

141 The basis of worldly existence, the garden of passions, a meal offered to all diseases,

142 The remnants of the dish of death, the body of desire, the highway of life and death,

143 A fund of deception, the outpouring of doubt, a cellar full of scorpions,

144 A den of tigers, the friend of prostitutes, the favorite device for the knowledge of sense objects,

145 The solicitude of a witch, a cool drink of poison, the trust placed in cunning thieves disguised as honest men,

146 The embrace of a leper, the softness of the serpent of death, the song of the hunter,

147 The hospitality of enemies, the respect of evil-doers, the ocean of calamity,

148 A vision seen in a dream, a forest watered by a mirage, or the sky filled with smoke—

149 Such a body is not obtained in a later birth by those who have become one with My limitless form.

आ ब्रह्मभुवनाल् लोकाः पुनरावर्तिनो ऽर्जुन ।
माम् उपेत्य तु कौन्तेय पुनर्जन्म न विद्यते ॥

ā brahmabhuvanāl lokāḥ
punarāvartino 'rjuna
mām upetya tu kāunteya
punarjanma na vidyate

16. Up to Brahma's realm of being, the worlds are subject to successive rebirths, Arjuna; but he who reaches Me is not reborn.

150 Even one who has attained the state of oneness with Brahma cannot escape from the cycle of birth and death. But just as a dead man cannot suffer from stomach pains,

151 Or just as a person on awaking is not drowned in the flood which he saw in his dream, in the same way those who have come to Me aren't even touched by worldly existence.

सहस्रयुगपर्यन्तम् अहर् यद् ब्रह्मणो विदुः ।
रात्रिं युगसहस्रान्तां ते ऽहोरात्रविदो जनाः ॥

sahasrayugaparyantam
ahar yad brahmano viduḥ
rātriṁ yugasahasrāntāṁ
te 'horātravido janāḥ

17. They who know that the day of Brahma extends as far as a thousand yugas, and that the night of Brahma ends only in a thousand yugas; they are men who know day and night.

152 Truly speaking the world of Brahma is at the head of the entire universe of form, the chief of all permanent things, the loftiest peak of the mountain of the three worlds.

153 It is that place where a portion of an hour lasts longer than the life of Indra, and where a day is longer than the lives of fourteen Indras.

154 When a cycle of the four eons passes away a thousand times, that is a day of Brahma. Similarly, when another thousand have passed, that is the night of Brahma.

155 Those fortunate beings who do not die within the duration of such a day and night are the deathless ones of heaven.

156 Compared with these, what can be said of the hosts of gods? Consider the state of the great Indra—fourteen lives of Indra in one day of Brahma!

अव्यक्ताद् व्यक्तय: सर्वा: प्रभवन्त्य् अहरागमे ।
रात्र्यागमे प्रलीयन्ते तत्रैवाव्यक्तसंज्ञके ॥

avyaktād vyaktayaḥ sarvāḥ
prabhavanty aharāgame
rātryāgame pralīyante
tatrāivāvyaktasaṁjñake

18. From the unmanifest, all manifestations come forth at the arrival of (Brahma's) day; at the arrival of (Brahma's) night, they are dissolved, at that point to be known as the unmanifest again.

157 Those who witness the passing of the eight divisions of a day and night of Brahma are called knowers of day and night.

158 When the day breaks in the world of Brahma, countless worlds come into existence out of the unmanifested.

159 At the end, the four divisions of the day of Brahma pass away, the ocean of the manifest creation dries up, and again at dawn the waters begin to rise.

भूतग्राम: स एवायं भूत्वा भूत्वा प्रलीयते ।
रात्र्यागमे ऽवश: पार्थ प्रभवत्य् अहरागमे ॥

bhūtagrāmaḥ sa evāyaṁ
bhūtvā bhūtvā pralīyate
rātryāgame 'vaśaḥ pārtha
prabhavaty aharāgame

19. This multitude of beings, having come to be again and again, is dissolved helplessly at the arrival of night, Arjuna, and it comes into existence again at the arrival of day.

160 Just as at the beginning of the *sharada* season clouds disappear from the sky, and at the end of the hot season they again gather in the sky,

161 Similarly, at the beginning of a day of Brahma, multitudes of created beings come forth until a thousand of these periods of four *yugas* have passed.

162 After that, the night begins, and the universe remains absorbed in the unmanifested for a thousand years of Brahma, of four *yugas* each. Then when the dawn breaks, the process of creation begins again.

163 Why should I say all this, that in one day and night of Brahma the universe is destroyed and recreated?

164 See what glory there is in this! He is the reservoir of the seeds of the universe, yet he is the peak of the cycle of birth and death.

165 O Arjuna, this universe is an extension of the world of Brahma, which is spread out as soon as the day dawns.

166 Then nightfall comes, when everything by its own nature returns from where it came, to a state of equilibrium.

167 Just as a tree is inherent in a seed, or just as a cloud becomes one with the sky, the state in which diversity becomes merged in unity is called equilibrium.

168 Then there is neither likeness nor unlikeness, and no trace of created beings remains, just as milk which has become curds loses its name and form.

169 As soon as the world loses its form, it loses its own nature, but the unmanifest from which it arose remains.

170 Then it is called the unmanifest. When it again takes form, it is called the manifest. These two seem to be mutually dependent, but this isn't so.

171 When a metal is melted down, it is called a bar of metal, but it loses this form when it is made into ornaments.

172 The same thing happens in the case of gold. Similarly, the concepts of the manifest and the unmanifest are both inherent in the Absolute.

173 In itself it is neither manifest nor unmanifest, neither destructible nor indestructible. It is beyond both and is eternally self-existent.

174 It is perceived in the form of the universe, but when the universe is destroyed it is not destroyed, just as one may erase writing but its meaning remains.

175 Look! Waves rise and fall, but the water in them always remains. Similarly, what is in the perishable elements is itself imperishable.

176 When ornaments are melted down, the gold is not destroyed. In the same way, the immortal exists within the mortal body.

परस् तस्मात् तु भावो ऽन्यो ऽव्यक्तो ऽव्यक्तात् सनातन: ।
य: स सर्वेषु भूतेषु नश्यत्सु न विनश्यति ॥

paras tasmāt tu bhāvo 'nyo
'vyakto 'vyaktāt sanātanaḥ
yaḥ sa sarveṣu bhūteṣu
naśyatsu na vinaśyati

20. But higher than this state of being is another unmanifest state of being higher than the primeval unmanifest, which, when all beings perish, does not perish.

अव्यक्तो ऽक्षर इत्य् उक्तस् तम् आहुः परमां गतिम् ।
यं प्राप्य न निवर्तन्ते तद् धाम परमं मम ॥

avyakto 'kṣara ity uktas
tam āhuḥ paramāṁ gatim
yaṁ prāpya na nivartante
tad dhāma paramaṁ mama

21. This unmanifest is the imperishable, thus it is said. They call it the supreme goal, attaining which, they do not return. This is My supreme dwelling place.

177 Although it may be called the unmanifest, that is not a worthy name for it because it is beyond the reach of mind or reason.

178 Although it is manifest in form it doesn't lose its formlessness, and its eternality is not affected by the loss of form.

179 Therefore, it is called the unchangeable, a concept which is more easily understood. There is nothing beyond it. It is called the final beatitude.

पुरुषः स परः पार्थ भक्त्या लभ्यस् त्व् अनन्यया ।
यस्यान्तःस्थानि भूतानि येन सर्वम् इदं ततम् ॥

puruṣaḥ sa paraḥ pārtha
bhaktyā labhyas tv ananyayā
yasyāntaḥsthāni bhūtāni
yena sarvam idaṁ tatam

22. This is the supreme Spirit, Arjuna, attainable by one-pointed devotion, within which all beings stand, and by which all this universe is pervaded.

180 Pervading this body, it is dormant for it does not work, nor does it cause anything else to work.

181 Meanwhile, O Arjuna, none of the physical functions ceases. The activities of the ten sense organs continue.

182 The market of sense objects is opened, and the mind becomes a trade center in which transactions of pleasure and pain are carried on.

183 Just as the business of a kingdom doesn't stop while the king rests peacefully, for his subjects carry it on as they please,

184 It is the same with the activity of the intellect and the mind, the functioning of the sense organs, and the movement of the vital forces.

185 All the bodily functions continue without being activated by the Self, just as men carry on their work without being impelled by the sun.

186 In the same way, O Arjuna, the Purusha is asleep in the body.

187 It may be that He is called Purusha because He is faithful to His devoted wife Prakriti.

188 Even the greatness of the Vedas cannot see His courtyard. See how He covers all space.

189 Knowing Him to be like this, the greatest yogis describe Him as the highest of the high. He enters the house of those who take refuge in no other.

190 He is the fertile soil in which ripens the devotion of those who attend to nothing else with their body, speech or mind.

191 O Arjuna, He is the refuge of those who are convinced that the whole universe is the highest Purusha.

192 He is the glory of the humble, the realization of those who are beyond all attributes, and the highest happiness of the dispassionate.

193 He resembles the most delicious food set before the contented, and the heart of a mother for those helpless beings who have no worldly longings. He is a straight road for devotion to seek His abode.

194 O Arjuna, it is unnecessary to describe this in detail. When a person reaches Him, he attains the state of oneness.

195 Just as hot water becomes cold in a cool breeze, and just as darkness becomes light when the sun rises,

196 In the same way, O Arjuna, when a person arrives at that place, even worldly existence is transformed into liberation.

197 Just as fuel thrown into fire becomes fire and can never again be distinguished as wood,

198 Just as sugar cannot be reconverted into sugarcane,

199 Just as only the philosopher's stone may change iron into gold and no other substance can turn it back into iron again,

200 And just as ghee cannot again become milk; similarly, there is no return from the state of union with the Supreme.

201 That is truly My highest abode. I have now revealed to you this hidden secret.

यत्र काले त्व् अनावृत्तिम् आवृत्तिं चैव योगिनः ।
प्रयाता यान्ति तं कालं वक्ष्यामि भरतर्षभ ॥

yatra kāle tv anāvṛttim
āvṛttiṁ cāiva yoginaḥ
prayātā yānti taṁ kālaṁ
vaksyāmi bharatarṣabha

23. But at which times the yogins return or do not return, as they depart at death, of these times I shall speak, Arjuna.

202 In another way it is easy to understand this place where yogis go when they leave their bodies.

203 If they leave their bodies at an inauspicious time, they must return again to earthly existence.

204 If they leave their bodies at an auspicious time, they immediately become one with the Absolute.

205 Therefore, union and rebirth are dependent on time. I will now describe that time to you.

अग्निर् ज्योतिर् अहः शुक्लः षण्मासा उत्तरायणम् ।
तत्र प्रयाता गच्छन्ति ब्रह्म ब्रह्मविदो जनाः ।।

agnir jyotir ahaḥ śuklaḥ
ṣaṇmāsā uttarāyaṇam
tatra prayātā gacchanti
brahma brahmavido janāḥ

24. Fire, brightness, day, the bright lunar fortnight, the six months of the northern course of the sun: departing then, the men who know Brahman go forth to Brahman.

206 O Arjuna, listen to Me. At the crisis of death, the five elements leave the body last.

207 At the moment of death, if the intellect is not overcome by confusion, if the memory does not become blind, and if the mind is not deadened,

208 Then the organs of perception retain their vigor, and the experience of union with the Eternal becomes a protective sheath.

209 In this way the senses remain conscious, and this condition lasts until death occurs. This is only possible as long as the heat of the body is maintained.

210 Look, when a lamp is extinguished by the wind or by water, is our eyesight of any use, though we still have it?

211 Similarly, at death the body becomes full of mucus because of the action of the wind, and the spark of the inner fire is put out.

212 When the vitality of life is lost, what can reason do? Consciousness cannot remain active in the body without heat.

213 O Beloved, when the fire in the body is extinguished, then the body is no longer a body, but merely a lump of damp clay; and life struggles in vain to find its end in the darkness.

214 At this time, a person should preserve all his memories of the past and, leaving the body, attain union with God.

215 The perception of consciousness is drowned in the phlegm of the body, and all awareness of past and future ceases.

216 In this way, the benefit of previous yogic practice is lost even before death occurs, as though the lamp held in person's hand were extinguished before he found what he had lost.

217 Understand that the gastric fire is the basis of consciousness. This fire is the source of all strength at the moment of death.

218 Within, there should be the light of the gastric fire. Without, the time should be during the bright half of the month, during daylight, and during one of the six months of the northern path of the sun.

219 He who leaves his body under such auspicious conditions becomes one with the Eternal, for he is a knower of the Absolute.

220 Listen, O Arjuna. These conditions are very powerful; therefore, this is the straight path by which one can reach Me.

221 The gastric fire is the first step, the light of the fire the second, the daytime the third, and the bright half of the month the fourth.

222 The requirement that it be during one of the six months of the northern path of sun is the highest step of this ascent, by which the yogi reaches perfection and union with the Absolute.

223 This is known as the best time and is called the path of light. Now listen, and I will describe to you the inauspicious time.

धूमो रात्रिस् तथा कृष्णः षण्मासा दक्षिणायनम् ।
तत् चान्द्रमस ज्योतिर् योगी प्राप्य निवर्तते ।।

dhūmo rātris tathā kṛṣṇaḥ
ṣaṇmāsā dakṣiṇāyanam
tatra cāndramasaṁ jyotir
yogī prāpya nivartate

25. Smoke, night, the dark lunar fortnight, the six months of the southern course of the sun; attaining by these the lunar light, the yogin is born again.

224 At the moment of death, the heart is compressed in darkness because of the pressure of air and phlegm.

225 The sense organs are blocked, the memory is lost in confusion, the mind is bewildered, and the life force is constricted.

226 The gastric fire is extinguished and smoke pervades everything. For this reason consciousness is confined within.

227 Just as when heavy rain clouds hide the moon, there is neither brilliance nor darkness, but only a dim light.

228 In this case the person doesn't die, nor does he remain conscious. He becomes motionless, and his earthly life awaits the moment of death.

229 When a mist has spread over the sense organs, the mind, and the intellect, all the gains of life are lost.

230 When a person loses what he has possessed, what use is there in gaining anything more? Such is a person's state at the moment of death.

231 This is the condition within the body. Outwardly, the time is night, during the dark half of the month, and during one of the six months of the southern path of the sun.

232 If all these conditions, which bring about rebirth, come together at the moment of a person's death, how can he attain union with the Absolute?

233 A yogi who dies at such a time reaches the world of the moon, and then he descends again into earthly life.

234 O Arjuna, understand that I have spoken here of the inauspicious time. This is the dark path leading to rebirth.

235 The other, known as the path of light, is the straight and easy highway leading to Self-realization.

शुक्लकृष्णे गती ह्येते जगतः शाश्वते मते
एकया यात्य् अनावृत्तिम् अन्ययावर्तते पुनः ॥

śuklakṛṣṇe gatī hyete
jagataḥ śāśvate mate
ekayā yāty anāvṛttim
anyayāvartate punaḥ

26. These are the two paths, light and dark, thought to be eternal for the universe. By one he does not return; by the other he returns again.

236 O Arjuna, these are the two eternal paths, one straight and the other crooked. I have purposely pointed them out to you,

237 So that for your welfare you can see the right path and the wrong one, recognize the true and the false, and know what is good and what is harmful.

238 Is a person apt to plunge into deep water when he sees a good boat near him? Will he take a side path when he knows the right road?

239 Will a person who can distinguish between nectar and poison be able to give up the nectar? Likewise, one who sees a straight road won't take a side path.

240 A person should discriminate clearly between good and evil, and then he will avoid an inauspicious moment.

241 However, at the time of death there is a great danger inherent in the dark path, that the practice of an entire lifetime will be in vain.

242 If a yogi misses the path of light and happens to enter the path of darkness, he will be bound to the cycle of birth and death.

243 Seeing this great danger, I have clearly explained both yogic paths to you, so you may know once and for all how to avoid this.

244 By one path the yogi reaches the Eternal; by the other he returns to the cycle of rebirths. But he will take the path which he is destined to travel at the time of death.

नैते सृती पार्थ जानन् योगी मुह्यति कश्चन ।
तस्मात् सर्वेषु कालेषु योगयुक्तो भवार्जुन ॥

nāite sṛtī pārtha jānan
yogī muhyati kaścana
tasmāt sarveṣu kāleṣu
yogayukto bhavārjuna

27. Knowing these two paths the yogin is not confused at all. Therefore, at all times, be steadfast in yoga, Arjuna.

245 At that time a person cannot know this, and it is useless to ask what will happen. At the time of death, he doesn't know by which path he may attain the Absolute.

246 Yogis know that they are truly the Eternal whether they are in the body or out of it, just as they know a rope is a rope and not a snake.

247 Does water know whether it has waves or not? The water itself remains the same at all times.

248 The water is not born of the waves, nor does it disappear when they subside. Those who become the Absolute while still in the body are like disembodied beings.

249 For them, there remains no memory at all of the body. So when do they die?

250 Why then should they seek the right path? Is there ever anything to lose once a person

has become one with time, place, and everything else?
251 When a clay pot is broken, the space within it goes on its way and merges at once in all space. Otherwise, it would get lost.
252 Consider this also: only the form is lost. The space was in space even before the form of the pot appeared.
253 In this way, yogis who have realized their oneness with God are not concerned with whether the path is right or wrong.
254 For this reason, O Arjuna, you should become absorbed in yoga so that you will have perpetual evenness of mind.
255 In that state, whether a person keeps his body or casts it off at any time or in any place, he cannot be separate from his unlimited and perpetual union with the Eternal.
256 Such a person is not born at the beginning of a great world age, nor does he die at the end of an age, neither is he deluded by the temptations of heaven or worldly life.
257 A person who has become a yogi through this teaching knows that it is right. Having weighed this experience, he reaches Self-realization.
258 O Arjuna, he has rejected as worthless even the royal glory which Indra and all the other gods praise.

वेदेषु यज्ञेषु तपःसु चैव
दानेषु यत् पुण्यफलं प्रदिष्टम् ।
अत्येति तत् सर्वम् इदं विदित्वा
योगी परं स्थानम् उपैति चाद्यम् ॥

vedeṣu yajñeṣu tapaḥsu cāiva
dāneṣu yat puṇyaphalaṁ pradiṣṭam
atyeti tat sarvam idaṁ viditvā
yogī paraṁ sthānam upāiti cādyam

28. The yogin, having known all this, goes beyond the pure fruit of action which comes from study of the Vedas, sacrifices, austerities, and gifts, and goes to the supreme primal state.

259 Even if a person has studied the Vedas, or if sacrifice has borne fruit for him, or if he has accumulated riches from austerities and charity,
260 And if the plantation of all this merit were to yield abundant fruit, it cannot be compared with the realization of the pure Absolute.
261 This would not fall short if measured against the final beatitude, which the Vedas and sacrifices are the means to attain.
262 It neither decays nor fades away, it satisfies the desire of those who experience it, and becomes like a beloved brother of eternal bliss.
263 It would delight the divine eye, it is founded on unseen merit, and it cannot be obtained even by a thousand sacrifices.
264 When yogis measure heavenly joy with the divine eye, they find it to be of very little worth.
265 O Arjuna, they use it as a stepping stone to ascend to eternal bliss.
266 He who is the glory of the entire animate and inanimate creation, who is worthy to be worshiped by Brahma and Shiva, and who is the only wealth enjoyed by yogis,
267 Who is the art of all arts and the image of the highest bliss, the life and soul of the whole universe,
268 Who is the essence of omniscience, and the shining light of the Yadavas—that is, Krishna—spoke in this way to Arjuna.
269 Sanjaya related to the king this story of what happened on the field of Kurukshetra. Jnanadeva says, listen further to this story.

9

THE YOGA OF SOVEREIGN KNOWLEDGE

I PROMISE you that if you give me your attention, you will be worthy of enjoying all happiness.

2 In an assembly of wise people like you, I don't speak with arrogance. My loving request is that you pay attention to what I say.

3 For if I have such wealthy ones as you as my home, all my desires are satisfied and all my wishes fulfilled.

4 Seeing the cool shade of the garden of your favor, enriched by graciousness, I rest in it for I am weary.

5 All of you are the deep waters of the nectar of happiness, whose coolness we long for. If I am afraid to approach you here as a friend, where can I refresh myself?

6 Just as a child uses its own childish words and its steps are stumbling and unsure, still its mother looks on in wonder and delight,

7 Similarly, may you saintly people give me your love in some way. This is my great desire as I lovingly approach you.

8 Besides, am I worthy to speak before such wise listeners as you are? Does a son of the goddess of learning have to be taught how to study?

9 Listen! However large a firefly may be, could it ever equal the sun in brightness? How could this be? Who can prepare food worthy of being served in a dish of nectar?

10 Is there any need to fan the moon with its cool rays? Who would sing before the mystic sound? Can ornaments be further decorated? How could this be done?

11 Is there anything that perfume can smell? Where could the ocean go to bathe? What space could contain the whole firmament?

12 What person possesses the power of oratory which could satisfy your interest and entertain you well enough to make you applaud?

13 But is it wrong to worship the sun which illumines the world with a simple oil lamp? Shouldn't we pay respect to the ocean by offering a handful of water?

14 You are all the incarnations of the great Shiva, while I am a simple man serving you with devotion. So even though I offer only the leaves of the thorny *nirguda* bush, please accept them as if they were those of the sacred bela tree.

15 If a child approaches his father and offers him food from his plate, the father delightedly opens his mouth to eat it.

16 Similarly, although I, like a child, am boring you with my talk, because of your affection I feel sure you will be pleased.

17 You saintly people are moved by the power of your love for me, so you shouldn't be offended by my familiarity in speaking to you like this.

18 Notice how a cow's milk flows more freely when her calf strikes her. Similarly, anger against a loved one increases love for him.

19 I have spoken to you like this, believing that my childlike words have aroused your hidden compassion.

20 Can the moon be ripened like mangoes? Can anyone give motion to the wind? Can the heavens be bound by a cage?

21 One doesn't have to make water liquid, nor to churn butter with a churning staff, so my shyness prevents me from speaking before you.

22 Am I worthy to explain in Marathi the *Gita*, which is the bed upon which the words of the Vedas lie resting, wearied by their attempt to describe the eternal Truth?

23 Nevertheless, I am eager to do this. Besides,

I have the hope that through my boldness I may win your love.

24 I pray that you will satisfy my desire by giving me your attention, which is more cooling than the moon and more life-giving than nectar.

25 If you shower your kindly looks upon me, the seeds of explanation will germinate in my mind. Otherwise, if you remain indifferent, the tender shoots of knowledge will wither.

26 So listen to me, for when my power of speech is fed by attention, a wealth of exposition will come forth in my words.

27 The meaning waits on the words, meaning calls forth further meaning, and there is a full blossoming of feeling in the mind.

28 Therefore, when the favorable wind of dialogue begins to blow, clouds of learning gather in the sky of the heart. But if the listeners are inattentive, the essence of the explanation will melt away.

29 The moonstone melts, but it is due to the action of the moon. In the same way, a speaker cannot be a speaker without listeners.

30 Do grains of rice have to ask the eaters to sweeten them? Do puppets have to ask the puppeteer to make them move?

31 Does he make them dance for their own sake? Isn't it to display his own skill? So why should I behave in a similar way?

32 The Guru exclaimed, What is this all about? We have understood your request. Now tell us what Lord Krishna taught Arjuna.

श्रीभगवान् उवाच। *śrībhagavān uvāca*

इदं तु ते गुह्यतमं प्रवक्ष्याम्य् अनसूयवे।
ज्ञानं विज्ञानसहितं यज् ज्ञात्वा मोक्ष्यसे ऽशुभात्॥
idaṁ tu te guhyatamaṁ
pravakṣyāmy anasūyave
jñānaṁ vijñānasahitaṁ
yaj jñātvā mokṣyase 'śubhāt

The Blessed Lord spoke:

1. But this most secret thing I shall declare to you, who do not disbelieve: knowledge and realization combined, having learned which you shall be released from evil.

33 Now Arjuna, I will tell you the inner meaning of the cherished secret of My heart.

34 Jnaneshwar, the disciple of Nivritti, was delighted, and joyfully agreed saying, Listen to the words of the Lord!

35 If you wonder why I should reveal to you My innermost secret like this,

36 Then listen, O wise one: you are the very symbol of earnestness, and you never disregard what I teach you.

37 If the secrecy is to be broken, so be it. Let that be spoken which should be spoken; allow this secret of My heart to enter yours.

38 Although there is milk concealed in the udders, they don't know of its sweetness. The cow lets it be drawn, provided that it satisfies the one who wants it and who can get it from no other source.

39 If seed is taken from a jar and sown in tilled soil, is the seed wasted by being scattered about?

40 Therefore, I will gladly impart My most secret wisdom to those who are of good will, who have a pure mind, who are respectful, and who take refuge only in Me.

41 Because there is no one else like you endowed with these virtues, it isn't right for Me to keep this wisdom hidden from you, although it is secret.

42 If I keep on repeating, "This is secret," you will think it is strange; so I will explain to you wisdom combined with worldly knowledge,

43 To allow you to discriminate between true and false knowledge, which seem to be intermingled.

44 Just as a royal swan can separate milk from water with its beak, I will explain to you wisdom and knowledge separately.

45 Just as a gust of wind blows away the sifted chaff while the grains of corn fall together in a heap,

46 Similarly, knowing this wisdom, the knower is placed on the throne of liberation, and the things of this world are joined with worldly life.

47 Among all the branches of knowledge, this is worthy of the highest position. It is the foremost of all secrets, the sovereign of all pure things,

48 The abode of righteousness, and the best of the best. Once a person attains it, there is no question of any rebirth for him.

49 However small a part of it the Guru may reveal, the disciple spontaneously experiences that self-existent Being residing in the heart.

50 Moreover, a person may reach it by easy steps, and once he has attained it, all other experience falls away.

51 Besides, the mind rejoices in that wisdom even while standing on the border of enjoying it. It is so easily attained, yet it is also the highest Absolute.

राजविद्या राजगुह्यं पवित्रम् इदम् उत्तमम् ।
प्रत्यक्षावगमं धर्म्यं सुसुखं कर्तुम् अव्ययम् ॥

rājavidyā rājaguhyaṁ
pavitram idam uttamam
pratyakṣāvagamaṁ dharmyaṁ
susukhaṁ kartum avyayam

2. This is royal knowledge, a royal secret, a supreme purifier, plainly intelligible, righteous, easy to practice, imperishable.

52 It has still another characteristic: once it has been attained it doesn't perish. When a person experiences it, he never loses it, nor does he tire of it.

53 At this point you may wonder how such a treasure has escaped the hands of men.

54 It is holy and delightful, simple to attain, a natural joy, yet righteous. It is experienced within oneself.

55 Therefore, when it is desirable in every way, how have people let it escape them? Although such a doubt is reasonable, you shouldn't entertain it.

अश्रद्दधानाः पुरुषा धर्मस्यास्य परंतप ।
अप्राप्य मां निवर्तन्ते मृत्युसंसारवर्त्मनि ॥

aśraddadhānāḥ puruṣā
dharmasyāsya paraṁtapa
aprāpya māṁ nivartante
mṛtyusaṁsāravartmani

3. Men who have no faith in this knowledge, Arjuna, not attaining to Me, are born again in the path of death and transmigration.

56 The milk of the cow is sweet and pure and lies just beneath the skin. But doesn't a leech leave the milk and suck the impure blood?

57 Lotus roots and frogs live together in the same pond. Bees feed on the pollen of the lotus and leave the mud for the frogs.

58 Again, there may be thousands of gold coins buried under the house of an unfortunate person, yet he will starve and live in poverty.

59 In the same way, although I may be the garden of all joys, still a deluded person will look for sense pleasures.

60 Seeing a mirage, a person might spit out a mouthful of nectar just as he was about to swallow it, while another might cut off the philosopher's stone hanging around his neck for the sake of an oyster shell.

61 These wretched people are so preoccupied with their lower self that they fail to reach Me, and they are tossed back and forth between the banks of life and death.

62 What am I really like? I am not like the sun which at times is visible and at other times is hidden from sight. I don't fail like this.

मया ततम् इदं सर्वं जगद् अव्यक्तमूर्तिना ।
मत्स्थानि सर्वभूतानि न चाहं तेष्व् अवस्थितः ॥

mayā tatam idaṁ sarvaṁ
jagad avyaktamūrtinā
matsthāni sarvabhūtāni
na cāhaṁ tesv avasthitaḥ

4. This whole universe is pervaded by Me in My unmanifest aspect. All beings abide in Me; I do not abide in them.

63 Isn't this entire universe just the manifestation of My own Self? Just as curdled milk is naturally called curds,

64 Just as a tree grows from a seed, and just as gold is made into ornaments, in the same way, this universe is nothing but a manifestation of Me.

65 My nature is confined when it is unmanifest. It becomes diffused when it manifests in the form of the universe. Know that I, the form of the formless, am manifest in the three worlds.

66 All forms, from the subtlest elements to physical matter, are reflected in Me like foam on water.

67 But, O Arjuna, just as when a person looks inside foam he finds no water, or when he wakes up what he saw in a dream no longer exists,

68 In the same way, all these beings are reflected in Me, but I am not in them. I have already taught you all this,

69 So there is no need to go into anymore detail. Let your mind's eye remain fixed on My inner nature.

न च मत्स्थानि भूतानि पश्य मे योगम् ऐश्वरम् ।
भूतभृन् न च भूतस्थो ममात्मा भूतभावनः ॥

na ca matsthāni bhūtāni
paśya me yogam āiśvaram

bhūtabhṛn na ca bhūtastho
mamātmā bhūtabhāvanaḥ

5. And yet beings do not abide in Me. Behold my divine yoga! Sustaining beings and not dwelling in beings is my Self, causing beings to be.

70 If you will try to see, without misunderstanding, My real nature underlying all matter, you will then understand that it is wrong to say that beings are in Me, for I am everything.

71 But in the twilight of mental bewilderment, the eyes of intelligence are darkened for a time. My eternal form is dimly perceived, and beings appear to be different from one another.

72 Again, when this bewilderment passes and as soon as doubt is destroyed, My indivisible form can be seen. Similarly, the error of mistaking a rope for a snake is removed by clearer vision.

73 Do pitchers and jars spring up spontaneously like shoots from the earth? No, they are the offspring of the potter's mind.

74 Are waves stored up in the water of the ocean? Isn't this change in the water brought about by the wind?

75 Are there bundles of cotton within the cotton plant? In the weaver's eye, it has already been made into cloth.

76 When gold is fashioned into ornaments, it doesn't lose its nature as gold; but when it is seen by the person who wears it, it appears superficially to be an ornament.

77 Tell me, aren't an echo and the forms we see in a mirror really our own creations, or do they appear from somewhere else?

78 Whoever attributes the existence of beings to My nature, sees only their appearance in the world.

79 When matter, which produces these appearances, passes away, the illusion of created beings disappears. Only My pure and unchanging nature remains.

80 When a person spins around, everything appears to be revolving around him. Similarly, separate beings appear to exist in My indivisible form.

81 Get rid of these ideas. There is no basis for thinking that beings are in Me and I am in them, even in a dream.

82 Such statements as, "I alone am the supporter of all beings," and "I am in them," are simply delirious ravings of the imagination.

83 Listen, O Beloved! I am the Self which pervades the universe and also the refuge of all creatures of the illusory world of nature.

84 A mirage seems to exist because of the rays of the sun. Similarly, the concept that all beings are in Me is false. This is an illusion superimposed on Me.

85 I am the basis of this illusion of the existence of the world; yet I am in no way different from it, just as the sun and its radiance are one.

86 Now you have seen My supreme nature. Tell Me, what is the difference between Me and these beings?

87 It is clear, therefore, that beings are not different from Me, and don't think that I am different from them.

यथाकाशस्थितो नित्यं वायु: सर्वत्रगो महान् ।
तथा सर्वाणि भूतानि मत्स्थानीत्य् उपधारय ।।

yathākāśasthito nityaṁ
vāyuḥ sarvatrago mahān
tathā sarvāṇi bhūtāni
matsthānīty upadhāraya

6. As the mighty wind, going everywhere, dwells eternally in space, so all beings dwell in Me. Consider this!

88 The extent of the sky is the same as the extent of the wind within it. When the wind moves, it appears to be different from the sky; yet in reality they are the same.

89 Similarly, when a person thinks that all beings are in Me, something seems to exist. But in the absence of thought, nothing remains except Me, and I am everything.

90 Their existence and non-existence depend on thought. With its disappearance they vanish, and with it they again appear.

91 When that original thought is destroyed, where can existence or non-existence be found? Therefore, consider again My supreme nature.

92 Become like a wave in the ocean of the realization of this wisdom. Then, seeing all this animate and inanimate creation, you will see your own Self.

93 Then the Lord asked, Has this wisdom now been awakened in you? Haven't you realized that duality is a delusion?

94 If your understanding were overcome by the

slumber of such thoughts, your realization of unity would vanish, and you would fall into the dream of separateness.

95 I am now about to reveal a secret to you. When you know it, this sleep will never occur; and through the awakening of pure wisdom you will realize that you are one with all.

96 Therefore, O Arjuna, listen attentively to My words. It is illusion which creates all beings and again destroys them.

सर्वभूतानि कौन्तेय प्रकृतिं यान्ति मामिकाम् ।
कल्पक्षये पुनस् तानि कल्पादौ विसृजाम्य् अहम् ॥
sarvabhūtāni kāunteya
prakṛtiṁ yānti māmikām
kalpakṣaye punas tāni
kalpādāu visṛjāmy aham

7. All beings, Arjuna, go to My own material nature at the end of a kalpa; at the beginning of a kalpa, I send them forth.

97 It is called primordial matter and it is of two kinds, as I have told you; one is eightfold in form; the other is the life-element.

98 You have already heard all about this matter, O Son of Pandu, so there is no need to repeat it; this is primordial matter.

99 Now, at the end of a great world-age, all beings are reabsorbed into My unmanifest nature.

100 As owing to the extreme heat of summer all grass is reabsorbed into the earth,

101 Or as when the vehemence of the rainy season is over, the *Sharada* season sets in, and masses of clouds then disappear from the sky,

102 The wind calms down and vanishes from the dome of the sky, and the restlessness of waves subsides in the water.

103 When a person wakes up, his dream sinks back into his mind. In the same way, at the end of a world age everything formed of matter is reabsorbed into the primal matter.

104 Then, at the beginning of another world age, I again create everything. Listen while I explain this to you clearly.

प्रकृतिं स्वाम् अवष्टभ्य विसृजामि पुनः पुनः ।
भूतग्रामम् इमं कृत्स्नम् अवशं प्रकृतेर् वशात् ॥
prakṛtiṁ svām avaṣṭabhya
visṛjāmi punaḥ punaḥ
bhūtagrāmam imam kṛtsnam
avaśaṁ prakrteṛ vaśāt

8. Resting on My own material nature, I send forth again and again this entire multitude of beings, which is powerless, by the power of My material nature.

105 O Arjuna, I pervade all matter. It is My own, just as the texture of warp and woof can be seen in a piece of cloth.

106 During the process of weaving, small squares of crossing threads take the form of cloth. Similarly, matter appears in forms consisting of the five elements.

107 Because of the presence of a thickening agent, milk is transformed into curds. Nature is formed out of matter in the same way.

108 When a seed comes in contact with water, it germinates and branches, both large and small, grow from it. Similarly, all beings are created because of Me.

109 If you say that a town was built by a certain king, it's true. But did the king's hands really take part in its construction?

110 If you ask Me how I pervade matter, it's like a person waking from sleep.

111 O Arjuna, when a person wakes from sleep, do his legs feel pain? Do they actually travel in a dream?

112 You may ask what all this means. It is this: in the evolution of this created world, I don't have to do anything at all.

113 Just as the subjects of a king perform their individual jobs, I am related to matter in the same way. It performs all the actual work.

114 Look, at the sight of the full moon, the ocean rises to high tide. But, O Arjuna, does this involve any effort on the part of the moon?

115 Doesn't lifeless iron move when placed near a magnet? But is the magnet disturbed by the proximity of the iron?

116 Similarly, when I assume My natural form, the creation of beings then begins of its own accord.

117 O Arjuna, all these innumerable creatures are dependent on matter. Just as the earth is capable of producing plants and leaves from seeds,

118 Just as childhood and the other ages of man evolve under the direction of the body, just as the rainy season causes clouds to form in the sky,

119 Or just as sleep causes dreams, similarly, O Arjuna, matter directs the creation of all things.

120 Matter is the root of the whole creation,

animate and inanimate, gross and subtle.

121 Therefore, this whole process of the creation and maintenance of beings has no relation to Me.

122 Moonlight spreads over the water like a vine, but it doesn't cause the moon to grow larger. Similarly, though all actions rest in Me, they are apart from Me.

न च मां तानि कर्माणि निबध्नन्ति धनंजय ।
उदासीनवद् आसीनम् असक्तं तेषु कर्मसु ।।

na ca māṁ tāni karmāṇi
nibadhnanti dhanaṁjaya
udāsīnavad āsīnam
asaktaṁ teṣu karmasu

9. And these actions do not bind Me, Arjuna; I sit indifferently, unattached to these actions.

123 It would be impossible for a handful of salt to stem the onward rush of the ocean. Similarly, can actions which end in Me bind Me?

124 Can a cage made of smoke restrain the force of the wind? Can darkness enter the sun?

125 Are minerals in the heart of a mountain damaged by showers of rain? Similarly, actions performed by matter don't affect Me.

126 Understand that I am the sole cause underlying all the effects of matter. However, like a dejected person, I don't do anything, nor do I cause anything to be done.

127 A lamp in a house neither directs nor restrains anyone, nor does it know who is engaged in what work.

128 It is a disinterested witness of the household activities. In the same way, although I am unattached to all works that creatures do, I am nevertheless in those creatures.

129 What need is there to repeat this argument in different ways? You should always remember it, O Arjuna.

मयाध्यक्षेण प्रकृतिः सूयते सचराचरम् ।
हेतुनानेन कौन्तेय जगद् विपरिवर्तते ।।

mayādhyakṣeṇa prakṛtiḥ
sūyate sacarācaram
hetunānena kāunteya
jagad viparivartate

10. With Me as overseer, material nature produces all things animate and inanimate. From this cause, Arjuna, the universe revolves.

130 O Arjuna, just as the sun is merely the instrument of the activities of all beings, similarly, I am the cause which produces this universe.

131 Since matter, which I established, produces all moving and unmoving things, it follows that I am the cause of all this.

132 In the light of this, you may clearly understand this principle: all beings are in Me, but I am not in them.

133 And don't ever forget this: beings are not actually in Me, nor am I in them.

134 This is My deep secret, which I have revealed to you alone. Closing fast the doors of the senses, experience it in your heart.

135 O Arjuna, as long as a person hasn't fully grasped this secret, he won't understand My real nature, just as he can't find grains in husks.

136 He may think that he can learn it from inference, but does the earth become damp from a mirage?

137 When a net is thrown into the water, the reflection of the moon appears to be caught in it; but when the net is pulled to shore and is shaken, where is the moon?

138 Likewise, people uselessly envy the discussion of this experience, but when it is a question of direct experience, there is nothing.

अवजानन्ति मां मूढा मानुषीं तनुम् आश्रितम् ।
परं भावम् अजानन्तो मम भूतमहेश्वरम् ।।

avajānanti māṁ mūḍhā
mānuṣīṁ tanum āśritam
paraṁ bhāvam ajānanto
mama bhūtamaheśvaram

11. The deluded despise Me, clad in human form, not knowing My higher being as the great Lord of beings.

139 What more can I say? If you fear this earthly life and have a true longing for Me, remember carefully this secret.

140 A person suffering from jaundice will say that the moonlight is yellow. In the same way, there are some who see impurities in My pure form.

141 A person loses his sense of taste when he has a fever and finds milk like poison. Similarly, there are those who regard Me as human, when I have no human form.

142 So I say again, O Arjuna, be careful that you don't forget this truth. If you regard it with your grosser understanding, it is worthless.

143 Some see Me with their grosser vision, but

you must understand that their vision is like blindness, just as nectar found in a dream has no power to make a person immortal.

144 The foolish think that they knew Me completely by means of their earthly vision, but such knowledge actually becomes an obstacle to the attainment of true knowledge,

145 Just as a swan would perish, seeing the reflections of stars and entering the water in the hope of finding jewels.

146 Does a person lose anything by passing by a mirage, which can give no water? Can his wish be fulfilled if he resorts to the thorny babul tree, thinking it is the wish-fulfilling tree of the gods?

147 He might put out his hand to grasp a poisonous snake, imagining it to be a double-stranded necklace of sapphires. He might gather pebbles, thinking they are jewels.

148 He might pick up a live ember in his garment, thinking he has found a treasure. Or a lion might leap into a well, not realizing that what he sees in it is his own reflection.

149 Similarly, those who have jumped to the conclusion that I dwell here in earthly existence are like those who think the moonlight on water is the moon itself.

150 Their belief is as useless as that of a person who drinks broth, expecting it to have the effect of nectar.

151 How can I manifest Myself to those who believe that they see Me, the imperishable, in a destructible material form?

152 O Beloved, can a person reach the western shore of the ocean by setting out toward the east? O Arjuna, can he obtain grains of rice by threshing the husks?

153 Similarly, can he know My true nature by knowing this gross bodily form? If he takes foam in his mouth, has he drunk water?

154 Thus, people with deluded minds erroneously identify Me with this body and attribute birth and action to Me.

155 As a result, they attribute names to Me, the nameless; action to Me, the actionless; and a bodily form to Me, the bodiless.

156 They think that I, the formless, have form; they worship Me, the attributeless; and they believe that I perform rituals and duties though I am beyond scriptural injunctions.

157 They attribute caste to Me when I am without caste, they assign attributes to Me when I am beyond these, and feet and hands when I have none.

158 They measure Me, the infinite, and restrict Me, the all-pervasive, within the limits of place. Just as a person may see a forest even though he lies asleep in his bed,

159 In the same way they imagine Me to have eyes and ears when I have none; they think I have family descent when I am without it; and they assume that I, the formless, have form.

160 They suppose that I, the unmanifest, am manifest; they attribute desire to Me, the passionless; and they believe that I experience satisfaction though I am self-sufficient.

161 They give clothing to Me though I cannot be clothed, they give ornaments to Me though I cannot be adorned, and they imagine that I am the result of some cause though I am the cause of all.

162 Though I am uncreated, they think they create Me; though I am self-existent, they set up images of Me; and though I am timeless, they call Me into existence and then dismiss Me.

163 Though I am always complete within Myself and unvarying in form, they attribute to Me childhood, youth, and old age.

164 They infer that I, the One, am dual; that I, the actionless, perform actions; and state that I experience enjoyment, when I am indifferent to it.

165 They describe My ancestry when I have none, they grieve at My death though I am eternal, and they assume that I have friends and enemies though I am within all.

166 Though I am absorbed in the bliss of My own nature, they still think that I desire pleasure; and though I am all-pervasive, they believe that I belong to one place.

167 Though I am the one Self in all creatures, immanent in all, they say that I favor one person and kill another out of anger.

168 In short, their knowledge is so perverted that they attribute to Me all kinds of human qualities.

169 When they see an image, they worship it as a god. When it is broken, they throw it away, believing that it is not.

170 They regard Me as human in all these various ways, and thus their beliefs cloud their understanding.

मोघाशा मोघकर्माणो मोघज्ञाना विचेतसः।
राक्षसीम् आसुरीं चैव प्रकृतिं मोहिनीं श्रिताः॥
moghāśā moghakarmāṇo

moghajñānā vicetasaḥ
rākṣasīm āsurīṁ cāiva
prakṛtiṁ mohinīṁ śritāḥ

12. Those of vain hopes, vain actions, vain knowledge, devoid of discrimination, abide in a fiendish and demoniacal nature, which is deluding.

171 Therefore, they are born in vain, like the clouds which form outside the rainy season, or like the waves of a mirage seen from a distance.

172 They are no better than riders made of clay, ornaments produced by a magic trick, or walls of a celestial city seen in the clouds. All these are nothing but appearances.

173 They are like a silk-cotton tree which has grown very high, but is hollow inside and bears no fruit, or like the false teat on the neck of a female goat.

174 The life of such fools is like the fruit of a silk-cotton tree that can neither be given nor taken. For shame!

175 Whatever they have learned is like a coconut picked by a monkey, or a pearl which has fallen into the hands of a blind man.

176 Their scriptural knowledge is of as little use as a weapon in the hands of a girl, or as secret mantras taught to the unclean.

177 O Arjuna, the knowledge and actions of such people are useless, for they are stupid.

178 The demoness of the quality of darkness consumes their clear intellect and destroys their mind.

179 Overcome by this demoness, they are constantly troubled by anxiety and fall into the jaws of the quality of darkness.

180 In her mouth the saliva of hope flows, the tongue of slaughter rolls, and she endlessly chews morsels of the meat of contentment.

181 She licks her lips, thrusting out her tongue to reach her victims' ears, and filling the valley of the mountain of error with her intoxication.

182 Her jaws of hatred grind down wisdom, and to foolish people with a dull intellect, it is like being within the pitcher of Agastya.

183 All those who fall into the jaws of this fiend of darkness become immersed in the pitcher of confusion.

184 The hand of discrimination cannot reach those who fall in this way into the pit of ignorance. Moreover, they have left no trace to indicate where they have gone.

185 Enough of these unnecessary words. What use is there in describing a fool? To continue with their story can only tire the voice.

186 When Lord Krishna said these things, Arjuna replied, Yes, O Lord. Then Lord Krishna continued, Listen to the description of the good, which will rest the voice.

महात्मानस् तु मां पार्थ दैवीं प्रकृतिम् आश्रिताः।
भजन्त्य् अनन्यमनसो ज्ञात्वा भूतादिम् अव्ययम्॥

mahātmānas tu māṁ pārtha
dāivīṁ prakṛtim āśritāḥ
bhajanty ananyamanaso
jñātvā bhūtādim avyayam

13. But those whose souls are great, Arjuna, partaking of a celestial nature, worship Me single-mindedly, knowing Me as the origin of beings and as the imperishable.

187 These are the ones in whose pure hearts I permanently dwell, as in a sacred place. Nonattachment attends them even during sleep.

188 Religious duty reigns supreme over their ardent desire and good faith, and their minds are the essence of wisdom.

189 They have bathed in the river of wisdom and are satisfied with the food of perfection. Within them, new foliage sprouts on the tree of peace.

190 They are the tendrils of Self-realization, the pillars of the hall of fortitude, and pitchers filled to the brim with the ocean of joy.

191 Their devotion is so fervent that they even dismiss liberation as worthless, and their morality can be seen in all their activities.

192 Their senses are adorned with the ornaments of restraint, and their minds are a shelter for Me, the all-pervading.

193 These men of deep experience, the glory of the God-like nature, know that everything is a manifestation of Me.

194 These great-souled ones worship Me with ever-increasing love. Their attitude is such that they never even touch the sense of separation.

195 Becoming one with Me, O Arjuna, they serve Me alone. The wonder of this must be told, so listen!

सततं कीर्तयन्तो मां यतन्तश्च दृढव्रताः।
नमस्यन्तश्च मां भक्त्या नित्ययुक्ता उपासते॥

satataṁ kīrtayanto māṁ
yatantaśca dṛḍhavratāḥ
namasyantaśca māṁ bhaktyā

nityayuktā upāsate

14. Perpetually glorifying Me and striving with firm vows, and honoring Me with devotion, ever steadfast, they worship Me.

196 With sacred stories, drama, and dance, they have destroyed the necessity of all acts of repentance, and not even the name of sin exists any longer.
197 They have made restraint of the senses and control of the mind unimportant, they have removed places of pilgrimage from their high rank, and have put an end to condemning sinners to hell.
198 Restraint asks, "What is there for me to curb?" Control asks, "What is there for me to subdue?" Pilgrimages to holy places ask, "What is there for us to consume? There are no sins which our purity must wash away."
199 By praising My name, they remove all the pains of the world and fill the whole universe with the highest bliss.
200 They enable others to see even without the dawn, they give creatures life without nectar, and they enable them to see liberation with their own eyes without the practice of yoga.
201 They honor equally both king and peasant, they make no distinction between high and low, so they are always a source of bliss to the whole world.
202 Rarely does anyone reach heaven, but these saints have turned the whole earth into heaven. They have purified everything with the power of their chanting My name.
203 They are as radiant as the light of the sun, but the sun has the defect of setting. The moon also is only full at times, but these beings are eternally perfect.
204 Clouds give generously but they disappear, so such a comparison is inadequate. These devotees are true lions of compassion.
205 In order to utter My name only once, a person must live through a thousand births. My name dances with delight in their speech.
206 I do not dwell in heaven, nor am I seen in the orb of the sun. More than that, I transcend even the minds of yogis.
207 Yet, O Arjuna, though I am lost to others, I must be sought in those who unceasingly chant My name.
208 How content they are, singing of My qualities! They forget even time and place, and in the joy of their song they experience inner bliss.
209 They joyfully recite My names—Krishna, Vishnu, Hari, Govinda—and engage in many enlightened discussions on the Self.
210 I have said enough. O Arjuna, chanting My names in this way, they move about among all creatures.
211 O Arjuna, there are others who restrain their *prana* with great effort. Taking the mind as a guide,
212 And setting up a boundary of control and restraint, they build within it a wall of the *vajra* posture, on which they mount the cannons of breath control.
213 With the light of Kundalini and the aid of the mind and the *prana*, they capture the state of the realization of the ultimate Reality.
214 Self-control performs mighty deeds which silence passion, and the sense organs are bound and imprisoned within the heart.
215 The horses of self-control are massed together, all the elements are united, and the army of thoughts is destroyed.
216 Then, with victorious battle cries the drums of contemplation resound, and absorption in the Absolute reigns supreme.
217 Finally, in the joy of the kingdom of Self-realization, the glory of perfect union is enthroned and anointed with the experience of oneness with the Supreme.
218 O Arjuna, devotion to Me is so mysterious that I will now describe some other ways in which it is practiced.
219 Just as there is only one thread running through a piece of cloth from one end to the other, similarly, they recognize no one but Me in the whole universe.
220 From Brahma at the beginning to an insect at the end, they regard everything in the universe as a manifestation of Me.
221 They see no difference between great and small, animate and inanimate. Taking everything together, they know it is Me.
222 Unaware of their own greatness, they don't distinguish between the worthy and the unworthy. Putting all together in the same class, they like to bow down before everyone.
223 Just as water pouring from a height flows downward without effort, in the same way, it is their nature to pay respect to every

creature that they see.

224 Just as the branches of trees laden with fruit bend towards the earth, similarly, they humble themselves before all creatures.

225 They are always free from conceit. Humility is their wealth which they offer to Me with words of reverence.

226 Since they are always humble, honor and dishonor do not exist for them, and they easily become united with Me. Always absorbed in Me, they worship Me.

227 O Arjuna, I have described to you the highest form of devotion. Now listen while I tell you of those devotees who worship Me with the wisdom sacrifice.

228 O Arjuna, you already know the method of their worship, for I have described it earlier.

229 Arjuna replied, This is true, O Lord. It was an act of Your grace. However, can anyone become satiated when drinking nectar?

230 Hearing this, Lord Krishna knew that Arjuna was eager to listen to Him. So He swayed joyfully and said,

231 That is good, O Arjuna. Although this is not the time to repeat it, your eagerness makes Me speak.

232 Then Arjuna said, Why is this? Does the moon shine only for the chakora bird? Isn't it the nature of the moon to cool the whole world?

233 The chakora bird raises its beak towards the moon for its own satisfaction. Similarly, we are making only a small request, O Lord.

234 The clouds, out of their generosity, relieve the thirst of the earth. But how small is the thirst of the chataka bird, compared with the showers of rain that fall?

235 To obtain even a mouthful of water, a person must go to a river. So whether our desire is small or great, we must express it, O Lord.

236 The Lord replied, Say no more. After the pleasure that I have experienced, it would be impossible to bear any more praise.

237 You listen so attentively that you encourage My eloquence. In this way, the Lord spoke appreciatively of what Arjuna had said.

ज्ञानयज्ञेन चाप्य् अन्ये यजन्तो माम् उपासते ।
एकत्वेन पृथक्त्वेन बहुधा विश्वतोमुखम् ॥
jñānayajñena cāpy anye
yajanto mām upāsate
ekatvena pṛthaktvena
bahudhā viśvatomukham

15. And by the wisdom sacrifice, others, sacrificing, worship Me as the one and as the manifold, variously manifested, facing in all directions (i.e. omniscient).

238 This is the nature of the wisdom sacrifice. The primal thought is the sacrificial post, the five elements are the canopy, and the sense of separateness is the sacrificial beast.

239 The qualities of the five elements, the senses, and the vital force are the materials used in the sacrifice, and ignorance is the ghee poured over them.

240 The mind and the intellect are the vessel in which the fire of wisdom burns, and the evenly balanced mind is the sacrificial altar, O My friend.

241 Sharpness of intellect combined with discrimination are the proper mantras, restraint is the ladle, and the individual soul is the sacrificer.

242 That sacrificer, with the vessel of Self-realization, destroys the sense of separateness by means of the powerful mantra of discrimination, and with wisdom as the guardian of the fire.

243 At that moment, ignorance is removed. When the sacrificer has performed the purifying ablutions with the water of union with the Self, both the sacrificer and the sacrifice cease to exist.

244 No longer does he think of the five elements, the senses, or the sense objects as separate. Through Self-realization, he knows that all are one.

245 O Arjuna, just as a person who suddenly wakes up might exclaim, "While I was asleep, wasn't I that army that I saw in my dream?

246 Now there is no army and I alone am everything!" In this way he realizes his unity with the universe.

247 Then he loses the concept of the individual soul, and he is filled with the realization of the unity of all created things, beginning with Brahma himself. Realizing unity, he worships Me with the wisdom sacrifice.

248 This diversity, which makes all things different, has existed from the beginning of time. The names and forms of all things are unique.

249 Although there are differences in the world, there is no duality in their wisdom, just as the limbs may seem to be separate, but they belong to the same body.

250 There are large and small branches, yet they belong to one tree, just as there is only one sun although its rays are many.
251 Likewise, beings may be of many kinds, they may have many different names, and may possess various qualities, but I am known as the indivisible among all these separate creatures.
252 O Arjuna, these people perform the wisdom sacrifice, aware of this multiplicity. Having attained Self-knowledge, they do not become separated.
253 Whatever objects they may perceive, at any time or anywhere, they are aware that there is nothing except Me.
254 A bubble on the surface of the water, wherever it may be floating, has only water around it. Whether it floats or bursts, it is still in the water.
255 When the wind blows up particles of dust, they cannot lose their nature as earth. When they settle again, they rest on the same earth.
256 So wherever and of whatever nature a thing may be, whether it exists or not, it is in Me.
257 O Beloved, the extent of their experience of unity is as vast as My all-pervasiveness, although they become many and are active in many forms.
258 O Arjuna, just as the sun is visible to everyone, in the same way they are always seen before the world.
259 Their wisdom is not two-sided; it is like the wind that blows in all the four quarters of the sky.
260 O Arjuna, their faith is as great as My infinity. Even if such people do not actually worship Me, their worship is still accomplished.
261 I am all that is. Therefore, who doesn't worship Me? But without true knowledge, this worship cannot take place.
262 Now I have explained to you about those who worship Me with the sacrifice of true knowledge.
263 Whatever actions they may perform, they offer all of them to Me alone. But the foolish, unaware of this, cannot attain Me.

अहं क्रतुर् अहं यज्ञः स्वधाहम् अहम् औषधम् ।
मन्त्रो ऽहम् अहम् एवाज्यम् अहम् अग्निर् अहं हुतम् ॥
ahaṁ kratur ahaṁ yajñaḥ
svadhāham aham āusadham
mantro 'ham aham evājyam
aham agnir ahaṁ hutam

16. I am the ritual, I am the sacrifice, I am the offering, I am the medicinal herb, I am the sacred text, I am also the clarified butter, I am the fire, and I am the pouring out (of the oblation).

264 When this awareness is awakened, then one discovers that I am the basic scriptures and the practices arising from them.
265 O Arjuna, I am the sacrifice to be performed strictly according to the precepts.
266 I am also the oblations and the food offered to the ancestors. I am the juice of the soma plant and the other herbs. I am the ghee, the fuel, and the mantras.
267 I am the priest maintaining the fire, which is a form of Myself, and I am even the offerings.

पिताहम् अस्य जगतो माता धाता पितामहः ।
वेद्यं पवित्रम् ओंकार ऋक् साम यजुर् एव च ॥
pitāham asya jagato
mātā dhātā pitāmahaḥ
vedyaṁ pavitram oṁkāra
ṛk sāma yajur eva ca

17. I am the father of the universe, the mother, the establisher, the grandfather, the object of knowledge, the purifier, the sacred syllable "Om," the Rig, Sama, and Yajur Vedas.

268 I am the father who creates the worlds through My union with the eightfold primordial matter.
269 Just as in the play of Shiva in His *ardhanarishwara* form the man also plays the woman's role, I am also the mother of all animate and inanimate beings.
270 The universe is born in Me alone, it is maintained in Me, and it evolves in Me and in no other.
271 Throughout the three worlds, I am the grandfather of the universe. From My primal unconditioned mind, pure spirit and primordial matter were born.
272 I am the point to which the various paths of knowledge lead. O Arjuna, I am He whom the Vedas call "the One who should be known."
273 I am the holy place where all the different theories are unified, where the various philosophies become reconciled, and in which all forms of knowledge converge.
274 The seed of Brahma sends forth the shoot of the four levels of speech, and I am the sacred

syllable, the abode of this speech.

275 The letter A and all the rest are conceived in the womb of this syllable. As they are born, they give rise to the three Vedas.

276 I am these three, the Rig, Yajur, and Sama Vedas; and I am also everything that proceeds from these three.

गतिर् भर्ता प्रभुः साक्षी निवासः शरणं सुहृत् ।
प्रभवः प्रलयः स्थानं निधानं बीजम् अव्ययम् ॥
gatir bhartā prabhuḥ sākṣī
nivāsaḥ śaraṇaṁ suhṛt
prabhavaḥ pralayaḥ sthānaṁ
nidhānaṁ bījam avyayam

18. I am the goal, the supporter, the great Lord, the witness, the abode, the refuge, the friend, the origin, the dissolution and the foundation, the treasure house and the imperishable seed.

277 I am the highest goal. Primordial matter, in which the entire movable and immovable universe lies latent, becomes exhausted and finds rest in Me.

278 This matter lives in Me and, receiving support from Me, it gives birth to the universe. Moreover, through it the universe experiences the three qualities.

279 O Arjuna, I am the consort of Lakshmi, the wealth of the universe, and the Lord of all the three worlds.

280 It is My command that ether should pervade the entire universe, that the wind shouldn't stop blowing even for a moment, that fire should burn and the waters flow,

281 That the mountains shouldn't leave their foundations, that the ocean shouldn't go beyond its bounds, and that the earth should bear the burden of all creatures.

282 I cause the Vedas to speak, the sun to move in its course, and the vital air to stir, keeping the world in motion.

283 O Arjuna, all actions are performed at My command, and in accordance with My laws all creatures are overtaken by death.

284 I am the all-powerful Lord of this universe. I am also the Witness, like the ether.

285 I am that which pervades all names and forms, O Arjuna, I am also the refuge of them all.

286 Just as waves consist of water and water is also in waves, I establish all and I am the abode of all.

287 I am the One, yet many, with all the diversity of the attributes of matter. I am the life force which is active in all living beings in the world.

288 Just as the sun sheds its rays on all, not distinguishing between the ocean and the smallest pool, similarly, I am the friend of all, from Brahma to all creatures.

289 O Arjuna, I am the life essence of all three worlds, and I am the cause of the birth and death of all creation.

290 A seed sends forth branches, and the quality of developing into a tree lies in the seed. Similarly, everything is the product of thought and ultimately is reabsorbed into thought.

291 Unmanifested thought in the form of desire, which is the cause of the entire creation, is reabsorbed into Me at the end of the world age.

292 At that time everything that has name or form passes away, all classes and individuals vanish, and all differences cease to exist.

293 When space is no more, I am the dwelling place of the immortal gods, whose function is to recreate form through thought and desire.

तपाम्य् अहम् अहं वर्षं निगृह्णाम्य् उत्सृजामि च ।
अमृतं चैव मृत्युश्च सद असच् चाहम् अर्जुन ॥
tapāmy aham ahaṁ varṣaṁ
nigṛhṇāmy utsṛjāmi ca
amṛtaṁ cāiva mṛtyuśca
sad asac cāham arjuna

19. I radiate heat, I withhold and send forth the rain; and I am both immortality and death, being and non-being, Arjuna.

294 As the sun, I send out heat and dry up the earth. Again, as Indra, I send down rain and refresh the world.

295 All that is encompassed by death is a manifestation of Me, and I am the imperishable in all that does not die.

296 No more needs to be said. Take this in once and for all. Understand that I alone am all that is and is not.

297 Therefore, O Arjuna, is there any place where I am not? However, what is the fate of living beings who don't perceive Me?

298 Everything is filled with Me, both within and without. Truly, the whole universe is molded in My form; but because they are involved in the process of action, they say I don't exist.

299 Waves dry up when there is no water, and a flame cannot be kindled without a wick. How strange! I am them, but they think that they are not in Me.

300 If a person were to fall into a well of nectar, would he climb out onto the bank? What can be done for a person who doesn't attain Me?

301 O Arjuna, just as a blind man, running in search of food, stumbles and kicks aside a wishing stone in his blindness,

302 Similarly, when true knowledge forsakes a person, he is in a similar state. All action performed without wisdom is worthless.

303 Of what use would the wings of Garuda be to a blind person? In the same way, without wisdom every right action is wasted.

त्रैविद्या मां सोमपा: पूतपापा
यज्ञैर् इष्ट्वा स्वर्गतिं प्रार्थयन्ते ।
ते पुण्यम् आसाद्य सुरेन्द्रलोकम्
अश्नन्ति दिव्यान् दिवि देवभोगान् ।।

trāividyā māṁ somapāḥ pūtapāpā
yajñāir iṣṭvā svargatiṁ prārthayante
te puṇyam āsādya surendralokam
aśnanti divyān divi devabhogān

20. Those who know the three Vedas, the soma drinkers, those whose evils are cleansed, worship Me with sacrifices and seek to go to heaven. They, attaining the pure world of the Lord of the gods, enjoy in heaven the gods' celestial pleasures.

304 O Arjuna, in accordance with the duties prescribed for each stage of life, they become models for the performance of rites.

305 When they perform the sacrifice with ease, the three Vedas bow their heads, and ritual itself stands before them offering them the fruit of it.

306 Such dedicated men, drinkers of soma, become the incarnation of sacrifice. But realize that by acquiring merit, they actually incur sin;

307 For, knowing the Vedas and performing a hundred sacrifices, they lose sight of Me, the object of sacrifice, and prefer heaven.

308 O Arjuna, it is just as if a poor beggar, seated under the wish-fulfilling tree, were to tie up the corners of his begging cloth and set out to beg in poverty.

309 Worshiping Me with a hundred sacrifices, they seek the pleasures of heaven. Don't they really accumulate sin, rather than merit?

310 Therefore, the attainment of heaven without Me is just the path of merit resulting from ignorance. Wise men consider it the path of calamity and destruction.

311 Compared with the pains of hell, heaven may be a place of joy, but the pure bliss of the Eternal is My true form.

312 O Arjuna, when a person sets out to reach Me, heaven and hell are the two false paths, the ways of robbers.

313 People ascend to heaven by means of sin, which they consider merit. They descend to hell as a result of actual sin. But I can only be reached by pure merit.

314 O Arjuna, since all things are in Me, isn't it a lie to say that that which alienates Me from them is merit?

315 Enough for the moment! Now listen: dedicated men who perform sacrifices in worship of Me are only seeking the pleasure of heaven.

316 By means of that merit, which is sin and by which they cannot reach Me, they go to heaven,

317 Where immortality is their throne, their steed is like Airavata, and Amaravati is their royal palace.

318 There they enjoy treasures of the highest psychic powers, jars full of nectar, and possess herds of wish-fulfilling cows.

319 There the gods themselves are their servants, there are fields of wishing gems, and gardens of wish-fulfilling trees for their delight.

320 There are songs of heavenly poets and dances of celestial dancers like Rambha. Urvashi is head of the maidens who minister to their pleasure.

321 The god of love serves them in their bedchamber, where the moon sprinkles water, and messengers as swift as the wind do their bidding.

322 The heavenly priest Brihaspati himself is head of the brahmins who chant blessings, and they enjoy all things in the company of the gods.

323 Mounted troops of the princely guardians of the earth accompany them, and Ucchaishravas is the leader of the horses on which they ride.

324 Enough of this. They experience pleasures like those of Indra, as long as their store of merit lasts.

ते तं भुक्त्वा स्वर्गलोकं विशालं
क्षीणे पुण्ये मर्त्यलोकं विशन्ति ।
एवं त्रयीधर्मम् अनुप्रपन्ना
गतागतं कामकामा लभन्ते ॥
te taṁ bhuktvā svargalokaṁ viśālaṁ
kṣīṇe puṇye martyalokaṁ viśanti
evaṁ trayīdharmam anuprapannā
gatāgataṁ kāmakāmā labhante

21. Having enjoyed the vast world of heaven, they enter the world of mortals when their merit is exhausted. Thus conforming to the law of the three Vedas, desiring enjoyments, they obtain the state of going and returning.

325 But when their merit is exhausted, they fall again from that exalted realm of Indra and return to the world of mortals.
326 The state of these sacrificers is as shameless as that of a man who has spent all his wealth on prostitutes and doesn't even dare to knock at their doors. How can it be told?
327 Those who wanted to enjoy heaven through their accumulated merit miss Me, although I am always with them. Their immortality has become worthless, and they return to earthly existence.
328 O Beloved, just as a person may find a treasure in a dream but it vanishes when he awakes, so is the heavenly happiness of these knowers of the Vedas.
329 O Arjuna, although a person may know the Vedas, without knowing Me it is like husks of corn winnowed without the grain.
330 Without Me, the three rites described in the Vedas are meaningless. Knowing Me, you will attain happiness.

अनन्याश् चिन्तयन्तो मां ये जनाः पर्युपासते ।
तेषां नित्याभियुक्तानां योगक्षेमं वहाम्य् अहम् ॥
ananyāś cintayanto māṁ
ye janāḥ paryupāsate
teṣāṁ nityābhiyuktānāṁ
yogakṣemaṁ vahāmy aham

22. Those men who worship, directing their thoughts to Me, whose minds do not go elsewhere; for them, who are constantly steadfast, I secure what they lack and preserve what they already possess.

331 I Myself serve those who have offered their whole heart and mind to Me, just as a child in the womb knows nothing of striving.
332 I serve those who love Me alone, those who have devoted their lives to Me,
333 Who meditate on Me with one-pointed minds, and who worship Me alone.
334 As soon as they have become one with Me, they follow My path, and all thought for their welfare falls on Me.
335 The performance of all that they have to do is passed to Me, just as a mother bird lives only to sustain the life of her fledglings.
336 A mother has to do all that is good for her child before it knows hunger and thirst. Similarly, I don't hesitate to do everything for those creatures who follow Me.
337 If they desire union with Me, I satisfy their longing; to those who seek to serve Me, I give My love.
338 Whatever wish they have in their hearts, I grant them that first of all, and I give them support.
339 Their entire welfare is in My hands, O Arjuna, for I am their sole refuge.

ये ऽप्य् अन्यदेवताभक्ता यजन्ते श्रद्धयान्विताः ।
ते ऽपि माम् एव कौन्तेय यजन्त्य् अविधिपूर्वकम् ॥
ye 'py anyadevatābhaktā
yajante śraddhayānvitāḥ
te 'pi mām eva kāunteya
yajanty avidhipūrvakam

23. Even those who worship other gods with faith, also worship Me, Arjuna, though they do so in ignorance.

340 There are other traditional paths, but in them people don't know that I am all-pervasive. They worship me as fire, Indra, the sun, or the moon.
341 Their worship does reach Me, for I am all these. However, the way of their worship is not the straight path, but a crooked one.
342 Aren't the branches and leaves of a tree born of the same seed? It is the roots which absorb the water, so the roots must be watered.
343 Although the ten sense organs belong to the same body, only one person enjoys the sense objects experienced through them.
344 Should a person put well-cooked food in his ear? Should he bring flowers and attach them to his eyes?
345 Just as food must be tasted by the tongue and fragrance must be smelled by the nose,

similarly, I must be worshiped in My true nature, as Myself.

346 Worship performed without knowing Me is worthless and irrelevant. In the same way, knowledge, which is like the eyes of these acts, must be untainted.

अहं हि सर्वयज्ञानां भोक्ता च प्रभुर् एव च ।
न तु माम् अभिजानन्ति तत्त्वेनातश् च्यवन्ति ते ।।

ahaṁ hi sarvayajñānāṁ
bhoktā ca prabhur eva ca
na tu mām abhijānanti
tattvenātaś cyavanti te

24. For I am the enjoyer and the Lord of all sacrifices. But they do not recognize Me in truth; hence they fall.

347 Look, O Arjuna! Of all the sacrificial offerings, is there any other enjoyer than Me?

348 I am the source of all sacrifices, and I am also the end of them; yet people of perverted minds forget Me and worship other gods.

349 Just as the water of the Ganges is poured back into the Ganges in the name of the gods and ancestors, similarly, these men offer Me to Myself, but in various forms of faith.

350 Therefore, O Arjuna, they fail to reach Me and attain that state which they have desired.

यान्ति देवव्रता देवान् पितॄन् यान्ति पितृव्रताः ।
भूतानि यान्ति भूतेज्या यान्ति मद्याजिनो ऽपि माम् ।।

yānti devavratā devān
pitṝn yānti pitṛvratāḥ
bhūtāni yānti bhūtejyā
yānti madyājino 'pi mām

25. Those who are devoted to the gods go to the gods; those who are devoted to the ancestors go to the ancestors; those who are devoted to the spirits go to the spirits; those who worship Me come surely to Me.

351 Those who offer their devotion to the gods with their mind, speech, and senses, become gods as soon as they leave the body.

352 Also, those who faithfully observe the rites for the ancestors attain the state of those ancestors when they die.

353 Those whose deities are the lower divinities and elemental spirits, whom they worship with magic practices,

354 They themselves become elementals when the veil of the body is removed. So, in accordance with their thoughts, they receive the fruit of their actions.

355 On the other hand, there are those who see only Me with their eyes, who hear only Me with their ears, who have no thought except for Me, and who praise Me with their voices.

356 They prostrate everywhere before Me with their bodies, they give in charity and perform other practices for My sake.

357 They have studied My wisdom, both inwardly and outwardly they are satisfied by Me, and have taken birth only for My sake.

358 They proudly boast that they exist for the glory of God, and their only greed is their greed for Me.

359 They are filled with a passionate desire for Me, they are brimming with love for Me, they are fascinated by their attraction to Me and forget the world.

360 They know only Me as their sacred books, they recite hymns only to reach Me, and they worship Me in every action.

361 These people have become united with Me even before death, so at death, how could they pass on to any other state?

362 Therefore, those who have become worshipers of Me and have offered themselves to Me attain union with Me.

363 O Arjuna, no one can please Me without giving himself to Me. I cannot be reached by any other offering.

364 He who claims knowledge of Me doesn't know Me, he who boasts of his Self-realization is imperfect, and he who declares that he has reached his goal has attained nothing.

365 O Arjuna, sacrifices, charity, austerities, and any efforts that a person is proud of are worthless. They are as ineffective as a blade of grass.

366 Just think: is there anything superior in knowledge to the Vedas? Is there anyone who is a greater speaker than Shesha?

367 Even Shesha hides beneath My bed. The Vedas themselves withdraw saying, "Not this, not this," while Sanaka and other great sages are perplexed by My nature.

368 Among those who practice severe penance, who is worthy to be placed beside Shankara? Yet he humbly bears on his head the waters which flow from My feet.

369 Can anyone's greatness equal that of Lakshmi, who is waited upon in her house by such serving maids as success?

370 If they were to build toy houses for play and

call them Amarapura, wouldn't Indra and the other gods be their dolls?

371 When she becomes tired of these toys, she breaks them and Indra becomes destitute. Whatever trees they see are changed into wish-fulfilling trees.

372 Even Lakshmi, the chief mistress, in whose presence the household servants possess such power, is not worthy to be mentioned here.

373 By serving Me with her whole heart and humbling herself before Me, she has become worthy of the honor of washing My feet, O Arjuna.

374 All greatness should be set aside and all learning forgotten, for when a person has become lowly in terms of the world, he is close to Me.

375 O Arjuna, if the moon fades before the light of the sun with its thousand rays, how can a firefly boast of its light?

376 How can an ordinary wretched human being come to Me, when the glory of Lakshmi is of no use and even the penance of Shiva does not suffice?

377 Therefore, relinquish the body, cast away every virtue, and abandon all pride of wealth.

पत्त्रं पुष्पं फलं तोयं यो मे भक्त्या प्रयच्छति ।
तद् अहं भक्त्युपहृतम् अश्नामि प्रयतात्मनः ।।
pattraṁ puṣpaṁ phalaṁ toyaṁ
yo me bhaktyā prayacchati
tad ahaṁ bhaktyupahṛtam
aśnāmi prayatātmanaḥ

26. He who offers to Me with devotion and a pure heart a leaf, a flower, a fruit, or water, that offering of devotion I accept from him.

378 If a devotee, with the joy of boundless devotion, brings as an offering to Me a fruit from any tree he may choose,

379 When he shows it to Me, however small it may be, I hold out both hands to receive it, and without even removing the stalk I taste it respectfully.

380 Also, if a flower is given to Me in the name of devotion, I place it in My mouth, although I should actually smell it.

381 But why a flower, when even any leaf would be accepted? It doesn't matter whether it is fresh or dry or in any other condition.

382 If it is offered to Me with utmost love, even though it may be a mere leaf, I take it with the same delight as a hungry man would rejoice at a drink of nectar.

383 A leaf would do, but it may happen that one cannot be found. In that case, it isn't difficult to find water.

384 Water is found anywhere, without price, and one finds it even without searching for it. He who offers even that to Me in the spirit of the purest devotion,

385 Builds for Me a temple more spacious than Vaikuntha, and offers Me jewels more perfect than the Kaustubha diamond in My crown.

386 He makes for Me many bedrooms of milk as delightful as the Milky Ocean.

387 He gives Me sweetly scented delights such as camphor, sandalwood, and aloe wood, and places on Me with his own hand a garland of lights like the sun.

388 He offers Me vehicles like Garuda, gardens filled with wish-fulfilling trees, and herds of heavenly cattle.

389 Tasty dishes served to Me are sweeter than nectar, and the smallest drop of water delights Me.

390 But why should I say more, O Arjuna? You have seen with your own eyes how, with My own hands, I untied the knot in Sudama's cloth to take out a few grains of rice.

391 True devotion is the only thing I recognize; I make no distinction between great and small. I am ready to be welcomed by the devotion of any person.

392 Truly, a leaf, a flower, or a fruit is for Me only a means of devotion. What I desire is complete devotion.

393 O Arjuna, listen to Me! Gain control over your mind and then you will never forget Me, for I dwell in the temple of your heart.

यत् करोषि यद् अश्नासि यज् जुहोषि ददासि यत् ।
यत् तपस्यसि कौन्तेय तत् कुरुष्व मदर्पणम् ।।
yat karoṣi yad aśnāsi
yaj juhoṣi dadāsi yat
yat tapasyasi kāunteya
tat kuruṣva madarpaṇam

27. Whatever you do, whatever you eat, whatever you offer, whatever you give, whatever austerities you perform, Arjuna, do that as an offering to Me.

394 However you may act, whatever pleasures you may enjoy, whatever kinds of sacrifices you may perform,

395 Whatever gifts you may give to deserving

people who request them of you, whatever wages you may pay your servants, whatever austerities and vows you may observe,

396 All such actions, according to their own nature, which you may do with steadfast devotion, you should offer to Me.

397 But let there remain no memory in your mind of having performed these actions. Purified in this way you should offer every action to Me.

शुभाशुभफलैर् एवं मोक्ष्यसे कर्मबन्धनैः ।
सन्यासयोगयुक्तात्मा विमुक्तो माम् उपैष्यते ॥

śubhāśubhaphalāir evaṁ
mokṣyase karmabandhanāiḥ
saṁnyāsayogayuktātmā
vimukto mām upāiṣyate

28. You shall certainly be liberated from the bonds of action which produce good and evil fruits; liberated, with your mind disciplined by the yoga of renunciation, you shall come to Me.

398 Just as seeds thrown into a fire lose their power to germinate, similarly, neither good nor bad actions bear any fruit when they are offered to Me.

399 O Beloved, when actions are not offered in this way, they bear the fruit of either pleasure or pain, and a person must be reborn to experience these.

400 However, when actions are offered to Me, then birth and death cease, and all the troubles arising from birth also disappear.

401 O Arjuna, there is no need to spend time thinking this over, for I have told you the easy way of renunciation.

402 Don't fall into the bondage of the body, and don't become engulfed in the ocean of pleasure and pain. The experience of eternal bliss in Me will come to you.

समो ऽहं सर्वभूतेषु न मे द्वेष्यो ऽस्ति न प्रियः ।
ये भजन्ति तु मां भक्त्या मयि ते तेषु चाप्य् अहम् ॥

samo 'haṁ sarvabhūteṣu
na me dveṣyo 'sti na priyaḥ
ye bhajanti tu māṁ bhaktyā
mayi te teṣu cāpy aham

29. I am the same (Self) in all beings; there is none disliked or dear to Me. But they who worship Me with devotion are in Me, and I am also in them.

403 If you ask what My nature is, I will say that I am the same in all beings. For Me there is no distinction such as "I" and "another."

404 Those who know Me in this way and who destroy the seat of egoism, worship Me with their entire soul and in every action.

405 Though apparently acting in the body, they are not really in their bodies, but are rather in Me; and I dwell wholly in their hearts.

406 Just as the complete nature of a banyan tree lies hidden in each of its seeds, and the seeds live within the tree,

407 Similarly, they and I are mutually related, although externally we differ in name. Still, the inner truth of this is that they and I are one.

408 Just as borrowed jewelry is only worn on the outside of the body, in the same way, these devotees are indifferent to life in the body.

409 Just as when its fragrance is carried away by the wind, a flower remains abandoned on its stem, so the body of such people is only retained for the span of their earthly life.

410 Truly, O Arjuna, a person whose egoism is absorbed in devotion to Me enters into union with Me.

अपि चेत् सुदुराचारो भजते माम् अनन्यभाक् ।
साधुर् एव स मन्तव्यः सम्यग् व्यवसितो हि सः ॥

api cet sudurācāro
bhajate mām ananyabhāk
sādhur eva sa mantavyaḥ
samyag vyavasito hi saḥ

30. If even the evil doer worships Me with undivided devotion, he is to be thought of as righteous, for he has indeed rightly resolved.

411 Those who worship Me with devotion and love are not reborn in a body, no matter what caste they belong to.

412 O Arjuna, where their conduct is concerned, for the most part it was bad, but they spent their latter days at the meeting place of the four ways of devotion.

413 O Beloved, whatever the last thought is at the moment of death, so will a person's state be in the afterlife. Therefore, if in the end he leads a life of devotion,

414 Although his earlier conduct may have been sinful, he is the best of men. He is like a person who has fallen into a great flood, but emerges alive.

415 He reaches the other shore alive, and the possibility of drowning has passed. Similarly, as a result of a person's devotion in his

last years, none of his past sin remains.

416 Even if he was very wicked, he has bathed in the holy waters of repentance, and thus cleansed he comes to Me by his earnest devotion.

417 His family is also made holy, pure, and noble. Such a person certainly fulfills the purpose of his life.

418 He has acquired knowledge, practiced austerities, and studied the eightfold yoga.

419 In short, O Arjuna, he who is wholeheartedly devoted to Me has become free from the bonds of the fruit of action.

420 O Arjuna, he has collected all the activities of his heart and mind in one-pointed devotion and has offered it to Me.

क्षिप्रं भवति धर्मात्मा शश्वच्छान्तिं निगच्छति ।
कौन्तेय प्रतिजानीहि न मे भक्तः प्रणश्यति ॥

kṣipraṁ bhavati dharmātmā
śaśvacchāntiṁ nigacchati
kāunteya pratijānīhi
na me bhaktaḥ praṇaśyati

31. Quickly he becomes virtuous and goes to everlasting peace. Arjuna, know for certain that no devotee of Mine is ever lost.

421 You must know that in the course of time he will be united with Me. But how is it possible for anyone who lives on nectar to die?

422 As long as the sun doesn't rise, it is night. In the same way, isn't any action performed without love for Me a great sin?

423 O Arjuna, when a person's mind reaches Me, he has truly become one with Me.

424 When one lamp is lighted from another, it is difficult to say which was lit first. Similarly, he who worships Me with his whole heart becomes one with Me.

425 Then he remains in My eternal peace, which is his glory. In fact, he lives by My life.

426 O Arjuna, shall I tell you about this again and again? He who longs for Me must never cease practicing devotion.

427 He doesn't need to come from a pure family; he shouldn't praise nobility of birth. And why should he bear the burden of useless learning?

428 Fascination with beauty or youth and boasting of worldly wealth are just empty show without devotion to Me.

429 Of what use are ears of corn without the grain, however plentiful they may be? Of what value is a deserted city, however beautiful?

430 What is the good of a dry lake? If two distressed men meet in a forest, what can they do? What is the use of a tree whose flowers are sterile?

431 Riches and the pride of race and caste are equally vain. In fact, they are no better than a body with all its limbs but no head.

432 In the same way, a life is cursed without devotion to Me. After all, aren't there stones on the earth?

433 Just as a good person will avoid the shade of a harmful tree, similarly merit deserts a person who doesn't worship Me.

434 A neem tree may be breaking with the weight of its own seeds, but only the crows benefit from it. In the same way, a person without devotion has lived only for sin.

435 If well-cooked food were put in a dish and left at night at the crossroads, it would only be food for dogs.

436 The life of a person without devotion is similar to this. Not even in his dreams can he realize what good actions are. He is only offering hospitality to all the sorrows of worldly life.

437 The family in which a person is born doesn't need to be noble. A person might be born as an outcaste, or even the body of an animal would be acceptable.

438 Look! When the elephant was seized by the crocodile, he remembered Me; and in spite of his animal nature, he was able to reach Me.

मां हि पार्थ व्यपाश्रित्य येऽपि स्युः पापयोनयः ।
स्त्रियो वैश्यास् तथा शूद्रास् तेऽपि यान्ति परां गतिम् ॥

māṁ hi pārtha vyapāśritya
ye 'pi syuḥ pāpayonayaḥ
striyo vāiśyās tathā śūdrās
te 'pi yānti parāṁ gatim

32. They who take refuge in Me, Arjuna, even if they are born of those whose wombs are evil (i.e. those of low origin), women, Vaishyas, even Shudras, also go to the highest goal.

439 O Arjuna, even those who are born in the lowest caste, the utterance of whose names is pollution, the wombs of sin,

440 Even if such ignorant ones, as stupid as a stone, are devoted to Me with all their heart and soul,

441 If they chant My praises with their voices, contemplate only My form with their eyes, and think only of Me with their minds,
442 If their ears listen to nothing but My glory, if the only ornament of their bodies is service to Me,
443 If their consciousness is aware of no sense objects but knows only Me, and if they regard the attainment of such a state as life and all else as death,
444 If they have made Me the sole essence of their lives by their absolute devotion,
445 They may be born in the most degraded caste, and they may be entirely unlearned; yet, when measured against Me, they are not inferior.
446 Look! Because of the fullness of their devotion, the demons excelled the gods, and on account of their greatness I had to incarnate as the Lion-man.
447 O Arjuna, many have taken Prahlada in place of Me, and he has received what should have been given to Me.
448 It is true that he came from a family of demons, but even Indra couldn't surpass him in devotion. So caste is unimportant. What is essential is devotion.
449 If a person has a piece of leather stamped with the royal seal, he may obtain everything with it.
450 Again, even gold and silver in themselves have no value as money; it is the royal decree that gives them value. Even a piece of leather bearing the royal stamp can purchase anything.
451 Similarly, greatness and supreme knowledge are of value only when the mind and intellect are filled with love of Me.
452 Race, caste, and color are all meaningless. The goal of life can be reached only by union with Me, O Arjuna.
453 In whatever way a person practices devotion, he should direct his mind towards Me. Once he does that, all those other things are useless.
454 Small streams exist as streams only until they merge in the river Ganges. Once they have joined the river they become one with it.
454 The distinction between sandalwood and acacia exists only until they are thrown into the fire and become one.
456 The divisions of Kshatriyas, Vaishyas, women, Shudras, and outcastes remain different only until they worship Me.
457 Like grains of salt thrown into the ocean, such distinctions of caste and person pass away when people become united with Me through devotion.
458 Rivers are called by various names and flow east or west until they reach the ocean.
459 It is the same when a person's mind has entered into Me. Then he naturally becomes one with Me.
460 Even if a piece of iron is lifted only for the purpose of cutting, if it comes in contact with the philosopher's stone, at that very moment it will become gold.
461 Weren't the women of Vraja united with Me when, out of love, they came to meet Me?
462 Didn't Kansa come to Me through fear and Chaidya and others through their great hostility to Me?
463 O Arjuna, the Yadavas were united with Me through kinship, and Vasudeva and others through affection.
464 Just as Narada, Dhruva, Akrura, Shuka, and Sanatkumara were able to reach Me through their devotion, O Arjuna,
465 So the Gopis came to me through love, Kansa through the confusion of fear, and Shishupala and others through their wicked intent.
466 O Beloved, I am the final refuge of all, though they come by various ways, whether devotion, desire, dread, dispassion, or enmity.
467 Listen! There are many ways a person can enter into Me.
468 Let him be born in any caste; let him serve Me or oppose Me; whether he is a devotee or an enemy, he must become Mine.
469 Under whatever pretext a person enters into Me, he is certain to attain union with Me.
470 Therefore, O Arjuna, even an outcaste, a Vaishya, a Shudra, or a woman enter My abode when they worship Me.

किं पुनर् ब्राह्मणाः पुण्या भक्ता राजर्षयस् तथा ।
अनित्यम् असुखम् लोकम् इमं प्राप्य भजस्व माम् ॥

kiṁ punar brāhmaṇāḥ puṇyā
bhaktā rājarṣayas tathā
anityam asukhaṁ lokam
imaṁ prāpya bhajasva mām

33. *How much more easily then, the pure Brahmins and the devoted royal seers! Having attained this impermanent and unhappy world, devote yourself to Me.*

471 Then come the brahmins, the highest of all castes. For them heaven is a royal right, and they are the home of the knowledge of mantras.

472 They are gods on earth, austerity incarnate, and through them good fortune arises in all places of pilgrimage.

473 All sacrifices dwell in them forever. They are the armor of the Vedas, and all auspiciousness grows in the lap of their sight.

474 Virtue flourishes by their ardor, and truth lives through their thoughts.

475 Fire was given life at their bidding, and for love of them the ocean gave them its waters.

476 To approach them, I pushed Lakshmi to one side, took My divine necklace in My hand, and bared my breast to receive the dust of their feet.

477 I still bear the imprint of Bhrigu's foot in My heart, O Arjuna, to preserve My divine wealth, vast as the ocean.

478 O Arjuna, their wrath is the dwelling place of Rudra, who brings the final conflagration, and through their grace one acquires supernatural powers.

479 These brahmins are worthy of veneration for their great merit and are filled with devotion for Me. Is it necessary to prove that they attain union with Me?

480 The leaves of a neem tree, touched by the wind blowing through a nearby sandalwood tree, absorb its fragrance and are placed on the forehead of a deity.

481 Therefore, how can one think that the sandalwood tree itself cannot attain such a state? Would this be true only if it were proved that it had happened?

482 Hara himself wore the half moon on his head, hoping that it might cool his brow.

483 So why shouldn't a person apply to his body the paste of the sandalwood tree, which has the power to cool, and whose fragrance is superior to that of the moon?

484 If drainage water easily reaches the sea with the help of the river into which it flows, can the river do anything other than carry it to the sea?

485 Therefore, for royal sages and brahmins who take their sole refuge in Me, I am certainly their ultimate state and their very being.

486 How can a person be carefree when he sets out in a boat full of holes? How can he expose himself to a shower of weapons?

487 When stones are thrown at a person's body, mustn't a shield be held in front of it? Or if he is attacked by a disease, should he be reluctant to take medicine?

488 O Arjuna, shouldn't he escape when he is surrounded on all sides by a forest fire? So why shouldn't he worship Me when he is born into affliction? Is he able to rest carefree in his home or at leisure?

489 Has anyone so much strength that he can refuse to worship Me?

490 Can anyone trust happily in his knowledge or his youth and yet not worship Me?

491 O Beloved, all the pleasures of the world only gratify the body which eventually falls into the jaws of death.

492 Man has arrived at the marketplace of the end of the world, where the merchandise of sorrow has been brought in for sale and is being meted out by the measuring hand of death.

493 O Arjuna, can a happy life be bought there? Can a lamp be lit by blowing a heap of ashes?

494 Can the juice pressed out of poisonous roots, though someone may call it nectar, make a person immortal?

494 Objects in the mortal world are as useful as if the head were cut off and bound onto a wound in the leg.

496 Whoever hears a report of any true happiness in this mortal world? How could one sleep at ease on a bed of live coals?

497 The moon of this world is forever waning, the sun rises only to set, and sorrow harasses all people in the guise of happiness.

498 The tender shoot of well-being is at once withered by evil, and death seeks out even a child still in the womb.

499 People become anxious about what they cannot have. Even if they get it, it is carried off by demigods and no trace of it is left.

500 O Arjuna, though a person may search on every path, there is no trace of anyone who has returned. There are only stories of the numberless dead.

501 Listen! Even if one were to describe the impermanence of that world throughout a lifetime of Brahma, the tale would never be finished.

502 It seems strange that a person can be carefree when he has been born in a world in

which life is like this.

503 A person won't give a fraction of his wealth for spiritual purposes in the visible or invisible world, yet he will spend a fortune on something which can only bring him ruin.

504 A person who is absorbed in worldly pleasures is called happy, and one who bends under a burden of greed is called wise.

505 People honor as an elder one who has only a short time to live and whose strength and mental powers are deteriorating.

506 As a child grows in strength, his parents dance with joy, yet they don't regret that his life is becoming shorter.

507 Since the day of his birth, every day brings him nearer to death; yet they celebrate his advancing age by raising flags.

508 O Beloved, they couldn't bear to hear the phrase "May you die!" They weep for the dead, but because of their ignorance they don't value life while it is here.

509 Look! A frog which is about to be swallowed by a snake will still wave its tongue to catch flies. Similarly, creatures multiply their desires out of greed.

510 Shame on such evil! Everything in this world is distorted. O Arjuna, you happen to have been born in this world.

511 Leave it at once and follow the path of devotion, which will lead you to My perfect abode.

मन्मना भव मद्भक्तो मद्याजी मां नमस्कुरु ।
माम् एवैष्यसि युक्त्वैवम् आत्मानं मत्परायण: ।।

manmanā bhava madbhakto
madyājī māṁ namaskuru
mām evāiṣyasi yuktvāivam
ātmānaṁ matparāyaṇah

34. With mind fixed on Me, be devoted to Me; sacrificing to Me, make reverence to Me. Thus steadfast, with Me as your supreme aim, you yourself shall come to Me.

512 Let your mind be united with Me, devote your love to worshiping Me, and show reverence only to Me.

513 When, under My direction, a man's personal will is burned out, then he is called My true worshiper.

514 When you have become one with Me in this way, then you will enter into My form. I am telling you this secret of My heart.

515 Possessing these riches that I have kept hidden from all others, you will be happy forever.

516 Sanjaya said, This was said by Krishna, the great Soul, the tree that fulfills the wishes of His devotees, the dark-hued incarnation of the Supreme.

517 Look! The old king silently listened to this, just as a buffalo will lie still in a flood.

518 Then Sanjaya nodded his head and said to himself, Oh, what showers of nectar have fallen on us! Yet the king seems to have withdrawn somewhere else.

519 Because he is my patron, however, it wouldn't be proper for me to tell him this. It is his nature, and he cannot help it.

520 I am truly blessed. The divine sage Vyasa has preserved me so I can tell this story.

521 As he was saying this, with great effort and mental stress, he was overcome by uncontrollable emotion.

522 His mind was stupefied and he became speechless, while his body vibrated from head to toe.

523 Tears of joy flowed from his half-closed eyes, and waves of inner joy caused him to tremble all over.

524 Beads of perspiration formed on his skin like pure wheat grains so that he seemed to be covered with a net of pearls.

525 Although his life seemed to be passing away in the ecstasy of his joy, it was preserved by his task of narration which Vyasa had given to him.

526 Then he suddenly began to hear again the conversation between Krishna and Arjuna, and this brought him back to full consciousness.

527 Brushing away the tears from his eyes and wiping the perspiration from his body, he said to Dhritarashtra, Listen to me, O King.

528 Now the listeners will gather a rich harvest of great truths, for Krishna's words are choice seeds sown in the fertile soil of Sanjaya's mind.

529 O listeners, you should pay attention so that you may rise to the heights of joy. The good fortune of your ears has brought you this blessing.

530 The Lord of all perfected beings will now show Arjuna the place of His glory. Listen to this, said Jnanadeva, disciple of Nivritti.

10

THE YOGA OF MANIFESTATION

SALUTATIONS to you, O Guru, skillful in clarity of explanation, causing the lotus of knowledge to bloom, delighting in the beauty of the first level of speech as in a lovely maiden!

2 Salutations to you who are the sun in the darkness of worldly life, who possess the highest powers, who are endowed with youthfulness, and who delight in fostering your disciples' attainment of the highest Truth.

3 Salutations to you who are the protector of the whole world, the storehouse of jewels of auspiciousness, the sandalwood tree in the forest of righteous people, the object most worthy of worship.

4 Salutations to you who are to the wise like the moon to the chakora bird, the king of the realm of Self-realization, the ocean of the essence of the Vedas, the inspiration of the god of love.

5 O prince among Gurus! Salutations to you who are worthy of being worshiped by all the faithful, who have destroyed the temples of the elephant of this worldly existence, the source from which the whole universe has evolved.

6 Your grace is personified by Ganesh. Favored by him, even a child may enter every branch of learning.

7 When the beneficent voice of the Guru speaks a word of reassurance, a person reaches the island of the nine feelings.

8 Even a dumb person can rival Brihaspati, the lord of eloquence, in the art of composition when he is favored by your love, which is like the goddess Saraswati.

9 Moreover, a person on whom you cast your gracious glance, or on whose head you place your lotus-like hand, though he may be an individual soul, he becomes equal to the great Lord Shiva.

10 With what further words can I praise your greatness? Is there any need to make the sun shine more brightly?

11 Or to cause the wish-fulfilling tree to bear flowers? What feast can be offered to the Milky Ocean? Who would want to add fragrance to camphor?

12 What ointment can be applied to sandalwood? What need is there to cook nectar? Is it possible to place anything above the sky?

13 When such is the greatness of the Guru, how can anyone understand him? Realizing this, I silently salute him!

14 If I were to say that I could describe my revered Guru by the power of intelligence, it would be like adding luster to pearls.

15 But let this be. To say more would be like applying a touchstone to the finest gold. It is better to fall silently at his feet.

16 Then I said, O Master, because you have shown me such love, I have become like a banyan tree in the holy city of this meeting place of Krishna and Arjuna.

17 Once when Upamanyu asked for a cup of milk, Lord Shiva offered him the entire Milky Ocean in a bowl.

18 The Lord of Vaikuntha presented the discontented Dhruva with the gift of the position of the pole star.

19 In the same way, I have been able to sing in the *ovi* meter about the *Bhagavad Gita*, which is the crown of the philosophy of the Absolute and the seat of all sciences.

20 When I was wandering in the forest of language, I couldn't hear what the words said, the fruit borne by the trees. But you have

turned that speech into a wish-fulfilling vine of understanding.

21 My consciousness has now been transformed into a treasure house of spiritual joy, and my heart has become a couch of rest in the ocean of the meaning of the *Gita*.

22 Now through your grace I have been able to explain without difficulty the first part of the *Gita* in the *ovi* meter.

23 In the first chapter Arjuna's depression was described, in the second the yoga of action was explained, as well as the difference between the yoga of wisdom and the yoga of action.

24 In the third chapter the yoga of action was described, and in the fourth the yoga of action was shown in relation to the philosophy of wisdom. In the fifth chapter the secret of the eight branches of yoga was revealed.

25 The same yoga was explained in detail in the sixth chapter, beginning with a description of yogic posture. It is the yoga by which the individual soul attains union with the highest Self.

26 The same chapter taught the complete theory of the realization of union and the fate of those who fall away from this path.

27 After this, in the seventh chapter, first the renunciation of matter was explained, and then the nature of the four kinds of worshipers of the Supreme.

28 In the eighth chapter, after answering Arjuna's seven questions, the Lord explains all matters concerning people's condition at the time of death.

29 Whatever teaching is in all the Vedas can be found in the hundred thousand verses of the *Mahabharata*.

30 The entire teaching contained in the *Mahabharata* is found in the seven hundred verses of the conversation between Krishna and Arjuna, and the essence of all these is found in the ninth chapter.

31 I wouldn't dare to set my seal on the ninth chapter, claiming that its meaning had been fully explained. Why should I speak with such boldness?

32 Sugar and molasses are made from the same sugarcane juice, but they are very different in the sweetness of their taste.

33 Some chapters describe God, realizing that He is all-pervasive, while others help us to realize His immanence. When we try to understand still others, we become absorbed in Him with all our powers of perception.

34 Such are the chapters of the *Gita*, but the ninth surpasses all description. The fact that I have been able to explain it is the work of Your grace, O Lord.

35 Vasishtha's saffron cloth shone like the sun, Vishvamitra was able to create another world, and Nala brought stones to make a bridge so the monkey armies could cross the sea.

36 Maruti caught the sun in the heavens, and Agastya drained the ocean in one gulp. In the same way, You have enabled me, as ignorant as I am, to relate that indescribable chapter.

37 If one were to ask for a description of the fight between Rama and Ravana, their meeting on the battlefield should be narrated exactly as it happened.

38 So I say that Krishna's teaching in the ninth chapter of the *Gita* is as it is given here in the ninth chapter. Those learned people who understand the meaning of the *Gita* will realize this.

39 I have explained the first nine chapters according to my views. Now the second part of this book begins. Please listen to it.

40 In this chapter Lord Krishna will explain to Arjuna in a skillful and interesting way His special and His general powers.

41 With all the eloquence of our Marathi language, the feeling of tranquility will surpass the feeling of love, and the *ovi* meter will adorn the composition.

42 If a person carefully reads my Marathi version of the original Sanskrit *Gita* with a clear understanding of its meaning, he cannot say which is the original.

43 Because of the beauty of the body, it becomes an ornament to the very ornaments that it wears, and one cannot say which of the two beautifies the other.

44 In the same way, the Sanskrit and Marathi languages display their beauty in the place of honor in the *Gita*. Listen carefully.

45 If a person has to express the feelings which the *Gita* arouses in him, he needs showers of the nine feelings to enrich his literary skill.

46 So, taking the beauty of the Marathi language and adding to it the youth of the

feelings, the precious truths of the *Gita* are set forth.

47 Hear now what Lord Krishna said. He is the greatest teacher in the whole world and causes the minds of intelligent people to marvel.

48 Jnanadeva, disciple of Nivritti, says, Hear what Lord Krishna said: O Arjuna, your mind is well able to understand all these things.

श्रीभगवान् उवाच । *śrībhagavān uvāca*

भूय एव महाबाहो शृणु मे परमं वचः ।
यत् ते ऽहं प्रीयमाणाय वक्ष्यामि हितकाम्यया ॥
bhūya eva mahābāho
śṛṇu me paramaṁ vacaḥ
yat te 'haṁ prīyamāṇāya
vakṣyāmi hitakāmyayā

The Blessed Lord spoke:
1. Again, O Arjuna, hear My supreme word which I shall speak to you, who are beloved, with a desire for your welfare.

49 I wanted to see whether you had paid attention to the explanation of the truth that I had already given, and I find that you have done very well.

50 Just as by pouring a little water into a pot, a person can see whether it leaks and then add more, in the same way I have tested you to see whether I can teach you more.

51 If a person wishes to leave a stranger in charge of his possessions, he makes him treasurer only if he is honest. Now I can place My confidence in you, O Arjuna.

52 Thus the Lord of all spoke to Arjuna with respect, just as clouds, on perceiving a mountain, gather around it.

53 That Prince of all compassionate beings said, Listen, O Arjuna, I will explain again the truths which I have imparted to you.

54 When a field is sown every year and yields a crop, it will yield more and more if the farmer doesn't become tired of cultivating it.

55 Gold which is heated again and again in a crucible doesn't deteriorate, for its quality increases.

56 Similarly, O Arjuna, I am not speaking for your sake but for My own purposes.

57 When a child is adorned with ornaments, it doesn't really appreciate them. It is the mother who is delighted when she sees them.

58 In the same way, as this benefits you more and more, My love for you is doubled.

59 O Arjuna, enough of this explanation. Clearly I love you, and there is no end to My satisfaction in talking with you.

60 This is why I am repeating these things. Listen to Me with full attention.

61 O Arjuna, listen to this secret, My sublime teaching. It is the highest Absolute, taking on the form of words, which is coming to embrace you.

न मे विदुः सुरगणाः प्रभवं न महर्षयः ।
अहम् आदिर् हि देवानां महर्षीणां च सर्वशः ॥
na me viduḥ suragaṇāḥ
prabhavaṁ na maharṣayaḥ
aham ādir hi devānāṁ
maharṣīṇāṁ ca sarvaśaḥ

2. Neither the multitude of gods nor the great seers know My origin. In truth I am the source of the gods and the great seers.

62 O Arjuna, don't you truly know Me? It is I who am here; the universe is only a dream.

63 Here the Vedas are silent, the mind and the *prana* become powerless, and the sun and moon set in darkness though it isn't night.

64 Just as the child in the womb doesn't know its mother's age, similarly, the gods don't know Me.

65 Just as a fish cannot measure the ocean, and just as a gnat cannot fly across the whole sky, in the same way, even the great sages with all their wisdom cannot know Me.

66 Eons have passed while they have tried to understand who I am, how great I am, where I come from and when.

67 O Arjuna, though I am the primal source from which all the gods, the great *rishis*, and the entire creation have sprung, it is very difficult for them to know Me.

68 If water that has flowed downward could flow up again to a mountain, or if a grown tree could return to its own roots, then the world which has emanated from Me could know Me.

69 If it were possible for a banyan tree to be contained in one of its shoots, if the sea could be contained in a single wave, or if the whole earth could be stored in a single atom,

70 Then it might be possible for Me to be known by the souls of men, the great *rishis*, and the gods whom I have created.

यो माम् अजम् अनादिं च वेत्ति लोकमहेश्वरम् ।
असंमूढः स मर्त्येषु सर्वपापैः प्रमुच्यते ॥

yo mām ajam anādiṁ ca
vetti lokamaheśvaram
asaṁmūḍhaḥ sa martyeṣu
sarvapāpāiḥ pramucyate

3. He who knows Me, the birthless and the beginningless, the mighty Lord of the world, he among mortals is undeluded; he is released from all evils.

71 Though I am like this, a person who withdraws from worldly life and turns away from all the activities of the senses,
72 Even though he may be drawn back into these he can quickly recover and, giving up the life of the body, he can rise above the power of the elements.
73 With his mind firmly established in this way, through the light of his own Self, he realizes clearly that by nature I am unborn.
74 Compared with other stones, he is the touchstone. Compared with other liquids, he is nectar. He is a part of Me in human form.
75 He is the living image of wisdom, and the limbs of his body are like the offshoots of bliss. His human form is an illusion for ordinary people.
76 If by chance a diamond were found in a lump of camphor and water fell upon it, wouldn't it emerge with its form intact?
77 In the same way, although this person may seem to be an ordinary person, the weaknesses of nature are unknown to him.
78 Sins avoid him for fear of their lives. Just as a serpent leaves a burning sandalwood tree, similarly, desires pass by the person who knows Me.
79 Now if you want to learn how to know Me, hear what I am and what My states of being are.
80 These are spread throughout the whole world, expressing themselves in various creatures according to their individual natures.

बुद्धिर् ज्ञानम् असंमोहः क्षमा सत्यं दमः शमः ।
सुखं दुःखं भवो ऽभवो भयं चाभयम् एव च ॥
buddhir jñānam asaṁmohaḥ
kṣamā satyaṁ damaḥ śamaḥ
sukhaṁ duḥkhaṁ bhavo 'bhavo
bhayaṁ cābhayam eva ca

4. Intellect, knowledge, freedom from delusion, patience, truth, self-restraint, tranquility, pleasure, pain, birth, death, and fear and fearlessness,

अहिंसा समता तुष्टिस् तपो दानं यशो ऽयशः ।
भवन्ति भावा भूतानां मत्त एव पृथग्विधाः ॥
ahiṁsā samatā tuṣṭis
tapo dānaṁ yaśo 'yaśaḥ
bhavanti bhāvā bhūtānāṁ
matta eva pṛthagvidhāḥ

5. Non-violence, impartiality, contentment, austerity, charity, fame, disrepute, the manifold conditions of beings, arise from Me alone.

81 The first of these is intellect; then follow limitless wisdom, freedom from confusion, forbearance, forgiveness, and truth.
82 Then come tranquility and restraint, joy and grief, birth and destruction—all these exist in My nature.
83 O Arjuna, fear and fearlessness, harmlessness and equanimity, contentment, austerity, and charity,
84 Honor and disgrace, success and failure, all these moods which are found everywhere in all creatures emanate from Me.
85 Just as all people are different, think of these moods also in the same way. Some proceed from My wisdom, and some know nothing of Me.
86 Light and darkness are caused by the sun. When it rises light appears, and darkness comes when it sets.
87 Similarly, knowledge and ignorance of Me are due to creatures' destinies. For this reason, they are of different kinds.
88 O Arjuna, you should know that the whole world of sentient beings is involved in My nature.

महर्षयः सप्त पूर्वे चत्वारो मनवस् तथा
मद्भावा मानसा जाता येषां लोक इमाः प्रजाः ॥
maharṣayaḥ sapta pūrve
catvāro manavas tathā
madbhāvā mānasā jātā
yeṣāṁ loka imāḥ prajāḥ

6. The seven great seers of old, and also the four Manus, from whom have sprung these creatures of the world, originated from Me, born of My mind.

89 Now I will speak of eleven other manifestations of Myself, those which protect the created worlds and by whose power the worlds live.
90 There are the illustrious seven sages, Kashyapa and the others, most advanced in all

virtues and wisest among the sages.

91 I will mention fourteen Manus, of whom there are four main ones. Svayambhu is the chief of these.

92 O Arjuina, I conceived these eleven beings in My mind to conduct the affairs of the created worlds.

93 Before the order of mankind had evolved or individuality had developed, the group of primary elements were still undivided.

94 When these were created, they established the guardians of the worlds, and these created all the different groups of people.

95 These eleven are like kings, and the worlds are their subjects. Therefore, know that the manifestation of this whole world is Mine.

96 For example, first there is only a seed. From it there grows a stem, and branches shoot out of that.

97 From the main branches others appear, and the foliage grows from all of these.

98 Then the flowers and fruit develop. The whole tree grows in this way, and the seed is all this, if we consider it in the right way.

99 So in the beginning I alone was; then awareness of mind was born. The seven great rishis and the four Manus arose from that.

100 They created the guardians of the worlds, and these brought the various worlds into being. From the worlds, all mankind was created.

101 In this way, the whole universe has evolved from Me. Only through faith can a person realize this.

एतां विभूतिं योगं च मम यो वेत्ति तत्त्वतः ।
सो ऽविकम्पेन योगेन युज्यते नात्र संशयः ॥
etāṁ vibhūtiṁ yogaṁ ca
mama yo vetti tattvataḥ
so 'vikampena yogena
yujyate nātra saṁśayaḥ

7. He who knows in truth this, My manifested glory and power, is united with Me by unwavering yoga; of this there is no doubt.

अहं सर्वस्य प्रभवो मत्तः सर्वं प्रवर्तते ।
इति मत्वा भजन्ते मां बुधा भावसमन्विताः ॥
ahaṁ sarvasya prabhavo
mattaḥ sarvaṁ pravartate
iti matvā bhajante māṁ
budhā bhāvasamanvitāḥ

8. I am the origin of all; all proceeds from Me. Thinking thus, the intelligent ones, endowed with the faculty of meditation, worship Me.

102 O Arjuna, these are the aspects of My powers, which pervade the entire universe.

103 In this manner, from Brahma, the creator down to the ant, there is nothing but Me.

104 One who knows that this is true has attained the awakened state of wisdom, and is unaware of the illusion of distinctions between superior and inferior.

105 You should know, through the experience of oneness, that I Myself, these manifestations of Mine, and the different things contained in them are all one.

106 A person who is united with Me through the yoga of certainty has attained the goal. There is no doubt about this.

मच्चित्ता मद्गतप्राणा बोधयन्तः परस्परम् ।
कथयन्तश्च मां नित्यं तुष्यन्ति च रमान्ति च ॥
maccittā madgataprāṇā
bodhayantaḥ parasparam
kathayantaśca māṁ nityaṁ
tuṣyanti ca ramanti ca

9. Those who think of Me, who absorb their lives in Me, enlightening each other, and speaking of Me constantly, they are content and rejoice.

107 Just as if the sun were to encircle the sun with light, the moon embrace the moon, or two brooks of the same size meet,

108 Similarly, the streams of union with the Supreme meet. The quality of purity floats like leaves on the surface of the water. These devotees become like the image of Ganesh, seated in a group of four for discussion.

109 In their great delight, they leave the village of their bodies and begin to proclaim their joy in Me.

110 The great truth of the Absolute, which the Guru imparts to his disciples after withdrawing to a quiet place, these men proclaim like the clouds in heaven till it resounds.

111 Just as when the lotus bud opens it doesn't know how to keep its fragrance to itself, but offers it as a feast of fragrance to king and beggar alike,

112 Similarly, these enlightened beings speak of Me throughout the universe. In the joy of the telling they forget their tale, and in this forgetfulness they lose all awareness of body and soul.

113 In the fullness of their love, they know neither day nor night. They have become one with the perfect bliss of union with Me.

तेषां सततयुक्तानां भजतां प्रीतिपूर्वकम् ।
ददामि बुद्धियोगं तं येन माम् उपयान्ति ते ॥

teṣāṁ satatayuktānāṁ
bhajatāṁ prītipūrvakam
dadāmi buddhiyogaṁ taṁ
yena mām upayānti te

10. To those who are constantly steadfast, those who worship Me with love, I give the yoga of discrimination by which they come to Me.

114 They win for themselves the priceless gift, which I Myself grant them.
115 O Arjuna, compared with the path which they take, both heaven and final liberation are like a by-path.
116 That love which they have for Me is the gift I have to bestow, but they have made it their own even before I could grant it.
117 Therefore, all that remains to be done is to ensure that their love increases, and that the evil eye of death doesn't fall on them. This is what I always have to do.
118 O Arjuna, just as a mother follows her beloved child and watches over it lovingly while it plays,
119 And she turns into gold whatever game it wants to play, in the same way I encourage in them every kind of worship.
120 I take special delight in helping them along the path which brings them joyfully to Me.
121 I love all creatures that are devoted to Me as their only refuge. There are few lovers of this kind in My abode.
122 The two paths leading to heaven and to liberation have been made for them to travel. I Myself and My consort Lakshmi spend our time serving them.
123 But the supreme and selfless joy is reserved for those devotees who are united with Me through their loving devotion.
124 O Arjuna, I am so attached to them that I take them to Myself. These things shouldn't be revealed.

तेषाम् एवानुकम्पार्थम् अहम् अज्ञानजं तमः ।
नाशयाम्य् आत्मभावस्थो ज्ञानदीपेन भास्वता ॥

tesām evānukampārtham
aham ajñānajaṁ tamaḥ
nāśayāmy ātmabhāvastho
jñānadīpena bhāsvatā

11. Out of compassion for them, I, who dwell within their own beings, destroy the darkness born of ignorance with the shining lamp of knowledge.

125 Those who have made Me, the true Self, the only center of their lives and who think of nothing else but Me,
126 For those pure enlightened ones, I Myself am the torch bearer. I go before them with the torch of camphor.
127 I dispel the dense cloud of the night of ignorance, and I create the dawn for them.
128 When Krishna, who is supreme and the beloved of His faithful devotees, had spoken in this way, Arjuna said, My mind is at rest.

अर्जुन उवाच । *arjuna uvāca*

मरं ब्रह्मपरं धाम पवित्रं परमं भवान् ।
पुरुषं शाश्वतं दिव्यम् आदिदेवम् अजं विभुम् ॥

paraṁ brahma paraṁ dhāma
pavitraṁ paramaṁ bhavān
puruṣaṁ śāśvataṁ divyam
ādidevam ajaṁ vibhum

Arjuna spoke:
12. You are the supreme Brahman, the supreme abode, the supreme purifier, the eternal divine Spirit, the primal God, unborn and all-pervading.

129 O Lord, You have swept away the dust of worldly life, and I am freed from the pains of human birth and rebirth.
130 Today I have seen my spiritual birth and found my own true life. I am content.
131 Wisdom has been born, and the day of my good fortune has dawned, for I have received the grace of Your words from Your divine lips.
132 With the light of Your teaching the inner and outer darkness has been dispelled, and I see Your nature in its full reality.
133 You are the supreme Absolute, the resting place of the elements, the holiest abode, O Lord of all the worlds.
134 You are the highest of the three gods, the Spirit of the twenty-fifth principle, the divine One beyond all forms of matter.
135 You are without origin, O Lord, free from the grasp of birth and action. Today I have realized You.
136 You control this wheel of time, You govern

all life, and You rule over the cauldron of the universe. Now I understand this clearly.

आहुस् त्वाम् ऋषयः सर्वे देवर्षिर् नारदस् तथा ।
असितो देवलो व्यासः स्वयं चैव ब्रवीषि मे ॥

āhus tvām ṛṣayaḥ sarve
devarṣir nāradas tathā
asito devalo vyāsaḥ
svayaṁ cāiva bravīṣi me

13. Thus they call You, all the seers, the divine seer Narada, also Asita, Devala, and Vyasa, and You Yourself (now) tell me so.

137 In another way I see the greatness of this experience: the great sages of old have said this about You,

138 But through Your grace my heart understands the truth of all they taught.

139 Though Narada always came to us and sang of You, I merely enjoyed his singing, in spite of the fact that I didn't understand the meaning of his words.

140 If the sun shines on the homes of blind men, they feel its warmth, but how can they know its light?

141 Similarly, when the great sage sang of the Supreme, I enjoyed the sweetness of the melody but didn't understand anything else.

142 I also heard Asita and Devala speak of You, but then my mind was overpowered by the poison of sense desires.

143 Why mention others' names? Even when the great Vyasa came to us, he always spoke of Your nature.

144 His teachings were like a wish-fulfilling gem lying in the dark unnoticed, but when daylight comes it appears and we say it is here.

145 In this way, the teachings of Vyasa and other sages were a mine of precious truth for me, but they were wasted without You, O Krishna.

सर्वम् एतद् ऋतं मन्ये यन् मां वदसि केशव ।
न हि ते भगवन् व्यक्तिं विदुर् देवा न दानवाः ॥

sarvam etad ṛtaṁ manye
yan māṁ vadasi keśava
na hi te bhagavan vyaktiṁ
vidur devā na dānavāḥ

14. All this which You speak to me, Krishna, I believe to be true; indeed, neither the gods nor the demons, O Blessed one, know Your manifestation.

146 Now the rays of the sun of Your teachings have shone forth, and they have dispelled my ignorance of the paths that the sages spoke of.

147 Their teachings, the seeds of life, have fallen deep into the soil of my heart. Watered by Your grace, they have borne fruit in this conversation.

148 The discourse of Krishna has brought juice into the flowers, and these have given me delight.

149 The sayings of Narada and other saints are like rivers of devotion, and I am the ocean of the joy of this dialogue into which they flow.

150 O Guru, You have given to me what all the merit that I accumulated in past lives couldn't achieve.

151 I have often heard the elders speak of You, but until You bestowed Your grace on me, I couldn't understand anything.

152 When a person's fortune is favorable, whatever he undertakes prospers. Similarly, all that he hears or studies bears fruit through the Guru's grace.

153 A gardener spends his life working and tending his trees, but he sees the fruit only when spring comes.

154 When fever subsides, what is sweet tastes sweet again. Even medicine seems sweet when health returns.

155 Just as the senses, speech, and breath serve their purpose only when consciousness is active in the body,

156 Similarly, all scriptural study and yogic exercises can only bear fruit under the Guru's guidance.

157 When Arjuna realized this, he danced with the joy of conviction and said, O Lord, I know Your words are true.

158 O Blessed Lord, I have had the clearest realization that Your nature is beyond even the understanding of the gods and demons.

159 Now I realize that unless Your teaching is revealed to us, we can never understand it with our intelligence alone.

स्वयम् एवात्मना ऽत्मानं वेत्थ त्वं पुरुषोत्तम ।
भूतभावन भूतेश देवदेव जगत्पते ॥

svayam evātmanā 'tmānaṁ
vettha tvaṁ puruṣottama
bhūtabhāvana bhūteśa
devadeva jagatpate

15. Supreme Being, O Lord of the universe, You know Yourself through Yourself alone, highest of spirits, source of welfare of beings, Lord of beings, God of gods, O Lord of the universe.

160 Just as the sky is aware of its own vastness and the earth knows its own weight,
161 Similarly, You also know Yourself through Your omnipotence, O Krishna! The Vedas boast in vain of their knowledge of You.
162 How can the speed of the mind be outrun, or the wind be measured in feet? How can the primal void be crossed by swimming with human arms?
163 It is the same with the knowledge of You; there is no one who can grasp it. You alone are able to impart knowledge of Yourself.
164 You alone know Yourself and are able to reveal Yourself to others, so wipe from my brow once and for all the sweat of my desire to know.
165 Have You heard me, O Creator of all beings? You are like a lion to the elephant of worldly existence, and are revered by all gods and deities, O Lord of the universe.
166 If we see Your greatness, we know that we are not worthy to stand before You. Because of this unworthiness we are afraid to approach You, yet we have no other way.
167 Everywhere the oceans and rivers are full, but to the chataka bird they seem dry, for it only drinks when rain falls from the clouds.
168 Similarly, there are many teachers, O Krishna, but You alone are our refuge. Describe to me then, Your divine manifestations.

वक्तुम् अर्हस्य् अशेषेण दिव्या ह्य् आत्मविभूतयः ।
याभिर् विभूतिभिर् लोकान् इमांस् त्वं व्याप्य तिष्ठसि ॥
vaktum arhasy aśeṣeṇa
divyā hy ātmavibhūtayaḥ
yābhir vibhūtibhir lokān
imāṁs tvam vyāpya tiṣṭhasi

16. Please describe without reserve the divine self-manifestations by which You pervade these worlds, and abide in them.

169 Show me those manifestations of Yours which are most permeated with Your divinity.
170 O Krishna, reveal to me those principal manifestations which pervade all the worlds.

कथं विद्याम् अहं योगिंस् त्वां सदा परिचिन्तयन् ।
केषुकेषु च भावेषु चिन्त्यो ऽसि भगवन् मया ॥
kathaṁ vidyām ahaṁ yogiṅs
tvāṁ sadā paricintayan
keṣukeṣu ca bhāveṣu
cintyo 'si bhagavan mayā

17. How may I know You, O Yogin, constantly meditating on You? And in what various aspects of being are You to be thought of by me, O Blessed One?

171 How may I know You? If I were to say that You are everything, meditation on You would be impossible.
172 So describe to me once more in detail those manifestations that You referred to before.
173 Speak to me clearly of them all, so that I won't have any difficulty in meditating on You in them.

विस्तरेणात्मनो योगं विभूतिं च जनार्दन ।
भूयः कथय तृप्तिर् हि शृण्वतो नास्ति मे ऽमृतम् ॥
vistareṇātmano yogaṁ
vibhūtiṁ ca janārdana
bhūyaḥ kathaya tṛptir hi
śṛṇvato nāsti me 'mṛtam

18. Explain to me further in detail Your power and manifestation, O Krishna. I am never satiated with hearing Your nectar-like words.

174 O Lord of creation, I pray that You will tell me of all those manifestations of Yours that I have asked You about. If you ask why I'm repeating this request,
175 I will reply, don't misunderstand this, O Krishna. When a person is drinking nectar, he can never have enough.
176 After all, through fear of death the gods drank the nectar which they obtained from the same source as the Kalakuta poison, and yet fourteen lifetimes of Indra passed away in one day of Brahma.
177 Even so, anyone who thinks that this liquid from the Milky Ocean resembles nectar has such faith in it that he cannot refuse it.
178 It is self-existent and eternal, and can be easily obtained without having to turn Mount Mandara or churn the Milky Ocean.
179 It is neither liquid nor solid, it has no distinct taste, and anyone who merely remembers it can obtain it.
180 As soon as a person tastes its sweetness, earthly existence becomes meaningless for him, and he becomes immortal.
181 There is no further mention of birth and death, and he experiences the highest bliss throughout his whole being.

182 When by good fortune he tastes it, it leads him at once to Self-realization. Now when You Yourself give this to me, I cannot refuse it.

183 Your name is a great delight to me, Your acquaintance has become friendship, and besides this You are pleased to talk with me.

184 With what can I compare this joy? I cannot speak because of my delight. But this much I know: I would like You to repeat what You have said.

185 Does the sun ever grow stale? Does the moon ever shrink? Do the flowing waters of the Ganges ever become unclean?

186 Hearing what You have spoken with Your lips is for us like seeing the form of God. Today we are enjoying the fragrance of the flowers of sandalwood.

187 Krishna swayed with pleasure at Arjuna's words and thought, His heart is a vessel for the wisdom of devotion.

188 In the joy of His loved one, affection for Arjuna welled up in His heart but He controlled it. Then what did Krishna say?

श्रीभगवान् उवाच । *śrībhagavān uvāca*

हन्त ते कथयिष्यामि दिव्या ह्य् आत्मविभूतयः ।
प्राधान्यतः कुरुश्रेष्ठ नास्त्य् अन्तो विस्तरस्य मे ॥
hanta te kathayiṣyāmi
divyā hy ātmavibhūtayaḥ
prādhānyataḥ kuruśreṣṭha
nāsty anto vistarasya me

The Blessed Lord spoke:
19. Listen! I shall explain to you My divine self-manifestations; those only that are prominent, for there is no end to My extent.

189 When you know this, you will know everything, O Arjuna, just as a person who holds a seed in his hand holds the entire tree.

190 When a person has a garden, he may easily get flowers. Similarly, if you see all these manifestations, you can perceive the whole universe.

191 Knowing well that He Himself was the Father of the father of all, and yet at the time forgetting it, Krishna said, O Arjuna, My father, you have done well!

192 It is no surprise that He called Arjuna father, for wasn't he actually the son of Nanda?

193 Let this be. Such things are due to great love. Then He said, O Arjuna, listen to what I am about to say.

194 Those manifestations of Mine that you have asked Me about are countless. Although they are Mine, even I cannot keep track of them.

195 I Myself don't know clearly My own nature or how great I am. Listen while I tell you of My principal manifestations.

196 Truly, O Arjuna, there is no limit to everything that emanates from Me. I even contain the expanse of the heavens.

अहम् आत्मा गुडाकेश सर्वभूताशयस्थितः ।
अहम् आदिश्च मध्यं च भूतानाम् अन्त एव च ॥
aham ātmā guḍākeśa
sarvabhūtāśayasthitaḥ
aham ādiśca madhyaṁ ca
bhūtānām anta eva ca

20. I am the Self, Arjuna, abiding in the heart of all beings; and I am the beginning and the middle of beings, and the end as well.

197 Listen, O Arjuna. I am the Self in each and every created being.

198 I am enshrined within their hearts, and I am also like a sheath around them. I am the beginning, the middle, and the end of all.

199 Just as the sky surrounds the clouds above, below, and on all sides, and they are both of the sky and in it,

200 And when they disappear they merge with it, similarly, I am the origin, the existence, and the end of all creatures.

201 In this way, you may know My manifold and all-pervasive Being through My manifestations. Listen with your heart, with full attention.

आदित्यानाम् अहं विष्णुर् ज्योतिषां रविर् अंशुमान् ।
मरीचिर् मरुताम् अस्मि नक्षत्राणाम् अहं शशी ॥
ādityānām ahaṁ viṣṇur
jyotiṣāṁ ravir aṁśuman
marīci marutām asmi
nakṣatrāṇām ahaṁ śaśī

21. Of the Adityas, I am Vishnu; of lights, the radiant sun; I am Marichi of the Maruts; among the heavenly bodies I am the moon.

202 With these words Lord Krishna continued, Among the heavenly deities I am Vishnu, among the radiant worlds of light I am the sun,

203 Among the companies of winds I am Marichi, and of all the heavenly bodies I am the moon.

वेदानां सामवेदो ऽस्मि देवानाम् अस्मि वासवः ।
इन्द्रियाणाम् मनश्चास्मि भूतानाम् अस्मि चेतना ॥

vedānāṁ sāmavedo 'smi
devānām asmi vāsavaḥ
indriyāṇām manaścāsmi
bhūtānām asmi cetanā

22. And of the Rudras, I am Shankara; I am Kubera of the Yaksas and Rakshasas; I am fire of the Vasus and the Meru of mountains.

204 Among all the Rudras I am Shankara, the enemy of the god of love. Have no doubt about this.

205 Among the Yakshas and Rakshasas I am wealthy Kubera, friend of Shambhu. I, Krishna, say this.

206 Among the eight Vasus, know that I am fire, and I am Meru among the high-peaked mountains.

रुद्राणां शंकरश्चास्मि वित्तेशो यक्षरक्षसाम् ।
वसूनां पावकश्चास्मि मेरुः शिखरिणाम् अहम् ॥

rudrāṇām śaṁkaraścāsmi
vitteśo yakṣarakṣasām
vasūnāṁ pāvakaścāsmi
meruḥ śikhariṇām aham

23. Of the Vedas, I am the Sama Veda; of the gods, I am Vasava; and of the senses, I am the mind, I am the consciousness of beings.

207 Of the Vedas I am the Sama Veda. Among the gods I am known as the great Indra.

208 Of the senses I am the eleventh, the mind, and of every living creature I am the living spirit.

पुरोधसां च मुख्यं मां विद्धि पार्थ बृहस्पतिम् ।
सेनानीनाम् अहं स्कन्दः सरसाम् अस्मि सागरः ॥

purodhasāṁ ca mukhyaṁ māṁ
viddhi pārtha bṛhaspatim
senānīnām ahaṁ skandaḥ
sarasām 'asmi sāgaraḥ

24. Know that I am the chief of household priests, Brihaspati, Arjuna; of the commanders of armies, I am Skanda; of bodies of water, I am the ocean.

महर्षीणां भृगुर् अहं गिराम् अस्म्य् एकम् अक्षरम् ।
यज्ञानां जपयज्ञो ऽस्मि स्थावराणां हिमालयः ॥

maharṣīṇāṁ bhṛgur ahaṁ
girām asmy ekam akṣaram
yajñānāṁ japayajño 'smi
sthāvarāṇaṁ himālayaḥ

25. Of the great seers, I am Bhrigu; of words, I am the single syllable "Om;" of sacrifices, I am japa (silent repetition); of immovable things, the Himalayas.

209 I am Brihaspati, the prince among all priests, ministering to the heavenly throne, the primal storehouse of all knowledge.

210 O Arjuna, of all the generals in the three worlds I am Skanda, who was born of the union of fire with Shiva's semen in Krittika.

211 Of all bodies of water, I am that great store of water, the ocean. Of the great sages I am Bhrigu, the treasure house of austerity.

212 Among all speech I am that sacred syllable which contains the highest Truth. I, Krishna, say this.

213 Among all the forms of worship in this world, I am the repetition of God's names. Having abandoned action, I give rise to action and other forms of religious activities.

214 Of all immovable mountains, I am the most holy Himalayas, said Krishna.

अश्वत्थः सर्ववृक्षाणां देवर्षीणां च नारद ।
गन्धर्वाणां चित्ररथः सिद्धानां कपिलो मुनिः ॥

aśvatthaḥ sarvavṛkṣāṇāṁ
devarṣīṇāṁ ca nārada
gandharvāṇāṁ citrarathaḥ
siddhānāṁ kapilo muniḥ

26. Among all trees, I am the sacred fig tree; and of the divine seers, Narada; and of the Gandharvas, Chitraratha; and of the perfected, Kapila the sage.

उच्चैःश्रवसम् अश्वानां विद्ध माम् अमृतोद्भवम् ।
ऐरावतं गजेन्द्राणां नराणां च नराधिपम् ॥

uccāiḥśravasam aśvānāṁ
viddhi mām amṛtodbhavam
āirāvataṁ gajendrāṇāṁ
narāṇāṁ ca narādhipam

27. Know that I am Ucchaishravas of horses, born of nectar; Airavata of princely elephants; and of men, the king.

215 Among all trees such as the *kalpa*, *parijata*, and sandalwood, well known for their qualities, I am the *ashwattha* or fig tree.

216 O Arjuna, among all the heavenly sages, know that I am Narada; and of all the celestial singers I am Chitraratha.

217 O Arjuna, I am the chief of all enlightened beings, the venerable Kapila. Among all horses I am Ucchaishravas.

218 Of elephants, which are the adornment of

kings, I am Airavata, churned out of the Milky Ocean by the gods.

219 Among men, My special manifestation is the king, whom all people serve as his subjects.

आयुधानाम् अहं वज्रं धेनूनाम् अस्मि कामधुक् ।
प्रजनश्चास्मि कन्दर्पः सर्पाणाम् अस्मि वासुकिः ॥

āyudhānām ahaṁ vajraṁ
dhenūnām asmi kāmadhuk
prajanaścāsmi kandarpaḥ
sarpāṇām asmi vāsukiḥ

28. Of weapons, I am the thunderbolt; of cows, I am the wish-fulfilling cow; I am the progenitor Kandarpa; and of serpents, I am Vasuki.

अनन्तश्चास्मि नागानां वरुणो यादसाम् अहम् ।
पितॄणाम् अर्यमा चास्मि यमः संयमताम् अहम् ॥

anantaścāsmi nāgānāṁ
varuṇo yādasām aham
pitṝṇām aryamā cāsmi
yamaḥ saṁyamatām aham

29. I am Ananta of the Nagas; Varuna of the water creatures; of the ancestors, I am Aryaman; and Yama of the controllers.

220 O Arjuna, of all great weapons I am the thunderbolt, the weapon of Indra, performer of a hundred sacrifices.

221 Of cows I am the cow of plenty, of unlimited powers. Of progenitors, know that I am Madana.

222 Of all the serpents I am the foremost, Vasuki. Of the nagas I am Ananta.

223 Among those who inhabit the waters I am Varuna, the consort of the western quarter. I, Krishna, say this.

224 Of the ancestors I am Aryama, the divine forefather. I tell you this truly, O Arjuna.

225 Of those who record the virtues and vices of men, who search their hearts, and grant them liberation according to their deeds,

226 Of those who exercise control over mankind, I am Yama, the witness of men's deeds, I, Krishna, say this to you, O Arjuna.

प्रह्लादश्चास्मि दैत्यानां कालः कलयताम् अहम् ।
मृगाणां च मृगेन्द्रोऽहं वैनतेयश्च पक्षिणाम् ॥

prahlādaścāsmi dāityānāṁ
kālaḥ kalayatām aham
mṛgāṇāṁ ca mṛgendro 'haṁ
vāinateyaśca pakṣiṇām

30. I am Prahlada of the demons; time, of the calculators; of the beasts, I am the lion; and Garuda, of the birds.

227 I am Prahlada, of the race of demons. For this reason, he was never tainted by hatred or other demoniacal vices.

228 Among all those who persecute, I am death. Among all beasts, the lion is My manifestation.

229 Of all birds, know that I am Garuda. This is why he can carry Me safely on his back.

पवनः पवताम् अस्मि रामः शस्त्रभृताम् अहम् ।
झषानां मकरश्चास्मि स्रोतसाम् अस्मि जाह्नवी ॥

pavanaḥ pavatām asmi
rāmaḥ śastrabhṛtām aham
jhaṣānāṁ makaraścāsmi
srotasām asmi jāhnavś

31. Of purifiers, I am the wind; Rama of the warriors; of the sea monsters I am the alligators; and of rivers I am the Ganges.

230 O Arjuna, of those that can cross the world in a moment of time, I am that which can circle the earth in one leap.

231 Of all swiftly moving things, I am the wind. Among all who bear weapons, I am Rama.

232 When righteousness was in danger, He transformed Himself into a bow to defend it. In Treta Yuga He made the glory of success his goal.

233 Then, standing on the summit of Mount Suvela, He boldly presented Ravana's ten heads as an offering to those in heaven who were praying for His victory.

234 Rama restored to the gods their rightful dignity and reestablished righteousness, rising as the sun of the great Solar race.

235 Among all the bearers of weapons, I am Rama, consort of Janaki. Among all the creatures dwelling in the water, I am the alligator.

236 Of all rivers I am the Ganges, brought down from heaven by Bhagiratha, swallowed by Janhu, and brought forth again from his torn thigh.

237 O Arjuna, among all rivers, know that I am the Ganges, the only river of the three worlds.

सर्गाणाम् आदिर् अन्तश्च मध्यं चैवाहम् अर्जुन ।
अध्यात्मविद्या विद्यानां वादः प्रवदताम् अहम् ॥

sargāṇām ādir antaśca
madhyaṁ cāivāham arjuna
adhyātmavidyā vidyānāṁ
vādaḥ pravadatām aham

32. Of creations I am the beginning and the end, and also the middle, O Arjuna; of all knowledge, the knowledge of the supreme Self. I am the logic of those who debate.

238 If I tried to name all My various manifestations in the universe, a thousand births wouldn't be enough to mention even half.

अक्षराणाम् अकारो ऽस्मि द्वन्द्वः सामासिकस्य च ।
अहम् एवाक्षयः कालो धाताहं विश्वतोमुखः ॥

akṣarāṇām akāro 'smi
dvandvaḥ sāmāsikasya ca
aham evākṣayaḥ kālo
dhātāhaṁ viśvatomukhaḥ

33. Of letters I am the letter A, and the dual of compound words; I alone am infinite time; I am the Establisher, facing in all directions (i.e. omniscient).

239 If a person wanted to gather together all the stars, he would have to enclose the heavens in a cloth.
240 If he wished to count all the atoms composing the earth, he would have to hold it under his arm. Similarly, anyone who wishes to see all of My manifestations must first know Me.
241 If a person wanted to grasp all the branches, flowers, and fruit of a tree at the same moment, he would have to uproot it.
242 In the same way, if My different manifestations are to be known in their entirety, My faultless nature must first be known.
243 Otherwise, how many of these various forms can you listen to? Therefore, know once and for all, O Arjuna, that everything is truly Me.
244 O Arjuna, I am beginning, the middle, and the end of all creation, just as thread is woven throughout the warp and the woof of cloth.
245 When a person understands that I pervade everything, why does he need to know My separate manifestations? You are not yet worthy to realize this.
246 So, O Arjuna, since you have asked Me, listen while I tell you more of those manifestations. Of all the branches of knowledge, I am the knowledge of the Self.
247 Among speakers I am the discourse which has no end, in spite of the principles laid down in the traditional teachings.
248 It grows as the discussion develops, it adds strength to the power of imagination in all who listen, and adds value to the speaker's words.
249 I, Krishna, say this. I am the argument in all controversy. Of all letters I am the pure A.
250 Of compounds, know that I am the *dvandva*. I am the one who, as death, seizes all, from the smallest gnat to the creator himself.
251 O Arjuna, grasping the light of universal dissolution, I am the one who swallows up the winds, and into whose belly all space is absorbed.
252 I, the consort of Lakshmi, am death, the infinite, and again I recreate everything.

मृत्युः सर्वहरश्चाहम् उद्भवश्च भविष्यताम् ।
कीर्तिः श्रीर् वाक् च नारीणां स्मृतिर् मेधा धृतिः क्षमा ॥

mṛtyuḥ sarvaharaścaham
udbhavaśca bhaviṣyatām
kīrtiḥ śrīr vāk ca nārīṇām
smṛtir medhā dhṛtiḥ kṣamā

34. I am all-destroying death, and the origin of those things that are yet to be. Among the feminine qualities, I am fame, prosperity, speech, memory, wisdom, courage, and patience.

253 I sustain all created things; I am their very life. And at the end, when I destroy them all, I am death. Listen to this.
254 Now among feminine qualities, I have seven manifestations. Listen carefully, and I will tell you about them.
255 O Arjuna, fame, which is ever new, is the embodiment of Me. I am also generosity with wealth.
256 In all people I am intelligence accompanied by steadiness, and I am also universal fortitude and forbearance.
257 I am these seven feminine qualities. So said Krishna, who is like the lion to the elephant of earthly experience.

बृहत्साम तथा साम्नां गायत्री छन्दसाम् अहम् ।
मासानां मार्गशीर्षो ऽहम् ऋतूनां कुसुमाकरः ॥

bṛhatsāma tathā sāmnāṁ
gāyatrī chandasām aham
māsānāṁ mārgaśīrṣo 'ham
ṛtūnāṁ kusumākaraḥ

35. Of chants I am the Brihatsaman; of meters I am the Gayatri; of months, the Marga-shirsha; and of seasons, the spring, abounding with flowers.

258 O Beloved, of the wealth of Vedic hymns I am the much loved Brihatsaman. I, the Lord of Lakshmi, say this.

259 Of all meters, the Gayatri is My own form. Know this for certain.

260 Of months I am Margashirsha, and of seasons I am the flower-laden spring. I, Krishna, say this.

द्यूतं छलयताम् अस्मि तेजस् तेजस्विनाम् अहम् ।
जयो ऽस्मि व्यवसायो ऽस्मि सत्त्वं सत्त्ववताम् अहम् ॥
dyūtaṁ chalayatām asmi
tejas tejasvinām aham
jayo 'smi vyavasāyo 'smi
sattvaṁ sattvavatām aham

36. I am the gambling of the dishonest, the splendor of the splendid; I am victory, I am effort, I am the goodness of the good.

वृष्णीनां वासुदेवो ऽस्मि पाण्डवानां धनंजयः ।
मुनीनाम् अप्य् अहं व्यासः कवीनाम् उशना कविः ॥
vṛṣṇīnām vāsudevo 'smi
pāṇḍavānāṁ dhanamjayaḥ
munīnām apy ahaṁ vyāsaḥ
kavīnām uśanā kaviḥ

37. Of the Vrishnis, I am Vasudeva; of the sons of Pandu, Arjuna; of the sages, moreover, I am Vyasa; of poets, the poet Ushana.

261 O wise Arjuna, among all gambling I am the dice. For this reason, no one should be turned away if there is theft in the marketplace.

262 I am the light of all brilliant things; believe this. In all undertakings I am success.

263 My nature is at the heart of all dealings where justice prevails, said the Lord of all gods.

264 I am the goodness in all good things, and I am the glory of all the Yadavas. I, Krishna, say this.

265 I am He who was born to satisfy the wish of Devaki and Vasudeva, who went to Gokula to please the Gopis, and who, nursing at her breast, drew the life force out of Putana with her milk.

266 I am He who even in His boyhood rid the earth of demons, and who, holding up the Govardhana Mountain in His hand, humbled the greatness of Indra.

267 I am He who destroyed the serpent piercing the heart of Kalindi, who saved Gokula from being burned, and who, for the sake of the cattle, drove Brahma mad.

268 I am He who in early youth easily destroyed such huge monsters as Kansa.

269 What more shall I say about this? You yourself have seen and heard it all. But still, you should know that I have manifested among the Yadavas.

270 Of all the Pandavas of the Lunar race, I am you, Arjuna. Because of this, our friendship endures.

271 Among the sages I am Vyasa, and of the great poets I am Ushana, the abode of all fortitude, said the Lord of the Yadavas.

दण्डो दमयताम् अस्मि नीतिर् अस्मि जिगीषताम् ।
मौनं चैवास्मि गुह्यानां ज्ञानं ज्ञानवताम् अहम् ॥
daṇḍo damayatām asmi
nītir asmi jigīṣatām
māunaṁ cāivāsmi guhyānāṁ
jñānaṁ jñānavatām aham

38. Of punishers, I am the scepter, and I am the guidance of those desirous of victory; of secrets, I am silence and the knowledge of the wise.

272 Of all instruments of punishment I am the scepter, which restrains all, from the smallest insect to the creator himself.

273 Of all the sciences which decide between good and evil and uphold righteousness, I am the science of ethics.

274 O My friend, I am the silence in every secret thing. Even the creator remains ignorant in the presence of those who don't speak.

275 Understand that I am the knowledge of those who know. But let this be enough. There is no end to these manifestations.

यच् चापि सर्वभूतानां बीजं तद् अहम् अर्जुन ।
न तद् अस्ति विना यत् स्यान् मया भूतं चराचरम् ॥
yac cāpi sarvabhūtānāṁ
bījaṁ tad aham arjuna
na tad asti vinā yat syān
mayā bhūtaṁ carācaram

39. And also I am that which is the seed of all creatures, Arjuna; there is nothing that could exist without existing through Me, whether moving or not moving.

276 Can you count the streams of rain, O Arjuna, or the number of blades of grass on the earth?

277 Just as no one can tell how many billows the ocean has, in the same way My forms are countless.

नान्तो ऽस्ति मम दिव्यानां विभूतीनां परंतप ।
एष तूद्देशतः प्रोक्तो विभूतेर् विस्तरो मया ॥
nānto 'sti mama divyānāṁ

vibhūtīnāṁ paraṁtapa
eṣa tūddeśataḥ prokto
vibhūter vistaro mayā

40. There is no end to My divine manifestations, Arjuna. This has been declared by Me as an example of the extent of My manifestations.

278 O Arjuna, I have now told you about seventy-five of my principal manifestations, yet it seems very little.
279 It is impossible to keep count of My manifestations. Could you hear them all, or could I tell them?
280 For this reason, I will now reveal to you My great secret: I am the seed from which all created beings arise and grow.
281 Therefore, you should regard Me as everything that is, without considering such concepts as great or small, high or low.
282 Listen now to one more simple sign by which you can recognize a manifestation of Me.

यद् यद् विभूतिमत् सत्त्वं श्रीमद् ऊर्जितम् एव वा ।
तत् तद् एवावगच्छ त्वं मम तेजोंऽशसंभवम् ॥
yad yad vibhūtimat sattvaṁ
śrīmad ūrjitam eva vā
tat tad evāvagaccha tvaṁ
mama tejo'ṁśasaṁbhavam

41. Whatever manifested being that is glorious and vigorous, indeed, understand that in every case he originates from a fraction of My splendor.

283 O Arjuna, wherever wealth and compassion are found together, you should know that they are part of Me.
284 Just as there is only one sun in the heavens, yet its light shines throughout all worlds, similarly, all people obey My law alone.
285 Don't say that He is alone nor call Him poor. Does the cow of plenty have to carry anything with her in order to satisfy desires?
286 She immediately begins to bring forth whatever a person may ask at any time. In the same way all powers are granted to Me.
287 O Arjuna, by this sign you may know that those people whose commands are obeyed by all are manifestations of Me.

अथवा बहुनैतेन किं ज्ञातेन तवार्जुन ।
विष्टभ्याहम् इदं कृत्स्नम् एकांशेन स्थितो जगत् ॥
athavā bahunāitena
kiṁ jñātena tavārjuna
viṣṭabhyāham idaṁ kṛtsnam
ekāṁśena sthito jagat

42. But what is this extensive knowledge to you, Arjuna? I support this entire universe constantly with a single fraction of Myself.

288 It is wrong to think that one is common and another good, for I alone pervade the entire universe.
289 Why should we imagine distinctions such as ordinary or good? Why let our minds be unnecessarily contaminated by the thought of differences?
290 What need is there to churn butter? Why reduce nectar by pressing it? Is there such a thing as left or right in a shower of rain?
291 We could ruin our sight by looking for the front or the back of the sun. Similarly, in My form there is no such thing as general and particular.
292 My manifestations are infinite. How will you measure My limitless form? You already know enough, O Arjuna.
293 This universe is permeated with one fragment of Myself; so setting aside all distinctions, worship Me one-pointedly.
294 So spoke the glorious Lord Krishna, who is like spring in the garden of the wise, the beloved of the dispassionate.
295 Then Arjuna said, O Lord, You spoke inconsistently when You said that we who must abandon difference are separate from that difference.
296 Does the sun tell the earth to drive away darkness? But it would be presumptuous to call You thoughtless.
297 O Lord, when a person utters Your name or hears it even once, all idea of separateness vanishes from his mind.
298 Can a person who is in the center of the moon feel heat? You have spoken impetuously, O Krishna.
299 The Lord was pleased. He embraced Arjuna closely and said, Beloved, don't be angry at what I say.
300 I have told you about My manifestations in terms of diversity in order to see whether you have understood unity.
301 In order to know this, I spoke for a moment in terms of outer appearances. Then you understood My manifestations.
302 Arjuna said, O Lord, You truly know. I see

that You have brought into being the whole universe.

303 When Sanjaya told Dhritarashtra that Arjuna had experienced Self-realization, the king remained unmoved.

304 Sanjaya, with a sad heart, said to himself, Isn't it strange that he should throw away such good fortune? I thought that he had good understanding, but now I find him to be blind inwardly as well as outwardly.

305 But let's leave what Sanjaya said. Arjuna's respect for nonduality had increased so much that he was eager to hear more.

306 Following this desire to see with his own eyes what he had experienced in his heart, the thought arose in his mind

307 That he should perceive with his eyes Krishna's cosmic form. It was his great good fortune which brought him this longing.

308 Arjuna is like a branch of the wish-fulfilling tree, which bears no sterile flowers. Whatever he may ask for, Krishna will surely grant him.

309 Krishna, who became poison for the sake of Prahlada, has been given to Arjuna as his Guru.

310 In the next chapter, I will describe the manner in which Arjuna asks to see Krishna's cosmic form. So says Jnanadeva, the disciple of Nivritti.

11

THE VISION OF THE COSMIC FORM

SALUTATIONS to Lord Ganesh!

1 Now in the eleventh chapter, the story in which Arjuna will experience Krishna's cosmic form is permeated by two of the feelings.

2 In it, the feeling of wonder has come as a guest to the house of tranquility, and the other feelings have received the honor of being invited to the feast.

3 Just as at the wedding of a bride and bridegroom, the relatives wear fine clothes and jewelry, similarly, all the feelings are carried in the procession on the palanquin of the Marathi language.

4 But here tranquility and wonder predominate, like Hari and Hara affectionately embracing each other.

5 These two feelings are united here, just as on the day of the new moon the orbs of the sun and moon meet.

6 The two feelings flow together like the confluence of the Ganges and the Jamuna rivers, so that the whole world may bathe there and be purified.

7 The *Gita* is the hidden stream of Saraswati, and the other two feelings are like the two visible rivers. In this way, O fathers, they form this great triple confluence.

8 It is easy to enter this holy place by means of the ear. Jnanadeva says, The grace of my Guru has brought this about.

9 Overcoming the difficult ascent of the steep banks of Sanskrit, Nivrittideva, the treasure house of all righteousness, has made a ladder of Marathi words

10 So that anyone can bathe here and behold Krishna's cosmic form, just as He can be seen at Prayaga. In this way, one can be freed from worldly existence.

11 I have said enough. The feelings are fully developed here, and the highest delight of hearing is given to the world.

12 It isn't enough to say that the feelings of tranquility and wonder can clearly be seen here, for all the others acquire added beauty. Here is the highest bliss.

13 This eleventh chapter is the Lord's resting place, and Arjuna is the most fortunate for he has arrived here.

14 But why should I say that Arjuna alone is so fortunate? This opportunity is available today to everyone, now that the *Gita* is explained here in Marathi.

15 So now listen to my request that all you good people should pay close attention.

16 It is improper for me to be so familiar in your presence, but you must treat me lovingly as your own child.

17 After all, if we teach a parrot and it learns well, we nod in approval. Isn't a mother delighted when her child does as she tells it?

18 O masters, whatever I can say is only what you yourselves have taught me, so you should certainly listen to it.

19 You yourselves have planted this sweet tree of knowledge, so you should nourish it with the nectar of attention.

20 Then it will produce the flowers of the feelings and bear the fruit of meaning. In this way, the whole world will benefit through your devotion.

21 Everyone was pleased with these words and exclaimed, We're delighted! You have done well.

22 Then the disciple of Nivritti said, How can an ordinary man like me tell of the dialogue between Krishna and Arjuna? You must help me tell it.

23 Ravana's defeat was brought about by the monkeys, eaters of the forest leaves. Couldn't

Arjuna alone defeat the eleven armies of the Kauravas?

24 Can it be said that whatever a competent person can do, others cannot? So you saints can enable me to explain the *Gita*.

25 Please listen now to this clear explanation of the *Gita*, which comes from the mouth of Lord Krishna.

26 Blessed is the *Gita*, for Krishna who is spoken of in the Vedas, is its author.

27 How can I describe the greatness of something which even Shambhu failed to grasp? You should greet that with a reverent heart.

28 Now listen to the way in which Arjuna, fixing his gaze on the cosmic form of the Supreme Being, began to speak about it.

29 All things are a manifestation of the Almighty. Arjuna now wished to see with his own eyes the experience of his beloved Lord.

30 Being hesitant to express his wish to the Lord, how can he suddenly ask to be shown the mystery of the cosmic form?

31 Arjuna said, How can I mention that which not even a loved one has ever asked for?

32 Although I am His dear friend, am I closer to Him than His mother? Yet even she was afraid to speak to Him about this.

33 However deep my devotion to Him may have been, can it be compared with that of Garuda? But he didn't dare to speak of this either.

34 Am I closer to Him than Sanaka and the other sages? Yet they didn't dare ask for this. Am I dearer to Him than the women of Gokula?

35 Some failed to recognize Him, misled by His youthful form. Another underwent the experience of birth, yet wasn't granted the vision. It hasn't been revealed to anyone.

36 The mystery of His Being, hidden deep within His heart, is profound. How can I be impatient and demand this?

37 Nevertheless, if I don't ask for it, there will be no joy in my heart, perhaps I cannot even go on living.

38 I will approach it tentatively and will do whatever the Lord wishes. So Arjuna, with some fear, began to speak.

39 But he spoke in such a way that the Lord, after answering him once or twice, would reveal His divine form to him without reservation.

40 A cow, moved by love, stands up when she sees her calf. Won't her milk flow as soon as its mouth touches her udders?

41 The Lord ran to help the Pandavas in the forest as soon as He heard their name. Will He disappoint Arjuna when he asks Him about this?

42 The Lord is the very incarnation of love, and Arjuna has aroused this love. When these two come together, how can any sense of difference remain?

43 Therefore, as soon as Arjuna speaks, the Lord will immediately manifest His cosmic form. Now I ask you to listen.

अर्जुन उवाच । *arjuna uvāca*

मदनुग्रहाय परम गुह्यम् अध्यात्मसंज्ञितम् ।
यत् त्वयोक्तं वचस् तेन मोहो ऽयं विगतो मम ॥
madanugrahāya paramam
guhyam adhyātmasaṁjñitaṁ
yat tvayoktaṁ vacas tena
moho 'yam vigato mama

Arjuna spoke:
1. As a favor to me, You have spoken about the highest secret known as the supreme Self. With this my delusion is gone.

44 Then Arjuna said to the Lord, O Compassionate One, for my sake You have spoken to me of what is inexpressible.

45 When the elements had been reabsorbed into the Absolute, and beings and matter no longer existed, then God alone remained. That is the ultimate end.

46 It is this knowledge which You have kept hidden within the depths of Your heart like a miser, and which was withheld even from the Vedas.

47 You have opened Your heart to me today. To gain this secret, Shankar laid aside His glory.

48 O Lord, You have granted this to me in a moment, yet how can I say that I am one with You?

49 When You saw that I was submerged in the flood of the great illusion, You, Krishna, plunged into it and rescued me.

50 There is no other beside You in the whole world, but just look at our fate—we imagined ourselves as existing apart from You.

51 Filled with pride in my personality, I thought that I was Arjuna and said that the Kauravas were my relatives.

52 In addition, I had an evil dream that I would

kill them. Then what would I do? But the Lord woke me from my sleep.

53 It was as though I had abandoned a celestial home and was trying to drink water from a mirage, O Krishna.

54 Or it was as though a person touched a snake made of cloth and could actually feel waves of its poison. O Krishna, You saved the soul of one who was about to die in a similar delusion.

55 A lion, not recognizing its own shadow, thinks it sees another lion and may jump into a well. O Krishna, You have saved me from a similar plight.

56 Until now I had resolved not to fight against my kinsmen, even if all the seven seas should merge into one.

57 Even if the whole world were submerged and the skies crashed down, still I wouldn't fight with my kinsmen.

58 In this way, in an excess of egoism, I had leapt into the waters of self-will. It is good that You were near.Otherwise,who would have saved me?

59 Though I am no one, I thought I was a person and called people my relatives who in reality didn't exist. You have saved me from this great madness.

60 You have already rescued me from burning in a fire of wax, but then only the body was in danger. Now it is a fire of another kind, and my soul is also threatened.

61 The Hiranyaksha of wrong understanding carried away under his arm the earth of my reason to a cave in the ocean of infatuation.

62 Through Your power, my reason has been restored to me. For this, You had to take another incarnation as the boar.

63 In this way, Your deeds on my behalf have been endless. How can I describe them all with only one voice? You gave Your very life for my sake.

64 However, none of this has been in vain, for You have overcome everything, O Lord. You have completely dispelled my illusion.

65 How could a person have anything to do with illusion if Your eyes, which are like lotuses in a lake of joy, have become for him the temples of Your grace?

66 How meaningless is all this? How could a flood of mirages extinguish the great fire in the depths of the ocean?

67 And yet even I, O Lord, am permitted to enter the innermost chamber of Your grace and eat the food of the Absolute.

68 Is it any wonder that my infatuation has been dispelled? I vow at Your feet that You have saved me.

भवाप्ययौ हि भूतानां श्रुतौ विस्तरशो मया।
त्वत्तः कमलपत्त्राक्ष माहात्म्यम् अपि चाव्ययम्॥

bhavāpyayāu hi bhūtānāṁ
śrutāu vistaraśo mayā
tvattaḥ kamalapattrākṣa
māhātmyam api cāvyayam

2. *The origin and the dissolution of beings have been heard in detail by me from You, O Krishna, and also Your imperishable majesty.*

69 O Lord of the lotus eyes, as brilliant as countless suns, O great God, today I have heard from You

70 How all things came to be and how they passed away. You have explained to me the whole process of creation.

71 Not only have You described nature to me, but You have also shown me the place of the Self, whose greatness forms the clothing of the Vedas.

72 The Vedas live and increase, and the jewel of religion has taken birth. All this is due to the power of worshiping at Your feet.

73 Your might is unfathomable, it is the goal to be attained by all paths, and the supreme delight of the experience of Self-realization. You have shown this to me.

74 When the sky is clear of clouds the sun is revealed, and when weeds are cleared away from a pond the water can be seen.

75 When a serpent is removed from a sandalwood tree a person can touch it, and when an evil spirit has left a hidden treasure one can unearth it.

76 Similarly, when the Lord dispelled the illusion clouding my mind, He revealed the great Truth to me.

77 O Lord, my heart is convinced of this, and yet another desire has arisen in my mind.

78 Although I might remain silent from a feeling of awe, whom else can I ask? Is there any other refuge but You?

79 Don't aquatic creatures depend on water? O Krishna, if a child draws back from its mother's breast, is there any other way it can live?

80 So, setting aside my fear, I will tell You

what I wish to say. Then the Lord said, Enough. Ask Me whatever you wish.

एवम् एतद् यथात्थ त्वम् आत्मानं परमेश्वर।
द्रष्टुम् इच्छामि ते रूपम् ऐश्वरं पुरुषोत्तम॥

evam etad yathāttha tvam
ātmānaṁ parameśvara
draṣṭum icchāmi te rūpam
āiśvaram puruṣottama

3. *Thus, as You have described Yourself, O supreme Lord, I desire to see Your divine form, O Supreme Spirit.*

81 Then Arjuna said, My intuition has been satisfied by what You have told me.
82 That by whose thought all these worlds have been created and destroyed, and that about which You say, "I am this,"
83 That is Your original form. From that form You have incarnated from time to time as two-armed and four-armed beings in order to carry out the purposes of the gods.
84 When you had finished Your manifestation as Vishnu sleeping on the ocean, You gathered up Your attributes in the forms of the Fish and the Tortoise, just as a juggler does at the end of his performance.
85 This is that which the Upanishads sing, which yogis perceive in their hearts, and which Sanaka and other sages have embraced.
86 O Lord, my mind is eager to see that unfathomable cosmic form of which I have heard.
87 Now that You have dispelled my fear, if in Your love for me You were to ask what I wish, then I would say that this is my greatest desire:
88 That You show me Your cosmic form. This is the deepest longing of my heart.

मन्यसे यदि तच्छक्यं मया द्रष्टुम् इति प्रभो।
योगेश्वर ततो मे त्वं दर्शयात्मानम् अव्ययम्॥

manyase yadi tac chakyaṁ
mayā draṣṭum iti prabho
yogeśvara tato me tvaṁ
darśayātmānam avyayam

4. *If You think it possible for me to see this, O Lord of Yogins, then show me Your imperishable Self.*

89 I have one doubt, O Krishna. Am I worthy to behold that form?
90 I don't know this myself, and if You should ask me why, I would answer, "Does a sick man know the cause of his illness?"
91 Just as a person impelled by a strong desire forgets his own worth, or a thirsty man thinks that the whole ocean wouldn't satisfy him,
92 Similarly, in the confusion of my powerful longing, I haven't been able to keep a proper sense of my worth. Therefore, just as a mother knows the true nature of her child,
93 You should consider my worthiness, O Krishna, and then show me the vision of Your cosmic form.
94 If I am worthy, grant me this favor. Otherwise, tell me that it isn't possible. How can one give the pleasure of music to a deaf person?
95 The clouds give rain not only to satisfy the chataka bird but for the whole world, yet the shower is wasted if it falls on rocky ground.
96 The chakora bird draws nectar from the moonlight. Are others prevented from doing the same? Yet, because they are blind, the moonlight is wasted.
97 I trust that You will show me Your cosmic form. Aren't You always revealed anew to the intelligent as well as to the unintelligent?
98 Your generosity isn't conditioned by the person who asks for it; You don't distinguish between the worthy and the unworthy. You have granted to Your enemies even such a sacred thing as salvation.
99 Liberation is truly difficult to attain. Yet it also serves at Your feet and, like a servant, goes wherever You send it.
100 To Putana, who angrily came to kill You with poison in her breast, You gave the state of union with Yourself which was worthy of the sage Sanaka.
101 How You were dishonored and abused with many evil words in the presence of the three worlds, gathered together at the time of the Rajasuya sacrifice!
102 Yet, O Krishna, You gave a place to that wicked Shishupala. Did the young son of Uttanapada want to be raised to the place of the pole star?
103 He withdrew to the forest so that he might sit on his father's lap. Nevertheless, You honored him like the sun and moon.
104 You are especially merciful towards those who are overcome with distress. You granted union with Yourself to Ajamila, who ut-

tered Your name when he saw his son of the same name.

105 O generous Krishna, You still bear on Your breast the imprint of Bhrigu's kick, and You don't abandon the body of Your enemy.

106 In all these ways You have given help to those who have done evil to You, and You have been generous even to the unworthy. You begged a gift from Bali, for which You became his doorkeeper.

107 You bestowed the joy of Vaikuntha on that courtesan who didn't even know how to worship You, but merely uttered Your name when calling her parrot.

108 Considering these trivial pretexts on which You have granted the gift of Your presence, will You then turn me away?

109 Can the calves of the celestial wish-fulfilling cow be left hungry when she satisfies the needs of the whole world with her plentiful milk?

110 Surely the Lord won't refuse to show me what I have requested, but He will make me worthy to see it.

111 If You think that my eyes can contemplate Your cosmic form, then satisfy my desire to see it, O Lord.

112 When Arjuna had finished expressing his plea in this way, Krishna was unable to restrain Himself.

113 He was like a cloud full of the nectar of compassion, while Arjuna was like the approaching monsoon. Or Krishna was like the kokila bird, for whom Arjuna was the spring.

114 Just as the tides of the sea begin to rise at the sight of the full moon, similarly, the Lord was joyful in His growing love for Arjuna.

115 Swaying in delight, the compassionate Lord said, O Arjuna, see all My infinite forms!

116 Arjuna had only desired to see His cosmic form, but the Lord showed Him the whole universe as a manifestation of Himself.

117 How abundant is the Lord's grace! He always gives Himself a thousandfold to one who seeks Him.

118 That innermost secret which was kept from Shesha, which was hidden from the Vedas, and which wasn't even shown to Lakshmi, His most beloved,

119 Will now be revealed in many forms to Arjuna. How great is Arjuna's good fortune!

120 Just as when a person falls asleep he seems to become everything he experiences in a dream, in the same way, the Lord appeared in the form of the infinite bowl of the universe.

121 He laid aside His mortal form and removed the veil from Arjuna's sight. Then He displayed the glory of His yogic power.

122 Giving no thought to whether Arjuna would be able to bear the sight or not, He explained in the ecstasy of love, Look!

श्रीभगवान् उवाच । *śrībhagavān uvāca*

पश्य मे पार्थ रूपाणि शतशो ऽथ सहस्रशः ।
नानाविधानि दिव्यानि नानावर्णाकृतीनि च ।।

paśya me pārtha rūpāṇi
śataśo 'tha sahasraśaḥ
nānāvidhāni divyāni
nānāvarṇākṛtīni ca

The Blessed Lord spoke:
5. Behold, Arjuna, My forms, a hundredfold, a thousandfold, various, divine, and of various colors and shapes.

123 O Arjuna, you have asked Me to show you one form, but that would hardly be worth granting. See now all that is contained in My cosmic form.

124 Some are thin, some fat, some short, others large. Some are massive, others are delicate, and some are limitless.

125 Some are wild, others calm; some active, others motionless; some are indifferent, others affectionate, and still others are fierce.

126 Some are senseless, others alert; some are simple, others profound. Some are generous, others miserly, and some are angry.

127 Some are tranquil, others riotous; some are quiet, others joyful. Some are loud, others silent, and some are gentle.

128 Some are lustful, others passionless; some awake, others asleep; some are contented, others anxious, and still others are serene.

129 Some carry weapons, others are unarmed; some submissive, others daring; some threatening, others friendly, and some are contemplative.

130 Some revel in the sport of creation, others protect by their love, some destroy with their fervor, and others are merely spectators.

131 Thus these forms are infinite in shape and variety, and brilliant with light. No two are

of the same color.

132 Some are the color of molten gold, some tawny, and some are red like the clouds at sunset.

133 Some scintillate with beauty as though the universe were adorned with rubies. Others are the color of red turmeric like the dawn.

134 There are some as clear as pure crystal, some are tinted with the sapphire blue of Indra, others are as black as collyrium, and some are of the color of Krishna.

135 Some are as yellow as shining gold; others as black as a storm cloud. Some are pale like champak flowers; others are green.

136 Some are red like heated copper; others are as clear as the whiteness of the moon. See My forms of many and varied hues!

137 Just as the colors are of every variety, so are the shapes. Some are so beautiful that even the god of love would be put to shame.

138 Some have shapes of incomparable beauty, and others have exquisite bodies, as if the treasure house of the goddess of wealth were opened.

139 Some have fleshy bodies with heavy limbs, others are emaciated and ugly, some as clear as light, and others massive.

140 Thus, O Arjuna, My forms are of infinite shapes; there is no end to them. You can see an entire world in each part of this cosmic form.

पश्यादित्यान् वसून् रुद्रान् अश्विनौ मरुतस् तथा ।
बहून्य् अदृष्टपूर्वाणि पश्याश्चर्याणि भारत ॥

paśyādityān vasūn rudrān
aśvināu marutas tathā
bahūny adṛṣṭapūrvāṇi
paśyāścaryāṇi bhārata

6. Behold the Adityas, the Vasus, the Rudras, the two Asvins, the Maruts too; many wonders unseen before, behold, Arjuna!

141 Whenever I open my eyes, there appear whole worlds of suns; and when I close them, all these vanish.

142 From the breath of My mouth everything is filled with flames, and from these emerge fire and the multitudes of Vasus.

143 When My eyebrows come together in anger, groups of Rudras come forth.

144 In My benign aspect, countless Ashwin gods appear, and many winds rush out of My ears.

145 Races of gods and adepts are brought forth from My simplest action. See all these great and infinite forms!

146 The Vedas stammer when they speak of them, and even the whole span of time wouldn't be enough to see them all.

147 Now see those infinite manifestations of Mine which are not known even to the divine trinity. Experience joyfully the glory of this wonder.

इहैकस्थं जगत् कृत्स्नं पश्याद्य सचराचरम् ।
मम देहे गुडाकेश यच् चान्यद् द्रष्टुम् इच्छसि ॥

ihāikasthaṁ jagat kṛtsnaṁ
paśyādya sacarācaram
mama dehe guḍākeśa
yac cānyad draṣṭum icchasi

7. Behold now the entire universe, with everything moving and not moving, standing together here in My body, Arjuna, and whatever else you desire to see.

148 O Arjuna, just as tender shoots of grass sprout around the trunk of the wish-fulfilling tree, see the created worlds springing from the roots of the hair of this form.

149 Just as we see particles floating in space because of air currents, in the same way universes hover around each joint of My limbs.

150 See a universe spread out in each part of My body, and if you wish to see what lies beyond this universe,

151 You will have no difficulty, for you can see whatever you wish in this body.

152 When Krishna in His cosmic form spoke like this, full of compassion, Arjuna remained silent, without saying whether he could see it or not.

153 Krishna looked at Him, wondering why he didn't speak, and realized that Arjuna was still absorbed in his desire for the vision.

न तु माम् शक्यसे द्रष्टुम् अनेनैव स्वचक्षुषा ।
दिव्यं ददामि ते चक्षुः पश्य मे योगम् ऐश्वरम् ॥

na tu mām śakyase draṣṭum
anenāiva svacakṣuṣā
divyaṁ dadāmi te cakṣuḥ
pasya me yogam āiśvaram

8. But you are not able to see Me with your own eyes. I give to you a divine eye; behold My majestic power!

154 Then Krishna said, His eagerness hasn't diminished, but he hasn't yet found the way to happiness. It has been clearly shown to

him, yet he cannot comprehend it.

155 The Lord smiled and said to Arjuna, who was still gazing at Him, I have shown you My cosmic form, yet you cannot perceive it.

156 At this, the wise Arjuna replied, Whose fault is this? You are feeding moonbeams to a heron!

157 You are holding a mirror before a blind man, O Krishna, or singing a song to a deaf person.

158 You are deliberately offering a meal of honey to a frog! Why then should You be angry, O Krishna?

159 You are placing before my human sight that which is beyond the reach of the senses and is visible only to the eye of wisdom. How could I see it?

160 But I shouldn't criticize You. It would be better for me to bear with it. Then the Lord said, O Beloved, I agree with that.

161 If I wanted to show you the vision of My cosmic form, I should first have given you the power to see it. But speaking with you lovingly, I was thoughtless.

162 What would be the use of sowing seed in a field without first plowing it? It would be a waste of time. But now I will give you the vision that will enable you to perceive My cosmic form.

163 O Arjuna, with that sight you can see the majesty of My divine power and know it from direct inner experience.

164 Thus spoke the Lord, the object of all the knowledge in the Upanishads, the source of all universes, and the Beloved of all the world.

संजय उवाच । *sañjaya uvāca*

एवम् उक्त्वा ततो राजन् महायोगेश्वरो हरिः ।
दर्शयम् आस पार्थाय परमं रूपम् ऐश्वरम् ॥

evam uktvā tato rājan
mahāyogeśvaro hariḥ
darśayam āsa pārthāya
paramam rūpaṁ āiśvaram

Sanjaya spoke:

9. Having spoken thus, O King, the great Lord of yoga, Hari (Krishna), revealed to the Arjuna His majestic supreme form.

165 Sanjaya continued, O Emperor of the Kurus, I have often wondered if there is anyone in all the three worlds more fortunate than Lakshmi.

166 Show me anything that can compete with the Shrutis in the statement of eternal truths. And is there any servant more devoted than Shesha?

167 Among yogis who tire themselves with their ceaseless devotion, who can be compared with Garuda?

168 However, all this has changed since the birth of the Pandavas, in whom the joy of the Lord is centered.

169 But among the five Pandavas, it is to Arjuna that Krishna willingly yields, just as a lover is under the influence of a woman.

170 A trained bird wouldn't talk so easily, nor would a tame animal behave so well. Who knows how such good fortune has come to Arjuna?

171 Today his sight is so blessed that he can experience the highest God. See how indulgently the Lord treats Arjuna's words!

172 When Arjuna is angry, the Lord quietly bears with Him. When Arjuna is displeased, He coaxes him. He seems to be strangely infatuated with Arjuna.

173 Great masters like Shuka, who even before birth had conquered desire, became Krishna's poets and sang about His adventures in love.

174 O King, it astonishes me that He who is the wealth of yogis' concentration should be so captivated by Arjuna.

175 Then Sanjaya continued, O King, is this any reason for wonder? For great good fortune comes to a person whom Krishna accepts.

176 Then the Lord of all gods said to Arjuna, I will give you that vision whereby you can see My cosmic form.

177 As soon as Krishna spoke these words, the darkness of ignorance passed away.

178 Then the eye of wisdom shone forth, Arjuna was endowed with supernatural sight, and the Lord displayed to him His glory.

179 All these incarnations of Krishna are like waves on the ocean. The whole universe is a mirage arising from His radiance.

180 Krishna displayed His form against the eternal background on which the picture of all created things is imprinted.

181 Once in His childhood Krishna ate some mud, and His mother Yashoda picked Him up angrily;

182 But when He opened His mouth to show her what He had eaten, He revealed to her all the fourteen worlds within it.

183 Another time, when Krishna was in the Madhu forest and touched Dhruva on the cheek with His conch, Dhruva began to utter His praises in such a way that even the Vedas were silenced.

184 O King, Krishna showed Arjuna such kindness that Arjuna wondered where his confusion had gone.

185 Suddenly the light of Krishna's glory dawned on all sides, as though a miraculous deluge had poured forth, and Arjuna's mind was submerged in a sea of wonder.

186 Just as Markandeya alone had swum in the waters up to the creator's heaven, in the same way Arjuna floated in the ocean of Krishna's cosmic form.

187 He exclaimed, The firmament was here. Who has carried it away? What has become of all created things and the elements?

188 The four quarters have disappeared, and I can no longer see above or below. All the worlds have vanished, just as a dream disappears on waking.

189 Just as in the bright light of the sun the moon and stars become invisible, similarly, the whole world is engulfed by this cosmic form.

190 Then Arjuna's mind ceased to function, his reason couldn't be restrained, and his senses were withdrawn into his heart.

191 He remained in deep silence, paralyzed by astonishment, as though his thought had been struck by a weapon.

192 While he was gazing at the vision, overcome with amazement, the four-armed figure of Krishna assumed many forms and spread out in all directions.

193 Just as during the rainy season clouds spread over the whole sky, and at the final dissolution the light of the sun envelops everything, similarly, nothing remained but that form.

अनेकवक्त्रनयनम् अनेकाद्भुतदर्शनम् ।
अनेकदिव्याभरणं दिव्यानेकोद्यतायुधम् ।।
anekavaktranayanam
anekādbhutadarśanam
anekadivyābharaṇaṁ
divyānekodyatāyudham

10. Of many mouths and eyes, of many wondrous aspects, of many divine ornaments, of many uplifted divine weapons.

194 Then Arjuna saw many faces as resplendent as Krishna's royal mansions, or like the treasury of Lakshmi's beauty.

195 The faces of Krishna which he saw were so beautiful that they resembled gardens of joy in full bloom, or like beauty itself endowed with royalty.

196 Others came forth which were infinitely terrible, like the legions of death on the night of universal destruction.

197 Perhaps these were the very faces of death, fortresses built of fear, or cauldrons blazing with the fire of the final holocaust.

198 Thus Arjuna beheld many faces, wonderful, terrible, or gentle; some ordinary and some beautiful.

199 With his divine eye he gazed at these faces, but there was no end to them. Then, in wonder, he began to look at the eyes.

200 Arjuna saw eyes like gardens of blooming lotuses of many colors, shining like clusters of suns.

201 Under the eyebrows he saw, among masses of dark clouds, yellow fire like flashes of lightning on the day of final destruction.

202 While Arjuna was watching these marvels in astonishment, the great variety in this one form unfolded before Him.

203 Wondering where the arms, the legs, and the crowns on the head could be seen, Arjuna began to long even more intensely for the vision.

204 Is it possible that the desire of Arjuna, who is the very storehouse of good fortune, won't be fulfilled? Could there be any useless arrow in the quiver of Shiva, who wields the Pinaka bow?

205 Can the four-faced Brahma utter a faulty word? Therefore Arjuna saw the whole extent of this limitless universe.

206 With his own eyes, Arjuna enjoyed in a moment a vision of every limb of that One whose path even the Vedas do not know.

207 He saw the glory of the full stature of that cosmic form shining with jeweled ornaments.

208 How can I describe those ornaments which the Supreme fashioned out of Himself to adorn His body?

209 They had a radiance of light which could illumine even the sun and moon, like the innermost center of that sun which lights the whole world.

210 The Lord adorned Himself with a brilliance

that was beyond the conception of any mind. This is how Arjuna saw Him.

211 Then, when Arjuna looked with his supernatural vision at the Lord's extended hands, he saw shining in them weapons that would strike down the flames of the holocaust at the end of the world.

212 The stars were parched by the fierceness of this radiance and even fire, scorched by its brilliance, longed to cast itself into the ocean.

213 He saw innumerable hands with raised weapons, as though engulfed in waves of Kalakuta poison, or like great forests of ignorance.

दिव्यमाल्याम्बरधरं दिव्यगन्धानुलेपनम् ।
सर्वाश्चर्यमयं देवम् अनन्तं विश्वतोमुखम् ॥

divyamālyāmbaradharaṁ
divyagandhānulepanam
sarvāścaryamayaṁ devam
anantaṁ visvatomukham

11. Wearing divine garlands and apparel, with divine perfumes and ointments, made up of all marvels, the resplendent Lord, endless, facing in all directions.

214 When Arjuna looked aside in fear and saw the neck and crown, he noticed that they were like the stems of divine trees.

215 He saw lotuses set in the crown which were as pure and fragrant as those on which Lakshmi rested when she was tired. Here the great supernatural powers have their origin.

216 On the crown of the head were bouquets of flowers arranged as though for worship, and superb garlands hung around the neck.

217 Around the loins was a garment of yellow silk, as though the heavens had clothed themselves in the light of the sun, or as if Mount Meru were covered with gold.

218 His body was like that of Shankar anointed with camphor, or Mount Kailas covered with quicksilver, or like the Milky Ocean covered with milk.

219 He saw the whole body covered with sandalwood paste, as though a garment of moonlight had been unfolded and wrapped as a cloak around the heavens,

220 With a fragrance which adds luster to light itself, which assuages the intensity of the bliss of union with the Absolute, and which gives life to the earth.

221 Who can describe that pure ointment used by the Lord and smeared on His body by the god of love?

222 Perceiving the beauty of each adornment, Arjuna was awestruck and could not tell whether the Lord was seated, standing, or lying down.

223 Then, opening his physical eyes, he saw that the whole of space was pervaded by this form. Reluctant to look at it, he remained silent, but he saw the same thing with his inner vision.

224 He saw before him countless shapes. In fear he turned his back on them; but there too, he saw the same faces, hands, and feet of that form.

225 Is there any wonder that he could see the vision with open eyes? But it is marvelous that he could see it even with his eyes closed.

226 See the Lord's gracious work! Arjuna perceived that He pervaded all things not only when he looked but also when he wasn't looking.

227 Scarcely had he reached the shore after being immersed in the waters of one marvel, than he plunged into the sea of another.

228 In this way, the Lord encompassed Arjuna with the miraculous vision of His manifold forms.

229 This form faced in all directions. It was this that Arjuna had asked the Lord to reveal to him. Now he saw the Lord as everything there is.

230 The Lord gave Arjuna a power of sight which would endure whether the light of a lamp or of the sun shone forth or was dimmed.

231 In this way, Arjuna was able to see both in the light and in the dark. Sanjaya related all this to King Dhritarashtra in Hastinapura.

232 He said, O King, you have heard how Arjuna saw that wonderful all-pervasive form adorned with many ornaments.

दिवि सूर्यसहस्रस्य भवेद् युगपद् उत्थिता ।
यदि भाः सदृशी सा स्याद् भासस् तस्य महात्मनः ॥

divi sūryasahasrasya
bhaved yugapad utthitā
yadi bhāḥ sadṛśī sā syād
bhāsas tasya mahātmanaḥ

12. If a thousand suns should rise all at once in the sky, such splendor would resemble the splendor of that great Being.

233 O King! How can I describe the splendor of

the Lord's form? It is said that on the day of final destruction, twelve suns will rise together in the sky.

234 But even if thousands of such resplendent suns were to appear at the same moment, could they be compared with the splendor of that vision?

235 If all lightning were brought together in one flash, if fuel were gathered for the final holocaust, and if the ten great heavenly bodies were added to it,

236 Even then that brilliance would be insignificant beside the splendor of the Lord's appearance. It could never be that radiant.

237 In this way, Krishna displayed the radiance of His cosmic form. I was able to see it by the grace of the sage Vyasa.

तत्रैकस्थं जगत् कृत्स्नं प्रविभक्तम् अनेकधा ।
अपश्यद् देवदेवस्य शरीरे पाण्डवस् तदा ॥

tatrāikasthaṁ jagat kṛtsnaṁ
pravibhaktam anekadhā
apaśyad devadevasya
śarīre pāṇḍavas tadā

13. There Arjuna then beheld the entire universe established in one, divided in many groups, in the body of the God of Gods.

238 There in that cosmic form the whole world was seen in its abundance, just as bubbles appear separately on the surface of the great ocean,

239 Or just as imaginary cities appear in the heavens, as ants build their nests in the earth, or as small particles lie on Mount Meru.

240 In this way, Arjuna saw at that time the whole universe in the body of the Lord of Lords.

ततः स विस्मयाविष्टो हृष्टरोमा धनंजयः ।
प्रणम्य शिरसा देवं कृताञ्जलिर् अभाषत ॥

tataḥ sa vismayāviṣṭo
hṛṣṭaromā dhanaṁjayaḥ
praṇamya śirasā devaṁ
kṛtāñjalir abhāṣata

14. Then Arjuna, who was filled with amazement, whose hair was standing on end, bowing his head to the Lord with joined palms, said:

241 The faint sense of duality which remained between him and the universe faded away, and his heart was absorbed in the vision.

242 He was filled with ecstasy, while outwardly his limbs lost their strength, and his whole body trembled from head to toe.

243 His hair stood on end, just as tender blades of grass shoot forth when the first monsoon rains pour down a mountain side.

244 His body was covered with beads of perspiration, just as water begins to ooze from the moonstone when the moon's rays touch it.

245 When a cluster of bees is caught in a lotus bud, it begins to sway on the water. Similarly, Arjuna trembled with waves of inner bliss.

246 Tears began to fall from his eyes, just as camphor drips from a camphor tree when its folds open with the fullness of the sap.

247 All the eight elements of the state of purity vied with one another in their eagerness to possess him, and the supreme bliss of God arose in his heart.

248 Waves of joy swelled within him, just as the ocean rises to full tide with the rising moon.

249 After this experience of joy, the human sight which perceived duality was restored to Arjuna and, sighing deeply, he waited.

250 Then, turning to where Krishna was seated, he bowed his head and with folded hands he spoke.

अर्जुन उवाच । *arjuna uvāca*

पश्यामि देवांस् तव देव देहे
सर्वांस् तथा भूतविशेषसंघान् ।
ब्रह्माणम् ईशं कमलासनस्थम्
ऋषींश्च सर्वान् उरगांश्च दिव्यान् ॥

paśyāmi devāṅs tava deva dehe
sarvāṅs tathā bhūtaviśeṣasaṁghān
brahmāṇam īśaṁ kamalāsanastham
ṛṣīnśca sarvān uragāṅśca divyān

Arjuna spoke:
15. I see the gods, O God, in Your body, and all kinds of beings assembled; Lord Brahma on his lotus seat, and all the seers and divine serpents.

251 O Lord, glory be to You! Through Your wonderful grace I, an ordinary man, have seen Your cosmic form.

252 It is good, O Lord, and I have great satisfaction in seeing that the whole universe is contained in You.

253 I perceive many worlds within Your body, just as forests full of beasts are seen everywhere on Mount Mandara.

254 In the heavens there are innumerable clusters of stars, and nests of birds are found on a huge tree.
255 Similarly, O Krishna, in Your cosmic form I see heaven and all the gods.
256 In it I also see many groups of the five primal elements, and numberless creatures of many worlds come forth.
257 In Your body I see Satyaloka, and isn't this Brahma himself? On another side, there is also Mount Kailas.
258 Mahadeva with His consort Bhavani is in one part of Your body, and I also see You Yourself there, O Krishna.
259 In this form I also see the long lineage of all the sages, with Kashyapa, and there is also the nether world with all the serpents.
260 In short, O blissful Lord, the fourteen worlds are pictured on the walls of each of Your limbs, as though they were supported by them.
261 And when I look at the people of those worlds depicted in Your form, I see Your incomparable depth.

अनेकबाहूदरवक्त्रनेत्रं
पश्यामि त्वां सर्वतो ऽनन्तरूपम् ।
नान्तं न मध्यं न पुनस् तवादिं
पश्यामि विश्वेश्वर विश्वरूप ॥

anekabāhūdaravaktranetraṁ
paśyāmi tvāṁ sarvato 'nantarūpam
nāntaṁ na madhyaṁ na punas tavādiṁ
paśyāmi viśveśvara viśvarūpa

16. I see You everywhere, infinite in form, with many arms, bellies, faces, and eyes; not the end, nor the middle, nor yet the beginning of You do I see, O Lord of all, whose form is the universe.

262 When I glance around with that divine eye, I see space stretching forth in Your strong arms.
263 Then I see all things accomplished eternally and simultaneously by Your hands alone.
264 In Your body I perceive countless bellies, as if all divine bliss had opened up the treasury of the created world.
265 As though countless images of the thousand-headed One appeared in one moment, or the great Creator as a tree were weighed down with fruit in the form of faces,
266 I see Your form having numberless mouths and countless rows of eyes.
267 Your form pervades everything. One can no longer tell whether it is heaven or hell, earth, or a distant firmament.
268 The universe is so completely filled with You that I search in vain for a single atom anywhere that isn't pervaded by You.
269 O Krishna, I see that You permeate all the primal elements gathered together and all created beings.
270 Where do You come from? Are You seated or standing? What womb were You born from? What is Your stature?
271 Of what nature are Your form and limbs? What is beyond You? On what do You rest?
272 When I began to ponder these things, then I understood that You are everything. You were born of no one; You are self-existent and without beginning.
273 You are neither standing nor seated, neither of great nor small stature. You extend far above and below Yourself.
274 You are Your own form and Your own age, O Lord. You are Your own Self before and behind.
275 O Krishna, I have now seen again and again that You are everything.
276 If there is anything that You lack, it is only that in Your form there is neither beginning, middle, nor end.
277 I have searched everywhere, but I have found no trace of any of these three things.
278 O infinite Lord of the universe, I have truly seen Your form without beginning, middle, or end.
279 Many individual forms are depicted within the body of this great form. You seem to have clothed Yourself in various kinds of garments.
280 You are like an immense ocean heaving with the waves of infinite shapes, or a huge tree bearing them as its fruit.
281 Just as the surface of the earth is covered with trees and the heavens are studded with stars, similarly, Your form is filled with these created forms.
282 In each of these shapes, the universe arises and disappears. It is merely the hair on Your body.
283 When I considered the extent of the universe within You and asked who You are, I realized that it is You who are my charioteer.
284 O Krishna, when I see all these things, I understand that You are eternally all-perva-

sive; but through compassion for Your devotees, You assume bodily form.

285 What is Your azure-hued, four-armed body which satisfies both our mind and our sight and which, if we reach out to it, we can grasp in our arms?

286 O Lord of the cosmic form, You have appeared in this beautiful body, but our mortal sight is so blurred that we see it imperfectly.

287 But now our sight is purified. You have endowed me with divine vision, and I have seen Your greatness as it truly is.

288 Now I have seen clearly that it is You who have assumed Your cosmic form. You are the charioteer seated behind the yoke of my chariot.

किरीटिनं गदिनं चक्रिणं च
तेजोराशिं सर्वतो दीप्तिमन्तम् ।
पश्यामि त्वां दुर्निरीक्ष्यं समन्ताद्
दीप्तानलार्कद्युतिम् अप्रमेयम् ॥

kirīṭinaṁ gadinaṁ cakriṇaṁ ca
tejorāśiṁ sarvato dīptimantam
paśyāmi tvāṁ durnirīkṣyaṁ samantād
dīptānalārkadyutim aprameyam

17. Crowned, armed with a club and bearing a discus, a mass of splendor, shining on all sides, with the immeasurable radiance of the sun and blazing fire, I see You, who are difficult to behold.

289 O Krishna! Isn't that Your crown placed on Your head? But now its luster and glory are wondrously enhanced.

290 O Lord of the cosmic form, there in Your uplifted hand is the discus, ready to be thrown. The sight of it is unmistakable.

291 O Krishna, isn't that Your mace in the other hand? Aren't Your lower hands, free of weapons, used for holding the horses' reins?

292 O Lord of the universe, I know that in Your eagerness You immediately assumed Your cosmic form to satisfy my desire.

293 What wonder is this! My astonishment is boundless, and my imagination is bewildered by the marvel of it.

294 Trying to perceive whether Your form is here or not leaves me breathless. The luster of Your body pervades all space.

295 In its light one's sight is scorched. Its light is so fierce that even the sun is lost in it like a firefly.

296 It is as though the whole created world had become submerged in the ocean of the great light, or as though the heavens were enveloped in the lightning of the last day.

297 Or it is as though the flames of the final holocaust had broken loose and had built for themselves a stage in the firmament. Even with the eye of wisdom, I am unable to look.

298 It grows brighter and brighter, burning with fierce flames, so that even my supernatural sight cannot bear to gaze at it.

299 It may be described as the consuming fire of the day of destruction, or the bursting forth of the hidden third eye of Rudra, the destroyer.

300 The spreading of this light forms a whirlpool of the five forms of fire, and the universe is reduced to cinders.

301 Never before in my life have I seen You as this wonderful blaze of light. No one can realize how limitless You are.

त्वम् अक्षरं परमं वेदितव्यं
त्वम् अस्य विश्वस्य परं निधानम् ।
त्वमव्ययः शाश्वतधर्मगोप्ता
सनातनस् त्वं पुरुषो मतो मे ॥

tvam akṣaraṁ paramaṁ veditavyaṁ
tvam asya viśvasya paraṁ nidhānam
tvam avyayaḥ śāśvatadharmagoptā
sanātanas tvaṁ puruṣo mato me

18. You are the unchanging, the supreme object of knowledge; You are the ultimate resting place of all; You are the imperishable defender of the eternal law; You are the primeval Spirit, I believe.

302 O Lord, You are unchanging and beyond the mystery of the sacred syllable. The Vedas search for You.

303 You are the origin of all form, the treasure house of the entire universe, unmanifest, unfathomable, and imperishable.

304 You are the essence of all religion, uncreated and ever new. I know that You are the supreme Self beyond the thirty-six principles.

अनादिमध्यान्तम् अनन्तवीर्यम्
अनन्तबाहुं शशिसूर्यनेत्रम् ।
पश्यामि त्वां दीप्तहुताशवक्त्रं
स्वतेजसा विश्वम् इदं तपन्तम् ॥

anādimadhyāntam anantavīryam
anantabāhuṁ śaśisūryanetram
paśyāmi tvāṁ dīptahutāśavaktraṁ
svatejasā viśvam idaṁ tapantam

19. With infinite power, without beginning,

middle, or end, with innumerable arms, the moon and sun being Your eyes, I see You, the blazing fire Your mouth, burning all this universe with Your radiance.

305 Your power is infinite, without beginning, middle, or end. You are the limitless hands and feet of the whole universe.

306 The sun and moon are Your eyes, through which You show anger and compassion. O Krishna, You show displeasure to one, and You protect another.

307 This is truly You that I see. Your mouth seems to have the fire of the final destruction flaming in it.

308 Your tongue rolling in Your mouth is licking Your teeth in the same way that the rising flames of a conflagration envelop a mountain.

309 With the heat from Your mouth and the radiant glory of Your whole body, the scorched universe is writhing in distress.

द्यावापृथिव्योर् इदम् अन्तरं हि
व्याप्तं त्वयैकेन दिशश्च सर्वाः ।
दृष्ट्वाद्भुतं रूपम् उग्रं तवेदं
लोकत्रयं प्रव्यथितं महात्मन् ॥

dyāvāpṛthivyor idam antaraṁ hi
vyāptaṁ tvayāikena diśaśca sarvāḥ
dṛṣṭvādbhutaṁ rūpam ugraṁ tavedaṁ
lokatrayaṁ pravyathitaṁ mahātman

20. This space between heaven and earth, is pervaded by You alone in all directions. Seeing Your marvelous and terrible form, the three worlds tremble, O great Being.

310 The created world, the nether regions, the earth, the firmament, and the horizon surrounding the ten quarters,

311 I see with wonder that they are all filled with You. It is as though all the heavens were engulfed by some horror,

312 Or as though the fourteen worlds were surrounded by great and miraculous waves. How can I comprehend such a marvel?

313 Your vast extent cannot be encompassed, and the fierceness of its brilliance is intolerable. All my joy is gone, and only with great difficulty can the world continue to exist.

अमी हि त्वां सुरसंघा विशन्ति
केचिद् भीताः प्राञ्जलयो गृणन्ति ।
स्वस्तीत्य् उक्त्वा महर्षिसिद्धसंघाः
स्तुवन्ति त्वां स्तुतिभिः पुष्कलाभिः ॥

amī hi tvāṁ surasaṁghā viśanti
kecid bhītāḥ prāñjalayo gṛṇanti
svastīty uktvā mahārṣisiddhasaṁghāḥ
stuvanti tvāṁ stutibhiḥ puṣkalābhiḥ

21. The throngs of gods enter into You, some, terrified, with reverent gestures praise You; saying "Hail," the throngs of great seers and perfected ones extol You with abundant praises.

314 O Lord, I don't know where this tide of fear comes from when I see You, or why the three worlds would be engulfed by waves of grief.

315 On the contrary, why should the sight of You, Exalted One, inspire fear and distress? But I realize why this vision brings me no joy.

316 As long as people haven't seen Your form, they take delight in the things of the world. But now that I have seen You, I am troubled by a loss of all interest in pleasure.

317 Can I immediately embrace You whom I have seen? If I cannot, how can I remain in this plight?

318 If I turn back, the life of birth and death confronts me. Yet You are before me, unrestrainable, and I cannot grasp You.

319 It is clear to me now that the three worlds are tormented, like parched grain, between these dangers.

320 Just as a man burned by fire rushes to the sea to alleviate his pain, and then is even more afraid of the force of the waves,

321 So is the state of restlessness into which the world is thrown at the sight of You. Look, over there are groups of sages.

322 These wise men have been absorbed into Your being through their devotion. The radiance of Your body has burned up the seeds of their actions.

323 Others, who are fearful by nature, pray to You with folded hands, always keeping Your vision before them.

324 O Lord, we are drowning in the ocean of ignorance and are entangled in the snare of worldly pleasure. We are trapped between heaven and earthly existence.

325 Who except You can set us free? We turn to You with all our heart and soul.

326 Sages, adepts, and the hosts of demigods all bless and praise You.

रुद्रादित्या वसवो ये च साध्या
विश्वे ऽश्विनौ मरुतश्चोष्मपाश्च ।

गन्धर्वयक्षासुरसिद्धसंघा
वीक्षन्ते त्वां विस्मिताश्चैव सर्वे ।।

rudrādityā vasavo ye ca sādhyā
viśve 'śvinău marutaścoṣmapāś ca
gandharvayakṣāsurasiddhasaṁghā
vīkṣante tvāṁ vismitāścāiva sarve

22. The Rudras, Adityas, Vasus, the Sadhyas, the Vishve devas, the two Ashvins, the Maruts, and the Ushmapas, the throngs of Gandharvas, Yakshas, Asuras, and perfected ones, all behold You, amazed.

327 The hosts of Rudras and Adityas, the Vasus, and all the Sadhyas, the Ashwins, the devas, and the wind,
328 The fire, the Gandharvas, all the hosts of demons, Indra with his gods, and the Siddhas,
329 All these eagerly look at Your divine vision, each from his own world.
330 Every moment as they gaze at You with their hearts amazed, they worship You, O Lord, encircling You with their crowns.
331 The heavens resound with their cries of "Victory to You!" They bow before You with their folded hands raised to their foreheads.
332 In the form of the pure quality, the season of spring has come to the forest full of trees of humility. You are the fruit growing in the tender leaves of their hands joined in salutation.
333 The day of good fortune has dawned for the eyes of these who have seen Your unfathomable cosmic form, and an abundance of joy has come to their minds.
334 Even the gods were filled with awe at the vision of that form, which pervades the whole world and can be seen from every direction.

रूपं महत् ते बहुवक्त्रनेत्रं
महाबाहो बहुबाहूरुपादम् ।
बहूदरं बहुदंष्ट्राकरालं
दृष्ट्वा लोकाः प्रव्यथितास् तथा ऽहम् ।।

rūpaṁ mahat te bahuvaktranetram
mahābāho bahubāhūrupādam
bahūdaraṁ bahudaṁṣṭrākarālaṁ
dṛṣṭvā lokāḥ pravyathitās tathā 'ham

23. Having seen Your great form, which has many mouths and eyes, which has many arms, thighs, and feet, which has many bellies, and mouths gaping with many tusks, O Krishna, the worlds tremble, and so do I.

335 Though it is only one, it has strange and terrible mouths, innumerable eyes, and countless arms holding weapons.
336 It has many legs and many bellies of various colors. See how all the mouths are full of fury!
337 It is as though at the end of a world age these mouths were scattered abroad with flames of fire in them.
338 These flames are like the missiles of Shiva, destroyer of Tripura, or all the Bhairavas on the day of dissolution. Or they are like the powers of destruction which strike down all creatures at the end of an age.
339 Your terrible mouths are seen in every direction, and Your fierce teeth cannot be restrained within them, like lions roaming in a valley.
340 In the dark night at the end of time, devouring spirits come out into the open. We see in Your mouths, as in theirs, jaws smeared with the blood of the final day of destruction.
341 Your faces are as terrible to look at as the god of death challenging to battle, or the widespread slaughter on the last day.
342 If one glances around this pitiful universe, it seems like a tree growing on the banks of the Jamuna river, full of the waters of distress.
343 The ship of the life of the three worlds is being tossed on the waves of the storm of anguish in the ocean of death, and You are that ocean.
344 O Lord, if You were suddenly to ask me, in anger, what I think of this world, saying that I should experience the joy of realization,
345 What could I say? I myself am full of dread. The distress of this world is only a thin veil concealing my own fear.
346 Even I, who was feared by Rudra and from whom the god of death hid himself, have been filled with terror by Your form.
347 This is a great calamity! It is strange that it should be called Your cosmic form, for it has the power to defeat even fear itself.

व्यात्ताननं दीप्तविशालनेत्रम् ।
नभःस्पृशं दीप्तम् अनेकवर्णं
दृष्ट्वा हि त्वां प्रव्यथितान्तरात्मा
धृतिं न विन्दामि शमं च विष्णो ।।

nabhaḥspṛśaṁ dīptam anekavarṇaṁ

vyāttānanam dīptaviśālanetram
dṛṣṭvā hi tvāṁ pravyathitāntarātmā
dhṛtiṁ na vindāmi śamaṁ ca viṣṇo

24. Having seen You touching the sky, blazing, many colored, gaping-mouthed, with enormous fiery eyes; I tremble indeed in my heart, and I find neither courage nor tranquility, O Vishnu!

348 Some of Your mouths are so fierce that they challenge even the god of death. Their vastness dwarfs the whole of space.

349 The wide expanse of heaven cannot contain them, nor can the winds of the three worlds encircle them. See how even fire itself is consumed by the vapor pouring out of them!

350 No two of them are alike, and they are of many different colors. Their flames assist in the work of universal destruction.

351 Their glow is so fierce that it burns the three worlds to ashes. In all those mouths, there are both large and small teeth.

352 Gales are added to the wind, and deluge to the ocean. The fire which lies beneath the ocean has come to meet the fire of poison.

353 Look! The glow in Your mouth is as fierce as if it had drunk the Kalakuta poison and death had set fire to death.

354 Who can tell their vastness? It is as though space had broken open, or the sky were split asunder.

355 It is like the cavern of the nether world opened by Shiva when the demon Hiranyaksha escaped into a cave with the world under his arm.

356 These mouths are so wide, and the tongues within them are so ravenous, that the whole world would be too small a mouthful to satisfy them.

357 In the hollows of the mouths, the tongues are spread out like the poisonous flames emitted by the hissing serpents of the nether regions, which rise up to the heavens.

358 The tips of those teeth, protruding beyond the lips, are like flashing lightning illuminating the heavens on the day of destruction.

359 Those huge eyes in their sockets below the forehead fill even fear with terror, as though they were waves of the great death lying in wait.

360 I don't know why You have assumed this terrifying form, but I am suddenly filled with the fear of death.

361 I have longed to see this form of Yours, and my desire has been fulfilled. I have seen with my own eyes, and they are satisfied.

362 This earthly body will die. Who cares? But now I am beginning to wonder whether my spirit will survive.

363 My limbs are trembling with fear, and if this increases, it will affect my mind. My intelligence is failing, and I have lost all self-respect.

364 Even more than this, my inner soul, the essence of all bliss, is overcome by fear.

365 O Beloved, I truly yearned for the vision of Your form; but now my understanding has left me, and our relationship of Guru and disciple can scarcely endure.

366 O Lord, I have striven courageously to overcome the weakness which has come into my heart after seeing this vision.

367 I had already lost courage, and now I have had this vision of Your form. Let that be. Your teaching has greatly bewildered me.

368 My weary spirit has fled in every direction hoping to find rest, but there is none to be found anywhere.

369 This terrifying vision has afflicted the whole universe. How could I not speak to You about this, O Krishna?

दंष्ट्राकरालानि च ते मुखानि
दृष्ट्वैव कालानलसंनिभानि ।
दिशो न जाने न लभे च शर्म
प्रसीद देवेश जगन्निवास ॥

daṁṣṭrākarālāni ca te mukhāni
dṛṣṭvāiva kālānalasaṁnibhāni
diśo na jāne na labhe ca śarma
prasīda deveśa jagannivāsa

25. And having seen Your mouths, bearing many tusks, glowing like the fires of universal destruction, I lose my sense of direction, and I do not find comfort. Have mercy! Lord of Gods, abode of the universe!

370 Along with Your huge eyes, Your vast mouths spread out as though they were shattered vessels of the great fear.

371 The teeth are so thickly set that the lips of each mouth cannot cover them. They seem like dense rows of the weapons of the final destruction.

372 It is as though the great serpent Takshaka were filled with poison. It is like the time when spirits wander abroad on the darkest

night, or fiery shafts of lightning are brandished in the sky.

373 Not only are Your mouths huge, but the fury within them pours out, engulfing us in the waves of death.

374 What can survive when the hurricane of the day of doom and the fire of the final holocaust come together?

375 My courage fails when I see these devouring mouths. I am confused and have lost all sense of direction. I no longer even know who I am.

376 Even after a brief glimpse of Your form, all my joy has left me. I beg You, remove this huge, limitless form of Yours!

377 If I had realized Your intention, would I have asked You to show this to me? I beg You, save me now from this vision!

378 O Krishna, if You are my Master, protect my life from this danger. Draw this display of deadly destruction back into Yourself.

379 Hear me, O Krishna! Your energy sustains the whole universe, but You have forgotten this and have begun to destroy it.

380 So be gracious, O Lord! Withdraw Your mystic power and save me from this terror.

381 I have experienced such dread of this form that again and again I have implored You to be merciful and remove it.

382 When Amaravati was attacked, didn't I alone save it? I'm not afraid to meet death face to face.

383 But this is quite different, O Lord. Rivaling death itself, You are about to engulf us with Your universal form.

384 How can it be that although this isn't the time of the universal dissolution, yet even now You are among us as death, and the life of this wretched world is nearing its end?

385 O perverse fate! Calamity has come even while we were seeking peace. Alas! The universe is passing away. You have begun to consume it.

386 Don't I see that with Your wide open mouths You are swallowing up our armies in all directions?

अमी च त्वां धृतराष्ट्रस्य पुत्राः
सर्वे सहैवावनिपालसंघैः ।
भीष्मो द्रोणः सूतपुत्रस् तथासौ
सहास्मदीयैर् अपि योधमुख्यैः ।।

amī ca tvāṁ dhṛtarāṣṭrasya putrāḥ
sarve sahāivāvanipālasaṁghāih
bhīsmo dronah sūtaputras tathāsāu
sahāsmadīyāir api yodhamukhyāiḥ

26. And entering into You, all the sons of Dhritarashtra, along with the throngs of kings, Bhishma, Drona, and Karna, the son of the charioteer, and also with our chief warriors,

387 Aren't the youths of the Kauravas, the sons of the blind Dhritarashtra, with all their friends and followers, being drawn into these mouths?

388 And all those kings of different countries who have come to support them are being swept away. None will be left to tell the tale.

389 You seize herds of raging elephants and swallow up everything on the battlefield.

390 Troops firing with cannons and foot soldiers armed with clubs are lost in Your mouth.

391 All the numberless weapons as destructive as death are being seized. Even one of them could swallow up the universe.

392 O Krishna, what pleasure does it give You to swallow whole these armies, their followers, and their horse-drawn chariots?

393 Who can compare with Bhishma in bravery and truthfulness? Alas! Even he and Drona, the brahmin, are being devoured.

394 Now the brave Karna, son of the sun, has disappeared! I see that all of us are brought to nothing like dead leaves.

395 Alas! How strange is the Lord's favor! My request has brought this fate to the poor world.

396 The Lord explained to me before in various ways some of His divine manifestations, but I wasn't satisfied with that and urged Him to show me His cosmic form.

397 We cannot avoid our destiny, and our mind brings about what is to be. I am fated to bring about the destruction of the world. How can it be avoided?

398 In earlier times the gods obtained nectar by churning the ocean, but they didn't stop there, and eventually they stirred up the Kalakuta poison.

399 However, in one way little harm was done, for a solution was found and Shiva overcame the calamity.

400 But now, how can this tempest of fire be controlled? Who can swallow the heavens filled with poison? Who can wrestle with death?

401 In this way, Arjuna was distressed and lamented in his heart. He couldn't understand the Lord's motives in doing this.

402 He was overwhelmed by the belief that he was the slayer and that the Kauravas had died by his hand. But it was to remove this illusion that Krishna gave him the vision of His form.

403 The Lord revealed through that vision that no person is killed by another, for He Himself is the only destroyer.

404 But Arjuna, unable to understand His intention, grieved in vain and his fear increased.

दंष्ट्राकरालानि भयानकानि ।
वक्त्राणि ते त्वरमाणा विशन्ति
केचिद् विलग्ना दशनान्तरेषु
संदृश्यन्ते चूर्णितैर् उत्तमाङ्गैः ॥

vaktrāṇi te tvaramāṇā viśanti
daṁṣṭrākarālāni bhayānakāni
kecid vilagnā daśanāntareṣu
saṁdṛśyante cūrṇitāir uttamāṅgāiḥ

27. They quickly enter Your fearful mouths, which gape with many tusks; some are seen with crushed heads, clinging between Your teeth.

405 Again Arjuna exclaimed, Look! Both armies at once are completely engulfed in Your mouth, just as clouds merge into the sky.

406 Just as the end of a great age, the god of death, angered at the world, seizes hell and the twenty-one heavens;

407 Or just as when a miser's luck has run out, he loses his hoarded treasure;

408 All the armies gathered here are drawn at once into Your jaws, and not one is able to escape. See the work of destiny!

409 As all these men enter Your mouth they are as nothing, like the shoots of an ashoka tree when stripped off by a camel.

410 See how their crowned heads have fallen into Your jaws and are being ground to powder!

411 The jewels of their crowns are caught in the crevices of the teeth, and their powder sticks to the tongue. The edges of some of the teeth are smeared with it.

412 And yet, although Your form as death has seized their bodies, the heads of the bodies have been preserved.

413 The heads, the spiritual part of the bodies, have been left intact though they are in the mouths of the great death.

414 Then Arjuna said, One who has been born can have no other fate. For that reason, the whole world is moving towards the cavities of these mouths.

415 All the created worlds are pouring into these mouths, and You silently swallow them as they come.

416 Brahma and the highest spiritual beings are rushing into the higher mouths, and ordinary people into the closer ones.

417 Other creatures are seized at the moment of their birth. Truly, nothing can escape the clutches of these jaws.

यथा नदीनां बहवो ऽम्बुवेगाः
समुद्रम् एवाभिमुखा द्रवन्ति ।
तथा तवामी नरलोकवीरा
विशन्ति वक्त्राण्य् अभिविज्वलन्ति ॥

yathā nadīnāṁ bahavo 'mbuvegāḥ
samudram evābhimukhā dravanti
tathā tavāmī naralokavīrā
viśanti vaktrāṇy abhivijvalanti

28. As the many torrents of the rivers flow toward the ocean, so those heroes of the world of men enter Your flaming mouths.

418 This world pours into Your mouths from all directions, just as great rivers flow swiftly into the ocean.

419 Hastening through the span of their earthly lives on the ladder of day and night, all creatures move onward to meet these mouths.

यथा प्रदीप्तं ज्वलनं पतङ्गा
विशन्ति नाशाय समृद्धवेगाः ।
तथैव नाशाय विशन्ति लोकास्
तवापि वक्त्राणि समृद्धवेगाः ॥

yathā pradīptaṁ jvalanaṁ pataṅgā
viśanti nāśāya samṛddhavegāḥ
tathāiva nāśāya viśanti lokās
tavāpi vaktrāṇi samṛddhavegāḥ

29. As moths enter a blazing flame to their destruction with great speed, so also, these creatures swiftly enter Your mouths to their destruction.

420 All of these fall into Your mouths, just as moths fly into the crevices of a blazing mountain.

421 Whatever enters Your mouths is swept away leaving no trace, just as water vanishes when it falls on heated iron.

लेलिह्यसे ग्रसमानः समन्ताल्
लोकान् समग्रान् वदनैर् ज्वलद्भिः ।

तेजोभिर् आपूर्य जगत् समग्रं
भासस् तवोग्राः प्रतपन्ति विष्णो ॥

lelihyase grasamānaḥ samantāl
lokān samagrān vadanāir jvaladbhiḥ
tejobhir āpūrya jagat samagraṁ
bhāsas tavogrāḥ pratapanti viṣṇo

30. You lick up , swallowing on all sides all the worlds, with Your flaming mouths. Filling all the universe with splendor, Your terrible rays blaze forth, O Vishnu!

422 Having consumed the whole world for Your meal, why are you still hungry? What is this extraordinary power to consume?

423 Just as a sick person recovering from a fever and a beggar in time of famine are overcome with hunger, in the same way, the tongues of Your mouths are licking Your lips.

424 How wonderful is Your insatiable hunger! Nothing that can be eaten escapes from Your mouths.

425 Do You wish to swallow the ocean in one gulp, to consume a mountain in one mouthful, or to sink Your teeth into the whole universe?

426 Such is Your voracity that You swallow up all the corners of the globe, and with one lick of Your tongue You wipe away the stars.

427 Just as desire increases with enjoyment, and a fire grows fiercer with fuel, similarly, as Your mouths eat they search for more.

428 Even one of these mouths is so vast that the three worlds could hang on the tip of its tongue, as though an apple were thrown into the great fire beneath the sea.

429 Your mouths are so numerous that there aren't enough worlds to fill them all. There is no reason to multiply them when there is no food for them.

430 Alas! This poor world is caught in the flames of Your mouths, just as animals are surrounded by a forest fire.

431 The universe is in such a plight that You are no longer its God. An evil fate has come upon it as though it were a fish floundering in the net of death.

432 How can any creature escape from the radiance of Your body? These are not mouths; for the world they are like wax houses.

433 Fire doesn't know its own power to burn because it cannot be burned, yet whatever it touches cannot escape from it.

434 Does a weapon know how its sharpness can destroy? Does poison know its power to kill?

435 Similarly, You are unaware of Your fierceness, yet here Your mouths have devoured the whole world.

436 O Lord, You are the one all-pervasive Spirit. Why have You become the god of death for us?

437 I have given up all desire for life. Tell me please, without hesitation, what is in Your mind.

438 How much more will You spread out Your terrifying form? Remember Your divine nature, or at least have mercy on me!

आख्याहि मे को भवान् उग्ररूपो
नमो ऽस्तु ते देववर प्रसीद ।
विज्ञातुम् इच्छामि भवन्तम् आद्यं
न हि प्रजानामि तव प्रवृत्तिम् ॥

ākhyāhi me ko bhavān ugrarūpo
namo 'stu te devavara prasīda
vijñātum icchāmi bhavantam ādyaṁ
na hi prajānāmi tava pravṛttim

31. Tell me who You are, of so terrible a form. Salutations to You, O Best of Gods; have mercy! I wish to understand You, primal One; indeed, I do not comprehend what You are doing.

439 O Lord, known to us in the Vedas, existing before all worlds, worshiped by the whole universe, listen to my plea.

440 With these words Arjuna bowed low at the feet of the Lord and said, Listen, O Lord of lords.

441 I asked You to show me Your cosmic form so that I might be satisfied, but You immediately began to swallow up the universe.

442 Who are You, and why have You assembled all these terrible faces? Why do You carry those weapons in every hand?

443 Why do You angrily grow even greater than the sky? Why do You terrify us by producing these horrifying eyes?

444 Why do You become the rival of the god of death? Will You explain all this to me?

445 To this Krishna replied, You ask Me who I am, why I have spread out My form in this way, and what this violence is.

श्रीभगवान् उवाच । *śrībhagavān uvāca*

कालो ऽस्मि लोकक्षयकृत् प्रवृद्धो
लोकान् समाहर्तुम् इह प्रवृत्तः ।
ऋते ऽपि त्वां न भविष्यन्ति सर्वे

ये ऽवस्थिताः प्रत्यनीकेषु योधाः ।।

kālo 'smi lokakṣayakṛt pravṛddho
lokān samāhartum iha pravṛttaḥ
ṛte 'pi tvāṁ na bhaviṣyanti sarve
ye 'vasthitāḥ pratyanīkeṣu yodhāḥ

The Blessed Lord spoke:
32. I am Time, the mighty cause of world destruction, who has come forth to annihilate the worlds. Even without any action of yours, all these warriors who are arrayed in the opposing ranks, shall cease to exist.

446 I am clearly the god of death, and My form is spread out like this for the destruction of the world. For this purpose these mouths are spread out: I will devour everything that is.

447 Arjuna replied, Alas! I was greatly confused, so I implored Your help. Then all these misfortunes arose.

448 Feeling that harsh words would discourage Arjuna, Krishna said, But there is another thing.

449 You, Arjuna, have been spared from this great calamity. At this, Arjuna, about to give up, gradually recovered his spirits.

450 As the fear of this great destruction passed, Arjuna came to himself and began to pay attention to the Lord's words.

451 The Lord continued, O Arjuna, only you are Mine. I am about to destroy all the others.

452 You have seen the whole world drawn into My mouths and consumed like an offering cast into the fire in the depths of the ocean.

453 Certainly none of this will remain, but see how these armies vainly boast!

454 These armies arrayed here arrogantly claim, with all the power of their warrior-like qualities, that their elephant troops are superior even to the god of death.

455 They say that they can create worlds upon worlds, and claim that they could even slay death itself and swallow the whole universe in one gulp.

456 They boast that they will devour the whole earth, burn up all space, and nail down the wind with their arrows.

457 Elated by their achievements, they try to excel the great death with the wealth of their weapons.

458 Their words are sharper than their weapons and fiercer than fire. Compared with their destructive power, the Kalakuta poison is sweet.

459 But all these warriors seem to be hollow masses of plaster or fruit painted in a picture.

460 These figures parading in grand attire are like the waters of a mirage. They are not armies, but resemble a snake made of cloth.

तस्मात् त्वम् उत्तिष्ठ यशो लभस्व
जित्वा शत्रून् भुङ्क्ष्व राज्यं समृद्धम् ।
मयैवैते निहताः पूर्वम् एव
निमित्तमात्रं भव सव्यसाचिन् ।।

tasmāt tvam uttiṣṭha yaśo labhasva
jitvā śatrūn bhuṅkṣva rājyaṁ samṛddham
mayāivāite nihatāḥ pūrvam eva
nimittamātraṁ bhava savyasācin

33. Therefore stand up and attain glory! Having conquered the enemy, enjoy prosperous kingship. These have already been struck down by Me; be the mere instrument, O Arjuna.

461 I have already consumed all the power which activates them. They are as lifeless as figurines in a pottery shop.

462 They are like puppets at the end of stick which tumble down in all directions as soon as the string which moves them is broken.

463 It would take Me only a moment to overcome these armies. So arise! Come to your senses!

464 When the Kauravas stole Virata's cattle, you struck them unconscious with your magic weapon, so that even the timid Uttara grabbed hold of them and stripped off their clothes.

465 These armies are even more worthless than those enemies. Now that they have come to this battlefield, kill them and win for yourself the glory of having conquered them single-handed.

466 This is no empty glory, O Arjuna. The whole kingdom will be yours, so act as a weapon in My hand.

द्रोणं च भीष्मं च जयद्रथं च
कर्णं तथान्यान् अपि योधवीरान् ।
मया हतांस् त्वं जहि मा व्यथिष्ठा
युध्यस्व जेतासि रणे सपत्नान् ।।

droṇaṁ ca bhīṣmaṁ ca jayadrathaṁ ca
karṇaṁ tathānyān api yodhavīrān
mayā hatāṅs tvaṁ jahi mā vyathiṣṭhā
yudhyasva jetāsi raṇe sapatnān

34. Drona, Bhishma, Jayadratha, and Karna too, others also, warrior heroes, have been killed by Me. Do not hesitate! Kill! Fight! You shall conquer the enemy in battle.

467 Don't be afraid of Drona or Bhishma. And why should you hesitate to take up arms against Karna?

468 Don't be concerned about killing Jayadratha and all those other renowned warriors.

469 Consider them as merely painted lions, to be wiped out with your hand.

470 O Arjuna, What is this great battle array? It is merely an outer show, for I already hold it in My hand.

471 At the moment when you saw them caught in My mouth, their lives were ended. Now they are like empty husks.

472 So arise at once and slay those whose lives I have already taken. Don't give way to senseless grief.

473 Realize that you are merely an instrument. Shoot them down like a man who, as a game, piles up wooden blocks and knocks them down again.

474 Beloved, those who have come forward to oppose you were already dead at the moment of their birth, so enjoy fame with the conquest of this kingdom.

475 Arjuna, in his bravery, destroyed his kinsmen, who were filled with pride and drunk with their worldly power.

476 O Arjuna, write these words on the tablet of the world's records and be victorious.

संजय उवाच । *sañjaya uvāca*

एतच् छ्रुत्वा वचनं केशवस्य
कृताञ्जलिर् वेपमानः किरीटी ।
नमस्कृत्वा भूय एवाह कृष्णं
सगद्गदं भीतभीतः प्रणम्य ॥
etac chrutvā vacanaṁ keśavasya
kṛtāñjalir vepamānaḥ kirīṭī
namaskṛtvā bhūya evāha kṛṣṇaṁ
sagadgadaṁ bhītabhītaḥ praṇamya

Sanjaya spoke:
35. Having heard this utterance of Krishna, Arjuna, with joined palms, trembling, prostrating himself, terrified, and bowing down, thus spoke in a choked voice to Krishna:

477 Sanjaya narrated this whole story to the king of the Kurus, who listened to it eager to hear more. So says Jnanadeva.

478 Then Krishna spoke with a sonorous voice, like the rushing of the Ganges pouring down from the highest heaven.

479 Like the roaring of heavy clouds sending down their torrents of rain, or the crashing of the Milky Ocean as it was being churned with Mount Mandara,

480 Similarly, Krishna, the source of the universe, unknowable and of infinite form, spoke to Arjuna in deep resounding tones.

481 Arjuna had scarcely heard it when his whole body began to tremble, whether with intense joy or grief, it would be hard to know.

482 Bowing very low and joining his hands in salutation, he touched the Lord's feet again and again with his forehead.

483 When he tried again to speak, his throat was choked with emotion. We can only imagine whether this was through joy or fear.

484 This was Arjuna's condition, brought about by the Lord's words. This is how I interpret the verses of the story.

485 Full of fear, again he bowed his head at the Lord's feet and said, O Lord, this is what You said:

अर्जुन उवाच । *arjuna uvāca*

स्थाने हृषीकेश तव प्रकीर्त्या
जगत् प्रहृष्यत्य् अनुरज्यते च ।
रक्षांसि भीतानि दिशो द्रवन्ति
सर्वे नमस्यन्ति च सिद्धसंघाः ॥
sthāne hṛṣīkeśa tava prakīrtyā
jagat prahṛṣyaty anurajyate ca
rakṣāṁsi bhītāni diśo dravanti
sarve namasyanti ca siddhasaṁghāḥ

Arjuna spoke:
36. Rightly, O Krishna, the universe rejoices and is gratified by Your praise. The demons, terrified, flee in all directions; and all the throngs of the perfected ones bow before You.

486 O Arjuna, I am death, and it is My play to devour all. This saying is unalterable.

487 But I cannot understand why You who should preserve are destroying every thing today.

488 How can youth be removed from the body and premature age be brought in? Therefore, what You claim to do is impossible.

489 O Krishna, can the sun ever set at noon, before the day has come to an end?

490 For You, who are endless time, there are three states, each one all-powerful in its own time.

491 When existence begins, continuation and dissolution cease to be. During the continuation of existence, creation and dissolution do not take place.

492 And at the moment of dissolution, creation and existence cease. This system is eternal and immutable.

493 For this reason, I cannot understand how You can devour the world while it is experiencing the state of existence.

494 Then the Lord gestured to Arjuna as if to say, I have shown you how these two armies are doomed, and the destruction of others will happen in due time.

495 Krishna had hardly spoken when Arjuna saw that the worlds had been restored to their previous state.

496 Arjuna said, O Lord, You hold the strings which control the puppet show of the universe. See, the world has returned to its former state.

497 I remember how it is said that You save those who have fallen into the ocean of sorrow.

498 Whenever I remember this, I experience the highest bliss and seem to float in the waves of the nectar of joy.

499 O Lord, this world is filled with love for You because of its very existence; but the wicked, on the other hand, suffer increasing destruction.

500 O Krishna, You are a source of terror to the demons who flee from You beyond the confines of the world,

501 While the gods, perfected beings, and the kinnaras—the entire animate and inanimate creation—salute You with great joy.

कस्माच् च ते न नमेरन् महात्मन्
गरीयसे ब्रह्मणो ऽप्य् आदिकर्त्रे ।
अनन्त देवेश जगन्निवास
त्वम् अक्षरं सद् असत् तत्परं यत् ।।
kasmāc ca te na nameran mahātman
garīyase brahmaṇo 'py ādikartre
ananta deveśa jagannivāsa
tvam akṣaraṁ sad asat tatparaṁ yat

37. And why should they not bow to You, O great One, who are the original Creator, greater even than Brahma! Infinite Lord of Gods, you are the dwelling place of the universe, the imperishable, the existent, the non-existent, and that which is beyond both.

502 O Krishna, why should the demons flee at the sight of You, instead of taking refuge in You?

503 Why should I ask You this? This much we know. How can darkness remain after the sun rises?

504 Because You, the storehouse of the light of the soul, have made Yourself visible to us today, it is only natural that the demons should flee.

505 This was hidden from me for a long time, O Krishna, but now I have seen Your profound greatness.

506 Your divine desire has brought forth the supreme Spirit, from whom proceed entire series of worlds and all manner of created beings.

507 You, O Lord, are that which is eternally limitless, the One who is not confined by the qualities, the same throughout all time. You are truly the whole process of speech in its four stages.

508 You are the essence sustaining all the worlds, O Krishna. You are indestructible, being and non-being, and all that is beyond these two.

त्वम् आदिदेव: पुरुष: पुराणस्
त्वम् अस्य विश्वस्य परं निधानम् ।
वेत्तासि वेद्यं च परं च धाम
त्वया ततं विश्वम् अनन्तरूप ।।
tvam ādidevaḥ puruṣaḥ purāṇas
tvam asya viśvasya paraṁ nidhānam
vettāsi vedyaṁ ca paraṁ ca dhāma
tvayā tataṁ viśvam anantarūpa

38. You are the primal God, the ancient Spirit; You are the supreme resting place of all the universe; You are the knower, the object of knowledge, and the supreme state. All the universe is pervaded by You, O One of infinite forms.

509 You are the source of both spirit and matter, the great first Principle, without beginning, self-existent, the ancient One.

510 You are the life of the whole universe, the storehouse of the life of the world. The knowledge of past and future is in Your hands.

511 Through the eyes of the Vedas we see the joy of union with You, O You who are one with the universe. You are the highest refuge of the three worlds.

512 Therefore, You are called the ultimate ref-

uge, for at the end of the world even the supreme Spirit merges into You.

513 In short, You pervade the entire universe. Who can describe Your infinite form?

वायुर् यमो ऽग्निर् वरुणः शशाङ्कः
प्रजापतिस् त्वं प्रपितामहश्च ।
नमो नमस् ते ऽस्तु सहस्रकृत्वः
पुनश्च भूयो ऽपि नमो नमस् ते ।।

vāyur yamo 'gnir varuṇaḥ śaśāṅkaḥ
prajāpatis tvaṁ prapitāmahaś ca
namo namas te 'stu sahasrakṛtvaḥ
punaśca bhūyo 'pi namo namas te

39. You are Vayu, Yama, Agni, Varuna, the Moon, the Lord of creatures, and the great grandfather. Salutations to You a thousand times, and again saluations, salutations to You!

नमः पुरस्ताद् अथ पृष्ठतस् ते
नमो ऽस्तु ते सर्वत एव सर्व ।
अनन्तवीर्यामितविक्रमस् त्वं
सर्वं समाप्नोषि ततो ऽसि सर्वः ।।

namaḥ purastād atha pṛṣṭhatas te
namo 'stu te sarvata eva sarva
anantavīryāmitavikramas tvaṁ
sarvaṁ samāpnoṣi tato 'si sarvaḥ

40. Salutations to You from in front and behind, salutations to You on all sides also, O All. You are infinite valor and boundless might. You pervade all, therefore You are all.

514 Aren't You the One? Is there any place where You are not? Hail to You and all that You are.

515 O Krishna, You are the god of the wind and of death, who is the punisher of all. You are the fire residing in all things.

516 You are the god of the waters and of the moon; Brahma, the creator of all; and Prajapati, the great progenitor of all.

517 Salutations to You, O Lord of the world! We hail You as all that You are, whether You are with or without form.

518 In this way, Arjuna praised the Lord and saluted Him again and again with devotion.

519 Once more looking at the Lord's form from head to toe, he cried, Hail, hail to You, O Lord!

520 Having observed all the animate and inanimate forms that were seen in His body, Arjuna exclaimed again, O Lord, salutations to You!

521 At the sight of the even stranger forms and marvels that were appearing, Arjuna was filled with amazement and exclaimed again and again, All hail to You!

522 He could think of no other words of praise, nor could he remain silent. He began to shout in the fervor of his love.

523 Thus he saluted the Lord a thousand times and exclaimed again, I bow down to You, O Krishna, who are here before me!

524 What does it matter to us whether You have front or back? From behind, I salute You!

525 There is no end to Your limbs and forms. So hail to You, who pervade all!

526 I salute You who have all mighty power and immeasurable force. You are always the same One manifest in all lands.

527 You are all in all and pervade all just as in the sky the whole space is sky.

528 You are all this, just as in the Milky Ocean every wave is of milk.

529 In no way are You different from all this. Now I realize that You Yourself are everything.

सखेति मत्वा प्रसभं यद् उक्तं हे कृष्ण हे यादव हे सखेति ।
अजानता महिमानं तवेदं मया प्रमादात् प्रणयेन वापि ।।

sakheti matvā prasabhaṁ yad uktaṁ
he kṛṣṇa he yādava he sakheti
ajānatā mahimānaṁ tavedaṁ
mayā pramādāt praṇayena vāpi

41. Whatever I have said impetuously as if in ordinary friendship, "Oh Krishna, Oh Son of Yadu, Oh Comrade," in ignorance of Your majesty, through negligence or even through affection,

530 I never realized that You were like this, O Lord, so I behaved towards You like a close friend.

531 How great was my impropriety! It was as if I had used nectar to wash the ground, or given away the wish-fulfilling cow in exchange for a bull,

532 Or as if, having found a touchstone, I had broken it up unwittingly to use it in building, or cut down the wish-fulfilling tree to make a hedge for a field,

533 Or as if, having found a mine of wish-fulfilling gems, I had not recognized them and had thrown them at unruly cattle to drive them away. Similarly, even while You were so near, we rejected You as a friend.

534 Considering the present situation, this war

after all is not important; yet I have used You, the highest God, as my charioteer!

535 O Generous One, we sent You as a mediator to the Kauravas, using You, the living Lord, as a common go-between.

536 What a fool I am! How couldn't I recognize You, the bliss of the highest attainment of yogis? And yet before Your very face, I have treated You discourteously.

यच् चावहासार्थम् असत्कृतो ऽसि
विहारशय्यासनभोजनेषु ।
एको ऽथवाप्य् अच्युत तत्समक्षं
तत् क्षामये त्वाम् अहम् अप्रमेयम् ॥
yac cāvahāsārtham asatkṛto 'si
vihāraśayyāsanabhojaneṣu
eko 'thavāpy acyuta tatsamakṣaṁ
tat kṣāmaye tvām aham aprameyam

42. And if, with humorous purpose, You were disrespectfully treated, while at play, resting, while seated or while dining, when alone, O Krishna, or even before the eyes of others, for that I ask forgiveness of You, immeasurable One.

537 You are the eternal origin of the universe, and yet we played with You on familiar terms as friends gathered together.

538 When at times we visited Your home, You received us with respect; yet, disregarding this, we would take offense.

539 O Krishna, to appease us You had to touch our feet, and we slighted You in many ways.

540 As though You were one of us, we turned our backs on You. O Krishna, in all these ways we behaved badly.

541 We crossed swords with You, wrestled with You constantly, in chess we treated You with scorn, and quarreled fiercely with You.

542 We demanded the best of everything, offered You advice, and at times treated You as of no account.

543 Our fault is so great that the three worlds cannot contain it; but touching Your feet, we assure You that we didn't understand.

544 The Lord would lovingly remember me at meals, but shamelessly I would remain silent.

545 Thoughtlessly I played in the Lord's room and rested beside Him on the couch.

546 I would call out to You, "Krishna!" I looked on You as a Yadava, and I would swear at You when You went away.

547 We would sit together and I would disregard Your words. Many such things happened through our familiarity. What more can I say?

548 O Krishna, how much more shall I tell? I am nothing but a mass of offenses.

549 Whatever faults I have committed either in Your presence or behind Your back, O Lord, take them all upon Yourself just as a mother would do.

550 Whenever rivers flow with their turbid waters into the ocean, doesn't it have to receive them, or can it reject them?

551 So, O Krishna, You should forgive me for all I have said against You, whether out of love or thoughtlessness.

552 Through Your forgiving nature, the earth has been able to bear all these creatures on its surface. Therefore, O Highest Being, is there any need to plead with You?

553 O You who are immeasurable, I have sought refuge in You. Forgive me for all my faults.

पितासि लोकस्य चराचरस्य
त्वम् अस्य पूज्यश्च गुरुर् गरीयान् ।
न त्वत्समो ऽस्त्य् अभ्यधिकः कुतो ऽन्यो
लोकत्रये ऽप्य् अप्रतिमप्रभाव ॥
pitāsi lokasya carācarasya
tvam asya pūjyaśca gurur garīyān
na tvatsamo 'sty abhyadhikaḥ kuto 'nyo
lokatraye 'py apratimaprabhāva

43. You are the father of the world, of all things moving and motionless. You are to be adored by this world. You are the most venerable Guru. There is nothing like You in the three worlds. How then could there be another greater, O Being of incomparable glory?

554 Now, O Lord, I have realized Your true greatness. You are the origin of the entire creation.

555 You are the highest deity of all the gods, Hari, Hara, and all others. You are the primal Guru, teaching even the Vedas.

556 You are profound, O Krishna, the only home of all creatures, the image of all virtues, the One without a second.

557 What need is there to state that no one is equal to You? Isn't the whole world contained in the space You created?

558 One should hesitate to say that there is anyone who can equal You. How then could one say that another is greater than You?

559 You are the only One in the universe, and

there is no one equal to or greater than You. Your incomparable greatness cannot be told.

तस्मात् प्रणम्य प्रणिधाय कायं
प्रसादये त्वाम् अहम् ईशम् ईड्यम् ।
पितेव पुत्रस्य सखेव सख्युः
प्रियः प्रियायार्हसि देव सोढुम् ॥

tasmāt praṇamya praṇidhāya kāyaṁ
prasādaye tvām aham īśam īḍyam
piteva putrasya sakheva sakhyuḥ
priyaḥ priyāyārhasi deva soḍhum

44. Therefore, bowing down, prostrating my body, I ask forgiveness of You, O Lord; as is a father to a son, a friend to a friend, a lover to a beloved, please, O God, be merciful!

560 Being filled with pure reverence, Arjuna said this and prostrated himself before the Lord.

561 Then he exclaimed in a choked voice, I beg You to have mercy and save me from the ocean of my faults.

562 Thinking of You, the friend of the whole world, as a personal relation, I didn't treat You with proper respect, but behaved arrogantly towards You, the Lord of all gods.

563 You Yourself are worthy of praise, but through Your affection for me You have praised me before others, and in my excitement I boasted more and more.

564 There is no limit to such mistakes, O Krishna. Save me, save me from my faults.

565 How can I be worthy to ask this of You? But I speak with familiarity, as a child to its father.

566 When a person meets a close friend, he doesn't hesitate to tell him freely of the troubles that have happened to him in the world.

567 If a faithful wife has surrendered herself wholeheartedly to her husband, she cannot conceal from him what is in her heart when he meets her.

568 In the same way, O Lord, I beg Your forgiveness. There is one more thing I would like to say to You.

अदृष्टपूर्वं हृषितो ऽस्मि दृष्ट्वा भयेन च प्रव्यथितं मनो मे ।
तद् एव मे दर्शय देव रूपं प्रसीद देवेश जगन्निवास ॥

adṛṣṭapūrvaṁ hṛṣito 'smi dṛṣṭvā
bhayena ca pravyathitaṁ mano me
tad eva me darśaya deva rūpaṁ
prasīda deveśa jagannivāsa

45. Having seen that which has never been seen before, I am delighted, and yet my mind trembles with fear. Show me that form, O God, in which You originally appeared. Have mercy, Lord of Gods, dwelling of the universe.

569 I took the liberty of begging You to reveal to me Your cosmic form and You, my father and mother, lovingly fulfilled my desire.

570 I wanted to have wish-fulfilling trees planted in my courtyard and wanted You to give me a calf of the wish-fulfilling cow to play with.

571 I wanted to play dice with the stars and to have the moon for a ball. You have fulfilled all these desires, O my mother!

572 Like the four months of the rainy season, You have showered nectar, a small particle of which one can obtain only with difficulty. Preparing the soil, You have sown wish-fulfilling gems in every furrow.

573 In this way, You have fulfilled the longing of my life, You have treated me indulgently, and have shown me Your form, of which Shiva and Brahma have never even heard, much less seen.

574 You have unraveled for me the knot of that secret which even the Upanishads failed to discover.

575 Even in all the lives through which I have passed from the beginning of the age until now,

576 Searching through them all, I cannot find that this has ever been seen or heard of.

577 The knowledge of the intellect has been unable to penetrate even its outer courtyard, nor can the heart imagine it.

578 How then can it be said that the eyes have ever seen it? Never before has anyone seen or heard of it.

579 This is that cosmic form which You revealed to me, and it has gladdened my heart.

580 But now I long to talk with You, to enjoy Your company, to embrace You.

581 How is this possible with that cosmic form of Yours? To which of Your faces shall I speak? Whom shall I embrace, as there is no end to Your form?

582 How can a person run with the wind, embrace the sky, or play in the ocean?

583 Great dread of that form has arisen in my heart, so grant me this favor—withdraw this vision.

584 Just as a person sees with pleasure the entire created world, then remains happily at home,

in the same way, Your four-armed form is our refuge.

585 If we practice yoga, it leads to the experience of Your finite form. We may study all the scriptures, but we attain the same end.

586 Whatever activities we perform, they are rewarded with this same fruit. This is the goal of all pilgrimages to holy places.

587 The works we perform in charity, the merit we acquire, all bring as a reward the vision of Your four-armed form.

588 My heart longs for that, but it is difficult to see it. Quickly, remove my distress!

589 O You who know our hearts, who establish the whole universe, who are to be worshiped, God of gods, have mercy on me.

किरीटिनं गदिनं चक्रहस्तम्
इच्छामि त्वां द्रष्टुम् अहं तथैव ।
तेनैव रूपेण चतुर्भुजेन
सहस्रबाहो भव विश्वमूर्ते ॥

kirīṭinaṁ gadinaṁ cakrahastam
icchāmi tvāṁ draṣṭum ahaṁ tathāiva
tenāiva rūpeṇa caturbhujena
sahasrabāho bhava viśvamūrte

46. I desire to see You wearing a crown, armed with a club, discus in hand, as before; become that four-armed form, O thousand armed One, O You who have all forms.

590 See how that form tints the blue lotuses, adds color to the azure sky, and gives luster to the sapphire.

591 It is as though the emerald were endowed with fragrance, as though arms were to grow on the body of joy, and as though all these were to lend beauty to the god of love himself.

592 There is a crown on Your head, but Your head is like a crown to the crown. Your body itself is the ornament of ornaments which adorn it.

593 O Krishna, You give Your necklace Vaijayanti added radiance, like clouds in the sky set in the rainbow.

594 How noble is Your mace, which gives the bliss of heaven to the demons with the force of its blow, and Your discus glows with a gentle radiance, O Krishna.

595 O Lord, I beg You to assume now that familiar form that I am so eager to see.

596 Having experienced the joy of Your cosmic form, my eyes are satisfied and long now to see You again as Krishna.

597 I only desire to see Your finite form. If my eyes cannot see that, they can no longer appreciate that other form.

598 For us, this simple form is our only source of joy and means of liberation. So withdraw Your cosmic form and become again the embodied Krishna.

श्रीभगवान् उवाच । *śrībhagavān uvāca*

मया प्रसन्नेन तवार्जुनेदं
रूपं परं दर्शितम् आत्मयोगात् ।
तेजोमयं विश्वम् अनन्तम् आद्यं
यन् मे त्वदन्येन न दृष्टपूर्वम् ॥

mayā prasannena tavārjunedaṁ
rūpaṁ paraṁ darśitam ātmayogāt
tejomayaṁ viśvam anantam ādyaṁ
yan me tvadanyena na dṛṣṭapūrvam

The Blessed Lord spoke:
47. By My grace toward you, Arjuna, this supreme form has been manifested through My own power, this form of Mine, made up of splendor, universal, infinite, primal, which has never before been seen by other than you.

599 The Lord of the cosmic form, wondering at Arjuna's words, said, I have never before seen anyone so foolish.

600 What a wonderful thing you have obtained! Yet you take no joy in it. Like an obstinate man, you don't know, in your fear, what you're saying.

601 At times, when I have been pleased, I have been willing even to give My body for My devotees. But to whom does one offer one's whole heart?

602 For you today I have given all of Myself to prepare for you this vision of My form.

603 My love for you is so great that I have displayed the banner of the supreme secret before the world.

604 This is My incomparable, highest form, out of which proceed incarnations like that of Krishna.

605 It is infused with the pure light of wisdom, pervading all worlds, eternal, immovable, the source of all.

606 O Arjuna, except for you, never before has this happened, nor can it be obtained by any means or practices.

न वेदयज्ञाध्ययनैर् न दानैर्
न च क्रियाभिर् न तपोभिर् उग्रैः ।

एवंरूपः शक्य अहं नृलोके
द्रष्टुं त्वदन्येन कुरुप्रवीर ।।

na vedayajñādhyayanāir na dānāir
na ca kriyābhir na tapobhir ugrāiḥ
evaṁrūpaḥ śakya ahaṁ nṛloke
draṣṭuṁ tvadanyena kurupravīra

48. Not by Vedic sacrifice nor (Vedic) recitation, not by gifts, and not by ritual acts nor by severe austerities, can I be seen in such a form in the world of men by any other than you, Arjuna.

607 When the Vedas set out to find it, they became silent. Sacrifice turned back from heaven in despair.

608 Seekers who encountered many difficulties abandoned the practice of yoga, and study of the sacred scriptures is ineffective where this matter is concerned.

609 The highest and most meritorious works pursued it eagerly, but in spite of all their efforts, most of them couldn't reach beyond the seventh heaven.

610 They saw heaven and immediately abandoned their austerities. The means of penance also failed them; the goal was beyond their reach.

611 Without any such effort you have seen this cosmic form, which no one else in the mortal world has been able to see.

612 You alone have been found worthy of this, the goal of meditation. Even the creator himself has not been this blessed.

मा ते व्यथा मा च विमूढभावो
दृष्ट्वा रूपं घोरम् ईदृङ्ममेदम् ।
व्यपेतभीः प्रीतमनाः पुनस् त्वं
तद् एव मे रूपम् इदं प्रपश्य ।।

mā te vyathā mā ca vimūḍhabhāvo
dṛṣṭvā rūpaṁ ghoram īdṛṅ mamedam
vyapetabhīḥ prītamanāḥ punas tvaṁ
tad eva me rūpam idaṁ prapaśya

49. Have no fear or confusion on seeing this terrible form of Mine; be again free from fear and cheered in heart. Behold, My (previous) form!

613 Be happy that you have seen this form. Have no fear of it, and don't consider anything to be good except this.

614 If a person were suddenly to come upon an ocean filled with nectar, would he abandon it for fear of drowning in it?

615 If he should find a mountain of gold, would he pass it by, thinking it was too heavy to be moved?

616 If by good fortune he were to wear a wish-fulfilling gem, would he reject it as a burden? Would he drive away the wish-fulfilling cow because he was unable to feed her?

617 If the moon were to appear in his house, would he say, "Leave! Don't bring heat"? Would he say to the sun, "Depart! You cast shadows"?

618 Today you have been given the glorious vision of the great light. Why should you be so disturbed?

619 O Arjuna, ignorant one, you don't understand. But should I be angry with you? You abandon the real body and cling to the shadow.

620 Isn't this form truly Me? In your timidity you give your love to what appears to be Me in My four-armed form.

621 O Arjuna, give up your previous concepts and don't remain attached to that form.

622 Though that cosmic form is fierce, terrifying, and vast, let it be the only goal of your desire.

623 A miser's whole heart is bound up in his treasure. He lives outwardly only as a body.

624 A mother bird leaves her heart in the nest with her unfledged young ones when she flies away into the sky.

625 Although a cow roams on the mountain, her love remains with her calf. Similarly, O Arjuna, focus your love on My form alone.

626 Enjoy My four-armed form for the sake of outer pleasure,

627 But, O Arjuna, again and again I urge you never to forget My words, that you shouldn't withhold your devotion from My cosmic form.

628 Because you have never seen this vision before, you are afraid. Give up this fear and give your love wholly to this form.

629 Then Krishna said, I will do as you say. I will gladly give you again the vision of My four-armed form.

संजय उवाच । *sañjaya uvāca*

इत्य् अर्जुनं वासुदेवस् तथोक्त्वा
स्वकं रूपं दर्शयाम् आस भूयः ।
आश्वासयाम् आस च भीतम् एनं
भूत्वा पुनः सौम्यवपुर् महात्मा ।।

ity arjunam vāsudevas tathoktvā

svakaṁ rūpaṁ darśayām āsa bhūyaḥ
āśvāsayām āsa ca bhītam enaṁ
bhūtvā punaḥ sāumyavapur mahātmā

Sanjaya spoke:
50. Having spoken thus to Arjuna, Krishna revealed His own (previous) form again. Having resumed His gentle, wonderful appearance, He calmed Arjuna, who was terrified.

630 As soon as He had spoken these words, the Lord resumed His human shape. See how wonderful is His love for Arjuna!

631 Lord Krishna is the highest bliss, and in the vision of His cosmic form, He gave Himself completely; yet Arjuna was not content with it.

632 He was like a person who accepts something and then throws it away, like one who finds fault with a jewel, or who sees a beautiful girl and rejects her.

633 See how Lord Krishna showed His great love by displaying His cosmic form! In this way, He gave to Arjuna the essence of all His teaching.

634 Just as gold ornaments made according to a person's wish are again melted down if the ornaments do not please him,

635 Similarly, Krishna, who out of love for His disciple had transformed Himself into His cosmic form, assumed again His personal form when Arjuna wasn't pleased.

636 Seeing this, we wonder where there could be any teacher so patient with the demands of his disciple. Sanjaya said, I don't understand such love.

637 Then the divine radiance which had been revealed, the cosmic form embracing all things, was drawn back into the personal form of Krishna.

638 Just as the concept of "you" is embraced by the broader concept of "That", just as the seed is contained in the tree,

639 Or just as the fantasy of a dream is destroyed when a person awakens, in the same way, Lord Krishna withdrew His cosmic form.

640 Just as the light of the sun is held within the sun's disk, as clouds form part of the sky, and as the full tide lies in the bed of the ocean,

641 Similarly, to please Arjuna, the Lord spread out like the folds of a new garment that cosmic form which had been concealed within His personal form.

642 When Arjuna, like a customer, had examined its measure and its color, it didn't please him; so the Lord again folded it and put it away.

643 In this way the cosmic form, which overpowers the world by its vastness, changed again into the gentle and beautiful finite form.

644 Perhaps Krishna returned to His lesser form in order to reassure the frightened Arjuna.

645 Then Arjuna was filled with amazement, just like a person who suddenly awakens from a dream in which he has been in heaven.

646 Arjuna looked at Krishna in the same way as a person whose interest in worldly matters has disappeared and through the grace of his Guru suddenly realizes the eternal Truth.

647 It seemed good to him that the cosmic form, which had been like a veil between them, had been withdrawn.

648 Then, just like a man who had overcome death, or had escaped from a terrible storm, or had crossed the seven seas by the strength of his own arms,

649 Arjuna rejoiced that after the cosmic form was removed, he could see Krishna as before.

650 Then, just as after sunset the stars appear again in the sky, Arjuna began to see the two armies on the field.

651 He looked around and saw the battlefield with the Kauravas and his relatives arrayed on the two sides, and as before, the warriors hurling masses of weapons against each other.

652 His chariot was still standing there as though under a canopy of the enemies' arrows, with Krishna seated at the front of his chariot and himself on the ground.

अर्जुन उवाच *arjuna uvāca*

दृष्ट्वेदं मानुषं रूपं तव सौम्यं जनार्दन।
इदानीम् अस्मि संवृत्तः सचेताः प्रकृतिं गतः॥

dṛṣṭvedaṁ mānuṣaṁ rūpaṁ
tava sāumyaṁ janārdana
idānīm asmi saṁvṛttaḥ
sacetāḥ prakṛtiṁ gataḥ

Arjuna spoke:
51. Seeing Your gentle human form, O

Krishna, now I am composed and my mind is restored to normal.

653 When everything had been restored to its previous state, Arjuna said, My mind has been restored!

654 Knowledge, abandoning intelligence, had strayed in fear into the wilderness; and my mind, accompanied by egoism, was wandering from place to place.

655 My senses had become inactive and my speech had ceased; such was the state of disorder within my body.

656 These have now been restored to their proper functioning, revitalized by the sight of Your gentle form.

657 Feeling such joy, Arjuna said to Krishna, Again I can see Your human form.

658 O Lord, by showing it to me, You have treated me just as a mother would coax an erring child and nurse it.

659 I was immersed in the ocean of Your cosmic form, struggling through the waves one by one with my hands. Now I have arrived at the shore of Your personal form.

660 O Krishna, this is no mere gift. It is as though You had showered down rain upon me, a withering tree.

661 I was overcome with thirst; now I have come upon an ocean of nectar. Confidence in my understanding has now been restored.

662 You have planted the vine of happiness in the garden of my heart, and have renewed my experience of joy.

श्रीभगवान् उवाच । *śrībhagavān uvāca*

सुदुर्दर्शम् इदं रूपं दृष्टवान् असि यन् मम ।
देवा अप्य् अस्य रूपस्य नित्यं दर्शनकाङ्क्षिणः ।।

sudurdarśam idaṁ rūpaṁ
dṛṣṭavān asi yan mama
devā apy asya rūpasya
nityaṁ darśanakāṅkṣiṇaḥ

The Blessed Lord spoke:

52. This form of Mine which you have beheld is difficult to see; even the gods are constantly longing to behold it.

663 After Arjuna had said this, Lord Krishna said, Focus your love on My universal aspect,

664 And then you may turn to this finite form for outer worship only. O Arjuna, have you forgotten all my teaching?

665 Once a person possesses even Mount Meru, he will consider it of little value. Such false dreams we have!

666 Even with all his penance, Shiva wasn't able to have the vision of that cosmic form which I have shown you.

667 Arjuna, yogis become weary through the practice of yogic discipline, but they don't have that vision.

668 The gods themselves spend their entire lives in the hope that one day they may catch a glimpse of it.

669 Just as the chataka bird looks up to the clouds with longing, holding out the cup of hope,

670 Similarly, the gods and men, with eager desire, repeat day and night their prayer for that vision.

671 Yet, you have seen so easily, face to face, this cosmic form which no one had seen even in a dream.

नाहं वेदैर् न तपसा न दानेन न चेज्यया ।
शक्य एवंविधो द्रष्टुं दृष्टवान् असि मां यथा ।।

nāhaṁ vedāir na tapasā
na dānena na cejyayā
śakya evaṁvidho draṣṭum
dṛṣṭavān asi mām yathā

53. Not through study of the Vedas, not through austerity, not through gifts, and not through sacrifice can I be seen in this form as you have beheld Me.

672 Look, O Arjuna! This vision cannot be reached by any road, and the Vedas have turned back in their search for it.

673 O Arjuna, My cosmic form cannot be reached through the practice of manifold penances;

674 Nor can that vision which you have seen with so little effort, be won by gifts, by austerities, or by sacrifices.

675 You should know that there is only one path to reach Me: the heart must be filled with devotion.

भक्त्या त्व् अनन्यया शक्य अहम् एवंविधो ऽर्जुन ।
ज्ञातुं द्रष्टुं च तत्त्वेन प्रवेष्टुं च परंतप ।।

bhaktyā tv ananyayā śakya
aham evaṁvidho 'rjuna
jñātuṁ draṣṭuṁ ca tattvena
praveṣṭuṁ ca paraṁtapa

54. By undistracted devotion alone can I be known, and be truly seen in this form, and be entered into, Arjuna.

676 This devotion must be like showers of rain

which have no other place to go, apart from the earth;

677 Or like the river Ganges, which with its abundant waters again and again seeks out the ocean, which is its only refuge.

678 In such a way, a devotee lives his life in Me with wholehearted and unswerving love, becoming one with Me.

679 Just as I am like the Milky Ocean, which from shore to shore consists only of milk,

680 Have no doubt that from Me down to the ant, there is no other to be worshiped in the entire creation.

681 As soon as you believe this, you will know My true nature; and when you know this, it follows that you will see Me.

682 When fire is lit from fuel, the fuel becomes fire and is lost from sight.

683 The sky remains dark as long as the sun hasn't risen, but when it appears, the light shines forth.

684 Similarly, through direct experience of Me, egoism vanishes; and with the disappearance of egoism, duality passes away.

685 Thus, I am all that is; I am by nature the only one who exists. What more can I say? A person who knows this is absorbed in union with Me.

मत्कर्मकृन् मत्परमो मद्भक्तः सङ्गवर्जितः ।
निर्वैरः सर्वभूतेषु यः स माम् एति पाण्डव ॥

matkarmakṛn matparamo
madbhaktaḥ sañgavarjitaḥ
nirvāiraḥ sarvabhūteṣu
yaḥ sa mām eti pāṇḍava

55. He who does all work for Me, considers Me as the Supreme, is devoted to Me, abandons all attachment, and is free from enmity toward any being, comes to Me, Arjuna.

686 A devotee who performs every action for My sake, and for whom there is no one in the world as dear as I am,

687 For whom I am the only goal among all things visible and invisible, who has chosen Me as the ultimate purpose of his existence,

688 Who has forgotten the language of created beings, and who reveres all things because he sees Me in all and is therefore free from enmity,

689 He becomes united with Me when he leaves his mortal body, O Arjuna.

690 Sanjaya said, O King! The Lord who contains the whole universe within Himself spoke in this way with words full of compassion.

691 Then Arjuna, endowed with the riches of supreme joy, and in all the world the one most fit to serve at Krishna's feet,

692 Saw both of the Lord's manifestations; but he preferred Krishna in His human form to the vision of the cosmic form.

693 However, Krishna didn't approve of Arjuna's choice, for the finite is not superior to the infinite.

694 In support of this, the Lord gave him several explanations.

695 Hearing these, Arjuna said to himself, Now I will ask which of the two is better.

696 With this thought in mind, Arjuna found appropriate ways to ask Krishna about it. Now listen to the continuation of the story.

697 Jnanadeva says, This story will now be told in an interesting way in the simple ovi meter by the grace of Nivritti.

698 At the feet of the Lord's cosmic form, I now offer the open flowers of my ovi verses, held in the hands of my pure devotion.

12

THE YOGA OF DEVOTION

Hail to you, O grace-bestowing power, who are pure, famous for your generosity, and always pouring out showers of joy!

2 When a person is overcome by the grasp of the serpent of sense pleasures, its bite is made harmless by one glance of your grace.

3 If you flow over us with the waves of your favor, whom can the heat of passion burn or the fire of grief consume?

4 O blessed grace, you reveal to your disciples the bliss of yoga, and you satisfy their yearning for Self-realization.

5 You rear them lovingly in the lap of the power seated in the *muladhara chakra* and rock them to sleep in the cradle of the heart.

6 You encircle them with the light of discrimination, you give them mind control and the vital force as toys for their play, and you wrap them in the clothing of the bliss of the Self.

7 You nurse them with the supreme Self, sing them songs of the mystic unstruck sound as lullabies, and lull them to sleep by telling them of the final absorption in the Self.

8 Thus you are the mother of spiritual seekers, and all knowledge matures at your feet. Therefore, I will not leave the shadow of your protection.

9 O grace of the Guru, one who is supported by your favor becomes like the creator of the whole world of knowledge.

10 Therefore, O wealthiest of mothers and wish-fulfilling tree for your devotees, command me to expound this work.

11 O mother, let the ocean of the nine feelings fill my speech, create mines of the finest figures of speech, and raise mountains of the interpretation of the meaning.

12 I beg of you, open up in the soil of the Marathi language a gold mine of literary composition, and cultivate it in vines of discernment.

13 Jnaneshwar says, Plant in it dense gardens ever full of the abundant fruit of the discussion of philosophical problems.

14 Break up the ravines of heresy, destroy the bypaths of controversy, and slay the evil beasts of false reasoning.

15 Make me always remain seated at the feet of Lord Krishna, and set the listeners on the throne of hearing.

16 Let the blessed day of the knowledge of the Absolute come to the city of the Marathi language, and let the world trade only in the bliss of union.

17 Clothe me in your blessed favor, and I will soon accomplish all of this.

18 Hearing the prayer of his disciple, the gracious Guru looked at him and told him to say no more but to begin at once the exposition of the *Gita*.

19 Jnaneshwar, filled with joy, exclaimed, Lord, Lord, I will do this! Then he said to his listeners, I will now begin to expound the work. Listen!

अर्जुन उवाच । *arjuna uvāca*

एवं सततयुक्ता ये भक्तास् त्वां पर्युपासते ।
ये चाप्य् अक्षरम् अव्यक्तं तेषां के योगवित्तमाः ॥

evaṁ satatayuktā ye
bhaktās tvāṁ paryupāsate
ye cāpy akṣaram avyaktam
teṣāṁ ke yogavittamāḥ

Arjuna spoke:

1. The constantly steadfast devotees who worship You with devotion, and those who worship the eternal unmanifest; which of these has the better knowledge of yoga?

20 Then Arjuna, the greatest of all warriors and the victorious leader of the Lunar race, began to speak.
21 He said to Krishna, Have You heard? You showed me Your cosmic form, and I was terrified by that marvelous vision.
22 Being familiar with Your human form as Krishna, my desire at once turned to that, but You forbade me to have such a wish.
23 O Lord, You are indeed both the manifest and the unmanifest. The manifest is reached through devotion, and the unmanifest is attained by yoga.
24 These are the two paths which lead to You, O Krishna, and the manifest and the unmanifest are the two thresholds which open onto them.
25 Look, when a bar of gold of a hundred grains is tested with a touchstone, the effect is the same as it would be with a piece of one grain. In the same way, both the limited and the limitless have the same value.
26 The power that lies in an ocean of nectar is found equally in a handful taken from one of its waves.
27 I truly believe this from my experience, but there is one question which I wish to ask You, O Krishna.
28 Will You tell me, O Lord, whether that cosmic form which You assumed for a time is real, or merely a display of Your power?
29 Those devotees whose actions are dedicated to You, for whom You are the highest goal, whose hearts are wholly given to devotion,
30 And who in many other ways worship You, O Krishna, with all their heart and soul;
31 And on the other hand those wise ones who worship You, the unmanifest, who are beyond even the sacred syllable and inexpressible in speech, untouched by any bondage,
32 The imperishable One, unmanifest, beyond space or definition;
33 Of these two, the devotees and the wise—who, O Eternal One, are more truly the knowers of yoga?
34 Krishna was pleased with these words of Arjuna and said, Your question is a good one.

श्रीभगवान् उवाच । *śrībhagavān uvāca*

मय्यावेश्य मनो ये मां नित्ययुक्ता उपासते ।
श्रद्धया परयोपेतास् ते मे युक्ततमा मताः ।।
mayyāveśya mano ye māṁ
nityayuktā upāsate
śraddhayā parayopetās
te me yuktatamā matāḥ

The Blessed Lord spoke:
2. Those who are eternally steadfast, who worship Me, fixing their minds on Me, endowed with supreme faith; I consider them to be the most devoted to Me.

35 Just as the sun's rays follow it as it reaches the border of the western mountain,
36 So is the devotion of those who, with their senses merged in Me, serve Me without awareness of day or night.
37 Similarly, their love abounds just as the waters of the Ganges seem to increase even after they have poured into the ocean.
38 Just as the waters of a river rise in the rainy season, O Arjuna, their devotion seems to increase more and more.
39 Such devotees, who devote themselves entirely to Me, I consider to be the ones who are the most perfected in yoga.

ये त्व् अक्षरम् अनिर्देश्यम् अव्यक्तं पर्युपासते ।
सर्वत्रगम् अचिन्त्यं च कूटस्थम् अचलं ध्रुवम् ।।
ye tv akṣaram anirdeśyam
avyaktaṁ paryupāsate
sarvatragam acintyaṁ ca
kūṭastham acalaṁ dhruvam

3. But those who honor the imperishable, the indefinable, the unmanifest, the all-pervading and unthinkable, the unchanging, the immovable, the eternal,

40 O Arjuna, there are also those whose minds, filled with the thought of oneness with the Absolute, reach out for that which is formless, imperishable, and indivisible;
41 That One whom the mind is unable to grasp, who cannot be perceived by the intellect nor apprehended by the senses;
42 Who, being neither confined by space nor limited by form, is even beyond the reach of meditation;
43 Who exists in every place, in every form, and at all times; in contemplating whom the mind is utterly confused;
44 Who comes into being and yet does not become, who exists yet is non-existent, and to reach whom all means are useless;
45 Who neither moves nor sways, who is neither diminished nor sullied, and whom these devotees, by their spiritual power, have made their own.

संनियम्येंद्रियग्रामं सर्वत्र समबुद्धयः ।
ते प्राप्नुवन्ति माम् एव सर्वभूतहिते रताः ॥
saṁniyamyendriyagrāmaṁ
sarvatra samabuddhayaḥ
te prāpnuvanti mām eva
sarvabhūtahite ratāḥ

4. Controlling all the senses, even-minded on all sides, rejoicing in the welfare of all creatures, they also attain Me.

46 Burning up the whole army of sense pleasures in the great fire of dispassion, they have brought their scorched passions under control.

47 Driving them back with the noose of self-restraint, they confine them within the inner depths of the heart.

48 Constraining the downward-moving breath with the help of the proper yogic posture, they build up the fortress of *mulabandha.*

49 They break the bonds of desire, remove the rocks of timidity, and dispel the darkness of sleep.

50 They burn the fluids of the body in the flames of the thunderbolt, making an offering of all diseases at the altar of the six *chakras* of the body.

51 They set the torch of Kundalini at the *muladhara chakra*, and with this light they find the way to the *sahasrara* at the crown of the head.

52 Closing fast the nine doors of the body with the strong bar of self-control, they open the window of the *sushumna nadi.*

53 With the help of the goddess of the vital force, they kill the sheep of ideas and sacrifice it along with the buffalo of the mind.

54 Bringing together the *ida* and *pingala nadis* and thus calling forth the unstruck sound, they rise swiftly to the source of the vital principle.

55 Through the central channel of the *sushumna*, they climb the stairway and reach the peak of the *brahmarandhra.*

56 Again, ascending the steps of *makara* and passing beyond the abyss, they support themselves by the heavens and become absorbed in the Absolute.

57 In this way, those who have an evenly balanced mind capture the boundless fortresses of yoga in order to attain union with the Absolute.

58 Thus, O Arjuna, in exchange for their self-renunciation, they attain the unmanifest and are united with Me.

59 It is not that they obtain anything more by these practices of yoga; rather, for them much more effort is required.

क्लेशो ऽधिकतरस् तेषाम् अव्यक्तासक्तचेतसाम् ।
अव्यक्ता हि गतिर् दुःखं देहवद्भिर् अवाप्यते ॥
kleśo 'dhikataras teṣām
avyaktāsaktacetasām
avyaktā hi gatir duḥkhaṁ
dehavadbhir avāpyate

5. The trouble of those whose minds are fixed on the unmanifest is greater, for the goal of the unmanifest is attained with difficulty by embodied beings.

60 For those who have abandoned the path of devotion and have set their minds on the unmanifest, the self-existent One, the source of the welfare of all beings,

61 Aspirations to the highest heavenly rank are like highway robbers. They are laid low by the combined assault of prosperity and psychic powers.

62 Many disturbances arise from desire and anger, and the body has to wrestle with the Spirit.

63 Their thirst they must quench with thirst, and when hungry they must feed on hunger. Day and night they strive to measure the wind with the span of their arms.

64 Wakefulness is their rest, for pleasure they have only restraint, and their only fellowship is with trees.

65 They wear cold as a garment, clothe themselves with heat, and dwell in the rain as in a house.

66 In short, O Arjuna, such practices are like the constant self-immolation of a widow.

67 In this, the purpose of the husband is not served, nor is there fulfillment of family duty. It is merely an ever-recurring struggle with death.

68 Is it possible to drink boiling poison more searing than death itself? Wouldn't the mouth that swallowed a mountain be torn to pieces?

69 Therefore, O Arjuna, there will be many difficulties in the path of those who set out on the way of yoga.

70 If a toothless man were to chew pieces of iron, would they satisfy his hunger, or wouldn't it mean certain death?

71 Can a man swim across the ocean by the strength of his arms? Can he walk on air?
72 Can a man going into battle expect to reach heaven without a single wound?
73 O Arjuna, it is as difficult for an embodied man to reach the unmanifest as it would be for a lame man to compete with the wind.
74 Even if they summon all their courage and ardently seek the unmanifest, only distress will befall them.
75 O Arjuna, this is the lot of those who resort to the path of yoga.

ये तु सर्वाणि कर्माणि मयि संन्यस्य मत्पराः ।
अनन्येनैव योगेन मां ध्यायन्त उपासते ।।
ye tu sarvāṇi karmāṇi
mayi saṁnyasya matparāḥ
ananyenāiva yogena
māṁ dhyāyanta upāsate

6. But those who, renouncing all actions in Me, and regarding Me as the Supreme, worship Me, meditating on Me with undistracted yoga,

76 Those who, according to their caste, fulfill peacefully their duties through the organs of action,
77 Who carry out prescribed actions and offer them to Me, omitting those that are forbidden, and burning up the fruits of their actions,
78 O Arjuna, when they surrender them all to Me, they annul the fruits of those actions.
79 Furthermore, all actions performed by the body or the mind have no other goal but Me.
80 Those who serve only Me, who by always worshiping and contemplating Me have become My abode,
81 Who consider all pleasure and enjoyment as well as the hope of liberation to be worthless, these devotees ever commune with Me in love.
82 How can I tell what I do for those who have sold wholly to Me their bodies and souls?

तेषाम् अहं समुद्धर्ता मृत्युसंसारसागरात् ।
भवामि नचिरात् पार्थ मय्यावेशितचेतसाम् ।।
teṣām ahaṁ samuddhartā
mṛtyusaṁsārasāgarāt
bhavāmi nacirāt pārtha
mayyāveśitacetasām

7. Of those whose thoughts have entered into Me, I am soon the deliverer from the ocean of death and transmigration, Arjuna.

83 To be brief, O Arjuna, you know how close a relationship there is between a mother and the child born from her womb.
84 So it is with My devotees and Me, O Arjuna. In whatever state they may be, I have promised to overcome death for them.
85 Besides this, My devotees have no need to be anxious on account of their worldly affairs. Does the wife of a rich man have to beg for food?
86 Know that they are like members of My own family. I do not feel ashamed of anything that I do for them.
87 Seeing this world of nature struggling in the surging waves of life and death, I felt thus in My heart:
88 What man would not feel afraid in an ocean? It is no wonder then that My devotees should feel overcome with fear.
89 O Arjuna, this is why I have become incarnate and come quickly to them.
90 Those who were unattached I told to meditate on Me. To those with families, I recommended the repetition of My names.
91 With My many names as boats in the ocean of worldly life, I have become the ferryman.
92 With My love bound to them like a safety raft, I have led them to the other shore of liberation.
93 In this way, I have made all My devotees, from animals to mankind, worthy of the throne of My heaven.
94 Thus My devotees suffer no anxiety, for I always uplift them.
95 When they devote their hearts to Me, they bind Me to themselves.
96 Therefore, O Arjuna, if you are determined to follow this path,

मय्य् एव मन आधत्स्व मयि बुद्धिं निवेशय ।
निवसिष्यसि मय्येव अत ऊर्ध्वं न संशयः ।।
mayy eva mana ādhatsva
mayi buddhiṁ niveśaya
nivasiṣyasi mayyeva
ata ūrdhvaṁ na saṁśayaḥ

8. Keep your mind on Me alone, your intellect on Me. Thus you shall dwell in Me hereafter. There is no doubt of this.

97 Concentrate your mind and will earnestly on My nature,
98 And when your mind and will have entered into Me through your loving devotion, you will attain union with Me.

99 When the mind and the will have both merged in Me, how can there remain any distinction of "I" and "you"?
100 When a lamp is extinguished, its light fades away. When the sun sets, daylight vanishes.
101 When the vital force leaves the body, the senses also depart with it. In the same way, awareness of oneself follows wherever the mind and will go.
102 So fix your mind and will firmly on Me, and you will certainly be one with Me, the all-pervading One.
103 I solemnly promise you that there is no other teaching than this.

अथ चित्तं समाधातुं न शक्नोषि मयि स्थिरम् ।
अभ्यासयोगेन ततो माम् इच्छाप्तुं धनंजय ॥

atha cittaṁ samādhātuṁ
na śaknoṣi mayi sthiram
abhyāsayogena tato
mām icchāptuṁ dhanaṁjaya

9. Or if you are not able to keep your mind steadily on Me, then seek to attain Me by the constant practice of yoga, Arjuna.

104 But if with your whole will and mind you are unable to fix your attention entirely on Me,
105 Devote to this concentration at least a brief period during the twenty-four hours of the day.
106 Then as long as the mind contemplates My joy, sense pleasures will not appeal to it.
107 Just as at the end of the rainy season the rivers begin to subside, your mind will withdraw itself from worldly activities.
108 Just as the moon begins to wane from the day of the full moon and is no longer visible by the day of the new moon,
109 In the same way, withdrawing itself from sense pleasures and entering into Me, your mind will gradually be united with Me, O Arjuna.
110 O Beloved, this is known as the yoga of constant practice. There is nothing that cannot be obtained by this method.
111 Some are able to pass through the air through the power of this yoga; others have been able to tame tigers and serpents.
112 Some can consume poison without harm; others may walk on water. Still others, through this yoga, have found it a simple matter to study even the Vedas.
113 In fact, there is nothing which is too difficult to achieve by means of this practice, so strive to reach Me by this path.

अभ्यासे ऽप्य् असमर्थो ऽसि मत्कर्मपरमो भव ।
मदर्थम् अपि कर्माणि कुर्वन् सिद्धिम् अवाप्स्यसि ॥

abhyāse 'py asamartho 'si
matkarmaparamo bhava
madartham api karmāṇi
kurvan siddhim avāpsyasi

10. If you are incapable even of practice, be intent on My work; even performing actions for My sake, you shall attain perfection.

114 If you are unable to follow this path of practice, then continue in your present way of life.
115 Do not restrain your senses, do not give up the enjoyment of pleasure, nor relinquish your pride of caste.
116 Carry out your family duties, perform prescribed actions, and avoid those that are prohibited. In this way you will be free to act as you wish.
117 But do not say that you yourself are the doer of your thoughts, words, and actions.
118 Realize that only the supreme Self, by whom the whole universe is created, knows what is to be done and what is not to be done.
119 Do not concern yourself with abundance and lack, but carry on the life appropriate to your caste.
120 Your life should be conducted like the water which flows quietly in the channel made for it by the gardener.
121 O Arjuna, is a chariot concerned with whether the road is straight or crooked?
122 Do not take on the burden of daily activities or giving them up. Let your mind be solely directed towards Me.
123 Whatever action you perform, surrender it wholeheartedly to Me, and do not consider whether it is great or small.
124 Fixing your heart on Me in this way with renunciation of the body, you will certainly attain the state of perfect union with Me.

अथैतद् अप्य् अशक्तो ऽसि कर्तुं मद्योगम् आश्रितः ।
सर्वकर्मफलत्यागं ततः कुरु यतात्मवान् ॥

athāitad apy aśakto 'si
kartuṁ madyogam āsritaḥ
sarvakarmaphalatyāgaṁ
tataḥ kuru yatātmavān

11. But if you are unable even to do this,

then, resorting to devotion to Me, and abandoning all the fruits of action, act with self-restraint.

125 If you cannot offer all your actions to Me, O Arjuna, then worship Me in this manner.
126 O Arjuna, if it is hard for you to fix your heart on Me before intending to act, or before or after the action,
127 Let this be. Set aside remembering Me, and direct your mind towards controlling the senses.
128 Just as trees and plants drop their fruit that is ripe, in the same way do not consider the result of any action when it is completed.
129 Do not worry about fixing your mind on Me or doing actions for My sake. Get rid of this thought.
130 Just as nothing comes from rain which falls on a rock or seed which is thrown into a fire, regard your actions as though they were a dream.
131 Just as a father's love for his daughter is free from passion, you should remain unaffected by the fruit of any action.
132 Just as flames of fire vanish as they rise in the air, let your actions end in nothing.
133 To give up the fruit of action may appear easy, yet this yoga is superior to all others.
134 By giving up all attachment to their outcome, actions cease to bear fruit, like the bamboo tree which bears seed only once.
135 In this manner there can be no rebirth of the body, and the cycle of birth and death comes to an end.
136 O Arjuna, through climbing the ladder of practice one acquires understanding, and through understanding one can reach the stage of meditation.
137 When all levels of feeling are merged in meditation, all activity is laid aside.
138 When action ceases one abandons its fruits, and through abandoning the fruits one attains peace.
139 Therefore, O Arjuna, these are the stages in the attainment of supreme peace. For this reason, you should begin with the yoga of practice.

श्रेयो हि ज्ञानम् अभ्यासाज् ज्ञानाद् ध्यानं विशिष्यते ।
ध्यानात् कर्मफलत्यागस् त्यागाच् छान्तिर् अनन्तरम् ॥
śreyo hi jñānam abhyāsāj
jñānād dhyānaṁ viśiṣyate
dhyānāt karmaphalatyāgas
tyāgāc chāntir anantaram

12. Knowledge is indeed better than practice; meditation is superior to knowledge; renunciation of the fruit of action is better than meditation; peace immediately follows renunciation.

140 Knowledge is deeper than practice, O Arjuna, but meditation transcends knowledge.
141 Selfless action is higher than meditation, but enjoyment of peace is even better than selfless action.
142 These are the stages on the road by which one reaches peace, O great warrior.

अद्वेष्टा सर्वभूतानां मैत्रः करुण एव च ।
निर्ममो निरहंकारः समदुःखसुखः क्षमी ॥
adveṣṭā sarvabhūtānāṁ
māitraḥ karuṇa eva ca
nirmamo nirahaṁkārah
samaduḥkhasukhaḥ kṣamī

13. He who hates no being, friendly and compassionate, free from attachment to possessions, free from egotism, indifferent to pain and pleasure, patient,

143 Such a person harbors no feeling of hatred for any creature, just as the spirit of life has no sense of "myself" or "another";
144 Just as earth does not say, "I will welcome the best man and reject the worst";
145 Just as life, ever kind, does not say, "I will treat well the body of a king and thrust aside that of a beggar";
146 Just as water makes no distinction nor says, "I will quench the thirst of a cow but kill a tiger by turning into poison";
147 Or just as a lamp does not give light to one household and leave others in darkness.
148 This person gives his friendship equally to every creature and is the very source of compassion.
149 In his mind the idea of "I" and "he" has no place. He calls nothing his own and is indifferent to either pleasure or pain.
150 His power of forgiveness is like that of the earth, and he holds contentment in his lap.

संतुष्टः सततं योगी यतात्मा दृढनिश्चयः ।
मय्य् अर्पितमनोबुद्धिर् यो मद्भक्तः स मे प्रियः ॥
saṁtuṣṭaḥ satataṁ yogī
yatātmā dṛḍhaniścayaḥ
mayy arpitamanobuddhir
yo madbhaktaḥ sa me priyaḥ

14. The yogin who is always contented and balanced in mind, who is self-controlled, and whose conviction is firm, whose mind and intellect are fixed on Me, and who is devoted to Me, is dear to Me.

151 Even without the rainy season the sea is full of water; in the same way a person is full of contentment, though he may not strive for it.
152 He has promised to retain control over his heart and carries out his every resolution.
153 In the palace of his heart, the individual self and the Supreme are seated together in splendor.
154 Being thus perfected in yoga, he merges his mind and will entirely in Me.
155 He is purified both inwardly and outwardly in yoga and is wholly devoted to Me.
156 Such a person, O Arjuna, is a true devotee, a perfect yogi, and has found liberation. His love for Me is like that of a wife for her husband.
157 He is dearer to Me than life itself, but even this is a poor comparison.
158 The story of the beloved is enchanting, and though it cannot be told, my love for you forces Me to speak of it.
159 For this reason, such a simile came to My mind. Otherwise, what comparison can be found?
160 This is enough, O Arjuna. Love is intensified by speaking of the beloved.
161 If the speaker has a loving listener, can delight ever fade?
162 O Arjuna, you are both the beloved and the listener, and the time has come to speak of this love.
163 For that reason, I will speak. It is good that we have come to this happy occasion. Speaking in this way, Krishna began to sway with joy.
164 Then again He said, Listen now to the qualities possessed by those devotees whom I hold in My heart.

यस्मान् नोद्विजते लोको लोकान् नोद्विजते च यः ।
हर्षामर्षभयोद्वेगैर् मुक्तो यः स च मे प्रियः ।।

yasmān nodvijate loko
lokān nodvijate ca yaḥ
harṣāmarṣabhayodvegāir
mukto yaḥ sa ca me priyaḥ

15. He from whom the world does not shrink, and who does not shrink from the world, who is freed from joy, envy, fear, and distress, is dear to Me.

165 Just as creatures living in the water are not afraid of the sea nor the sea of them,
166 Similarly, such a person is not distressed by the pleasure-loving world, and the world does not weary of him.
167 Just as the body never tires of its own limbs, in the same way he is never tired of any creature, considering it his own Self.
168 In fact, it is as though the world is his own body, so that he is free from all likes and dislikes and from joy and anger.
169 He who is free from the pairs of opposites, from fear and depression, always remains devoted to Me.
170 Such a person is very dear to Me. How can I describe him? He lives in My life.
171 He is content with inner bliss, and the Supreme dwells in him. He is the lord of fulfillment.

अनपेक्षः शुचिर् दक्ष उदासीनो गतव्यथः ।
सर्वारम्भपरित्यागी यो मद्भक्तः स मे प्रियः ।।

anapekṣaḥ śucir dakṣa
udāsīno gatavyathaḥ
sarvārambhaparityāgī
yo madbhaktaḥ sa me priyaḥ

16. He who is free from wants, pure, capable, disinterested, free from anxiety, who has abandoned all undertakings and is devoted to Me, is dear to Me.

172 Such a person, O Arjuna, is free from ambition, and his very existence causes joy to increase.
173 The Ganges is pure, and all sin and passion are purified in its waters, but one must sink in them.
174 It is well known that Benares generously bestows liberation, but those who go there have to sacrifice the life of their bodies.
175 All impurities disappear when one goes to the Himalayas, but it involves risking one's life. There is no such danger to the purity of a good person.
176 The depths of devotion cannot be known unless a person drowns in them. Liberation is attained immediately even without death.
177 The impurities of the Ganges are removed by the touch of saints. Then how great must be the purity derived from the company of such devotees?
178 Let that be! A good person imparts his pu-

rity even to holy places and dissipates entirely all impurities of the mind.

179 Both inwardly and outwardly he is as pure as the light of the sun. Just as a fortunate person is born with clairvoyance, he is endowed with the vision of the highest Truth.

180 Just as the sky is limitless yet indifferent, so such a person's mind reaches everywhere; yet nothing can sully it.

181 A bird which has escaped from a snare no longer has any fear. Similarly, he is free from worldly distress and regards everything with indifference.

182 A person who is always contented is free from anxiety, just as a dead man feels no shame.

183 When he undertakes anything he does so without self-consciousness, just as a fire without fuel will die out.

184 He who is at peace within himself is already on the threshold of liberation.

185 Filled with the sense of his oneness with God, he is about to reach the further bank of the ocean of dualism, O Arjuna.

186 Then, in order to enjoy the bliss of devotion, he divides himself as it were into two parts, assuming the role of devotee.

187 The other part he calls Me and thus points out the path of devotion to those yogis who do not serve Me.

188 Such a person is very dear to Me. He is My dwelling place, and I am not happy until I reach him.

189 For his sake I must become incarnate, and for him I must live in this world. I feel that I should embrace him with My very life.

यो न हृष्यति न द्वेष्टि न शोचति न काङ्क्षति ।
शुभाशुभपरित्यागी भक्तिमान् यः स मे प्रियः ।।

yo na hṛṣyati na dveṣṭi
na śocati na kāṅkṣati
śubhāśubhaparityāgī
bhaktimān yaḥ sa me priyaḥ

17. He who neither rejoices nor hates, nor grieves nor desires, has renounced good and evil, and is full of devotion, is dear to Me.

190 He considers knowledge of the Self the highest attainment, so he is not carried away by the enjoyment of worldly pleasures.

191 Being at one with the whole world, he is free from any sense of separateness. Consequently, he doesn't feel any hatred.

192 Recognizing that what is really his own can never be lost even at the end of a world age, he does not grieve for anything he may lose in this world.

193 He recognizes that he has within himself that which is more precious than anything else, and he has no further desire.

194 He makes no distinction between evil and good, just as the sun does not think about light and darkness.

195 A person who has attained the highest Self-realization and who still lives in devotion to Me,

196 Is more beloved to Me than the dearest relative. I assure you that this is true.

समः शत्रौ च मित्रे च तथा मानापमानयोः ।
शीतोष्णसुखदुःखेषु समः सङ्गविवर्जितः ।।

samaḥ śatrāu ca mitre ca
tathā mānāpamānayoḥ
śītoṣṇasukhaduḥkheṣu
samaḥ saṅgavivarjitaḥ

18. Alike toward enemy and friend, the same in honor and disgrace, alike in cold and heat, pleasure and pain, freed from attachment,

197 O Arjuna, he has no sense of inequality; friends and enemies are alike to him.

198 A tree gives the same shade to the man who planted it as to the one who strikes at its roots to fell it.

199 Sugarcane is sweet to the one who cultivates it and equally sweet to the one who extracts its juice.

200 A person who has the same attitude toward friends and enemies, or honor and shame,

201 Does not vary in heat or cold, just as the sky remains the same throughout the seasons.

202 O Arjuna, just as Mount Meru bears the north and the south winds equally, in the same way such a person remains steady whether joy or sorrow come to him.

203 He has the same attitude towards all creatures, just as moonlight shines with sweetness on both a king and a beggar.

204 Just as everyone on this earth desires water, similarly, all three worlds seek him out.

205 Laying aside all contact with inner and outer objects, he lives apart with his soul absorbed in God.

तुल्यनिन्दास्तुतिर् मौनी संतुष्टो येन केनचित् ।
अनिकेतः स्थिरमतिर् भक्तिमान् मे प्रियो नरः ।।

tulyanindāstutir māunī

saṁtuṣṭo yena kenacit
aniketaḥ sthiramatir
bhaktimān me priyo naraḥ

19. Indifferent to blame or praise, silent, content with anything whatever, homeless, steady-minded, full of devotion; this man is dear to Me.

206 Just as the sky is not affected by pollution, similarly, such a person is neither offended by scorn nor elated by praise.

207 Regarding praise and blame with equal indifference, he moves among people or in seclusion as freely as the air.

208 Indifferent as to whether truth or untruth is spoken, he remains silent for he is absorbed in his state of freedom from illusion.

209 He takes no delight in the satisfaction of desires, nor is he disappointed by any loss, just as the sea does not dry up when there is no rain.

210 Just as the wind has no fixed abode, he seeks no refuge.

211 He believes that everywhere is his home and regards himself as one with all movable and immovable things.

212 Furthermore, O Arjuna, if he also worships Me, I place him on my head as a crown.

213 Is it strange that people should bow their heads before such a great being? Even the three worlds revere the water that has touched his feet.

214 Only if Shiva Himself were a person's teacher could he know how to appreciate such great devotion.

215 But enough of Shiva! In praising Him I would be praising Myself.

216 This is not an adequate illustration, for I carry him upon my head.

217 Bearing in his hands the fourth attainment of human life, Self-realization, he treads the path of devotion, bestowing his gift on the world.

218 Though he is able to give others the highest bliss, he takes the lowest place like water.

219 Let us bow to him, placing him like a crown upon our heads and his feet upon our breasts.

220 Let us beautify our speech with the jewels of his praise and adorn our ears with his fame.

221 Desiring to see him, I have taken human eyes and worship him with a lotus in My hand.

222 I have assumed My four-armed body so that I may embrace him.

223 To delight in his company, I, the formless One, have become incarnate. My love for him is truly incomparable.

224 Is it any wonder that he is so dear to Me? Those who listen to the story of his life,

225 Those who praise the lives of the saints, are dearer to Me than My very soul.

226 O Arjuna, what I have explained to you is the entire yoga of union through devotion.

227 It is a state so high that those who attain it are very dear to Me. I meditate on them and hold them in the highest esteem.

ये तु धर्म्यामृतम् इदं यथोक्तं पर्युपासते ।
श्रद्दधाना मत्परमा भक्तास् ते ऽतीव मे प्रियाः ॥
ye tu dharmyāmṛtam idaṁ
yathoktaṁ paryupāsate
śraddadhānā matparamā
bhaktās te 'tīva me priyāḥ

20. Those who honor this immortal law described above, endowed with faith, devoted and intent on Me as the Supreme; they are exceedingly dear to Me.

228 Those who listen to this teaching which is full of beauty, sweet as a stream of nectar, and leads to righteousness, and who understand it through experience;

229 Who have the proper state of mind, which has already been described as a seed in well-tilled soil;

230 Who with perfect faith in its truth allow it to grow within them and practice it with all their heart;

231 These, O Arjuna, are My beloved devotees. They alone are true yogis in this world, and for them I feel the deepest love.

232 They are the true holy streams and sacred places. In this world those men alone are pure who give themselves up to devotion.

233 They are the helpers of the gods and delight in caring for the world. They take pleasure in protecting those who resort to them.

234 They are ever beneficent to their devotees and are open-hearted to those who love them. They are supporters of truth and are a storehouse of all arts.

235 Let us contemplate them as the deity whom we worship. Nothing is more pleasing to Me than such devotees.

236 They are My delight, My treasure, and the source of My contentment.

237 O Arjuna, I also regard as My highest deity

those who speak of this devotion.

238 These things were said by Krishna, the giver of joy to all His people, the source of all created things.

239 O King, He who is the pure, perfect, and merciful protector of all those who take refuge in Him;

240 Who shines with the luster of His glory and righteousness and is famed for His boundless charity; who by His incomparable strength bound the powerful Bali;

241 Krishna, the supreme sovereign of Vaikuntha, spoke in this way and Arjuna listened to what he said.

242 Sanjaya said to Dhritarashtra, Listen now to what I will describe after this.

243 This story, full of interest, will be told in the Marathi language. Listen to it earnestly.

244 Jnanadeva says, My Guru Nivrittinath has taught me how I should entreat you saintly men.

13

THE YOGA OF DISTINCTION BETWEEN THE FIELD AND THE KNOWER OF THE FIELD

SALUTATIONS to the holy feet of my Guru! Remembering them leads to the attainment of all branches of knowledge.
2 Thinking of them, one attains the power of literary composition, and all learning comes readily to the tongue.
3 Eloquence surpasses even nectar in its sweetness, and the nine feelings wait upon the words.
4 The symbols reveal deep meaning, and truths can be discerned and understood.
5 When a person remembers in his heart the feet of his Guru, good fortune is added to wisdom.

अर्जुन उवाच । *arjuna uvāca*

प्रकृतिं पुरुषं चैव क्षेत्रं क्षेत्रज्ञम् एव च ।
एतद् वेदितुम् इच्छामि ज्ञानं ज्ञेयं च केशव ॥

prakṛtiṁ puruṣaṁ cāiva
kṣetraṁ kṣetrajñam eva ca
etad veditum icchāmi
jñānaṁ jñeyaṁ ca keśava

Arjuna said:
1. Prakriti and Purusha, the field and the knower of the field, knowledge and the knower of knowledge, I wish to know about these, Krishna.

6 Then Arjuna said, I wish to learn from You about nature and Spirit, the field and the Knower of the field.
7 Jnaneshwar says, I will bow to them. Krishna, the Father of the creator and the husband of Lakshmi, said:

श्रीभगवान् उवाच । *śrībhagavān uvāca*

इदं शरीरं कौन्तेय क्षेत्रम् इत्य् अभिधीयते ।
एतद् यो वेत्ति तं प्राहुः क्षेत्रज्ञ इति तद्विदः ॥

idaṁ śarīraṁ kāunteya
kṣetram ity abhidhīyate
etad yo vetti taṁ prāhuḥ
kṣetrajña iti tadvidaḥ

The Blessed Lord spoke:
2. This body, Arjuna, is said to be the field; he who knows this is called the knower of the field by those who are wise in such things.

8 Listen, O Arjuna. The body is called the field, and he who knows it is called the Knower of the field.

तत् क्षेत्रं यच् च यादृक् च यद्विकारि यतश्च यत् ।
स च यो यत्प्रभावश्च तत् समासेन मे शृणु ॥

kṣetrajñaṁ cāpi māṁ viddhi
sarvakṣetreṣu bhārata
kṣetrakṣetrajñayor jñānaṁ
yat taj jñānaṁ mataṁ mama

3. Know also that I am the knower of the field in all fields, Arjuna; knowledge of the field and of the knower of the field, that is considered by Me to be true knowledge.

9 I am He who is known as the Knower of the field and the supporter of all fields.
10 To understand clearly what this field is and who it is that knows it, is to My mind true knowledge.

क्षेत्रज्ञं चापि मां विद्धि सर्वक्षेत्रेषु भारत ।
क्षेत्रक्षेत्रज्ञयोर् ज्ञानं यत् तज् ज्ञानं मतं मम ॥

tat kṣetraṁ yac ca yādṛk ca
yadvikāri yataśca yat
sa ca yo yatprabhāvaśca
tat samāsena me śṛṇu

4. This field, what it is, and of what kind, what its modifications are and whence they come, and who he (the knower of the field) is, and what are his powers, that, in brief, hear from Me:

11 Now I will explain fully to you why this body

is referred to as the field.
12 I will tell you why it is called the field, and how and where it is born.
13 Does it measure three and a half arm lengths? What is its size? Is it barren or fertile? To whom does it belong?
14 Listen and I will tell you about all the properties of this field.
15 The Vedas frequently speak of its place, and there has been constant speculation about it.
16 The six philosophies have exhausted themselves discussing it, and their conflicting views have reached no agreement.
17 All the sciences have failed to agree concerning it, and discussions on this subject have spread throughout the world.
18 No two people agree about it, and opinions contradict one another. Arguments and vain talk flourish.
19 Nothing is known about who inhabits it, but the intensity of the dispute is so great that everywhere people come to blows.
20 In order to refute the agnostics, the Vedas have risen in rebellion. Seeing this, the heretics have raised their voices.
21 They say, You have no foundation in truth; your arguments are false. If you deny this, we challenge you.
22 Naked ascetics, tearing out their hair, laid fallacious arguments before the heretics, but they also fell to the ground.
23 Yogis, fearing that death would overtake them with the problem still unsolved, came forward to join the quest.
24 Fearing death, they withdrew to the forest to practice severe austerities to the very end.
25 Out of his deep respect for this field, Shiva abandoned His heavenly kingdom, regarding it as an obstacle, and resorted to the burning ground of penance.
26 With a firm resolve to pursue this quest, He stripped himself of everything and burned to ashes the god of love, who had tempted Him.
27 Brahma, the lord of Satyaloka, had the advantage of having four faces, but even he failed to understand the nature of this field.

ऋषिभिर् बहुधा गीतं छन्दोभिर् विविधैः पृथक् ।
ब्रह्मसूत्रपदैश्चैव हेतुमद्भिर् विनिश्चितैः ॥
ṛṣibhir bahudhā gītaṁ
chandobhir vividhāiḥ pṛthak
brahmasūtrapadāiścāiva
hetumadbhir viniścitāiḥ

5. Sages have sung of it in many ways, distinctly, in various sacred (Vedic) hymns, and with quotations concerning Brahman, full of reasoning.

28 There are those who say that this field is basically the home of the living spirit, and the vital force is the occupant.
29 In this house, the four pranas as brothers work as laborers, and the mind directs the work.
30 This life has under its command a team of ten oxen in the form of ten senses, who labor unceasingly in the field of sense objects, ignoring observances of the new moon day or dawn.
31 If a person avoids the practice of prescribed duties, sows the seed of unrighteousness, and cultivates the soil with evil actions,
32 Then, according to the nature of the seed, there results a plentiful harvest of sins, from which he suffers misery throughout countless lives.
33 On the other hand, he may sow good seed in the tilled soil of prescribed duties and enjoy happiness throughout hundreds of lives.
34 Others say that this isn't true; the individual soul is not the master of the field. It is we who should be consulted about the field.
35 The soul is a stranger here, a traveler on a long journey, and the vital force is the supervisor of the field.
36 The Sankhyas describe the eternal *mulaprakriti*, primordial matter, as the hereditary owner of this field.
37 She owns all the equipment and directs the cultivation of the field.
38 She gives birth to the three qualities, who are the primal cultivators of the land.
39 *Rajas* or passion sows the seed, *sattva* or purity preserves it, and *tamas* or ignorance alone gathers in the harvest.
40 Making the intellect a threshing floor, with the help of the ox called Kaluga, she threshes out the corn from which arises the great mass of unmanifest nature.
41 Other philosophers, despising this explanation, state that the theory is meaningless and of recent origin.
42 They say, What is matter compared with the Absolute, which is all in all? Listen quietly to our explanation of the field.
43 Once all-powerful thought slept on the soft-

est cushions in the bedroom of the primal void.

44 Suddenly he awoke, but always being fortunate in his affairs, he obtained the treasure of the created world according to his desire.

45 Through him, the garden of the Supreme, vast as the three worlds, came into being.

46 Placing the five elements together, he separated the fallow land into four parts in the fourfold division of creatures.

47 Then, binding together the five elements, he made from them the human body with its five functions.

48 On both sides, he built a wall of action and inaction, and made a barren region of the unproductive creatures.

49 In order to pass back and forth between these regions, the primal thought made the beautiful path of life and death.

50 He formed the intellect and combined it with the sense of individuality to guide the whole created world.

51 Thus in the great void there grew the branches of the tree of thought, which is the origin of this worldly existence.

52 Others examined these theories as pearls of wisdom and said, You are very wise, aren't you?

53 If you assume that thought exists in the Absolute, why shouldn't you also accept that matter is included in it too?

54 You needn't trouble yourselves any further, however, for everything will now be explained to you.

55 Who is it that stores the water in the rain clouds? Who holds the stars in the heavens?

56 Who has spread out the wide canopy of the sky? Who is it that makes the wind blow?

57 Who makes the hair grow on your body? Who fills the ocean and sends down showers of rain?

58 This field of the body is a natural phenomenon and belongs to no one. He who tills it receives its fruits; others gain nothing.

59 Then other philosophers came forward and angrily said, What you say is all very well, but how is it then that time dominates the whole field?

60 We believe that death is like an angry lion in a cave. Why do you argue uselessly like this?

61 The hand of death will surely strike, but still they all assert their own opinions.

62 This lion of death suddenly reaches beyond the cycle of time and attacks even the elephant in the form of the highest of all worlds.

63 Entering the heavenly forest, he destroys the guardian deities and companies of the elephants of the four quarters.

64 Through the wind of their passing bodies, beasts in the form of human souls perish and are left wandering in the pit of the cycle of life and death.

65 See how widespread is the grasp of time, in which he holds this elephant representing the universe of form!

66 It is true to say that time rules everything in this universe. O Arjuna, these are the various opinions held about the field of this body.

67 The seers held frequent discussions in the Naimisha forest, to which the Puranas testify.

68 Poetic discourses in various forms of verse are still quoted arrogantly in support of these opinions.

69 The verses of the great Sama Veda, the holiest from the standpoint of insight, didn't understand what this field is.

70 Many great and wise sages have devoted their minds to this quest.

71 But no one has been able to explain clearly what it is, how great it is, or to whom it belongs.

72 I will now explain this field to you as fully as possible.

महाभूतान्य् अहंकारो बुद्धिर् अव्यक्तम् एव च।
इन्द्रियाणि दशैकं च पञ्च चेन्द्रियगोचराः॥

mahābhūtāny ahamkāro
buddhir avyaktam eva ca
indriyāṇi·daśāikaṁ ca
pañca cendriyagocarāḥ

6. The great elements, egoism, intellect and the unmanifest, the senses, ten and one, and the five objects of the senses,

इच्छा द्वेषः सुखं दुःखं संघातश्चेतना धृतिः।
एतत् क्षेत्रं समासेन सविकारम् उदाहृतम् ॥

icchā dveṣaḥ sukhaṁ duḥkhaṁ
saṁghātaścetanā dhṛtiḥ
etat kṣetraṁ samāsena
savikāram udāhṛtam

7. Desire, hatred, pleasure, pain, the body, intelligence, steadfastness—this briefly is described as the field with its modifications.

73 The five great cosmic elements, the ego, the intellect, unmanifest matter, and the ten senses,

74 Also the mind, the activities of the ten sense organs; pleasure, pain, and aversion; the whole range of desire;
75 Consciousness and fortitude—I have told you that all these constitute the field.
76 Now I will tell you one at a time which are the five great elements, the sensory activities, and the sense organs.
77 Earth, water, fire, air, and ether are the five great elements. I have told you this.
78 Just as during the waking state the dream state disappears, or as the moon is hidden on the day of the new moon,
79 As youth lies latent in early childhood, as fragrance is hidden in the bud until it expands into the full-blown flower,
80 And as fire lies dormant within fuel, similarly, O Arjuna, consciousness lies latent in the womb of primal matter.
81 A fever lying within the body awaits the pretext of an unsuitable diet. Then what was already inside pervades the body outside as well.
82 When the five elements unite and take the form of a body, the ego causes it to function.
83 Now, intellect is known by these signs. Listen and I will tell you, said Krishna.
84 Impelled by the god of passion, the activity of the senses overcomes the sense objects.
85 When the individual soul has to give an account of its experiences of pleasure or pain, the intellect enables it to determine which is better.
86 By using the intellect, it is able to discriminate between pleasure and pain, good and evil actions, purity and impurity.
87 It enables it to distinguish between base and noble, high and low, and to examine sense objects.
88 It causes the development of the sense organs, stores up the quality of harmony, and establishes the union between the Self and the individual soul.
89 O Arjuna, know that one can recognize the intellect by these things. Now listen to the ways of recognizing the unmanifest.
90 O Arjuna, what the Sankhya philosophers called primordial matter is also referred to as the unmanifest.
91 I have already explained to you the nature of this primordial matter as it is expounded by the Sankhya philosophy.
92 O Arjuna, the condition of the individual soul, called the lord of heroes, is also known as the unmanifest.
93 At dawn the light of the stars disappears from the sky, and at sunset the activities of all creatures cease.
94 O Arjuna, when the physical body is cast off, all its activities and conditions are hidden in the individual's karma.
95 The entire tree lies hidden in its seed, just as woven cloth lies in the threads which will make it.
96 Similarly, the great elements and the beings which have proceeded from them become subtle and fade away when they leave their material forms.
97 O Arjuna, this is known as the unmanifest. Now listen to the description of the sense organs.
98 The ear, eye, skin, nose, and tongue are the five organs of perception.
99 By means of this system, the intellect can express its experience of pleasure and pain through the five organs.
100 The mouth, hands, feet, and the excretory and sexual organs are the five organs of action.
101 The Lord says that these should be known as the organs of action.
102 The power of activity, which is the wife of the life principle, enters and leaves the body by these five ways.
103 The Lord said, In this way I have described to you the ten sense organs. Now listen and I will tell you clearly what the mind is.
104 It forms a link between the organs and the intellect and hovers on the shoulders of passion.
105 The mind is like the blueness of the sky or the illusory waves of a mirage.
106 When the male semen meets the sexual fluid of the female, the combination of the ten elements is produced.
107 Through the power inherent in the bodily functions, these ten settle into their appointed roles.
108 In these, there is only one power of activity, which is the basis of passion.
109 This power is outside the control of the will, but dominates the realm of ego-awareness.
110 This activity is wrongly called mind; it is really thought. Through thoughts, the universal Spirit assumes the condition of individuality.

111 This is the source of all tendencies and the ground of all passion. It activates ego-awareness.
112 It increases desire, encourages hope, and fosters fear.
113 It awakens the sense of duality, fortifies ignorance, and plunges the senses into contact with sense objects.
114 It first intends to create, then brings about destruction. It builds a pile of fantasies and then shatters them.
115 It is like a cave of delusion, the heart of the element of air, and it conceals all the channels of the intellect.
116 O Arjuna, this is what is known as the mind. Now listen to the names of the various sense pleasures.
117 Touch, sound, form, taste, and smell are the faculties of the five organs of perception.
118 Through the doors of these five organs, perception reaches out of the body just as cattle stray towards green pastures.
119 Breathing and speaking, accepting and rejecting objects, walking, and the action of the sexual and excretory organs,
120 These are the functions of the five organs of action. From the creation that they build, all action is carried on.
121 These are the ten functions of the body. Now it is necessary to explain desire.
122 Its activity is awakened by remembering past experience, or by hearing the words of others.
123 Supported by passion, it is aroused as soon as the senses come in contact with sense objects.
124 When it is awakened, the mind rushes here and there, and the senses are thrust towards undesirable objects.
125 Through its love of activity, the mind is disturbed by its delight in sense objects. This is desire.
126 But if the senses don't find the satisfaction they desire, the disappointment they experience leads to hatred.
127 Now let's consider what pleasure is like. By experiencing it, a person becomes oblivious to all things.
128 When bodily actions, speech, and thought cease and all awareness of the body is lost,
129 The *prana* becomes subdued and the state of harmony is intensified.
130 Then all sense activity is withdrawn to the cave of the heart, and peaceful sleep follows.
131 In brief, pleasure is a state in which the soul can realize union with the Self.
132 O Arjuna, the condition in which a person doesn't experience this state is called pain.
133 These states are not brought about by any intention. They arise naturally, and they are the bases of pleasure and pain.
134 Now the power of the Self in the body, the detached witness of all that happens, is called Consciousness, O Arjuna.
135 From the toenails of the feet to the hair of the head, it is alert in the body and remains unchanged throughout the three stages of life.
136 It gives freshness to the mind, the will, and other functions, like the eternal sweetness of spring in the forest of the world of matter.
137 It is this Consciousness which is the motive force in both organic and inorganic matter. I am not deceiving you.
138 A king doesn't know every one of his subjects, and yet at his command, they overthrow the invading enemy. At the full moon, the waters of the ocean rise to high tide.
139 Contact with a magnet sets fragments of iron in motion. The rising of the sun arouses all people to work.
140 The tortoise feeds her young one when she sees it, not waiting for its mouth to touch her.
141 Similarly, O Arjuna, inorganic matter is infused with life through the presence of the Self in the body.
142 This, then, is called Consciousness, O Arjuna. Listen now to the explanation of steadfastness.
143 The elements, by their very nature, are at enmity with one another.
144 Heat dries up water, wind fights with fire, and the firmament devours the wind.
145 Ether doesn't mingle with any other elements. Though it penetrates all, it is entirely separate from everything.
146 In this way, all these five elements contend with one another. Yet, when they come together in one body,
147 They set aside their differences, live in unity, and even nourish one another with their own particular qualities.
148 The strength which holds these elements together, in spite of their natural antagonisms, is call steadfastness.
149 O Arjuna, together with the individual soul, this aggregate of thirty-six elements consti-

tutes the field.

150 In this way, I have clearly explained to you all the thirty-six components which form the body.

151 O Arjuna, when the parts of a chariot are assembled, they are called a chariot. Similarly, the combined upper and lower parts of the body are referred to as the body.

152 Again, an assembly of horses and elephants constitutes an army, and groups of syllables are called sentences.

153 Masses of clouds are referred to as the sky, and the various peoples on the earth make up the world.

154 Oil, wick, and fire held together are known as a lamp.

155 Similarly, these thirty-six elements grouped together are called the field.

156 Through cultivating the body, crops of merit and demerit are produced. So we call it figuratively, the field.

157 According to some it is called the body, but let this be. Its names are countless.

158 Gods, men, and serpents are all born according to their kind, and find themselves caught within the system of particular qualities and set duties.

159 From the supreme Spirit down to inanimate matter, whatever exists and then dies is part of the field.

160 O Arjuna, I will speak later about these qualities. Here I will explain the nature of knowledge.

161 I have already described to you in detail the characteristics of the field and its modifications. Now listen to what I have to say about knowledge.

162 In order to obtain knowledge, yogis overcome all obstacles to reach heaven, and swallow up the ether in the sacred center between the eyebrows.

163 They don't care about spiritual attainment, nor do they have any regard for worldly prosperity. They despise such austerities as yogic practices.

164 They surmount the fortresses of penance, and set aside the merits of performing hundred of sacrifices.

165 Some adopt various forms of worship, others roam about naked, while yet others enter the depth of the *sushumna nadi.*

166 To acquire knowledge, great sages in their ardent search wander from page to page in the leaves of the great tree of the Vedas.

167 O Arjuna, they vow to spend their lives in the service of their Gurus.

168 This knowledge dispels ignorance and brings abut the union of the individual soul with the supreme Self.

169 It closes the doors of the sense organs, takes away the power from outgoing activities, and removes the poverty of the mind.

170 When this knowledge is obtained, the famine of duality comes to an end and the abundant life of unity follows.

171 It leaves no trace of pride, overcomes all illusion, and leaves no room for the thought of oneself and others.

172 It uproots worldly existence, washes away the mire of thoughts, and makes it possible to grasp the unattainable goal of the highest knowledge.

173 By its light the eyes of the intellect are opened, and the soul can enjoy the highest bliss.

174 This is knowledge, the treasure of all holiness, which purifies the unclean mind.

175 Contact with knowledge immediately heals a soul suffering from the disease of pride.

176 It is impossible to describe knowledge, though it will be described. When heard, it can be discerned only by reason. It is not visible to the eye.

177 When this knowledge appears in the body, the eyes can perceive it, for it expresses itself through the activities of the sense organs.

178 Its presence may be recognized in the same way that the coming of spring is noticed by the freshness of the trees.

179 When water is poured on the roots of a tree, its effect is shown in the sprouting of leaves on the branches.

180 The softness of the earth is proved by the tender shoots of the plants. A person's noble behavior is evidence of good breeding.

181 A person's friendly nature is expressed in his acts of hospitality; and when the mere sight of a person brings comfort, we know that he is good.

182 The presence of camphor in a tree is recognized by its fragrance. The light of a lamp enclosed in a glass is seen outside it.

183 Now listen carefully while I tell you how signs are also visible in the body when this knowledge dwells in the heart.

अमानित्वम् अदम्भित्वम् अहिंसा क्षान्तिर् आर्जवम् ।

आचार्योपासनं शौचं स्थैर्यम् आत्मविनिग्रहः ॥

amānitvam adambhitvam
ahiṁsā kṣāntir ārjavam
ācāryopāsanaṁ śāucaṁ
sthāiryam ātmavinigrahaḥ

8. Absence of pride, freedom from hypocrisy, non-violence, patience, rectitude, service of the teacher, purity, constancy, self-restraint,

184 Such a person doesn't strive for success in any worldly matter and feels any honor to be a burden.

185 If people praise his qualities, if they show him respect, or if they recognize his greatness,

186 He feels embarrassed, like a deer trapped by a hunter, or a swimmer caught in a whirlpool.

187 O Arjuna, in the same way he is disturbed by expressions of respect, and won't accept any mention of his greatness.

188 He doesn't want to see any sign of his worthiness, or to hear any word of fame. He prefers that others not remember him as having any special qualities.

189 Such a person has no wish to receive respect or honor. He prefers death to receiving a salutation.

190 Like Brihaspati, he possesses all knowledge, yet for fear of greatness he hides among madmen.

191 He conceals his knowledge, makes no use of his high attainments, and prefers to be considered mad.

192 Worldly fame distresses him, he dislikes learned discussion, and chooses to live in silence.

193 He prefers to be ignored and doesn't want his own relatives to notice him. This is the way he likes to live.

194 He behaves in such a way that people will consider him lowly. Humility is like a jewel to him.

195 He tries to live in such a way that people will be unaware of whether he is alive or dead.

196 He desires that people should never know whether he walks by himself or whether he is propelled by the wind.

197 He prefers that his existence should be hidden and his name unknown, so that no creature will fear him.

198 A person who has taken such vows always lives in seclusion and delights in the idea of solitude.

199 He is content with the company of the wind, takes pleasure in conversing with the sky, and loves trees as his own life.

200 A person in whom these characteristics are found is the intimate companion of knowledge.

201 A person's humility is known by these characteristics. Now I will tell you how to recognize unpretentiousness.

202 This quality is like the mind of a miser who refuses to reveal his hidden treasure, even though his life may be threatened.

203 Similarly, O Arjuna, an unpretentious person will never reveal by word or gesture, even at the risk of his life, any good action that he may perform.

204 O Arjuna, a vicious cow drives her calf away, a prostitute tries to conceal her advancing age,

205 A rich man overtaken in a forest hides his wealth, a girl of noble birth conceals her limbs,

206 And a farmer covers the seed sown in the ground. In the same way, such a person remains silent about his charitable deeds.

207 He doesn't adorn his body to impress others, he abstains from flattery, and he doesn't boast of his righteousness.

208 He doesn't speak of the good he has done to others. He doesn't display his knowledge, nor will he sell it for the sake of fame.

209 He is miserly concerning bodily pleasure; yet when it comes to charity, he doesn't count the cost.

210 There is always poverty in his household and his body is very thin, but when there is a need for charity, he rivals the wish-fulfilling tree.

211 He is noble in performing his duty and is generous when the occasion demands. He is skillful at discussing the Self, yet at other times he appears to be mad.

212 The trunk of the plantain tree seems to be light and hollow, yet when the fruit is formed it is firm and sweet.

213 Clouds may look light in weight and may be easily driven before the wind, yet they can send down torrents of rain.

214 If one studies such a person closely, one sees that he is completely satisfied, although outwardly he seems to lack everything.

215 I have said enough. Understand that a person in whom these qualities are fully present has acquired wisdom.

216 All this is called unpretentiousness. Now listen to the signs of harmlessness.

217 Listen how different schools of thought have described this quality according to their various opinions.
218 As if a person should break off the branches of a tree to build a fence around the trunk,
219 Cut off his arm and sell it in order to satisfy his hunger, or demolish a temple and use the stones to build a wall around the deity,
220 Similarly, the ritualists hold that harmlessness can be cultivated by slaughtering animals as a sacrifice.
221 When the earth is suffering from a lack of water, they offer various sacrifices so it will rain.
222 The basis of these sacrifices is the slaughter of animals. How can harmlessness be practiced in this way?
223 If the taking of life is the seed that is sown, how can harmlessness spring from it? O Arjuna, how great is the presumption of those ritualists!
224 O Arjuna, the whole science of Vedic medicine is equally strange in this respect, for in order to save one life it prescribes the taking of another.
225 When people suffer from disease and groan with pain, this science prescribes medicine to remove it.
226 To prepare this treatment, plants are dug up or entirely uprooted.
227 Sometimes trees are cut through to the center, or the bark may be removed. Sometimes the center is boiled in a cauldron.
228 O Arjuna, some who know nothing of enmity are struck in such a way that they wither and die.
229 Sometimes bile is taken from the bodies of animals and used for treating other suffering creatures.
230 All this is like tearing down good houses to build temples and shrines, or robbing traders to set up houses for the free distribution of food.
231 It is as though a person were to wrap a cloth around his head and leave the rest of his body naked, or as if a house were demolished to build a large shed.
232 It is like a person who sets his clothes on fire in order to warm himself, or like the bathing of an elephant.
233 It is like selling cattle to build a cattle pen, or setting a parrot free and then making a cage to keep it in. Are such things done seriously or as a joke? Should we laugh at them?
234 Some people strain the water they drink as a religious practice, and many lives are lost in the process.
235 There are others who refuse to cook grain for fear of doing harm. In this way they torment the body, and that is also harmful.
236 O wise Arjuna, harmlessness and destruction both amount to the same thing in the code of the ritualists. You should realize this.
237 When I began to explain harmlessness, I intended to describe its true characteristics.
238 Then I thought I shouldn't avoid mentioning these different views regarding it, so that you could know them also.
239 This is all inherent in the subject. Otherwise, you will be led astray.
240 Moreover, O Arjuna, in order to establish fully one's point of view, one must also understand others' opinions.
241 This is the method of explanation. Now listen carefully, for this is the most important point.
242 I will now express My own views so that you may understand the inner meaning of harmlessness.
243 Whether or not a person has fully understood the nature of harmlessness may be judged from his daily life, just as a touchstone reveals any inferior quality in gold.
244 As soon as the mind and knowledge come together, the mind receives the imprint of harmlessness.
245 Avoiding any disturbance of the waves, without breaking the ripples with its legs or agitating the calm surface,
246 A crane passes through the water swiftly but cautiously watching its prey.
247 A bee alights gently on a lotus flower, so that the pollen won't be disturbed.
248 In the same way, a person who is imbued with harmlessness, believing that the smallest atom is full of minute lives, walks over the ground softly and with compassion.
249 He bestows kindness as he goes and spreads good will in all directions, protecting other creatures with his own life.
250 O Arjuna, a person who walks with such care is beyond praise, and no words do justice to him.
251 A mother cat lovingly carries her kittens in her mouth, and although her sharp teeth touch them, they are not hurt.

252 When an affectionate mother waits for her child, her eyes fill with tenderness.
253 When a person gently fans himself with a lotus leaf, the cool wind refreshes his eyes.
254 Similarly, a person who practices harmlessness steps gently upon the ground and joy comes to all mankind.
255 O Arjuna when such a person, walking quietly, notices a worm or an insect in his path, he turns back.
256 He feels that if he should tread heavily, he might disturb someone's sleep and interrupt his peace.
257 In his compassion, he would turn back and wouldn't harm anyone.
258 He doesn't step on a blade of grass, for there is life within it. How then could he unwittingly cause harm to any creature?
259 Just as it would be impossible for an ant to cross over Mount Meru or a gnat to swim across the ocean, similarly, he couldn't step on any creature he might meet.
260 His behavior is like the fruit of kindness, and his speech is full of compassion.
261 His breathing is calm, his face is the source of all affection, and even his teeth seem to send forth sweetness.
262 Even before he begins to speak love springs from him, and compassion expresses itself before he says a word.
263 He prefers not to speak, for fear that he may hurt someone's feelings.
264 He avoids speaking unnecessarily, so that no one will be distressed or caused to suffer doubts,
265 So that his words may not distract anyone from his work, or cause anyone to fear or scorn him.
266 He maintains silence so that he won't hurt others' feelings or cause them to frown. This is his attitude.
267 If he is ever requested to speak, he speaks with affection, and those who listen feel he is their parent.
268 His words sound like the resonant voice of God, or the waters of the Ganges. They are as chaste as a virtuous wife who has grown old.
269 His words are tender and true, moderate and sincere, like waves of nectar.
270 His speech is free from sarcasm, hurting no one, never provoking ridicule or wounding deeply.
271 In his speech there is no agitation or haste, no guile or false hope, doubt, or deceit. He avoids such faults.
272 O Arjuna, his look is steady and his brow unwrinkled.
273 He believes that the universal Spirit is in all beings, so he usually avoids looking at them lest this Spirit be harmed.
274 If his inner kindliness compels him to look at another,
275 His glance brings comfort, just as moonbeams, though invisible, bring satisfaction to the chakora bird.
276 The effect of his look on all creatures is such that even the tortoise doesn't know the depth of its tenderness.
277 You will see that the hands of a person who looks at another in this way are equally harmless.
278 His hands are as still as those of a person who has attained his goal and has no further desire.
279 Just as something that cannot last is given up, as a fire without fuel ceases to burn, or as a mute person must remain silent,
280 Similarly, this man's hands apparently have nothing to do, so they remain at rest.
281 He doesn't move his hands lest the wind receive a shock, or the sky be pierced by his nails.
282 Then how could he brush away a fly settling on his body or gnats buzzing around his eyes? How could he frighten birds or beasts with his glance?
283 O Arjuna, how could he pick up a weapon when he is unwilling to grasp even a stick in his hand?
284 He avoids playing with a lotus, or tossing a garland of flowers, as this would seem to him like playing with a sling.
285 He won't pass his hand over his body lest he cause the hair on it to tremble, and he allows his nails to grow until they wrap around his fingers.
286 Normally his hands are inactive, but if he has occasion to use them, he folds them.
287 He raises them to reassure the fearful, to raise the fallen, or to help the distressed.
288 Even though he does this reluctantly, he helps those in distress or fear. Even moonbeams cannot know the tenderness of his touch.
289 Compared with the gentleness with which he touches animals, even the breeze from the Malaya mountains would seem harsh.
290 His hands are always empty and free like the

sandalwood tree, which cannot be called barren though it bears no fruit.

291 But I have said enough. The hands of a good person are gentle, like his character.

292 Now if I were to tell you truly about such a person's mind, I would say, "Of whose activity have I spoken?"

293 Aren't the branches one with the tree? Can there be an ocean without water? Is there any difference between the sun and its light?

294 Are the limbs of a body separate from it in any way? Are water and wetness different from each other?

295 Similarly, all these outer expressions which I have described are only manifestations of the mind.

296 Just as the seed sown in the ground becomes a tree, the mind manifests itself through the senses.

297 If harmlessness has no place in the mind, how can it find any outer expression?

298 O Arjuna, whatever inclination may arise, it is first awakened in the mind. Then it is passed on either to the speech, the eye, or the hand.

299 How can anything that isn't first in the mind express itself through the body? Can a sprout grow in the ground without a seed?

300 How can a stream flow if its source dries up? How can a lifeless body be active?

301 In the same way, as soon as the mind stops functioning, the senses become inactive, just as puppets are motionless when there is no puppeteer holding the strings.

302 O Arjuna, the mind is the mainspring of all sensory activities, and it works through the channel of the senses.

303 Whenever there is any impulse in the mind, it is expressed through the channel of the senses.

304 When harmlessness is established in the mind, it radiates outward just as fragrance pours out of a flower.

305 In this way the senses carry out the activity of harmlessness, spending freely its abundant riches.

306 Just as the water of the ocean at high tide flows into every inlet, similarly, the mind pours out its wealth through the senses.

307 Enough! Just as a teacher holds a child's hand and easily writes a line of words,

308 In the same way, the mind transmits its kindliness to the hands and feet, and through them it brings about harmlessness.

309 Therefore, O Arjuna, know that by describing the activity of the senses, the activity of the mind is also described.

310 When you see that a person has entirely renounced harmfulness in speech, thought, or outer action,

311 Understand that he is a storehouse of wisdom. Truly, he is the very incarnation of wisdom.

312 If you want to understand harmlessness, which is heard, spoken, and written of in books, you only have to look at such a person.

313 Jnanadeva says, I should have told you in a few words what the Lord said. Forgive me for explaining this at such length.

314 Cattle which are put to graze in a green pasture constantly move onwards, leaving what lies behind. Birds flying with the wind, are lost in the sky.

315 Similarly, inspired by the theme and tempted by poetic feeling, my mind was carried away.

316 But listen! There is a better reason for this explanation. Otherwise, the word harmlessness itself consists of only a few syllables.

317 Harmlessness seems like a small thing, but one can explain it clearly only when one considers all the views regarding it.

318 If I were to explain harmlessness without referring to the various opinions held about it, you wouldn't accept my explanation.

319 If a common stone were taken to an expert jeweler, he would throw it away. It would be futile to praise it.

320 Just think, in a market where they judge the scent of camphor, could anyone sell flowers as a substitute?

321 Gentlemen, in an assembly such as this, a flow of eloquent words would elicit no response.

322 You would listen to me only if I spoke of both the general and particular theories about this subject.

323 Moreover, if I mingled the purity of the explanation with the turbid waters of doubt, your attention would be distracted.

324 Do swans seek out water covered with weeds?

325 The chakora bird won't open its beak to feed on moonbeams if the moon shines through a cloudy sky.

326 Likewise, if my explanation weren't beyond dispute, not only would you reject it, but it would provoke your anger.

327 If this discourse didn't help you to understand or dispel your doubts, you wouldn't accept it.
328 I have undertaken all this writing for the purpose of pleasing you saintly people.
329 Knowing how deeply interested you are in understanding the *Gita*, I have held it faithfully in my heart.
330 I feel sure that you are ready to give all you have and to abandon everything in order to gain the knowledge of the teachings of the *Gita*. For this reason, my work is a pledge of your kindness.
331 On the other hand, if you only consider your own interest and disregard the search for liberation, then listen: the *Gita* and I will meet the same fate.
332 In short, I wish to win your favor, and I have written this book for that purpose.
333 I decided to speak of the various opinions about this doctrine so that I could find a discourse which would appeal to you appreciative listeners,
334 So I have made this digression and set aside the meaning of the verses. Forgive me for this, for I am your child.
335 It takes time to remove sand from rice, but there is no fault in that, for it must be removed.
336 If a child delays coming home in order to avoid running into a thief, should his mother be angry with him or should she perform the ceremony to preserve his life?
337 But my discourse hasn't been like this, and it is good that you have been tolerant with me. Now listen to what the Lord said.
338 O Arjuna, if you want to have the vision of wisdom, pay attention to Me. I will explain to you how to recognize wisdom.
339 You may recognize wisdom in a person who has patience without intolerance.
340 He is like a lotus on the surface of a deep lake, or wealth in the house of a fortunate person.
341 O Arjuna, I will tell you clearly the characteristics of one who possesses forebearance.
342 He patiently bears all things, just as a person wears his favorite ornaments.
343 Even if calamity should come to him, he wouldn't be overwhelmed by it.
344 His attitude is one of glad acceptance, whether he obtains what he wants or what he doesn't want.
345 He bears with equanimity both honor and shame, he is the same in happiness and in sorrow, and he isn't affected differently by praise or blame.
346 He isn't scorched by heat, nor does he shiver with cold. He isn't intimidated by anything.
347 Just as Mount Meru doesn't feel the weight of its own peaks, nor does the boar feel the burden of the earth,
348 And just as the entire creation doesn't weigh down the earth, in the same way, he doesn't sweat under the pressure of the pairs of opposites.
349 Just as the ocean swells to receive the water of all the rivers flowing into it,
350 Similarly, there is nothing that such a person cannot bear with equanimity, and he has no memory even of what he has suffered.
351 Whatever happens to his body he accepts as his own, and he takes no credit for what he suffers.
352 O Arjuna, he who practices such quiet endurance adds greatness to wisdom.
353 O Arjuna, that person is the essence of wisdom. Now listen as I tell you about uprightness.
354 It is like the generosity of the vital force, which has the same attitude of benevolence towards all.
355 The sun sheds its light without discrimination. The sky, too, gives its space to all.
356 Similarly, this person's attitude doesn't change with different people. His behavior is the same towards all.
357 The whole world seems familiar to him, as if all men were his close friends. He has no thought of "himself" and "others."
358 He meets with everyone, just as water mixes with anything. His mind turns against no one in any matter.
359 Like the swiftly moving wind, his mind is straightforward. Doubt and hope don't exist for it.
360 Just as a child doesn't hesitate to come to its mother, such a person freely expresses his thoughts to others.
361 O Arjuna, he doesn't spend his life in concealment, but lives as a full-blown lotus which freely spreads its fragrance.
362 Like a pure jewel whose luster shines from its surface, his pure mind always goes ahead of his actions.
363 He doesn't need to think ahead. He is satisfied in the experience of union, and his heart

is free and candid.

364 His glance is frank and open, his speech is sincere, and he bears malice toward no one.

365 All his senses are pure, and his five *pranas* are unrestricted throughout the twenty-four hours of the day.

366 His heart is as honest as a stream of nectar. Truly, he is the very source of honesty.

367 O Arjuna, such a person is the embodiment of uprightness, and wisdom has made its home in him.

368 Now, O Arjuna, I will explain to you the nature of devotion to the Guru.

369 How devotion is the mother of prosperity, and how it makes even a distressed person reach the Absolute,

370 I will now explain to you. Pay close attention.

371 Just as the Ganges enters the ocean with all the wealth of its waters, just as the scriptures all culminate in the Supreme,

372 Just as a wife surrenders her whole being to her husband, with all her virtues and faults,

373 Similarly, a person who is devoted to his Guru offers to him all that he has, and makes of himself a temple of devotion.

374 Just as a wife parted from her husband constantly thinks of him, the devotee always remembers the place where his Guru lives.

375 He runs to welcome the breeze that blows from his Guru's house and meeting it he begs it to enter his own home.

376 Carried away by love, he takes delight in directing his speech only toward the Guru's house, for in his mind that is where he resides.

377 He lives in his own home only to obey the Guru's command, like a calf tied with a rope.

378 He continually wonders when the rope will break so he can see his Guru. His separation from his Guru seems longer than a world age.

379 If anyone should come to him from his Guru or brings a message from him, he feels like a dead person brought back to life.

380 Like parched sprouts that are showered with nectar, like a small fish from a pond that finds itself in the ocean,

381 Like a poor man who sees a hidden treasure, a blind man who recovers his sight, or a beggar who is raised up to the throne of Indra,

382 The mention of his Guru's house fills him with joy, and he expands so much that he can easily embrace the whole sky.

383 When you see a person who has this kind of love for his Guru's house, you will realize that wisdom itself is his servant.

384 Through the force of love in his heart, he worships and meditates on his Guru's form.

385 In his pure heart, he makes a temple for his Guru and sets him in the place of honor. With his heart and soul, he himself becomes everything that is needed for worship.

386 In the courtyard of his awareness, within the temple of his joy, he sprinkles the image of his Guru with the nectar of meditation.

387 When the sun of enlightenment dawns, he fills the basket of his intelligence with the flowers of pure feelings and offers them to Shankar in the form of his Guru.

388 At all three appointed times for worship, he burns the incense of his inner Self and waves around it the lamp of wisdom.

389 He constantly offers to his Guru the food of union with the Self. He becomes the worshiper and makes his Guru the object of his worship.

390 It is as though his inner heart were the bed on which the Guru, as a husband, enjoys union with him, and he delights in that love.

391 When at times his heart overflows with love, it resembles the Milky Ocean.

392 For him, the bliss of meditation on his Guru is like the bed of the cobra Shesha on which his Guru is sleeping.

393 He becomes Lakshmi, bathing the feet of Vishnu in the form of his Guru, or he may become Garuda, standing in his presence.

394 In his love for his Guru he pictures himself as Brahma, being born from the navel of Vishnu. Through this desire, he experiences the bliss of meditation.

395 Sometimes in the intensity of his love, he imagines that his Guru is his mother, and he is lying in her lap while being fed.

396 O Arjuna, he may think of his Guru as a cow standing under the tree of consciousness and picture himself as her calf.

397 At times he imagines himself as a fish swimming in the waters of his Guru's love,

398 Or he may feel like a plant being showered with the nectar of the Guru's grace. There is no end to the fantasies that arise in his mind.

399 Sometimes his love is so boundless that he imagines himself as a fledgling bird and the Guru as the mother bird.

400 Again, he imagines his Guru as the mother

bird feeding him with her beak, or he pictures the Guru as a boat to which he is clinging for support in the water.

401 Just as wave after wave arises on the ocean, similarly, one meditation follows another through the depth of his love.

402 In this way, he always enjoys contemplating the Guru's image in his heart. Now I will tell you how he serves the Guru outwardly.

403 He always feels, I will serve my Guru so well that he will become pleased with me and tell me to ask him for a boon.

404 When my Guru becomes pleased with my devotion, I will humbly ask him,

405 O Master, I want to become all your servants.

406 I want to become all the things you need for worship.

407 This is the boon that I would ask of him. If he agreed, I would minister to his every need.

408 If I myself became all the things he needs for worship, he would appreciate my devotion to him.

409 Although the Guru is the mother of all his disciples, I will put such pressure on him through serving him in all ways that he will be my mother alone.

410 I will draw his love so strongly that he will be like a husband devoted to only one wife. In this way, I will make him take the vow of remaining in only one place, and the Guru's love will always be directed to me alone.

411 Just as the winds can never pass beyond the limits of the four quarters, I will become a cage to ensnare all of my Guru's benevolence.

412 All the ornaments of my virtues I will offer to his service as to a queen, and I will be the only vessel of devotion to him.

413 I will become the deep earth on which the Guru's love falls like showers of rain.

414 I will become the Guru's house. I will be his servant and do all his work.

415 I will be the threshold of the door over which my Guru passes when entering or leaving his house. I will both be the door and his doorkeeper.

416 I will become his shoes and will also put them on his feet. I will become his umbrella as well as the one who holds it.

417 I will be his herald and the one who holds his fly whisk. I will be his forerunner.

418 I will prepare his betel nut and serve his personal needs. I will make the preparations for his bath.

419 I will become the seat on which he rests, his garments, his ornaments, sandalwood paste, and all other articles for his use.

420 I will be his cook, will serve his food, and will myself become the lamp which is waved before him.

421 When my Guru takes his meals I will be his companion, and when the meal is over I will come forward to offer him his betel nut roll.

422 I will remove the dishes, make his bed, and massage his feet.

423 I will become his throne. Thus I will serve him in every way.

424 I will be the subject on which he meditates.

425 I will be all the words that may fall on his ear, and the sensation he feels when something touches his body.

426 I will become whatever object the Guru looks at with love.

427 I will become whatever taste his tongue savors, and whatever fragrance pleases his nose.

428 In this way, becoming everything in the world, I will surround my Guru with every conceivable form of service.

429 As long as my body lasts, I will serve him in this way; and after death I will still long to do so.

430 I will mix the earth element of my body with the earth on which the feet of my Guru walks.

431 I will mix the water element of my body with the water touched by my Guru's hand.

432 I will merge the fiery element of my body with the flame of the lamp that lights my Guru's house and with the flame that is waved before him in worship.

433 I will place my vital force by my Guru's fan so I will serve his body.

434 I will merge the etheric element of my body into the space wherever my Guru's form may be.

435 Alive or dead, I will never stop serving my Guru, nor let anyone else serve him even for a moment. For many lifetimes I will serve him like this.

436 A disciple has this kind of eagerness, and he is incomparable in his service.

437 When he is serving, he doesn't think about day or night, nor does he regard any service as either greater or less. The harder the work the Guru gives him, the happier he becomes.

438 When the Guru calls him to work he feels greater than the sky, and he takes delight in serving alone.

439 The moment he receives the Guru's command to perform any service, his body outruns his mind, competing with it to finish the work quickly.
440 At any time he is ready to sacrifice his entire life for the slightest whim of his Master.
441 His body may become emaciated by this service to his Guru, but he is nourished by his love for the Guru and is the abode of his Guru's command.
442 He is noble by virtue of the nobility of his Guru's family, he is kind through their kindness, and he is diligent because of his preoccupation with serving his Guru.
443 He regards as his daily duties those things that belong to his Guru's religious tradition, and devotes himself solely to serving him.
444 He regards the Guru as a holy place, his deity, mother, and father, and knows no other path than service to him.
445 It is the joy of his life to live in his Guru's house, and he loves others who serve the Guru as his own brothers.
446 The repetition of the Guru's name is his only prayer, and his only scripture is his Guru's words.
447 For him the water that touches his Guru's feet embraces all the holy places in the three worlds.
448 If he should find some of the leftovers of his Guru's meal, they would be a feast far more sumptuous for him than even the bliss of *samadhi.*
449 O Arjuna, he would take a speck of the dust raised by his Guru's feet as the price with which to obtain eternal joy.
450 What more can I say? His devotion is boundless. Out of overpowering inspiration, I have described it in this way.
451 A person who has this kind of devotion and who enjoys nothing but serving the Guru
452 Is a treasure house of wisdom. Wisdom is even honored by his existence. He is a god and wisdom is his devotee.
453 Wisdom enters him through open doors and lives in him. It is enough to satisfy the whole world.
454 Jnanadeva says, My soul takes delight in serving my Guru. This is why I have explained it in such detail.
455 Otherwise, if I am not occupied in serving him, I am helpless even though I have hands, I am blind to worship even though I have eyes, and I am less able than a lame man to walk around the temple.
456 I am mute in praising his glory even though I have a voice, an idler who eats other's food. Yet in my heart I have the sincere desire to serve him.
457 This is what has compelled me to become involved in this long explanation.
458 I, Jnanadeva, ask you to forgive me and allow me to serve you. Now I will continue this explanation in a better way.
459 Listen, O Arjuna. Lord Krishna, the incarnation of Vishnu and the bearer of the weight of the earth, spoke as follows:
460 Now I will speak of purity. The body and mind of a pure person are as pure as camphor.
461 He is as clear as a jewel and as radiant as the sun.
462 His good actions make his body clean, while inwardly he is enlightened by his wisdom. Thus he is full of purity.
463 According to the rules of the Vedas, water and earth cleanse a person outwardly.
464 The dust on the mirror of the mind is cleansed by the intellect, just as stains on cloth are removed by the washerman's soap.
465 Similarly, a person is pure if he is outwardly clean and has the light of wisdom in his heart.
466 Otherwise, O Arjuna, if the heart is not pure, the display of outer effort serves only to deceive others.
467 It would be like adorning a dead body, bathing a donkey in a holy river, sprinkling a bitter pumpkin with sugar,
468 Hanging flags on a deserted house, pasting food on the body of a starving man, or putting kum-kum on a widow.
469 A gilded dome is hollow and its glitter is worthless. What is the use of painting an imitation fruit made of cow dung?
470 This is how it is with an impure man and his outer actions. Inferior merchandise cannot be sold for a high price.
471 When wisdom enters the heart, outer cleanliness naturally follows. How can wisdom arise merely by performing external actions?
472 The body is purified through spiritual practices, and inner impurities are cleansed through wisdom.
473 Then the distinction between outside and inside vanishes, and purity alone remains.
474 The pure qualities of the inner Self shine

through the senses, like a flame enclosed in a crystal lamp.

475 Even if such a person sees, hears, or encounters things that ordinarily give rise to doubts and evil thoughts or sow the seeds of bad actions,

476 They don't affect his mind any more than the sky is tainted by the color of the clouds.

477 Although his senses may enjoy sense objects, he is not contaminated by passion.

478 He remains completely untouched by these things, just as a high caste and a low caste woman meet on the road without coming in contact with each other.

479 A woman embraces both her husband and her son, yet her son arouses no passion in her.

480 In the same way, good and evil desires never seep into a pure-hearted person. He knows which actions are right and which are wrong.

481 Just as water cannot permeate a diamond and sand cannot be cooked in boiling water, his heart cannot be contaminated by any kind of evil thought.

482 O Arjuna, this state is known as purity, and you should know that wisdom dwells here.

483 A person in whom steadfastness resides is the life of wisdom.

484 His body may perform many kinds of actions, but the equanimity of his mind is never disturbed.

485 A cow doesn't lose her affection for her calf even when she wanders in a forest. A devout wife who burns herself on her husband's funeral pyre takes no pleasure in the ornaments she is wearing.

486 The heart of a miser remains with his buried treasure no matter how far he may go from it. Similarly, the mind of a steadfast person is not disturbed when his body moves from one place to another.

487 The sky doesn't move with the fleeting clouds, the pole star remains fixed while the other stars revolve around it,

488 And when travelers walk, the road itself doesn't move, nor do the trees leave their places, O Arjuna.

489 In the same way, even while his body is being activated by the five elements, the mind of a pure person is not disturbed by waves of feelings.

490 Just as the earth is not shaken by the force of a hurricane, likewise, such a person is not disturbed by the swirl of calamity.

491 He is not distressed by the misery of poverty, he is never overwhelmed by fear or sorrow, nor does he dread the death of the body.

492 His mind remains steady and is not swayed by hope, anxiety, disease, or old age.

493 Not even a hair of his body is disturbed when he is assaulted by contempt and dishonor, or confronted with passion and desire.

494 Even though the sky may fall on him or the earth crumble, his mind remains unshaken.

495 Just as an elephant isn't driven away by throwing flowers at it, likewise, he isn't wounded by the arrows of harsh words.

496 Mount Mandara isn't moved by the waves of the Milky Ocean, and the sky isn't consumed by a forest fire.

497 Similarly, no matter how many waves of passion may arise, his mind isn't disturbed. He remains courageous and patient even if the world comes to an end.

498 O Arjuna, this state of mind which I have described in such detail is called steadfastness.

499 A person whose heart and mind acquire this kind of steadfastness is an open treasure of wisdom.

500 A greedy man thinks only of his home, a warrior clutches his weapons, a miser clings to his wealth,

501 A mother thinks only of her child, and a bee is always greedy for honey.

502 Similarly, O Arjuna, such a person keeps strict watch over his mind and doesn't allow it to stand at the threshold of the senses.

503 He always fears that some passionate creature or some fiend of desire may hear, see, and take hold of his heart.

504 Just as an outraged husband confines his unruly wife to the house, so a pure person keeps watch over his mental tendencies.

505 He controls his senses, mortifies his body, and performs all actions with restraint.

506 At the doorway of his mind, he turns his senses within and restrains his activities.

507 In the three centers—*muladhara* at the base of the spine, *manipura* at the navel, and *vishuddha* at the throat—he performs the three yogic *bandhas—mula, uddiyana, and jalandhara*—and focuses his mind at the junction of the *ida* and *pingala nadis.*

508 He puts meditation to sleep on the couch of *samadhi*, and his mind becomes one with Consciousness.

509 Know that such a person has mastered his heart. When this happens wisdom rises supreme.
510 A person whose heart obeys his every command should be considered wisdom incarnate.

इन्द्रियार्थेषु वैराग्यम् अनहंकार एव च ।
जन्ममृत्युजराव्याधि- दुःखदोषानुदर्शनम् ॥
indriyārtheṣu vāirāgyam
anahaṁkāra eva ca
janmamṛtyujarāvyādhi-
duḥkhadoṣānudarśanam

9. Indifference to the objects of sense, and absence of egotism; keeping in view the evils of birth, death, old age, disease, and pain;

511 Complete indifference to sense objects occupies his mind.
512 The tongue doesn't like vomited food, and there is no pleasure in embracing a corpse.
513 No one wants to take poison, to enter a burning house, or to live in a tiger's den.
514 A person wouldn't leap into molten iron, or use a serpent as a pillow.
515 In the same way, O Arjuna, such a person avoids all contact with sense objects and doesn't allow his thoughts to stray in their direction.
516 Although his mind is utterly indifferent to sense pleasures and his body is emaciated, he still has a great desire to practice self-control.
517 O Arjuna, he practices all manner of penance, and finds the company of others as intolerable as the end of the world.
518 He is strongly attracted to yoga, wishes to live in seclusion, and cannot bear even the mention of others' company.
519 To him, the enjoyment of worldly pleasures is like lying on a bed of arrows or rolling in mud.
520 Even the mere idea of heaven seems to him like the decaying flesh of a dog.
521 This is dispassion and the good fortune of Self-realization. Through it, the soul becomes worthy of the bliss of union with God.
522 Wisdom is found in a person who has such a strong dislike for the pleasures of this world or of heaven.
523 Like a person who hasn't renounced passion, he performs his religious duties, but he clings to no sense of merit.
524 He carries out all his family obligations and religious rites, but without personal involvement in them.
525 His mind isn't disturbed by the feeling that he is the one who has performed them.
526 The wind blows in any direction, the sun shines with no sense of its own importance,
527 The Vedas speak spontaneously, and the Ganges flows without a sense of purpose. In the same way, this person acts without pride.
528 He performs actions just as trees bear their fruit in due season, not knowing what they do.
529 The illusion of egoism is absent from his heart, deeds, and speech, like a necklace from which the string has been removed.
530 Just as clouds float in the sky without being attached to it, so are the actions of such a person.
531 He is like the clothing worn by a drunkard, a weapon in the hand of a clay image, or books tied to the back of a bull.
532 Similarly, he has no awareness of being involved in worldly life. This is what is called selflessness.
533 When these signs are present in a person, understand that wisdom dwells in him. There is no doubt of this.
534 He is able to understand birth, death, sorrow, disease, old age, and sin, even before they approach him.
535 A person with special powers protects himself against evil spirits, yogis take precautions against obstacles, a mason uses a plumb-line,
536 And a serpent retains its enmity even from a former birth. In the same way, this person is always mindful of the sins of past lives.
537 Just as a grain of sand doesn't melt into the eye, and as a weapon inserted into a wound is not absorbed in it, similarly, he never forgets the pain of a former life.
538 He exclaims, Alas! I have fallen into the mud, I took birth through the lowest passage, and I tasted sweat as my mother nursed me.
539 In this way, he is disgusted when he remembers his birth, and declares that he will never allow it to happen again.
540 A gambler plays another game to make up for his losses, a son will avenge a wrong done to his father,
541 And a younger brother will seek revenge for the murder of his elder brother. In the same way, such a person strives to avoid rebirth.
542 The shame of his birth never leaves him, just as a noble man cannot tolerate dishonor.

543 Although his death is still in the future, he is as vigilant as if it might occur that very day.

544 O Arjuna, when a swimmer is told that the river is deep, he adjusts his clothing while still on the bank.

545 A warrior about to go into battle makes careful preparations and wards off the blows with his shield before they strike him.

546 A traveler anticipates the danger of finding thieves at his next stop. Before a person dies, medicine is brought for him.

547 What is the use of digging a well when one's house is already on fire?

548 When a person has fallen like a stone into deep water and is drowning, who will respond to his cries for help?

549 A man who has a powerful enemy must always be armed with weapons,

550 An engaged girl must be ready to leave her father's house, and a person renouncing the world must sever all ties. In the same way, such a person always meditates on the idea of death, even before it comes to him.

551 Thus, even in this life he wards off rebirth, he overcomes future death by dying to earthly existence, and he lives only in his true nature.

552 In such a person, there is an abundance of wisdom. The thorns of anxiety about life and death no longer pierce his heart.

553 In this way, he thinks of death while still in the fullness of youth, before his body is worn out with old age.

554 He says to himself, Right now my body is well-fed, but eventually it will become as thin as a piece of dried fruit.

555 My limbs will become useless, like a bankrupt business or a kingdom which has lost its power for lack of a minister.

556 Although my nose now takes delight in the fragrance of flowers, it will become as insensitive as a camel's knee.

557 My head will become like the sore hooves of a restless cow stamping in the cow pen.

558 My eyes that now rival lotus blossoms will then be as lusterless as a dry gourd.

559 My eyelids will droop like the dry bark of a tree, and my chest will waste away under the falling of my tears.

560 My face will be smeared with saliva, like the trunk of the babul tree, sticky with the secretions of chameleons.

561 Mucus will collect around my nose like the droppings at the foot of a cooking stove.

562 My mouth, now red with betel nut juice, will then be clogged with phlegm.

563 The teeth which show as I laugh and which I now use for elegant speech, will have fallen out.

564 My tongue won't be able to move, like a farmer caught in the meshes of debt, or cattle sunk in the mud after a rainstorm.

565 The hair on my face will fall off like dry straws blown away by the wind.

566 The spit will run from my mouth, just as rain water rushes down a mountain creek at the first downpour of the monsoon.

567 My speech will fail, my ears will lose their power of hearing, and my body will be like that of an old monkey.

568 Just as a grass scarecrow shakes in the wind, my whole body will tremble.

569 My legs will totter, my arms will be weighed down, and my body will become a travesty of its former state.

570 I will lose control of my bodily organs, and people will pray for my death.

571 If I don't die soon, people will spit on me and my relatives will be tired of me.

572 Children will call me a ghost, women will faint when they see me, and everyone will hate me.

573 When a fit of coughing overcomes me in the night, my sleeping neighbors will say, That old man exhausts everyone.

574 Therefore, when the wise man is still young he worries about old age, and the thought of it fills him with revulsion.

575 He says to himself, Youth will pass away and old age will overtake me. Then what will I have left?

576 Therefore, before I lose my hearing, I will spend my time listening to what is worthwhile. Before I become lame, I will visit holy places.

577 Before my sight fails, I will see all that is worth seeing. Before I lose my power of speech, I will say good things.

578 I know my hands will become weak, so now I will use them for charity and good works.

579 When this condition overtakes me, my mental powers will deteriorate, so I will spend my time now thinking of the Self.

580 Just as people should conceal their wealth so

thieves won't seize it, and they should hide everything in the evening before the lights go out,

581 Similarly, it is wise to do everything that should be done now, so it won't be left undone when old age comes.

582 If a traveler walks until nightfall, when birds are returning to their nests, and then stops, exhausted, in a place surrounded by forts, he is likely to be robbed.

583 Similarly, if old age comes to a person whose life has been useless, can it be said that he still has a long life to live?

584 The pods of sesame seeds that have been threshed don't yield more seeds if they are threshed again. Can a fire burn once it has become ashes?

585 A wise person bears in mind the thought of old age and tries to rob it of its grimness.

586 He takes every precaution to prevent disease from attacking his body.

587 A sensible person will reject anything that has fallen from a serpent's mouth.

588 Such a person becomes indifferent and gives up the attachment that leads to separation, pain, disaster, and distress.

589 He uses stones of self-control to block the doors of the senses through which sin might thrust itself.

590 In short, the person who uses all these possible means is a master of the wealth of wisdom.

591 Listen, O Arjuna. I will now speak of another characteristic of such a person.

असक्तिर् अनभिष्वङ्ग पुत्रदारगृहादिषु ।
नित्यं च समचित्तत्वम् इष्टानिष्टोपपत्तिषु ॥
asaktir anabhiṣvaṅga
putradāragṛhādiṣu
nityaṁ ca samacittatvam
iṣṭāniṣṭopapattiṣu

10. Non-attachment, absence of clinging to son, wife, home, and so on, and constant even-mindedness toward desired and undesired events;

592 He is as indifferent to his body as a person living in a hotel.

593 He regards the shade of a tree with the same interest as he feels for his own house.

594 Just as a person is unaware of his shadow, he is desireless towards his wife.

595 He cares no more for his children than for a stranger who comes to his house, or than a tree cares for the cattle lying under it.

596 O Arjuna, surrounded by his possessions, he is as indifferent as a mere passer-by.

597 He is as fearful of the authority of the Vedas as a parrot locked in a cage.

598 The man who has no attachment to his wife, children, or home is the source of all wisdom.

599 Good and evil mean as little to him as the hot or rainy seasons mean to the ocean.

600 His mind is unaffected by good or bad things, just as the sun doesn't change with the morning, noon, or evening.

601 Where there is complete equanimity, as there is in the sky, there you may see true wisdom.

मयि चानन्ययोगेन भक्तिर् अव्यभिचारिणी ।
विविक्तदेशसेवित्वम् अरतिर् जनसंसदि ॥
mayi cānanyayogena
bhaktir avyabhicāriṇī
viviktadeśasevitvam
aratir janasaṁsadi

11. And unswerving devotion to Me with single-minded yoga, frequenting secluded places, distaste for the society of men,

602 In body, speech, and mind he desires only Me.

603 He has drunk fully of the conviction that I am his sole refuge. He has no other.

604 His mind has become so merged in Me that he and I live together.

605 Just as a woman feels no restraint with her husband either in her heart or in her body, he is completely one with Me.

606 When the river Ganges reaches the ocean, it merges with it. Similarly he is united with Me, and worships Me with all his soul.

607 The sunlight rises and sets with the sun. It is one with the sun and enhances its brilliance.

608 Water sparkles and plays on the surface of the ocean. People call it waves, but it is really only water.

609 Similarly, the person who is devoted to Me and has become one with Me is wisdom incarnate.

610 He is drawn to holy places, to the banks of sacred rivers, to pure groves where penance is practiced, and to caves where he can retire.

611 He likes to live in mountain caves and on the shores of lakes, and prefers to avoid cities.

612 He loves solitude and grows weary of people's company. He is wisdom in human form.

613 O wise Arjuna, I will also explain to you other features of wisdom.

अध्यात्मज्ञाननित्यत्वं तत्त्वज्ञानार्थदर्शनम् ।
एतज् ज्ञानम् इति प्रोक्तम् अज्ञानं यद् अतो ऽन्यथा ॥
adhyātmajñānanityatvaṁ
tattvajñānārthadarśanam
etaj jñānam iti proktam
ajñānaṁ yad ato 'nyathā

12. Constancy in knowledge of the supreme Spirit, observing the goal of knowledge of the truth; this is declared to be true knowledge. Ignorance is what is contrary to this.

614 He realizes that the highest Self is the only reality,
615 And he is convinced that the knowledge of heaven and earthly life is merely ignorance.
616 Therefore, he gives up the goal of reaching heaven, he rejects worldly life, and with complete faith plunges into the knowledge of the Self.
617 When a traveler reaches a point where the road divides, he avoids a by-path and continues along the highway.
618 Similarly, the wise man lays ignorance aside and directs his mind and intellect toward the knowledge of the supreme Self.
619 He says that this alone is the truth and everything else is delusion, and he is as firm as Mount Meru in this conviction.
620 In his certainty regarding knowledge of the Self, he is as fixed as the pole star.
621 Knowledge dwells in him. A person whose mind is devoted to knowledge is one with it.
622 Just as the act of sitting doesn't happen merely by talking about it, it is the same with knowledge.
623 There is one result which is attained from pure knowledge of the Self: the object of knowledge. This is where he has fixed his gaze.
624 If the object of knowledge isn't attained, that knowledge is useless.
625 What good is a lamp in the hands of a blind man? In the same way, all knowledge is futile if it doesn't result in Self-realization.
626 If the mind cannot reach the supreme Self with the light of knowledge, the urge toward it is blind.
627 Therefore, a person's insight must be purified so that he recognizes as God whatever knowledge reveals to him.
628 Insight grasps the object revealed by pure knowledge.
629 His reason develops along with this knowledge, and he doesn't need to state that he himself is knowledge.
630 His mind grasps reality with the light of knowledge, and he easily reaches the highest Truth.
631 O Arjuna, is it strange that such a person should be described as the incarnation of knowledge? Does one need to say that the sun is the sun?
632 Then those who were listening said, You have said enough. Don't digress too far, for you are diverting our interest in your explanation.
633 You have already entertained us generously and eloquently, by expounding what knowledge is.
634 There shouldn't be too much feeling, and you are using too many poetic devices. You will only lose our interest.
635 If a hostess removed all the dishes as soon as her guest sat down to eat, what good would her hospitality be?
636 Who will feed a cow which only kicks and won't let anyone sit near her at milking time?
637 You have done well; you are not like those writers who talk idly without first filling their minds with knowledge.
638 To attain even a little of that knowledge, a person will practice many austerities, and your explanation of it has been good.
639 Would a person complain if nectar showered down on him continuously for a week? And who would take the trouble to count the days if his happiness lasted for thousands of years?
640 Would the chakora bird ever tire of looking at the moon even if there were a whole age of full moon nights?
641 Similarly, listening to a discourse on knowledge, full of poetic feeling, who would say, "That is enough!"
642 If a fortunate guest were served by a beautiful woman, he would be reluctant to finish the meal.
643 It is the same with us: we desire knowledge, and you also have great love for it.
644 For this reason, your explanation has great inspiration. No one can deny that you have deep insight into knowledge.
645 So, inspired by wisdom, you should explain the meaning of the verses.
646 In response to these words of his saintly listeners, Jnanadeva said, This was my intention.
647 Now that you have commanded me, I will waste no more words.
648 Now listen to the eighteen characteristics of

knowledge, about which the Lord spoke to Arjuna.

649 Then Krishna said, True knowledge has been explained by Me and by many other wise men.

650 I have made knowledge as clear to you as if it were a fruit in the palm of your hand.

651 O Arjuna, I will now tell you plainly what the characteristics of ignorance are.

652 Now that you have a clear understanding of knowledge, it will be easy for you to see that what isn't knowledge is ignorance.

653 When the day is over, night takes its place. There is no third possibility.

654 Similarly, where there is no knowledge, there is ignorance. But I will tell you some of its features.

655 A person who lives for greatness, who seeks esteem, and who is pleased when others honor him,

656 Whose pride is like a mountain peak, and who won't climb down from his importance, is full of ignorance.

657 In his speech he displays his righteousness like a rope tied to a tree, and sets it up like a broom on a temple roof.

658 He proclaims his learning, makes a great show of his good deeds, and does everything that may bring him fame.

659 Although he smears his body with ash and deceives others, he is a mine of ignorance.

660 His conduct is painful to all, and is like a fire raging through a forest consuming everything in its path.

661 His words are more harmful than an iron bar, and his motives are deadlier than poison.

662 He is a storehouse of ignorance, and his life is the dwelling place of destruction.

663 Just as a bellows first swells up and then collapses, such a person is elated by good fortune and depressed by misfortune.

664 When people praise him, he leaps with joy like dust blown into the air by a whirlwind.

665 At the slightest rebuff he is cast down, just as earth is dampened by a few drops of rain but is dried by the wind.

666 A person who is so hypersensitive to praise and blame is full of ignorance.

667 Although he seems to behave with frankness, he keeps his thoughts to himself. He mingles with everyone while deceiving them in his heart.

668 Such a person behaves outwardly in a friendly way, but inwardly he is against everyone, just as a hunter spreads out food as bait to catch birds.

669 Like a stone covered with moss or a ripe neem fruit, his deeds appear superficially to be good.

670 Believe me, such a person is a storehouse of ignorance. This is the truth.

671 He is ashamed of his Guru's house, cares nothing for serving him, and treats disrespectfully the one from whom he has gained his knowledge.

672 To speak of him is like eating the food of a low-caste person, but it cannot be avoided when describing such a man.

673 I will now speak of devotion to the Guru, which will expiate this sin of speech. The mention of a person who serves his Guru is like the light of the sun.

674 To speak of such a person saves one from sin and wards off even the worst of evil deeds.

675 It even destroys the fear of sin. Now listen to other signs of the ignorant person.

676 He neglects performing good deeds, and his mind is full of doubts. He is like an abandoned well in a forest.

677 The opening of the well is overgrown with thorns, and it is full of bones. An evil person is like this.

678 He sees no difference between his own wealth and that of another person. He is like a dog which, to satisfy its hunger, makes no distinction between food that is exposed and food which is covered.

679 Just as a pig will mate anywhere, such a person is careless in his relationships with women.

680 He doesn't care if he misses the proper time to perform his duties or his religious practice.

681 He is shameless about committing sin, is indifferent to doing good deeds, and his mind is full of evil thoughts.

682 His eyes are always fixed on acquiring wealth. Such a person is the image of ignorance.

683 For even the smallest gain he will swerve from the path of steadfastness, like a blade of grass bent by an ant.

684 He is disturbed by the slightest hint of fear, just as water in a pond becomes muddy at the first footstep.

685 He is distracted by sorrow in the same way that mist is scattered in every direction by the wind.

686 His mind is carried away by his desires, just as a gourd that falls into flood waters.
687 Like the wind, he cannot rest in a holy place or by a holy river.
688 He wanders aimlessly about, like an excited chameleon running up and down a tree.
689 Just as a clay pot can stand only where it is placed on the ground, he stays wherever he happens to be. Otherwise, he roams from place to place.
690 Such a person is full of ignorance and is as fickle as a monkey.
691 O Arjuna, his mind completely lacks self-control.
692 He is no more concerned about committing wrong actions than a stream in flood would be hindered by a sandbank.
693 He disregards vows and violates religious duty and ethical conduct.
694 He never tires of sin, he rejects right action, and uproots all the boundaries of shame.
695 He turns his back on family duties, ignores the injunctions of the Vedas, and cannot discriminate between right and wrong action.
696 He is like a wild bull, the wind blowing freely, an overflowing stream in the forest,
697 A blind elephant running amok, or a wildfire spreading on a mountain. In this way, his mind wanders among sense pleasures.
698 What cannot be thrown on a heap of garbage? Who may not run into an animal on the loose? Who may not cross over the limits of a village?
699 Just as anyone may eat the food cooked for brahmins, as power may fall into the hands of indifferent men, or anyone may enter the shop of a merchant who is giving away his goods,
700 So is the heart of such a person. Ignorance thrives in him.
701 He doesn't give up his desire for sense pleasures either in life or in death, and he seeks to enjoy them even in heaven.
702 He constantly strives for pleasure and is addicted to acting with selfish motives; yet if he sees someone who has renounced these, he bathes to purify his body and his clothes.
703 Although sense pleasures fade away, he neither tires of them nor guards against them. He is like a leper eating with unclean hands.
704 Even though a female donkey doesn't allow the male to approach her and kicks him on the muzzle, he still doesn't leave.
705 Such a person will jump into a blazing fire to experience pleasure, and boasts of his addiction as though it were an ornament.
706 A deer will exhaust itself following a mirage, and never realize that it is an illusion.
707 Similarly, such a person will pursue sense pleasures all his life; but instead of becoming weary of them, his passion increases.
708 In his childhood he is devoted to his father and mother, but when he grows up he indulges in relationships with women.
709 As old age approaches, he transfers this love to his children.
710 Just as a woman who has a blind child always remembers him, he never stops longing for sense pleasures either in life or in death.
711 Understand that he is filled with boundless ignorance. Now I will tell you some other characteristics of his.
712 He acts from a firm identification with his body.
713 Whether he finishes his work or not, he displays it before everyone.
714 Just as an exorcist bears the burden of the responsibility given to him, this person is weighed down by his age and his learning.
715 He feels that he alone exists, that the greatest wealth is in his own home, and that his conduct is superior to all others'.
716 He thinks that no one else is as great as he is, and that he is supremely learned. In this way, he is full of arrogance.
717 Just as sense pleasures shouldn't be shown to a sick person, he is unable to tolerate the good in others.
718 The wick of a lamp is burned as well as the oil, and it leaves soot wherever it is placed.
719 If it is sprinkled with water it will splutter, if it is fanned it will be blown out, if it is placed near straw it will burn up,
720 And it gives little light and warmth. Such a person is like this lamp.
721 If milk is given to a patient with a fever, it only increases his fever. If it is given to a serpent, it turns into poison.
722 In the same way, this person envies virtuous people. He is vain about his learning, and is puffed up with pride in his wisdom and his austerities.
723 He is as arrogant as a low-caste man who has been given a seat of honor, or as a snake who has swallowed a pillar.
724 He is as stubborn as a beam or a rock, and as

cunning as a snake which escapes from the snake charmer.

725 I tell you that ignorance continually increases in such a person.

726 Moreover, O Arjuna, being engrossed in his house, his family, and his possessions, he gives no thought to his former births.

727 He forgets them just as an ungrateful person forgets obligations, as a thief forgets money loaned to him, or as a shameless person disregards praise.

728 A dog that has had its ears and tail cut off and has been driven away for doing harm, will return to the house to do more.

729 A frog in a snake's mouth is unaware of its fate and is only interested in catching flies.

730 Although this person's body has lost its vitality and is decaying with disease, he isn't troubled by the thought of how this happened.

731 He lay nine months in his mother's womb, among layers of filth,

732 And he remembers nothing of the pain he suffered during birth.

733 He is neither troubled nor disgusted at the sight of a child being born from the womb.

734 Hasn't his former birth passed away? And won't another one come? He doesn't consider these questions.

735 Even while watching the whole panorama of his life unfold, he gives no thought to death.

736 He has such confidence in life that he doesn't recognize death, which it implies.

737 A fish that lives in shallow water assumes that it won't dry up and doesn't seek a deeper part of the river.

738 A deer lured on by the hunter's song doesn't notice the hunter himself. A fish swallows the bait, unaware of the hook it conceals.

739 A moth doesn't know that the glittering flame of a lamp will destroy it.

740 A foolish person who is asleep doesn't see that his house is on fire, or he may mix poison with his food.

741 Absorbed in the pleasures of passion, he doesn't realize that death comes disguised as life.

742 He considers as real the strength of his body, the sequence of day and night, and the intensity of sense pleasures.

743 Such a person is wretched and doesn't realize that all this is like surrendering himself to a prostitute; it will squander all his wealth.

744 Associating with a thief may bring about death. A painting on a wall can be easily washed off.

745 When a body swells up with jaundice it appears well-nourished, but it means it is close to death. Similarly, a deluded person doesn't know that a life of eating and sleeping leads to death.

746 For a person running toward a stake, death draws nearer with every step.

747 In the same way, as such a person's body ages and as he continues to enjoy sense pleasures,

748 Death gradually gains mastery over his life, just as salt gradually dissolves in water.

749 As life passes by, death approaches. He fails to recognize this continuous process.

750 In short, O Arjuna, deluded by pleasure, he doesn't see that death is gradually approaching.

751 O mighty Arjuna, he is the king of the land of ignorance. There is nothing more to say.

752 Engrossed in the pleasures of life, he doesn't notice death. Youth doesn't concern itself with old age.

753 He doesn't see that old age is before him, any more than a wagon falling over a cliff or a rock slipping off a mountain top is aware of its end.

754 He is carried away by the passions of youth, just as a stream becomes swollen in a flood, or as two buffaloes fight and become enraged.

755 His body shrinks, his attractiveness fades, his head begins to tremble,

756 And his beard turns gray. Yet he refuses to acknowledge all this, and still seeks to fulfill his desires.

757 A blind man doesn't know what is in front of him until he runs into it. A lazy person is pleased when he is overcome with drowsiness.

758 In the enjoyment of youth, he doesn't see that old age is approaching. He is truly ignorant.

759 Whenever he sees a person who is decrepit and bent over, he makes fun of him, not realizing that that will be his own condition later.

760 Even when the mark of death is already stamped on him, the illusion of youth doesn't leave him.

761 Believe me, such a person is the dwelling place of ignorance. Now listen to more of his qualities.

762 A bull which has grazed in a forest full of tigers and through luck has returned safely, will confidently go back to the same place.

763 A person who happens to find a hidden treasure in a serpent's hole concludes that there is no serpent there.
764 After he visits the treasure several times, he becomes convinced that there is none.
765 If a person assumes his enemies are sleeping, that all bad feeling has come to an end, he and his family will lose their lives.
766 Similarly, an ignorant person has no anxiety about disease as long as his health is good and he gets food and sleep.
767 He acquires more wealth and enjoys the company of his wife, children, and other relatives. Through this pleasure, he loses his insight.
768 He doesn't foresee that in a sudden tragedy he may lose his wife and children or his wealth.
769 O Arjuna, understand that he is ignorant, for he encourages his senses in every way.
770 In the heat of youth and with the aid of his wealth, he impulsively enjoys all sorts of pleasures.
771 He does what he shouldn't do, and he allows his mind to dwell on improper thoughts.
772 He goes where he shouldn't go, asks for what he shouldn't have, and mentally and physically he touches forbidden things.
773 He looks at things he shouldn't see, eats what he shouldn't eat, and relishes it.
774 He keeps bad company, maintains relations with people he should avoid, and follows the wrong path of action.
775 He listens to what he shouldn't hear, says things that should be left unsaid, and is unaware that he is doing the wrong thing.
776 He is swayed by his inclinations, disregards good and evil, and acts haphazardly, without considering what he should or shouldn't do.
777 He doesn't stop to think that he is committing sin and that later he will have to suffer the pain of hell.
778 Because of him, ignorance increases in the world; and through contact with him, even wise people may be affected by it.
779 There are still other signs that mark such people, so you may clearly know what ignorance is.
780 He is attached to his home and family, just as a bee is drawn to the pollen of a newly opened flower.
781 Just as a fly cannot leave a mound of sugar, such a person's mind is always occupied with thoughts of women.
782 He is like a frog caught in a pond, a fly stuck in slime, or a beast sunk deep in mud.
783 He doesn't stir from his house either in life or in death, just as a dead snake stays on the ground.
784 He holds fast to his body, just as a wife clings to her husband.
785 He guards his house diligently, like a bee in search of honey.
786 Just as a beloved child born to parents in their old age means everything to them,
787 In the same way, O Arjuna, he is devoted to his house, and he treasures his wife above all else.
788 When a saint attains union with God, worldly activities cease for him;
789 But this man lives only for women and doesn't realize who he is or what he ought to do.
790 The man whose desires are focused on women doesn't care about loss, shame, or criticism.
791 He strives to please his wife and waits on her like a monkey dancing around its master.
792 Just as a greedy person exhausts himself and alienates his friends while he amasses wealth,
793 Such a person cuts down on charitable acts, deceives his relatives, satisfies his wife's every whim, and deprives her of nothing.
794 He is negligent about worship, deceives his Guru, and pretends to be poor before his parents.
795 On the other hand, he never lacks money where his wife's pleasure is concerned, and buys for her all the good things that he sees.
796 He serves his wife as devotedly as one who worships God.
797 He thinks that the whole world would collapse if anyone looked at his wife or opposed her.
798 He gives her the most precious things, while he provides nothing to maintain others.
799 Just as a person is careful to keep a vow he has made to the god Naga for fear of getting ringworm, in the same way he satisfies all his wife's desires.
800 O Arjuna, his wife means everything to him, and he loves the children who are born to her.
801 All her possessions are dearer to him than his life.
802 Such a man is the root of all ignorance, and ignorance is strengthened through him. Truly, he is ignorance incarnate.
803 Just as boats on a stormy sea are tossed about by the waves,

804 He is overwhelmed with delight when he gets what he wants, and is plunged into depression if any misfortune happens to him.
805 O Arjuna, a person who is agitated by joy or misery is truly ignorant.
806 Concerning his devotion to Me, it is prompted only by his desire for its fruit. He will make a show of devotion to gain money.
807 He is like an unfaithful wife who behaves lovingly with her husband in order to continue her relationship with her lover.
808 O Arjuna, he begins to worship Me, but his mind is focused on pleasure.
809 If he should fail to get what he wants through worship, he abandons it, saying it is an illusion.
810 He goes from one deity to another, just as a peasant cultivates one field and then another.
811 He follows the Guru whom he considers eminent, takes a mantra from him, and ignores everything else.
812 He is unkind to all living creatures. He professes devotion to the image of a deity, but without a steady purpose.
813 He makes an image of Me, puts it in a corner of his house, and then goes on pilgrimages to worship other gods and goddesses.
814 Sometimes he worships Me, at other times he worships his family deity, and at still other times he prostrates before other gods.
815 Although he has an altar to Me in his home, he makes vows to other gods, and on special days he worships his ancestors.
816 He feels as much devotion for Me as he does for the serpent god on the day of Naga Panchami, the snake festival.
817 At dawn on the fourth day of the month he worships Ganesh, and on the fourteenth he worships Durga.
818 On the day when the goddess Chandi is worshiped, he sets aside his regular practices and offers his devotion to her, while on Sundays he offers food at the feet of Shiva.
819 On Mondays he goes to the Shiva temple and offers leaves of the bel tree. In this way, he shows devotion to all manner of gods.
820 He worships all continuously, without a moment of silence, just as a prostitute sits at the city gates.
821 The person who seeks to follow every deity is the incarnation of ignorance.
822 He too is ignorant who dislikes holy places of seclusion, groves where penance is performed, places of pilgrimage, or the shores of lakes.
823 Though a person may be learned, if he scorns the knowledge by which Self-realization is attained he is also ignorant.
824 He won't read the Upanishads, has no interest in yoga, and pays no attention to the knowledge of the supreme Self.
825 He refuses to acknowledge the importance of spiritual discussion, and his mind is undisciplined.
826 Another person is well versed in rituals, knows the Puranas by heart, and is an expert in astrology.
827 He is knowledgeable in the art of sculpture, skilled at cooking, and knows all the rituals in the Atharva Veda.
828 He is well versed in treatises on love, has read the complete *Mahabharata*, and has mastered all the scriptures.
829 He understands the science of ethics and medicine, and is unrivaled in his knowledge of poetry and drama.
830 He is versed in the Smritis, knows the secrets of the juggler, and has at his command the whole glossary of Vedic roots.
831 He is a master of grammar and proficient in logic; nevertheless, he is blind to the understanding of the supreme Self.
832 In every science except that of the Self, he may be like the earth which creates all the basic principles. But because he is ignorant of the Self, he is like a child whom no one will look at because he was born at an inauspicious time.
833 He is as useless as the numerous eyes on a peacock's feathers, for they are sightless.
834 If even a tiny portion of a life-restoring root is found, what is the use of cartloads of other herbs?
835 Similarly, all sciences are invalid without the supreme science of the Self.
836 Therefore, O Arjuna, understand that a person who doesn't know the scriptures, who doesn't study this science with determination,
837 Has a body in which the seed of ignorance is growing, and his learning is like the vines that spring from it.
838 Everything he says is merely the flower of ignorance, and any meritorious actions he performs are its fruit.
839 It goes without saying that a person who doesn't believe in this science can never real-

ize the highest Truth.

840 How can anyone learn about the opposite bank of a river if he runs away even from this bank?

841 Can a person know what is inside a house if his feet are bound together on the threshold?

842 Similarly, how can a person realize the supreme Truth if he knows nothing of the science of the Self?

843 It is not necessary to tell you that such a person cannot possibly understand the one Reality.

844 When a pregnant woman is fed, her unborn child is nourished at the same time. In the same way, the characteristics of knowledge were described earlier, and the characteristics of ignorance are implied in the same description.

845 When a blind man is invited to dinner, someone else must go with him. Similarly, the signs of ignorance don't need to be described separately from those of knowledge.

846 The characteristics of knowledge, such as humility and others, are contrary to those of ignorance, and have already been explained in previous verses.

847 When the eighteen signs of knowledge are inverted, the nature of ignorance becomes obvious.

848 Lord Krishna has already said in earlier verses that ignorance is the opposite of knowledge.

849 For this reason I have been careful to expand on this subject. Otherwise, it would have been like adding water to increase the quantity of milk.

850 So without any useless talk and keeping within the boundaries of the texts, I have been inspired to expand the original.

851 The listeners then exclaimed, Wait! Why all this explanation? What are you afraid of?

852 Lord Krishna has told you to reveal those difficult matters that He Himself has kept concealed.

853 You are actually explaining to us the hidden thoughts of the Lord. The thought of this might inhibit your mind,

854 So we will say no more. We have been given the joy of hearing about the boat of knowledge in which one can cross the ocean of this world.

855 Without further delay, tell us what Lord Krishna said.

856 When his saintly listeners said this, the disciple of Nivritti answered, Now listen to what the Lord said.

857 O Arjuna, all these characteristics which you have heard represent ignorance.

858 Turn away from all these things, and set your heart firmly on attaining knowledge.

859 Then you will be able to penetrate with a clear mind the object of all knowledge. Arjuna expressed a desire to know this.

860 Lord Krishna, aware of his desire, said to him, Listen while I tell you what you must know.

ज्ञेयं यत् तत् प्रवक्ष्यामि यज् ज्ञात्वा ऽमृतम् अश्नुते ।
अनादिमत् परं ब्रह्म न सत् तन् नासद् उच्यते ॥
jñeyaṁ yat tat pravakṣyāmi
yaj jñātvā 'mṛtam aśnute
anādimat paraṁ brahma
na sat tan nāsad ucyate

13. I shall declare that which has to be known, knowing which, one attains immortality; it is the beginningless supreme Brahman, which is said to be neither existent nor non-existent.

861 God is the object of all knowledge, and knowledge is the only means to comprehend Him.

862 When He is known, there is nothing else to know. That knowledge alone brings the knower into union with Him.

863 When He is known, all worldly activities cease for the knower, who becomes absorbed in eternal bliss.

864 That One, the object of knowledge, is without beginning and is called the Supreme.

865 If one says that He doesn't exist, one must understand that He is one with the universe; but if one says that He Himself is the universe, this is illusion.

866 He has no manifest form and no color, nor can anyone see Him. How can anyone say that He exists?

867 If one says that He doesn't exist, then how did all the elements come into existence? In whom do they have their being? Is there anything but Him?

868 Therefore, it is meaningless to say that He is or is not. It is impossible to attain Him through thought.

869 Just as earth can be seen in the form of clay pots, in the same way God is everything and in everything.

सर्वतःपाणिपादं तत् सर्वतो ऽक्षिशिरोमुखम् ।
सर्वतःश्रुतिमल् लोके सर्वम् आवृत्य तिष्ठति ॥
sarvataḥpāṇipādaṁ tat

sarvato 'kṣiśiromukham
sarvataḥśrutimal loke
sarvam āvṛtya tiṣṭhati

14. Having hands and feet everywhere, eyes, heads and faces everywhere, having ears everywhere, That stands, enveloping everything in the world,

870 In all times and places, He remains unchanged by time and space. His hand alone produces the activity of both the gross and subtle elements.

871 For this reason, He is called the One who has arms on all sides; for in all actions and in all times, it is He who acts.

872 Because He is everywhere at the same time, O Arjuna, He is called the all-pervasive One, with feet everywhere.

873 Just as the sun has no body or eyes, yet illumines everything, similarly, He is in all and sees all.

874 Thus the Vedas in their wisdom called the sightless Absolute the One who has eyes everywhere.

875 Just as the body of the sacrificial fire is one with the mouth which consumes the oblations, in the same way the Supreme Being partakes of everything through Its presence in all beings.

876 Therefore, O Arjuna, the Vedas call Him the One with mouths on all sides.

877 Just as ether pervades everything, so His ears hear every word that is spoken.

878 Because He pervades everything, we call Him the One with ears everywhere.

879 O Arjuna, the Shrutis describe Him as having eyes everywhere to indicate His all-pervasive nature.

880 Otherwise, any reference to His hands, ears, or feet is meaningless; for by nature He is without attributes.

881 One wave appears to swallow up another, but is one separate from the other?

882 Similarly, when there is only one Being, can it be said that one pervades and another is pervaded? Yet, when speaking of these things, one must make such a distinction.

883 In order to indicate zero, one has to use the figure for zero. In the same way, one has to use the language of duality to describe nonduality.

884 Otherwise, O Arjuna, the Guru-disciple relationship would be impossible and speech would be silenced.

885 Therefore, the Shrutis have adopted the language of duality to express nonduality.

886 Now listen to the way in which God pervades everything by means of sight and the other senses.

सर्वेन्द्रियगुणाभासं सर्वेन्द्रियविवर्जितम् ।
असक्तं सर्वभृच्चैव निर्गुणं गुणभोक्तृ च ।।

sarvendriyaguṇābhāsaṁ
sarvendriyavivarjitam
asaktaṁ sarvabhṛc cāiva
nirguṇaṁ guṇabhoktṛ ca

15. Shining by the function of the senses, yet freed from all the senses, unattached yet maintaining all, free from the qualities yet experiencing the qualities;

887 O Arjuna, like the ether He pervades all space. He is also like the thread in cloth.

888 Just as moistness is in water, or light in a lamp,

889 As the quality of camphor is in camphor, as activity manifests in the body,

890 And as gold exists in every piece of gold, similarly, the Absolute is all and is in all, O Arjuna.

891 The gold nugget has all the properties of gold. Although it is in a nugget, it is still only gold.

892 When a stream winds, the water in it seems to bend; yet the water flows without bending. When iron is heated by fire, the fire doesn't become iron.

893 Space appears to be round when it is enclosed in a pot, and square when it is in a house.

894 But just as the ether doesn't cease to exist when the forms which enclose it are destroyed, similarly, God doesn't experience change although He exists in forms that are subject to change.

895 O Arjuna, He appears to have a mind and sense organs, as well as the three qualities.

896 But just as the sweetness in a lump of sugar has nothing to do with its form, in the same way, the sense organs and the qualities are clearly not God.

897 O Arjuna, ghee takes the form of milk as long as it is milk, but after it is made into *ghee* it is no longer milk.

898 Similarly, you should understand that in spite of all these modifications, God Himself undergoes no modification. An ornament is a form of gold, but it is still gold.

899 So I'm telling you in plain language, O Arjuna, that there is a great difference between God

and the qualities and the sense organs.

900 Such modifications as name, form, relationship, kind, activity, and separateness belong entirely to the outer form.

901 God is not the qualities, nor is He connected with them, though they may appear to belong to Him.

902 Because of this, O Arjuna, a deluded person imagines that they are attributes of God.

903 To think in this way is like believing that the sky is one with the clouds, that a mirror is one with the image reflected in it,

904 That the sun is one with its reflection in water, or that a mirage is the same as the sunlight which causes it.

905 It is utterly false to say that the Absolute is one with the attributes which appear to be superimposed on Him, for He has no associations.

906 To say that God has attributes is as foolish as saying that a poor man is a king just because he dreams that he is.

907 Therefore, it is incorrect to say that God is related to the attributes or that He enjoys them.

बहिर् अन्तश्च भूतानाम् अचरं चरम् एव च।
सूक्ष्मत्वात् तद् अविज्ञेयं दूरस्थं चान्तिके च तत्॥
bahir antaś ca bhūtānam
acaraṁ caram eva ca
sūkṣmatvāt tad avijñeyaṁ
dūrasthaṁ cāntike ca tat

16. Outside and inside beings, those that are moving and not moving, because of its subtlety This is not comprehended. This is far away and also near.

908 O Arjuna, God is in everything, both movable and immovable, just as heat is the same in all forms of fire.

909 Know that the Being which is the object of knowledge is subtle and indestructible, and is in all things.

910 He is within and without, near and yet far. He is One without a second.

अविभक्तं च भूतेषु विभक्तम् इव च स्थितम्।
भूतभर्तृ च तज् ज्ञेयं ग्रसिष्णु प्रभविष्णु च॥
avibhaktaṁ ca bhūteṣu
vibhaktam iva ca sthitam
bhūtabhartṛ ca taj jñeyaṁ
grasiṣṇu prabhaviṣṇu ca

17. Undivided yet remaining as if divided in all beings, This is to be known as the sustainer of beings, their devourer and creator.

911 Just as the sweetness of the Milky Ocean is not greater at the center and less near the shore, in the same way this Being is the same everywhere.

912 He is immanent in all beings of every kind, without exception.

913 O Arjuna, the reflection of the moon is the same in every vessel which contains water.

914 There is a salty taste in every grain of salt, and there is sweetness in every piece of sugarcane.

915 O Arjuna, He alone pervades the whole creation and is the sole cause of the universe.

916 The Supreme is the support of all the forms which proceed from Him, just as the sea supports the waves within it.

917 When the body passes through the three stages of childhood, youth, and adulthood, it still remains a body. In the same way He is unchanging throughout the beginning, middle, and end of creation.

918 He remains unchanging just like the sky throughout the morning, noon, and evening.

919 O Arjuna, at the time of manifestation He is called Brahma, the creator; during the period of existence He is called Vishnu, the sustainer;

920 And when all forms are dissolved He is called Rudra, the destroyer. And when these three qualities cease to be active in Him, He is the great void.

ज्योतिषां अपि तज् ज्योतिस् तमसः परम् उच्यते।
ज्ञानं ज्ञेयं ज्ञानगम्यं हृदि सर्वस्य विष्ठितम्॥
jyotiṣāṁ api taj jyotis
tamasaḥ param ucyate
jñānaṁ jñeyaṁ jñānagamyaṁ
hṛdi sarvasya viṣṭhitam

18. Also This is said to be the light of lights that is beyond darkness; it is knowledge, the object of knowledge and that which is to be attained through knowledge. It is seated in the hearts of all.

921 From this Being come the flame of fire and the light of the moon, and through Him the sun is visible.

922 He is the origin of all origins, the growth in everything that grows, the intelligence in all minds, and the life in everything that lives.

923 Through Him the stars shed their light and the sun sends forth its brilliance.

924 He is the activity in all minds. Through Him the eyes see, the nose perceives scent, and the tongue utters speech.
925 He is the breath in breathing and the source of all motion and activity.
926 He gives form to everything and is the origin of all expansion and destruction.
927 He forms the substance of earth and of water, and everything that has luster derives its radiance from Him.
928 He is the breath of the wind; He is the space of the firmament. All manifestation appears through Him.
929 In short, O Arjuna, He is all in all, so there remains no place for duality.
930 When insight is awakened, He is revealed as both the seer and the seen. This brings about the state of union with God.
931 He is simultaneously the knower, the known, and the process of knowing, and the goal is also reached through Him.
932 When a calculation has been completed, it results in one figure. Similarly, the goal and the means of reaching it become one.
933 O Arjuna, there remains no trace of duality in Him, and He is found in every heart.

इति क्षेत्रं तथा ज्ञानं ज्ञेयं चोक्तं समासतः।
मद्भक्त एतद् विज्ञाय मद्भावायोपपद्यते ॥

iti kṣetraṁ tathā jñānaṁ
jñeyaṁ coktaṁ samāsataḥ
madbhakta etad vijñāya
madbhāvāyopapadyate

19. Thus the field, knowledge, and the object of knowledge have been briefly described. My devotee, understanding this, enters into My state of being.

934 Thus, O friend, I have clearly explained to you the field, that which is known.
935 Afterwards, O Arjuna, I told you about the nature of knowledge in a way that you could understand.
936 I have also clearly explained the nature of ignorance in order to satisfy your longing.
937 Furthermore, I have clearly described the object of all knowing.
938 O Arjuna, by meditating on these things, My devotees, full of faith, become united with Me.
939 Going beyond the need to control their bodies and minds, they have found their true heritage in Me.
940 O Arjuna, knowing that I am all this, they have become one with Me.
941 Now listen to the main way in which a person can reach Me. I have made an easy path for this,
942 Just as steps are carved out of a hillside, a wooden scaffold is constructed to reach high places, and a boat is built to cross over deep water.
943 Otherwise, O Arjuna, if I told you that all this is the Self, your mind would be unable to grasp it.
944 Therefore, realizing how difficult it is to understand this, I have divided the subject into four parts.
945 Just as a child is fed only a little at a time, in the same way I have described the One to you in four parts.
946 First there is the field, then knowing, what is to be known, and finally ignorance. Knowing how much you can understand, I have made these four categories.
947 O Arjuna, if you still don't understand this method of explanation, I will present the subject to you once again.
948 I won't speak in terms of four sections or of one only, but of the Self and the non-Self.
949 For this, you should give Me what I ask of you: that you listen with complete concentration.
950 When he heard these words of Krishna's Arjuna trembled with joy. The Lord said, That is good, but don't let yourself be overwhelmed by this.
951 Restraining Arjuna's emotion in this way, He said, Now listen to the two divisions of Spirit and matter.
952 I will now describe to you the path of knowledge known to yogis as Sankhya. In order to proclaim it, I incarnated as the sage Kapila.
953 Listen carefully to the explanation of Spirit and matter, the Supreme Being said to Arjuna.

प्रकृतिं पुरुषं चैव विद्ध्य् अनादी उभाव् अपि।
विकारांस् च गुणांस् चेंच विद्धि प्रकृतिसंभवान् ॥

prakṛtiṁ puruṣaṁ cāiva
viddhy anādi ubhāv api
vikārāṇś ca guṇāṅś cāiva
viddhi prakṛtisaṁbhavān

20. Know that material nature and Spirit are both beginningless, and know also that the modifications of the field, and the qualities, too, arise from material nature.

954 The Spirit is eternal and so is matter. The two

are united like day and night.

955 The shadow is attached to the body like a phantom, and the grain and husk of a seed grow closely together, O Arjuna.

956 In the same way, matter and Spirit are inseparable, two in one, both existing eternally.

957 What I have previously described as the field should be understood as matter,

958 And what I have called the Knower of the field is Spirit, or the Self. This cannot be denied.

959 Though these two are given different names, their description is the same. You shouldn't forget these as the discussion proceeds.

960 O Arjuna, Spirit is pure being, and matter is the name given to all activity.

961 The intellect, the sense organs, and the heart, with all their modifications as well as the three qualities—*sattva, rajas,* and *tamas*—

962 The combination of all these things arises from matter, and matter causes all action.

कार्यकारणकर्तृत्वे हेतु: प्रकृतिर् उच्यते ।
पुरुष: सुखदु:खानां भोक्तृत्वे हेतुर् उच्यते ।।

kāryakāraṇakartṛtve
hetuḥ prakṛtir ucyate
puruṣaḥ sukhaduḥkhānāṁ
bhoktṛtve hetur ucyate

21. Material nature is said to be the cause in the producing of cause and effect. The Spirit is said to be the cause in the experiencing of pleasure and pain.

963 Matter first creates desire and intellect along with ego, which arouses the longing for satisfaction.

964 O Arjuna, the effect is what activates the means of satisfaction.

965 The force of desire awakens the mind, and the mind impels the senses to act. This is called action.

966 Understand that matter is the origin of cause, effect, and action. Krishna, the Prince of adepts, said this.

967 With the union of these three, matter takes the form of action, which is performed according to the predominant quality.

968 Actions prompted by the quality of goodness are called virtuous deeds, those springing from passion are called mixed, or pure and impure,

969 And those that arise solely from darkness are considered unrighteous and evil.

970 Therefore, you can see that good and evil actions spring from matter and result in happiness and misery.

971 Evil actions breed sorrow, and good actions produce joy. The Spirit experiences both of these.

972 In describing this interaction of Spirit and matter there is an inconsistency: the wife labors but the husband enjoys the fruits.

973 As long as happiness and misery arise, activity belongs to matter and experience to Spirit.

974 In this case the husband and the wife are not united, and yet the wife gives birth to the world. Now listen to this strange thing.

पुरुष: प्रकृतिस्थो हि भुङ्क्ते प्रकृतिजान् गुणान् ।
कारणं गुणसङ्गो ऽस्य सदसद्योनिजन्मसु ।।

puruṣaḥ prakṛtistho hi
bhuṅkte prakṛtijān guṇān
kāraṇaṁ guṇasaṅgo 'sya
sadasadyonijanmasu

22. For the Spirit, abiding in material nature, experiences the qualities born of material nature. Attachment to the qualities is the cause of its birth in good and evil wombs.

975 The Spirit is formless, alone, the most ancient of ancient things.

976 He is called the Spirit, and yet He is neither male nor female. In fact, it cannot be said what He is.

977 He is without eyes, ears, hands, or feet. He has neither form, color, or name.

978 Though He has no attributes, He is the husband of matter and experiences happiness and misery.

979 He is inactive, indifferent, and without the capacity for experience. It is His wife who makes Him capable of experience.

980 With the slightest movement of her form and attributes, she can bring about any activity.

981 For this reason she is called the one who possesses attributes. She is truly the embodiment of the qualities.

982 She is continually renewed, she is all forms and qualities, and her force activates even lifeless substances.

983 Names are known through her, love is love through her, and the sense organs derive their activity from her.

984 Isn't the mind neuter? Yet her power is so wonderful that she causes it to be active in all the three worlds.

985 She is the great island of delusion, the essence of the power to pervade everything, and the creator of an infinite variety of moods.

986 She is like an arbor made of the vine of desire, or spring in the forest of infatuation. She is known as the Divine Illusion.

987 She inspires literature, she gives form to the formless, and she is the indestructible force behind all worldly existence.

988 All art and learning spring from her; and she gives birth to desire, knowledge, and action.

989 She is the chamber in which all sound is produced and the treasure house of all marvels. All things arise from the play of her power.

990 Creation and dissolution are her morning and evening; in short, she is the great enchantress.

991 She is the counterpart of the One, the companion of the detached Spirit, and dwells with Him in the great void.

992 Her good fortune is so powerful that she is able to control the One who is beyond control.

993 He has no attributes or moods; she herself becomes all these things for Him.

994 She makes birth possible for the One, who is self-existent. She is the manifestation of the unmanifest, and the condition and location of the One who is unconditioned and all-pervasive.

995 She is desire in the One who is desireless, satisfaction in the One who is complete, and caste and lineage in the One who transcends all definitions.

996 She is the visible sign of the indescribable, she measures the immeasurable, and she is the mind and intellect of the One who transcends the mind.

997 She is the form of the formless, the activity of the unmoving, and the individuality of the one who transcends individuality.

998 She is the name of the nameless, the birth of the unborn, and action in the One who is beyond all action.

999 She gives attributes to the attributeless, feet to the One who is without feet, ears to the One who is without ears, and eyes to the One who is without eyes.

1000 She gives feeling to the One who is passionless and limbs to the limbless. In fact, she is all things for Him.

1001 In this way, with her power to pervade all things, she gives attributes to the attributeless.

1002 Because of her there are male and female. Just as the light of the moon is dimmed at the time of the new moon,

1003 As even a grain of alloy lessens the value of pure gold,

1004 As an evil spirit leads a good person to commit sin, as clouds in the sky spoil a clear day,

1005 As milk is concealed in a cow's udder, as fire is latent in a piece of wood, as the luster of a diamond is hidden in a cloth,

1006 As a king is conquered by his enemy, and as a lion is weakened by disease, similarly, the Spirit loses His inherent splendor when He is in contact with matter.

1007 Just as a person who falls asleep becomes a victim of the experiences in his dreams,

1008 Similarly, the Spirit in contact with matter is affected by the qualities, just as a dispassionate man can be disturbed by contact with a woman.

1009 As long as there is contact with the qualities, the unborn Spirit is subject to birth and death.

1010 Nevertheless, O Arjuna, all this is like saying that fire suffers the blows when heated iron is struck with a hammer.

1011 Or that there are many moons because of the countless reflections on the ripples of a lake.

1012 A face seems to be double when it is close to a mirror, and red powder makes crystal look red.

1013 Similarly, the unborn Spirit appears to have taken birth through contact with the qualities, yet He is never born.

1014 People think that He takes birth in a noble or lowly family, just as an ascetic might dream that he was born an outcaste.

1015 In the same way, in pure Spirit, there is neither birth nor experience. The contact with the qualities causes all this.

उपद्रष्टानुमन्ता च भर्ता भोक्ता महेश्वरः ।
परमात्मेति चाप्य् उक्तो देहे ऽस्मिन् पुरुषः परः ॥
upadraṣṭānumantā ca
bhartā bhoktā maheśvaraḥ
paramātmeti cāpy ukto
dehe 'smin puruṣaḥ paraḥ

23. *The highest Spirit in this body is called the witness, the consenter, the supporter, the experiencer, the great Lord, and also the supreme Spirit.*

1016 Spirit is always present in matter. They are like a vine and the trellis on which it grows. Spirit and matter are related to each other like the earth and the sky.

1017 O Arjuna, the Spirit is like Mount Meru on

the bank of the river of matter. It is reflected in the water but cannot be carried away by the current.

1018 Matter forms and dissolves, but Spirit exists eternally. Therefore, Spirit is the ruler of creation from Brahma downwards.

1019 Matter lives through Spirit and through her power gives birth to the world, so Spirit is the husband of matter.

1020 O Arjuna, the universe exists in matter for countless ages and is dissolved into Spirit at the end of a great world age.

1021 Spirit is the great Lord of matter and directs the course of the universe. The visible world is measured by His infinite Being.

1022 When it is said that the great Spirit inhabits the human body, you should understand it in this way.

1023 O Arjuna, the belief that there is a Being beyond matter refers to this Spirit.

य एवं वेत्ति पुरुषं प्रकृतिं च गुणैः सह ।
सर्वथा वर्तमानो ऽपि न स भूयो ऽभिजायते ।।

ya evaṁ vetti puruṣaṁ
prakṛtiṁ ca guṇāiḥ saha
sarvathā vartamāno 'pi
na sa bhūyo 'bhijāyate

24. He who in this way knows the Spirit and material nature, along with the qualities, in whatever stage of transmigration he may exist, is not born again.

1024 If a person truly knows this Spirit and knows that the activity of the qualities is derived from matter,

1025 In the same way that he must be able to tell the difference between an object and its shadow, or water and a mirage,

1026 And if he has arrived at a clear distinction between Spirit and matter,

1027 Then, O Arjuna, he may perform any act whatsoever while he is in the body and yet be no more contaminated by action than the sun is by smoke.

1028 The person who, while living in the body, doesn't let himself be deluded by its activities is not reborn after death.

1029 This is what he receives from that knowledge which discriminates between Spirit and matter.

1030 Now listen to the different ways in which this discrimination may be awakened so that it may shine in your heart like the sun.

ध्यानेनात्मनि पश्यन्ति केचिद् ग्रात्मानम् ग्रात्मना ।
ग्रन्ये सांख्येन योगेन कर्मयोगेन चापरे ।।

dhyānenātmani paśyanti
kecid ātmānam ātmanā
anye sāṁkhyena yogena
karmayogena cāpare

25. Some perceive the Self in the Self by the Self through meditation; others by the discipline of Sankhya and still others by the yoga of action.

1031 O Arjuna, there are some who burn in the fire of discrimination the impure mixture of the non-Self and the pure Self.

1032 They break through the thirty-six principles of creation and extract from them the pure essence of the Self.

1033 O Arjuna, through the insight that comes in meditation, these see themselves within the supreme Self.

1034 Others, according to their destiny, concentrate on the Self through Sankhya yoga, and yet others seek Him by relying on the path of karma yoga.

ग्रन्ये त्व् एवम् ग्रजानन्तः श्रुत्वान्येभ्य उपासते ।
ते ऽपि चातितरन्त्य् एव मृत्युं श्रुतिपरायणाः ।।

anye tv evam ajānantaḥ
śrutvānyebhya upāsate
te 'pi cātitaranty eva
mṛtyuṁ śrutiparāyaṇāḥ

26. Yet others, not knowing this, worship, having heard it from others, and they also cross beyond death, devoted to what they have heard.

1035 In these various ways they pass beyond the confusing fear of worldly existence.

1036 There are others who overcome their pride and trust the teachings of a Guru,

1037 One who knows what is good and what is harmful, who compassionately removes all loss, and who dispels weariness and brings them joy.

1038 They listen with respect to whatever the Guru says and follow him devotedly.

1039 In order to listen to him, they leave all other activity and honor his words with all their heart.

1040 O Arjuna, these people cross easily over the ocean of death.

1041 You can see that there are many ways to realize the Absolute.

1042 But I have said enough. Let Me give you the essence of all these teachings.

1043 O Arjuna, in this way you may come to experience true Self-knowledge and find no difficulty in what lies beyond.
1044 So let's consider this well, refute all the diverse views, and clarify the inner meaning.

यावत् संजायते किंचित् सत्त्वं स्थावरजङ्गमम् ।
क्षेत्रक्षेत्रज्ञसंयोगात् तद् विद्धि भरतर्षभ ॥

yāvat saṁjāyate kiṁcit
sattvaṁ sthāvarajaṅgamam
kṣetrakṣetrajñasaṁyogāt
tad viddhi bharatarṣabha

27. Know, Arjuna, that any being whatever that is born, moving or unmoving, arises from the union of the field and the knower of the field.

1045 I have revealed Myself to you as the Knower of the field and have fully described the field.
1046 All creatures evolve from the union of these two, just as waves arise on the surface of water through the force of the wind.
1047 Just as the rays of the sun shining on a desert create the illusion of a mirage, O Arjuna,
1048 Or as showers of rain falling on the earth cause a variety of plants to spring up,
1049 In the same way, know that all movable and immovable creatures, in fact, everything that lives, evolves from the union of these two.
1050 Therefore, O Arjuna, all beings are not separate in any way from the supreme Knower of the field.

समं सर्वेषु भूतेषु तिष्ठन्तं परमेश्वरम् ।
विनश्यत्स्व् अविनश्यन्तं यः पश्यति स पश्यति ॥

samaṁ sarveṣu bhūteṣu
tiṣṭhantaṁ parameśvaram
vinaśyatsv avinaśyantaṁ
yaḥ paśyati sa paśyati

28. He who sees the Supreme Lord, existing alike in all beings, not perishing when they perish, truly sees.

1051 Just as woven cloth is not in the same state as the threads of which it is made, yet it is dependent on them, it is the same with this union. Consider this carefully.
1052 All creatures evolve from the One and are one, but they appear to be various.
1053 Their names are different and they behave in different ways. Their outer forms also vary.
1054 But seeing this, O Arjuna, if you were to think that they are inherently different, you couldn't escape from the clutches of rebirth.
1055 Just as a gourd plant will bear fruit that is long, curved, or round, due to various influences,
1056 And just as the same jujube tree has both crooked and straight branches, similarly, there may be a variety of forms, but the Spirit within them is the same.
1057 The one Lord pervades all beings, just as the same heat exists in every particle of fire.
1058 He exists in all created forms, just as the rain falling from the sky consists only of water.
1059 Although creatures may be varied, the essence within them is the same, just as the same space fills both a pot and a house.
1060 Even though all these creatures are subject to dissolution, the Self within them is imperishable, in the same way that the gold in bracelets and other ornaments isn't destroyed when they are melted down.
1061 Therefore, he who sees that the attributeless One is not separate from all creatures is the most perceptive of all seers.
1062 O Arjuna, among all those who have the inner vision of wisdom, his is the clearest. This is not empty praise; such a person is truly fortunate.

समं पश्यन् हि सर्वत्र समवस्थितम् ईश्वरम् ।
न हिनस्त्य् आत्मना ऽत्मानं ततो याति परां गतिम् ॥

samaṁ paśyan hi sarvatra
samavasthitam īśvaram
na hinasty ātmanā 'tmānaṁ
tato yāti parāṁ gatim

29. Seeing indeed the same Lord established everywhere, he does not injure the Self by the self. Thereupon he goes to the supreme goal.

1063 This body is like a bag containing the senses and dualities, a blend of fluids, and the terrible group of five elements.
1064 It is like a scorpion with five tails, stinging in five places, or a lion which has come upon the lair of a deer.
1065 Though all this is true, there is no one who thrusts the knife of knowledge of the Eternal into the vitals of knowledge of the perishable.
1066 O Arjuna, a person shouldn't become his own destroyer while he is in the body; then he will ultimately reach the Absolute.
1067 Yogis, relying on their knowledge and yogic practice, and having passed through thousands of lives, plunge into union with the Absolute, knowing that they will never return.

1068 That is the opposite shore of the river of form, the home of highest contemplation, the last boundary of sound. It is the supreme God.
1069 All conditions, including final liberation, come to rest there, just as rivers like the Ganges find their refuge in the ocean.
1070 Those people who recognize the diversity of all creatures, yet mentally preserve the sense of unity, experience supreme bliss even while they are still in the body.
1071 The same Lord is present in all, just as there is only one light that shines in a thousand lamps.
1072 O Arjuna, one who lives with the perception of the unity underlying all things is not caught in the grip of life and death.
1073 For this reason, I have described again and again the fortunate person who rests in the understanding of unity.

प्रकृत्यैव च कर्माणि क्रियमाणानि सर्वशः।
यः पश्यति तथात्मानम् अकर्तारं स पश्यति ॥
prakṛtyāiva ca karmāṇi
kriyamāṇāni sarvaśaḥ
yaḥ paśyati tathātmānam
akartāraṁ sa paśyati

30. He who sees that all actions are performed exclusively by material nature, and thus the Self is not the doer, truly sees.

1074 An enlightened being knows that all actions proceed from the five sense organs, the mind, the intellect, and the five organs of action, and that they are all prompted by matter.
1075 Just as the people living in a house are all active though the house itself remains inactive, and just as clouds pass across the sky while the sky remains undisturbed,
1076 In the same way matter, activated by the light of the Spirit, sports in various ways according to the qualities, while the Spirit remains as motionless as a pillar.
1077 A person who understands this and who has seen his own inner light has truly realized that the Spirit is actionless.

यदा भूतपृथग्भावम् एकस्थम् अनुपश्यति।
तत एव च विस्तारं ब्रह्म संपद्यते तदा ॥
yadā bhūtapṛthagbhāvam
ekastham anupaśyati
tata eva ca vistāraṁ
brahma saṁpadyate tadā

31. When he perceives the various states of being as resting in the One, and from That alone spreading out, then he attains Brahman.

1078 O Arjuna, a person is blessed with the knowledge of the Absolute when he understands that all these diverse forms are contained within one unity.
1079 Just like waves in water, atoms and grains of sand in the earth, rays of light in the sun,
1080 Like the limbs of the body, feelings in the mind, and sparks in fire,
1081 In the same way, all created forms rest in the One. When this vision of unity is awakened, a person crosses the ocean of life in the ship of the wealth of the Supreme.
1082 Wherever he looks he sees only God and enters into infinite bliss.
1083 O Arjuna, I have explained to you step by step the nature of Spirit and matter by means of experience.
1084 You should value this experience as though it were a handful of nectar, or as though you had found a hidden treasure.
1085 Besides this, O Arjuna, with this experience you can build the house of Truth in your mind, but not yet. That will come later.
1086 I will now explain other deep truths. Pay close attention to Me so you can understand them.
1087 Saying this, the Lord began to speak further, while Arjuna listened with all his heart and soul.

अनादित्वान् निर्गुणत्वात् परमात्मायम् अव्ययः।
शरीरस्थोऽपि कौन्तेय न करोति न लिप्यते ॥
anāditvān nirguṇatvāt
paramātmāyam avyayaḥ
śarīrastho 'pi kāunteya
na karoti na lipyate

32. This imperishable supreme Self is beginningless and without qualities; even though situated in the body, Arjuna, it does not act, and is not tainted.

1088 Know that this is the nature of the Supreme. It is like the sun which, though reflected in water, doesn't become wet.
1089 The sun existed before the water, O Arjuna, and will continue to exist after the water dries up. It seems to be in the water, and this is the way others see it.
1090 Similarly, it is untrue to say that the Spirit exists in bodily form. It is everywhere.
1091 Just as we say that a face is reflected in a

mirror, this is how the Spirit dwells in the body.

1092 It is wrong to say that the Spirit can come in contact with a body. How could one say that wind and sand can be blended together?

1093 How could a thread be made from fire and a feather? How could the sky be united with a stone?

1094 Can a person setting out towards the east meet another who has set out towards the west?

1095 The relationship between the Spirit and the body is like the relationship between the living and the dead, or between light and darkness.

1096 There is no more bond between them than there is between day and night or gold and cotton.

1097 The body is the product of the five elements, strung on the thread of action, and it spins around tied to the wheel of birth and death.

1098 Like a lump of butter it is thrown into the fire of time, and perishes as swiftly as a fly moves its wings.

1099 If it falls into the fire, it is instantly reduced to ashes. If it is thrown to the dogs, it becomes soil.

1100 If it escapes these two fates, it is consumed by worms. Its end is vile, O Arjuna.

1101 Such is the condition of the body; but the Spirit is eternal, self-existent, and without beginning.

1102 The Spirit is neither divided nor whole, neither active nor inactive, neither fine nor gross. It is without attributes.

1103 It is neither perceived nor unperceived, neither shining nor dark, neither small nor large. It has no form.

1104 It is neither empty nor full, neither with possessions nor without them, neither with form nor formless. It is the void.

1105 It neither experiences joy nor sorrow, it is neither one nor many, it is neither free nor bound. It is the Self.

1106 It cannot be measured, it is neither self-created nor created by another, it neither speaks nor is silent. It has no outer sign.

1107 It neither comes into existence when the universe is created, nor is it destroyed with universal destruction. It is the final resting place of being and non-being.

1108 It is immeasurable and indefinable, it neither increases nor diminishes, it is eternal and inexhaustible. It is without substance.

1109 Beloved Arjuna, those who declare that the Self is confined in the body are like those who say that space can be confined in a pot.

1110 O wise Arjuna, it neither assumes nor abandons bodily form. It is eternally the same.

1111 Just as day and night appear in the sky and then vanish, in the same way bodies come and go by the power of the Spirit.

1112 In the body it neither acts nor causes action, nor does it produce spontaneous events.

1113 It is not subject to increase or decrease. It is present in the body, yet untouched by it.

यथा सर्वगतं सौक्ष्म्याद् आकाशं नोपलिप्यते ।
सर्वत्रावस्थितो देहे तथात्मा नोपलिप्यते ॥
yathā sarvagataṁ saukṣmyād
ākāśaṁ nopalipyate
sarvatrāvasthito dehe
tathātmā nopalipyate

33. As the all-pervading ether, because of its subtlety, is not tainted, so the Self, seated in the body, is not tainted in any case.

1114 O Beloved, where doesn't space exist? In what place isn't it present? Yet it remains unaffected by anything.

1115 The Spirit is present in all bodies at all times, but it is not contaminated by contact with them.

1116 Again and again this characteristic of the Self is clearly seen. You should realize that the Knower of the field is not involved with the field itself.

1117 A piece of iron moves when it comes in contact with a magnet, but the iron itself is not magnetic. The same difference exists between the field and the Knower of the field.

1118 The light of a lamp makes it possible for activities to take place within a house, but there is a great difference between the lamp and the house.

1119 O Arjuna, fire lies latent in a piece of wood, but the fire is not the wood. The Self should be understood in this way.

1120 It is like the difference between the sky and the clouds, or between the sun and a mirage.

यथा प्रकाशयत्य् एकः कृत्स्नं लोकम् इमं रविः ।
क्षेत्रं क्षेत्री तथा कृत्स्नं प्रकाशयति भारत ॥
yathā prakāśayaty ekaḥ
kṛtsnaṁ lokam imaṁ raviḥ
kṣetraṁ kṣetrī tathā kṛtsnaṁ
prakāśayati bhārata

34. As the sun alone illumines this entire

world, so the Lord of the field illumines the entire field, Arjuna.

1121 I have said enough! Just as the sun in the heavens illuminates the entire earth from moment to moment,

1122 In the same way, the knower of the field illuminates all forms of the field. Don't ask any further questions. Have no doubt about it.

क्षेत्रक्षेत्रज्ञयोर् एवम् अन्तरं ज्ञानचक्षुषा ।
भूतप्रकृतिमोक्षं च ये विदुर् यान्ति ते परम् ॥

kṣetrakṣetrajñayor evam
antaraṁ jñānacakṣuṣā
bhūtaprakṛtimokṣaṁ ca
ye vidur yānti te param

35. They who know, through the eye of knowledge, the distinction between the field and the knower of the field, as well as the liberation of beings from material nature, go to the Supreme.

1123 True wisdom is the vision by which one realizes the difference between the field and the knower of the field.

1124 Those who are eager to understand this difference follow the wise beings who know this truth.

1125 O wise Arjuna, for the sake of this knowledge, they seek the riches of peace and nourish the scriptures in their homes as if they were milk-giving cows.

1126 With this hope, some eagerly climb the heights of the heaven of yoga.

1127 They regard their bodies and possessions as worthless, and with their whole hearts become the lowliest servants of saints.

1128 By using all the different methods of gaining knowledge, they become convinced within themselves.

1129 Let us salute the enlightenment of those beings who perceive the difference between the field and the knower of the field.

1130 They understand the illusory nature of matter, dispersed in countless forms among the elements.

1131 Though they aren't caught up in this illusion like the frightened parrot standing on a revolving bar, yet they appear to be caught.

1132 They know that a necklace is a necklace although it may look like a serpent, and the illusion of the serpent is dispelled.

1133 They know that a seashell is recognized for what it is when the illusion that it is silver is destroyed.

1134 Such beings know in their hearts the truth that matter is totally different from Spirit, and in this way they attain union with God.

1135 God is more pervasive than space. He is the further shore of the unmanifest, where no confusion about differences remains.

1136 There all form disappears, all individuality ceases, duality passes away, and only the One remains.

1137 O Arjuna, they become united with God, the highest Truth, for they can discriminate between the Self and the non-Self, just as the royal swan can separate milk from water.

1138 Thus the Lord gave His beloved Arjuna the full explanation of Spirit and matter.

1139 He gave Himself to Arjuna just as a person pours water from one pot to another.

1140 Yet who gave to whom? For Arjuna is Man incarnate and Krishna is Narayana, and Krishna had said that He was Arjuna.

1141 But this is irrelevant; I am speaking without being asked. In fact, the Lord gave Arjuna all that He had.

1142 However, Arjuna's mind wasn't satisfied and he craved to know more.

1143 The more oil is fed to a lamp, the larger the flame will be. It was the same with Arjuna's heart as he listened.

1144 When a woman is an expert cook and serves generously, and when she has appreciative guests, everything combines to make a good meal.

1145 This is how Krishna felt when He saw the sharpness of Arjuna's attention. His explanation became more and more eager.

1146 Just as favorable winds cause rain clouds to gather, and as the ocean tide rises with the full moon, in the same way, a teacher is inspired by the eagerness of his listeners.

1147 Sanjaya said, O King, now listen to the words with which the Lord will fill the universe with joy,

1148 And about which the sage Vyasa with his great intellect has spoken in the Bhishma Parva of the *Mahabharata.*

1149 I will now continue the story of the conversation between Krishna and Arjuna in Marathi in the *ovi* meter.

1150 I will tell this story with the feeling of tranquility, which is more beautiful than the feeling of love.

1151 I will tell it in the beautiful Marathi language, and it will be an ornament to literature, for it is sweeter than nectar.

1152 In its coolness it will rival the moon, and the beauty of its feeling will even surpass the divine resonance.

1153 On hearing it, streams of purity will spring up even in the heart of an evil spirit, and a good person will experience the joy of deep meditation.

1154 Its eloquence will pour forth and fill the whole world with the meaning of the *Gita*, and it will raise a canopy of joy over the entire universe.

1155 It will remove any lack of discrimination, the life of the ear and the mind will be renewed, and anyone who wishes it will discover a mine of Self-knowledge.

1156 The eye will have the vision of the highest Truth, the festival of joy will dawn, and the world will enter into the abundance of the knowledge of the Absolute.

1157 Because my holy Guru Nivritti supports me, all this will now come to pass, and I will say it well.

1158 With words full of meaning and abundant similes, I will clarify the meaning of the *Gita* verse by verse.

1159 My revered Guru has endowed me with all learning.

1160 Therefore, through his grace, whatever I say will be acceptable, and I will explain the *Gita* to this gathering of saintly people.

1161 I have come here to sit at your feet so that there is no barrier between us.

1162 The goddess of learning couldn't possibly give birth to a mute child, and the goddess of wealth could hardly be without auspicious signs.

1163 Then how could ignorance exist in your presence? So I will shower down upon you all the nine feelings.

1164 O Masters, grant me this opportunity! I will then begin my explanation, said Jnanadeva.

14

THE YOGA OF THE DIFFERENTIATION OF THE THREE QUALITIES

HAIL to you, O Guru, greatest of all the gods, rising sun of pure intellect, and dawn of happiness.
2 O refuge of all, delight of the realization of union with God, you are the ocean on which the waves of the various worlds arise.
3 Hear me, O brother of the afflicted, ocean of eternal compassion, and husband of the bride of pure knowledge.
4 You reveal the whole universe to those from whose sight you are hidden, and you make manifest to them all that is.
5 The juggler may deceive the spectator, but the illusion by which you conceal yourself is wonderful.
6 You alone are the whole universe; but while some have found true wisdom, others are still living in illusion. I bow to you, who have this mysterious power.
7 We know that water has moisture, but it owes its quality of wetness to you. The earth also derives its stability from you.
8 The sun and moon illumine the three worlds, but the light within them shines by the brilliance of your light.
9 Through your divine power the wind blows, and the sky appears and disappears within your being.
10 You enlighten both the great illusion as well as knowledge. But this is enough description, for the Vedas have striven to explain this.
11 They are skillful in describing you, as long as your form is not seen. When you are known, everything becomes silent.
12 In the final flood of the ocean of destruction, no single drop of water can be seen. Then how can the great rivers be distinguished?
13 When the sun rises, the moon appears to be a firefly. In the same way, we men and the Vedas are both insignificant in your presence.
14 Then the power of duality is reduced to nothing, and speech is helpless. How then can the tongues of men describe you?
15 So, I will stop praising you. It is better for me to prostrate myself silently at your feet.
16 I salute you as you are, O great Guru. Be my source of wealth so that my task of explaining the *Gita* may flourish.
17 Bestow the riches of your grace, fill the purse of my intelligence, and strengthen me with this poem full of wisdom.
18 In this way I will be able to make earrings for the saints and adorn them with the signs of discrimination.
19 Apply to my intellect the lotion of your love, so that my mind can draw on the treasure of the *Gita*.
20 Let the pure sun of your compassion rise, so that the eyes of my intellect can see the world of speech.
21 O you who are the crown of compassion, be my spring, so that the vine of my intelligence may bring forth the fruit of poetry.
22 Shower your grace abundantly, so that the Ganges of my understanding may be flooded with the waters of the truth.
23 O you who are the sole refuge of the universe, may the moon of your kindness be like the full moon of my inspiration.
24 If you regard me in that way, the full tide of the nine feelings will rise in the ocean of my knowledge to inspire me.
25 Then his Guru, being pleased with these words said, We see that by expressing your plea in the guise of praise, you have fallen into duality.
26 Stop making these irrelevant remarks. Explain to us this book which explains the pure knowledge contained in it, and don't let your listeners lose interest.

27 Jnaneshwar said, O honored Master, I was waiting until you told me to begin.
28 The roots of durva grass are by nature immortal; and in addition to this, a flood of nectar washes over its blades.
29 So by the same grace I will explain the original text,
30 In such a way that the boat of doubt within the heart will sink and the desire to listen will increase.
31 As I come begging for alms of grace at my Guru's door, may my words express true sweetness.
32 In the thirteenth chapter Krishna explained to Arjuna this truth:
33 That this universe evolves from the union of the field and the Knower of the field, and that the Self enters into worldly existence through contact with the qualities.
34 This contact with matter is the cause of the experience of pleasure and pain. Apart from this, the Self is beyond all qualities.
35 How can the free soul be in bondage? What is the union of the field and the Knower of the field? How can the Spirit experience pleasure and pain?
36 What are the qualities and how many are there? How do they affect the Self? What are the characteristics of the Self, which transcend these qualities?
37 The explanation of all these things is the subject of the fourteenth chapter.
38 So listen to Lord Krishna's teachings on this subject.

श्रीभगवान् उवाच । *śrībhagavān uvāca*

परं भूयः प्रवक्ष्यामि ज्ञानानां ज्ञानम् उत्तमम् ।
यज् ज्ञात्वा मुनयः सर्वे परां सिद्धिम् इतो गताः ॥

paraṁ bhūyaḥ pravakṣyāmi
jñānānāṁ jñānam uttamam
yaj jñātvā munayaḥ sarve
parāṁ siddhim ito gatāḥ

The Blessed Lord spoke:
1. I shall declare, further, the highest knowledge, the best of all knowledge, having known which all the sages have gone from here to supreme perfection.

39 Krishna said, O Arjuna, summon your entire power of attention, and grasp this knowledge.
40 I have already explained to you in various ways all these theories, but you haven't fully understood them.
41 So I will explain to you again that knowledge which the Vedas called the highest.
42 This knowledge is rightfully ours, but because we have taken pleasure in this life and in the heaven world, it has become foreign to us.
43 For this reason, I call this the best of knowledge. It is like fire, while all other forms of knowledge are like grass.
44 Other forms of knowledge teach men about earthly life and life in heaven. They especially approve of sacrifice, and they teach duality.
45 All such forms of knowledge are like a dream when compared with true knowledge. They are like gusts of wind which are eventually swallowed up by the sky,
46 Or like the moon which fades before the rising sun, or like rivers which disappear in the final deluge.
47 Similarly, O Arjuna, when true knowledge is awakened, all forms of ignorance vanish. Therefore, it is the highest.
48 Through this knowledge, O Arjuna, we can find that liberation which was ours from the beginning.
49 Because of their awareness of this knowledge, all great men refuse to allow earthly existence to overcome them.
50 When the mind is controlled, it turns away from desire and a person attains peace. Even while he is alive, his body has no power over him.
51 Then he transcends all bodily limitations and in every respect becomes equal to Me.

इदं ज्ञानम् उपाश्रित्य मम साधर्म्यम् आगताः ।
सर्गे ऽपि नोपजायन्ते प्रलये न व्यथन्ति च ॥

idaṁ jñānam upāśritya
mama sādharmyam āgatāḥ
sarge 'pi nopajāyante
pralaye na vyathanti ca

2. Resorting to this knowledge, and arriving at a state of identity with Me, even at the creation of the world they are not born, nor do they tremble at its dissolution.

52 O Arjuna, those who have entered into Me, the Eternal, share in My fullness.
53 They are eternally joyful and filled with truth, as I am, and are not separate from Me.
54 They are completely united with Me, just as the space in a pot is one with the surrounding space when the pot is broken.

55 A fire may have many small flames which appear to be one.
56 In the same way, O Arjuna, when duality comes to an end, they and I live in one place, with one name.
57 For this reason there is no need for them to be reborn even when all things are created anew.
58 How is it possible for those who are not subject to the bonds of the body at the time of creation to die when all the worlds are dissolved?
59 Therefore, O Arjuna, those who have followed the path of union with Me have transcended birth and death.
60 The Lord praised knowledge in this way so that Arjuna would be attracted to it.
61 Then a change came over Arjuna, and his whole body became like a listening ear. He became full of rapt attention.
62 As Krishna was pouring His love upon him, His explanation was marvelous beyond words.
63 Then Krishna said, O Arjuna, today My speech has surpassed itself because it has found in you a listener who is worthy of it.
64 Now I will explain to you how I, the One, have become ensnared in the nets of bodily life, trapped by hunters in the form of the three qualities.
65 Listen as I tell you how these worlds came into being through contact with the field,
66 And how matter is called the field because it brings forth all creatures through the seed of contact with Me.

मम योनिर् महद् ब्रह्म तस्मिन् गर्भं दधाम्य् अहम् ।
संभवः सर्वभूतानां ततो भवति भारत ॥

mama yonir mahad brahma
tasmin garbhaṁ dadhāmy aham
saṁbhavaḥ sarvabhūtānāṁ
tato bhavati bhārata

3. Great Brahma is My womb. In it I place the seed. The origin of all beings exists from that, Arjuna.

67 Matter is called the great Brahma, for it is the home of the great primary elements.
68 O Arjuna, it is called the great Brahma because the whole extent of manifestation takes place through it.
69 Those who believe in non-manifestation call it the unmanifest, while according to the Sankhya belief it is matter.
70 O Arjuna, the Vedantists call it illusion. What need is there to quote any others? Matter is truly ignorance.
71 It is called ignorance because through it arises that forgetfulness of the Self as our true nature, O Arjuna.
72 When discrimination develops, ignorance cannot exist, just as a lamp isn't used to see darkness.
73 When milk is undisturbed cream gathers on its surface, but it isn't visible when the milk is shaken.
74 Similarly, in deep sleep there is neither wakefulness nor dreams, neither is there awareness of form.
75 Before the wind blows, space is barren and void. Ignorance is like this.
76 A man may be uncertain whether what stands before him is a pillar or a man; he doesn't know what he sees.
77 In the same way, through ignorance an object doesn't appear as it really is; it is seen as something else.
78 Just as twilight is neither day nor night but lies between the two, in the same way ignorance is neither perception of the Self nor the opposite of that state.
79 This is known as ignorance, and the insight hidden within it is called the Knower of the field.
80 You should understand that it is characteristic of the Knower of the field to make ignorance increase as long as it is unaware of its own true nature.
81 O Beloved, understand that this is the union of the Knower of the field with the field. It is the natural condition of existence.
82 The eternal Self sees itself as ignorant and doesn't realize the many forms it assumes.
83 A deluded person may say, "Look, here I come, the king." Another, having fainted, may think he has gone to heaven.
84 In the same way, when a person lacks insight, whatever he perceives he thinks it is the creation which he himself has brought about.
85 This complex matter I will explain later in various ways, but in the meantime try to experience this.
86 This ignorance is My wife, eternal yet ever youthful and of indescribable qualities.
87 While I sleep she is awake, and through union with My being she conceives.
88 Then in the womb of matter, the great Brahma develops the fetus of the eight common elements.

89 Her nature is non-existence, and yet her dwelling place is boundless. She draws near to those who sleep in ignorance, but remains far from the awakened.

90 The union of these two gives birth first to the intellect, which in turn produces the mind.

91 The young wife of the mind brings into being the ego, and out of this principle arise the primary elements.

92 As these elements naturally intermingle with the senses and their objects, these also come into being at same time.

93 When they stir and become active, the three qualities arise. Then they immediately enter the womb of desire.

94 The tree lies within the seed, which sprouts as soon as it comes in contact with water.

95 In the same way, through contact with Me, ignorance begins to send forth the shoots of many worlds.

96 O Arjuna, listen to how the form of that fetus then develops.

97 Then the various species appear, born of eggs, sweat, earth, or the womb.

98 The preponderance of ether and air produces the egg-born species.

99 The sweat-born are produced when there is darkness and passion in the womb. They are nourished with water and heat.

100 The earth-born ones are formed from darkness and all the evil that pertains to it. They are fed on water and earth.

101 Creatures possessing the five organs of action, the five senses of perception, mind, and intellect, are born of the womb.

102 Having these four species as its hands and feet, gross matter as its head,

103 Worldly activity as its belly, cessation of action as its back, the gods as its chest,

104 The heavens as its neck, the realm of death as its torso, and the nether world as its hips,

105 A child was born of matter, and its growth produces the three worlds.

106 The eight million, four hundred thousand species are the joints of its limbs, and its strength increases day by day.

107 Matter adorns all the parts of its body with names, as if they were jewels, and it is nourished by the breast of delusion.

108 The various worlds are the fingers of its hands and the toes of its feet, on which it wears rings of pride.

109 In this way, matter greatly magnifies itself by giving birth to this mighty child in the form of the inconceivably beautiful universe.

110 For this child, Brahma is the dawn, Vishnu is the midday, and Shiva is the evening.

111 When its play ends, it sleeps on the bed of final dissolution and reawakens in its delusion at the beginning of a new age.

112 O Arjuna, in this way, the child runs about with delight in the house of illusion throughout the cycle of the four world ages.

113 Desire is his friend and egoism is his playmate. He is destroyed when true knowledge appears.

114 In short, the great illusion gives birth to a universe and fulfills My power.

सर्वयोनिषु कौन्तेय मूर्तयः संभवन्ति याः ।
तासां ब्रह्म महद् योनिर् अहं बीजप्रदः पिता ॥

sarvayoniṣu kāunteya
mūrtayaḥ saṁbhavanti yāḥ
tāsāṁ brahma mahad yonir
ahaṁ bījapradaḥ pitā

4. Whatever forms are produced in any womb, Arjuna, the great Brahma is their womb, and I am the seed-sowing father.

115 For this reason, O Arjuna, I am the Father, the great Brahma is the mother, and the child is the manifest universe.

116 Seeing these innumerable bodies, don't let your mind think in terms of diversity. Mind, intellect, and the other elements are all one.

117 Aren't they different parts of the same body? In the same way, you should see this varied universe as one.

118 Just as many branches, some high and others low, grow from the same seed,

119 In the same way, I am related to everything. Just as a pitcher is a child of the earth and cloth is the grandson of cotton,

120 As all waves are the children of the same ocean, similarly I am related to all living and inanimate things.

121 Just as flames are nothing but fire, in the same way I am the whole universe and this relationship is a delusion.

122 If I am hidden beneath the form of this world, then who manifests through its existence? Is a ruby hidden under its own luster?

123 Is gold lost when it is made into ornaments? Isn't a lotus still a lotus when it is in full bloom?

124 Tell me, O Arjuna, is a body concealed by its own organs? Aren't the organs themselves

the body?

125 Is a grain of corn lost when it develops into the full ear, or has it become more grains?

126 If this universe is drawn aside, I am seen behind it. It isn't different from Me. In fact, I am all that is.

127 O Arjuna, establish this great truth firmly in your mind.

128 Thus, I manifest in different bodies and appear to be diverse. I seem to be bound by the qualities of nature.

129 O Arjuna, a person may dream of his own death and suffer the pain of it.

130 When a man is suffering from jaundice his eyes turn yellow, and everything he sees also appears to be yellow.

131 We see a cloud only when it is illuminated by the light of the sun. Even when it hides the sun, it is visible to us because of the sun.

132 A man may be frightened by his own shadow, but is the shadow something apart from him?

133 In the same way, manifesting all these various bodies, I remain different from them. However, I create the impression that I am bound by the qualities just as they are.

134 Because of ignorance, people don't know whether I am bound or not.

135 O divine Arjuna, listen to the way in which I seem to be bound.

136 First learn how many qualities there are, their names and natures, their forms, and how they are produced.

सत्त्वं रजस् तम इति गुणाः प्रकृतिसंभवाः ।
निबध्नन्ति महाबाहो देहे देहिनम् अव्ययम् ।।
sattvaṁ rajas tama iti
guṇāḥ prakṛtisambhavāḥ
nibadhnanti mahābāho
dehe dehinam avyayam

5. *Sattva, rajas, tamas, thus, the qualities born of material nature, bind fast in the body, O Arjuna, the imperishable embodied One (the atman).*

137 These three qualities are called purity, passion, and darkness, and they are born of matter.

138 Of these three, purity is the best, passion is intermediate, and darkness is the lowest.

139 These three qualities are inherent in mental tendencies, just as the three stages of childhood, youth, and old age are inherent in the body.

140 The weight of gold increases as more alloys are mixed with it, but its value is reduced by half.

141 When lethargy prevails over wakefulness, a person falls into deep sleep.

142 In the same way, the mood of the mind succumbs to ignorance, and darkness emerges out of purity and passion.

143 Arjuna, you should know that these are the three qualities. I will now explain how they bring about bondage.

144 As soon as the Self enters the body as the Knower of the field, he identifies with the body.

145 He commits himself to all the different bodily conditions from birth to death,

146 Just as a fisherman jerks the hook as soon as a fish takes the bait in its mouth,

तत्र सत्त्वं निर्मलत्वात् प्रकाशकम् अनामयम् ।
सुखसङ्गेन बध्नाति ज्ञानसङ्गेन चानघ ।।
tatra sattvaṁ nirmalatvāt
prakāśakam anāmayam
sukhasañgena badhnati
jñānasañgena cānagha

6. *Of these, sattva, free from impurity, illuminating and free from disease, binds by attachment to happiness and by attachment to knowledge, Arjuna.*

147 Purity, like a hunter, throws the net of happiness and knowledge over the Self and draws him in just as a hunter traps a deer.

148 He becomes excited by his knowledge, destroys his happiness, and ends by casting aside the joy of Self-realization.

149 He rejoices in learning, delights in recognition, and boasts that he has everything he wants.

150 He says to himself, "How fortunate I am! My happiness is unrivaled!" He is puffed up with the various modifications of goodness.

151 He is bound by the evil spirit of the pride of learning.

152 He feels no sorrow at losing the understanding that he embodies spiritual light, and his knowledge of worldly affairs becomes as vast as the heavens.

153 A king may dream that he is a beggar wandering through the city, and if he is given a few grains of rice he feels like Indra.

154 In the same way, the bodiless Self encased in a body gathers knowledge of the external world, O Arjuna.

155 He masters all worldly knowledge, under-

stands all about sacrifices, and even knows what happens in heaven.

156 Then he boasts that no one is learned except him, and that his mind is the sky in which the moon of wisdom shines.

157 In this way, purity drives the individual soul with the reins of happiness and knowledge, just as a beggar leads his bull.

158 I will now tell you how the Self is bound by passion. Listen.

रजो रागात्मकं विद्धि तृष्णासङ्गसमुद्भवम् ।
तन् निबध्नाति कौन्तेय कर्मसङ्गेन देहिनम् ।।

rajo rāgātmakaṁ viddhi
tṛṣṇāsaṅgasamudbhavam
tan nibadhnāti kāunteya
karmasaṅgena dehinam

7. Know that rajas is characterized by passion arising from thirst and attachment. This binds fast the embodied one, Arjuna, by attachment to action.

159 Even if the soul is only slightly affected by pleasure, it madly seeks gratification and mounts the wind of anxious craving.

160 Passion knows how to give the greatest pleasure to the soul. It is the eternal pleasure-seeking youth.

161 When clarified butter is poured onto a fire and it blazes like lightning, can it be said that the fire is either greater or less than it was before?

162 When desire is aroused, sense objects are thought to be sweet, although they are tinged with pain. Even the glory of Indra cannot satisfy desire.

163 Desire becomes so intense that even if a person possessed Mount Meru it would only urge him on to acquire more.

164 If he spends all that he has today he is concerned about tomorrow, so he embarks on great undertakings.

165 A person is ready to throw away his life for even the smallest gain, and he thinks he has attained his goal if he gets a blade of grass.

166 He is anxious about what he will eat if he goes to heaven, so he rushes to all kinds of sacrifices.

167 He carries out one rite after another, but he undertakes only what will bring him personal gain.

168 O Arjuna, just as at the end of the hot season the wind is never still, similarly such a man doesn't stop working day or night.

169 He is more restless than a fish or the glance of a woman in love. Even a flash of lightning doesn't move that fast.

170 He plunges into the fire of action in pursuit of earthly or heavenly profit.

171 The Self, though different from the body, binds itself with the chains of desire and bears around its neck the burden of worldly affairs.

172 This is the terrible bondage of passion, chaining the embodied Self. Now listen to the deception of darkness.

तमस् त्व् अज्ञानजं विद्धि मोहनं सर्वदेहिनाम् ।
प्रमादालस्यनिद्राभिस् तन् निबध्नाति भारत ।।

tamas tv ajñānajaṁ viddhi
mohanaṁ sarvadehinām
pramādālasyanidrābhis
tan nibadhnāti bhārata

8. Know indeed that tamas is born of ignorance, which confuses all embodied beings. This binds fast, Ajuna, with negligence, indolence, and sleepiness.

173 The veil of darkness which dulls earthly life is like the black clouds of the night of infatuation.

174 It is the essence of ignorance, and because of this alone the world dances in delusion.

175 Lack of discrimination is its magical charm. It is a cup filled with the wine of folly, and it acts as a weapon which numbs the Self.

176 O Arjuna, the nature of darkness is that it securely binds anyone who identifies with the body.

177 When this quality begins to grow within all living and non-living creatures, nothing else can exist there.

178 The senses are dulled, stupidity enters a person's mind, and he becomes lazy.

179 His body deteriorates, he has little inclination to work, and he yawns continuously.

180 O Arjuna, even with his eyes open he doesn't see, and without being addressed he will rise and call out.

181 Just as a fallen stone can't turn itself over, he is unable to change his posture.

182 Even if the earth descended into the nether regions or if the sky fell down on him, it wouldn't occur to him to rise.

183 Lying inert, with no thought of what is appropriate or inappropriate, he only feels like rolling from side to side.

184 He rests his cheeks on his hands, and places his head on his knees.

185 The only desire of his heart is for sleep, and as he falls asleep even the bliss of heaven would give him less pleasure.
186 He would like to sleep for an entire day of Brahma, and he has no other desire.
187 If he should lie down while walking along a road, he wouldn't even care for nectar. He would only want to sleep.
188 If he were ever compelled to work, he would fly into a rage.
189 He doesn't know when or how to act, with whom or how to speak, or what he is able or unable to do.
190 Like a deluded moth that thinks it can put out a forest fire with its wings,
191 He recklessly performs improper actions and delights in doing the wrong thing.
192 In this way, darkness is the force of lethargy, laziness, and negligence, which binds the originally pure and free soul.

सत्त्वं सुखे सञ्जयति रजः कर्मणि भारत ।
ज्ञानम् आवृत्य तु तमः प्रमादे सञ्जयत्य् उत ॥
sattvaṁ sukhe sañjayati
rajaḥ karmaṇi bhārata
jñānam āvṛtya tu tamaḥ
pramāde sañjayaty uta

9. Sattva causes attachment to happiness, rajas to action, Arjuna; tamas, obscuring knowledge, causes attachment to negligence.

रजस् तमश्चाभिभूय सत्त्वं भवति भारत ।
रजः सत्त्वं तमश्चैव तमः सत्त्वं रजस् तथा ॥
rajas tamaścābhibhūya
sattvaṁ bhavati bhārata
rajaḥ sattvaṁ tamaścaiva
tamaḥ sattvaṁ rajas tathā

10. When prevailing over rajas and tamas, sattva arises, Arjuna; rajas prevailing over sattva and tamas also comes to be; likewise tamas prevailing over sattva and rajas.

193 Just as fire appears to take the form of a log, as the space inside a jar seems to take the shape of the jar,
194 And as the moon is reflected in the water of a lake, in the same way the Self seems to be the qualities which bind it.
195 When bile predominates over phlegm and wind and spreads through the body, it increases the heat in the body.
196 When the rains give way to the cool season, the whole sky looks chilly.
197 When both the waking state and the dream state end, deep sleep follows and for a time there is deep contentment.
198 Similarly, when goodness overcomes passion and darkness, goodness causes the Self to say, "Don't I feel happy now?"
199 Then, when goodness and passion recede, darkness predominates and a person falls into error.
200 Likewise, when passion overcomes goodness and darkness,
201 The Soul that lives in the body thinks that nothing is as beautiful as action.

अप्रकाशो ऽप्रवृत्तिश्च प्रमादो मोह एव च ।
तमस्य् एतानि जायन्ते विवृद्धे कुरुनन्दन ॥
sarvadvāreṣu dehe 'smin
prakāśa upajāyate
jñānaṁ yadā tadā vidyād
vivṛddhaṁ sattvam ity uta

11. When the light of knowledge shines through all the gates of this body, then it should be known that sattva is dominant.

सर्वद्वारेषु देहे ऽस्मिन् प्रकाश उपजायते ।
ज्ञानं यदा तदा विद्याद् विवृद्धं सत्त्वम् इत्य् उत ॥
lobhaḥ pravrttiṛ ārambhaḥ
karmanām aśamah sprhā
rajasy etāni jāyante
vivṛddhe bharatarṣabha

12. Greed, activity and the undertaking of actions, restlessness, desire; these are born when rajas is dominant, Arjuna.

लोभः प्रवृत्तिर् आरम्भः कर्मणाम् अशमः स्पृहा ।
रजस्य् एतानि जायन्ते विवृद्धे भरतर्षभ ॥
aprakāśo 'pravṛttiśca
pramādo moha eva ca
tamasy etāni jāyante
vivṛddhe kurunandana

13. Darkness and inertness, heedlessness and confusion; these are born when tamas is dominant, Arjuna.

यदा सत्त्वे प्रवृद्धे तु प्रलयं याति देहभृत् ।
तदोत्तमविदां लोकान् अमलान् प्रतिपद्यते ॥
yadā sattve pravṛddhe tu
pralayaṁ yāti dehabhṛt
tadottamavidāṁ lokān
amalān pratipadyate

14. When an embodied being goes to dissolution (death) under the dominance of sattva, then he attains the stainless worlds of those who know the highest.

रजसि प्रलयं गत्वा कर्मसङ्गिषु जायते ।
तथा प्रलीनस् तमसि मूढयोनिषु जायते ॥

rajasi pralayaṁ gatvā
karmasaṅgiṣu jāyate
tathā pralīnas tamasi
mūḍhayoniṣu jāyate

15. He who goes to dissolution (death) when rajas is dominant, is reborn among those attached to action; likewise, dissolved (dying) when tamas is dominant, he is reborn from the wombs of the deluded.

कर्मणः सुकृतस्याहुः सात्त्विकं निर्मलं फलम् ।
रजसस् तु फलं दुःखम् अज्ञानं तमसः फलम् ॥

karmaṇaḥ sukṛtasyāhuḥ
sāttvikaṁ nirmalaṁ phalam
rajasas tu phalaṁ duḥkham
ajñānaṁ tamasaḥ phalam

16. They say the fruit of good action is sattvic and without impurity, but the fruit of rajasic action is pain, and the fruit of tamasic action is ignorance.

202 When goodness increases and overcomes passion and darkness, these are the signs by which it is known:

203 Just as in spring lotuses give out their fragrance, in the same way knowledge overflows the mind and spreads beyond it.

204 Discrimination is applied to the senses, and the hands and feet seem to be endowed with sight.

205 When a mixture of milk and water is placed before a royal swan, it separates one from the other with the tip of its beak.

206 Similarly, the senses are able to distinguish between right and wrong, and sense control is their helper, O Arjuna.

207 The ears avoid whatever they shouldn't hear, the eyes shun what they shouldn't see, and the tongue refrains from uttering what it shouldn't say.

208 Just as darkness is dispelled by a lamp, whatever is forbidden doesn't appear before the senses.

209 Just as a river overflows its banks in the rainy season, the intellect of such a person comprehends all sciences.

210 Just as moonlight spreads throughout the sky on the night of the full moon, the intellect easily grasps all knowledge.

211 Desire is directed towards God, mental activity subsides, and the mind is not attracted to pleasure.

212 Thus goodness increases. If death should occur while a person is in such a state,

213 Why shouldn't he attain glory and a place in heaven, according to the wealth of his family and their generous tendencies?

214 If it is a time of abundance and a feast is held, the beloved ancestors from heaven will come to it.

215 O Arjuna, in such favorable circumstances, what other outcome could there be? Where else could such a pure person go?

216 The person in whom goodness predominates takes that quality with him when he casts off his body, the home of worldly enjoyment.

217 Anyone who dies suddenly in this state is born again into goodness, or into a wise family.

218 Tell me, O Arjuna, would a reigning monarch be less regal if he retired to a hilltop?

219 O Arjuna, isn't a lamp of this village still a lamp even if it is carried to a neighboring village?

220 In the same way, the purity of goodness grows as knowledge increases, and intellect floats on the surface of discrimination.

221 He meditates on the nature of the intellect and of the other elements, and ultimately becomes absorbed in the Absolute.

222 He who is the thirty-seventh principle beyond the other thirty-six, the twenty-fifth element beyond the other twenty-four, or the fourth quality beyond the other three,

223 This is the Absolute, the One who is all and the highest of all; and such a person easily reaches Him. He is born into a body that is beyond comparison.

224 Now consider what happens when passion predominates over goodness and darkness.

225 When passion runs riot in the body, the following characteristics can be seen:

226 Just as a traveling whirlwind gathers up all kinds of objects in its wake, in the same way the senses wander freely among the sense objects.

227 Associating indiscriminately with women, a passionate person disregards prohibitions and behaves like a sheep that feeds on whatever it finds.

228 His greed is so unrestrained that only what is beyond his reach escapes his grasp.

229 O Arjuna, he doesn't hesitate to undertake any venture which may come his way.

230 He conceives the boldest projects, such as building a temple or performing the horse sacrifice.

231 He wants to establish cities, to plant great forests of trees, and to create reservoirs of water.
232 He undertakes these great projects, while his desire for worldly and heavenly enjoyments is never satisfied.
233 His lust is so overwhelming that even the ocean would overflow with it and fire couldn't consume it.
234 His eagerness runs ahead of his thought, he competes in a race with desire, and he treads the whole universe underfoot.
235 These are some of the characteristics found in a person in whom passion is dominant. If he dies in this condition,
236 He will enter another body accompanied by these traits, and will be reborn in a human womb.
237 Even if a beggar were to live in a palace and enjoy all its luxury, would that make him a king?
238 A bull feeds on straw. He wouldn't be given anything else to eat even if he were to pull a cart in a rich man's wedding procession.
239 Such a person would have to live with people who are occupied with worldly undertakings without rest, by day or by night.
240 Moreover, a person who dies in the depths of passion may be born among those who engage in selfish actions.
241 On the other hand, when darkness overcomes goodness and passion, and becomes the dominating influence,
242 These are its characteristics. Listen with careful attention.
243 A person's mind becomes as dark as the sky on the night before the new moon, when neither the sun nor the moon is visible.
244 His heart is also desolate and without inspiration or intelligent thought.
245 His intellect is heavier than a stone, and his memory wanders aimlessly about.
246 Lack of discrimination takes possession of his whole being, and stupidity is active within him.
247 The signs of depravity are visible in the courtyard of his senses, and his evil deeds continue even after his death.
248 One can see that he delights in wrongdoing, just as an owl can see in the dark.
249 He enjoys performing prohibited actions, and his sense organs run towards their objects.
250 His body sways though he hasn't drunk any wine, he talks wildly though he's not delirious, and raves like a madman though he's not in love.
251 He may stare into space, not because he has attained liberation, but because he is infatuated.
252 In short, these are the signs of darkness, which increases by its own efforts.
253 If death should occur in these circumstances, that person will be reborn with all these dark tendencies.
254 When a mustard plant dies, having passed on its essence to its seeds, can the seeds grow into anything other than mustard plants?
255 If a lamp is lit from a flame, won't the fire continue to exist in the new flame?
256 In the same way, a person who dies while his thoughts are burdened with darkness is reborn with this same quality.
257 What more can be said? If a person dies when darkness is dominant, he may be reborn as a beast, a bird, a tree, or an insect.
258 For this reason, the Vedas define good action as whatever arises from the quality of goodness.
259 The fruit of happiness and knowledge, which is born of pure actions, is descried as *sattvic*, or good.
260 Action which has the quality of passion is like ripe indravani fruit, outwardly pleasing but leading to sorrow.
261 Such action is like the fruit of the neem tree, which looks sweet but tastes bitter.
262 Action arising from darkness can bear only ignorance as its fruit, just as poisonous plants can produce only poison.

सत्त्वात् संजायते ज्ञानं रजसो लोभ एव च ।
प्रमादमोहौ तमसो भवतो ऽज्ञानम् एव च ।।

sattvāt saṁjāyate jñānaṁ
rajaso lobha eva ca
pramādamohau tamaso
bhavato 'jñānam eva ca

17. From sattva knowledge is born, and from rajas desire; negligence and delusion arise from tamas, and ignorance too.

263 O Arjuna, goodness awakens knowledge just as the sun brings daylight.
264 Similarly, passion is the source of greed, just as forgetfulness of oneself leads to unity.
265 O wise Arjuna, darkness is the root of the sins of infatuation, ignorance, and negligence.
266 Now I have shown you the qualities as clearly

as you could see a fruit in the palm of your hand.

267 You have seen that passion and darkness lead to degradation, while only goodness leads to knowledge.

268 There are some people who practice goodness all their lives. They leave everything else and practice the fourth form of devotion through knowledge.

ऊर्ध्वं गच्छन्ति सत्त्वस्था मध्ये तिष्ठन्ति राजसाः ।
जघन्यगुणवृत्तिस्था अधो गच्छन्ति तामसाः ॥

ūrdhvaṁ gacchanti sattvasthā
madhye tiṣṭhanti rājasāḥ
jaghanyaguṇavṛttisthā
adho gacchanti tāmasāḥ

18. Those established in sattva go upward; the rajasic stay in the middle; the tamasic, established in the lowest quality, go downward.

269 Those who live and die in the practice of goodness become the lords of heaven when they leave their physical bodies.

270 In the same way, those who live and die in passion are reborn as human beings in this mortal world.

271 Here they all eat from the same dish a mixture of pleasure and pain. Having fallen into the path of death, they don't arise from it.

272 Those who are dominated by darkness and enjoy physical pleasures inherit the land of hell.

273 In this way, O Arjuna, I have explained to you the power of the one reality, the Absolute who is the cause of the three qualities.

274 The Real lives entirely as reality, unchanging; but it manifests according to the way in which the qualities produce their effects.

275 Just as a king may dream that he is conquering another king, or that he himself is being defeated,

276 In the same way, the highest, the intermediate, and the lowest states are different because of the activity of the qualities. When this is laid aside, only the pure Absolute remains.

277 We won't go into this any further, but don't think it is irrelevant. Now listen as I tell you more about what I have already said.

नान्यं गुणेभ्यः कर्तारं यदा द्रष्टानुपश्यति ।
गुणेभ्यश्च परं वेत्ति मद्भावं सोऽधिगच्छति ॥

nānyaṁ guṇebhyaḥ kartāraṁ
yadā draṣṭānupaśyati
guṇebhyaśca paraṁ vetti
madbhāvaṁ so 'dhigacchati

19. When the seer perceives no doer other than the qualities, and knows that which is higher than the qualities, he attains My being.

278 Understand that the three qualities, each according to its power, naturally come into action through contact with the body.

279 Just as fire appears to take the shape of the fuel it consumes, or as the watery element in the earth takes the form of a tree,

280 As milk is changed into curds, or as sweetness manifests in sugarcane,

281 Similarly, the three qualities, along with the heart, make up the body and are the cause of bondage.

282 O Arjuna, it is incredible that liberation can still be attained in spite of all these entanglements.

283 Though the three qualities, according to their special properties, affect the activities of the body, they don't diminish the power of that which transcends them.

284 Now I will explain to you why this liberation is natural, for you are like a bee on the lotus of knowledge.

285 This is the principle that I have already explained to you: the Self, though involved with the qualities, is not of them.

286 The enlightened perceive this, O Arjuna, just as a person who awakes from sleep realizes that he had a dream.

287 If a man stands on the bank of a lake and looks at his reflection in the water, it will seem to be fragmented because of the movement of the waves.

288 Just an actor isn't deceived by the role that he's playing, in the same way, we should understand the qualities without identifying with them.

289 The sky contains the three seasons, yet it preserves its separate existence.

290 Similarly, when the Absolute, beyond the qualities, enters into the realm of the qualities, it maintains its identity in spite of being limited by individuality.

291 Regarding everything in this way, the soul says, I am the witness; I am not the doer. It is the qualities which cause all activity.

292 The whole field of action arises from the three qualities of goodness, passion, and darkness. Actions are merely the modifications

caused by these three.

293 Among them I remain like springtime in a forest, the cause of all the wealth of its beauty.

294 The stars vanish, the sun-crystal flashes, the lotuses blossom, and darkness is dispelled,

295 Yet the sun itself doesn't bring about all these changes. In the same way, I am present in the body, but not as the doer.

296 Manifesting through Me, the qualities become evident. They increase because of Me, and when they pass away I am what remains.

297 He who has attained enlightenment, O Arjuna, transcends the qualities and proceeds on the upward path.

गुणान् एतान् अतीत्य त्रीन् देही देहसमुद्भवान् ।
जन्ममृत्युजरादुःखैर् विमुक्तो ऽमृतम् अश्नुते ॥

guṇān etān atītya trīn
dehī dehasamudbhavān
janmamṛtyujarāduḥkhāir
vimukto 'mṛtam aśnute

20. When an embodied being transcends these three qualities, which are the source of the body, released from birth, death, old age, and pain, he attains immortality.

298 Then he knows that the One who is without attributes is different from the qualities, for wisdom has taken up residence in him.

299 In short, O Arjuna, he attains My nature just as a river merges into the ocean.

300 Like a parrot that has escaped from its perch and is sitting on the branch of a tree, he is overcome by the awareness of oneness with God.

301 He is like a man who has been snoring in the deep sleep of ignorance and suddenly awakens to the knowledge of his real nature.

302 The mirror of delusion falls from his hand, O Arjuna, and he is freed from the reflection of the world.

303 When the wind of concern with the body ceases to blow, O Arjuna, the soul attains union with God just as waves merge into the ocean.

304 Such a person immediately becomes one with Me. Just as clouds are absorbed into the sky at the end of the rainy season,

305 He truly becomes united with Me. Then, although he remains in the body, he is no longer at the mercy of the qualities which produce the body.

306 Just as the light of a lamp isn't dimmed when it is encased in a glass container, and as the fire at the bottom of the ocean isn't extinguished by the waters,

307 Similarly, his intellect isn't tainted by the flux of the qualities. He lives in the body just as the moon is reflected in water.

308 Even though the three qualities play fully in his body, he doesn't allow himself to be aware of them.

309 When he reaches this state, he concentrates firmly on his heart and remains unaware of what his body is doing.

310 When a serpent has shed its skin, it retires beneath the earth and is no longer concerned with what will happen to the skin.

311 When the fragrance of a lotus goes forth and mingles with the air, it doesn't return to the flower.

312 Similarly, when such a person attains union with the Self, he isn't concerned with the nature or state of his body.

313 Therefore, conditions such as birth, old age, and death affect only the body. They don't touch the enlightened being.

314 When the pieces of a broken pot are thrown away, the space which was inside the pot is absorbed by the space outside.

315 In the same way, if a person remembers his true nature, he experiences nothing but union, and awareness of the body passes away.

316 Such a person has transcended the qualities, having attained enlightenment while still in the body.

317 These words of the Lord pleased Arjuna greatly, like a peacock hearing the sound of a thunderbolt.

अर्जुन उवाच । *arjuna uvāca*

कैर् लिङ्गैस् त्रीन् गुणान् एतान् अतीतो भवति प्रभो ।
किमाचारः कथं चैतांस् त्रीन् गुणान् अतिवर्तते ॥

kāir liṅgāis trīn guṇān etān
atīto bhavati prabho
kimācāraḥ kathaṁ cāitāṅs
trīn guṇān ativartate

Arjuna spoke:
21. By what marks is he recognized who has transcended these three qualities, O Lord? What is his conduct? And how does he go beyond these three qualities?

318 Then Arjuna, full of joy, asked the Lord about the signs of a person who had experienced enlightenment.

319 After transcending the qualities, how does he

behave? In what way does he remain free from them? You are the abode of grace; tell me this.

320 Listen how the Lord will answer Arjuna's question.

321 The Lord said, It is strange, O Arjuna, that you should ask such a question. It is like asking how a moving object can remain still.

322 A person who has risen above the qualities can't be subject to them. Even if he comes in contact with them, he can easily escape from their grasp.

323 How can a person know whether he is bound by the qualities or not when he is entangled in them?

324 If this is the reason for your question, you should ask me freely. Listen while I explain this.

श्रीभगवान् उवाच । *śrībhagavān uvāca*

प्रकाशं च प्रवृत्तिं च मोहम् एव च पाण्डव ।
न द्वेष्टि संप्रवृत्तानि न निवृत्तानि काङ्क्षति ।।

prakāśaṁ ca pravṛttiṁ ca
moham eva ca pāṇḍava
na dveṣṭi saṁpravṛttāni
na nivṛttāni kāṅkṣati

The Blessed Lord spoke:
22. He neither hates nor desires the presence or the absence of light or activity or delusion, Arjuna.

325 When someone is under the power of passion, the impulse to act is awakened. When he is enmeshed in it,

326 A person who has transcended the qualities isn't intoxicated with the pride that he is performing action, nor is he depressed if that action fails.

327 When goodness predominates, knowledge shines through all the senses. Yet his mind isn't carried away by the thought of his learning, nor is he depressed if he lacks knowledge.

328 When darkness increases in him he isn't overcome by delusion and infatuation, nor is he troubled by ignorance. He simply doesn't accept it.

329 When confusion overtakes him, he doesn't seek knowledge. When he gains wisdom he disregards action, yet he feels no remorse if he finds himself engaged in it.

330 He is like the sun, which is not affected by the three periods of the day: morning, noon, and evening.

331 Does he need any other light with which to acquire wisdom? Is the ocean filled up by rain?

332 Does he consider himself a man of action because of the work he does? Do the Himalayas tremble under the snow which lies on them?

333 When infatuation comes upon him, will he be annoyed? Can he be consumed by the heat of the hot season?

उदासीनवद् आसीनो गुणैर् यो न विचाल्यते ।
गुणा वर्तन्त इत्य् एव यो ऽवतिष्ठति नेङ्गते ।।

udāsīnavad āsīno
guṇāir yo na vicālyate
guṇā vartanta ity eva
yo 'vatiṣṭhati neṅgate

23. He who is seated as if indifferent, who is not disturbed by the qualities, thinking "the qualities are operating," and who stands firm and does not waver,

334 Knowing that the qualities and their operation are all a part of himself, he isn't disturbed when one or the other is present.

335 Having this conviction, when he enters a body he is like a traveler who encounters an obstacle.

336 He is like a battlefield which of itself neither wins a victory nor suffers a defeat, for he neither overcomes the qualities nor is he overcome by them.

337 Therefore, O Arjuna, he isn't disturbed when the qualities come or go, just as the waves of a mirage cannot sway Mount Meru.

338 What more can I say? Just as the sky isn't shaken by the wind, and the sun isn't swallowed up by darkness,

339 In the same way, he is not affected by the qualities, just as a person who is awake isn't deluded by a dream. Understand this.

340 He isn't influenced by them and sees them only from afar, like a man judging the merits and demerits of a puppet show.

341 The quality of goodness leads to good actions, passion engages a person in the pursuit of sense pleasures, while darkness promotes confusion and infatuation.

342 You should understand clearly that the activities of the qualities come about through the power of such a person, just as the power of the sun promotes the activities of all people in the world.

343 The tide of the ocean rises, the moonstone oozes moisture, and the moon lotuses open

their blossoms; yet the moon itself remains silent.

344 Although the wind may rise and subside, the sky remains motionless. Similarly, such a person is undisturbed by the play of the qualities.

345 O Arjuna, one who has transcended the qualities can be recognized by these signs. Now listen to the way he lives.

समदुःखसुखः स्वस्थः समलोष्टाश्मकाञ्चनः ।
तुल्यप्रियाप्रियो धीरस् तुल्यनिन्दात्मसंस्तुतिः ॥

samaduḥkhasukhaḥ svasthaḥ
samaloṣṭāśmakāñcanaḥ
tulyapriyāpriyo dhīras
tulyanindātmasaṁstutiḥ

24. To whom pain and pleasure are equal, who dwells in the Self, to whom a clod, a stone, and gold are the same, to whom the loved and the unloved are alike, who is steadfast, to whom blame and praise of himself are alike,

346 Just as a piece of cloth is nothing but threads, O Arjuna, in the same way, such a person sees the whole world as infused with My form.

347 Whether he suffers pain or joy, his mind remains steady, just as the Lord gives gifts to both His devotees and His enemies.

348 As long as he swims like a fish in the waters of earthly existence, naturally he has to experience pleasure and pain.

349 Nevertheless, he disregards them both and remains established in his true nature, just as a seed is separated from the husk.

350 Just as the river Ganges, having run its course, merges in the ocean and leaves behind its turbulent flow,

351 Similarly, O Arjuna, the person who dwells in the Self equally accepts pain and pleasure.

352 Just as night and day are the same to a pillar, similarly, the pairs of opposites inherent in life don't exist for the person who is one with the Self.

353 A sleeping man doesn't care whether a snake or a heavenly nymph is lying near him. Similarly, these pairs of opposites don't affect the person who is united with God.

354 For him cowdung isn't different from gold, nor does he see any difference between a jewel and a stone.

355 His enjoyment of union with the Self never fades, whether heaven enters his house or a tiger attacks him.

356 Just as what is dead cannot come back to life and what has been burned cannot grow again, in the same way, his evenness of mind cannot be disturbed.

357 He cannot be praised as though he were God, nor can he be scorned as though he were lowborn, just as ashes cannot be burned as fuel.

358 Praise and blame are of no consequence to him, just as the sun is untouched by darkness or light.

मानापमानयोस् तुल्यस् तुल्यो मित्रारिपक्षयोः ।
सर्वारम्भपरित्यागी गुणातीतः स उच्यते ॥

mānāpamānayos tulyas
tulyo mitrāripakṣayoḥ
sarvārambhaparityāgī
guṇātītaḥ sa ucyate

25. To whom honor and dishonor are equal, dispassionate toward the side of friend or foe, renouncing all undertakings—he is said to transcend the qualities.

359 Whether he is worshiped as a deity or condemned as a thief, whether he is made a king or is surrounded by bulls and elephants,

360 Whether friends approach him or enemies attack him, it is the same to him, just as the light of the sun is indifferent to night or dawn.

361 Just as the sky remains unaffected by the various seasons, similarly, his mind is unaware of differences.

362 He has another characteristic: he seems to be detached from all action.

363 He remains separate from every undertaking, earthly activity appears not to exist for him, and he himself is the fire in which the fruit of all action is consumed.

364 Such ideas as heaven or earth do not arise in his mind, and he enters naturally into whatever experience comes to him.

365 He is unaffected by pleasure or fatigue as if he were a stone, and his mind has abandoned all decisions to act or not to act.

366 Why explain this any further? A person who acts in this way has transcended the qualities.

367 Lord Krishna said, Now listen to the way this can be achieved.

मां च यो ऽव्यभिचारेण भक्तियोगेन सेवते ।
स गुणान् समतीत्यैतान् ब्रह्मभूयाय कल्पते ॥

māṁ ca yo 'vyabhicāreṇa
bhaktiyogena sevate
sa guṇān samatītyāitān
brahmabhūyāya kalpate

26. And he who serves Me with the yoga of unswerving devotion, transcending these qualities, is ready for absorption in Brahman.

368 A person who serves Me with an unswerving mind through the path of devotion is able to overcome the qualities.

369 I must explain to you clearly who I am, what devotion is, and what error is.

370 Listen, O Arjuna, I am in this universe just as luster is inherent in a jewel.

371 Moisture is in water, space is in the sky, sweetness is in sugar. There is no separation between these things.

372 Flames and fire are one, lotus petals are one with the flower, and the branches and the fruit of a tree are the tree itself.

373 The snow which falls on a mountain becomes part of it, and curds are nothing but curdled milk.

374 Similarly, the entire universe is Me. There is no reason to strip the moon; one would find only the moon itself.

375 Ghee is clarified butter in spite of its solidity, and though a bracelet isn't melted down, it is still gold.

376 Even if a garment isn't unraveled, it is still nothing but woven threads. One doesn't have to crush a clay pot to see that it is earth.

377 Therefore, don't think that I can only be found by dissolving the universe, for I am everything.

378 To realize Me in this manner is called one-pointed devotion. If any sense of difference appears, it is a mistake.

379 So, laying aside all sense of duality, and with an undivided mind, you may know Me as one with yourself.

380 O Arjuna, just as gold and the ornament that is made from it are one, similarly you shouldn't consider yourself as different from the Self.

381 When light emits a ray, the ray is the light itself. This is how you should think of Me.

382 You should realize that you are in Me, like a particle of dust on the earth or a snowflake on a mountain.

383 However small a wave may be, it isn't different from the ocean. In the same way, there isn't any difference between Me and the Universal Self.

384 When a person's vision is illuminated by the experience of oneness, we call this devotion.

385 This vision is the excellence of knowledge and the essence of yoga.

386 O Arjuna, this process is as continuous as the flow of water between a raincloud and the ocean.

387 Just as there is no boundary between the space inside a well and the sky above it, similarly, such a person becomes united with the Supreme.

388 This union of the soul with God is like the light of the sun which extends from its reflection in water right up to the sun itself.

389 When this experience of union takes place, even the sense of union itself is lost.

390 When a grain of salt has melted into the water of the ocean, O Arjuna, the process of melting ceases with it.

391 When fire has consumed grass, the fire itself burns out and all awareness of duality is lost.

392 Any thought such as, I am beyond the qualities while My devotee is not, passes away. The sense of timeless union becomes clear.

393 There is no longer any meaning in saying that such a person overcomes the qualities, O Arjuna. The knot of his individuality has been severed.

394 In short, O wise one, this state is the nature of God. One who worships Me in this way attains it.

395 For a person who possesses these attributes and who is devoted to Me, this state of oneness with God is like that of a devoted wife.

396 When the turbulent waters of the Ganges flow onward, they have no other end but to merge with the ocean.

397 Similarly, O Arjuna, a person who serves Me with this enlightened vision is the crest jewel on the crown of the state of union with God.

398 O Arjuna, this state is that of absorption in God, which is the last of the four goals of human life.

399 Worshiping Me is the ladder to reach this state. Although it may seem to you that I am a means to that end,

400 Don't let such a thought enter your mind, for God is not different from Me.

ब्रह्मणो हि प्रतिष्ठाहम् अमृतस्याव्ययस्य च ।
शाश्वतस्य च धर्मस्य सुखस्यैकान्तिकस्य च ॥
brahmaṇo hi pratiṣṭhāham

amṛtasyāvyayasya ca
śāśvatasya ca dharmasya
sukhasyāikāntikasya ca

27. For I am the abode of Brahman, of the immortal and the imperishable, of everlasting virtue, and of absolute bliss.

401 O wise one, just as the moon and its sphere are not different, I am not separate from God.
402 O Beloved, God is eternal, unchanging, the essence of righteousness, limitless joy, and the One without a second.
403 I am that goal which is the end of the path of discrimination, the boundless essence of truth. I am truly all this.
404 In this way, Krishna, the matchless friend of devotees, spoke to Arjuna. Listen, O King.
405 Then Dhritarashtra said, O Sanjaya, why have you told all this to me without my asking you?
406 Remove my anxiety and bring me news of victory. Sanjaya said, Don't be concerned about this.
407 Then Sanjaya, surprised, sighed and said impatiently to himself, How far the king is from the divine!
408 May the gracious Lord have mercy on him. May he be filled with discrimination and be healed of this great sickness of confusion.
409 Reflecting in this way and listening to the discussion between the Lord and Arjuna, great joy poured into Sanjaya's heart.
410 With great delight, he will continue to tell what the Lord said.
411 Jnanadeva, the disciple of Nivritti, says, Listen to me and I will impress on your mind the meaning of the Lord's words.

15

THE YOGA OF THE SUPREME BEING

NOW on the altar of my heart I will place my Guru's feet.

2 Pouring my senses as flowers into the cupped hands of the experience of union with the Supreme, I offer a handful of these flowers at his feet.

3 My desire, washed clean by the pure water of devotion, will be the sandalwood paste.

4 Making anklets of the pure gold of my love for him, I will adorn his beautiful feet.

5 My strong, pure, and one-pointed devotion to him will be a pair of rings for his toes.

6 I will place on them the bud of pure emotions with the fragrance of bliss, and the full-blown eight-petalled lotus.

7 Then I will burn before him the incense of egoism, I will wave before him the lamp of union with the Self, and I will embrace him with the experience of oneness with the Absolute.

8 I will put on his holy feet the sandals of my body and my vital force, and I will wave around them the neem leaves of experience and liberation.

9 May I be worthy of the Guru's feet! Through them I may attain all the goals of human life,

10 Through them I will gain that pure knowledge which leads to rest in God, and through them speech is transformed into an ocean of nectar.

11 This good fortune brings forth such eloquence that thousands of full moons should salute it.

12 Just as the sun, rising in the east, sheds its glorious rays of light over the earth, in the same way, language becomes a festival of the light of knowledge for the listeners.

13 Through this good fortune, such eloquence arises that it diminishes the divine resonance. The highest beatitude cannot compare with its beauty.

14 In the arbor of the joy of hearing, the world enjoys the springtime of wisdom, and the vine of speech blossoms forth.

15 Words then reveal the nature of that divine Being who causes speech and mind to withdraw having failed to comprehend Him. What a marvelous thing this is!

16 That Being who is beyond knowing, unattainable by meditation, and imperceptible to the senses, is revealed in his words.

17 When the devotee receives the blessing of the pollen falling from the Guru's lotus feet, this wonderful power of speech comes to him.

18 Nothing more needs to be said. Jnaneshwar says, This good fortune has come to me,

19 For I am like the tender child of my Guru, who has no other son, and he pours out his whole blessing on me.

20 Just as a cloud showers down its rain for the chataka bird, my Guru has done the same thing for me.

21 My untrained tongue has been set free and has been touched by the sweetness of the *Gita*.

22 For a fortunate person, even sand is transformed into jewels. If a person is destined to remain alive, even one who is about to kill him will treat him with affection.

23 If the Lord wishes to save a hungry person, even sand boiled in water will turn into the sweetest rice.

24 Similarly, when the Guru accepts a person as his own, this earthly existence becomes for him a life of liberation.

25 See how the Lord, the primeval One worshiped by the entire universe, removed all of Arjuna's shortcomings.

26 Similarly, my Guru, Shri Nivrittiraja, has raised my ignorance to the state of knowledge.
27 But enough of this! My love for him grows more intense as I speak. Where can one find the knowledge to describe the glory of the Guru?
28 By his grace, I will touch the feet of you saintly people with my explanation of the *Gita*.
29 The Lord of liberation has discussed this subject at the end of the fourteenth chapter.
30 Only he who has found spiritual wisdom can attain liberation, just as a person who performs a hundred sacrifices can reach heaven.
31 Only one who performs Brahmanic rites for a hundred lifetimes attains the world of Brahma. No one else can achieve this.
32 Just as only a person who can see is able to enjoy the sunlight, similarly the sweetness of liberation can be tasted only through this wisdom.
33 When we consider who is worthy to attain this knowledge, we see that there is only one such person.
34 In order to discover treasures hidden in the earth, a person must apply a special lotion to his eyes, but even then he must have been fortunate enough to have been born with his feet first.
35 It is also true that knowledge will enable a person to attain liberation. Nevertheless, his mind must be pure so that it will remain with him.
36 Without dispassion, knowledge cannot last. The Lord established this truth after much thought.
37 Now the omniscient Lord has shown us the nature of that dispassion which takes possession of the mind.
38 If a person who is eating realizes that the food is poisoned, he will push away the dish.
39 Similarly, when a person realizes how transitory this earthly existence is, he turns to dispassion.
40 In the fifteenth chapter the Lord of the universe will explain the nature of impermanence, using the parable of a tree.
41 This tree of worldly existence is not an ordinary tree that falls down when it is uprooted and soon dries up.
42 By means of this simile, the Lord removes the necessity of the cycle of birth and death.
43 The fifteenth chapter will show the deceptive nature of worldly existence, and the way in which one can merge one's individuality in God.
44 This is the essence of the teachings given in this chapter. As I explain them, I beg you to listen with all your heart.
45 Lord Krishna, the ocean of the highest joy, the moon of the full-moon day says:

श्रीभगवान् उवाच । *śrībhagavān uvāca*

ऊर्ध्वमूलम् अधःशाखम् अश्वत्थं प्राहुर् अव्ययम् ।
छन्दांसि यस्य पर्णानि यस् तं वेद स वेदवित् ।।

ūrdhvamūlam adhaḥśākham
aśvatthaṁ prāhur avyayam
chandāṁsi yasya parṇāni
yas taṁ veda sa vedavit

The Blessed Lord spoke:
1. They speak of the eternal ashvattha tree, having its roots above and branches below, whose leaves are the (Vedic) hymns. He who knows this is a knower of the Vedas.

46 O Arjuna, the delusion of the universe, which prevents the seeker from reaching his home of Self-realization,
47 Should be thought of as a huge tree, and not as life in the form of an extended universe.
48 It is not like an ordinary tree, having its roots in the earth and its branches pointing upward. For this reason, no one can describe it.
49 When the trunk of an ordinary tree is struck with an axe or burned by fire, no matter how large it is, what will happen to its upper branches?
50 When its roots are torn out, the entire tree will fall. But the tree of worldly existence is different; it isn't brought down so easily.
51 O Arjuna, it is truly wonderful that this tree grows downward.
52 No one knows how high the sun is, and yet its rays descend in every direction. This tree of earthly existence is the same, with its branches growing downwards.
53 It penetrates everything that is and is not, just as the sky will be submerged in the final deluge.
54 This tree pervades all space, just as after sunset the night is filled with darkness.
55 O Arjuna, it has neither fruit to taste nor

flowers to give out fragrance, and yet this tree is all that is.

56 Though its roots point upwards, it is not uprooted and it is always green.

57 Though it is true that its roots extend upwards, it also has many roots which grow downwards.

58 It has roots which grow from its branches, like the pipal tree or the banyan tree, and it spreads in all directions.

59 O Arjuna, in this way the tree of worldly existence not only has branches which grow downwards,

60 But, strangely enough, it also has groups of well-developed branches which grow upwards.

61 It is as if space had grown into a vine, as if the wind itself had assumed the shape of a tree, or as if the three states of waking, dreaming, and deep sleep had set in.

62 So the whole universe has taken on the form of a great tree with its roots extending upwards.

63 Now what are the characteristics of the upward- growing roots, and also those of the downward-growing branches?

64 And what are the roots of the tree below and the branches above?

65 Why has it been called the ashwattha tree, the name given to it by those who delight in the knowledge of God?

66 I will explain all this to you in a simple way so you may understand it.

67 So listen, O fortunate Arjuna. You are worthy to hear this. Let your body be all ears, and listen with all your heart.

68 When Lord Krishna had spoken these words, Arjuna was moved by His love and became the embodiment of attention.

69 What the Lord said seemed almost insignificant compared with Arjuna's eagerness to listen, as though the heavens were embraced by the ten directions.

70 He was like a second Agastya, in that he strove to drink in one gulp the whole ocean of Krishna's explanation.

71 When Krishna saw Arjuna's overwhelming eagerness, He encircled him with His own delight.

72 Then Krishna said, O Arjuna, the Supreme is the upper part of this tree. It is said to be uppermost only in relation to the rest of the tree.

73 In reality, there are no such distinctions as upper, lower, or middle. There is only indivisible unity in the Absolute.

74 Pure knowledge is the inaudible essence of all sounds, the fragrance of flowers which is imperceptible to the senses, the joy which is beyond sense pleasures;

75 It is the same both near and far, in front, and behind. It is the invisible witness of all, and yet is without sight.

76 It becomes manifest in the world of name and form, and is affected by illusion.

77 This is pure knowledge, without either the knower or the object known. It is heaven filled with the essence of joy.

78 This is the Absolute, the upper part of the tree. All the branches of the tree sprout from this part.

79 These branches are known as Maya, or illusion, but Maya both is and is not. She is as impossible to describe as the child of a barren woman.

80 She neither exists nor does not exist, and she cannot tolerate the idea of thought. This is her nature, which is considered eternal.

81 She is the seed of the tree of earthly existence, the soil in which it is planted. She is the lamp of all wrong understanding.

82 She is the treasure chest of all forces, the sky in which the cloud of the universe appears, and the fold of the cloth of all that has form.

83 Maya abides in the Supreme and both is and is not. Only through her does the splendor of the Supreme become manifest.

84 Just as a person who falls asleep loses consciousness, just as soot obscures the light of a lamp,

85 Or as a young wife sleeping beside her husband may suddenly awaken him and embrace him while she is dreaming and thus excite his passion,

86 Similarly, O Arjuna, Maya arises in the Absolute. Ignorance is the failure to recognize from where she comes, and it is the first root of this tree.

87 This lack of awareness of God, the true Reality, is the root set deep in the upper part of the tree. In Vedanta this is described as the seed.

88 The deep sleep of ignorance is called the seed state, while the dream and waking states are the fruit.

89 This is how Vedanta explains it. But let this be. Here we consider ignorance to be the root.

90 Above, in the pure Spirit, roots sprout upwards and downwards, held in the firm grip of Maya.

91 Then the innumerable forms of thought arise, and their shoots grow downward on all four sides.

92 In this way the tree of existence has its roots firmly established in the upper part, and offshoots appear from those clusters of roots.

93 Then the first of the great principles, intellect, sprouts in Consciousness and a leaf grows from it.

94 Out of this springs a branch with three leaves, growing downwards as the individual consciousness with its three qualities: *sattva*, *rajas*, and *tamas*.

95 From this grows the branch called reason. The sense of duality develops, and the branch called the mind shoots forth from it.

96 When the root has gained strength from the sap of thought, there grow from it four tender shoots which are the four psychic instruments: the mind, intellect, subconscious mind, and ego.

97 After these, there grow the stems of the five elements: ether, air, fire, water, and earth.

98 From these five stems grow the tender leaves of the five senses of hearing, sight, touch, taste, and smell.

99 First sound appears, and the sense of hearing eagerly reaches out towards it.

100 Then the vine of the skin sends out the tendril of touch, and from this there arise all manner of new sensations.

101 Following this a leaf of form develops, and the eye reaches out to enjoy it, spreading confusion.

102 As sprigs of taste grow, leaves of various desires are excited in the tongue.

103 Then, when fragrance sprouts, shoots of the sense of smell grow strong, arousing intense desire.

104 In this way, the ego, the mind, and the primary elements, the bonds of worldly life, develop from the great first Principle.

105 Although this tree expands throughout all the various divisions of nature, it is like a seashell which appears to be silver.

106 The waves of the ocean reach only as far as its shores. Similarly, the Absolute manifests in the form of this tree, which springs from ignorance.

107 This whole tree is only the one Absolute manifested outwardly. It is like a dream in which a person may become many, although he is really only one.

108 This is enough. In this way this strange tree grows and sends forth its branches in the form of the intellect and the other principles of matter.

109 Now listen and I will explain why the wise call this the ashwattha tree.

110 The syllable *shwa* in *ashwattha* means 'tomorrow' and the prefix *a* is negative, for it doesn't last. This tree of worldly life isn't permanent.

111 Just as clouds in the sky continually change their color, as lightning is never still even for an instant,

112 As a drop of water on a trembling lotus petal cannot remain steady, and as the mind of a troubled person is restless,

113 It is the same with the condition of this tree. It is in a constant state of degeneration, so it is said "not to remain until tomorrow."

114 Ashwattha is also the name given to the pipal or fig tree, but the Lord doesn't use it in this sense.

115 Although it isn't inappropriate to call it the fig tree, let that be. We are not concerned here with popular usage.

116 Instead, listen to its mystery. It is called *ashwattha* because it is transitory.

117 Another important point is that it is also known as *avyaya*, the imperishable one. The inner meaning of this is as follows:

118 Since on the one hand clouds draw their water from the ocean, and on the other hand rivers replenish it,

119 The volume of the ocean neither increases nor decreases, but seems to remain constant. But this is so only as long as the rivers and clouds work together in this way.

120 This tree is called *avyaya* because its creation and destruction happen constantly and are therefore imperceptible.

121 Just as a charitable person seems to be saving money while he is spending it, similarly, even in its constant destruction this tree seems to be indestructible.

122 Because of their great speed, the wheels of a vehicle appear not to be moving.

123 Similarly, as time passes, some branches of

the tree wither and fall off, while countless other shoots spring forth.

124 Yet it is impossible to say when one disappears or when others sprout, like the clouds in the sky during the monsoon.

125 In the same way, at the end of a great age existing worlds pass away, and multitudes of others spring up in their place.

126 The fierce whirlwinds of the final dissolution destroy the trees of earthly life during one cycle, and thousands of new trees spring up in the next cycle.

127 The era of one progenitor follows that of another and races succeed one another, just as in sugarcane one joint rises above another as the stalk grows.

128 At the end of Kali Yuga the dry bark of the trees falls off, and at once the great trees of Krita Yuga begin to appear.

129 As one year passes away the next is ushered in, just as one day follows another; yet a person is hardly aware of it.

130 He cannot tell at what point one breeze passes into another, nor can he tell how many branches of the tree fall off and how many others take their place.

131 As soon as one branch, in the form of a body, breaks off, another one grows. This makes the tree of existence seem to be eternal.

132 Just as a stream of water flows quickly on and joins another stream, similarly, the growth of this tree of existence is unreal, though people think it is real.

133 In the wink of an eye, countless waves rise and fall on the ocean, although it looks like one continuous wave.

134 A crow has only one eye with a pupil, but when it moves its eyes in both directions, people are deluded into thinking that it has a pupil in both eyes.

135 When a top is spinning rapidly, it seems to be fixed to the ground. It is the speed which gives this impression.

136 Enough! When a burning torch is swung around in the dark, it looks like a circle of fire.

137 In the same way, to the ignorant this tree of earthly existence appears to be indestructible, though it is constantly being created and destroyed.

138 However, the person who recognizes that this is due to speed and that it is transitory, realizes that countless worlds arise and pass away in a single moment.

139 He knows that this tree has no other source but ignorance and that its existence is an illusion.

140 Such a person is wise, O Arjuna. He should be revered as though he were the sacred teaching itself.

141 He alone is worthy to experience the fruit of yoga. Truly, wisdom itself dwells in him.

142 I have said enough. Who can possibly describe the person who has realized the illusory nature of this tree of existence?

गुणप्रवृद्धा विषयप्रवालाः ।
अधश्चोर्ध्वं प्रसृतास् तस्य शाखा
अधश्च मूलान्य् अनुसंततानि
कर्मानुबन्धीनि मनुष्यलोके ॥

adhaścordhvaṁ prasṛtās tasya śākhā
guṇapravṛddhā viṣayapravālāḥ
adhaśca mūlāny anusaṁtatāni
karmānubandhīni manuṣyaloke

2. Below and above its branches spread, nourished by the qualities, with objects of the senses as sprouts; and below its roots stretch forth engendering action in the world of men.

143 On this tree of worldly existence with its branches growing downwards, there are also many branches growing upwards.

144 Those spreading downwards serve as roots, and vines and leaves sprout from them.

145 I already explained all this at the beginning, but now listen while I explain it in simpler language.

146 Gathering up ignorance, the binding root, the power of the elements, and the greatness of the Vedas,

147 From the trunk of the tree grow four great branches: the species born of sweat, seed, egg, and the womb.

148 From each of these branches, eight million, four hundred thousand smaller species come into being, and innumerable shoots of individual lives grow from them.

149 These four large branches also produce cross branches, which are creatures of various smaller classes.

150 Then there appear clusters of men, women, and creatures without gender, their bodies quivering with the burden of their passions.

151 Just as the rain spreads throughout the sky in rain clouds, in the same way the vine of

all these forms spreads through ignorance.
152 Bending from the weight of the branches, they become entangled, and this gives rise to the winds of excitement through the qualities.
153 Because of the struggle among the qualities, the upward-growing roots spread in three directions.
154 When the wind of passion blows strongly, small branches in the form of human beings thrive.
155 These shoot neither upwards nor downwards, but remain in the center and grow as cross branches of the four castes.
156 These branches then send out the foliage of prescribed duties and prohibited actions, and the fresh leaves of the Vedic laws enhance their beauty.
157 The forests of desire and passion arise from them, and the momentary pleasure derived from them.
158 Through the desire of Maya to expand, the shoots of good and evil deeds develop, and innumerable offshoots of actions appear.
159 Then as human bodies fall away like decaying tree trunks, exhausted by past experiences, other sprouts of new bodies take their place.
160 The beauty of the foliage of sense objects is constantly renewed by beautiful sounds and other sensory experiences.
161 In this way, with the strong wind of passion, the branches representing human life proliferate. This is known as the world of men.
162 As soon as the wind of passion dies down, the hurricane of darkness begins to blow.
163 Then evil desires appear from those human branches, sending out shoots of bad actions.
164 Twisted shoots of laziness break out, and leaves and tendrils of error appear.
165 On the tips of the leaves, the rules and prohibitions of the Rig Veda, Yajur Veda, and Sama Veda are heard humming.
166 These produce the vine of desire in the form of the laws of the Atharva Veda, which teach about killing and incantations.
167 Meanwhile, strong roots of evil actions are forming, and the branches of rebirth are flourishing.
168 Deluded evildoers are trapped by the branches of all kinds of wickedness, such as those deeds which lower caste people commit.
169 Then there are side growths of still lower species such as birds, pigs, tigers, scorpions, and snakes.
170 O Arjuna, branches grow out on all sides, and their fruit is the perpetual experience of hell.
171 More and more shoots emerge from recurring births due to evil deeds such as violence and sexual indulgence.
172 These in turn become trees, grass, metal, clods of earth, or stone. Such is the fruit of these branches.
173 Listen, O Arjuna. In this way, the downward growth of the tree ranges from human beings to the inanimate world.
174 Therefore, humanity may be regarded as the downward-growing roots of the tree of worldly existence.
175 On the other hand, O Arjuna, if we look at the chief root growing upwards, we will find that its origin is the middle branch of humanity.
176 Between the downward and upward growing branches are found those produced by good and evil deeds resulting from the qualities of purity and dullness.
177 O Arjuna, the leaves of the three Vedas cannot grow anywhere except here, for their precepts are only relevant to human beings.
178 Although in terms of the human body these upward-growing roots are branches, in terms of the development of action they are roots.
179 The roots of ordinary trees deepen as the branches grow and the branches spread out as the roots develop.
180 The same is true of the body: as long as there is activity the body remains in the world, and as long as there is a body there is activity. This cannot be denied.
181 For this reason the Father of all men has said that the human body is the cause of all activity. There is no doubt about this.
182 At times when the fierce gale of darkness ceases, the whirlwind of goodness rushes in.
183 Then this root of the human body produces blades of good desire, which grow into sprouts of good actions.
184 Through the awakening of knowledge and with the force of right understanding, the intellect immediately sends out many offshoots.
185 From this shining foliage of respect, pregnant with the sap of understanding, limbs of

righteousness sprout.
186 Boughs of good conduct spring from these, and the sound of Vedic hymns vibrates through them.
187 The discipline prescribed by the Vedas and sacrificial rites are the leaves growing from these branches.
188 On the branches of self-control and mastery of the senses appear clusters of penance, spreading gently over the boughs of detachment.
189 The shoots of special vows rise upwards with the speed of creation.
190 Among these there is the thick foliage of the Vedas, which resounds with right knowledge as the strong wind of righteousness blows through it.
191 The branch of religious duty spreads out along with the branch of life in the world, bearing on its cross branches the fruit of heavenly enjoyment.
192 Next to these the limb of dispassion emerges, and also the bough of dharma and liberation on which tender new leaves unfold.
193 On the outer cross branches are the sun, moon, and planets, the ancestors, seers, and demigods.
194 Above these are the great boughs of Indra and the other gods, their stems laden with fruit.
195 Still higher are those of the sages Marichi, Kashyapa, and others who attained the highest rank of penance and wisdom.
196 In this way the branches rise higher and higher, with small stems and pointed tips, bearing abundant fruit.
197 O Arjuna, from the fruit-laden boughs above these upper branches come the tender shoots of Brahma and Shiva.
198 Weighed down by fruit, the upper branches bend downwards so that they rest on the roots.
199 Trees bend low when the branches are laden with fruit,
200 And with increasing knowledge this tree of life bends down to rest on its own roots.
201 The soul doesn't grow beyond Brahma and Shiva, for above them there is only the Absolute.
202 Those branches cannot be compared to the root of Maya, from which this tree springs.
203 The topmost branches representing Sanaka and other sages rise upwards unimpeded, for they have already reached the Absolute.
204 This tree grows from its roots in humanity and extends upwards to the highest level, which are Brahma and other deities.
205 Thus humanity is called the root because Brahma evolves from it.

न रूपम् अस्येह तथोपलभ्यते
नान्तो न चादिर् न च संप्रतिष्ठा ।
अश्वत्थम् एनं सुविरूढमूलम्
असङ्गशस्त्रेण दृढेन छित्त्वा ॥

na rūpam asyeha tathopalabhyate
nānto na cādir na ca saṁpratiṣṭhā
aśvattham enaṁ suvirūḍhamūlam
asaṅgaśastreṇa dṛḍhena chittvā

3. *Its form is not perceptible here in the world, not its end, nor its beginning, nor its existence. Cutting this ashvattha tree, with its well grown root, by the strong axe of non-attachment,*

206 I have now described to you this wonderful tree of worldly existence.
207 I have also fully explained to you those roots which grow downwards. Now listen to the way this tree can be uprooted.
208 You may wonder how it is possible to uproot such a great tree.
209 How can it be that the highest branches reach up to Brahma, and yet the roots are above in the formless Spirit?
210 The lowest branches reach down into the depths of inorganic matter, while other roots of humanity grow in the middle.
211 Who could destroy such a vast tree? But don't concern yourself with such an idle question.
212 Is any effort necessary to uproot this tree? One doesn't have to rush here and there to save a child from its fear of a ghost.
213 Does a person have to destroy castles in the clouds, break off the horns of a hare, or pick a flower growing in the sky?
214 In the same way, O Arjuna, this tree of existence has no reality, so why should you be anxious to uproot it?
215 My description of its network of roots and branches is like the description of a house full of the children of a barren woman.
216 When we wake up, of what use are the words we said in our dream? All talk of this tree is as meaningless as a fairy tale.
217 O Arjuna, this tree as I have described it is an illusion. It would be like serving a king

with ghee made from a tortoise's milk.

218 Ignorance, the root of the tree, is unreal. So how can its effects be real? How can the tree really exist?

219 Some say that the tree has no end, and in one sense this it is true.

220 If there were no waking, sleep would never end. If night didn't pass, there would be no dawn.

221 Similarly, O Arjuna, until discrimination arises, there will be no end to this tree of earthly existence.

222 It isn't incorrect to say that it has no beginning.

223 How can you ask who is the mother of a child who hasn't been born? How can something exist which doesn't have a beginning?

224 Then why consider the effort to uproot this tree, since it has neither beginning, end, existence, or form?

225 O Arjuna, this illusory tree thrives because of our ignorance, so strike it down with the sword of Self-knowledge.

226 If you use any other means except Self-knowledge, you will only become more deeply entangled in it.

227 How far will you wander up and down through branch after branch? Strike down ignorance with true knowledge.

228 Otherwise, you will be like a person weighed down with sticks he has collected to beat a rope which he thinks is a snake.

229 It would be like a person drowning in a river while he is running around a forest looking for a boat to cross over a mirage.

230 Similarly, O Arjuna, when a person strives to find a way to destroy this illusion of worldly life, his own true nature is hidden and he is overcome by frustration.

231 O Arjuna, the only remedy for a wound inflicted in a dream is to wake up. In this case, too, knowledge is the only weapon to destroy ignorance.

232 For the sword of knowledge to be effective, the mind must be governed by strong and enduring dispassion.

233 When a person develops dispassion, he will abandon the pleasures of the three worlds, just as a dog vomits its food.

234 O Arjuna, his dispassion must be so strong that he will feel disgusted with all worldly enjoyment.

235 Draw this sword from the sheath of egoism, and hold it in the hand of Self-knowledge.

236 Sharpen it on the stone of discrimination, give it a keen edge with the awareness of union with God, and polish it with perfect understanding.

237 Hold it firmly in the grip of determination, and observe it closely. Test it well in meditation.

238 When this sword of dispassion and the awareness of the Self become united in constant meditation, there will be nothing left to strike.

239 The sword of Self-knowledge, strengthened by the radiance of the belief in nonduality, will not allow this tree of existence to survive anywhere.

240 Then this tree will disappear, along with its whole network of branches and roots, just as a mirage vanishes in the moonlight.

241 Therefore, O Arjuna, strike down this tree of worldly existence with the sword of Self-knowledge.

ततः पदं तत् परिमार्गितव्यं
यस्मिन् गता न निवर्तन्ति भूयः ।
तम् एव चाद्यं पुरुषं प्रपद्ये
यतः प्रवृत्तिः प्रसृता पुराणी ॥

tataḥ padaṁ tat parimārgitavyaṁ
yasmin gatā na nivartanti bhūyaḥ
tam eva cādyaṁ puruṣaṁ prapadye
yataḥ pravṛttiḥ prasṛtā purāṇī

4. Then that goal is to be sought from which, having gone, no one returns. In that primal Spirit I take refuge, whence the primeval energy streamed forth.

242 Then a person feels a oneness with things which he formerly experienced as different from himself, and he becomes aware of his true nature.

243 Don't be like a fool who looks at his face in a mirror and sees two when there is only one.

244 In this way, I am telling you clearly how you should see yourself from the viewpoint of nonduality.

245 That which is seen without seeing and known without knowing is the Absolute, the primal Being.

246 The Vedas take their stand on limitation and strive to describe Him in long drawn-out sentences, speaking vainly of name and form.

247 Those who are weary of earthly and heav-

enly pleasures and who seek liberation set out to find Him, turning to yogic practice and knowledge, so they won't have to return to worldly existence.

248 Fleeing from attachment to worldly life in the boat of dispassion, they reach the shore of the Absolute and escape from the bonds of karma.

249 Shaking off all moods and egoism, the wise take a passport to their original home.

250 Ignorance of God has led to the false knowledge which has spread throughout the world, giving rise to the concept of duality.

251 From Him there develop these expanding worlds, which are like the empty hopes of an unlucky man.

252 O Arjuna, we should realize that God is our own Self, as though cold could shiver with its own coldness.

253 O Arjuna, there is another sign by which a person can recognize this state: once he attains it, there is no rebirth for him.

254 Those who are filled with the knowledge of the Self, like the fullness of the waters at the time of the final deluge, reach the state of the Supreme.

निर्मानमोहा जितसङ्गदोषा
अध्यात्मनित्या विनिवृत्तकामाः ।
द्वन्द्वैर् विमुक्ताः सुखदुःखसंज्ञैर्
गच्छन्त्य् अमूढाः पदम् अव्ययं तत् ॥

nirmānamohā jitasaṅgadoṣā
adhyātmanityā vinivṛttakāmāḥ
dvandvāir vimuktāḥ sukhaduḥkhasaṁjñāir
gacchanty amūḍhāḥ padam avyayaṁ tat

5. Without arrogance or delusion, with the evils of attachment conquered, dwelling constantly in the supreme Self, with desires turned away, released from the dualities known as pleasure and pain, the undeluded go to that imperishable goal.

255 Those people have freed their minds of all confusion, just as the clouds vanish from the sky at the end of the rainy season.

256 They have thrown off the grip of passion, just as the family of a hard-hearted man hates him when he is poverty-stricken.

257 Those who earnestly seek Self-realization turn away from all action, just as a plantain tree falls after it has borne fruit.

258 All desires leave them, just as birds fly away from a burning tree.

259 They are completely unaware of the concept of separateness, the soil from which all kinds of evil weeds sprout.

260 Egoism and ignorance leave them, just as night flees when the sun rises.

261 Just as a lifeless body suddenly releases the soul, the ignorance of duality departs from them.

262 For them, the sense of duality is like a famine. In the same way the touchstone destroys iron, and the sun and darkness cannot coexist.

263 The pairs of opposites such as pleasure and pain, which are experienced in earthly life, cannot exist in the presence of such beings.

264 When a man is awake, the dream that he had of possessing a kingdom doesn't make him happy, and his dream of death doesn't make him sad.

265 Such people cannot be caught up in experiences of pleasure or pain, which produce good and bad karma, just as an eagle cannot be grasped by a snake.

266 They are like royal swans, feeding on the milk of Self-knowledge, having separated it from the water of the non-Self.

267 Just as the sun, having poured down its radiance on the earth, draws it back into itself through its rays,

268 Similarly, the vision of the Self brings back into unity that one Spirit which appeared to be scattered everywhere in countless beings, because of confusion about its true nature.

269 Just as a river merges into the ocean, in the same way, in these people discrimination is absorbed into the certainty of Self-realization.

270 Those who have realized that the one Self exists in all have no more desires, just as the sky has no need to move from one place to another.

271 Just as seeds cannot germinate in a mountain of fire, similarly, no feeling can arise in their minds.

272 But why continue this any further? Sense objects are helpless before them, just as particles of dust are helpless before a strong wind.

273 Those who have sacrificed all their desires in the fire of wisdom are united with the fire, just as gold unites with gold in one ornament.

274 If you should ask where they go, I will tell you that they go where there is no loss.

275 It cannot be seen by the eye, it cannot be known, nor can it be described.

न तद् भासयते सूर्यो न शशाङ्को न पावकः ।
यद् गत्वा न निवर्तन्ते तद् धाम परमं मम ॥

na tad bhāsayate sūryo
na śaśāṅko na pāvakaḥ
yad gatvā na nivartante
tad dhāma paramaṁ mama

6. The sun does not illumine, nor the moon, nor fire, that place to which, having gone, no one returns; that is My supreme abode.

276 No flame can illumine That, neither can moonlight, nor the brilliance of the sun.

277 All things are seen by this light which itself is not seen. The world is illumined by its hidden light.

278 If a shell is covered with silver, it appears to be silver rather than a shell. If a rope is hidden under a snake, it appears to be a snake.

279 The light by which the sun, moon, and planets give forth their brightness, and even by whose darkness they shine,

280 That Supreme Being is light itself, active within all creatures. It also radiates in the heart of the sun and moon.

281 Compared with God's effulgence, the light of the sun and moon is darkness. The brilliance of all lights is the body of God.

282 In the light of That, the whole universe with all its suns and moons vanishes, just as the light of the moon and stars fades away when the sun rises.

283 In the same way, the images in a dream pass away when a person awakes and mirages disappear in the evening.

284 Understand that My main abode is that invisible place of the Supreme.

285 Those who have gone to that place never return, like the rivers which flow into the sea.

286 An elephant made of salt and placed in the sea can never resume its form.

287 Flames rising into the sky don't descend again, and water coming in contact with hot iron ceases to exist as water.

288 Similarly, those who reach union with Me through pure knowledge can never return to this world.

289 Hearing these words, Arjuna said, O Lord, I have a question. Please listen attentively.

290 Are those who attain union with You and don't return separate from You or one with you?

291 It is inconsistent to say that those who were originally separate from you don't return. Do bees that enter flowers ever become flowers?

292 Arrows that are separate from a target hit it and then fall away. In the same way, surely those who reach You will return.

293 But if they are one with You by nature, who merges into whom? Can a weapon pierce itself?

294 Therefore, it cannot be said that souls are either united with You or separate from You. Are the limbs separate from the body?

295 Those who are basically different from You can never become united with You. Then why is there any confusion as to whether they return or not?

296 O You who face in all directions, explain this to me. Who are those who don't return, once they have been united with you?

297 When he heard Arjuna's question and realized his intelligence, the Lord, the highest jewel of the wise, was delighted.

298 Then the Lord said, O Arjuna, among those who reach Me and don't return, there are two kinds of people: those who are one with Me and those who are separate from Me.

299 Although superficially they may seem to be different from Me, deeper insight will show that they are one with Me.

300 Waves on the surface of the ocean may seem to be different from the ocean, but they consist of the same water.

301 The gold in ornaments appears to be different from gold nuggets, yet when a person examines them, he sees that all are gold.

302 Similarly, O Arjuna, to the eye of wisdom, all beings are one with Me. This separateness arises from ignorance.

303 From the standpoint of reality, how can there be anything other than Me, the One? If there is, it arises from the duality of oneness and difference.

304 When the sunlight swallows up all space and pervades the world, how can its individual rays be separately distinguished?

305 O Arjuna, when the final deluge takes place at the end of an age, is it possible to distinguish separate streams? In the same way, can there be separate parts of Me, the changeless One?

306 When a river winds, its water appears to be bent. When the sun is reflected in water, it seems to be double.
307 Can you say that the firmament is either round or square? Yet it may be so when it is enclosed in a house or in a jar.
308 While a man is dreaming, he becomes a king. Doesn't he alone fill the whole world?
309 When gold is mixed with an alloy it loses some of its value, although the gold itself is still pure. In the same way, when I, the pure One, am surrounded by the illusion which I create, then ignorance predominates.
310 Because of this people wonder who I am, and they identify Me with the body.

ममैवांशो जीवलोके जीवभूत: सनातन: ।
मन:षष्ठानीन्द्रियाणि प्रकृतिस्थानि कर्षति ।।
mamāivāṁśo jīvaloke
jīvabhūtaḥ sanātanaḥ
manaḥ ṣaṣṭhānīndriyāṇī
prakṛtisthāni karṣati

7. Merely a fragment of Myself, becoming an eternal (individual) soul in the world of the living, draws to itself the senses, of which the sixth is the mind, that exist in material nature.

311 When knowledge of the Self is limited to the body, it seems that the Self is a part of Me.
312 When the sea rises in waves, driven by the wind, they appear to be small parts of it.
313 Similarly, O Arjuna, people think I am the individual soul giving life to the body and generating egoism.
314 All the visible activities which Consciousness produces are called the world of living beings.
315 The belief in the reality of birth and death is inherent in the world of living creatures.
316 You should understand that in this world I am like the moon: although it is reflected in water, the moon is unaffected by it.
317 O Arjuna, a crystal lying on a red powder seems to be red, but it isn't really so.
318 In the same way, although My eternal nature is never affected, nor is My unchanging state disturbed, through delusion people think I am the one who acts and experiences.
319 When the pure Spirit comes in contact with nature, it assumes the qualities that belong to nature.
320 It accepts as its own the mind, the senses, and their activities, and then the individual soul becomes involved in action.
321 Just as an ascetic dreams that he has a family, becomes deluded, and begins to engage in worldly activities,
322 Similarly, the Self forgets its true nature, imagines that it is matter, and serves it accordingly.
323 Seated in the vehicle of the mind and passing through the gateway of the ear, it finds itself in a forest of words.
324 Taking the bridle of matter, it enters the jungle of touch through the path of the skin.
325 At times it goes out through the doors of the eyes and wanders over the hills of sense objects.
326 O Arjuna, it passes along the path of the tongue and enters the valley of taste.
327 The Lord of the body strays into the desert of fragrance through the gate of the nose.
328 In this way it enjoys the senses, taking with it the mind, the leader of all the senses.

शरीरं यद् अवाप्नोति यच् चाप्य् उत्क्रामतीश्वर: ।
गृहीत्वैतानि संयाति वायुर् गन्धान् इवाशयात् ।।
śarīraṁ yad avāpnoti
yac cāpy utkrāmatīśvaraḥ
gṛhītvāitāni saṁyāti
vāyur gandhān ivāśayāt

8. When the Lord acquires a body, and also when He departs from it, He goes, taking them along, like the wind blowing perfumes from their source.

329 The Self appears to engage in action only when it possesses a body.
330 O Arjuna, just as a prince's way of life is known only when he begins to live in a palace,
331 Similarly, egoism and action increase, and sense pleasures run wild only when the Self enters a body. Know that this is true.
332 When it leaves the body, it carries all the senses away with it,
333 Just as puppets stop dancing when their strings are removed or just as a host's merit is destroyed if he insults a guest.
334 People's vision is carried away by the setting sun, and the fragrance of flowers is dispersed by the wind.
335 Similarly, O Arjuna, as the Self leaves the body, it takes with it the mind and the five senses.

श्रोत्रं चक्षुः स्पर्शनं च रसनं घ्राणम् एव च ।
अधिष्ठाय मनश्चायं विषयान् उपसेवते ।।

śrotraṁ cakṣuḥ sparśanaṁ ca
rasanaṁ ghrāṇam eva ca
adhiṣṭhāya manaścāyaṁ
viṣayān upasevate

9. Presiding over hearing, sight and touch, taste and smell, as well as the mind, He (i.e. the fragment of the Lord incarnated as the individual soul) enjoys the objects of the senses.

336 Whenever the Spirit enters a body, whether on earth or in heaven, it is endowed with a mind and the five senses.
337 O Arjuna, when a lamp is extinguished, it takes its light with it. When it is relit, it gives out light again.
338 But this process seems to take place only to the sight of the unenlightened, O Arjuna.
339 They believe that when the Spirit enters a body, it experiences sense pleasures; then it leaves the body.
340 Actually, birth, death, action, and enjoyment are functions of matter, not of the Self.

उत्क्रामन्तं स्थितं वापि भुञ्जानं वा गुणान्वितम् ।
विमूढा नानुपश्यन्ति पश्यन्ति ज्ञानचक्षुषः ।।

utkrāmantaṁ sthitaṁ vāpi
bhuñjānaṁ vā guṇānvitam
vimūḍhā nānupaśyanti
paśyanti jñānacakṣuṣah

10. When He departs, remains, or enjoys (sense objects) while accompanied by the qualities, the deluded do not perceive Him. Those with the eye of knowledge see Him.

यतन्तो योगिनश्चैनं पश्यन्त्य् आत्मन्य् अवस्थितम् ।
यतन्तो ऽप्य् अकृतात्मानो नैनं पश्यन्त्य् अचेतसः ।।

yatanto yoginaścāinaṁ
paśyanty ātmany avasthitam
yatanto 'py akṛtātmāno
nāinaṁ paśyanty acetasaḥ

11. The yogins, striving, see Him (the embodied fraction of the Lord) situated in the Self, but the unthinking, those of unperfected selves, strive but do not see Him.

341 As soon as a body is born and is endowed with consciousness, deluded people think that the Self has entered the body.
342 Furthermore, O Arjuna, when the senses become active in their own ways, people think that the Self experiences them.
343 When the body loses its ability to enjoy and dies, they say that the Spirit has gone because they cannot see it.
344 O Arjuna, could a person say that the wind is blowing only when a tree sways, and that when there is no tree there is no wind?
345 Should we think that we exist only when we see our reflection in a mirror, and that before then we didn't exist?
346 Or if the reflection is hidden, do we say that we no longer exist?
347 Although sound is a property of space, thunder is attributed to the clouds; and people think the moon makes the clouds move.
348 Similarly, those who are blinded by lack of discrimination attribute the birth and death of the body to the changeless Spirit.
349 There are others, though, who recognize that the soul is of God and the properties of life belong to the body.
350 With the eye of wisdom they see beyond the sheath of the body. Like the fierce rays of the sun in the hot season,
351 These wise beings are able to concentrate on God through the development of insight and to recognize the Spirit.
352 The firmament is full of countless stars, which are reflected in the sea; but this doesn't mean that the sky has fallen to pieces.
353 The sky is still the sky; it is the reflection that is unreal. In the same way, these people think that the Spirit is encased in the body.
354 The movement of a flowing stream is in the stream itself, and moonlight is constant within the moon.
355 Whether a pool is dry or full, the sun is still the same. Similarly, they recognize Me whether the body is born or dies.
356 Even though clay pots and people's houses are created and destroyed, the space that they enclose remains unchanged.
357 In the same way, the wise recognize as the eternal Spirit what the ignorant identify with the transitory body.
358 Through the recognition of the Self they know that the Spirit neither grows nor diminishes, neither acts nor promotes action.
359 Even if a person masters all knowledge, accounts for every particle of matter, and grasps all the scriptures,
360 He cannot reach Me, the all-pervasive One,

unless he develops dispassion.

361 O Arjuna, even if a person is filled with all knowledge, he can never reach Me, the purest of all beings, as long as he has any desire for pleasure in his heart.

362 Can a person free himself from the entanglement of worldly life with knowledge he acquires in a dream? Is handling books a substitute for reading them?

363 Could a blindfolded man smell the quality and value of pearls?

364 Similarly, as long as egoism remains in the heart, no one can reach Me, even by diligently studying the scriptures throughout innumerable lives.

365 I am He who pervades all living creatures. Listen while I explain to you this manifestation of Mine.

यद् ग्रादित्यगतं तेजो जगद् भासयते ऽखिलम् ।
यच् चन्द्रमसि यच् चाग्नौ तत् तेजो विद्धि मामकम् ।।
yad ādityagataṁ tejo
jagad bhāsayate 'khilam
yac candramasi yac cāgnau
tat tejo viddhi māmakam

12. That brilliance which resides in the sun, which illumines the entire universe, which is in the moon and which is in fire, know that brilliance to be Mine.

366 The brilliance of the sun that illumines the whole universe is eternally Mine.

367 O Arjuna, the light of the sun which dries up water and the light of the moon which sheds moisture both are Mine.

368 The heat of the fire which gives people warmth and cooks their food is also Mine.

गाम् ग्राविश्य च भूतानि धारयाम्य् ग्रहम् ग्रोजसा ।
पुष्णामि चौषधीः सर्वाः सोमो भूत्वा रसात्मकः ।।
gām āviśya ca bhūtāni
dhārayāmy aham ojasā
puṣṇāmi cāuṣadhīḥ sarvāḥ
somo bhūtvā rasātmakaḥ

13. Entering the earth, I support all beings with energy, and, having become the watery moon, I cause all the plants to thrive.

369 I have entered into the earth, and that is why its clods don't disintegrate in the waters of the ocean.

370 Because I am in the earth sustaining it, it can support the entire creation.

371 O Arjuna, I am the moon, a moving lake of nectar in the sky.

372 With moonbeams pouring down in limitless streams, I nourish all vegetation.

373 In this way, crops of all kinds of grain are produced that give food to every living creature.

ग्रहं वैश्वानरो भूत्वा प्राणिनां देहम् ग्राश्रितः ।
प्राणापानसमायुक्तः पचाम्य् ग्रन्नं चतुर्विधम् ।।
ahaṁ vāiśvānaro bhūtvā
prāṇināṁ deham āśritaḥ
prāṇāpānasamāyuktaḥ
pacāmy annaṁ caturvidham

14. Having become the digestive fire of all men, I abide in the body of all living beings; and joining with the prana and apana, I (digest) the four kinds of food.

374 How can the food produced in this way be digested, so that it may satisfy those who eat it?

375 For this purpose, O Arjuna, I have lit a fire around the navel of each living being, and I am that fire in the belly.

376 Fanning this fire with the bellows of the incoming and outgoing breaths, great quantities of food can be consumed in the belly day and night.

377 Whether food is dry or juicy, well cooked or burned, I digest the four kinds of food.

378 In this way I am all creatures, the life which supports them, and the inner fire which is the chief means of life.

379 How is it possible to describe the mystery of My all-pervasiveness? You should know that I am everywhere, and there is nothing else but Me anywhere.

380 Then how does it happen that some beings are always happy and others are miserable?

381 If the evening is illumined by only one lamp in an entire city, won't there be some who cannot see?

382 I will try to remove all doubt from your mind.

383 Though I am in all and this cannot be otherwise, each being realizes Me according to his own intelligence.

384 You are concerned about this. Listen. There is only one sound in space, yet different instruments are played which produce different notes.

385 Although there is only one sun which rises, it serves many different purposes as people go about their various activities.

386 For plants to grow, water is needed accord-

ing to the kind of seed. Similarly, My form develops in different ways in each creature.

387 A necklace of blue beads looks different to a wise person and to an ignorant one; it brings joy to the wise while the ignorant may think it is a snake.

388 Just as the water in the Swati constellation becomes pearls in a shell but is poison to a serpent, in the same way I am a source of joy for the wise and misery for the ignorant.

सर्वस्य चाहं हृदि संनिविष्टो
मत्तः स्मृतिर् ज्ञानम् अपोहनं च ।
वेदैश्च सर्वैर् अहम् एव वेद्यो
वेदान्तकृद् वेदविद् एव चाहम् ।।

sarvasya cāhaṁ hṛdi saṁniviṣṭo
mattaḥ smṛtir jñānam apohanaṁ ca
vedāiśca sarvāir aham eva vedyo
vedāntakṛd vedavid eva cāham

15. I have entered into the hearts of all beings; from Me come memory and knowledge, as well as their loss. I alone am that which is to be known in all the Vedas; I am the author of the Vedanta and the knower of the Vedas.

389 O Arjuna, I am truly that knowledge in the heart of each human being which makes him perpetually aware of his individuality.

390 But through the company of saints, the practice of yoga, the acquisition of knowledge, service of the Guru, and dispassion,

391 Ignorance completely disappears, and the individual soul finds rest in God.

392 When through Me he sees that I am his own Self, he is happy forever. Can this realization be attained through anyone else?

393 O Arjuna, when the sun rises, it is seen by means of its own light. In the same way, I am known through Myself.

394 On the other hand, if people associate with those who seek sense pleasures and listen only to the praises of worldly life, with their egoism centered in the body,

395 If they chase along the path of action after the enjoyments of this life and the next, they can only inherit great sorrow.

396 Nevertheless, O Arjuna, I Myself am the cause of this ignorance, just as a person is the cause of his own sleep and dreams.

397 It is daylight which makes people aware that the day is darkened by clouds. Similarly, I am the cause of that ignorance which makes people unaware of Me and makes them perceive sense objects.

398 O Arjuna, isn't it the waking state that causes us to be aware of sleep? Similarly, I am the root of both knowledge and ignorance in mankind.

399 O Arjuna, the Vedas, which have been divided into three branches, do not know Me as I am, but they strive to learn about Me.

400 But I, the pure One, am known in all the three branches, just as all rivers flowing from the east or the west empty into the ocean.

401 The Vedas with all their words culminate in the highest Truth, just as fragrance borne upward on the wind is lost in the sky.

402 When all the Vedas are lost in shame, then I reveal the Truth as it is.

403 I alone have knowledge of the Self, in which both the Vedas and the universe are finally absorbed.

404 When a person awakes from sleep, he knows that there was no one except himself in his dreams, and he realizes his own oneness.

405 I am aware of My oneness without duality, and I Myself bring about that awareness.

406 O Arjuna, when camphor is burned, neither soot nor fire remains.

407 Similarly, when the knowledge that destroys ignorance is itself absorbed, it is impossible to say whether there is anything or whether there isn't.

408 Who can catch that thief who has stolen the universe, leaving no trace? I am that pure state and that One.

409 After the Lord of heaven had explained in this way to Arjuna how he pervades all things, He ended His discourse.

410 This teaching was reflected in Arjuna's heart, just as the rising moon is mirrored on the ocean.

411 Just as a picture may be reflected on a wall in front of it, similarly the teachings of Lord Krishna were reflected in Arjuna.

412 The more a person realizes the knowledge of the Self, the greater is his joy. Therefore Arjuna, whose perception was deep, said to Krishna,

413 O You who are infinite, while explaining to me Your immanence in the universe, You have spoken from time to time of Your nature, which has no attributes.

414 I ask You now to explain this fully to me. Then Krishna replied, Your question is a good one.

415 O Arjuna, I am always delighted to explain this truth, but what can I do? I rarely find someone who asks Me.

416 Now that I have met you and you have questioned Me eagerly, My desire has been fulfilled.

417 You have helped Me to experience what can be enjoyed beyond unity. You have brought Me joy by asking about My true nature.

418 When a mirror is placed before a person, he sees himself reflected in it. In this way, you are the ideal partner in discussion.

419 O friend, there is no formality in this. You simply ask what you don't know, and I listen attentively.

420 With these words the Lord embraced Arjuna, and regarding him graciously said to him,

421 Your questions and My answers are as complementary as the two lips which produce speech, or the two feet which produce walking.

422 The two of us, you who ask and I who answer, should be considered as one.

423 Speaking in this way, the Lord was overcome by His great love for Arjuna, and He stood there embracing him. Then He became afraid that such an expression of feeling might be improper.

424 Just as sugarcane juice is spoiled by adding salt, in the same way the joy of this conversation would be spoiled by intimacy.

425 Just like Nara and Narayana, there is no separation between us, but this emotion which I feel must be restrained.

426 With this thought in mind, the Lord said, O Arjuna, what was your question?

427 Arjuna, who had been drawn into the Lord's consciousness, came to himself again. Then he began to listen to the answers to his questions.

428 Overcome with feeling, Arjuna said, My Lord and Master, I asked You to tell me about Your limitless nature.

429 At this, Krishna began to explain the condition of limitation in two ways.

430 If anyone were to wonder why He spoke of conditioned existence when He was asked about unconditioned existence, consider these examples:

431 When butter is to be extracted from milk, buttermilk must first be separated. To obtain pure gold, the alloy must first be removed.

432 When weeds are removed, pure water appears. When the clouds are blown away, the sky can be seen.

433 As soon as the husks are threshed and separated, the pure grain can be gathered.

434 Similarly, if a person reflects on it, once conditioned existence has been described, he needn't ask any further about the unconditioned.

435 A young bride, when asked to say her husband's name, will reject all other names; but when the forbidden name is mentioned, she reveals it by her silence.

436 By speaking first of what can be described rather than of what cannot, Krishna explained unconditioned existence.

437 A tree branch is used to describe the new moon on New Year's Day. Similarly, conditioned existence must first be described.

द्वाव् इमौ पुरुषौ लोके क्षरश्चाक्षर एव च ।
क्षरः सर्वाणि भूतानि कूटस्थो ऽक्षर उच्यते ॥

dvāv imāu puruṣāu loke
kṣaraścākṣara eva ca
kṣaraḥ sarvāṇi bhūtāni
kūṭastho 'kṣara ucyate

16. There are these two spirits in the world —the perishable and the imperishable. All beings are the perishable; the unchanging is called the imperishable.

438 The Lord continued, O Arjuna, there are only two inhabitants of this city of worldly life.

439 Just as day and night are the two occupants of the sky, in the same way there are only two in the city of this world.

440 There is still a third, but he cannot bear even the mention of the others' names. When he arrives, he destroys them along with the entire city.

441 Let us leave this till later. For now, listen to the description of the first two who have come to live in the city of this world.

442 One is blinded by ignorance, deranged, and crippled, and the other is healthy, and with his limbs intact. They have come together by living in this city.

443 The first one is called the perishable, and the other is the imperishable. These two possess the city of worldly existence.

444 Now I will clearly explain how the perishable and the imperishable are to be known.

445 O Arjuna, from the highest level of self-

consciousness down to the smallest blade of grass,

446 The large and the small, the movable and immovable, everything that is perceived by the mind and the intellect,

447 Everything composed of the five elements, all that has name and form and that is under the control of the three qualities,

448 Every form of living being, which is like a gold coin that time uses as a counter in his game of dice,

449 Everything that is understood through false knowledge, and everything that is created and lost in a moment,

450 That which builds the entire structure of matter with the forest of illusion, in fact, everything that is known as the universe,

451 That which has already been described as matter in all its forms, and what has been described as the field with its thirty-six divisions—

452 But why should I repeat here what I have already described using the metaphor of the tree—

453 Realizing that all these various forms are its dwelling, Consciousness has entered each of them.

454 Just as a lion, seeing his reflection in a well, is infuriated and leaps into the well,

455 Or as the sky is reflected in water, which originated from the sky, similarly, the non-dual Consciousness becomes dual.

456 O Arjuna, in the same way the Spirit, in the sleep of forgetfulness, regards the city of forms as His dwelling place.

457 Just as a person may see a bed in his dream and lie down on it, similarly, this city seems to the Spirit to be a bed.

458 Then he snores in deep sleep, thinking he is happy or miserable, and immersed in egoism he calls out,

459 Imagining that someone is his father, that someone else is his mother, that he is handsome, low, or blameless; or that he has a son, a wife, or wealth.

460 Carried away by these dreams and wandering through the jungle of earth and heaven, this aspect of Consciousness is known as the perishable man, O Arjuna.

461 Now listen to the description of the one that is called the Knower of the field, and the state of the individual soul.

462 The Self which sets aside Its own nature and takes on the form of living creatures is called the perishable One.

463 In His true nature He is perfect and is called Purusha. He is endowed with personality, and He dwells asleep in the city of the body.

464 Because He has taken on the limitations of life in the body, the quality of perishability has been falsely attributed to Him.

465 Because of these same limitations, He appears to be impermanent, just as the moon appears to move when its reflection is tossed about on the waves of the ocean.

466 When the waves subside, the reflection of the moon disappears. Similarly, when the limitations are destroyed, the limited Self is no longer apparent.

467 Thus through these limitations the idea of impermanence is attributed to Him, and because of this apparent defect He is called the perishable One.

468 Therefore, all individual souls are called perishable. Now I will explain the nature of the imperishable One.

469 O Arjuna, this other Purusha, the imperishable Self, stands in the middle just as Mount Meru is central among mountains.

470 Mount Meru is the same throughout the three levels: earth, the nether world, and heaven. Similarly, knowledge and ignorance are inseparable.

471 He is not perceived through right knowledge, nor is He considered dual through false knowledge. His true nature is found in the absence of all knowing.

472 He is the intermediate state, just as a clod of earth is neither the original dust nor the vessels made from it.

473 When the water of the sea dries up, neither water nor waves remain. In the same way, this imperishable One exists in a state which has no form.

474 O Arjuna, it is like the frontier of sleep, when a person is neither awake nor dreaming.

475 The imperishable One is like a state of non-perception, just as when the world passes away but realization of the Self hasn't yet been awakened.

476 On the new moon day, the various phases of the moon are invisible, and yet the moon itself remains. The imperishable One can be regarded in this way.

477 Just as the life of a tree lies latent in the seed

of the ripe fruit, similarly, this state emerges after all limitations have been destroyed.
478 Thus the state which infuses the conditioned existence of all beings is called the unmanifest.
479 Vedanta speaks of this state as the seed state, and the imperishable One dwells in this.
480 From this state, false knowledge spreads out into the waking and dream states and enters the jungle of the multiplicity of forms.
481 O Arjuna, the imperishable One is that from which the individual soul comes forth, creating the universe; and it is also That which causes them both to pass away.
482 The other, the perishable One, is active in the waking and dream states, conditions to which He himself gave birth.
483 But that state of deep sleep in ignorance falls short of the state of union with God.
484 O Arjuna if this weren't so, and if consciousness didn't return to the waking and dream states, this state of deep sleep might be identified with absorption in God.
485 However, both Spirit and matter are clouds in the sky of deep sleep, and the field and the Knower of the field are only phenomena perceived in the dream state.
486 In short, the imperishable One is the root of the tree of worldly existence with its downward-growing branches.
487 He is called the imperishable One because he lies in deep sleep in the city of illusion.
488 This state is called deep sleep because in it there are no changing moods and no false knowledge.
489 This condition doesn't pass away of itself, nor can it be destroyed without knowledge.
490 For this reason, the great philosophy of Vedanta calls it imperishable.
491 You should know that this imperishable One is the cause of individual life, characterized by illusion.
492 The two states of false knowledge, waking and dreaming, are absorbed into that dark ignorance.
493 That ignorance also becomes absorbed into true knowledge and dies out, just as fire dies out when it has consumed all the fuel.
494 In this way, when knowledge dispels ignorance, and that knowledge ends in the realization of the one Reality, pure Consciousness remains without any way to perceive it.

उत्तमः पुरुषस् त्व् अन्यः परमात्मेत्य् उदाहृतः।
यो लोकत्रयम् आविश्य बिभर्त्य् अव्यय ईश्वरः॥

uttamaḥ puruṣas tv anyaḥ
paramātmety udāhṛtaḥ
yo lokatrayam āviśya
bibharty avyaya īśvaraḥ

17. But the highest Spirit is another, called the supreme Self, who, entering the three worlds as the eternal Lord, supports them.

495 That is the highest state, the third, which is different from the other two that have already been described.
496 Just as the waking state is different from the states of dreaming and deep sleep,
497 Just as the sun is different from its rays or the mirage they cause, similarly, this highest state is different from the others.
498 It is different from both the perishable and the imperishable, just as fire is different from the fuel it consumes.
499 When the deluge takes place at the end of the world, the oceans overflow their boundaries and all are merged in one great ocean.
500 Just as day and night are swallowed up in the blaze of the final conflagration, neither deep sleep, dreaming, nor waking exist.
501 Here it isn't even known whether unity or duality exist or not. All perception is lost.
502 This is the highest state, known as the supreme Spirit.
503 O Arjuna, the individual soul calls Him by this name because here there can be no such thing as union with Him. Just as a person standing on the riverbank can speak about someone else who has drowned in the water,
504 Similarly, O Arjuna, the Vedas, being the bank of thought, can speak of what is near and what is far.
505 On this side of the Spirit are the perishable and imperishable states. What is beyond these is called the highest Self.
506 O Arjuna, you should know that God and the supreme Spirit are the same.
507 Here all speech becomes silence, knowledge is merely ignorance, and existence and nonexistence are one. Such is the one Reality.
508 Here even the awareness of oneness with the Supreme fades away, the speaker and the spoken merge, and the seer and the seen become one.

509 Though a person cannot see the light which is between the sun and its reflection, he cannot say that it doesn't exist.
510 He cannot deny that fragrance passes between a flower and his nose, even though it isn't visible.
511 When both the seer and the seen are lost, who can say what is or is not? In this realization, one can know the nature of the Self.
512 He is light which is illumined by no other. He is the Lord of all, controlled by none, and He fills all space with His own nature.
513 He is the sound which produces all other sounds, the essence of taste, and the delight with which pleasure is experienced.
514 He is joy added to joy, the luster in all that is lustrous, and the great void in which all space is lost.
515 He is the Supreme Being, the culmination of perfection, the haven of rest of the peaceful.
516 He remains after the creation of the universe, and survives in His perfection after it has been swallowed up. He is greater than all things.
517 He is like mother-of-pearl, which looks like silver to those who don't know its nature.
518 Although the gold in jewelry isn't hidden it isn't recognized as gold. Similarly, He sustains the universe although He is not the universe.
519 Just as water and waves aren't different from each other, in the same way, He is the existence and the light that penetrate the world.
520 O Arjuna, His nature causes both the expansion and the contraction of the universe, just as the moon reflected in water appears to increase and decrease.
521 He doesn't come into being when the universe is created, nor does He perish when it passes away, just as the sun isn't different by day and by night.
522 In this way, He can never be measured or compared with anyone. He can only be compared with Himself.

यस्मात् क्षरम् अतीतो ऽहम् अक्षराद् अपि चोत्तमः ।
अतो ऽस्मि लोके वेदे च प्रथितः पुरुषोत्तमः ॥

yasmāt kṣaram atīto 'ham
akṣarād api cottamaḥ
ato 'smi loke vede ca
prathitaḥ puruṣottamaḥ

18. Since I transcend the perishable and am higher than the imperishable, therefore I am, in the world, and in the Vedas, celebrated as the supreme Spirit.

523 O Arjuna, what more can I say? I am self-illumined and without a second,
524 Beyond limitation, the Supreme beyond both the perishable and the imperishable. Therefore, the Vedas call Me the Supreme Being.

यो माम् एवम् असंमूढो जानाति पुरुषोत्तमम् ।
स सर्वविद् भजति मां सर्वभावेन भारत ॥

yo mām evam asaṁmūḍho
jānāti puruṣottamam
sa sarvavid bhajati māṁ
sarvabhāvena bhārata

19. He who, thus undeluded, knows Me as the supreme Spirit, he, all-knowing, worships Me with his whole being, Arjuna.

525 In short, O Arjuna, the person in whom the sun of knowledge has risen knows that I am the Supreme Being.
526 When a person wakes from sleep, his dream vanishes. Similarly, when he attains knowledge, he knows the world is an illusion.
527 When a man picks up a garland, the delusion that it is a serpent disappears. In the same way, true perception of Me destroys all illusion.
528 If a person recognizes that ornaments are gold, he is not deluded by their shape as ornaments. Similarly, when I am known, the sense of duality passes away.
529 Then the person who knows he is one with Me exclaims, I am the self-manifested One who is existence, consciousness, and bliss!
530 When the sense of duality has left, it is inadequate even to say that he knows all that is.
531 O Arjuna, only such a person is worthy to worship Me, just as the sky alone can embrace the sky.
532 Only the Milky Ocean can provide a feast for the Milky Ocean. Only nectar can be blended with nectar.
533 Only pure gold can be mixed with pure gold. Similarly, only when a person is united with Me is he fit to worship Me.
534 If the Ganges were different from the ocean, how could its waters merge into the ocean? Similarly, how can one who isn't united with Me worship me?
535 Listen, O Arjuna! A person who worships

Me isn't different from Me, just as waves aren't different from the sea.

536 There is no difference between the sun and its brilliance. Similarly, such a person's worship should be considered worthy.

इति गुह्यतमं शास्त्रम् इदम् उक्तं मया ऽनघ ।
एतद् बद्ध्वा बुद्धिमान् स्यात् कृतकृत्यश्च भारत ॥
iti guhyatamaṁ śāstram
idam uktaṁ mayā 'nagha
etad buddhvā buddhimān syāt
krtakṛtyaśca bhārata

20. Thus this most secret doctrine has been taught by Me, O Arjuna; having awakened to this, a man becomes wise and fulfills all his duties, Arjuna.

537 Everything that I have related from the beginning is like the fragrance of the lotus petals of the ten Upanishads, and can only be understood by studying the scriptures.

538 The *Gita* is the purest essence of the milk of the Vedas, which I have churned out with the help of the sage Vyasa's intellect.

539 It is the Ganges of the nectar of wisdom, the seventeenth digit of the moon of bliss, and Lakshmi rising from the Milky Ocean in the form of thought.

540 It cannot be known except through Me. I am the life in its meaning and in each syllable and word.

541 These two, the perishable and the imperishable, approached Lakshmi, but she rejected them and gave everything to Me, the Supreme Being.

542 So this *Gita* which you have just heard is My devoted bride in this world.

543 Truly, it isn't a learned science but a weapon with which to conquer this worldly existence, and its words are the mystic means by which it unveils the Spirit.

544 O Arjuna, the *Gita* that I have taught you is My hidden wealth. I have brought it out for your sake.

545 O Arjuna, with your devotion to Me you have become the sage Gautama, drawing out of My head, as from Shiva, the Ganges of My secret treasure.

546 O Arjuna, you have made Me a mirror in which you can clearly see your whole nature before you.

547 Just as the moon and stars fill the sky and they also fill the ocean with their reflection, in the same way you have drawn Me into your heart with the *Gita*.

548 Having cleansed yourself from the impurity of sin, you have become a dwelling fit for Me and for the *Gita*.

549 What more can I say? The *Gita* is the blossoming vine of My wisdom. He who knows it is freed from all deception.

550 O Arjuna, just as the river of nectar removes all a person's diseases and makes him immortal,

551 Similarly, when he understands the *Gita*, it will not only remove all his delusion, but through Self-realization it will unite him with Me.

552 In the state of Self-realization, all karma is dissolved and passes away forever.

553 O Arjuna, when something that was lost is found, the search ends. When knowledge is attained, it rises to the pinnacle of the temple of action.

554 Therefore, all action ceases for the enlightened being, said Krishna, the friend of the helpless.

555 The nectar of Lord Krishna's words flooded Arjuna's heart, and through Vyasa's kindness Sanjaya received it.

556 Sanjaya gave this to Dhritarashtra to drink so he wouldn't be burdened with confusion at the end of his days.

557 When he heard the *Gita* he felt unworthy of it, but at the end he found enlightenment.

558 When a grapevine is watered with milk it seems to be wasteful, but it causes the vine to bear abundant fruit.

559 Sanjaya reverently told Dhritarashtra the words spoken by Lord Krishna, and the blind king finally became happy.

560 With my limited understanding, I have explained these things as clearly as possible in Marathi.

561 When those who lack understanding see the shevanti plant they are unimpressed, but the bee which sucks its honey knows its fragrance.

562 Similarly, you should accept whatever appeals to you and return to me whatever you find deficient, for ignorance is a natural characteristic of a child.

563 A child's parents take endless delight in it and caress it although it has no knowledge.

564 In the same way, you saints are my parents, and when you see me you should treat me lovingly. Accept this book as a token of my

love for you.

565 Jnanadeva says, O Nivrittinath, my Guru, soul of the universe, accept my worship in the form of these words.

16

THE YOGA OF THE DISTINCTION BETWEEN THE DIVINE AND THE DEMONIACAL

HAIL to the Guru, that resplendent sun which has risen, dispelling the illusion of the universe and causing the lotus of nonduality to unfold its petals!

2 He swallows up the night of ignorance, removes the illusion of knowledge and ignorance, and brings in the day of enlightenment for the wise.

3 At the dawning of the day, the eyes of Self-knowledge are opened, and birds in the form of individual souls leave their nests of identification with the body.

4 As he rises, the bee of Consciousness, held in the lotus of the subtle body, gains its freedom.

5 On the opposite banks of the river of duality, which springs from the conflicting teachings of the scriptures, intellect and understanding cry out like a pair of geese in the distress of their separation.

6 This light of the world, set in the firmament of Consciousness, brings to them the consolation of union.

7 At the rising of the sun, the dark night of thieves passes away, and traveling yogis set out on the path of spiritual experience.

8 Touched by its rays of discrimination, the sparks of the sun-crystal of intellect burst into flames and consume the forests of worldly existence.

9 His scorching rays settle in the desert of the Self, and the mirage of psychic powers arises.

10 When this sun reaches its zenith of Self-knowledge and shines in the noontide of union with God, it hides itself in the shadow of delusion concerning the nature of the individual soul.

11 When the night of illusion has faded away, who will remember the sleep of wrong understanding, with its dreamlike delusion of the universe?

12 In the city of unity-awareness, the market is surfeited with bliss, and then dealings in worldly pleasures fall away.

13 His glory gives perpetual light to the experience of the highest bliss of a liberated being.

14 When this great sovereign of the sky rises forever, the cycle of rising and setting disappears along with the four quarters of the earth.

15 Both appearance and disappearance vanish; and God, who was concealed beneath outer forms, is revealed. What more is there to say? This dawn is beyond description.

16 Who can see that sun of knowledge which is beyond day and night, which is self-illumined and sheds abundant light?

17 To Nivritti, that sun of Consciousness, I bow again and again. There are no words which can express his praises.

18 When one considers the greatness of the deity, the praise is sublime only if the praiser and the praised are merged with it into one.

19 He is known only through not knowing, he is described only in silence, and he is brought to us only when we become nothing.

20 In praise of him, the four stages of speech—*para*, *pashyanti*, *madhyama*, and *vaikhari*—are powerless.

21 I, your servant, humbly adorn you with the jewel of my hymn. Even though it is inadequate, accept it, O joy of union!

22 A beggar, finding a sea of nectar, doesn't realize what is appropriate and hastens to offer it a meal of vegetables.

23 The offering of vegetables should be appreciated, but the eagerness with which it is given is the real value. When a person wor-

ships the sun with a tiny lamp, it is his intense devotion which we should consider.

24 If a child knew everything that was right, what would childhood mean? But its mother delights in it because of its childishness.

25 If drainwater were to flow into the Ganges, would the river refuse to receive it?

26 How great was the offense that Bhrigu committed! Yet Krishna accepted it gladly as a blessing.

27 If the sky filled with clouds appeared in the presence of the lord of the day, would he tell it to move away?

28 Bear with me, O Master, if in the language of duality I have weighed you on the scale of comparison with the sun,

29 You whom yogis perceive with the eye of meditation, and whom the Vedas praise! What you have suffered in this, make me also suffer the same thing.

30 Today I have delighted in praising your merits, so don't blame me. Do what you will; I won't stop until I am fully satisfied with this feast of praise.

31 I have been allowed to describe the sweet nectar of your grace in the form of the *Gita*, and in this way my good fortune has doubled.

32 My tongue must have practiced the penance of right speech throughout many lives. The fruit of this is that I have come to possess this great island of the *Gita*, O Lord.

33 I must have performed very special deeds of merit, for I am set free by being allowed to describe your virtues.

34 In the forest of this life, I was caught in the village of death. Today that adversity has totally disappeared.

35 I have been permitted to describe your fame, which is known as the *Gita* and which has conquered ignorance.

36 If great prosperity comes to dwell in the house of a poor man, should he be called poor?

37 If the sun were to enter the house of darkness, wouldn't that darkness become the light of the world?

38 Although the universe is a mere speck compared with the greatness of God, don't His devotees receive according to their devotion?

39 My explanation of the *Gita* is like an attempt to smell a flower in the sky, but you with your power have fulfilled my desire.

40 Jnanadeva says, O my Master, by your grace I will clearly explain the deep verses of the *Gita*.

41 In the fifteenth chapter, Krishna explained to Arjuna the whole doctrine of the *Gita*.

42 Just as a good physician diagnoses an illness, in the same way the Lord described the entire world of conditioned existence by the illustration of the ashwattha tree.

43 He spoke of the imperishable, the highest Spirit, as the Supreme Being; and at the same time he showed how Consciousness is connected with matter.

44 Afterwards, the Lord explained the true nature of the universal Self by speaking of it as the Supreme Being.

45 Then He spoke clearly of that strong inner wisdom, the means of Self-realization.

46 So in this chapter there remains no topic for discussion, except that mutual love of the Guru and his disciple.

47 This has been explained fully to the wise, but seekers of liberation still search for understanding.

48 O wise Arjuna, if a person through knowledge reaches Me, the Supreme Being, he knows all things and is the summit of devotion.

49 The Lord of the three worlds said this in a verse in the last chapter, and there He described knowledge at length and with great joy.

50 While a person renounces the pleasures of this world, he should realize the Supreme Being. Then he will sit on the throne of supreme joy.

51 There is no other means to reach this high state, said the Lord, and right understanding is the supreme method.

52 Now all the seekers of knowledge were delighted and reverently offered their salutations with uplifted hearts.

53 Because of the nature of love, the beloved is constantly in the mind of the lover.

54 Therefore, until seekers of knowledge have truly experienced it, they are preoccupied with the question of how to obtain it and how to preserve it.

55 They know how to make this knowledge their own and how to increase it.

56 They also want to find out what prevents them from attaining it, or what works against this knowledge, leading it into the wrong

path.
57 A person should avoid everything that prevents it from arising, and faithfully keep in mind everything that promotes it.
58 Now Lord Krishna will resume His explanation, so that the desire which you seekers have in your minds may be fulfilled.
59 He will now describe the divine wealth that causes right knowledge to take birth and how your peace may increase.
60 The source of good and evil actions lies in these two forces. This subject has already been discussed in the ninth chapter.
61 This explanation should properly have been given there, but another subject intervened. The Lord will now proceed with this matter.
62 According to the arrangement of what has gone before, this chapter should be considered the sixteenth.
63 I have said enough about that. These two forms of wealth are able either to promote knowledge or to hinder it.
64 Now listen first to the description of that divine force which helps people along the path of knowledge, and which is the lamp of dharma in the night of confusion.
65 When one thing helps another, and when all meet together in a group, this is what people call wealth.
66 That force which produces spiritual happiness and supports the divine qualities is called divine wealth.

श्रीभगवान् उवाच । *śrībhagavān uvāca*

अभयं सत्त्वसंशुद्धिर् ज्ञानयोगव्यवस्थितिः ।
दानं दमश्च यज्ञश्च स्वाध्यायस् तप आर्जवम् ॥

abhayaṁ sattvasaṁśuddhir
jñānayogavyavasthitiḥ
dānaṁ damaśca yajñaśca
svādhyāyas tapa ārjavam

The Blessed Lord spoke:
1. Fearlessness, purity of being, perseverance in yoga and knowledge, giving, self-restraint and sacrifice, study of sacred texts, austerity, and uprightness,

67 Now, of all these divine qualities, fearlessness holds the highest place. Listen to what it is.
68 A person who doesn't leap into a flood has no fear of drowning, nor does he dread illness if he lives a temperate life.
69 Similarly, the person who doesn't allow egoism to arise in connection with good and bad actions, who abandons the anxieties of worldly life,
70 And who knows that all others are one with him through his realization of nonduality, casts out all fear.
71 When salt is thrown into water, it becomes one with the water. Similarly, he who realizes his unity with everything destroys fear.
72 O Beloved, this is what is called fearlessness. You should know that it is the servant of true perception.
73 Now learn about purity of understanding, which is recognized by the following signs: like embers that are neither burning nor extinguished,
74 Or like the subtle form of the moon immediately preceding the day of the new moon, so is true perception.
75 When the rainy season is over and the hot season hasn't yet begun, the form of a river becomes visible.
76 In the same way, when the force of desire and doubt has come to an end and the burden of passion and darkness has been removed, there remains only that understanding which loves to experience its own true nature.
77 This kind of understanding remains undisturbed, however much the senses may tempt it with pleasant or unpleasant objects.
78 When the husband of a devoted wife leaves her, she is troubled by the separation and doesn't notice what gain or loss may come to her.
79 In the same way, the understanding which continuously delights in the Self is called pure.
80 Now, devote all your desire to attaining Self-realization, whether you choose the path of knowledge or the path of yoga.
81 Apply your whole mind to it, just as a detached person offers a full oblation to the sacrificial fire.
82 Just as when a man of noble birth gives his daughter in marriage to another noble family, or when Lakshmi becomes the bride of Vishnu,
83 Similarly, when a person attains his goal of union through yoga or knowledge, he knows steadfastness, said Lord Krishna.
84 One who never avoids another in distress,

even if he is an enemy, but helps him in word, deed, thought, and with all his wealth,

85 Just as a tree withholds nothing from a traveler, neither its flowers, fruit, shade, leaves, nor roots, O Arjuna,

86 Such a person goes to help someone in trouble, when the occasion arises, and will offer him everything, from his heart to his worldly wealth.

87 This is called charity, the magic lotion that grants the vision of liberation. Now listen to the characteristics of self-control.

88 This quality destroys the union of the sense organs with their objects, separating them from each other just as alum clarifies muddy water.

89 The person who is self-controlled doesn't permit the wind of sense objects to blow through the gateways of his senses, but binds them with self-restraint and hands them over to discipline.

90 He lights the fire of dispassion at all the ten gates of his body, causing all tendencies to turn back into the recesses of his mind.

91 He observes many vows more severe than breath control, and though he zealously practices them day and night, he isn't satisfied.

92 This is known as self-control. Now I will briefly explain the meaning of sacrifice.

93 At the highest level are the brahmins, and at the lowest are women and *shudras*. Others are in between, each caste with its own special status.

94 Each one should faithfully follow the form of worship prescribed for him, according to what is best for him.

95 The brahmin performs the proper rites while the *shudra* salutes him, and in this way they both reap the benefits of their respective sacrifice.

96 Similarly, each person performs sacrifice in his own way according to his status, but he shouldn't desire the fruits of it.

97 Moreover, he shouldn't allow the thought that he is the doer to enter his mind through the door of egoism. He must be present and the sacrifice must be carried out according to the prescribed Vedic rites.

98 O Arjuna, you should understand that this is the meaning of the word sacrifice. Krishna, Master of the knowledge of the path of liberation, spoke in this way.

99 A person throws a ball to the ground so it can return to his hand. He sows seed in a field to reap a crop.

100 He lights a lamp to see what is hidden, and he waters the roots of a tree so it will give forth branches and fruit.

101 If he wants to see his reflection in a mirror, he must clean it often.

102 Similarly, in order to realize the Divine, a person should constantly study the Vedas.

103 In order to reach the supreme Self, the twice-born should study the Brahma Sutras, while others may study hymns or repeat the divine names.

104 O Arjuna, this is what is meant by the study of Vedas.

105 Charity means giving all that one has. To keep one's wealth leads to death. A plant bears its fruit and then dies.

106 Charity should be given in the same way as incense is burned up in fire, as impure gold loses weight when it is heated, or as the moon wanes in the dark half of the month when the spirits of the ancestors feed on it.

107 O Arjuna, austerity is the state in which the vital force, the senses, and the body are mortified in order to attain the Self.

108 It is like the swan thrusting its beak into milk to separate it from the water.

109 In the same way, austerity is differentiating the body from the Self as soon as a person is born, and thus awakening discrimination in his heart.

110 When a person turns within towards the Self, the activity of reason is restricted, just as dreams vanish on waking.

111 O Arjuna, when discrimination is focused on the Self, that is true austerity.

112 Uprightness is kindness towards every living thing, just as Consciousness is inherent in all creatures and as mother's milk is essential for all infants.

अहिंसा सत्यम् अक्रोधस् त्यागः शान्तिर् अपैशुनम् ।
दया भूतेषु अलोलुप्त्वं मार्दवं ह्रीर् अचापलम् ॥

ahiṁsā satyam akrodhas
tyāgaḥ śāntir apāiśunam
dayā bhūteṣv aloluptvaṁ
mārdavaṁ hrīr acāpalam

2. Non-violence, truth, absence of anger, renunciation, serenity, absence of calumny, compassion for all beings, freedom from desire, gentleness, modesty, absence of fickleness,

113 Harmlessness is shown by using one's body, speech, and mind for the good of the world.

114 A jasmine bud has a sharp point, yet it is soft. Moonbeams give light though they are cool.

115 Although medicine can cure disease, at the same time it has a bitter taste. To what can it be compared?

116 Water is so soft that it may touch the eye without damaging it, yet it can break up rocks.

117 True speech is sharper than a sword when it comes to resolving doubts, but it brings sweetness to the ears.

118 When listening to it, the ears long for mouths with which to taste it; yet by the power of its integrity, it can even pierce the Absolute.

119 No one is deceived by its sweetness, nor is anyone hurt by it.

120 A hunter's music is pleasing to the ear, yet it is a threat. Fire burns openly, but shame on the kind of speech that hurts!

121 That speech which charms the ear while its meaning wounds the listener's heart isn't sweet, but demonic.

122 A mother pretends to be angry when her children do wrong, but otherwise she is as tender as a flower.

123 Similarly, that speech which both brings joy to the listener and results in good conduct is known as truth.

124 A stone will never send forth a shoot even though it is watered, nor can butter be produced by churning rice water.

125 Striking the head of a sloughed snake skin won't make it spread its hood, nor can spring flowers ever grow in the sky.

126 Even Rambha's beauty couldn't arouse passion in Shuka, nor can ashes rise in flames even if ghee is poured on them.

127 Even if such a person were assailed by curses which would enrage young men,

128 Yet, O Arjuna, he wouldn't be filled with anger, just as a man whose life is over can't be revived even by falling at the feet of the creator.

129 This state of mind is called freedom from anger, said Krishna.

130 A jar is destroyed by breaking up the clay of which it is made, a piece of cloth by tearing apart the threads of which it is woven, and a tree by destroying its seed.

131 A painting is spoiled by ruining the canvas on which it is painted, and dreams vanish when sleep comes to an end.

132 Waves disappear when water dries up, clouds pass away when the rainy season ends, and enjoyment ceases when wealth is renounced.

133 In the same way, wise people should give up all sense of individuality; then they can abandon attachment to worldly affairs.

134 This is what is called renunciation, said the Lord. Accepting this teaching, Arjuna then said,

135 Please explain to me the characteristics of tranquility. The Lord replied, Listen carefully to Me.

136 Tranquility is that state in which knowledge is attained, and then both the knower and the known cease to exist.

137 When the final deluge engulfs the entire universe, it alone remains.

138 When neither rivers, their currents, nor the ocean into which they flow exist any longer, who is there to be aware that everything has become water?

139 Similarly, O Arjuna, when knowledge is attained and the process of knowing ceases, the state which remains is called tranquility.

140 When a patient is tormented by a disease, a good physician isn't concerned about whether he is a stranger until after the patient has recovered.

141 When a cow is stuck in the mud, a person is anxious for her and doesn't consider whether she gives milk or not.

142 A compassionate person will save the life of a drowning man without asking first whether he is of a high or low caste.

143 A good man who finds a naked woman in a forest doesn't look at her until he has clothed her.

144 Also, to those who are suffering from ignorance and error, who are cursed with an evil fate, or held down by vulgarity,

145 A good person gives all that he has to remove the distress that torments them.

146 He looks at them only after he has cleansed them with his own pure glance.

147 Just as a god should be seen only after being worshiped, as a person must sow his field before he can reap, and he must satisfy a guest before asking him for a blessing,

148 In the same way, a good person looks upon

unfortunate people only after he has removed all their faults with his own virtues.

149 Moreover, he won't hurt anyone's feelings or lead anyone into evil ways, nor will he refer to a person's faults.

150 He will raise up those who have fallen and won't wound their hearts.

151 O Arjuna, he won't make comparisons between high and low, nor call anyone evil.

152 This is known as absence of fault-finding, and it is an excellent way to seek liberation.

153 Now I will explain compassion. It is like the full moon that bestows its cooling rays on high and low without distinction.

154 When a compassionate person relieves someone's distress out of pity, he doesn't take his status into account.

155 He acts in this world like water that pours itself out to save the life of dying plants.

156 He is moved by compassion for those in distress and considers it a small thing to give himself to their aid.

157 Just as water cannot flow on without filling a hole that lies in its path, he cannot pass by without refreshing a weary person he meets.

158 He is tormented by the sufferings of others, just as a person feels pain when a thorn has pierced his foot.

159 Just as when a person's feet are cooled his eyes are also refreshed, in the same way he always rejoices in others' happiness.

160 Just as the purpose of water is to quench thirst, similarly, the purpose of his life is to help those in distress.

161 O Arjuna, such a person is kindness incarnate. I consider Myself indebted to him, for all compassion springs from him.

162 A lotus faithfully responds to the sun, but the sun doesn't receive its fragrance.

163 During springtime all the wealth of a forest assembles like an army, but the season passes without taking any part in it.

164 Although Lakshmi approaches with all her magical powers, the great Vishnu disregards her.

165 Even if all earthly and heavenly pleasures were the servant of this person's desire, still he wouldn't long for them.

166 His heart has no desire for sense objects. This is called freedom from desire.

167 Just as a hive is a bee's haven, as water is a refuge to the animals that live in it, as birds are free in the sky,

168 As a mother's love is focused on her child, as the wind is gentle in spring,

169 As the beloved is dear to the eye, and as the sight of a mother tortoise delights her brood, similarly, a desireless person is tender-hearted towards all creatures.

170 Camphor is soft to the touch, pleasant to taste, fragrant to smell, and pure when applied to the body.

171 If it weren't harmful when eaten, one could compare it to tenderness.

172 The tender-hearted person is like the sky, which holds all the elements and yet is contained in the tiniest atom.

173 What can I say? He lives only for the creatures of the world. This is what I called tenderness of heart.

174 A king would be overcome with shame if he were defeated in battle, and a self-respecting person would be distressed if he did something mean.

175 An ascetic would feel humiliated if he entered the home of an outcaste out of lust for a woman.

176 Running away from the battlefield is a disgrace for a warrior, and a devoted wife would be appalled if she were addressed as a widow.

177 If a person were attacked by leprosy he would consider it a reproach, and if a respectable person were slandered he would consider it a humiliation worse than death.

178 Having to live like a corpse in a body and from time to time being born, dying, and being reborn,

179 Being molded into a body through all the processes of pregnancy and birth,

180 A pure-minded person thinks that nothing is more shameful than having a name and a form in a human body.

181 Such a person, in these evil conditions, is disgusted with the body; yet to the shameless it is a delight.

182 Just as a puppet cannot move when its strings are broken, similarly, the activity of the sense organs ceases when the breath fails.

183 When the sun sets its rays are withdrawn; similarly, when mental control is lost the organs of perception no longer function.

184 In the same way if the mind and breath are restrained, all the ten sense organs lose their power. You should know that this is cessation of activity.

तेजः क्षमा धृतिः शौचम् अद्रोहो नातिमानिता ।

भवन्ति संपदं दैवीम् अभिजातस्य भारत ।।

tejaḥ kṣamā dhṛtiḥ śāucam
adroho nātimānitā
bhavanti saṁpadaṁ dāivīm
abhijātasya bhārata

3. Vigor, forgiveness, fortitude, purity, freedom from malice, freedom from pride; these are the endowment of those born to a divine destiny, Arjuna.

185 If some evil as bad as death itself should befall a widow about to mount her husband's funeral pyre, she would consider it as nothing for her husband's sake.

186 In the same way, a person will hurry along the narrow path to the Absolute with great resolution, destroying all obstacles in the form of poisonous sense objects.

187 He pays no attention to religious injunctions or prohibitions; neither do psychic powers have any attraction for him.

188 In this way his mind turns naturally towards the Supreme. This is called spiritual light.

189 When a person lacks the pride that he is able to bear all things, just as the body is unaware of carrying the hair that grows on it, this is called patience.

190 Even if the force of the senses is very powerful or if through fate disease comes, even if unpleasant things may happen to him and pleasant things are taken away from him,

191 And even if all these things should overtake him simultaneously, he would face them as courageously as if he were Agastya.

192 Just as a gentle breeze can easily disperse a large column of smoke rising into the sky,

193 Similarly, O Arjuna, such as person easily overcomes all difficulties, whether they arise from physical or spiritual sources or from destiny.

194 When a person remains courageous and undisturbed in the midst of mental agitation, this is called fortitude.

195 Purity is like a jar of pure refined gold filled with the holy waters of the Ganges.

196 When a person's actions are without desire and true discrimination is in his heart, then he is the image of purity.

197 Just as the Ganges on its way to the ocean removes people's sin and distress and also nourishes the trees on its bank,

198 Or just as the sun encircles the earth, dispelling the world's darkness and opening up the temple of nature's wealth,

199 In the same way, such a person frees those who are in bondage, rescues the drowning, and removes the sufferings of the distressed.

200 In short, he works night and day for the happiness and welfare of humanity, and also attains his own goal.

201 Moreover, the thought of working for himself at other's expense doesn't enter his mind.

202 This is called freedom from malice, O Arjuna, and I have explained it to you in such a way that you can clearly recognize it.

203 O Arjuna, just as the Ganges humbly withdrew when it reached Shiva's head, similarly, the sense of modesty when honor is bestowed on one is called humility.

204 I have already explained this to you, so is there any need to repeat it?

205 In this way spiritual wealth consists of these virtues, and it is the royal reward of those who excel among seekers of liberation.

206 This divine wealth is the holy Ganges of the liberated sons of Sagara, surrounded by these virtues which resemble sacred places.

207 These virtues are like a garland of flowers that the bride of liberation hangs around the necks of those who are entirely free from worldly attachment.

208 They are also like a lamp of twenty-four flames lit by the *Gita* as a bride, which she waves around the head of her bridegroom, the divine nature.

209 This wealth also resembles a sacred shell in the ocean of the *Gita*, which produces the pure pearls of these virtues.

210 It is needless to elaborate on this, for I have described the virtues which compose this wealth in such a way that they will reveal themselves.

211 In this explanation I must now describe demoniacal wealth, which is the hidden vine of sorrow covered with the thorns of all the vices.

212 Even though it is worthless and you should discard it, in order to do so you must recognize it so listen closely with your full attention.

213 This demoniacal wealth is the collection of all the horrible vices that result in the terrifying pains of hell.

214 Just as the Kalakuta poison is made up of all other poisons, in the same way this wealth

is the combination of all vices.

दम्भो दर्पो ऽभिमानश्च क्रोधः पारुष्यम् एव च।
अज्ञानं चाभिजातस्य पार्थ संपदम् आसुरीम्॥

dambho darpo 'bhimānaśca
krodhaḥ pāruṣyam eva ca
ajñānaṁ cābhijātasya
pārtha saṁpadam āsurīm

4. Hypocrisy, arrogance, pride, anger, insolence, and ignorance, are the endowment of those born to a demoniacal destiny, Arjuna.

215 Among these demoniacal qualities is ostentation, O Arjuna, which is boasting of one's own greatness.

216 If a man were to bring shame to his mother before men, even if she were as pure as a holy place, it would be a degradation.

217 If a person were to proclaim in public the knowledge taught by his Guru, it would be harmful even though the teaching in itself is valuable.

218 If a drowning man were to carry on his head the boat which could take him to the shore, he would drown.

219 O Arjuna, food sustains life, but when it is taken in excess it can become poison.

220 Similarly, if a person were publicly to proclaim his religion, which is his support in this world and the next, the very thing that brings salvation would become a cause of evil.

221 A religious life becomes irreligious if it is openly spoken of in public. This is the meaning of ostentation, O Arjuna.

222 A fool gains a little knowledge and is then unable to appreciate the learning of an assembly of brahmins.

223 To a well-trained horse of a horseman, the size of an elephant is insignificant. To a chameleon on a thorny bush, the heavens seem to be low.

224 A fire fed by grass rises to the sky in flames, and a fish swimming in a pool scorns the sea.

225 Similarly, a man may become vain about his wife, his wealth, his learning, his reputation, or his social standing. A beggar may be proud of the meal he gets at someone else's home.

226 An unfortunate person tears down his house and takes the shadow of the clouds for shelter. A fool, seeing a mirage, tears down the wall of his water tank.

227 When a person is full of conceit about his worldly possessions, this is arrogance. There is no need to say more.

228 The world believes in the Vedas, the Supreme Being is worshiped with faith, and the sun is the only source of light to the world.

229 A man's highest desire is to rise to an emperor's throne, and everyone desires freedom from death.

230 If anyone were to praise God joyfully for such gifts, the arrogant person would be filled with envy.

231 He would exclaim, I will destroy God, and I will poison the Vedas! In his pride, he destroys his own power.

232 A moth dislikes a flame, a firefly cannot bear the sun, and to the titavi bird the ocean is an enemy.

233 Similarly, a person infatuated with pride and egoism cannot bear even to hear the name of God and claims to rival the Vedas.

234 He is inflated with conceit about his worthiness. Full of arrogant pride, he is on the road to hell.

235 The sight of others' joy makes the poison of anger arise in his mind.

236 Oil burns more fiercely when it comes in contact with cold water, and a jackal becomes excited when it sees the moon.

237 The sinful owl is enraged at dawn when it sees the rising sun, which enlightens the life of the world.

238 Daybreak, which is the joy of mankind, is an evil worse than death to robbers; and milk is poison to a snake.

239 The great fire beneath the ocean, drinking its waters, doesn't subside but burns even more fiercely.

240 When a person becomes enraged at the good fortune of his fellow men in learning, happiness, and prosperity, this is called anger.

241 The mind of such a person is like a viper's nest, his sight is like the shot of an arrow, his speech is like a shower of live coals,

242 And his actions are like a sharp saw. In this way, his whole nature is harsh.

243 He is the lowest of men and the embodiment of violence. Now listen to the characteristics of ignorance.

244 A stone cannot distinguish between heat and cold, and day and night are the same to a blind man.

245 Fire will consume without distinction every thing it touches, and the touchstone cannot distinguish iron from gold.
246 Although a ladle is put in various sauces, it cannot discern their taste.
247 The wind doesn't consider the direction in which it should blow. Similarly, baseness doesn't concern itself with good and bad actions.
248 A child puts into its mouth whatever it sees, without knowing whether it is clean or dirty.
249 Similarly, the ignorant person randomly intermingles sin and righteousness, and doesn't distinguish the bitterness or sweetness of the two.
250 This is ignorance; there can be no other name for it. I have now told you the characteristics of the six vices.
251 Demoniacal wealth is supported by these six vices, just as a powerful poison may exist in the small body of a serpent.
252 The conflagration of the final day may seem insignificant, but the oblation of the entire world won't be enough to satisfy it.
253 When there is an excess of the three bodily fluids, it will invariably bring about a person's death even if he appeals to the creator. But these six vices are twice as evil as they are.
254 Even though this group consists of only six vices, this demoniacal wealth shouldn't be underestimated.
255 It is as though all the harmful planets were in conjunction in the same sign of the zodiac, as though every possible sin were to assail a slanderer,
256 As if many diseases should attack a person doomed to die, or as if all unfavorable omens should meet together at an inauspicious moment.
257 A person who possesses all these vices is like a dying goat stung by a seven-tailed scorpion.
258 If a person were to discover that a man he had trusted was a thief, or if an exhausted person were thrown into a flood, that would be like the effect of these vices.
259 If such a person were to approach the path of liberation, he would cry out, "I won't leave this world!" and he would plunge into worldly affairs.
260 O Arjuna, he descends into lower and lower births and eventually reaches the lowest order of inanimate beings.
261 Enough of this. Together, these six vices produce in a person what is called demoniacal wealth.
262 In this way, I have described to you the two kinds of wealth with their various characteristics.

दैवी संपद् विमोक्षाय निबन्धायासुरी मता।
मा शुचः संपदं दैवीम् अभिजातो ऽसि पाण्डव ॥

dāivī sampad vimokṣāya
nibandhāyāsurī matā
mā śucaḥ sampadaṁ dāivīm
abhijāto 'si pāṇḍava

5. The divine destiny leads to liberation; the demoniacal to bondage, it is thought. Do not grieve! You are born to a divine destiny, Arjuna.

263 The first of these two, the divine, is the dawn of the joy of liberation.
264 The other, the demoniacal, is the chain of greed and infatuation that binds the soul.
265 But don't let these words frighten you. Is the night afraid of the moonlight?
266 O Arjuna, this demoniacal wealth is bondage for one who turns to these six vices.
267 But you are fortunate to have been endowed with all the divine qualities.
268 O Arjuna, since you are the master of this divine wealth, you may attain the joy of final beatitude.

द्वौ भूतसर्गौ लोके ऽस्मिन् दैव आसुर एव च।
दैवो विस्तरशः प्रोक्त आसुरं पार्थ मे शृणु ॥

dvāu bhūtasargāu loke 'smin
dāiva āsura eva ca
dāivo vistaraśaḥ prokta
āsuraṁ pārtha me śṛṇu

6. There are two classes of created beings in this world—the divine and the demoniacal. The divine has been explained at length; now hear from Me, Arjuna, about the demoniacal.

269 People's endowment with either divine or demoniacal wealth is eternally appointed.
270 Demons carry on their activities by night; human beings and other creatures should perform their proper actions by day.
271 In this way, O Arjuna, the two orders of beings, the divine and the demoniacal, carry on their activities according to their nature.
272 Earlier, while describing knowledge, I fully

explained divine wealth.

273 Now I will describe for you the nature of those who have demoniacal wealth. Give Me your full attention.

274 Without articulated sound there can be no word, just as there can be no honey where there are no flowers.

275 Similarly, the demoniacal nature cannot manifest unless it has a human body.

276 Just as fire can be produced because it lies latent in wood, this nature manifests through a human body.

277 Just as sugarcane gives more juice as it grows, the demoniacal nature intensifies when it enters a human form.

278 O Arjuna, I will now describe for you the characteristics of those people in whom the demoniacal forces are at work.

प्रवृत्तिं च निवृत्तिं च जना न विदुर् आसुराः ।
न शौचं नापि चाचारो न सत्यं तेषु विद्यते ॥

pravṛttiṁ ca nivṛttiṁ ca
janā na vidur āsurāḥ
na śaucaṁ nāpi cācāro
na satyaṁ teṣu vidyate

7. Demoniacal men do not understand when to act and when to refrain from action. Neither purity, nor good conduct, nor truth is found in them.

279 Their minds are like the darkness of night when it comes to performing good deeds and abstaining from evil deeds.

280 A silkworm, preoccupied with weaving its cocoon, doesn't think about entering it or leaving it.

281 A fool will lend money to a thief without considering whether he will be repaid.

282 In the same way, demoniacal people have no knowledge of doing good and abstaining from evil. They have no understanding of purity even in a dream.

283 Coal might lose its blackness, a crow might become white, or a demon might even turn against animal food;

284 But, O Arjuna, there can be no more purity in a devilish person than there is holiness in a bottle of liquor.

285 Such people cannot develop a desire for sacred rites, nor honor the way of life of their elders, nor have any knowledge of right action.

286 Their actions are as haphazard as the grazing of goats, the blowing of the wind, or the burning of fire.

287 Acting solely on impulse, they behave like demons and are always at enmity with the truth.

288 They can no more speak truthfully than a scorpion's tail can tickle the skin.

289 Truth cannot come to them any more than a sweet smell can come from the breath.

290 Even though they may do nothing, their very nature is evil. Now I will tell you of the strange way in which they speak.

291 These devilish people are like a camel's body, which has no straight part. Listen to this:

292 Their speech is like a chimney pouring out columns of smoke. I will tell you about this so that you can clearly understand it.

असत्यम् अप्रतिष्ठं ते जगद् आहुर् अनीश्वरम् ।
अपरस्परसंभूतं किम् अन्यत् कामहैतुकम् ॥

asatyam apratiṣṭhaṁ te
jagad āhur anīśvaram
aparasparasaṁbhūtaṁ
kim anyat kāmahāitukam

8. "The universe," they say, "is without truth, without basis, without a God; brought about by a mutual union. How else? It is caused by lust alone."

293 This universe is eternal and is controlled by the Supreme Being; and the Vedas decree, as in a public hall, what is just and what is unjust.

294 Those who are judged to be sinful suffer punishment in hell, while the just live happily in heaven.

295 This is the eternal organization of this universe. Nevertheless, these people declare that all this is false.

296 They say that people are fascinated by sacrifice and are deceived by it, that some are overly pious and are deluded by the images that they worship, and that those who wear the saffron robes of the yogi, attracted by the experience of *samadhi*, are misled.

297 They ask, "Can we gain merit in any other way than through enjoying our worldly possessions?"

298 If some people are too weak to accumulate possessions and are tormented by the lack of sense pleasures, they say this is sinful.

299 It is a sin to take the life of a rich man, but if by doing so a person can possess the rich man's wealth, isn't that the reward of merit?

300 If it is a sin for the strong to destroy the

weak, they why aren't fish exterminated?

301 If it is good to look into a family's heredity, to choose a young woman in order to have children, and to find an auspicious time for the marriage,

302 Then why hasn't a similar procedure been established for the mating of birds and animals, which produce limitless offspring?

303 If stolen money comes into a person's possession, does it turn to poison? If a man commits adultery, does he become a leper?

304 As the Ruler of this universe, God causes people to experience both right and wrong; and according to a person's desire, he will experience life in the hereafter.

305 But since we cannot see either God or the hereafter, they must be unreal. Also, when a person dies and leaves no trace, who is left to experience anything?

306 A mere worm can be as happy crawling around in hell as Indra can be in heaven accompanied by a celestial maiden.

307 Neither is heaven the result of merit, nor is hell the result of sin, for in both these places pleasure is the result of desire.

308 A man and a woman come together out of desire, and from this the whole world is born.

309 Whatever a person craves for his own interest he nourishes with his desire. Later, through mutual hatred, desire destroys the world.

310 In this way, these demoniacal people claim that this world has no other basis than desire.

311 I will now leave this tiresome subject and not expand it further, for it is a waste of words.

एतां दृष्टिम् अवष्टभ्य नष्टात्मानो ऽल्पबुद्धयः ।
प्रभवन्त्य् उग्रकर्माणः क्षयाय जगतो ऽहिताः ।।

etām dṛṣṭim avaṣṭabhya
naṣṭātmāno 'lpabuddhayaḥ
prabhavanty ugrakarmāṇaḥ
kṣayāya jagato 'hitāḥ

9. Holding this view, these men of lost souls, of small intelligence, and of cruel actions, come forth as enemies of the world for its destruction.

312 Not only do they speak blasphemously of the Supreme Being, but they are convinced that He does not exist.

313 Their hearts are openly filled with heresy, and the arrows of atheism are thrust deep into their souls.

314 Respect for heaven and fear of hell have been burned up in them.

315 O My friend, such people are imprisoned in the body and, like bubbles in dirty water, they are sunk in the mire of sense pleasures.

316 When death draws near, disease attacks their bodies just as fishermen approach the deep waters.

317 Just as the rising of a comet augurs calamity in the world, similarly, these people are born to destroy mankind.

318 As evil grows, it thrusts out its shoots. In the same way, these people are walking memorials of sin.

319 Just as fire knows nothing else but to burn everything that comes in contact with it, similarly, they can only oppose everyone they meet.

320 Krishna said to Arjuna, Now listen to the state of delusion which produces these actions.

कामम् आश्रित्य दुष्पूरं दम्भमानमदान्विताः ।
मोहाद् गृहीत्वा ऽसद्ग्राहान् प्रवर्तन्ते ऽशुचिव्रताः ।।

kāmam āśritya duṣpūraṁ
dambhamānamadānvitāḥ
mohād gṛhītvā 'sadgrāhān
pravartante 'śucivratāḥ

10. Attached to insatiable desire, full of hypocrisy, arrogance, and pride, having accepted false notions through delusion, they work with unclean resolves,

321 A net cannot be filled with water, nor can a fire ever be satisfied with fuel; yet these people are even more insatiable than this.

322 O Arjuna, harboring desire in their hearts, they add to it deception and conceit.

323 Just as crazed elephants would become even more infuriated if they were given liquor, similarly, with age these people become more and more arrogant.

324 Their obstinacy is equally strong and aided by their folly. How can there be any stable resolution in them?

325 Their actions distress others and even cause the ruin of those around them. These are the practices which they constantly engage in.

326 They boast of their actions, treat the whole world with contempt, and spread the net of lust in every direction.

327 Through such actions they commit great sins, just as a cow which is set free may dig up the crops at random.

चिन्ताम् अपरिमेयां च प्रलयान्ताम् उपाश्रिताः ।
कामोपभोगपरमा एतावद् इति निश्चिताः ॥
cintām aparimeyāṁ ca
pralayāntām upāśritāḥ
kāmopabhogaparamā
etāvad iti niścitāḥ

11. Clinging to immeasurable anxiety, ending only in death, with gratification of desire as their highest aim, convinced that this is all;

328 Their only objective is to carry out their own intentions, and they are more concerned with this than with their lives.
329 They are deeper than hell and higher than the heavens. For them, even the universe is smaller than an atom.
330 The endless anxiety in their hearts is like the ceaseless practice of yoga. They cling to it just as a virtuous wife refuses to leave her husband even in death.
331 This anxiety continues to grow beyond all bounds as they set their hearts on worthless sense objects.
332 They love to hear women sing, to enjoy the sight of their bodies, and to embrace them with all the pleasure of their senses.
333 They value the company of women more highly than nectar.
334 To experience it they would rush into hell, ascend to heaven, or fly beyond the boundaries of the earth.

आशापाशशतैर् बद्धाः कामक्रोधपरायणाः ।
ईहन्ते कामभोगार्थम् अन्यायेनार्थसंचयान ॥
āśāpāśaśatāir baddhāḥ
kāmakrodhaparāyaṇāḥ
īhante kāmabhogārtham
anyāyenārthasaṁcayān

12. Bound by a hundred snares of hope, devoted to desire and anger, they seek to obtain, by unjust means, hoards of wealth for the gratification of their desires.

335 Just as a fish is likely to swallow the hook as well as the bait, in the same way these people are caught up in the desire for pleasure.
336 Their desires are not fulfilled, and the seed of vain hopes multiplies like the silkworm.
337 This increasing lust remains unfulfilled and turns to hatred. Then only lust and anger remain as their purpose in life.
338 O Arjuna, just as a watchman walks around all day and still has to remain awake at night, they get no rest either by day or by night.
339 Such people are cast down from the heights by desire and dashed onto the rocks of anger below. Because of their love of pleasure, their anger and hatred are out of control.
340 They harbor in their hearts a craving for sense objects, but doesn't it need wealth to satisfy it?
341 Therefore, in order to obtain enough money, they rob and cheat everyone.
342 Some they kill, others they rob of all their possessions, and for still others they find other methods of destruction.
343 Just as hunters setting out to hunt in the hills take with them nooses, sacks, snares, dogs, falcons, sticks, and spears,
344 Similarly, in order to feed themselves these people slaughter many creatures and perform other evil deeds.
345 By taking the lives of others, they amass wealth. But once they obtain it, how can their hearts feel satisfied?

इदम् अद्य मया लब्धम् इदं प्राप्स्ये मनोरथम् ।
इदम् अस्तीदम् अपि मे भविष्यति पुनर् धनम् ॥
idam adya mayā labdham
idaṁ prāpsye manoratham
idam astīdam api me
bhaviṣyati punar dhanam

13. This has been obtained by me today; this desire I shall attain; this is mine, and this wealth also shall be mine.

346 See how blessed I am? The wealth that once belonged to many people is now mine.
347 Elated by such self-praise, their hearts desire more and they say, I will take even more of others' possessions.
348 With what I have already acquired, I will be able to get everything else in the world.
349 Then I will be the lord of all wealth; I will possess all that the eye can see.

असौ मया हतः शत्रुर् हनिष्ये चापरान् अपि ।
ईश्वरो ऽहम् अहं भोगी सिद्धो ऽहं बलवान् सुखी ॥
asāu mayā hataḥ śatrur
haniṣye cāparān api
īśvaro 'ham ahaṁ bhogī
siddho 'haṁ balavān sukhī

14. "That enemy has been slain by me, and I shall slay others too; I am a lord, I am the enjoyer, I am successful, powerful, and happy,

350 I have destroyed these people, but they are not enough. I will kill more so that only I will remain in my greatness.

351 I will destroy everyone except those who serve me. In fact, I am the lord of all.

352 I am the king of the land of enjoyment. I am the center of all pleasure. Compared with me, even Indra is insignificant.

353 Whatever I do with my mind, body, or speech, must be fulfilled. Who else can command but me?

354 The god of death seems mighty only as long as people are unaware of my infinite power. I am a huge mountain of happiness.

आढ्यो ऽभिजनवान् अस्मि को ऽन्यो ऽस्ति सदृशो मया ।
यक्ष्ये दास्यामि मोदिष्य इत्य् अज्ञानविमोहिताः ॥
āḍhyo 'bhijanavān asmi
ko 'nyo 'sti sadṛśo mayā
yakṣye dāsyāmi modiṣya
ity ajñānavimohitāḥ

15. "I am wealthy and high born. Who else is equal to me? I shall sacrifice, I shall give, I shall rejoice." Thus, they are deluded by ignorance.

355 The god Kubera may be wealthy, but he doesn't experience the enjoyment that I do. Even Vishnu Himself is not worthy of my riches.

356 Compared with my illustrious family and my relatives, even Brahma is inferior.

357 They boast of being called gods, but they cannot compare with me. Who can?

358 Magical incantations are no longer used, but I will revive them and reestablish sacrificial rites to injure others.

359 I will give whatever they want to those who sing songs praising me and to those who entertain me with dancing.

360 I will be the embodiment of pleasure in all three worlds, eating delicious food, drinking, and keeping the company of young women.

361 But I have said enough about this! All those who have become mad through their demoniacal nature are like people who try to smell flowers growing in the sky.

अनेकचित्तविभ्रान्ता मोहजालसमावृताः ।
प्रसक्ताः कामभोगेषु पतन्ति नरके ऽशुचौ ॥
anekacittavibhrāntā
mohajālasamāvṛtāḥ
prasaktāḥ kāmabhogeṣu
patanti narake 'śucāu

16. Led astray by many imaginings, enveloped in a net of delusion, attached to the gratification of desires, they fall into a foul hell.

362 It is as if the dust of ignorance, caught up by the whirlwind of hope, were swept around and around in the sky of desire.

363 Just as a feverish person talks wildly in his delirium, they chatter about their desires.

364 Just as clouds mass together in the rainy season, and as waves rise incessantly on the surface of the ocean, in the same way these people desire endless pleasures.

365 A thick cluster of desires is formed within them, and their inner being is broken to pieces or mutilated like lotuses dragged over thorny bushes.

366 O Arjuna, if a pitcher falls on a stone, it will be broken into fragments. In the same way their hearts are shattered.

367 Just as the darkness deepens as the night passes, similarly, delusion develops in their hearts.

368 As this delusion increases, their desire for sense pleasures grows more intense, and this leads to hell.

369 They amass so many sins that even during their lives they experience the horrors of hell.

370 O wise Arjuna, those devilish people who harbor evil desires descend to live in hell.

371 In that awful place there are trees with leaves like swords, mountains of live coals, and oceans of boiling oil.

372 Ever increasing agonies and tortures imposed by the god of death pursue those demoniacal beings who inhabit hell.

373 Yet these people who are doomed to inherit hell continue to perform sacrifices in their delusion.

आत्मसंभाविताः स्तब्धा धनमानमदान्विताः ।
यजन्ते नामयज्ञैस् ते दम्भेनाविधिपूर्वकम् ॥
ātmasambhāvitāḥ stabdhā
dhanamānamadānvitāḥ
yajante nāmayajñāis te
dambhenāvidhipūrvakam

17. Self-conceited, stubborn, filled with the

pride and arrogance of wealth, they perform sacrifices only in name, with hypocrisy, and not according to Vedic injunction.

374 O Arjuna, sacrificial rites are valuable, but these people make them fruitless because they perform them like actors in a play.

375 In the same way, prostitutes take lovers and enjoy in their imagination the pleasures of married life.

376 They hold themselves in high esteem and are inflated with limitless pride.

377 They show no sign of humility but stand as erect as an iron column, or a mountain which soars aloft in the sky.

378 Rejoicing in their own superiority, they regard all others as being more worthless than grass.

379 O Arjuna, intoxicated in this way by the wine of wealth, they aren't concerned about good and evil actions.

380 How can such people, filled with these ideas, perform sacrifices? But such madmen will do anything.

381 At times, intoxicated with stupidity, they pretend to perform sacrifices.

382 They don't prepare an altar, a shelter, or a sacrificial mound; nor do they assemble the proper materials. In this way, they reject all prescribed rules.

383 They won't tolerate even the mention of God or of brahmins, so how can God or a brahmin attend their sacrifices?

384 An experienced cowherd will place a stuffed calf near a cow so he can milk her.

385 Similarly, these men invite people to be present at their sacrifices and rob them of their possessions for sacrificial offerings.

386 In this way they perform sacrifices for the sake of their own profit, while desiring everyone else's destruction.

अहंकारं बलं दर्पं कामं क्रोधं च संश्रिताः ।
माम् आत्मपरदेहेषु प्रद्विषन्तो ऽभ्यसूयकाः ॥

ahaṁkāraṁ balaṁ darpaṁ
kāmaṁ krodhaṁ ca saṁśritāḥ
mām ātmaparadeheṣu
pradviṣanto 'bhyasūyakāḥ

18. Clinging to egotism, force, insolence, desire, and anger, those malicious people hate Me in their own and others' bodies.

387 They proclaim their sacrificial skill to the world with drums and banners and vainly announce their greatness to everyone.

388 Thus, as though smearing darkness with soot, these vulgar people become even more swollen with pride because of their fame.

389 Their folly increases, and their arrogance, egoism, and lack of consideration are doubled.

390 Their strength grows more formidable as they strive to annihilate everyone else in the world.

391 As their selfishness and power combine, the ocean of arrogance swells beyond all limits.

392 With this upsurge of pride, lust turns into bad temper, and through the heat of this fire anger is ignited.

393 Just as in summer a store of oil and ghee may be set on fire and a strong wind may arise,

394 Similarly, as such people grow more egotistical, arrogance is added to the combination of lust and anger.

395 Then, O Arjuna, whom won't they try to destroy in the pursuit of their own pleasure?

396 They wouldn't hesitate to sell their own flesh and blood to practice magic.

397 In this way they burn up those very bodies in which I dwell, wounding Me, the Self.

398 Because I am the consciousness in all creatures, I suffer harm in all those who are injured by those who practice magic.

399 If anyone happens to escape from the danger of this magic, they hurl at him the stones of slander.

400 Virtuous men and women, charitable men and priests, famous ascetics and recluses,

401 Devotees and great beings in whom I dwell and who are purified by sacrifice, the study of the Vedas, and other practices,

402 Are the targets of their arrows of abuse, smeared with the poison of hatred.

तान् अहं द्विषतः क्रूरान् संसारेषु नराधमान् ।
क्षिपाम्य् अजस्रम् अशुभान् आसुरीष्व् एव योनिषु ॥

tān ahaṁ dviṣataḥ krūrān
saṁsāreṣu narādhamān
kṣipāmy ajasram aśubhān
āsurīṣv eva yoniṣu

19. Those cruel haters, the worst of men, I constantly hurl into the wombs of demons in the cycles of rebirth.

403 Now listen to the way in which I deal with all those sinners who treat Me as an enemy.

404 Those who are born in a human body, hating this world, I deprive of their human

state and reduce to a lower condition.

405 I commit these wicked people to the lowest order of life, to the dung hill of trouble in the city of worldly existence.

406 I transform them into tigers and wolves in a desert in which not even grass will grow to sustain them.

407 There they are tormented by hunger and tear off their flesh for food. Dying again and again, they are reborn in the same condition.

408 Or they may be born as serpents confined in their holes, where their skins are burned up by the heat of their own poison.

409 O Arjuna, I don't let these wicked people rest even for the time it takes to breathe in and out.

410 I leave them in these torments for such a vast amount of time that a million world ages would seem short in comparison.

411 This is just the first stage on the road they have to travel. There are no experiences more terrible than those which come to them.

आसुरीं योनिम् आपन्ना मूढा जन्मनि जन्मनि ।
माम् अप्राप्यैव कौन्तेय ततो यान्त्य् अधमां गतिम् ॥

āsurīṁ yonim āpannā
mūḍhā janmani janmani
mām arāpryāiva kāunteya
tato yānty adhamāṁ gatim

20. Having entered the wombs of demons, those who are deluded, not attaining Me in birth after birth, Arjuna, from there go to a condition still lower than that.

412 Now listen to the state of degradation which those demoniacal people attain.

413 Even birth in the darkest womb of such animals as the tiger provides a slight relief through the support of a body,

414 But I even deprive them of this comfort. Then there follows a continuous darkness in which even darkness itself would be blackened.

415 Such darkness would arouse loathing in sin, it would fill hell with terror, and create a weariness which would cause even weariness itself to faint.

416 Through it impurities become even more impure, heat is scorched, and fear is stuck with terror.

417 O Arjuna, those who enter wombs of darkness have to undergo the most evil degradation in the universe.

418 Speech weeps when describing it, and the mind shrinks from the memory of it. Alas, what a hell those fools have brought upon themselves!

419 Why do they encourage this demoniacal wealth, which has brought about such a terrible fall?

420 O Arjuna, don't go near the place where these demoniacal people dwell.

421 It is not necessary to tell you that you should avoid all those who embody these six vices.

त्रिविधं नरकस्येदं द्वारं नाशनम् आत्मनः ।
कामः क्रोधस् तथा लोभस् तस्माद् एतत् त्रयं त्यजेत् ॥

trividhaṁ narakasyedaṁ
dvāraṁ nāśanam ātmanaḥ
kāmaḥ krodhas tathā lobhas
tasmād etat trayaṁ tyajet

21. This is the threefold gate of hell, destructive of the self: desire, anger, and greed. Therefore one should abandon these three.

422 Know that every form of evil thrives where the three vices of lust, anger, and greed are found together.

423 O Arjuna, all the sorrows have provided guides to show the way that leads to them.

424 They are the sins which cause wicked people to be cast into hell.

425 As long as these three vices haven't arisen in a person's heart, he only hears of hell indirectly.

426 They bring harm and cause pain. Through them loss isn't simply loss; they are the very embodiment of loss.

427 O Arjuna, what more can I say? These are three spikes set on the threshold of the lowest hell.

428 One who associates with desire, anger, and greed is condemned to the city of the lower regions.

429 Therefore, O Arjuna, I tell you again and again to get rid of these three vices which are the most evil of all.

एतैर् विमुक्तः कौन्तेय तमोद्वारैस् त्रिभिर् नरः ।
आचरत्य् आत्मनः श्रेयस् ततो याति परां गतिम् ॥

etāir vimuktaḥ kāunteya
tamodvārāis tribhir naraḥ
ācaraty ātmanaḥ śreyas
tato yāti parāṁ gatim

22. Released from these three gates to darkness, Arjuna, a man does what is best for himself. Then he goes to the highest goal.

430 Until a person has freed himself from these, it isn't possible to discuss dharma or the other three goals of life.

431 The Lord said, No one can find happiness as long as these three vices are active in his heart.

432 Anyone who is concerned about himself and who fears self-destruction should be careful to avoid them.

433 Swimming across the ocean with a stone tied to your body, or living on meals of Kalakuta poison

434 Wouldn't be more impossible than attaining your goal in the company of lust, anger, and greed. Therefore, wipe out every trace of them.

435 If a person is able to suddenly break this threefold chain, he will continue joyfully on his way.

436 Just as when the body is cleansed of the three bodily fluids, a city has been freed from immorality, or a heart has been released from affliction,

437 Similarly, when a person has freed himself of these vices, he experiences happiness in the world and finds the company of good people on the road to liberation.

438 Then he can pass through the dangerous forest of life and death supported by the company of the good and sustained by the scriptures.

439 Then he reaches the city of the Guru's grace, where the joy of the Self lives forever.

440 There he will meet his mother, the eternal Self, the summit of all desirable things; and in a moment the clamor of worldly life will cease.

441 He reaches that place where lust, anger, and greed are utterly destroyed, and he comes to possess the great gift.

यः शास्त्रविधिम् उत्सृज्य वर्तते कामकारतः।
न स सिद्धिम् अवाप्नोति न सुखं न परां गतिम्॥

yaḥ śāstravidhim utsṛjya
vartate kāmakārataḥ
na sa siddhim avāpnoti
na sukhaṁ na parāṁ gatim

23.He who acts under the impulse of desire, casting aside the injunctions of the scriptures, does not attain perfection, nor happiness, nor the highest goal.

442 A person who doesn't care about these things and who is obsessed with evil is a traitor to the Self.

443 If a person disregards the Vedas, which are compassionate to all mankind and are a light revealing good and evil;

444 If he pays no attention to prescribed actions and doesn't consider what is good for him, but indulges more and more in sense pleasures;

445 If he refuses to give up lust, anger, and greed, but remains faithful to them and resorts freely to the jungle of unrestrained conduct;

446 What will happen to him when the bonds of worldly life fall away? He won't even experience the pleasures of earthly life.

447 He cannot get close enough to the river of liberation to drink its water. He cannot approach it even in a dream.

448 If a brahmin, desiring fish, were to enter the water along with the fisherman, he would immediately become an outcaste.

449 In the same way, death carries off a person who casts away the bliss of heaven for the sake of sense pleasures.

450 In this way, he attains neither heavenly bliss nor earthly pleasures. Then what possibility does he have of finding liberation?

451 Therefore, a person who, out of lust, desires to enjoy sense objects will have neither pleasure nor heaven, nor will he attain liberation.

तस्माच् छास्त्रं प्रमाणं ते कार्याकार्यव्यवस्थितौ।
ज्ञात्वा शास्त्रविधानोक्तं कर्म कर्तुम् इहार्हसि॥

tasmāc chāstraṁ pramāṇaṁ te
kāryākāryavyavasthitāu
jñātvā śāstravidhānoktaṁ
karma kartum ihārhasi

24. Therefore, determining your standard by the scriptures, as to what is and what is not to be done, knowing the scriptural injunction prescribed, you should perform action here in this world.

452 Therefore, O My friend, a person who seeks his own welfare shouldn't disregard the command of the scriptures.

453 A devoted wife will easily do what is good for her if she follows her husband's instructions.

454 A disciple will be able to enter the mansion of Self-realization if he pays attention to the teachings of his Guru.

455 A man will use a lamp when he wants to

find his hoarded wealth.

456 In the same way, O Arjuna, a person who is anxious to realize all the goals of human life should respect the Vedas and the scriptures.

457 Whatever the scriptures tell us to give up, we should do so. We should consider even a kingdom to be as worthless as grass. And whatever they tell us to accept, we should take it without objection, even if it were poison.

458 O Arjuna, misfortune will never strike a person who is devoted to the Vedas.

459 The Vedas protect us from evil and give us what is good. There is no mother in the world who is better than they are.

460 They bring us to union with God, so no one should disregard them. O Arjuna, you should especially respect them.

461 Through the power of your merit, you have been born to fulfill the purposes of the sacred scriptures, O Arjuna.

462 Being the younger brother of righteousness, you should behave only in that way.

463 A person should take the scriptures as his authority in discriminating between right and wrong, and he should give up everything that is forbidden as evil.

464 You should carry out faithfully with all your strength whatever you must do.

465 O wise one, the seal of universal authority has been given to you. You are supremely worthy to be the leader of mankind.

466 In this way, the Lord explained to Arjuna the nature of the demoniacal qualities and how a person may escape from them.

467 Now listen with the ear of understanding to the way in which Arjuna will earnestly question Him.

468 Just as under Vyasa's direction Sanjaya entertained the king by narrating all this to him, similarly, with Nivritti's blessing I will continue this story.

469 O good people, if you favor me with your grace, I will fulfill your expectations.

470 Jnanadeva said, Therefore grant me the favor of your attention, which will give me strength.

17

THE YOGA OF THE THREEFOLD DIVISION OF FAITH

SALUTATIONS to my revered Guru, who is to me like the god Ganesh, through whose ritual gestures in deep meditation the universe is sent forth to blossom!

2 Shiva, the Self, surrounded by the demon Tripura as the three cities of the qualities and confined to the fortress of existence, was delivered by you as Ganesh because you remembered him.

3 Therefore, you are superior in greatness to Lord Shiva; yet as a boat to carry us over the waters of this life of illusion, you are light in weight.

4 Those who are ignorant of you call you the twisted-faced one, but the wise see that you look straight ahead.

5 Although your divine eyes seem to be small, by opening and closing them you bring about the creation and destruction of the world.

6 When you move your ear, representing activity, a breeze blows, fragrant with the moisture emanating from your temples. Bees in the form of individual souls gather around as if worshiping you with blue lotuses.

7 When you move your other ear, representing inactivity, the worship ceases. Then the ornaments on your body are displayed.

8 In the playful dance of your consort, the illusion of creation, you reveal the skill of your movements.

9 I have said enough, O creator of wonders. Those whom you befriend are set free from the bonds of all relationships.

10 You are called the brother of the whole world, for you release all worldly bonds. So let us worship you in this form.

11 O Lord, in this worship, a person who thought he was separate from you finds that his separateness, perceived through duality, no longer exists.

12 You remain far away from those who regard you as separate from themselves and who seek the way to find you.

13 You are not found in the hearts of those who try to reach you through meditation, but you love those who forget even meditation.

14 You don't accept a person who truly doesn't know you but who parades about as if he were all-knowing, even though his words may be as numerous as those of the Vedas.

15 Your zodiacal name is Silence. Why then should I try to praise you? How can I worship you when all appearance is illusion?

16 Even if I wish to be your servant, doesn't that make me guilty of duality? So I shouldn't enter into any relationship with you.

17 When all these things have passed away, I will attain union with you. Then I will know your inner meaning, O you who are worthy of all worship.

18 When salt is placed in water, no distinction is left. So is my salutation to you. What more can I say?

19 An empty pitcher put into the sea overflows with water. When the wick of a lamp is lighted, it becomes a lamp.

20 In the same way, by my salutation to you I have become perfect in you, O Shri Nivritti, so I am able to explain the meaning of the *Gita*.

21 In the last verse of the sixteenth chapter, the Lord has clearly given the following teaching:

22 O Arjuna, in order to discriminate properly between right and wrong actions, the scriptures should be your sole authority.

23 At this point Arjuna said to himself, How is

it that there is no other source of authority than the scriptures for performing action?

24 How could a person remove a jewel from the hood of a serpent, or pluck a hair from the lion's nose?

25 Is it that only he who can get the jewel and string it on the hair can have such a necklace? Otherwise, will his neck have to remain bare?

26 Who could compile all the various scriptural teachings? And who would profit from this?

27 Even if uniformity were achieved, would anyone have time to apply it? Would anyone live that long?

28 Even if someone were to have the means, time, and place to study all the texts, this wouldn't be possible for everyone.

29 It is impossible for everyone to study the scriptures. So what will be the fate of those seekers of liberation who are ignorant?

30 The subject of the seventeenth chapter will be Arjuna's inquiry concerning this matter.

31 Arjuna disliked all sense objects. He was skilled in all arts and was a marvel even in Krishna's eyes, a second Krishna in the form of Arjuna.

32 He was the foundation of all bravery, the jewel of the kingly line of the Lunar race, and he took delight in bestowing happiness and other benefits.

33 He was the beloved consort of pure intellect, the treasury of the knowledge of the Absolute, and the faithful follower of the Lord.

अर्जुन उवाच । *arjuna uvāca*

ये शास्त्रविधिम् उत्सृज्य यजन्ते श्रद्धयान्विताः ।
तेषां निष्ठा तु का कृष्ण सत्त्वम् आहो रजस् तमः ।।

ye śāstravidhim utsṛjya
yajante śraddhayānvitāḥ
teṣāṁ niṣṭhā tu kā kṛṣṇa
sattvam āho rajas tamaḥ

Arjuna spoke:
1. Those who sacrifice casting the injunctions of the scriptures aside, but filled with faith, what is their condition, Krishna? Is it sattva, rajas, or tamas?

34 Then Arjuna said, O Krishna, You whose complexion is as dark as the tamal tree, who are God in a form that our senses can perceive, Your words leave me in doubt.

35 On what grounds did the Lord say that it is impossible for a person to attain liberation except according to the scriptures?

36 There might not be a place where a person could practice their teachings, he might not have time, and there might not be anyone to teach him.

37 There might not be any aids available for his study.

38 His former births might not provide sufficient merit, or his intelligence might be inadequate. In these ways, the scriptures might be beyond his reach.

39 In any of these circumstances, he might give up all consideration of the scriptures, being unable to grasp their meaning.

40 There are holy beings who, having understood the scriptures and followed their sacred laws, now dwell in heaven.

41 We earnestly wish to become like them and to follow their example.

42 O generous Krishna, just as a child copies letters from a model, and as a person who is unwell sends a guide before him,

43 Similarly, people follow with faith the actions of a person who is learned in the scriptures.

44 They worship Shiva and other gods, give land and other things in charity, and devotedly perform such rituals as burning the sacrificial fire.

45 O highest Lord, will you tell me what is the condition of such people, whether it is *sattvic, rajasic,* or *tamasic*?

46 Then Lord Krishna, who dwells in Vaikuntha, who is the pollen of the lotus of the Vedas, to whom the universe is like the shadow to the body,

47 Who is the vastness of time, mighty and beyond all conception, the invisible One without a second, and full of joy,

48 Who is worthy of all glory and through whose power everything exists, spoke in the following way:

श्रीभगवान् उवाच । *śrībhagavān uvāca*

त्रिविधा भवति श्रद्धा देहिनां सा स्वभावजा ।
सात्त्विकी राजसी चैव तामसी चेति तां शृणु ।।

trividhā bhavati śraddhā
dehināṁ sā svabhāvajā
sāttvikī rājasī cāiva
tāmasī ceti tāṁ śṛṇu

The Blessed Lord spoke:
2. The faith of embodied beings is of three kinds, born of their innate nature; it is sattvic, rajasic, and tamasic. Now hear of this.

49 O Arjuna, I understand your point, that you consider the study of the scriptures as an obstacle.
50 O wise one, you seek to take by storm the highest state simply by faith, but that is not an easy matter.
51 O Arjuna, you shouldn't rely on faith alone to reach this state. If a brahmin comes in contact with an untouchable, doesn't he himself become an untouchable?
52 Consider this: if water from the Ganges were poured into a wine bottle, no one would accept it.
53 Sandalwood is cooling. Yet, when it is set on fire, can't it burn the hand which holds it?
54 If gold fell into a vessel of base metal, wouldn't a person be deceived if he took it as pure gold?
55 In the same way, all forms of faith are pure in themselves; but when someone has faith,
56 It is affected by the nature of the person, who is in turn influenced by matter and conditioned by the three qualities.
57 In every person, two of the qualities are weakened and one predominates. Then this one quality affects the tendencies of the mind.
58 As the tendency is, so is the desire. As the desire is, so the person acts. And according to his action, he is born into another body after death.
59 A seed dies when it grows into a tree, and the tree dies and carries on in the seed. This process continues eternally, and the species is never destroyed.
60 Similarly, a person passes through countless births, but the action of the three qualities inherent in him never changes.
61 So you should realize that the faith which a person has is affected by these three qualities.
62 It may be that pure goodness predominates in him and he seeks knowledge, but the other two qualities are in opposition.
63 Faith which is sustained by goodness leads to the fruit of liberation. Then why do passion and darkness remain inactive?
64 If passion undermines the power of goodness and becomes predominant, then faith will be reduced to dust.
65 When the flames of darkness rise, faith is destroyed and one is ready to enjoy any undesirable pleasure.

सत्त्वानुरूपा सर्वस्य श्रद्धा भवति भारत ।
श्रद्धामयो ऽयं पुरुषो यो यच्छ्रद्धः स एव सः ॥
sattvānurūpā sarvasya
śraddhā bhavati bhārata
śraddhāmayo 'yam puruṣo
yo yacchraddhaḥ sa eva saḥ

3. Faith is in accordance with the truth (nature) of each, Arjuna. Man is made of faith. Whatever faith he has, thus he is.

66 O wise Arjuna, among human beings there is no faith which is unaffected by goodness, passion, and darkness.
67 Faith is inevitably imbued with the three qualities and is therefore threefold, having the quality of either goodness, passion, or darkness.
68 Water gives life, but when in contact with poison it becomes deadly, mixed with pepper it becomes pungent, and combined with sugarcane it becomes sweet.
69 Similarly, if a person is born and dies while dominated by darkness, his faith will come to have that quality.
70 Then, just as soot and black ink have the same color, in the same way his faith is identical with darkness.
71 In the case of a passionate person, faith takes on that nature; and when a person is good, it is entirely good.
72 Therefore, this world is molded out of faith.
73 Under the influence of these three qualities, faith is stamped with this threefold nature. You should understand this.
74 Just as a tree is recognized by its flowers, as a person's mind is revealed by his speech, or as his actions in a previous birth can be known by his experience in this life,
75 In the same way, the threefold nature of faith can be recognized by the three characteristics which I will now describe to you.

यजन्ते सात्त्विका देवान् यक्षरक्षांसि राजसाः ।
प्रेतान् भूतगणांश्चान्ये यजन्ते तामसा जनाः ॥
yajante sāttvikā devān
yakṣarakṣāṁsi rājasāḥ
pretān bhūtagaṇāṅścānye
yajante tāmasā janāḥ

4. The sattvic worship the gods, the rajasic worship the Yakshas and demons; the others, the tamasic men, worship the ghosts and the hordes of nature spirits.

76 The minds of those whose faith is pure are generally directed towards heavenly happiness.
77 They study all the arts and sciences, they choose the proper sacrifices, and they reach heaven.
78 O Arjuna, those whose faith is passionate worship fiends and demons.
79 Those who offer human sacrifices and worship after dark the hosts of evil spirits and corpses in the burning grounds,
80 Are created of the essence of darkness and are the home of dark faith.
81 These are the signs of the three kinds of faith. I have described them to you for the following reason:
82 So that people should hold fast to pure faith and abandon the two kinds which are opposed to it.
83 O Arjuna, a person whose mind is steadfast in pure faith doesn't need to fear concerning ultimate bliss.
84 It doesn't matter if he doesn't study the Brahma Sutras, master all the scriptures, or have insight into philosophical doctrines.
85 Those elders who have become the very incarnation of the scriptural teachings, giving them to the world by their own practice of them,
86 He follows the conduct of those people, walking in pure faith, and he is assured of the same fruit.
87 If someone manages to light a lamp with great effort and another lights his lamp from the first one, is the second person's lamp any less effective in giving light?
88 If someone builds a mansion at great expense, won't a temporary occupant also enjoy it?
89 Does a water tank only quench the thirst of the person who builds it? Doesn't a cook prepare food for others as well as for himself?
90 What more should I say? Did the sage Gautama bring down the Ganges for himself alone, while everyone else must be content with an ordinary stream?
91 Even if a person is a fool, he will attain liberation if, according to his ability, he follows the conduct of those who are learned in the scriptures, provided that he has faith.

अशास्त्रविहितं घोरं तप्यन्ते ये तपो जनाः ।
दम्भाहंकारसंयुक्ताः कामरागबलान्विताः ॥

aśāstravihitaṁ ghoraṁ
tapyante ye tapo janāḥ
dambhāhaṁkārasaṁyuktāḥ
kāmarāgabalānvitāḥ

5. Men who undergo terrible austerities not enjoined by the scriptures, accompanied by hypocrisy and egotism, along with desire and passion,

92 There are other people who cannot even utter the names of the scriptures, and they won't allow a person who knows the scriptures to come near them.
93 They mock the religious practices of their elders and scoff at learned men.
94 Proud of their riches and power, they perform unauthorized acts of penance.
95 Thrusting a knife into whatever lies before them, they fill sacrificial vessels with blood and flesh.
96 They pour them into the flames of the sacrificial fires, offer them to evil spirits, and even make offerings of little children for vows they have made.
97 They will fast for weeks on end in an excess of zeal for some inferior deity.
98 In this way, O My friend, they sow the seed of injury to themselves and others in the field of darkness. Later, they reap what they have sown.
99 O Arjuna, they are like an armless man in the sea who refuses to get into a boat,
100 Or like a sick man who gets angry with the physicians and kicks away the medicine. How can he be cured of his illness?
101 They are like a person who, out of envy for another who has sight, tears out his own eyes and is confined to his own room by blindness.
102 Those who have a demoniacal nature are like these men. They despise the teachings of the scriptures and wander at random along the paths of infatuation.
103 They do whatever their lust dictates and kill anyone whom their anger impels them to kill. Truly, they torment Me with the stones of suffering.

कर्षयन्तः शरीरस्थं भूतग्रामम् अचेतसः ।
मां चैवान्तः शरीरस्थं तान्विद्ध्य् आसुरनिश्चयान् ॥

karṣayantaḥ śarīrasthaṁ
bhūtagrāmam acetasaḥ
māṁ cāivāntaḥ śarīrasthaṁ
tān viddhy āsuraniścayān

6. The unthinking, torturing within the body the aggregate of elements, and also torturing Me thus within the body, know them to be of demoniacal resolves.

104 I Myself have to bear whatever pain they cause to their own bodies and to those of others.
105 One shouldn't even speak through a curtain to such sinners, but I must mention them so that you will avoid them.
106 A corpse must be taken out of a house. Also, a person may have to speak with an untouchable, but then he must wash the dirt from his hands.
107 For the sake of cleanliness, one mustn't refuse to recognize dirt. Similarly, I must refer to these people so that you can avoid them.
108 O Arjuna, when you see such people, remember Me. There is no other way to cleanse this stain.

आहारस् त्व् अपि सर्वस्य त्रिविधो भवति प्रियः ।
यज्ञस् तपस् तथा दानं तेषां भेदम् इमं शृणु ॥
āhāras tv api sarvasya
trividho bhavati priyaḥ
yajñas tapas tathā dānaṁ
teṣāṁ bhedam imaṁ śṛṇu

7. But also the food preferred by all is of three kinds, as are their sacrifices, austerities, and gifts. Hear now the distinction between them.

109 You should strive in every way to maintain your pure faith.
110 You should associate with people whose company encourages goodness, and you should eat food which will help to increase your purity.
111 In fact, there is nothing as helpful to the cultivation of a pure nature as suitable food.
112 O Arjuna, a person, in full awareness, may take an intoxicating drink and immediately become drunk.
113 If someone, while eating his food, is overcome by wind and phlegm or suffers from fever, will he cure this by drinking milk?
114 Just as drinking nectar leads to immortality while drinking poison causes death,
115 In the same way, the state of the bodily fluids varies according to the food a person eats, and these fluids affect his inner nature.
116 Just as water heated in a jar becomes hot, similarly, a person's moods are controlled by his bodily fluids.
117 Therefore, when he eats pure food, he encourages the quality of goodness; and when he eats food which is of a passionate or of a dark nature, he develops the corresponding qualities.
118 Now listen closely, and I will explain which food is pure and which leads to passion and darkness.
119 O Arjuna, I will clearly show you that there are three kinds of food that a person can eat.
120 Dishes are prepared according to the taste of the one who eats them, and he is dominated by the three qualities.
121 A person both experiences and acts, and his nature and actions are threefold according to the way in which he is affected by the qualities.
122 His food is of three kinds, he performs sacrifices in three ways, and his acts of penance and his charitable gifts are also of three kinds.
123 First I will describe the different kinds of food, as I have told you, and I will make it quite clear.

आयुः सत्त्वबलारोग्य- सुखप्रीतिविवर्धनाः ।
रस्याः स्निग्धाः स्थिरा हृद्या आहाराः सात्त्विकप्रियाः ॥
āyuḥsattvabalārogya-
sukhaprītivivardhanāḥ
rasyāḥ snigdhāḥ sthirā hṛdyā
āhārāḥ sāttvikapriyāḥ

8. Promoting life, virtue, strength, health, happiness, and satisfaction, which are savory, smooth, firm, and pleasant to the stomach; such foods are dear to the sattvic.

124 Those fortunate people who are endowed with the quality of goodness are attracted to sweet foods,
125 Those which are juicy, sweet, succulent, and ripe.
126 Not too large, soft to the touch, tasty and pleasing to the tongue,
127 Food which is full of juice and at the same time soft, moist, and which cannot be spoiled by heating,
128 Which is also small in size but, like the Guru's word, powerful in its effect, so that even a small quantity of it will satisfy.
129 Those who have the quality of goodness like all foods which are not only sweet to

the taste but also beneficial to the health.

130 These are the properties of the foods which promote goodness and which protect and renew life.

131 When the clouds of such good food rain down into a person's body, the river of his life flows more fully day by day.

132 O wise Arjuna, this is the food which maintains goodness, just as the sun sustains the well-being of the day.

133 All these foods are a source of strength to both the body and the mind. How then could there be any place for disease in those who eat them?

134 When a person eats this kind of food, his body is fortunate enough to enjoy good health.

135 All the activities of his body result in prosperity, and happiness becomes his constant companion.

136 This is the effect of pure food on the body. It brings happiness both within and without.

137 Now I will tell you about the foods which are preferred by those of a passionate nature.

कट्वम्ललवणात्युष्ण तीक्ष्णरूक्षविदाहिनः ।
आहारा राजसस्येष्टा दुःखशोकामयप्रदाः ॥
kaṭvamlalavaṇātyuṣṇa-
tīkṣṇarūkṣavidāhinaḥ
āhārā rājasasyeṣṭā
duḥkhaśokāmayapradāḥ

9. Causing pain, misery, and sickness, bitter, sour, salty, excessively hot, pungent, dry, and burning; such foods are desired by the rajasic.

138 They like food which is deadlier and more bitter than the Kalakuta poison, sour, and which burns more fiercely than lime.

139 It is filled with as much salt as the water needed to make dough.

140 A passionate person likes extremely salty foods, and in terms of hot seasoning, eating this food is like swallowing fire.

141 It gives out such hot steam that a candle could be lit from it. This is the kind of hot food that a passionate person likes.

142 He eats food so pungent that it could pierce rocks, though it passes through him without causing any injury.

143 He likes food that is drier than ashes, and he enjoys the sting of it on his tongue.

144 He enjoys eating food that he has to grind between his teeth.

145 Even though the ingredients of this food are already pungent, he adds mustard to it so that when he eats it, heat passes through his mouth and nose.

146 He loves food which is so highly seasoned that it would repel the heat of fire.

147 Not being satisfied with this, his appetite runs riot and he would even eat flaming fire.

148 As a result, he is always in a feverish heat and cannot rest either on the ground or in bed. The drinking glass never leaves his mouth.

149 What he has eaten is not food; it is a stimulant he has taken which arouses in him sleeping serpents in the form of disease.

150 Disease and trouble arise in him and rival each other. In this way, the food of a passionate quality results in suffering.

151 O Arjuna, I have now described the food of a passionate kind and its many effects.

152 I will now tell you the kind of food which is preferred by those of a dark nature. Don't let it fill you with disgust.

यातयामं गतरसं पूति पर्युषितं च यत् ।
उच्छिष्टम् अपि चामेध्यं भोजनं तामसप्रियम् ॥
yātayāmaṁ gatarasaṁ
pūti paryuṣitaṁ ca yat
ucchiṣṭam api cāmedhyaṁ
bhojanaṁ tāmasapriyam

10. Stale, tasteless, putrid, rotten, and refuse as well as the impure, is the food which is dear to the tamasic.

153 The person of a dark nature doesn't think that decaying food will do him any harm, just as a buffalo will eat mash.

154 He will eat in the afternoon food that was cooked in the morning, and will even go so far as to eat it the next day.

155 He also eats food which is either half-cooked or burned and which has no flavor.

156 If something is well cooked or succulent, he doesn't consider it food.

157 If he happens to be given food, he will leave it until it rots, as a tiger does.

158 Or he will take food that is several days old and has lost its flavor, or which is dried up, rotten, and full of worms.

159 His children knead this into a mass with their hands, or he sits down with his wife and family to eat from the same dish.

160 After he has eaten this impure food, he feels

that he has had a good meal, but the sinner is still not satisfied.

161 Then see what happens! He eats substances which are forbidden and which are sinful and full of evil.

162 He uses impure water and unsuitable dishes. All this serves to increase his eagerness for food of the quality of darkness.

163 O Arjuna, such is the taste of these people of darkness, and it isn't long before it bears its consequences.

164 As soon as this unholy food touches his lips, he is liable to commit sin.

165 Moreover, what he eats cannot be called food, for he is filling his body with suffering.

166 Why should a person want to experience having his head cut off, or walking into fire? You should realize how this person suffers.

167 The Lord said, O Arjuna, it isn't necessary to describe the consequences of eating food of a dark nature.

168 Now hear how sacrifice is also of three kinds, just as food is.

169 O Arjuna, listen to the nature of the first form of sacrifice, which has the quality of goodness.

अफलाकाङ्क्षिभिर् यज्ञो विधिदृष्टो य इज्यते ।
यष्टव्यम् एवेति मनः समाधाय स सात्त्विकः ।।
aphalākāṅkṣibhir yajño
vidhidṛṣṭo ya ijyate
yaṣṭavyam eveti manaḥ
samādhāya sa sāttvikaḥ

11. Sacrifice which is offered, observing the scriptures, by those who do not desire the fruit, concentrating the mind only on the thought "this is to be sacrificed;" that sacrifice is sattvic.

170 A faithful wife doesn't allow her desire to turn towards anyone but her husband.

171 The Ganges doesn't flow beyond the ocean into which it merges, and the Vedas become silent when they perceive the Self.

172 In the same way, those who are concerned for their own welfare don't allow themselves to be egotistically interested in the fruits of their actions.

173 When water reaches the roots of a tree, it doesn't turn back but is absorbed into the tree.

174 In the same way, those people who are completely absorbed in their determination to perform sacrifices desire nothing.

175 The best sacrifice is performed by those who have given up all desire for reward and who care for nothing but their duty.

176 Just as a person can see his own face in a mirror, and with a lamp he can see a jewel held in his hand,

177 And just as when the sun rises he can clearly see the road he wants to follow, similarly, these people rely on the authority of the Vedas.

178 They make fire pits, shelters, and altars, and gather the necessary materials for the sacrifice according to the prescribed rituals.

179 Just as each limb of the body has its own appropriate ornaments, these people arrange all the materials correctly.

180 How can I describe this? The embodiment of the art of sacrifice is richly adorned and displayed in this kind of sacrifice.

181 Such a sacrifice is complete in every way and is free from any desire for self-aggrandizement.

182 The tulsi plant is tended and watered although it has neither fruit nor flowers and gives no shade.

183 In the same way, understand that a sacrifice which is carefully performed without any desire for the fruit has the quality of goodness.

अभिसंधाय तु फलं दम्भार्थम् अपि चैव यत् ।
इज्यते भरतश्रेष्ठ तं यज्ञं विद्धि राजसम् ।।
abhisaṁdhāya tu phalaṁ
dambhārtham api cāiva yat
ijyate bharataśreṣṭha
taṁ yajñaṁ viddhi rājasam

12. But sacrifice which is offered with a view to the fruit, Arjuna, and also for the purpose of ostentation; know that to be rajasic.

184 O Arjuna, a similar kind of sacrifice may be performed which is like inviting a king to a ceremony in honor of the ancestors.

185 If the king attends the ceremony it will be very profitable, for the ceremony will be carried out and the host will also become famous.

186 Entertaining such a desire, a person will perform a sacrifice hoping to reach heaven and to become famous as an expert in sacrificial rites.

187 O Arjuna, the performance of a sacrifice for the sake of its fruits and in order to acquire

worldly fame has the quality of passion.

विधिहीनम् असृष्टान्नं मन्त्रहीनम् अदक्षिणम् ।
श्रद्धाविरहितं यज्ञं तामसं परिचक्षते ।।

vidhihīnam asṛṣṭānnaṁ
mantrahīnam adakṣiṇam
śraddhāvirahitaṁ yajñam
tāmasaṁ paricakṣate

13. Sacrifice devoid of faith, contrary to scriptural ordinances, with no food offered, without mantras and without gifts (to the presiding priest), they regard as tamasic.

188 Just as no priest is required for birds and beasts to mate, but only the instinct, similarly all sacrifices which have the quality of darkness are based on desire.

189 Just as the wind doesn't blow in a particular path, death doesn't wait for an auspicious moment, and fire isn't afraid to burn something that is prohibited,

190 In the same way, O Arjuna, the conduct of a person of darkness isn't restrained by prescribed rites, so it is undisciplined.

191 He has no respect for proper rites, nor does he use mantras. He is like a fly which eats any and every kind of food.

192 He dislikes brahmins, so there is no question of giving gifts to them.

193 Like fire combined with a hurricane, he squanders all he has. He is without faith, just as the house of a man without an heir is robbed.

194 So sacrifice performed only for the sake of outward appearances is the sacrifice of darkness, said Krishna.

195 Although the water of the Ganges is one, as it flows in different streams, it may be polluted in one and remain pure in another.

196 Likewise, penance is threefold in its nature, corresponding to the three qualities. The practice of one leads to sin, while the practice of the other brings liberation.

197 O wise Arjuna, if you want to know why this is so, first you must understand what penance is.

198 First I will show you the nature of penance; then I will speak of it as divided according to the three qualities.

199 There are also three kinds of penance: physical, mental, and verbal.

200 First listen to the explanation of physical penance, according to whether a person chooses to worship Shiva or Vishnu.

देवद्विजगुरुप्राज्ञ पूजनं शौचम् आर्जवम् ।
ब्रह्मचर्यम् अहिंसा च शारीरं तप उच्यते ।।

devadvijagurुprājña-
pūjanaṁ śaucam ārjavam
brahmacaryam ahiṁsā ca
śārīraṁ tapa ucyate

14. Worship of the gods, the twice-born, teachers, and wise men; purity, rectitude, celibacy, and non-violence; these are called austerities of the body.

201 Day and night his feet make pilgrimages to the shrine of his chosen deity.

202 His hands are occupied in beautifying the courtyard of the temple and supplying the articles for worship.

203 As soon as he sees an image of Shiva or Vishnu, he does a full prostration like a pole.

204 He gives due service to brahmins and the elders because of their virtues of learning and humility.

205 He brings relief to those who are worn out from traveling or afflicted with suffering.

206 He offers his body to the service of his parents, whom he considers to be superior to all other holy places.

207 He serves his Guru, who is compassionate and gives knowledge. The very sight of him removes the sorrows of this terrible earthly existence.

208 O Arjuna, in order to remove the dirt of his egoism, he pours it onto the sacrificial fire of his own duty, and covers it with the repetition of sacred texts.

209 He salutes all creatures as being permeated with the Self, he is zealous in doing good to others, and he practices restraint with women at all times.

210 His only contact with a woman's body was at birth; since then he has always remained chaste.

211 He doesn't injure even a blade of grass, for he considers it to be a living creature. In fact, he avoids all injury and all sense of difference.

212 When all his behavior is like this, his penance may be called complete.

213 O Arjuna, because all this behavior principally involves bodily action, I call it the penance of the body.

214 In this way I have described the nature of physical penance. Now hear about the pure

penance of speech.

अनुद्वेगकरं वाक्यं सत्यं प्रियहितं च यत् ।
स्वाध्यायाभ्यसनं चैव वाङ्मयं तप उच्यते ॥
anudvegakaraṁ vākyaṁ
satyaṁ priyahitaṁ ca yat
svādhyāyābhyasanaṁ cāiva
vāṅmayaṁ tapa ucyate

15. Words that do not cause distress, truthful, agreeable, and beneficial; and practice in the recitation of sacred texts; these are called austerities of speech.

215 The philosopher's stone transforms iron into gold without reducing its size or weight.
216 Such goodness is found in the speech of a person who practices this penance that he never hurts his neighbor. He only gives pleasure to those around him.
217 Just as water is poured mainly for a tree, but at the same time keeps the grass alive, similarly, if he speaks to one person, all others benefit.
218 If a person came upon a river of divine nectar he would become immortal, and by bathing in it all his sin and trouble would be removed. In addition, it would be sweet to drink.
219 In the same way, his speech dispels ignorance and people realize their eternal nature. However much people listen to his speech, they never grow tired of it, as if it were nectar.
220 A person who practices the penance of speech speaks whenever he is asked a question. Otherwise, he recites the Vedas or repeats the name of God.
221 He establishes within his speech a temple for the three Vedas, and his mouth is like a school of the Supreme.
222 When the tongue is always occupied in repeating the name of Shiva or Vishnu, this is known as the penance of speech.
223 I will now explain to you mental penance. Listen, said the Lord of all the gods of the three worlds.

मन:प्रसाद: सौम्यत्वं मौनम् आत्मविनिग्रह: ।
भावसंशुद्धिर् इत्य् एतत् तपो मानसम् उच्यते ॥
manaḥprasādaḥ sāumyatvaṁ
māunam ātmavinigrahaḥ
bhāvasaṁśuddhir ity etat
tapo mānasam ucyate

16. Peace of mind, gentleness, silence, self-restraint, purity of being; these are called austerities of the mind.

224 Just like a lake with no ripples on its surface, the sky without clouds, a grove of sandalwood trees free from serpents,
225 The moon without changing phases, a king free from anxiety, or the Milky Ocean without Mount Mandara to churn it,
226 Similarly, when the mind is freed from the meshes of doubt, it rests in the Self.
227 The mind itself is like light without heat, food that is tasty yet not heavy, or the sky without emptiness;
228 For it knows that its well-being lies in escaping from its natural tendencies, as though a chilled limb didn't allow itself to shiver.
229 The pure beauty of the mind is like the clear, unwaning orb of the full moon.
230 The wounds inflicted by dispassion are healed, all disturbing mental activity subsides, and the soul is prepared for Self-realization.
231 The tongue, which is usually engaged in reciting the scriptures, is released from its reins.
232 When it attains union with the supreme Self, the mind ceases to carry out its normal functions, just as salt becomes one with water.
233 When this is so, how can those moods arise in the mind which drive it along the road of the senses until it reaches the village of sense objects?
234 In this way the mind becomes purified of its normal tendencies, just as the palm of the hand is free from hair.
235 O Arjuna, what need is there to say more? When the mind reaches this state, it becomes fit for mental penance.
236 The Lord said, I have fully explained to you the characteristics of mental penance.
237 I have told you of penance in general and of its threefold division into the penance of the body, speech, and mind.
238 Now listen with all your power of understanding to the way in which this threefold nature of penance arises from the three qualities.

श्रद्धया परया तप्तं तपस् तत् त्रिविधं नरै: ।
अफलाकाङ्क्षिभिर् युक्तै: सात्त्विकं परिचक्षते ॥
śraddhayā parayā taptaṁ
tapas tat trividhaṁ narāiḥ

aphalākāṅkṣibhir yuktāiḥ
sāttvikaṁ paricakṣate

17. This threefold austerity practiced with the highest faith by men who are not desirous of fruits and are steadfast, they regard as sattvic.

239 O wise Arjuna, you should practice with full faith the three kinds of penance which I have shown you, without any desire for the fruit of it.

240 When it is performed with a pure heart and with faith in the authority of the scriptures, the wise say that it has the quality of goodness.

सत्कारमानपूजार्थं तपो दम्भेन चैव यत् ।
क्रियते तद् इह प्रोक्तं राजसं चलम् अध्रुवम् ॥
satkāramānapūjārthaṁ
tapo dambhena cāiva yat
kriyate tad iha proktaṁ
rājasaṁ calam adhruvam

18. Austerity which is practiced with hypocrisy for the sake of honor, respect, and reverence; that, here in the world, is declared to be rajasic, unsteady, and impermanent.

241 On the other hand, penance that is performed in the spirit of duality to prove a person's austerity and to establish him on the highest pinnacle of superiority,

242 So that the world may honor him alone and give him the highest place at feasts,

243 So that the world may praise him and all people will make pilgrimages to him,

244 So that he alone may be the object of all forms of worship and he will enjoy all the pleasures that accompany greatness,

245 Putting on a show of austerity in body and speech in order to win favor, just as a prostitute adorns herself to attract attention,

246 This kind of penance, practiced in the hope of gaining wealth and respect, has the quality of passion.

247 If a cow is diseased, she gives no milk after giving birth to a calf. If crops have been grazed, there is nothing left to harvest.

248 Similarly, that penance which is performed with great effort in the hope of winning fame bears no fruit.

249 Besides being fruitless, O Arjuna, it is given up while still unfinished. Thus it has no stability.

250 Untimely clouds which gather in the sky may seem to shatter the world with thunder, but how long do they stay?

251 In the same way, this passionate kind of penance is fruitless and isn't practiced continuously.

252 Now when penance is performed according to the way of darkness, a person loses both earthly fame and life in heaven.

मूढग्राहेणात्मनो यत् पीडया क्रियते तपः ।
परस्योत्सादनार्थं वा तत् तामसम् उदाहृतम् ॥
mūḍhagrāheṇātmano yat
pīḍayā kriyate tapaḥ
parasyotsādanārthaṁ vā
tat tāmasam udāhṛtam

19. Austerity which is performed with deluded notions and with self-torture, or with the aim of destroying another, is declared to be tamasic.

253 O Arjuna, some people with foolish minds consider their bodies as enemies.

254 They light the five fires around their bodies so they may be burned up as fuel.

255 They burn balsam on their heads, thrust hooks into their backs, and scorch their bodies with flaming wood.

256 They restrain their breath, fast unnecessarily, and hang upside down over a fire, swallowing mouthfuls of smoke.

257 They stand in cold water up to their necks, or sit on rocks or river banks where they tear at their flesh.

258 O Arjuna, in these and in many other ways they inflict wounds on their bodies, performing austerities in order to harm others.

259 It is like a rock which, loosened by its own weight, falls and shatters and at the same time crushes to powder whatever comes in its way.

260 O Arjuna, these austerities, which are evil practices performed with skill, have the quality of darkness.

261 These people inflict pain on themselves in their desire to overcome others who are living happily.

262 In this way I have shown you that there are three kinds of penance, related to the three qualities.

263 Now the time has come for me to explain to you the threefold nature of charity.

264 The giving of gifts is also threefold, corresponding to the three qualities. First, listen to the kind of charity which is called good.

दातव्यम् इति यद् दानं दीयते ऽनुपकारिणे ।
देशे काले च पात्रे च तद् दानं सात्त्विकं स्मृतम् ।।

dātavyam iti yad dānaṁ
dīyate 'nupakāriṇe
deśe kāle ca pātre ca
tad dānaṁ sāttvikaṁ smṛtam

20. The gift which is given only with the thought "it is to be given," to a worthy person who has done no prior favor, at the proper place and time; that gift is held to be sattvic.

265 Whatever a person has received through performing his duty, he should respectfully give again to others.

266 This kind of charity is rare, just as good seed and fertile soil are seldom found at the same time.

267 A person may find a valuable jewel, but there may not be gold for the setting, and there may be no one to wear it.

268 We are truly fortunate if we have wealth and friends to invite to a feast when a holiday comes.

269 When charity and goodness come together, the place, time, means, and a deserving person will be available.

270 In the first place, if possible a person should be in Kurukshetra or any other part of the world that is equally holy.

271 Secondly, the time should be at the conjunction of the sun, moon, and Rahu, or a similarly auspicious occasion.

272 Then, at that time and place there should be a person worthy to receive the gift, someone who is the incarnation of purity,

273 Who has become the source of good conduct, the market where Vedic knowledge is distributed, and the purest jewel among brahmins.

274 To such a person the gift should be given, renouncing all of one's right to it, just as a wife gives herself fully to her husband.

275 Just as someone returns to a person what he has been keeping for him, or as a king's servant carrying his box of spices offers it to him,

276 Similarly, a person should offer gifts with the same detachment and spirit of service. In short, no desire should arise in the giver's heart.

277 Furthermore, the giver should make sure that the one who receives the gift is in no way able to reciprocate.

278 If a person shouts up into the sky there will be no echo, and he can see nothing in a mirror from behind it.

279 If he throws a ball onto the surface of water, it won't rebound into his hand.

280 Just as a bull dedicated to a temple makes no return for the food given to it, and as an ungrateful person doesn't repay a benefit conferred on him,

281 Similarly, when a gift has been given to someone who cannot give anything in return, the giver should remain indifferent about it.

282 O Arjuna, the giving of gifts in this way is the highest form of giving and is called pure;

283 For in it there is the combination of the right time, the right place, a worthy recipient, and a pure gift given with propriety.

यत् तु प्रत्युपकारार्थं फलम् उद्दिश्य वा पुनः ।
दीयते च परिक्लिष्टं तद् दानं राजसं स्मृतम् ।।

yat tu pratyupakārārthaṁ
phalam uddiśya vā punaḥ
dīyate ca parikliṣṭaṁ
tad dānaṁ rājasaṁ smṛtam

21. But that gift which is given grudgingly, with the aim of recompense or gain, with regard to fruit, is considered rajasic.

284 If a person feeds his cow so that she may give him milk, or builds a storehouse and then goes out to sow the crop,

285 If he invites his friends to a feast so he will receive gifts, or sends presents to a friend who has taken a vow not to accept them,

286 If he lends money to a neighbor after deducting the interest paid for it, or gives medicine to a sick person only after it has been paid for,

287 Gifts offered with such motives, in the hope that the giver will gain enjoyment as a result of them, are of a passionate nature.

288 O Arjuna, if such a person meets a good brahmin, who is unable to give him anything in return,

289 He gives him a small gift so that in return the sins of his relatives may be forgiven.

290 He hopes to gain all kinds of heavenly pleasures from it, although the alms he has given wouldn't be enough to provide food for even a single person.

291 Moreover, when a brahmin accepts his offering, the giver is overcome with grief, as

though thieves had robbed him of all of his possessions.

292 O wise Arjuna, there is no need to say anymore. Gifts given in this spirit are known as passionate.

अदेशकाले यद् दानम् अपात्रेभ्यश्च दीयते ।
असत्कृतम् अवज्ञातं तत् तामसम् उदाहृतम् ।।

adeśakāle yad dānam
apātrebhyaśca dīyate
asatkṛtam avajñātaṁ
tat tāmasam udāhṛtam

22. That gift which is given at the wrong place and time to the unworthy, without paying respect, or with contempt, is declared to be tamasic.

293 In places where nonbelievers live, in forests inhabited by strange tribes, among tent-dwellers, or in the marketplaces of towns,

294 Where people gather at dusk or at night, and where stolen goods are freely distributed,

295 To ballad singers, jugglers, prostitutes, gamblers, and those under magic spells—

296 Those people who offer gifts under these conditions are delighted with dances, and their ears are enchanted when they hear songs of their own praise.

297 Besides this, when they smell the fragrance of balsam, they become confused and act like demons.

298 This kind of giving is of a dark nature. There is still another thing that may happen through misfortune.

299 Just as an insect may bore holes in wood and they may appear to form letters, or as a crow may accidentally be caught when one claps one's hands, a person of the dark quality may come upon a holy place at an auspicious moment.

300 There, a worthy person may ask him for alms. Then he becomes confused with pride,

301 And because there is no faith in his heart, he doesn't bow his head, offer worship, or show reverence; nor does he ask the other person to do so.

302 He doesn't spread a seat for him or offer him kum-kum or grains of rice. This is the behavior of an ignorant person.

303 He places a small sum in his hand, as though he were a creditor, and dismisses him with contempt.

304 He makes insulting remarks to him, saying that he isn't worthy of a greater gift, and pushes him away with abusive language.

305 I will say no more. This kind of charity is known everywhere as having the quality of darkness.

306 Now I have explained to you the characteristics of all three kinds of giving. Notice particularly those that have the qualities of passion and darkness.

307 O Arjuna, I know that with your clear mind you will raise a question here.

308 Since there is only one kind of action, that of goodness, which releases a person from the bonds of earthly life, why should we speak of the opposite ones, which are sinful?

309 To obtain a hidden treasure, a person must first overcome the evil spirit that guards it. When a lamp is lit, there will be smoke.

310 Similarly, passion and darkness are doors barring the way to pure goodness. Is it wrong to remove them from the world?

311 Every action derived from the virtues which I have described, from faith to charity, is dominated by the three qualities.

312 Don't think that I wanted to speak of all three. But in order to explain goodness, it was necessary to define the other two.

313 When two are set aside, the third can be seen more clearly, in the same way that the twilight is seen better between day and night.

314 Similarly, by removing passion and darkness, the third quality of goodness remains and stands out clearly.

315 So in order to show you the quality of goodness, I have described passion and darkness. Now you can avoid them and attain goodness.

316 If you perform sacrifices and all other duties in the spirit of pure goodness, you will attain the goal of your life as easily as if it were in the palm of your hand.

317 What can't we see, if the sun shows us everything there is? So if we do everything in the spirit of goodness, what fruit can't we obtain?

318 Goodness has the ability to satisfy all our desires. But concerning the means to attain liberation,

319 That is a deeper matter. When we are helped to attain this, we can enter the state of liberation.

320 Although a certain amount of gold is worth fifteen rupees, without the royal seal it can-

not be used as a coin.

321 Water may be clear, cool, sweet, and pleasant; but its holiness depends on its presence in sacred places.

322 A river may be large or small, but once it flows into the Ganges it is carried to the ocean.

323 Similarly, O Arjuna, no obstacle can possibly come in a person's way once his good works have led him to liberation.

324 As soon as Arjuna heard these words, his heart couldn't contain his eagerness to know about this and he exclaimed, O Lord, please tell me about this!

325 Then the compassionate Lord replied, Listen to that which enables a person to obtain the jewel of liberation.

ओं तत् सद् इति निर्देशो ब्रह्मणस् त्रिविधः स्मृतः ।
ब्राह्मणास् तेन वेदाश्च यज्ञाश्च विहिताः पुरा ॥

oṁ tat sad iti nirdeśo
brahmaṇas trividhaḥ smṛtaḥ
brāhmaṇās tena vedāśca
yajñāśca vihitāḥ purā

23. "Om tat sat"—this has been taught as the threefold designation of Brahman. By this the brahmins, the Vedas, and the sacrifices were created in ancient times.

326 The eternal, supreme Self, the origin and dwelling place of the universe, has one name, which is threefold.

327 Although He is beyond all name and class, the Vedas have given Him a symbol so that people may recognize Him in the dark night of pride and ignorance.

328 Those who are weighed down by the sorrows of this world turn to God in supplication, and the name to which He answers is this symbol.

329 In their mercy, the Vedas have given a sacred word so that the one God may break His silence and meet duality.

330 When God is invoked by this name, what was formerly hidden is revealed.

331 However, only those who are worthy to sit with God in the city of the Upanishads on the mountain peak of the Vedas know the meaning of this name.

332 Moreover, the power of creation that lies in the creator emanates from this one name.

333 O Arjuna, before the creation of the world, Brahma was alone and in an undifferentiated state.

334 He was not conscious of Me, nor could he create, but this name gave him the power to do so.

335 When he meditated inwardly on the meaning of this name and repeated the threefold word, he was endowed with the power of creating the universe.

336 Then he created the brahmins, gave them the Vedas to guide them, and established sacrifices and other rites as a way of life.

337 After this, he created countless living beings and gave them the gift of the three worlds.

338 Lord Krishna said, Now hear from Me the form of that invocation which endowed the creator with the power to create:

339 Om, the prince of all invocations, is the first syllable, *Tat* is the second, and *Sat* is the third.

340 These three—*Om*, *Tat*, and *Sat*—compose the threefold name of the Supreme. The Upanishads enjoy the fragrance of this flower.

341 When a person unites himself with this name and performs actions which are pure and good, then he seizes the final beatitude as if it were a servant in his house.

342 Through good luck a person may be given ornaments of camphor, but the difficulty lies in knowing how to wear them.

343 Similarly, a person may perform good actions while repeating God's name, yet if he doesn't know the secret of how to use it,

344 It is as useless as bringing home a group of sages when one doesn't know how to entertain them properly.

345 If a person tied up all his jewels and gold in a cloth and hung it around his neck,

346 It would be as futile as if he performed good actions while repeating God's name, but without knowing the proper way to do it.

347 A hungry child will starve, even with food nearby, if it doesn't know how to feed itself.

348 O Arjuna, a person may have oil, a wick, and fire in his house; but if he doesn't know how to use them, there will be no light.

349 Similarly, when the moment arrives for a person to act and he remembers the invocation, it will still be fruitless if he doesn't repeat it in the correct way.

350 So learn from Me the proper way to repeat the threefold name of God.

तस्मादो इत्य् उदाहृत्य यज्ञदानतपःक्रियाः ।
प्रवर्तन्ते विधानोक्ताः सततं ब्रह्मवादिनाम् ॥

tasmād om ity udāhṛtya
yajñadānatapaḥkriyāḥ
pravartante vidhānoktāḥ
satataṁ brahmavādinām

24. Therefore, acts of sacrifice, giving, and austerity are always begun uttering the syllable "Om" by the students of Brahman, as prescribed in the Vedic injunctions.

351 This name of God should be uttered at the beginning, in the middle, and at the end of action.
352 O Arjuna, this is the method by which knowers of the Absolute receive the knowledge of the Absolute.
353 Those who speak from scriptural knowledge, in their desire for union with God, never neglect the practice of sacrifice and other rites.
354 First, they form a clear impression of *Om* in their minds through meditation, and then they utter the word.
355 Meditating on it and uttering it aloud, they begin to perform action.
356 The repetition of the sacred *Om* at the beginning of all actions is like an unfailing light in the darkness, or a strong companion in a forest.
357 In this way, people offer abundant wealth through the fire or through brahmins, so that it may reach the deity for whom it is intended.
358 They also offer to the fire oblations in the form of renunciation, observing the proper rituals.
359 By performing various kinds of sacrifice, they free themselves from all undesirable limitations.
360 At the proper time and place, they offer to worthy people land and money which they have obtained by honest means.
361 They abstain from alternate meals with great severity, and they eat and fast according to the waxing and waning of the moon, performing austerities which dry up the fluids of their bodies.
362 So they easily attain liberation by the methods of sacrifice, charity, and penance, which are usually thought of as forms of bondage.
363 When a boat is drawn up on the shore it is heavy, but once it is launched a person can cross the ocean in it. In the same way, a person can free himself from the bondage of action by using this name properly.
364 All actions are effective when they are performed with the repetition of *Om*.
365 When a person finds that he is entering into the fruit of his action, he repeats the word *Tat*.

तद् इत्य् अनभिसंधाय फलं यज्ञतपःक्रियाः ।
दानक्रियाश्च विविधाः क्रियन्ते मोक्षकाङ्क्षिभिः ॥

tad ity anabhisaṁdhāya
phalaṁ yajñatapaḥkriyāḥ
dānakriyāśca vividhāḥ
kriyante mokṣakāṅkṣibhiḥ

25. Uttering "tat" and without aiming at fruits, acts of sacrifice and austerity and acts of giving of various sorts are performed by those who desire liberation.

366 The word *Tat* refers to that which transcends the universe, which alone sees all and is beyond all.
367 O wise Arjuna, meditating on God as the primal source of all, they express it by the word *Tat*.
368 Then they say, May all our actions and the fruits of our actions be dedicated to God, and may there be nothing left for us to experience in the world.
369 So with the repetition of *Tat*, referring to the Supreme, they offer all their actions to Him. Saying, This is not mine, they cleanse themselves from the taint of action.
370 In this way, the action which they undertake with the repetition of *Om* and offer up with *Tat* is transformed into the nature of the Absolute.
371 Although the action takes on the form of God, it isn't complete as long as the performer remains separate from God.
372 Salt becomes one with water when mixed with it, yet its saltiness remains. Similarly, although the action has merged into the Absolute, duality remains in the one who performed it.
373 The more duality grows, the more fear of earthly life increases. The Lord has said this both here and in the Vedas.
374 So that the sense of separateness from God may give way to a sense of unity, the Lord has given the word *Sat*.
375 If an action has merged with the Supreme through the words *Om* and *Tat* and has been praised as excellent,
376 The word *Sat* applies to it. I will now explain this to you.

सद्भावे साधुभावे च सद् इत्य् एतत् प्रयुज्यते ।
प्रशस्ते कर्मणि तथा सच्छब्दः पार्थ युज्यते ॥

sadbhāve sādhubhāve ca
sad ity etat prayujyate
praśaste karmaṇi tathā
sacchabdaḥ pārtha yujyate

26. "Sat" is used in its meaning of "reality" and in its meaning of "goodness." Also the word "sat" is used for an auspicious act, Arjuna.

377 The word *Sat* refers to that perfect nature of reality, by which all unreality loses its value, like a counterfeit coin.
378 This reality is unaffected by time and place and remains undivided in its own essence.
379 The entire world of form is unreal. Once a person perceives this, he attains union with the Supreme.
380 Because of this, a worthy action merges with God, and should be seen with the awareness of oneness with God.
381 An action which has become one with God through the words *Om* and *Tat* is immediately absorbed into the supreme Self.
382 This is the essence of the use of the *Sat*. It is Krishna who says this, not I, Jnaneshwar.
383 If I were to say that I am the one who says this, it would impute duality to Him, and this would detract from His greatness. Therefore, I say that these are the Lord's words.
384 There is still another way to use the word *Sat*, which is helpful to one who performs good deeds.
385 If a person performs good actions according to his position, but there is some defect in carrying them out,
386 Then, just as the body cannot move properly if one limb is defective, or a carriage cannot be driven if one of its parts is missing,
387 Similarly, a good action loses its value if one virtue is lacking when the action is performed.
388 However, if the word *Sat* is repeated after *Om* and *Tat*, this rescues the action from being worthless.
389 Because of its power of purification, the word *Sat* will nullify the defect in performing the action and restore its validity.
390 Just as a divine medicine can cure a patient, and help can be given to one who is overwhelmed, in the same way the word *Sat* can restore perfection to an action which was carried out imperfectly.
391 By mistake, an action may overstep the boundaries of what is forbidden,
392 Just like a traveler who loses his way, or an expert who is mistaken. Don't such things happen in the world?
393 So when through carelessness an action passes beyond the boundary and is called unrighteous,
394 Then the use of this word, which is more powerful than the other two, makes the action a worthy one.
395 Just like the contact of iron with the philosopher's stone, the mingling of a stream with the waters of the Ganges, or a shower of nectar over a dead person,
396 Such is the effect of the word *Sat* on an imperfect action, O Arjuna. This is the power of this name.
397 When you consider this name and have understood its secret, you will know that it is truly the Supreme.
398 You should know that the repetition of these three words, *Om*, *Tat*, and *Sat*, leads to God, from whom the entire visible world has manifested.
399 This name is the hidden symbol of the Absolute, the pure Supreme.
400 This name is supported by God, just as the sky is its own support. The name and the named are inseparable.
401 When the sun rises in the heavens, it shines by its own light. In the same way, God reveals this threefold symbol.

यज्ञे तपसि दाने च स्थितिः सद् इति चोच्यते ।
कर्म चैव तदर्थीयं सद् इत्य् एवाभिधीयते ॥

yajñe tapasi dāne ca
sthitiḥ sad iti cocyate
karma cāiva tadarthīyaṁ
sad ity evābhidhīyate

27. Steadfastness in sacrifice, austerity, and giving is also called "sat," and action relating to these is likewise designated as "sat."

402 This name isn't just a threefold symbol; it is God Himself, so know that whatever action you may undertake,
403 Whether it is a sacrifice, a gift, or some severe penance, it may remain defective or incomplete;
404 But if it is offered to God, it is transformed into His nature. There is no question of the

quality of the gold produced by contact with the philosopher's stone.

405 In the Absolute, the complete and the incomplete can no longer be distinguished, just as rivers cannot be separated once they have flowed into the sea.

406 O Arjuna, I have explained to you the power of God's name.

407 I have also explained to you the proper way to repeat these syllables.

408 Such is the greatness of this name of God. Have you understood this mystery?

409 Therefore, from now on let your faith in this name always increase. It will set you free from all bonds.

410 Whatever action is accompanied by the proper use of this name is comparable to the recitation of all the Vedas.

अश्रद्धया हुतं दत्तं तपस् तप्तं कृतं च यत् ।
असद् इत्य् उच्यते पार्थ न च तत् प्रेत्य नो इह ॥

aśraddhayā hutaṁ dattaṁ
tapas taptaṁ kṛtaṁ ca yat
asad ity ucyate pārtha
na ca tat pretya no iha

28. An oblation offered or an austerity practiced without faith is called "asat," Arjuna, and is nothing in the hereafter or here in the world.

411 If a person were to leave this path, lose his faith, and let his own self-will increase,

412 Then even if he performed countless horse sacrifices, gave away alms that would fill the world with jewels, or performed thousands of austerities standing on one toe,

413 All of these efforts would be as irrelevant as creating new oceans as reservoirs of water.

414 It would be as useless as showers of rain falling on rocky ground, pouring oblations onto dead ashes, or embracing a shadow.

415 O Arjuna, from the very beginning such undertakings would be as ineffective as trying to beat the sky with one's hands.

416 It would be like grinding stone in an oil-mill. Instead of producing oil, it would only lead to poverty.

417 If a traveler makes a bundle of broken pieces of pottery and takes it along for food, he will starve to death, for they serve no purpose either in his own country or anywhere else.

418 Similarly, any action performed without faith brings no worldly happiness. Then how could it bring any hope for joy in heaven?

419 Any action undertaken without faith in the name of God brings only weariness in this world and the world beyond.

420 Lord Krishna, the lion who destroys the elephant of sin, the dispeller of darkness of misery, the best of warriors, said these things.

421 Arjuna was absorbed in the bliss of the Self, as if the moon were lost in its own light.

422 A battlefield is like a merchant who uses arrows as his tally to count the lives of men, as though they were pieces of flesh.

423 Even at this terrible time, Arjuna experienced the bliss of union with the Self. No one else has ever had such incomparably good fortune.

424 Sanjaya said to the king of the Kauravas, One delights in seeing these virtues in the enemy, Arjuna. He is a Guru who brings us heavenly joy.

425 If Arjuna hadn't questioned Him, the Lord wouldn't have revealed these mysteries. Then how could we have witnessed this experience of union with God?

426 We would be groping in the darkness of ignorance in the cycle of birth and death. However, we have been brought into the temple of the light of the Self.

427 The favor that he has bestowed on us is so great that he is like a brother to the great Vyasa in his power of teaching.

428 At this point, Sanjaya thought that his praise of Arjuna wouldn't please the king and that he was saying too much.

429 So he left this subject and began to speak of what Arjuna had asked Krishna.

430 Jnanadeva, the disciple of Nivritti, says, I will now relate all this to you. Please listen.

18

THE YOGA OF LIBERATION BY RENUNCIATION

HAIL to You, O God, pure and always merciful to Your devotees. You dispel like the storm wind the clouds of birth and old age!

2 Victory to You, O God, mighty One, destroyer of all that is inauspicious. You are the fruit of the tree of the Vedas and also the giver of the fruit.

3 Hail to You, O God, all in all, compassionate towards those who have freed themselves from worldly attachment, overcoming the relentless grasp of death, beyond all limitation.

4 Victory to You, O God, immutable, whose belly is swollen from feeding on those of fickle mind. You delight in the constant play of the evolution of the universe.

5 Hail to You, O God, undivided One. You inspire the fullness of joy, destroy all sin forever, and are the source of all creatures.

6 Victory to You, O God, self-luminous One, the sky which bears the world as a cloud, pillar of support for the creation of the universe from its very beginning, and destroyer of worldly existence.

7 Hail to You, O God, pure One, ocean of mercy, elephant in the garden of the dawn of knowledge. You destroy the passion of lust by the practice of restraint.

8 Victory to You, O God, One and indivisible. You have overcome the power of the serpent of the god of love, You are the light in the house of Your devotees, the remover of all trouble.

9 I salute You, who are without a second, sole object of the love of the dispassionate, worthy of the worship of those who have attained You, beyond the reach of illusory matter.

10 Hail to You, O God and Guru. You are like the wish–fulfilling tree which is beyond the power of thought to imagine, the soil in which the seed of Self–knowledge grows.

11 O You who are supreme, how can I sing Your praises with all these various epithets?

12 That form of Yours which I have described in these words is invisible to us. Therefore, I am ashamed to speak to You in this way.

13 The ocean stays within its boundaries, but only as long as the moon doesn't rise.

14 The moonstone doesn't worship the moon by giving out its own moisture. It is the moon which draws it out.

15 Who can tell what causes the trees to send out fresh foliage at the coming of spring? The tree has no power to prevent this.

16 Does the lotus hesitate to open when it receives the rays of the sun? Doesn't salt lose its form when touched by water?

17 Similarly, when I remember You, I lose all thought of my own individuality. Just as a person who has eaten a full meal cannot refrain from belching,

18 In the same way, since You have filled me with Yourself, I have lost all awareness of myself, and my voice is wild with the desire to praise You.

19 On the other hand, if I were to praise You in full awareness, I would distinguish between You and Your qualities.

20 But You are the very image of oneness. How could I make a distinction between You and Your qualities? If a pearl is broken in two pieces, should the pieces be joined or left as they are?

21 If I call myself a servant, wouldn't that attribute to You the status of a Master? Why should I use for You such words implying

separateness?
22 It wouldn't be correct of say that You are my father or my mother, for this would wrongly imply the distinction of parent and child.
23 If I were to speak of You as the Spirit, pervading the universe, O giver of all, that would suggest that You who are within could also be outside.
24 Therefore, it seems that there is no proper form of praise in this world and that silence is the only ornament that is worthy of You.
25 Therefore, silence is the only praise, absence of action is the only way to worship, and cessation of separate existence is to be in You.
26 O my Mother, accept my praise though it may be like the irresponsible words of someone who is confused.
27 I pray that You will place the blessed seal of the *Gita* on my explanation so that it may be acceptable to this gathering of saintly people.
28 At this point Shri Nivritti exclaimed, Don't go on repeating the same thing. How long must a person go on rubbing a piece of iron with a touchstone?
29 Then Jnanadeva asked him to grant his blessing and listen to his discourse.
30 The *Gita* is like a jeweled temple, and its meaning is the jewel on its pinnacle. This chapter is the guide to its revelation.
31 As soon as a person sees the dome of a temple, he has a vision of the deity within it.
32 It is the same with this chapter; it enables one to understand the meaning of the whole *Gita*.
33 This is why I say that the eighteenth chapter is the pinnacle which Shri Badarayana placed on the temple of the *Gita*.
34 In a temple nothing is added after the pinnacle. Similarly, this chapter is the completion of the *Gita*.
35 Shri Vyasa is a great craftsman, for on that mountain of jewels known as the Vedas, he has marked the site of the meaning of the Upanishads.
36 In the soil were found innumerable stones, such as the goals of life, and with them he built a surrounding wall in the form of the *Mahabharata*.
37 In the center of this enclosure, he carved many stones in the form of knowledge of the Self, from the dialogue between Arjuna and Krishna.
38 Then with the plumb line of inaction, he erected the courtyard of liberation and added the essence of all the scriptures.
39 In this way, he built a temple consisting of the first fifteen chapters, from the purifying of the ground to the top layer of the fifteenth chapter.
40 The sixteenth chapter is the dome above it, while the seventeenth chapter is the base of its pinnacle.
41 The eighteenth chapter is the pinnacle which rises above it bearing the banner of Vyasa, author of the *Gita* and other sacred works.
42 Thus, all the previous chapters are layers rising one above the other, while this chapter shows the completion of the work.
43 The pinnacle shows clearly that the work is finished and the eighteenth chapter reveals the entire *Gita*.
44 In this way, the skillful Vyasa erected the temple of the *Gita*, providing shelter for all creatures.
45 Some wander around it by repeating it daily, and some enjoy the shade it gives by hearing it recited.
46 Others make offerings of betel leaves and money in the form of their complete attention, and enter the inner temple of the understanding of its meaning.
47 There, through enlightenment they at once meet the Lord, but in the temple of liberation all men are equal.
48 Thus the *Gita* is the temple of the followers of Vishnu, and the eighteenth chapter is its pinnacle. Here I have shown its special nature.
49 Now I will explain how, as I understand it, this chapter arises from the previous seventeen.
50 The androgynous form of Shiva shows that the body is one and the two forms are not separate.
51 The Ganges and the Jamuna rivers are separate because they flow in different streams, but because they are both of water, they are seen to be one.
52 During the bright half of the month the phases of the moon increase, but they don't appear as separate layers of the moon.
53 The four quarters of a verse seem to be sepa-

rate because they are divided into stanzas. Similarly, each chapter is separate only because the book is divided into chapters.
54 Where the meaning is concerned they are not separate, just as one thread holds together a necklace of jewels.
55 Pearls are strung together on a necklace, but in the beauty of their form they are one.
56 The flowers in a garland can be seen separately, but their fragrance merges into one. Verses and chapters may be regarded in this same way.
57 There are seven hundred verses and eighteen chapters in the *Gita*, but the Lord has taught only one truth.
58 I haven't departed from this method in expounding the *Gita*. Now listen to the explanation of this chapter in the same manner.
59 At the end of chapter seventeen, in the closing verses, the Lord said this:
60 O Arjuna, all actions which are performed without faith in the name of God are worthless.
61 Hearing these words of the Lord, Arjuna was pleased and said to himself, I think He has condemned all those who devote themselves to a life of action!
62 How can these poor people, who are blinded by ignorance and who don't see God, have any idea of the power of His name?
63 Without freedom from passion and darkness, faith is weak. How can it grasp the meaning of God's name?
64 Just as it is dangerous to grasp a spear, to run on a rope, or to play with the hood of a serpent,
65 Similarly, actions performed without faith are harmful. They lead to rebirth, and all kinds of evil lie in them.
66 Even if actions are properly performed, they only lead people as far as knowledge. Otherwise, they may lead them to hell.
67 If the life of action is filled with so many difficulties, how can people who perform them hope to reach liberation?
68 So let us set action aside, renounce everything, and resort to perfect detachment.
69 Then we won't have to be concerned about the bad effects of action, and we will attain knowledge of the Self.
70 These are the mystic words which evoke knowledge, the good soil in which the crop of knowledge ripens, and the ropes to capture it.
71 I would like to ask the Lord whether people would be liberated if they followed the way of renunciation and non-attachment.
72 With this thought in mind, Arjuna asked Krishna to explain clearly the nature of these two.
73 The answer which Krishna gave is the subject of the eighteenth chapter.
74 Thus, one chapter leads to another, just as one generation gives birth to the next. Now hear how Arjuna asked Krishna about this.
75 When Arjuna heard the final words of the Lord in the last chapter, his mind became agitated.
76 Though in reality he had thoroughly understood the teaching, he was troubled when Krishna remained silent.
77 When a cow has satisfied her calf, she doesn't wander away. This is the nature of true love.
78 Similarly, people long for their loved one to speak even without any cause, and they enjoy looking at each other again and again, increasing their delight.
79 This is the nature of true love. Because Arjuna was the embodiment of such love, he was troubled at this silence.
80 Through discussion a person may come to realize the Absolute, just as he can see his own image in a mirror.
81 But if the conversation ends, the opportunity for this experience is lost. Now that Arjuna had tasted this joy, how could he bear the loss of it?
82 So under the pretext of asking the Lord about renunciation and non-attachment, Arjuna reopened the subject of the *Gita*, just as one unrolls a piece of cloth.
83 This is not just chapter eighteen; it is the entire *Gita* contained in one chapter. When a calf wants milk, doesn't the cow respond immediately?
84 So when the discussion of the *Gita* was drawing to a close, Arjuna returned to the same subject. Can a master refuse to speak with his servant?

अर्जुन उवाच । *arjuna uvāca*

संन्यासस्य महाबाहो तत्त्वम् इच्छामि वेदितुम् ।
त्यागस्य च हृषीकेश पृथक् केशिनिषूदन ।।
saṁnyāsasya mahābāho

tattvam icchāmi veditum
tyāgasya ca hṛṣīkeśa
pṛthak keśiniṣūdana

Arjuna spoke:
1. I wish to know the truth of sannyasa, Krishna, and of renunciation, and the difference between them.

85 I have said enough. Addressing his question to Krishna, Arjuna said, O Lord, listen to my request!
86 O Master, these two terms seem to have the same meaning, just as company and group are synonymous.
87 Similarly, renunciation also expresses *sannyasa*. This is how I understand them.
88 If there is any difference in their meaning, will You make it clear? Then Lord Krishna said, They are certainly different.
89 Yet I agree with your opinion, O Arjuna, that these two words have only one meaning.
90 Both of these words do mean renunciation, but this is the difference between them:
91 *Sannyasa* means giving up all action, while renunciation implies giving up the fruit of the action.
92 I will now explain to you when one should renounce the fruit of an action and when one should give up the action itself. Pay attention to what I say.
93 Trees grow abundantly in forests and on mountains, but rice and garden shrubs don't grow naturally on their own.
94 Grass grows freely without being sown. On the other hand, rice won't grow without cultivation.
95 The human body grows by itself, but the ornaments that adorn it are made with skill. A river rises from its own source, but a well is made only by digging.
96 In the same way, daily actions and ceremonies take place naturally, but actions prompted by a desire for their results are performed with this motive.

श्रीभगवान् उवाच । *śrībhagavān uvāca*

काम्यानां कर्मणां न्यासं
संन्यासं कवयो विदुः ।
सर्वकर्मफलत्यागं
प्राहुस् त्यागं विचक्षणाः ॥

kāmyānāṁ karmaṇāṁ nyāsaṁ
saṁnyāsaṁ kavayo viduḥ
sarvakarmaphalatyāgaṁ
prāhus tyāgaṁ vicakṣaṇāḥ

The Blessed Lord spoke:
2. The relinquishment of actions prompted by desire the sages understand as sannyasa; the relinquishment of the fruit of all action the wise declare to be renunciation.

97 All actions performed with a desire for their fruits, such as the horse sacrifice,
98 Digging wells and tanks, planting gardens, donations of land and towns, and the observance of similar kinds of vows,
99 In fact, everything that is done for the sake of merit or benefit, prompted by desire, binds the person who does these actions to the experience of their fruits.
100 O Arjuna, when a person enters the village of this body, he cannot avoid the experiences of life and death.
101 What is appointed by destiny cannot by any means be avoided. A fair or dark complexion cannot be changed by washing.
102 A person must experience the fruit of every action that he performs with desire as its motive. It is like a debt from which he can never be freed except by payment.
103 O Arjuna, a person might suddenly commit an action without desire. Even without fighting, he might be struck by an arrow shot accidentally.
104 Sugar tastes sweet even if a person puts it in his mouth unintentionally. A live coal would burn him even if he thought it was ashes and held it in his hand.
105 Similarly, actions performed for their fruit have an inherent power, so one who seeks liberation should avoid them.
106 O Arjuna, an action of this kind is like poison that must be expelled from the stomach.
107 Giving up this kind of actions is called *sannyasa*. Thus spoke the Lord, who sees into everyone's heart.
108 When a person gives up his wealth, his fear vanishes. Similarly, when he renounces all actions motivated by desire, all his desires are eliminated.
109 When the sun and the moon are conjunct, it is the time to honor the ancestors. The *shraddha* ceremonies are performed on the anniversary of the death of one's father or mother.

110 When a guest arrives, certain things must be done. All these rites are recurring duties.
111 In the rainy season the sky is filled with clouds. In the spring the beauty of the forest increases, and youth adds beauty to the body.
112 The moonstone becomes moist under the moon, and the sun causes the lotuses to bloom.
113 If all those actions which are performed daily are carried out properly, they are called recurring rites.
114 Actions which are performed daily in the morning, at noon, and in the evening, are called daily actions. But just as the sight of the eyes is not superior to the eye itself,
115 As the power of walking is in the feet and not somewhere else, as light lies potentially in a lamp,
116 As fragrance lies hidden in the sandalwood tree and isn't given to it from some other source, in the same way the performance of an action is inherent in it.
117 O Arjuna, these actions are normally called daily actions. In this way, I have explained to you both daily actions and recurring rites.
118 Because both these kinds of action are performed of necessity, some consider them to be without fruit.
119 Nevertheless, just as a person who eats is satisfied and his hunger disappears, these daily and periodic duties produce their results.
120 If an alloy of gold is placed in the fire, the alloy disappears and the pure gold is left. Similarly, such actions will produce their corresponding fruit.
121 When a person performs these actions, all his sin is removed. Then his worthiness increases and the state of liberation comes within his grasp.
122 The fruit of daily actions and periodic rites is great, but one should abandon it just as one avoids a child born at an inauspicious time.
123 Vines blossom and mango trees send out new growth, but spring passes without even touching them.
124 Similarly, a person should carry out his daily duties and periodic rites with due attention and within the proper limits, and then he should give up the entire fruit as if it were vomit.
125 Wise people call renunciation giving up the fruit of such actions. Now I have explained to you both *sannyasa* and renunciation.
126 When a person attains renunciation, actions springing from desire cannot bind him, for he naturally avoids everything that is prohibited.
127 Actions become powerless when he abandons the desire for them, in the same way that the whole body becomes lifeless if the head is cut off.
128 Then all his actions fade away, just as a crop dies after it has ripened, and he easily attains Self-knowledge.
129 Thus, through practicing both these methods, he is raised to the place of honor in Self-knowledge.

त्याज्यं दोषवद् इत्य् एके कर्म प्राहुर् मनीषिणः ।
यज्ञदानतपःकर्म न त्याज्यम् इति चापरे ।।

tyājyaṁ doṣavad ity eke
karma prāhur manīṣiṇaḥ
yajñadānatapaḥkarma
na tyājyam iti cāpare

3. Some men of wisdom declare that action is to be abandoned and is full of evil, and others say that acts of sacrifice, giving, and austerity are not to be abandoned.

130 However, if a person doesn't do this diligently and practices renunciation in the wrong way, it is no longer renunciation and he falls into even greater entanglement.
131 Medicine taken without a proper diagnosis can be as harmful as poison. Food eaten by a person who isn't hungry may be dangerous for him.
132 So don't renounce what you shouldn't renounce, and don't become attached to what you should renounce.
133 If renunciation is done in the wrong way, it becomes a burden. Therefore, dispassionate people struggle against forbidden actions.
134 Some people are unable to give up the desire for the fruit of their actions, and they say that all action is bondage. They are like naked men who regard others as quarrelsome because they call them naked.
135 A greedy man who gets sick blames the food. A leper isn't angry with his body but with the flies that settle on it.
136 Similarly, those who cannot give up the fruit of action consider all actions evil and decide that they should give them up.
137 Others say that actions such as sacrifice

must be performed, for there is nothing else as purifying as these actions.

138 To attain a state of mental purity as quickly as possible, a person shouldn't be lazy about practicing those actions which strengthen it.

139 If gold is to be purified, one mustn't hesitate to put it in the fire. To keep a mirror clean, it must be scoured.

140 If a person wants to have clean clothes, he mustn't despise the washerman's caldron saying it is dirty.

141 Just as the only way to have tender food is to cook it, similarly, although actions may be difficult, they shouldn't be left undone.

142 Arguing in this way, some people say that one should never give up action, but their renunciation has become a subject of dispute.

143 Now pay attention to Me. I will explain how you can resolve this conflict and reach a decision on renunciation.

निश्चयं शृणु मे तत्र त्यागे भरतसत्तम ।
त्यागो हि पुरुषव्याघ्र त्रिविधः संप्रकीर्तितः ॥
niścayaṁ śṛṇu me tatra
tyāge bharatasattama
tyāgo hi puruṣavyāghra
trividhaḥ saṁprakīrtitaḥ

4. Hear My conclusion in this matter concerning renunciation, Arjuna. Renunciation is declared to be of three kinds:

144 O Arjuna, there are three kinds of renunciation. Now I will distinguish between them.

145 Though I may clarify these three kinds of renunciation, you should know what is the essence of them all.

146 First you should listen to what is clearly My opinion.

यज्ञदानतपःकर्म न त्याज्यं कार्यम् एव तत् ।
यज्ञो दानं तपश्चैव पावनानि मनीषिणाम् ॥
yajñadānatapaḥkarma
na tyājyaṁ kāryam eva tat
yajño dānaṁ tapaścaiva
pāvanāni manīṣiṇām

5. Acts of sacrifice, giving, and austerity are not to be abandoned, but rather to be performed; sacrifice, giving, and austerity are purifiers of those who are wise.

147 This is a matter which every seeker who is aware of the importance of his own liberation must understand completely.

148 A seeker can no more give up sacrifice, charity, austerity, and all duties which are considered obligatory, than a traveler can avoid taking step after step.

149 A person cannot give up his search for a lost object until he finds it, neither can he put aside a dish of food until he satisfies his hunger.

150 He cannot leave a boat until he reaches the opposite shore, he cannot cut down a plantain tree until it has borne fruit, and he cannot put away a lamp until he finds the object he is looking for.

151 Likewise, a person shouldn't be indifferent to the performance of sacrifice and other duties as long as his determination to gain Self-knowledge isn't firm.

152 On the contrary, he should carry out acts of sacrifice, charity, and austerity again and again, according to his capacity.

153 The faster he walks, the sooner he will be able to rest. Similarly, the more he practices these duties, the more rapidly he reaches the state of renouncing action.

154 The more medicine he takes, the sooner he will be free from disease.

155 In the same way, the more often he performs these actions in the proper way, the sooner he will drive out passion and darkness.

156 When one puts impure gold in a melting pot and adds salt, the alloy is removed and the gold is purified.

157 Similarly, when a person performs an action with devotion, it casts out passion and darkness and gives him the vision of pure goodness.

158 O Arjuna, for those who desire purity of mind, such actions are as effective as pilgrimages to holy places.

159 Just as if a stream of nectar were to come to a thirsty man in a desert, as if the sun were to shine on a blind man's eyes,

160 As if a river were to run to rescue a drowning man, the earth embrace a falling man, or death prolong the life of a person who is dying,

161 Similarly, O Arjuna, good actions free the seeker from the bondage of actions. Just as a dying man can be saved by poison used as medicine,

162 In the same way, O Arjuna, if a person skillfully performs actions, they will free him

from the bondage of action.

एतान्य् अपि तु कर्माणि सङ्गं त्यक्त्वा फलानि च ।
कर्तव्यानीति मे पार्थ निश्चितं मतम् उत्तमम् ॥

etāny api tu karmāṇi
saṅgaṁ tyaktvā phalāni ca
kartavyānīti me pārtha
niścitaṁ matam uttamam

6. These actions, however, are to be performed abandoning attachment to the fruits. This is My definite and highest belief, Arjuna.

163 Now, O Arjuna, I will explain to you how actions can annul the results which they bring about.

164 When a person properly performs sacrifices according to the rites, he takes no pride in being the doer.

165 If he goes on a pilgrimage at someone else's expense, he cannot take pride in the fact that he is making a pilgrimage.

166 If he captures a king by the power of the royal seal, he cannot boast that he is a victor.

167 If he crosses the water supported by someone else, he cannot claim that he is swimming. A priest who distributes gifts on another's behalf is not displaying his own generosity.

168 Therefore, a person should carry out all his actions at the proper time without being proud that he has performed them.

169 Furthermore, O Arjuna, once you have performed actions, don't let any desire for their fruit enter your mind.

170 O Arjuna, a person should give up all desire for the fruit of his actions before he performs them, just as one woman may nurse another woman's child.

171 He should perform his actions with indifference towards their results, just as he wouldn't water a holy fig tree with the hope of getting its fruit.

172 Just as a cowherd may round up the cows without any longing for their milk, similarly a person should have the same attitude towards the results of his own actions.

173 Whatever actions he carries out in this way bring him the blessing of Self-knowledge.

174 Therefore, My teaching is that one should perform actions after renouncing all attachment to their fruit and to bodily desire.

175 Anyone who is weary of the bondage of earthly life and who longs to be freed from it should observe this teaching.

नियतस्य तु संन्यासः कर्मणो नोपपद्यते ।
मोहात् तस्य परित्यागस् तामसः परिकीर्तितः ॥

niyatasya tu saṁnyāsaḥ
karmaṇo nopapadyate
mohāt tasya parityāgas
tāmasaḥ parikīrtitaḥ

7. But renunciation of obligatory action is not proper; the abandonment of it through delusion is proclaimed to be tamasic.

176 If a person were to avoid his prescribed duties because he hated activity, it would be like tearing his eyes out because he was angry with darkness.

177 In My opinion, this kind of renunciation has the quality of darkness, and it is like a man who cuts off his head because he has a headache.

178 If the road is difficult, a person can travel it on foot. Should he cut off his feet because of the fault of the road?

179 If a hungry man were to kick over a dish placed before him because the food was too hot, without thinking that he would then have to remain hungry,

180 He would be like a man of darkness who, in his confusion, doesn't know that defects in the performance of actions are overcome by performing them in the proper way.

181 If a person gives up actions that he should perform as a duty, he practices that renunciation which has the quality of darkness.

दुःखम् इत्येव यत् कर्म कायक्लेशभयात् त्यजेत् ।
स कृत्वा राजसं त्यागं नैव त्यागफलं लभेत् ॥

duḥkham ityeva yat karma
kāyakleśabhayāt tyajet
sa kṛtvā rājasaṁ tyāgaṁ
nāiva tyāgaphalaṁ labhet

8. He who abandons action merely because it is difficult, or because of fear of bodily suffering, performs rajasic renunciation. He does not obtain the fruit of that renunciation.

182 A person should understand his own capacity and recognize those rites which are obligatory, yet realize the difficulty of performing them.

183 The beginning of an action may at first appear difficult, just as one may feel it is a burden to carry provisions for a journey.

184 Just as a neem leaf is bitter to the taste, or herbs are sour at first, similarly, before a duty is completed it may seem hard to perform.

185 Even a cow has horns which are harmful, and a rose bush has a thorny stem. It is difficult to enjoy a meal if one has to cook it first.

186 In the same way, if the beginning of an action appears difficult, a person feels he needs to make an effort to perform it.

187 Just as he may drop a burning object, a person may begin an action because it is compulsory but abandon it when he has trouble doing it.

188 He may say to himself, I have gotten this body as a result of my good fortune! Why should I bother with rites which sinful people perform?

189 I don't want to enjoy later the fruits of the actions I perform now. Isn't it better to enjoy what I have already done?

190 O Arjuna, if a person gives up actions through fear of suffering, his renunciation is of a passionate nature.

191 Although he renounces actions, he doesn't get the real fruit of renunciation. When a liquid boils over onto the fire, this isn't an oblation.

192 If a person drowns, he cannot claim that he has offered up his life by submerging himself in water. He has merely suffered an unnatural death.

193 Similarly, if he gives up an action through attachment to the body, he doesn't get the fruit of real renunciation.

194 In short, when knowledge of the Self arises in the mind, then just as the dawn extinguishes the light of the stars,

195 In the same way, O Arjuna, all actions disappear with their causes. This kind of renunciation leads to liberation from the fruits of action.

196 O Arjuna, liberation doesn't come through the kind of renunciation which is born of ignorance. You shouldn't consider this as true renunciation; it is born of passion.

कार्यम् इत्येव यत् कर्म नियतं क्रियते ऽर्जुन ।
सङ्गं त्यक्त्वा फलं चैव स त्यागः सात्त्विको मतः ॥

kāryam ityeva yat karma
niyataṁ kriyate 'rjuna
saṅgaṁ tyaktvā phalaṁ cāiva
sa tyāgaḥ sāttviko mataḥ

9. When action is done because it is a duty, Arjuna, and abandoning attachment to the fruit, such renunciation is thought to be sattvic.

197 Listen now, while I tell you what kind of renunciation leads to liberation from the results of action.

198 A person who has the quality of goodness performs actions that have come to him naturally. According to his own capacity, he carries them out with due respect for the scriptures.

199 He renounces the notion that he is the doer of actions, and he doesn't hope for the results of what he does.

200 O Arjuna, if a man were to treat his mother with disrespect or have lustful thoughts about her, this would lead him to the deepest hell.

201 He should reject such impulses and worship her as his mother. Should he abandon a cow merely because her mouth is dirty?

202 Who would throw away his favorite fruit because its skin or pit has no juice?

203 The pride of being the doer of actions and the desire for their fruits are the two chains that bind a person to doing them.

204 Just as a father doesn't behave in either of these ways towards his child, similarly, no harm can come from performing prescribed duties in the spirit of renunciation.

205 Renunciation is the greatest of all trees, for the fruit of liberation grows on it. It is known throughout the worlds as having the quality of goodness.

206 Just as a tree is made barren if its seeds are burned, in the same way, by renouncing the fruits of action, one renounces action itself.

207 As soon as iron is touched by the philosopher's stone, its blackness is removed. Similarly, the impurities of passion and darkness disappear when an action becomes pure.

208 Through the pure quality of goodness the eyes of Self-knowledge are opened, just as the water of a mirage disappears in the evening.

209 Then the mind no longer perceives the illusion of the phenomenal world, just as the space of heaven is invisible.

न द्वेष्ट्य् अकुशलं कर्म कुशले नानुषज्जते ।
त्यागी सत्त्वसमाविष्टो मेधावी छिन्नसंशयः ॥

na dveṣṭy akuśalaṁ karma
kuśale nānuṣajjate
tyāgī sattvasamāviṣṭo
medhāvī chinnasaṁśayaḥ

10. The man of renunciation, the wise man whose doubt is cut away, filled with goodness, does not hate disagreeable action, nor is he attached to agreeable action.

210 Because of former births he has to perform both pleasant and unpleasant actions; however, for him they are like clouds fading out of the sky.
211 O Arjuna, for him all actions are equally pure, and therefore neither pleasure nor pain affects him.
212 Although he knows which actions are auspicious, do they elate him? And will he shrink from what is inauspicious?
213 He has no doubt about this, just as a person who is awake is not deluded by his dreams.
214 O Arjuna, he has no concept of duality between the doer and the action. This kind of renunciation has the quality of goodness.

न हि देहभृता शक्यं त्यक्तुं कर्माण्य् अशेषतः ।
यस् तु कर्मफलत्यागी स त्यागीत्य् अभिधीयते ॥
na hi dehabhṛtā śakyaṁ
tyaktuṁ karmāṇy aśeṣataḥ
yas tu karmaphalatyāgī
sa tyāgīty abhidhīyate

11. Indeed embodied beings are not able to abandon actions entirely; he, then, who abandons the fruit of action, is called a man of renunciation.

215 O Arjuna, if a person gives up actions in this way, he truly renounces them. If he gives them up in any other way, they bind him even more tightly.
216 O Arjuna, those people who have incarnated in a body yet are reluctant to perform actions are ignorant.
217 What would happen to a jar if it felt disgusted by clay? How can a garment get rid of the threads of which it is woven?
218 Heat is the property of fire. Can it become tired of it? Can a lamp hate its own light?
219 If asafetida is repelled by its own unpleasant smell, how can it acquire a sweet fragrance? What would be left if water cast away its own moisture?
220 Similarly, as long as a person has to remain embodied in a physical form, it is foolish for him to talk of giving up activity.
221 We place a sacred mark on our foreheads and can remove and replace it at will. But can we do the same thing with our foreheads?
222 Similarly, we may renounce the actions that we ourselves have undertaken, but can we give up that activity which is inherent in bodily life?
223 Even during sleep we breathe in and out without any effort on our part, and other functions also continue without our control.
224 Because of the life of the body, activity is inevitable and cannot cease either in life or after death.
225 There is only one way in which we can gain freedom from such activities: that is, not to let ourselves be overcome by the desire for their results.
226 When a person offers the fruit of his action to God, he attains enlightenment by God's grace. Then he loses all fear, just as a person who recognizes a rope as a rope is no longer afraid that it might be a snake.
227 Similarly, knowledge of the Self removes both ignorance and the necessity for action. O Arjuna, when this kind of renunciation is performed, it is true renunciation.
228 When a person carries on activity in the world in this way, I regard him as a true renunciant. Otherwise, he is like a sick man who mistakes fainting for taking a rest.
229 When a person grows tired of one kind of activity and begins another, he is like one who is beaten with a stick after receiving a blow from the fist.
230 In short, a true man of renunciation has made his actions ineffective through giving up their fruit.

अनिष्टम् इष्टं मिश्रं च त्रिविधं कर्मणः फलम् ।
भवत्य् अत्यागिनां प्रेत्य न तु संन्यासिनां क्वचित् ॥
aniṣṭam iṣṭaṁ miśraṁ ca
trividhaṁ karmaṇaḥ phalam
bhavaty atyāgināṁ pretya
na tu saṁnyāsināṁ kvacit

12. The fruit of action for those who have not renounced when they depart (die) is threefold: evil, good, and mixed; but for the renouncers there is none whatever.

231 On the other hand, O Arjuna, a person who

doesn't perform this renunciation has to experience three kinds of consequences.

232 When a father says that his daughter is not his and offers her in marriage to another, he withdraws from his responsibility and the son-in-law is in a difficult position.

233 Anyone who plants a field of poisonous plants and sells the drug lives on the profit, but those who buy the drug die from taking it.

234 Similarly, whether a person performs actions with the idea that he is the doer, or whether he does them without this idea and with no desire for their fruit, there is no way to escape activity.

235 The fruit of a tree by the roadside is for anyone who wants it. Similarly, the fruit of an action comes to the one who performs it.

236 But a person who renounces the fruit even after performing an action is not bound by the world, for the three worlds are nothing but the result of activity.

237 The gods, human beings, and inanimate creation make up the world. They are the three aspects of the effect of activity.

238 Of these three kinds of fruit one is desirable, another is undesirable, and the third combines both qualities.

239 All those who are addicted to worldly pleasures and indulge in prohibited activity, disregarding what is prescribed,

240 Are reborn into forms of the lowest levels: insects, worms, and clods of earth. This is called the undesirable fruit of actions.

241 Those who perform good actions according to the sacred tradition, with respect for their own duty and regard for their capacity,

242 Are reborn as Indra and other gods, O Arjuna. This form of rebirth is known as the desirable fruit of action.

243 Just as the mixture of sweet and sour flavors produces a third which is different from the others and replaces them;

244 As in yogic practice the exhalation can be suspended by blocking the nostrils; or as when truth and falsehood are blended in one, falsehood is defeated;

245 Similarly, when sinful and virtuous deeds are in equal proportion, a person is reborn in a human body. This is called mixed fruit.

246 So the results of action are threefold. He who desires pleasure doesn't renounce the fruits of action.

247 As long as his tongue can taste, a person will enjoy the pleasure of eating, but in the end he will die from too much food.

248 There is no threat of robbers as long as one doesn't enter a forest. A prostitute isn't dangerous if she isn't touched.

249 Similarly, if a person boasts of his importance while he performs actions, he will experience their fruit as soon as he dies.

250 When a powerful money-lender comes with a bill for payment, he won't be turned away. Similarly, the experience of the fruit of one's actions is inevitable.

251 When grains of wheat fall from the ear, they will produce new ears of wheat. This again falls and in turn produces more grain.

252 Similarly, when a person experiences the fruit of an action, this causes further activity, just as in walking one step follows another.

253 Just as a ferry boat goes back and forth from one bank to the other, likewise, there is no escape from the attraction of enjoying the fruits of one's actions.

254 The experience of the fruit of action depends on a person's goal and his means of reaching it, so one who renounces it is no longer caught up in worldly life.

255 Just as a jasmine flower begins to wither as soon as it opens, actions performed by one who renounces their fruit are as though they had never been performed.

256 If a farmer uses up all his seed for food, he cannot cultivate any further crops. Similarly, when one renounces the fruit of actions, he has no further desire for activity.

257 Such people, helped by their purified nature and by the shower of nectar of their Guru's grace, remove the misery of duality with the prosperity of true knowledge.

258 This destroys the threefold fruit which brings about the illusion of the universe, and both the subject and object cease to exist.

259 O Arjuna, those people who are guided by wisdom and who renounce in this way are relieved of the suffering of experiencing the fruit of their actions.

260 When a person attains the vision of the Self through this renunciation, he doesn't see action as something separate from himself.

261 When a wall falls down, the pictures painted on it are reduced to clay. When the dawn breaks, does the darkness of night remain?

262 When a person isn't standing, his body doesn't cast a shadow. Without a mirror, can a person's face be reflected?

263 When a person awakes from sleep, what are his chances of dreaming? Then who can say whether his dreams are true or false?

264 When renunciation has taken place, the root of ignorance cannot live. Who then can perform or renounce action which arises from it?

265 When renunciation has taken place, there can be no talk of performing action. But as long as ignorance remains in a person,

266 And he is concerned with whether his actions are auspicious or inauspicious, and his mind is obsessed with duality,

267 Then, O Arjuna, the Self is as far from activity as the east is from the west.

268 The sky and the clouds are entirely different from each other, like the sun and a mirage, or the wind and the earth.

269 Although the rocks in a river are covered by its water, you know very well that these two are completely different.

270 Although weeds float on the surface of the water, they are different from it. Can the soot of a lamp and its light be considered as one because they are found together?

271 Although there are dark spots on the moon, they are not the same as the moon. Sight and the eyes are quite different from each other.

272 A path and the person who walks along it are as different as a river and the bed in which it flows. Also, a mirror is distinct from the person who looks into it.

273 O Arjuna, in the same way activity is completely separate from the Self, but it is true that they are associated together through ignorance.

पञ्चैतानि महाबाहो कारणानि निबोध मे ।
सांख्ये कृतान्ते प्रोक्तानि सिद्धये सर्वकर्मणाम् ॥
pañcāitāni mahābāho
kāranāṇi nibodha me
sāṁkhye kṛtānte proktāni
siddhaye sarvakarmaṇām

13. Learn from Me, O Arjuna, these five factors, declared in the Sankhya doctrine for the accomplishment of all actions:

274 By blossoming on the lake, a lotus gives the impression that the sun has risen, and the black bee immediately feeds on the pollen.

275 I tell you again that the activity in which the Self appears to take part is derived from different causes. I will now explain these five causes.

276 Perhaps you already know these five causes, for the scriptures openly discuss them.

277 They have been proclaimed to the accompaniment of drums in the royal city of the Vedas and in the palaces of Vedanta and Sankhya.

278 They are the principal causes for the performance of all the actions in the world. Don't attribute this cause to the Self.

279 O Arjuna, they are widely known and discussed, and you should listen to them carefully.

280 Why should you take the trouble to learn about them from someone else when I, the jewel of wisdom, am here?

281 When a mirror is placed in front of a person, why should he ask someone else to tell him what he looks like?

282 I am here today as your playmate, just as when a devotee looks for something he always finds Me there within it.

283 While the Lord was speaking like this in the flow of His love for Arjuna, Arjuna's heart melted with joy and he forgot himself,

284 Just as in a flood of moonlight a mountain of moonstones would dissolve into a lake.

285 So, breaking through the barrier that separates joy from the experience of it, Arjuna's whole being was filled with bliss.

286 Then the all-powerful Krishna at once came to Himself and rescued Arjuna, who was about to be overwhelmed.

287 The flood of ecstasy was so intense that even a great being like Arjuna, with all his wisdom, could have been submerged.

288 Lifting him out of it, Krishna said, O Arjuna, come to yourself! Then Arjuna took a deep breath and bowed his head.

289 O generous Lord, You know that I was tired of our separate existence and was trying to enter into union with You.

290 If in Your love for me You want to satisfy this urgent desire, why do You raise this barrier of individuality between us?

291 Then Lord Krishna said, O foolish one, don't you know yet that there is no difference between us? Is there any separation between the moon and the moonlight?

292 I am afraid you will be angry if I speak like

this, but this only strengthens true love.
293 The difference which lies between us enables us to recognize each other and live together, so don't speak of this anymore.
294 O Arjuna, what were we discussing? Wasn't I telling you about the difference between activity and the Self?
295 Then Arjuna said, You had begun to satisfy my wish and explain this truth to me.
296 You promised to clarify for me the five causes of activity,
297 And You told me that the Self is in no way connected with activity. I beg You to continue with this subject, which I want to understand.
298 The Lord of the universe, feeling great pleasure, said, Where else could one find a man who is so persistent in his search?
299 O Arjuna, I will explain to you the inner meaning of our discussion, but I am even more indebted to you for your love.
300 Then Arjuna said, O Lord, have You forgotten what You said earlier? Why do You still say "you" and "I" in the language of duality?
301 The Lord continued, Is that so? Now pay close attention to what I am going to say.
302 O Arjuna, know that it is true that the whole structure of human activity results from five causes, which are quite separate from the Self.
303 Also, there are five purposes from which all activity proceeds.
304 In the midst of all this, the Self remains indifferent. It is neither the purpose nor the cause of activity, nor does it support the performance of any action.
305 Good and evil actions originate in the same way that day and night appear in the sky.
306 When water, heat, and vapor combine with the air, clouds appear in the sky; but the sky is unaware of it.
307 When a boatman rows a boat and the wind propels it, the water only witnesses its movement.
308 When a potter puts a lump of clay on a wheel, he makes it a pot by turning the wheel with a handle.
309 The potter uses his skill, but consider this: does it receive anything from the earth except its support?
310 When the world begins its activity at sunrise, does the sun play any part in this?
311 Similarly, when the five causes are combined, the vine of activity is planted, quite apart from the Self.
312 Now I will describe these five in detail, just as pearls are each weighed separately.

अधिष्ठानं तथा कर्ता करणं च पृथग्विधम् ।
विविधाश्च पृथक्चेष्टा दैवं चैवात्र पञ्चमम् ॥

adhiṣṭhānaṁ tathā kartā
karaṇaṁ ca pṛthagvidham
vividhāśca pṛthakceṣṭā
daivaṁ cāivātra pañcamam

14. The seat of action (the body), the doer, the various organs, and the various separate activities, with the presiding deities as the fifth;

313 Now listen carefully to the characteristics of these five causes of action, the first of which is the body.
314 It is called the seat of action because both the experience and what is experienced live in it.
315 Then the ten sense organs, busy day and night, are engaged in the activities which produce pain and pleasure.
316 The body is called the seat of action because a person has no other way to experience pleasure and pain.
317 It is the home of the twenty-four elements, and it is here that the knot of bondage and liberation is unraveled.
318 Besides this, O Arjuna, it is the foundation for the three states of consciousness: waking, dream, and deep sleep.
319 The second cause of action is the doer, the reflection of Consciousness.
320 When water from the sky falls to the earth it forms pools, and when the sky is reflected in them it seems to take the shape of a pool.
321 While sleeping, a king forgets he is a king and dreams he is a beggar.
322 In the same way, Consciousness forgets its own true nature, identifies itself with the body, and takes on that form.
323 In this sense, universal Consciousness is called the individual soul, and this soul promises to remain attached to the body in every respect.
324 Although matter performs actions, the individual soul takes credit for them out of delusion. For this reason, he is called the doer.
325 There is only one vision gazing through the

eyelashes, but it seems to be divided up as though by the hairs of a fly-whisk.

326 A single lamp in a house appears to be many because it is seen through different windows.

327 Similarly, the one knowledge of the intellect seems to be distributed throughout the senses because of the functioning of the different sense organs.

328 O Arjuna, the senses are the third cause of activity.

329 Just as rivers flowing from the east and the west empty into the same ocean and their water flows together,

330 Just as a single man portraying the nine different feelings appears to be many different people,

331 Similarly, the power of action that resides in the inexhaustible life force seems to be divided when it manifests through the various senses.

332 When it is expressed through the voice it is speech. When it moves through the hands it takes the form of giving and taking.

333 It is the force of movement in the feet, and in the lower organs it takes the form of excretion.

334 When it passes from the navel to the heart, uttering the sacred syllable, it is called *prana*, the vital force of the body.

335 When this force rises upward toward the head, it is called *udana*.

336 When it flows through the lower passages, it is called *apana*. Because of its diffused nature, pervading the whole body, it is called *vyana*.

337 With the essence of food it permeates the interior of the body as *samana*, passing into every joint, including the navel.

338 O Arjuna, after it has carried out all these functions, it flows evenly throughout the body.

339 When it manifests as yawning, sneezing, and belching, it is called respectively "serpent," "tortoise," and "lizard."

340 O Arjuna, in this way the activity of the vital force in the body is one, although it seems to be many because it expresses itself in various ways.

341 This force, manifesting through different functions, is the fourth cause of activity.

342 The best of all seasons is Sharada, when the moon is at its most beautiful and especially when the moon is full.

343 In springtime a garden is at its most delightful. Then a man enjoys the company of his beloved, and all circumstances are favorable.

344 O Arjuna, lotuses are at the height of their beauty when in full bloom, and their fragrance intensifies their loveliness.

345 Just as a poetic quality and elegance of style enhance speech, and the spirit inspires it,

346 Likewise, of all the senses, the intellect is the finest and has incomparable beauty.

347 Pure intellect holds the place of honor in the company of the senses, for it represents the group of presiding deities.

348 The sun and the other deities bestow their favor on each of the ten senses.

349 The Lord said, O Arjuna, this group of ten deities is the fifth cause of activity.

350 Here I have explained to you these five causes of activity in terms that you can easily understand.

शरीरवाङ्मनोभिर् यत् कर्म प्रारभते नरः ।
न्याय्यं वा विपरीतं वा पञ्चैते तस्य हेतवः ॥
śarīravāṅmanobhir yat
karma prārabhate naraḥ
nyāyyaṁ vā viparītaṁ vā
pañcāite tasya hetavaḥ

15. Whatever action a man undertakes with his body, speech or mind, either right or wrong, these are its five factors.

351 Now I will explain how this group of five causes increases in its effect, giving rise to the entire range of actions.

352 If spring suddenly arrives, it causes new foliage to sprout. This produces flowers which in turn form fruit.

353 The rainy season brings clouds, the clouds produce rain, and this leads to the joy of the harvest.

354 The east brings forth the dawn; then the sunrise follows the dawn and gives light to the whole day.

355 Similarly, O Arjuna, the mind gives rise to the thought of action, which then lights the lamp of speech.

356 That lamp of speech illumines the path of all kinds of activity. Then the doer begins to perform actions.

357 The entire body supplies the motive for bodily actions, just as iron objects are made of iron.

358 O Arjuna, just as threads are interwoven and form a piece of cloth,
359 In the same way, the various functions of the mind give rise to the actions of the mind, speech, and body, just as a diamond is used to cut another diamond.
360 Now if someone were to ask how the body, for instance, can be both a cause and a motive, let him listen to this explanation.
361 The sun is both the motive and the cause of sunlight, and one section of the sugarcane plant causes the growth of the next section.
362 To praise the goddess of speech, speech itself must be used. To establish the Vedas, they themselves must be used.
363 Similarly, although it is well known that the body and its senses are both the causes of activity, it must be understood that they are also the motives.
364 When the body and its senses are causes as well as motives, the whole world of activity comes into existence.
365 O Arjuna, if you follow the path sanctified by the scriptures, rightness itself is the motive of right conduct.
366 If a large amount of water fell on a rice field, it would serve a good purpose even though the earth would absorb it.
367 If a man leaves his house in anger and happens to find himself on the road to Dwarka, he may be weary but his steps won't have been in vain.
368 Similarly, right activity arises for the combined cause and motive through the insight given by the scriptures.
369 If milk boils over when it is needed for serving, it is lost and not used for any purpose.
370 Similarly, if an action performed without scriptural sanction isn't considered useless, one would have to regard stolen money and a gift as having equal value.
371 O Arjuna, is there any mystic verse which contains a letter beyond the fifty-two letters of the alphabet? Or is there any human being who doesn't utter one of these fifty- two letters?
372 But as long as a person doesn't understand the meaning of the verse, its recitation will be fruitless.
373 Similarly, activity which arises at random from cause and motive doesn't adhere to the teachings of the scriptures.
374 It is a kind of action, but it is ineffective and must be considered as sin arising from sinful causes.

तत्रैवं सति कर्तारम् आत्मानं केवलं तु यः।
पश्यत्य् अकृतबुद्धित्वान् न स पश्यति दुर्मतिः ॥

tatrāivaṁ sati kartāram
ātmānaṁ kevalaṁ tu yaḥ
paśyaty akṛtabuddhitvān
na sa paśyati durmatiḥ

16. This being so, he who sees his Self as the doer does not really see, because of the fact that he has not perfected his understanding.

375 In this way, O Arjuna, the five causes of action are also motives. Now consider the part that the Self plays in all this.
376 Just as the sun reveals objects to the eye, in the same way the Self reveals action although it is not the doer.
377 O Arjuna, a person who looks in a mirror is neither the mirror nor the reflected image, but he can account for both.
378 The sun is neither day nor night, but it causes both. Similarly, the Self, which is neither the doer nor the action, is the revealer of activity.
379 If a person is deluded by the individuality of the body and mentally identifies with it, he is as blind to the Self as the darkness of midnight.
380 If a person considers God, the limitless Spirit, in terms of the body and believes that the Self is the doer,
381 He doesn't realize that I, as the Self, am beyond all action and am only the witness of it.
382 He measures the boundless Self by the limits of the body. Isn't this strange? Does an owl turn day into night?
383 Wouldn't a person who had never seen the sun in the sky think that its reflection in a pool of water was the sun itself?
384 He believes that the sun exists when the pool is there, that it vanishes when it is not, and that it trembles when the water ripples.
385 As long as a sleeping man doesn't wake up, he thinks his dream is real. Is it any wonder that if a person doesn't recognize a rope, he will be afraid it is a snake?
386 When a person's eyes are affected by jaundice, he will see the moon as yellow. Isn't a deer deceived by a mirage?
387 Such a person will have nothing to do with

the scriptures or with a Guru, but lives his life in ignorance.

388 He casts the net of the body over the Self by thinking the two are identical, just as a jackal attributes the movement of the clouds to the moon.

389 O Arjuna, because of these false concepts, he becomes bound with the iron shackles of activity in the prison of the body.

390 His condition is like that of the poor parrot that thinks it is bound to a revolving pipe and won't remove its legs, which are actually free.

391 Similarly, anyone who attributes the activity of matter to the pure Self remains confined within the limits of activity for endless ages.

यस्य नाहंकृतो भावो बुद्धिर् यस्य न लिप्यते ।
हत्वापि स इमाँल् लोकान् न हन्ति न निबध्यते ॥

yasya nāhaṁkṛto bhāvo
buddhir yasya na lipyate
hatvāpi sa imāṁl lokān
na hanti na nibadhyate

17. He whose state of mind is not egoistic, whose intellect is not tainted, even though he slays these people, he does not slay, and is not bound (by his actions).

392 The Self is always in the midst of activity but is untouched by it, just as the waters of the ocean have no effect on the great fire in their depths.

393 Now I will show you how you may recognize a person who remains separate from his actions.

394 When we realize the nature of a liberated being, we attain our own liberation, just as we find a lost object when we look for it with a lamp.

395 When a mirror is cleaned, we see our own image in it. When salt is added to water, it is immediately absorbed by the water.

396 When a reflection in a mirror looks back at the original form, the action of seeing vanishes and only the real form is left.

397 Similarly, when we want to find our lost Self, we should seek the saints, in whom we see ourselves. For this reason, we should always praise the saints and listen to their teachings.

398 He who lives a life of activity but remains untouched by its good or bad effects, is like the sense of sight that is unaffected by the skin around the eye.

399 I will now carefully explain to you the characteristics of the person who is free from activity.

400 O Arjuna, Lord Vishnu lay in the deep sleep of ignorance and was having a dream of the entire activity of the universe.

401 He was suddenly awakened by the great Truth, as though the Guru's hand had struck his head.

402 All at once, awakened from His sleep and the illusion of His cosmic dream, He became conscious of the bliss of union with God.

403 The illusory flood of a mirage vanishes as soon as the moon rises.

404 A ghost doesn't trouble a person who is no longer a child. It is no longer possible to cook food after the fire has burned out.

405 O Arjuna, a person who has experienced this union loses his sense of individuality, just as after he wakes up he doesn't see his dreams.

406 Just as the sun cannot find darkness even if it were to search for it in a cavern,

407 Similarly, when a person who is filled with the awareness of the Self looks at objects, he recognizes them as visible forms.

408 Whatever is burned by fire becomes one with it; then the duality of the fire and fuel disappears.

409 In the same way, when a person stops attributing to the Self the responsibility for action,

410 Will he still identify himself with the body? Does the water of the great deluge consider itself a mere stream?

411 O Arjuna, can union be attained by identification with the body? Can the sun be held by grasping its reflection?

412 When butter has been churned out of milk, can it mix again with the buttermilk from which it was separated?

413 O Arjuna, when the fire has been removed from wood, can it be put in a wooden box?

414 When the sun emerges from the womb of night, does it know anything about the existence of night?

415 Likewise, once a person understands the relation between the knower and the known, how can he identify himself with the body?

416 Wherever space extends it is filled with space, for it is all-pervasive.

417 Similarly, when a person sees himself in everything that he does, what actions is he responsible for as the doer?
418 It would be like thinking that there is no place apart from the sky, no current in the ocean, or no fixed place for the pole star.
419 In this way his sense of individuality is transformed into enlightenment; yet as long as his body lives, action continues.
420 Even after the wind has stopped blowing, the trees may continue to sway. The fragrance of camphor may remain in a box even after the camphor has been used up.
421 Even when a chanting session is over, people are still moved by it. Moisture lies on the ground long after water has been poured over it.
422 After the sun has set, its light still blazes against the background of the sky.
423 Even after an arrow is shot through a target, it continues its flight until its momentum is lost.
424 When a potter removes from his wheel the pot he has made, the wheel continues revolving for some time.
425 Similarly, O Arjuna, even when there is no longer a sense of individuality, its inherent activity still produces action.
426 A dream may arise without any previous thought, trees may grow in a forest without being planted, and castles may appear in the air without being built.
427 Similarly, without the involvement of the Self, the five physical causes by their very nature initiate all kinds of activity.
428 Because of the effects of actions in past lives, these five causes and their accompanying motives produce many different activities.
429 Whether that activity destroys the whole universe or brings another into being is unimportant.
430 The sun doesn't observe how lotuses fade and how others bloom.
431 The earth may be shattered by a stroke of lightning, or showers of rain may cause it to bring forth fresh grass,
432 But the sky knows nothing of this. Such is the state of a person who lives in the body but is detached from it.
433 He is unaware of bodily actions, whether they create or destroy the world, just as a man doesn't remember his dream after he wakes up.
434 On the other hand, those who see the body only with their physical eyes believe that it is the originator of action.
435 A jackal thinks that a straw scarecrow set up in a field is a watchman.
436 Others have to take care that a madman is clothed and not left naked. Someone else has to count the wounds of a dead soldier.
437 A devoted widow about to immolate herself has no thought for the fire or her body or the people around her, while the onlookers only look at the jewelry she is wearing.
438 Similarly, a person who has realized his true nature and is no longer aware of the duality of the seer and the seen, knows nothing of the activity of the sense organs.
439 People on the shore may think that when large waves hide small ones, one wave swallows another.
440 But when we look at this from the point of view of the water, what has swallowed what? Similarly, there is no one who can destroy a person who has no sense of duality.
441 If a golden image of Chandrika kills a golden image of Mahisha with a golden spear,
442 A worshiper may think that this depicts a true story; but the goddess, the spear, and the demon are, after all, nothing but gold.
443 Water and fire may be painted in a picture, but they can neither moisten nor burn.
444 In the same way, the body of a person who has attained liberation acts according to the effects of his actions in past lives, while ignorant people consider him the doer.
445 Even if his actions destroyed the whole universe, it couldn't be said that he had done it.
446 Can it be said that first the sun sees the darkness and then tries to dispel it? For an enlightened man, there is nothing other than the Self. Then whom can it destroy?
447 His mind is unaffected by either sin or virtue, just as when a river enters the Ganges its impurities are removed.
448 O Arjuna, when two fires meet, does one burn the other? Can a weapon strike itself?
449 What can sully the pure intellect of a person who doesn't think of activity as being separate from himself?
450 Similarly, a person who considers action, the doer of action, and the performance of action as all one in the Self, isn't bound by action arising from the body and its senses.
451 The individual soul, which is the doer, skill-

fully digs five furrows with a plow made from the ten instruments of action.

452 Then, constructing a framework of prescribed and forbidden actions, he builds a mansion of activity.

453 The Self doesn't participate at all in this great work. You shouldn't even say that he plays a part in the beginning of it.

454 He is merely a witness, the essence of pure thought. Can he then have any thought of performing action?

455 He takes no part in the activities which are such difficult work for ordinary people.

456 Therefore, a person who has realized that he is one with the pure Self isn't bound to action.

ज्ञानं ज्ञेयं परिज्ञाता त्रिविधा कर्मचोदना ।
करणं कर्म कर्तेति त्रिविधः कर्मसंग्रहः ।।

jñānaṁ jñeyaṁ parijñātā
trividhā karmacodanā
karaṇaṁ karma karteti
trividhaḥ karmasaṁgrahaḥ

18. Knowledge, the process of knowing, and the knower are the threefold impulse to action; the instrument, the action, and the doer are the threefold basis of action.

457 When the picture of false knowledge appears on the canvas of ignorance, the painter is this group of three things.

458 This consists of knowledge, the knower, and the process of knowing. These three are the seed of this world, from which all actions spring.

459 O Arjuna, I will now explain to you the separate nature of these three.

460 The individual soul is the sun, whose rays of the five senses spread out and force open the buds of the lotuses of sense objects.

461 Or it is like a king who mounts an unsaddled horse and, with the senses as his troops, plunders the lands of the sense objects.

462 Enough of these images. The knowledge which works through the senses and which gives the soul the experience of joy and sorrow, becomes diminished in sleep.

463 O Arjuna, the soul is the knower, and what I have just explained is knowledge.

464 It is born from the womb of ignorance and immediately divides itself in three elements.

465 Placing the objects to be known in front, and behind them one's concept of oneself as the doer,

466 Between the knower and the objects which are known is the process of knowing, and they are related by mutual interaction.

467 When the process of knowing reaches the limit of the objects which are known, it gives names to all things.

468 This is ordinary knowledge. Now I will tell you the characteristics of the objects that are known.

469 Things that are known have five variations: sound, touch, form, smell, and taste.

470 The same mango is experienced differently by the various senses through its taste, color, smell, and touch.

471 In this way, although it is only one mango, it is known through the five senses so its nature is fivefold.

472 Just as the current of a river ceases when it enters the ocean, as a person stops walking when he reaches his destination, and as a plant dies when the grain has ripened,

473 Similarly, O Arjuna, when the process of knowing, operating though the senses, comes to an end, that goal is the object that is known.

474 In this way, O Arjuna, I have explained to you the characteristics of the knower, the known, and the process of knowing. These three things produce action.

475 The five aspects of knowing—sound,touch, form, smell, and taste—are either pleasant or unpleasant.

476 O Arjuna, as soon as the process of knowing brings objects to the knower, he either accepts or rejects them.

477 A heron spotting a fish, a beggar discovering a treasure, and a lustful man seeing a woman are all compelled to pursue their objects.

478 Water rushes down a slope, a bee flies toward a flower, and a calf runs to its mother at feeding time.

479 When men hear the heavenly nymph Urvashi, they try to reach her by setting up a ladder of sacrifices.

480 O Arjuna, when a pigeon soaring through the sky catches sight of his mate, he instantly plunges to her side.

481 When a peacock hears a clap of thunder, it tries to fly into the sky. All these are like the knower who is drawn to the object of knowledge.

482 O Arjuna, this is why the knower, the known, and the process of knowing are the

three forces that produce all activity.
483 If the knower especially likes the object, he cannot tolerate any delay in enjoying it.
484 However, if he happens to come across something unpleasant, he feels it will take him thousands of years to be rid of it.
485 If he finds a snake he is immediately filled with fear, but at the sight of a necklace he is overcome with joy.
486 He is affected in this way when he encounters pleasant and unpleasant objects, and he is always busy accepting and rejecting them.
487 A wrestler, even if he is the leader of an army, will get down from his chariot when he sees another wrestler.
488 Similarly, a knower becomes a doer of action. Then, just as a person who wishes to eat cooks himself some food,
489 As a bee might create for itself a flower garden, as a touchstone might go in search of metal, or as a god might set out to build himself a temple,
490 Similarly, O Arjuna, when the knower sets his senses in motion through his passion for objects, he becomes the doer of actions.
491 Once he is the doer, his process of knowing naturally becomes the cause, and the object known becomes the effect.
492 In this way, O Arjuna, the process of knowing undergoes a change, just as the beauty of the eyes changes at night.
493 Just as the pleasure of a rich man decreases when his fortune changes, and as the moon wanes after it has become full,
494 Similarly, through the activity of the senses, the knower becomes involved in action. Now listen to the characteristics of this state.
495 The inner psychic instrument consists of the functions of the intellect, the mind, thought, and ego.
496 The skin, the ear, the eye, the tongue, and the nose represent the five external sense organs.
497 The inner instrument, the doer, considers what is to be done; and if it believes that the particular activity will result in pleasure,
498 It sets in motion all ten sense organs.
499 It keeps them working until the activity has brought about the desired result.
500 If the doer sees that the activity will result in pain, he diverts all the sense organs into the process of rejection.
501 He exercises his senses day and night until the pain is relieved, just as a king will keep his men working day and night until the property tax is paid.
502 In this way, when the knower directs his senses towards the experience of pleasure and the avoidance of pain, he is called the doer.
503 I speak of the senses as instruments, because in all the actions of the doer their function is like that of a plow in farming.
504 All the actions that the doer performs through them make up a person's karma.
505 Ornaments are the proof of the goldsmith's skill, the rays of the moon spread out into the moonlight, and a vine is seen by the extent of its growth.
506 Light is permeated by its own radiance, sugarcane juice is filled throughout with sweetness, and the sky occupies all space.
507 Similarly, O Arjuna, everything that is involved in the activity of the doer is called karma. There is no other term.
508 In this way I have explained to you the characteristics of the doer, the action, and the instruments of action.

ज्ञानं कर्म च कर्ता च त्रिधैव गुणभेदतः।
प्रोच्यते गुणसंख्याने यथावच्छृणु तान्यपि ॥

jñānaṁ karma ca kartā ca
tridhāiva guṇabhedataḥ
procyate guṇasaṁkhyāne
yathāvac chṛṇu tāny api

19. It is declared in Sankhya that knowledge, action, and the doer are of three kinds, distinguished according to the qualities. Hear about these also:

509 In this way the knower, the known, and the process of knowing are the threefold cause of action, while the doer, the action, and the instrument make up the process of activity.
510 Just as smoke is inherent in fire, as a tree is latent in the seed, or as desire always lies dormant in the mind,
511 Similarly, the doer, the action, and the instrument are the vital forces in all activity, just as gold is found in a gold mine.
512 Therefore, O Arjuna, whenever a person feels that he himself is the doer of action, the Self is far removed from all action.
513 Why should I repeat to you that the Self is separate from action? You already know this well.
514 These three things—the instrument, the ac-

tion, and the doer of action—which I have described, can be distinguished by their three separate qualities.

515 O Arjuna, don't put your trust in these three things, for two of them lead to bondage and only one to liberation.

516 I will explain to you the difference in their qualities, as the Sankhya philosophy clearly teaches, so that you may understand the quality of goodness.

517 In the matter of discrimination this philosophy is like the Milky Ocean, and in Self-knowledge it is like the moon to the moon lotus. O Arjuna, it is the eye of knowledge for all philosophy.

518 It shows the difference between Spirit and matter, which are interwoven, just as the sun enables us to distinguish day from night.

519 It weighs worldly life with the measure of the twenty-four elements and brings people to the joy of union with the Supreme.

520 O Arjuna, here is the description of the distinctions of the qualities, as one reads about them in the texts of Sankhya.

521 These qualities have imprinted their threefold nature on the entire visible creation.

522 The power of the qualities of goodness, passion, and darkness is so great that it has divided into three classes everything in the entire creation down to the tiniest creature.

523 First of all I will explain that knowledge which divides all created things into classes through the distinction of these qualities.

524 Clear vision enables a person to see all things plainly. Similarly, with pure knowledge he can understand the true nature of things.

525 Lord Krishna, the treasure house of the highest bliss, said, I will describe that pure knowledge to you. Listen carefully.

सर्वभूतेषु येनैकं भावम् अव्ययम् ईक्षते ।
अविभक्तं विभक्तेषु तज् ज्ञानं विद्धि सात्त्विकम् ।।

sarvabhūteṣu yenāikaṁ
bhāvam avyayam īkṣate
avibhaktaṁ vibhakteṣu
taj jñānaṁ viddhi sāttvikam

20. That knowledge by which one sees one imperishable Being in all beings, undivided in separate beings; know that knowledge to be sattvic.

526 O Arjuna, through the development of *sattvic* knowledge, the knower and the known merge into one.

527 The sun can never see darkness, the ocean doesn't know rivers separately, and no one can embrace his own shadow.

528 It is the same with this knowledge, for through it all creation, from the highest gods to a blade of grass, is seen to be one.

529 A picture cannot be seen by feeling it, salt cannot be washed with water, and dreams don't occur after waking.

530 Similarly, the knower, the known, and the process of knowing cease to exist separately when one understands them with the help of this knowledge.

531 An intelligent person doesn't melt down gold ornaments to see whether they are made of gold, or strain waves to get water.

532 In the same way, *sattvic* knowledge is beyond the perception which sees differences in things.

533 If a person happens to look in a mirror, he sees his own image. Similarly, when the knower knows himself, the known disappears.

534 Pure knowledge is the storehouse of the wealth of liberation. Now I will explain the characteristics of *rajasic* knowledge.

पृथक्त्वेन तु यज् ज्ञानं नानाभावान् पृथग्विधान् ।
वेत्ति सर्वेषु भूतेषु तज् ज्ञानं विद्धि राजसम् ।।

pṛthaktvena tu yaj jñānaṁ
nānābhāvān pṛthagvidhān
vetti sarveṣu bhūteṣu
taj jñānaṁ viddhi rājasam

21. But that knowledge which sees in all beings separate entities of various kinds, by differentiation, know that knowledge to be rajasic.

535 Listen, O Arjuna. The knowledge which is bound by the idea of separateness is *rajasic.*

536 Because of this knowledge, which attributes variety to all creatures, we become separate parts of the whole. This even deceives the wise.

537 Just as sleep draws the curtain of forgetfulness over the real forms of things and sets in motion the process of dreaming,

538 Similarly, when Self-knowledge is surrounded by the network of false perceptions, the individual soul is deluded by the play of the three states of consciousness.

539 Just as a child doesn't recognize gold disguised in the form of ornaments, similarly, through *rajasic* knowledge the inherent

oneness is concealed in names and forms.
540 Just as an ignorant person doesn't recognize clay after it has been made into pots and jars, as fire isn't visible in a bright light,
541 As a foolish person doesn't distinguish threads if they are woven into cloth, or as a dull person hates the canvas on which a picture is painted,
542 In the same way, because of *rajasic* knowledge, created objects appear to be separate and the perception of unity is obscured.
543 Then, just as fire seems to be separate in different logs, as fragrance seems distinct in different flowers, and as a separate moon is reflected in every pool of water,
544 Similarly, *rajasic* knowledge perceives multiplicity in created things and distinguishes them as large and small.
545 Now I will explain to you *tamasic* knowledge, which has the quality of darkness, so you may know it and reject it just as one avoids the house of an outcaste.

यत् तु कृत्स्नवद् एकस्मिन् कार्ये सक्तम् अहैतुकम् ।
अतत्त्वार्थवद् अल्पं च तत् तामसम् उदाहृतम् ॥

yat tu kṛtsnavad ekasmin
kārye saktam ahāitukam
atattvārthavad alpaṁ ca
tat tāmasam udāhṛtam

22. That (knowledge), however, which is attached to one single effect as if it were all, and without reason, without a real purpose and small in significance, is declared to be tamasic.

546 O Arjuna, this kind of knowledge wanders naked, unclothed by scriptural authority, turning its back on tradition.
547 Other scriptures also cast it out so they won't be defiled, and drive it away toward the distant hills of infidel faiths.
548 This knowledge, possessed by the evil spirit of darkness, spins around like a madman.
549 It regards no person as a friend nor any food as prohibited. It is like a dog let loose in a desert village,
550 Which eats everything, leaving aside only what its mouth cannot reach, or what is hot enough to burn its tongue.
551 It is like a rat which steals some gold and cannot judge whether it is pure or alloyed, or like a meat eater who doesn't consider whether the meat is dark or white.
552 It is like a forest fire that doesn't spare anything, or a fly that will settle on anything, alive or dead.
553 A crow doesn't choose between vomit and newly served food, or between what is fresh and what is rotten.
554 Similarly, this knowledge in its lust for sense pleasure is unaware that what is prohibited should be avoided and what is prescribed must be respected.
555 Whatever it perceives it grasps for pleasure, whether it is relations with women or money for food.
556 Water may be holy or defiled, as long as it quenches the thirst.
557 Food may be sanctioned or forbidden, to be taken or rejected, but whatever is pleasing to the taste this knowledge regards as pure.
558 This kind of knowledge causes a man to see women only as a means of sense pleasure and seek their company.
559 It makes him look on all those who serve his own interest as relatives, and therefore he considers them to be unimportant.
560 Just as everything is food for death, and as all things are fuel for fire, in the same way the quality of darkness considers the whole world as its own possession.
561 It regards the world as an object of pleasure, and the nourishment of the body its sole purpose.
562 Its entire activity is directed towards satisfying the body, just as rain from the sky inevitably falls into the ocean.
563 The understanding that one reaches heaven by carrying out proper duties and hell by neglecting them is like the darkness of night to a person with this kind of knowledge.
564 His understanding cannot reach beyond the idea that the body is the Self and that a stone image is the Supreme.
565 He believes that when the body dies, the Self with all its activities ceases to exist. Then what is left to experience anything?
566 If God exists and causes us to experience the fruits of our actions, then how is it that people live by selling images of gods?
567 If the stone gods in a village temple can punish people, why do the stones of the neighboring hills remain silent?
568 If this kind of knowledge believes in a god at all, it will regard an idol as a god and the body as the spirit.
569 It considers virtue and sin as false ideas and,

like a fiery flame, devours everything it finds to serve its own ends.

570 All that the physical eyes can see and all that pleases the senses is the only real experience, as far as it is concerned.

571 O Arjuna, you will see that this way of life is as useless as a wisp of smoke rising into the sky.

572 It is as worthless as the *bhanda* tree, whether it is green or dry, growing or withering.

573 The ears of the sugarcane plant, a field of prickly cactus, and an impotent man are all equally useless.

574 The mind of a child, the hoarded wealth of a thief, and the false teat on a goat's neck serve no purpose.

575 Therefore, knowledge which is as empty and worthless as these things has the quality of darkness.

576 To call this knowledge would be as irrelevant as saying that the eyes of a blind man are large,

577 That the ears of a deaf man are well shaped, or that filthy water is good to drink. In the same way, *tamasic* knowledge is knowledge in name only.

578 But let this be. This shouldn't be regarded as knowledge but as the eyes of darkness.

579 So, Arjuna, I have shown you the three different kinds of knowledge and their characteristics.

नियतं सङ्गरहितम् अरागद्वेषतः कृतम् ।
अफलप्रेप्सुना कर्म यत् तत् सात्त्विकम् उच्यते ॥

niyataṁ saṅgarahitam
arāgadveṣataḥ kṛtam
aphalaprepsunā karma
yat tat sāttvikam ucyate

23. That action which is ordained and free from attachment, performed without desire or hate, with no wish to obtain fruit, is said to be sattvic.

580 Now, O Arjuna, actions can clearly be observed in the light of these three kinds of knowledge.

581 Actions follow three directions, just as water flows in the channels made for it.

582 Governed by the threefold nature of knowledge, action is also of three kinds. Now hear what actions are *sattvic*.

583 Pure action is performed according to a person's status and duty. It is as proper for him as the embrace of a faithful wife for a beloved husband.

584 A person's authority is enhanced by the performance of his daily duties, just as sandalwood paste improves a dark complexion or a black ointment increases the beauty of a young woman's eyes.

585 This daily duty, supported by periodic rites, is good and is like fragrance added to gold.

586 Just as a mother will devote all the strength of her body and life to caring for her child without thinking of her own weariness,

587 In the same way, a good person will perform his duty wholeheartedly, without a thought for its fruit, but offering it all to God.

588 Just as a person unstintingly gives hospitality to a friend who arrives at his house, in the same way, if the *sattvic* person should be interrupted in performing his duty,

589 He doesn't feel sorry because it is unfulfilled or give in to resentment; neither does he become elated when it is completed.

590 O Arjuna, an action performed in this manner is *sattvic.*

591 Now I will explain to you the nature of a *rajasic* action. Don't let your attention wander.

यत् तु कामेप्सुना कर्म साहंकारेण वा पुनः ।
क्रियते बहुलायासं तद् राजसम् उदाहृतम् ॥

yat tu kāmepsunā karma
sāhaṁkāreṇa vā punaḥ
kriyate bahulāyāsaṁ
tad rājasam udāhṛtam

24. But that action which is performed with a wish to obtain desires, with selfishness, or, again, with much effort, is declared to be rajasic.

592 A fool cannot speak a good word to his mother or father but he treats everyone else with respect.

593 A person who won't sprinkle water on the sacred *tulsi* plant may pour milk on the roots of a vine.

594 Similarly, a *rajasic* person who cannot even make the effort to rise and perform his obligatory daily and periodic duties

595 Would consider it as nothing to spend his body and all that he has for the sake of actions which bring him pleasure.

596 He is like a man who never tires of lending money at a high interest rate, or like a farmer who is never satisfied however many crops he may sow,

597 Like a person who has found a philosopher's stone but doesn't consider himself prosperous until he has spent all he has on iron to be transmuted into gold.

598 With his mind set on the fruits of his action, he performs difficult tasks which bring sense pleasures, but he is never satisfied.

599 He performs properly all those prescribed rites which will bring pleasurable results.

600 He publicly boasts of having performed these rites and makes them valueless by constantly speaking of them.

601 In this way, he is filled with pride and pays no respect to his father or to his Guru, just as typhus fever cannot be cured by any medicine.

602 Therefore, whatever a person does reverently, yet through egoism and the desire for the fruits of his action,

603 And with great exertion, it is like the performance of an acrobat by which he earns a living.

604 It is like a rat burrowing through an entire mountain to find a single grain, or a frog stirring up the ocean for a little moss.

605 Such a person is like a juggler who carries around a snake in order to earn more than he can get by begging. There are some people who enjoy such labor.

606 The efforts he makes to win heavenly pleasure are like those of a white ant which burrows down to hell in search of a particle of food.

607 *Rajasic* action is prompted by desire and filled with agitation. Now listen to the characteristics of *tamasic* action.

अनुबन्धं क्षयं हिंसाम् अनपेक्ष्य च पौरुषम् ।
मोहाद् आरभ्यते कर्म यत् तत् तामसम् उच्यते ॥

anubandhaṁ kṣayaṁ hiṁsām
anapekṣya ca pāuruṣam
mohād ārabhyate karma
yat tat tāmasam ucyate

25. That action which is undertaken because of delusion, disregarding consequences, loss, or injury to others, as well as one's own ability, is said to be tamasic.

608 *Tamasic* action is like the dark house of condemnation and the birthplace of all that is prohibited.

609 Once it has been performed, its result disappears from view like a line drawn across water.

610 It is like churning gruel, blowing dead ashes, or grinding sand in an oil-press. There is nothing to show for it.

611 It is as useless as winnowing chaff, shooting into the sky, or setting a trap to catch the wind.

612 All these actions are worthless, and after they are finished they produce no results.

613 On the contrary, the precious treasure of human life is spent performing them, and they destroy happiness.

614 If a net of thorns were dragged over a bed of lotus flowers, the net itself would be spoiled and the lotuses destroyed.

615 A moth dazzled by a flame not only burns its body, but also prevents people from seeing the light.

616 Similarly, this kind of action harms others as well as being useless and hurting the body.

617 A fly, by letting itself be swallowed, causes a person to vomit. This kind of action is like such disgusting experiences.

618 A *tamasic* person doesn't consider whether he has the capacity to perform actions, but continues to act blindly.

619 He doesn't ask himself, What skills do I have? What opportunities are there? What is the advantage of doing this?

620 He erases all such thoughts and completes all his actions, treading the path of ignorance.

621 Fire spreads at random, burning up the fuel which is its source. The ocean might rise and overflow its shores,

622 Spreading in all directions without regard for any obstacles whether small or large.

623 Similarly, by these traits you may recognize actions which have the quality of darkness. They take no thought for what is proper or improper and don't distinguish between what is their own and what is someone else's.

624 O Arjuna, I have now explained to you the nature and cause of the three kinds of action resulting from the three qualities.

मुक्तसङ्गो ऽनहंवादी धृत्युत्साहसमन्वितः ।
सिद्ध्यसिद्ध्योर् निर्विकारः कर्ता सात्त्विक उच्यते ॥

muktasaṅgo 'nahamvādī
dhṛtyutsāhasamanvitaḥ
siddhyasiddhyor nirvikāraḥ
kartā sāttvika ucyate

26. Released from attachment, free from ego, endowed with steadfastness and resolution, unperturbed in success or failure; such a doer is said to be sattvic.

625 The people who perform action, regarding themselves as the doer, are also of three kinds.

626 Just as a person appears in four different ways according to the four stages of life, in the same way those who perform actions are of three kinds because of the differences in activity.

627 Of these three, I will first describe to you the characteristics of the *sattvic* doer. Listen carefully.

628 Just as the finest sandalwood tree grows straight branches without any hope of bearing fruit,

629 And the *naga* vine fulfills its purpose without yielding any fruit, similarly, the *sattvic* person performs his daily and periodic duties in the same way.

630 These actions are not fruitless, even though they seem to bear no fruit. O Arjuna, how can that which in itself is fruit bear fruit?

631 As he faithfully performs his duties, no thought arises in his mind that he is the doer, just as the clouds gather silently in the rainy season.

632 In order to perform all his duties in a manner worthy of being offered to the Supreme,

633 He looks for an appropriate time and a proper place, and he evaluates all his actions in the light of scriptural teaching.

634 He brings under control his mental tendencies and sense organs, refrains from any thought of the fruit of his actions, and accepts the restrictions imposed by the scriptures.

635 In order to carry out his discipline, he remains alert and courageous.

636 Moreover, out of devotion to the Self, he renounces all physical pleasures while carrying out his duties.

637 The more he deprives himself of sleep, endures hunger, and denies himself physical pleasures,

638 The more ardent he becomes, just as gold decreases in weight but increases in value the more it is heated in the crucible.

639 Where there is true love, a person regards his life as of little worth. A devoted wife doesn't hesitate to immolate herself on her husband's funeral pyre.

640 Similarly, O Arjuna, if a person longs for such a precious thing as Self-realization, will he grieve because of physical discomfort?

641 The more detached he becomes from sense pleasures, the less concern he has for his body, and the greater joy he takes in performing his duty.

642 In this way he carries out what has to be done; but if an occasion arises where he must refrain from action,

643 He isn't affected by this interruption any more than a wagon is concerned if it falls over a precipice.

644 If he accomplishes an action perfectly, he doesn't parade his success.

645 O Arjuna, the doer in whom these traits are seen while he performs action, may truly be called *sattvic.*

रागी कर्मफलप्रेप्सुर् लुब्धो हिंसात्मको ऽशुचिः।
हर्षशोकान्वितः कर्ता राजसः परिकीर्तितः॥
rāgī karmaphalaprepsur
lubdho hiṁsātmako 'śuciḥ
harṣaśokānvitaḥ kartā
rājasaḥ parikīrtitaḥ

27. Passionate, desiring the fruits of action, greedy, violent-natured, impure, subject to joy or sorrow; such a doer is proclaimed to be rajasic.

646 The *rajasic* person is a storehouse of worldly desires.

647 Just as a sewer is the place where the refuse of a village is deposited, and the burying ground is the destination of everything that is impure,

648 Similarly, such a person is the receptacle for the greed of the whole world, like a place where people wash their feet.

649 He applies himself resolutely to any undertaking that he sees to be profitable.

650 When he gets what he wants, he doesn't waste the tiniest particle of it and is always ready to sacrifice his life to keep it.

651 He keeps as careful a watch on others' possessions as a miser does on his treasure and a heron does on fish.

652 If a person becomes entangled in a *boru* tree and struggles to free himself, its branches will scratch him and its fruit will burn his tongue.

653 Similarly, this kind of person acts violently towards others in thought, word, and deed,

and has no consideration for others while attaining his own ends.

654 Moreover, if he lacks the capacity or perseverance to carry out an action, he feels no dissatisfaction.

655 Just as the fruit of the thorn-apple tree contains within it intoxicating juice and on the outside has a thorny rind, such a person has no purity either within or without.

656 O Arjuna, if this person obtains the fruit of his actions, he laughs scornfully at the world in his joy.

657 On the other hand, if he fails to get any results from his undertaking, he is overcome with grief and curses all action.

658 In short, you may be certain that if his conduct reveals these characteristics, he is a *rajasic* person.

659 I will now describe to you the *tamasic* doer, the field in which evil deeds grow.

अयुक्तः प्राकृतः स्तब्धः शठो नैकृतिको ऽलसः ।
विषादी दीर्घसूत्री च कर्ता तामस उच्यते ॥

ayuktaḥ prākṛtaḥ stabdhaḥ
śaṭho nāikṛtiko 'lasaḥ
viṣādī dīrghasūtrī ca
kartā tāmasa ucyate

28. Undisciplined, vulgar, obstinate, wicked, deceitful, lazy, despondent, and procrastinating; such a doer is said to be tamasic.

660 Fire has no understanding that it will burn those things with which it comes in contact.

661 A weapon has no knowledge that its sharp edge can kill, and poison is unaware of its effects.

662 Similarly, O Arjuna, the *tamasic* doer performs evil actions which will harm himself as well as others.

663 While performing these actions, he doesn't care what effects they may have, just as a stormy wind blows at random.

664 O Arjuna, he sees no relation between the doer and his actions, and he is more deranged than any madman.

665 He sustains his life on all that sense pleasures can provide, just as a louse attaches itself to a bull's hind quarters.

666 He acts on the impulse of the moment, just as a child laughs and cries regardless of the occasion.

667 Controlled by his own nature, he cannot discriminate between proper and improper actions and swells up with satisfaction at whatever he does, just as a dung hill is built up on refuse.

668 He will not humble himself before those who should be held in reverence, not even before the Supreme. He is more obstinate and rigid than a mountain.

669 His mind is deceitful, his conduct is dishonest, and his appearance is like that of a prostitute.

670 In short, he is the embodiment of deceit, and his life is like a gambling den.

671 You should avoid his company. Doesn't he look like the village of a lustful tribesman?

672 If he does good to another person, it seems to him like a hostile act to himself, just as salt added to milk makes it undrinkable.

673 Even if frozen fuel is put into a fire, it will immediately become fire in the flames.

674 O Arjuna, the most delicious food taken in the body eventually becomes excrement.

675 Similarly, if such a person finds anything good in another, he begins at once to speak badly of him.

676 He turns all virtue into vice and nectar into poison, just as milk given to a serpent becomes venom.

677 Even when the opportunity arises for him to perform an action in this world which will benefit him in the next, he falls asleep.

678 However, when he is committing evil deeds, sleep deserts him like an unclean woman sitting to one side.

679 Just as the mouth of a crow is turned sour with the juice of grapes or sugarcane, and as an owl is blinded by daylight,

680 In the same way, when he has the opportunity to do good he is lazy, but he does whatever he likes in a careless manner.

681 He is forever full of despair, just as the fire burns eternally in the heart of the ocean.

682 Just as a fire burning dung smolders, and as the downward-moving air in the body has an unpleasant smell, similarly, at the end of his life he is filled with depression.

683 O Arjuna, he engages in lustful actions which he hopes will bear fruit for his enjoyment after many years.

684 He is full of anxiety about life beyond this world, although he is unlikely to obtain even the smallest fruit of his action.

685 In such a person, the incarnation of all sins,

you will clearly see the *tamasic* doer.

686 In this way, O Arjuna, I have explained to you the threefold characteristics of action, knowledge, and the doer.

बुद्धेर् भेदं धृतेश्चैव गुणतस् त्रिविधं शृणु ।
प्रोच्यमानम् अशेषेण पृथक्त्वेन धनंजय ।।

buddher bhedaṁ dhṛteścāiva
guṇatas trividhaṁ śṛṇu
procyamānam aśeṣeṇa
pṛthaktvena dhanaṁjaya

29. Now hear the threefold distinctions of intellect and also of firmness, according to the qualities, taught completely and separately, Arjuna:

687 Dwelling in the town of ignorance, clothed in illusion, and decked with all the ornaments of doubt,

688 The steady intellect, which mirrors the beauty of Self-realization, also has this threefold nature.

689 O Arjuna, consider this: is there anything in this world which isn't distinguished by the three *gunas*?

690 Is there any piece of wood in which fire isn't latent? In the same way, is there any object in the world which doesn't have these three qualities?

691 The intellect also has a threefold nature arising from the *gunas*; and steadiness, too, is of three kinds.

692 Now I will begin to tell you how they are distinguished by their characteristics.

693 O Arjuna, of these two, intellect and steadiness, I will first describe the different kinds of intellect.

694 O Arjuna, for all beings which enter worldly existence there are three ways of life: the best, the middle, and the lowest.

695 From these three—prescribed action, action with desire for its fruits, and prohibited action—arises people's fear of worldly life.

प्रवृत्तिं च निवृत्तिं च कार्याकार्ये भयाभये ।
बन्धं मोक्षं च या वेत्ति बुद्धिः सा पार्थ सात्त्विकी ।।

pravṛttiṁ ca nivṛttiṁ ca
kāryākārye bhayābhaye
bandhaṁ mokṣaṁ ca yā vetti
buddhiḥ sā pārtha sāttvikī

30. That intellect which knows when to act and when not to act, what is to be done and what is not to be done, and what is to be feared and what is not to be feared, along with the knowledge of bondage and liberation, Arjuna, is sattvic.

696 Daily duties, prescribed by the scriptures, are the only good actions and should be done according to a person's capacity.

697 In order to obtain the fruit of Self-realization, he should perform these actions, just as a person drinks water to quench his thirst.

698 By this kind of action, a person is delivered from the terrible dread of earthly life, and it is easy for him to find liberation.

699 A person who acts in this way does well, for he loses his fear of worldly life and attains the status of a seeker of liberation.

700 The person whose mind firmly believes in this path is as sure to attain liberation as if he had already reached it.

701 Therefore, shouldn't such a person plunge into a life of activity which acclaims renunciation of the fruits of action and condemns activity that is performed for the sake of its fruits?

702 Water gives life to a thirsty man, a boat can save a person drowning in a flood, and the sun's rays help one who has fallen into a dark well.

703 If good medicine and a proper diet are given, a person will recover from a severe illness. A fish will survive in water, whereas it will die without it.

704 Similarly, the person who carries out his duties cannot fail to attain liberation.

705 The clear knowledge which enables a person to recognize which actions are right and which are not is known as *sattvic*.

706 Those actions which are prompted by desire, which give rise to the fear of earthly life, and which are stained with error,

707 And undesirable actions which cause recurrence of birth and death,

708 Have the same result as jumping into a furnace, plunging into deep water, or grasping a red-hot weapon.

709 If a person sees a hissing snake, he shouldn't stretch out his hand to it; neither should he approach a tiger's den.

710 This is the kind of wisdom which unfailingly creates fear in a person when he sees improper actions.

711 If a person eats food cooked with poison, he will certainly die. Similarly, this understanding recognizes the bondage inherent in all prohibited actions.

712 Fearful of the bondage brought about by such actions, it avoids performing them.

713 This kind of understanding can discriminate between actions which are proper and those which are not, using the criterion of action and inaction, just as an expert can distinguish a true jewel from a false one.

714 The intellect which has this unlimited power of discrimination between desirable and undesirable actions is of a *sattvic* nature.

यया धर्मम् अधर्मं च कार्यं चाकार्यम् एव च ।
अयथावत् प्रजानाति बुद्धिः सा पार्थ राजसी ॥

yayā dharmam adharmaṁ ca
kāryaṁ cākāryam eva ca
ayathāvat prajānāti
buddhiḥ sā pārtha rājasī

31. That intellect which distinguishes incorrectly between the right and the wrong, and between that which is to be done and that which is not to be done, is rajasic, Arjuna.

715 Just as a heron will drink a mixture of milk and water, being unable to separate it, as a blind man cannot distinguish between day and night,

716 And as the same bee which tastes the honey in flowers may then bore a hole in wood, though this isn't consistent with the bee's nature,

717 In the same way, this kind of understanding cannot discriminate between right and wrong actions and duties.

718 If a person were to trade in pearls without a trained eye, he might by chance find one of value; but if not, he might as well not buy them.

719 Similarly, if he isn't forced to perform a bad action, he may leave it aside; but he regards both good and evil as the same.

720 Such understanding is clearly *rajasic*. It is like a person's inviting guests to a celebration without regard to their suitability.

अधर्मं धर्मम् इति या मन्यते तमसावृता ।
सर्वार्थान् विपरीतांश्च बुद्धिः सा पार्थ तामसी ॥

adharmaṁ dharmam iti yā
manyate tamasāvṛtā
sarvārthān viparītaṁśca
buddhiḥ sā pārtha tāmasī

32. That intellect which, enveloped in darkness, imagines wrong to be right, and all things to be perverted, is tamasic, Arjuna.

721 The royal highway is a dangerous road for a thief. Day must become night for a demon to be able to see.

722 A treasure found by an unlucky man would be worth no more to him than a heap of coal. Even though he possessed it, it would do him no good.

723 In the same way, this kind of understanding regards good actions as evil and confuses the true with the false.

724 It turns everything valuable into dross and treats all virtue as vice.

725 In short, it interprets whatever the scriptures have established as having the opposite meaning.

726 O Arjuna, that understanding is unquestionably *tamasic*, of the quality of darkness. What value can it have?

727 Thus, I have explained clearly the three different kinds of intellect or understanding to you, Arjuna. You are like the moon to the lotus in the form of Self-knowledge.

धृत्या यया धारयते मनःप्राणेन्द्रियक्रियाः
योगेनाव्यभिचारिण्या धृतिः सा पार्थ सात्त्विकी ॥

dhṛtyā yayā dhārayate
manaḥprāṇendriyakriyāḥ
yogenāvyabhicāriṇyā
dhṛtiḥ sā pārtha sāttvikī

33. The unswerving firmness by which, through yoga, one holds fast the functions of the mind, vital breath, and senses, that firmness, Arjuna, is sattvic.

728 The resolution which supports the understanding by which a person decides upon his course of action is also of three kinds.

729 Listen carefully while I explain the characteristics of the three aspects of resolution.

730 When the sun rises, the darkness which is necessary for thieves comes to an end. A royal command will put a halt to evil practices.

731 When the wind blows with all its might, the clouds with their thunder are dispersed.

732 At the sight of the Agastya star, the ocean becomes tranquil. At the rising of the moon, the sun lotuses begin to close their blossoms.

733 When an elephant is in rut, he cannot set down his raised foot even if a roaring lion should be in his path.

734 Similarly, when resolution is firm in the mind, mental and other activities cease.

735 O Arjuna, the knot that binds the senses to sense objects is easily loosened, and the ten senses return to the womb of their mother, the mind.

736 The *prana* ceases flowing up and down and, bound together with the other vital forces, it plunges into the *sushumna nadi.*

737 The mind is stripped of its garment of good and evil desires, and sits silently in its nakedness behind the pure intellect.

738 That royal resolution dismisses all the activities of the mind, the senses, and the *prana,* and their commerce with one another;

739 And with the skill of yogic practice, it confines them all within the inner chamber of meditation.

740 There, resisting all bribery, it holds them captive until it can deliver them into the hands of the great ruler, the Self.

741 Krishna said to Arjuna, This is *sattvic* resolution.

742 As long as he is in the body, such a person dwells both on earth and in heaven, satisfying his desires by three means.

यया तु धर्मकामार्थान् धृत्या धारयते ऽर्जुन ।
प्रसङ्गेन फलाकाङ्क्षी धृतिः सा पार्थ राजसी ॥
yayā tu dharmakamārthān
dhṛtyā dhārayate 'rjuna
prasañgena phalākāñkṣī
dhṛtiḥ sā pārtha rājasī

34. But the firmness by which one holds to duty, pleasures, and wealth, with attachment and desire for the fruits of action, that firmness, Arjuna, is rajasic.

743 He sails across the ocean of desires in the boat of religious duty, wealth, and passion, and with the help of resolution he carries on the trade of action.

744 His resolution supports his intention of obtaining fourfold interest on the capital, in the form of the fruits of his actions, which he invests.

745 O Arjuna, this kind of resolution is *rajasic.* Now hear about the third kind of resolution, which is *tamasic.*

यया स्वप्नं भयं शोकं विषादं मदम् एव च ।
न विमुञ्चति दुर्मेधा धृतिः सा पार्थ तामसी ॥
yayā svapnaṁ bhayaṁ śokaṁ
viṣādaṁ madam eva ca
na vimuñcati durmedhā
dhṛtiḥ sā pārtha tāmasī

35. That firmness by which a stupid man does not abandon sleep, fear, grief, depression, and conceit, is tamasic, Arjuna.

746 This kind of resolution is as full of the lowest quality as coal is of blackness.

747 Can one use the term "quality" for anything as vulgar and low as this? Yet, isn't there a class of demons named Punyajana?

748 Isn't the fiery planet called Mangala, the auspicious one? So the term "quality" is not out of place here.

749 O Arjuna, the person whose body is fashioned out of the quality of darkness is the home of all sin.

750 Unduly fond of idleness, he takes every opportunity to sleep. He is never free from grief because he nourishes sin.

751 He is pursued by fear because he is attached to pleasure and wealth, just as hardness cannot be separated from a stone.

752 He always has to live with sorrow, being bound by desire to objects of pleasure, just as sin always accompanies an ungrateful person.

753 Day and night he is filled with discontent, so depression is his constant companion.

754 Garlic never loses its smell, and a person who eats immoderately is never free from disease. Similarly, depression follows him until the hour of his death.

755 Youth, wealth, and desire increase his delusion, and he becomes the home of conceit.

756 Fire never loses its heat, viciousness is natural to a snake, and fear is the perpetual enemy of mankind.

757 Just as death is always inevitable for the body, in the same way infatuation is inseparable from the *tamasic* quality.

758 Indulgence in sleep and other faults are the marks of this quality, and the resolution with which they hold a person

759 Is known as *tamasic* resolution, said the Lord of the universe.

760 Thus, the threefold intellect first determines what action should be done, and resolution leads to its completion.

761 The sunlight makes a road visible, and then a person can walk along it, but to do so he must have resolution.

762 In the same way, the intellect directs activity and sets the senses in motion, but resolution is necessary for all this.

763 Thus, I have explained to you the three

kinds of resolution, which lead to the three kinds of action.

सुखं त्व् इदानीं त्रिविधं शृणु मे भरतर्षभ ।
अभ्यासाद् रमते यत्र दुःखान्तं च निगच्छति ।।
sukhaṁ tv idānīṁ trividhaṁ
śṛṇu me bharatarṣabha
abhyāsād ramate yatra
duḥkhāntaṁ ca nigacchati

36. *And now, hear from Me, Arjuna, the threefold happiness that one enjoys through practice, and in which one comes to the end of suffering.*

764 Happiness is also threefold because of the influence of action.
765 I will now explain to you in detail the three kinds of happiness, the fruits of actions, which are distinguished by the three qualities.
766 But how can this be done? You will say, let us understand it through speaking; yet the way you hear it may distort what the ear hears.
767 So listen with the inner ear of the heart. In this way, you can disregard the outer process of paying attention to what is said.
768 Saying this, the Lord began to explain the three kinds of happiness, on which I will now comment.
769 Now, O Arjuna, listen to the description of the three kinds of happiness, about which I have promised to speak.
770 I will show you that happiness which the individual soul experiences when it meets the Self.
771 A divine medicine is taken in small doses at stated times. Through the process of alchemy, tin is transmuted into silver.
772 Water is poured onto salt several times to make salt water.
773 Similarly, even the smallest amount of such happiness which the soul experiences through training must wipe out sorrow.
774 This bliss of the Self is threefold in nature, and I will now describe these aspects.

यत् तद् अग्रे विषम् इव परिणामे ऽमृतोपमम् ।
तत् सुखं सात्त्विकं प्रोक्तम् आत्मबुद्धिप्रसादजम् ।।
yat tad agre viṣam iva
pariṇāme 'mṛtopamam
tat sukhaṁ sāttvikaṁ proktam
ātmabuddhiprasādajam

37. *That which in the beginning is like poison but in the end like nectar; that happiness, born from the tranquility of one's own mind, is declared to be sattvic.*

775 The roots of a sandalwood tree are dangerous because of the presence of snakes, and there are demons at the mouth of a hole where a treasure is hidden.
776 A person must make arduous sacrifices before reaching the pleasures of heaven, and childhood is full of difficulties.
777 When a person lights a lamp he must endure its smoke, and when he takes medicine he may find it unpleasant to the taste.
778 O Arjuna, it is the same with this happiness which results from the difficult practice of controlling the mind and the senses.
779 When indifference to worldly things arises, removing all desire, then the boundaries between heaven and earth are removed.
780 For the sake of this, the intellect is deprived of its vitality by the rigorous discipline of listening to the teaching of true knowledge and the observance of severe vows,
781 And the *pranas* are absorbed into the *sushumna nadi*. These are the initial difficulties which a person encounters in attaining this happiness.
782 A pair of herons are distressed if they are separated, and a calf if it is taken away from the cow's udder. Isn't a beggar also upset if he is driven away from his meal?
783 A mother grieves when death takes her only child, and a fish cannot survive without water.
784 In the same way, it may take an entire world age to separate the senses from the sense objects, yet dispassionate people can bear such distress.
785 This kind of happiness is attained only after great initial difficulty, but from the churning of the Milky Ocean there came the reward of nectar.
786 When firm resolution, like that of Lord Shiva, has swallowed the poison of dispassion, then there follows the feast of the nectar of knowledge.
787 Unripe grapes may sting the tongue like burning coals, but when ripe they are full of sweetness.
788 Similarly, when dispassion is perfected by the light of the Self and every form of ignorance is destroyed,
789 Then the intellect becomes merged in the

Self just as the water of the Ganges flows into the ocean, and the vast storehouse of the bliss of union is opened.

790 Therefore, that happiness which is rooted in dispassion and which leads to the experience of union is called *sattvic.*

विषयेद्रियसंयोगाद् यत् तद् अग्रे ऽमृतोपमम् ।
परिणामे विषम् इव तत् सुखं राजसं स्मृतम् ॥

viṣayendriyasaṁyogād
yat tad agre 'mrtopamam
pariṇāme viṣam iva
tat sukhaṁ rājasaṁ smṛtam

38. That which in the beginning, through contact between the senses and their objects, is like nectar, and in the end like poison; that happiness is declared to be rajasic.

791 O Arjuna, when the senses are united with their sense objects, this kind of happiness overflows its banks.

792 When a ruler visits a town a festival is held, and money is borrowed to celebrate a marriage.

793 Sugar and plantains taste equally sweet to a sick man's tongue, and the poisonous *bacnaga* plant is pleasing to the eyes.

794 Just as the friendship of villains, the company of prostitutes, and the strange feats of jugglers are all attractive at first,

795 Similarly, a person's happiness is fed by the sin of the union of the senses with their objects, but the result is like that of a swan dashing against the rocks.

796 All such happiness comes to an end, life may even be destroyed, and all accumulated merit is wasted.

797 All the pleasures which a person has enjoyed vanish like a dream, leaving him struck down by disaster.

798 Thus, this kind of happiness brings about disaster in this world and turns to poison in the next.

799 If sense pleasures are given full rein, they burn up the field of religious duty and enjoy a feast of sensual indulgence.

800 Sin becomes established, and the sinner is cast into hell. Therefore, this kind of happiness is an obstacle to reaching heaven.

801 There is a poison which by name is sweet, but which proves deadly in its effects.

802 O Arjuna, it is the same with this *rajasic* happiness which is full of poison. Therefore, you should avoid any contact with it.

यद् अग्रे चानुबन्धे च सुखं मोहनम् आत्मनः ।
निद्रालस्यप्रमादोत्थं तत् तामसम् उदाहृतम् ॥

yad agre cānubandhe ca
sukhaṁ mohanam ātmanaḥ
nidrālasyapramādotthaṁ
tat tāmasam udāhṛtam

39. That happiness which both in the beginning and afterwards deludes the self, arising from sleep, indolence, and negligence, is declared to be tamasic.

803 The happiness which arises from indulging in drink, from eating undesirable food, and from the company of loose women,

804 From assault and robbery of others and from the praise of poets,

805 Which is fed by laziness and enjoyed in oversleeping, and which always leaves a person confused about the way he should live,

806 O Arjuna, this kind of happiness is truly *tamasic,* of the nature of darkness. I won't say much about it, for it can hardly be experienced as happiness.

न तद् अस्ति पृथिव्यां वा दिवि देवेषु वा पुनः ।
सत्त्वं प्रकृतिजैर् मुक्तं यद् एभिः स्यात् त्रिभिर् गुणैः ॥

na tad asti pṛthivyāṁ vā
divi deveṣu vā punaḥ
sattvaṁ prakṛtijāir muktaṁ
yad ebhiḥ syāt tribhir guṇāiḥ

40. There is no being, either on earth or yet in heaven among the gods, which can exist free from these three qualities born of material nature.

807 So according to the threefold nature of action, happiness is also of three kinds. I have made this clear to you.

808 There is nothing in the world, either gross or subtle, which isn't involved in these three things—the doer, the action, and the fruit of action.

809 O Arjuna, these three things are woven into the nature of the qualities like the warp and woof of cloth.

810 There is nothing in the world of nature, in the world of mortal men, or in heaven, which isn't ruled by the three qualities.

811 Could there be a blanket without wool, a lump of clay without earth, or waves without water?

812 There is no creature in all of nature which isn't composed of the three qualities.

813 Therefore, you should know that everything is fashioned from the three qualities.
814 Because of these qualities there are three gods and three worlds, and people belong to the four castes according to their various functions.

ब्राह्मणक्षत्रियविशां शूद्राणां च परंतप ।
कर्माणि प्रविभक्तानि स्वभावप्रभवैर् गुनैः ॥
brāhmaṇakṣatriyaviśāṁ
śūdrāṇāṁ ca paraṁtapa
karmāṇi pravibhaktāni
svabhāvaprabhavāir guṇāiḥ

41. The duties of the brahmins, the kshatriyas, the vaishyas, and of the shudras, Arjuna, are distributed according to the qualities which arise from their own nature.

815 Now if you should ask what these four castes are, I will tell you that the first and the foremost is the brahmins.
816 Of the others, both the *kshatriyas* and the *vaishyas* are regarded as equal to the brahmins, in that they are qualified to practice Vedic rites.
817 O Arjuna, the fourth caste, the *shudras*, have nothing to do with these rites, for they are obliged to serve the other three castes.
818 The *shudras* are called the fourth caste because of their close association with the brahmins and the others.
819 When a rich man smells a garland of flowers, he also smells the string which holds them together. Similarly, through their association with the twice-born castes, the *shudras* are also accepted by the Vedas.
820 O Arjuna, this is called the organization of mankind into the four castes. I will now explain their respective functions.
821 By means of the three qualities, the four castes can escape from the grip of the cycle of birth and death and reach the Supreme.
822 The three qualities born of the divine nature have allotted to each of the four castes their special functions.
823 A father divides his wealth among his children, the sun reveals various paths to travelers, and a master assigns different duties to his servants.
824 Similarly, the three qualities born of matter have appointed duties for each of the four castes.
825 The brahmins and the *kshatriyas* were assigned their functions by their greater and lesser degrees of the *sattva guna.*
826 The *vaishya* caste is established by the *rajo guna* with some *sattva guna*, and the *shudra* caste by *rajo guna* mixed with *tamo guna.*
827 In this way, O Arjuna, the human race consists of four different castes arising from the three qualities.
828 Thus, the scriptures explain the functions of the castes according to the difference of the qualities, just as with help of a lamp we can find an object that is hidden.
829 So listen, O Arjuna, while I tell you what the appointed duties of the castes are.

शमो दमस् तपः शौचं क्षान्तिर् आर्जवम् एव च ।
ज्ञानं विज्ञानम् आस्तिक्यं ब्रह्मकर्म स्वभावजम् ॥
śamo damas tapaḥ śāucaṁ
kṣāntir ārjavam eva ca
jñānaṁ vijñānam āstikyaṁ
brahmakarma svabhāvajam

42. Tranquility, restraint, austerity, purity, forgiveness, and uprightness, knowledge, wisdom, and faith in God are the duties of the brahmins, born of their innate nature.

830 When the intellect, gathering together the tendencies of all the senses, meets the Self, just as a wife meets her husband in a quiet place,
831 This is called tranquility, and it is the essential virtue for beginning all action.
832 Then, expelling all the outer senses with the whip of prescribed duties, not allowing them to follow the path of unrighteousness,
833 Self-control, the aid of tranquility, is the second virtue, enabling a person to carry out his duties properly.
834 Just as a lamp must be kept burning on the sixth night after the birth of a child, similarly, firm faith in God should be maintained.
835 This is called austerity, and it is the third virtue. Then there is sinless purity, which is of two kinds.
836 The mind should be filled with pure emotions and the body adorned with right actions. Thus one's entire life becomes gracious.
837 O Arjuna, this is called purity and it is the fourth virtue in the performance of duties. Just as the earth bears all burdens,
838 In the same way, forgiveness is the fifth virtue, just as the fifth note of the scale is the sweetest.

839 The Ganges flows on as a river though its course may wind. Sugarcane has the same sweetness throughout though its joints may be crooked.

840 In the same way, when a person is upright and straightforward even towards unpleasant people, this reveals the sixth virtue, uprightness.

841 A gardener diligently waters the roots of trees and sees the result in the fruit they bear.

842 Similarly, through wisdom a person obeys the teachings of the scriptures and finds God.

843 This is the seventh virtue, which is needed in the performance of action. Then comes knowledge, which we will now see.

844 When a person attains true inner purity, he can certainly find the Supreme either through meditation or through scriptural study.

845 This knowledge is good, and is the eighth among these virtues. The ninth is belief in the scriptures.

846 Just as people respect anyone bearing the royal insignia, similarly, belief in the scriptures involves the faithful following of those paths of conduct which the scriptures accept.

847 This is the ninth of these virtues which lead to right action.

848 The natural duty of a brahmin consists of this group of nine pure virtues, beginning with tranquility.

849 He is the ocean of these virtues, a garland of these nine jewels, and is as inseparable from them as is light from the sun.

850 Just as a champak tree is adorned with its flowers, as the moonlight adds to the brilliance of the moon, and as the value of the sandalwood tree is enhanced by its fragrance,

851 Similarly, these nine virtues are perfect ornaments of the brahmin and are inseparable from him.

शौर्यं तेजो धृतिर् दाक्ष्यं युद्धे चाप्य् अपलायनम् ।
दानम् ईश्वरभावश्च क्षात्रं कर्म स्वभावजम् ।।

śāuryaṁ tejo dhṛtir dākṣyaṁ
yuddhe cāpy apalāyanam
dānam īśvarabhāvaśca
kṣātraṁ karma svabhāvajam

43. Heroism, majesty, firmness, skill, not fleeing in battle, generosity, and lordly spirit are the duties of the kshatriyas, born of their innate nature.

852 Now, O Arjuna, listen with full understanding to the explanation of the proper duties of a *kshatriya*.

853 The sun sheds its light without any help, and a lion seeks no support from another.

854 Similarly, courage which is strong and self-reliant, which excels without the need for others' support, is the first and greatest virtue of a *kshatriya*.

855 In the light of the sun, countless stars are eclipsed. When the sun vanishes, the stars and the moon reappear.

856 In the same way, although the *kshatriya* may astonish the world with his bravery, he shouldn't allow himself to be carried away by it.

857 Confidence in all that he does is the second virtue, and steadfastness is the third.

858 Steadfastness is that courage through which a person wouldn't close the eye of clear perception, even if the heavens were to fall.

859 However deep the water may be, the lotus rises from the bottom and opens its blossoms, and the sky is able to rise above all heights.

860 In the same way, O Arjuna, a *kshatriya* should be able to triumph in all circumstances and to perceive the results through his wisdom.

861 The ability to act in this way is the fourth virtue, and the fifth is heroism in battle.

862 The *kshatriya* should always face an enemy in the same way that a sunflower looks up at the sun.

863 He should never turn his back on an enemy on the battlefield as a woman avoids her husband during her monthly periods.

864 This is the fifth of the great virtues which he should practice, just as devotion is the most important of the four goals of existence.

865 The flowers and fruit of a tree are free for everyone, and a lotus generously spreads its fragrance everywhere.

866 A person may enjoy as much moonlight as he wishes, and he may give to another according to his desire.

867 Such limitless generosity is the sixth virtue, as well as encouraging obedience to commands.

868 When our body is properly nourished, it will

function as we wish. Similarly, when the *kshatriya* protects his people, he is loved and served by them.

869 This is called leadership, which embodies all power. It is the seventh of the virtues and the ruler of them all.

870 A *kshatriya* is adorned with these seven virtues, just as the sky is made beautiful by the constellation of the seven stars of the seven sages.

871 The sacred duties which the *kshatriya* carries out in the world through these seven virtues constitute the essence of warriorship.

872 Truly, the *kshatriya* is no ordinary man. He is like Mount Meru in the form of the gold of goodness, and his duty is to support the heaven of these seven virtues.

873 His work isn't ordinary action but is like the earth surrounded by the seven oceans in the form of these virtues.

874 The stream of these seven virtues is like the Ganges, giving delight to the ocean which receives it.

875 In fact, the duties arising from these virtues are the essential functions of the *kshatriya* caste.

कृषिगौरक्ष्यवाणिज्यं वैश्यकर्म स्वभावजम् ।
परिचर्यात्मकम् कर्म शूद्रस्यापि स्वभावजम्

kṛṣigāurakṣyavāṇijyaṁ
vāiśyakarma svabhāvajam
paricaryātmakam karma
śūdrasyāpi svabhāvajam

44. Plowing, cow-herding, and trade are the duties of the vaishyas, born of their innate nature. Service is the duty of the shudras, born of their innate nature.

876 O Arjuna, now listen and I will tell you the proper functions of the *vaishya* caste.

877 They are as follows: earning interest on his wealth by means of the land, plowing, and sowing,

878 Living on the proceeds of agriculture and husbandry, and buying goods at a low price to sell them at a higher price.

879 The function of the *shudra* caste is to serve the brahmins, *kshatriyas*, and *vaishyas*, the twice-born castes.

880 The *shudra* has no other calling than the service of these castes. Now I have shown you the duties of the four castes.

स्वे स्वे कर्मण्य् अभिरतः संसिद्धिं लभते नरः ।
स्वकर्मनिरतः सिद्धिं यथा विन्दति तच् छृणु ॥

sve sve karmaṇy abhirataḥ
saṁsiddhiṁ labhate naraḥ
svakarmanirataḥ siddhiṁ
yathā vindati tac chṛṇu

45. Devoted to his own duty, a man attains perfection. Hear then how one who is devoted to his own duty finds perfection:

881 O Arjuna, these are the proper duties of the various castes, just as the ears and the other senses have their related objects.

882 Just as a river is the proper destination of rain falling from the clouds, and as the destination of the river is the ocean,

883 Similarly, the natural duties according to his caste are proper for each person, just as fairness of skin is a natural property of blonds.

884 O Arjuna, let your mind firmly resolve to perform your caste duties as ordained by the scriptures.

885 Just as a person needs the help of an expert to determine the value of a jewel, he must turn to the scriptures to know what his duty is.

886 Although we possess the power of sight, it cannot be used without light, and our feet are useless if we don't know what road to take.

887 In the same way, we should discover which are the duties proper to our caste through understanding the scriptures.

888 Then, O Arjuna, just as with the help of a lamp a person has no difficulty in finding his home in the dark,

889 Similarly, the scriptures confirm the work that comes naturally to a person. When he carries out his appointed duty,

890 Abandoning laziness, not thinking about the results, and devoting his whole body and mind to it,

891 Then he fulfills his function in an orderly way, like a stream of water which flows steadily in one channel.

892 O Arjuna, a person who performs his proper duties in this way reaches the gateway to liberation.

893 Such a person is free from any dread of earthly existence, for he never performs an unworthy action or one that is prohibited by the scriptures.

894 He isn't tempted to turn towards any action prompted by desire, just as he wouldn't willingly place his legs in the stocks even if they were made of sandalwood.
895 With regard to daily duties, he nullifies their effects by renouncing their fruits. In this way, he is able to reach the boundary of liberation.
896 Thus freed from good and evil actions in earthly life, he finds himself at the door of liberation in the form of dispassion.
897 To attain this dispassion is the height of good fortune, the assurance of liberation, and the end of all striving.
898 It is the certainty of the fruit of freedom and the flower of the tree of merit, on which the seeker of freedom settles like a bee.
899 This dispassion is the dawn that announces the coming of the day of Self-realization.
900 It is like the magic lotion which, when applied to the soul, gives the vision enabling one to find the treasure of Self-knowledge.
901 O Arjuna, performing his prescribed duties makes a person worthy of attaining liberation.
902 Therefore, these duties are our only support. To perform them is loving service rendered to Me, the Supreme Being.
903 A devoted wife surrenders herself wholeheartedly to pleasing her husband. In this way she practices penance.
904 A mother is the sole support of her child, so it is the child's foremost duty to depend on her.
905 A fish may regard the Ganges merely as water, but by remaining in it he obtains the blessings of all sacred places.
906 Similarly, there is no other way to liberation but the faithful performance of one's duties. In this way, the Lord of the world carries the burden.
907 The Supreme intends for each person to have his appointed duty, and in performing it he surely attains blessedness.
908 If a serving girl stands the test of her master's love, she may become his wife. A person who risks his life for his master goes down in history.
909 O Arjuna, to be diligent about pleasing one's master is truly to serve him. All else is like a merchant's business.

यतः प्रवृत्तिर् भूतानां येन सर्वम् इदं ततम् ।
स्वकर्मणा तम् अभ्यर्च्य सिद्धिं विन्दति मानवः ॥

yataḥ pravṛttir bhūtānāṁ
yena sarvam idaṁ tatam
svakarmaṇā tam abhyarcya
siddhiṁ vindati mānavaḥ

46. By worshiping with his own proper duty Him from whom all beings have their origin, Him by whom all this universe is pervaded, man finds perfection.

910 When a person performs his own duty, it isn't only that he has done that action, but that he has carried out the purpose of God from whom the entire creation arises.
911 The creator has wrapped around the individual soul a garment of ignorance, and he makes it dance like a puppet on the string of egoism, woven from the three qualities.
912 He pervades the entire universe, within and without, just as a lamp is filled with light.
913 O Arjuna, when a person offers God the flowers of his duty, God's joy is boundless.
914 Being pleased by his worship, the Lord bestows the attainment of dispassion on him as a further favor.
915 When a person in this state of dispassion is overcome by his longing for the Supreme, he feels utter aversion towards all the things of this world.
916 Just as a wife separated from her husband feels that her life is a burden, he regards all objects of pleasure as sources of misery.
917 As soon as true realization is awakened, he becomes absorbed in the Self and acquires the worthiness to receive further teaching.
918 Therefore, a seeker who is determined to attain liberation should apply himself diligently to performing his duty.

श्रेयान् स्वधर्मो विगुणः परधर्मात् स्वनुष्ठितात् ।
स्वभावनियतं कर्म कुर्वन् नाप्नोति किल्बिषम् ॥

śreyān svadharmo viguṇaḥ
paradharmāt svanuṣṭhitāt
svabhāvaniyataṁ karma
kurvan nāpnoti kilbiṣam

47. Better one's own duty, though imperfect, than the duty of another well performed; performing the duty prescribed by one's own nature, one does not incur evil.

919 O Beloved, even though his appointed duty may be difficult to perform, a person should consider its ultimate reward.
920 O Arjuna, if it is necessary for his own good to drink the juice of the neem tree, he

shouldn't be repelled by its bitterness.

921 He might be discouraged by the appearance of a plantain tree before it has borne fruit, but if he were to destroy it, how could he obtain its sweet fruit?

922 Similarly, if he were to reject his duty because it was difficult, he would deprive himself of the joy of liberation.

923 Although a mother may be deformed, her love for her children is genuine.

924 Other women may be more beautiful than Rambha, but what does this matter to her children?

925 Ghee has qualities that aren't found in water, but what would happen to a fish living in it?

926 What is poison to the whole world is like nectar to a worm; yet sugarcane juice, which is sweet to the world, would cause its death.

927 Therefore, a person must practice his own appointed duty, however difficult it may seem to be, for it frees him from the bondage of life.

928 If a person were to undertake someone else's duty, considering it to be better, it would be like trying to walk on his head instead of his feet.

929 Therefore, when a person carries out the duty given to him according to his nature, he overcomes the bondage of action.

930 So it is unnecessary to lay down the rule that a person ought to perform his own duty and leave that of another.

सहजं कर्म कौन्तेय सदोषम् अपि न त्यजेत् ।
सर्वारम्भा हि दोषेण धूमेनाग्निर् इवावृताः ॥

sahajaṁ karma kāunteya
sadoṣam api na tyajet
sarvārambhā hi doṣeṇa
dhūmenāgnir ivāvṛtāḥ

48. One should not abandon the duty to which one is born even though it be deficient, Arjuna. Indeed, all undertakings are enveloped by evil as fire is by smoke.

931 O Arjuna, a person doesn't stop performing action until he has experienced the vision of the Self, and where there is action there must first be effort.

932 If others initially find it difficult to perform their duty, why should a person think that this is a fault in his own duty?

933 If he walks along a straight road, his feet get just as tired as if he were walking along a jungle path.

934 O Arjuna, whether he carries stones or a bag of food on a journey, the burden is the same. Therefore he should carry something that will be useful when he stops to rest on the way.

935 Whether he is separating out grains or husks, the effort is the same. It takes as long to cook food for a dog as to cook materials for a sacrifice.

936 If it is just as expensive to support a wife as to keep a mistress, why should a man subject himself to criticism?

937 O Arjuna, it takes as much work to churn curds as to churn water, and grinding sesame seeds requires as much effort as grinding sand.

938 Since a person cannot avoid death by a blow in the back, shouldn't he face the enemy and receive it in front?

939 If a highborn woman is as likely to receive a beating in the house of another man there is no purpose in leaving her own husband.

940 Therefore, if a person cannot accomplish what he wishes without trouble, why should he consider his own duty to be a burden?

941 O Arjuna, if he could gain immortality by taking a little nectar, why shouldn't he spend all that he has to obtain it?

942 Why should he spend his money on poison with which to commit suicide?

943 If he were to spend his whole life accumulating sin by indulging his senses, the only result would be sorrow.

944 Therefore, let him perform his own duties, which will remove all his burdens and enable him to realize the supreme purpose of life.

945 For this reason, O Arjuna, no one should neglect the practice of his duty, just as he would never forget a magic word that rescues him in difficulty.

946 A person shouldn't let a boat loose at sea or refuse to take medicine during an illness. This should also be his attitude towards his duty.

असक्तबुद्धिः सर्वत्र जितात्मा विगतस्पृहः ।
नैष्कर्म्यसिद्धिं परमां संन्यासेनाधिगच्छति ॥

asaktabuddhiḥ sarvatra
jitātmā vigataspṛhaḥ
nāiṣkarmyasiddhiṁ paramāṁ
saṁnyāsenādhigacchati

49. With his intellect unattached at all times, with conquered self, free from desire, by renunciation, one attains the supreme state of freedom from action.

947 O Arjuna, then God is pleased with his worship in the form of his duty and cleanses him from passion and darkness.

948 Leading his desire along the way of purity, the Lord shows him that earth and heaven are like deadly poison.

949 Thus he reaches his goal in that perfection which was earlier described as dispassion.

950 Now I will tell you what he gains when he has reached this perfect dispassion.

951 The dispassionate person cannot be entangled by physical existence or the conditions of worldly life, just as the wind cannot be caught in a net.

952 His desire for earthly things grows weak, just as when a fruit is ripe it no longer clings to the stem.

953 He becomes detached from his wife, his children, and his wealth, not considering them his own, just as no one would claim to own poison.

954 His mind withdraws from sense pleasures as if it were burned by their touch, and he retires into inner silence.

955 His inner senses refrain from turning outward and breaking their resolution to avoid sense pleasures, just as a servant is afraid to disobey the command of her master.

956 O Arjuna, he places his mind securely within the grasp of union with the Self and drives it on with his longing for the Supreme.

957 Then every desire he had for worldly or heavenly enjoyment comes to an end, just as smoke vanishes when a fire is extinguished.

958 With his mind under control desire dies away, and he attains the condition of self-restraint.

959 O Arjuna, as a result his wrong understanding disappears.

960 In the same way that stored water is gradually used up, his accrued merit is spent and he acquires no new merit by further action.

961 O Arjuna, when he has gained this state of perfect equilibrium in action, he will find his Guru without difficulty.

962 When the four watches of the night are past, we can see the sun, the destroyer of darkness.

963 When a plantain tree has borne fruit, its growth ceases. Similarly, when a seeker meets his Guru, he is freed from the necessity of action.

964 Then, O Arjuna, by the grace of his Guru he will reach perfection, just as the moon becomes perfect on the day when it is full.

965 That grace dispels all ignorance, just as darkness passes away when the night is over.

966 With the death of ignorance all action comes to an end, and this brings about complete renunciation.

967 With this total renunciation of ignorance, all visible matter disappears and the Self is all that remains.

968 When a person wakes from sleep, will he try to rescue himself from the river in which he dreamed he was drowning?

969 Then the dream vanishes in which he thought he would eventually find knowledge, and he himself becomes that knowledge in which there is neither knower nor object known.

970 O Arjuna, when a mirror is taken away, the reflection disappears and only the observer is left.

971 Similarly, when ignorance is removed knowledge also disappears, and only pure knowledge which is free from action remains.

972 O Arjuna, because action isn't possible in that state, it is described as the state beyond action.

973 When the wind stops blowing over the sea, the waves subside. Similarly, when a person realizes that he is truly the Self,

974 The sense of inaction that arises is the perfect state of being beyond activity. This is the highest attainment.

975 The pinnacle of a temple represents its completion, the supreme goal of the Ganges is its union with the sea, and the highest value of gold is one hundred percent purity.

976 Likewise, the state in which knowledge dispels ignorance and then is itself dispelled,

977 Is not surpassed by any other. Therefore it is regarded as the supreme attainment.

सिद्धिं प्राप्तो यथा ब्रह्म तथाप्नोति निबोध मे ।
समासेनैव कौन्तेय निष्ठा ज्ञानस्य या परा ॥
siddhiṁ prāpto yathā brahma
tathāpnoti nibodha me

samāsenāiva kāunteya
niṣṭhā jñānasya yā parā

50. Learn from Me briefly, Arjuna, how one who has attained perfection also attains Brahman, which is the highest state of knowledge.

978 A person who has good fortune reaches this realization in time through the grace of his Guru.
979 When the sun rises, darkness is lost in the light. When camphor is put into a flame, it is also transformed into light.
980 When grains of salt are added to water, they dissolve immediately and become water.
981 When a person wakes up, his sleep and his dreams vanish, and he returns to the waking state.
982 Similarly, when by good fortune a person hears the teaching of his Guru, he overcomes duality and his mind is at rest.
983 Then is there any further need for action? Is the sky concerned with coming and going?
984 Truly, nothing else remains for him to do. However, there are some for whom it isn't possible
985 To experience union with God immediately when they hear the Guru's words, O Arjuna.
986 Such a person must first burn up passion and darkness in the fire of his own duty, with the fuel of actions which are prohibited or prompted by desire.
987 Any desire for children, wealth, or heavenly life must become like a servant in his house.
988 He must purify his senses in the holy waters of restraint, for they have been contaminated by wandering among sense objects.
989 He must offer up the fruit of his duties to the Supreme, and in this way he must remain firmly established in dispassion.
990 He must equip himself with all these means, so he can gain the true perception which leads to Self-knowledge.
991 Once he has done this, he must find a Guru who is sincere in his teaching.
992 When a person takes medicine his disease doesn't disappear right away. Does noon immediately follow dawn?
993 If good seed is sown in a well-irrigated field, a good harvest may be expected, but only in course of time.
994 Even if a person finds an excellent road and is in good company, it takes time for him to complete his journey.
995 Similarly, when a person attains dispassion, when he has found his Guru, and when the tender shoot of discrimination begins to grow in his mind,
996 He experiences with conviction the truth that there is only one God and all else is delusion.
997 That God is all-pervasive and is the highest state. Even liberation comes to an end in Him.
998 O Arjuna, this realization will continue to such an extent that he will no longer feel even the oneness of union as a separate experience.
999 All bliss that can be distinguished as a mental perception becomes merged in the Absolute. The subject, the object, and the link between them is lost in absolute union; and nothing remains.
1000 He then experiences in due course of time the state of oneness with God.
1001 If a hungry man is served delicious food, he becomes more and more satisfied with every mouthful.
1002 He is inspired by the wealth of the Self in the same way that the lamp of the mind is fed with the oil of dispassion.
1003 Then he acquires the worthiness to experience the full glory of God.
1004 Now I will tell you in order the steps to union with God and their inner meaning. Listen to this.

बुद्ध्या विशुद्धया युक्तो धृत्यात्मानं नियम्य च ।
शब्दादीन् विषयांस् त्यक्त्वा रागद्वेषौ व्युदस्य च ॥

buddhyā viśuddhayā yukto
dhṛtyātmānaṁ niyamya ca
śabdādīn viṣayāṅs tyaktvā
rāgadveṣāu vyudasya ca

51. Endowed with a pure intellect, controlling the self with firmness, abandoning sound and the other objects of sense, casting off attraction and hatred,

1005 Arriving at the holy place of discrimination by the road that his Guru has shown, he cleanses his mind of all stain.
1006 Then it is restored to its original purity, like the light of the moon when it is released from the grip of the demon Rahu.
1007 Just as a wife leaves the homes of both her mother and her father-in-law and follows her husband, he renounces the world of

duality and devotes himself to meditation.
1008 Then the various sense objects, which have been given too much importance by the sense organs, driving away the helpful friend of wisdom,
1009 Are deprived of their power through control of the senses, just as a mirage is dispelled by the setting sun.
1010 In the same way that one should vomit food eaten by mistake in the house of a lowborn person, one should detach the senses and feelings of desire from sense objects.
1011 The senses, which are withdrawn from their objects, are then purified by penance, as though by the waters of the Ganges.
1012 Then they are cleansed by the practice of pure resolution, and the mind perseveres in meditation.
1013 With his mind in this condition, if he meets with pleasure or pain as a result of past lives, he feels no resentment against unfortunate experiences;
1014 Neither does he allow desire to arise in his mind if pleasurable experiences come to him.

विविक्तसेवी लघ्वाशी यतवाक्कायमानसः ।
ध्यानयोगपरो नित्यं वैराग्यं समुपाश्रितः ॥
viviktasevī laghvāśī
yatavākkāyamānasaḥ
dhyānayogaparo nityaṁ
vāirāgyaṁ samupāśritaḥ

52. Dwelling in solitude, eating lightly, controlling speech, body, and mind, constantly devoted to yoga meditation, taking refuge in dispassion,

1015 O Arjuna, renouncing both love of pleasure and hatred of what is unpleasant, he withdraws to live in a cave or forest.
1016 He avoids all human activities and lives alone in a forest, with only himself for company.
1017 He practices control of the body and the mind, silence is his only conversation, and he is unaware of time in his meditation on the teachings of his Guru.
1018 Whether food will strengthen his body, satisfy his hunger, or be pleasant to the taste,
1019 He doesn't take these things into consideration when eating. Although he eats little, there is no limit to his satisfaction.
1020 Because the life force may be destroyed by feeding the inner fire, he eats only enough to sustain life.
1021 Just as a wife of a good family doesn't give up her body to another man's lust, he doesn't give in to sleep or laziness.
1022 His body touches the ground only when he prostrates himself before his deity. He doesn't lie down for the pleasure of sleeping.
1023 He uses his hands and feet only for the necessary movements of the body. In this way he has complete self-control.
1024 He never allows desire to cross the threshold of his mind, O Arjuna. For this reason, there is no opportunity for conversation.
1025 Having thus controlled his body, speech, and mind, he then encompasses the further regions of meditation.
1026 Just as a person may examine himself closely in a mirror, he becomes firmly convinced of the wisdom which the Guru's teachings have impressed on him.
1027 Listen! Although he himself is the one meditating, in the practice of meditation he realizes the essence of the three elements. This is the true method of meditation.
1028 O Arjuna, he continues his practice until meditation, the meditator, and the object of meditation have all merged into one.
1029 In this way, as the seeker turns to the practice of yoga, he becomes expert in attaining knowledge of the Self.
1030 O Arjuna, he presses with his heel the lower organs of the body in the yogic posture.
1031 Contracting the lower part of the trunk and combining three yogic postures, he unites three of the vital forces.
1032 He awakens Kundalini by opening the *sushumna nadi* and forces a way through from the lowest *chakra* to the highest.
1033 Now the cloud of the thousand-petaled lotus at the crown of the head showers a stream of nectar which flows through the body down to the *muladhara chakra*.
1034 In the earthen bowl of the deity of Consciousness, dancing on the holy mountain of the *sahasrara*, he serves a dish of the mixture of the mind and the vital force.
1035 In this way, the yogi thrusts forward an army of yogic practices and behind it completes his meditation on the Self.
1036 Yet before these two, yoga and meditation, can enter into uninterrupted realization of the Self,
1037 He must first become the friend of dispas-

sion and travel along the entire road in its company.

1038 If a person carries a light, will it take him a long time to find what he has lost?

1039 Similarly, as long as dispassion accompanies him, a person who has experienced liberation cannot fail to reach union with God.

1040 In this way, the person who has dispassion and who has acquired and practiced wisdom has become worthy of union with the Self.

1041 Therefore, if a man wears the armor of renunciation and mounts the steed of the highest yoga,

1042 If he holds the sword of meditation in the hand of discrimination and strikes down all obstacles, great or small,

1043 He enters the battlefield of worldly life like the rising sun and wins as his bride the glorious victory of liberation.

अहंकारं बलं दर्पं कामं क्रोधं परिग्रहम् ।
विमुच्य निर्ममः शान्तो ब्रह्मभूयाय कल्पते ॥

ahaṁkāraṁ balaṁ darpaṁ
kāmaṁ krodhaṁ parigrahaṁ
vimucya nirmamaḥ śānto
brahmabhūyāya kalpate

53. Relinquishing egotism, force, arrogance, desire, anger, and possession of property; unselfish, tranquil, he is fit for oneness with Brahman.

1044 There he defeats all his enemies, the vices which come in his path. The first of these is egoism, the sense of individuality associated with the body.

1045 This enemy won't set him free by killing him. Having brought him into this life, it won't let him live. It imprisons him within the physical body.

1046 O Arjuna, he captures the fortress of the body in which the enemy lives and then destroys his second enemy, power.

1047 This vice increases fourfold at the very mention of an object of pleasure, and it reduces the world to a state of death.

1048 It is the king of all vices and that deep source from which gushes the poison of sense pleasures, but it cannot withstand a blow from the sword of meditation.

1049 It rejoices when it obtains sense pleasures and delights in surrounding itself with them like a garment.

1050 It causes a person to wander from the right path, leads him into the by-paths of evil, and hands him over to the tiger of hell.

1051 Then the yogi destroys pride, which gives false confidence and brings terror to the hearts of those who practice penance.

1052 He also destroys anger, the greatest of vices, which becomes more empty the more it is fostered.

1053 As he removes all trace of desire, he eradicates anger along with it.

1054 Just as when the roots of a tree are cut the branches wither, similarly, when desire dies anger dies with it.

1055 So when the enemy called desire is killed in this battle, anger suffers the same fate.

1056 Just as a tyrant doesn't hesitate to make a criminal carry a load on his head even while his feet are shackled, similarly, a person's burden increases with his possessions.

1057 Greed lays a burden upon a man's head, gives rise to many faults, and places in his hand the staff of personal possession.

1058 It entices even a detached person into establishing hermitages and yogic training for the pleasure of explaining the scriptures to disciples.

1059 Sometimes a man abandons his family, returns into the forest, and even there, through greed, he becomes attached to the objects around him. It assails him even when he has abandoned his clothing.

1060 But the true seeker overcomes this powerful greed for possessions and triumphs over worldly life.

1061 Then humility and all the other great virtues of wisdom come out to meet him like princes of the land of highest bliss.

1062 They bestow on him the kingship of true knowledge and become the retinue which always accompanies him.

1063 As he walks along the highway of worldly activity, the three states of consciousness, like three maidens, wave around him the protective leaves of happiness at every step.

1064 The banner of enlightenment is carried before him, discrimination moves aside the throng of the visible world, and meditation accompanies him waving its lamp.

1065 Psychic powers gather together and shower him with flowers.

1066 When he approaches the kingdom of union with the supreme Self, all the three worlds are filled with joy.

1067 Then, O Arjuna, there is no sense of duality

left which would make him call one person his friend and another his enemy.

1068 He has become so free from duality that he doesn't claim anything as his own.

1069 O Arjuna, when he has brought the whole world under his command in this way, he dries out all sense of attachment to possessions.

1070 In this way he has overcome all his enemies and, having become one with the whole world, he brings to a halt the steed of yogic practices.

1071 He loosens for a while the tightly fitting armor of dispassion.

1072 And since that duality which he killed with the sword of meditation is no longer before him, the hand of activity casts it away.

1073 Then he becomes like a medicine which, having had its effect, dies with the disease.

1074 Just as a person stops running when he reaches the end of his journey, he gives up his yogic practices now that he has attained God.

1075 When a river flows into the ocean, the speed of its current is lost. A wife becomes calm in the presence of her husband.

1076 When a plantain tree has borne fruit, its growth stops. A road comes to an end when it reaches a village.

1077 Similarly, when a person attains union with the Self, he gradually sets aside the various means he used to reach that state.

1078 Therefore, O Arjuna, when union with God is attained, the means to attain it serve no further purpose.

1079 When the sun of dispassion sets, knowledge reaches maturity and the fruit of yoga ripens.

1080 A person then reaches the state of perfect peace and is worthy to become the Supreme, O Arjuna.

1081 The moon on the fourteenth day is just a little smaller than it is on the day of the full moon. The value of slightly impure gold is only a little less than that of pure gold.

1082 When a river reaches the ocean, it remains a river only as long as it flows with a current. When the current disappears, it becomes the ocean.

1083 The difference that separates God from a person who is worthy to become God is as slight as these differences. By reaching the state of peace, he very soon becomes God.

1084 He who realizes that he is the Supreme, even before he becomes the Supreme, is worthy to attain oneness with Him.

ब्रह्मभूतः प्रसन्नात्मा न शोचति न काङ्क्षति ।
समः सर्वेषु भूतेषु मद्भक्तिं लभते पराम् ॥

brahmabhūtaḥ prasannātmā
na śocati na kāṅkṣati
samaḥ sarveṣu bhūteṣu
madbhaktiṁ labhate parām

54. Absorbed in Brahman, he whose self is serene does not mourn, nor does he desire; impartial among all beings, he attains supreme devotion to Me.

1085 O Arjuna, the person who has reached this state of worthiness attains the blessed state of Self-realization.

1086 When cooked food cools down, one can enjoy it.

1087 The turbulent waters of the Ganges subside after the rainy season. At the end of a song, the accompanying drum dies down.

1088 In the same way, the stress and strain of striving for Self-realization ceases when one attains the goal.

1089 This state is known as the glory of Self- realization. O Arjuna, the person who is worthy of it enters into this experience.

1090 When he reaches complete equanimity, he loses any sense of personality which can be subject to grief or desire.

1091 When the sun rises, its brilliance dims the light of all the stars.

1092 Similarly, O Arjuna, when a person has reached Self-realization, he loses the sense of diversity in creatures; and he sees himself in all things.

1093 Just as letters written on a blackboard can be erased, in the same way, all forms of difference disappear in his sight.

1094 With this disappearance, both the waking and dreaming states, which arise from false knowledge, are lost in ignorance.

1095 Ignorance also passes away as enlightenment increases, and is absorbed in perfect Self-realization.

1096 As a person continues to walk, the distance of his journey grows less, and he stops walking at the end of it.

1097 As he eats a meal his hunger decreases, and when he is satisfied it passes away.

1098 Similarly, when he enters the waking state sleep is overcome, and when he is wide awake it is completely lost.

1099 When the moon is full its waxing ceases, and the bright half of the month is over.
1100 Similarly, when knowledge overcomes all known objects, it is absorbed into Me, the Supreme; and ignorance finally disappears.
1101 At the time of the final deluge the boundaries of all rivers and oceans break, and the whole universe is filled with water.
1102 When all pots and houses are destroyed, all space is one. When all fuel is burned up, only fire remains.
1103 When all ornaments are melted in a crucible only gold is left, and all names and forms disappear.
1104 When a person wakes up his dreams vanish, and only the person himself remains.
1105 Similarly, when a devotee sees nothing but Me, he has reached the fourth state of devotion.

भक्त्या माम् अभिजानाति यावान् यश्चास्मि तत्त्वतः ।
ततो मां तत्त्वतो ज्ञात्वा विशते तदनन्तरम् ॥

bhaktyā mām abhijānāti
yāvān yaścāsmi tattvataḥ
tato māṁ tattvato jñātvā
viśate tadanantaram

55. By devotion to Me he comes to know who I am in truth; then having known Me in truth, he enters Me immediately.

1106 This is called the fourth state of devotion. The other three are practiced by those who suffer, those who seek knowledge, and those who seek wealth.
1107 Yet is it neither one of these three nor the fourth, neither the first nor the last. Its true name is the devotion of oneness with Me.
1108 The fourth form illumines that ignorance which shows Me in a false light, and it leads people to worship Me everywhere.
1109 It is that uninterrupted light which reveals everything. Through it, each person sees an object according to his own individual perception.
1110 It is the light through which the universe comes into being and is dissolved, just as objects appear and disappear in a dream.
1111 O Arjuna, this light inherent in Me is therefore called devotion.
1112 For a person full of desire this devotion takes the form of desire, and he makes Me the object of his longing.
1113 O Arjuna, for those who seek wisdom it manifests as the search for knowledge, and I am the object of that search.
1114 O Arjuna, for those who seek wealth it takes the form of requests, and by identifying Me with wealth, it calls Me by that name.
1115 When people practice devotion to Me in these ways, prompted by ignorance, they convert Me, the seer, into the seen.
1116 It is true that in a mirror the face sees the face, but the mirror gives the false impression of duality.
1117 A person perceives the moon with his eyes, but through defective sight he may see two moons where there is only one.
1118 Similarly, I pervade all things through this devotion; but because of a person's ignorance, he is under the illusion that I can be seen.
1119 Finally this ignorance is dispelled, and I become one with My visible self, just as a reflection is one with the object reflected.
1120 Even though there is an alloy mixed with gold, the gold itself is pure. When the impurity is removed, only pure gold is left.
1121 Isn't the moon whole even before the day of the full moon? Yet on that day it appears to reach fullness.
1122 Similarly, through false knowledge I appear to be visible in various ways; but when this illusion of visibility is removed, My visible self and I are seen to be one.
1123 For this reason, O Arjuna, the fourth state of devotion transcends the other three, in which I am thought to be visible.
1124 You already know that the devotee who has attained union with Me through knowledge is truly one with Me.
1125 O Arjuna, in the seventh chapter I told you that the wise man is My very Self.
1126 At the beginning of the world I taught this to Brahma the creator, through the *Bhagavatam*, as the highest form of devotion.
1127 The wise call it Self-knowledge, the followers of Shiva say it is Shakti, but I call it the highest devotion.
1128 As soon as a yogi attains union with Me through the way of action, it bears fruit. He sees the world as entirely pervaded by Me.
1129 Then discrimination and dispassion vanish, bondage and liberation pass away, and the cycle of birth and death comes to an end.
1130 Just as what is near is lost in what is farther away, and as space envelops all the four elements,
1131 In the same way he experiences only Me, the pure One, limitless, and beyond the dis-

tinction of the goal of life and the means to attain it.

1132 Just as the waters of the Ganges still sparkle even after they have reached the sea, so is his enjoyment of union with Me.

1133 His joy in Me is like the light reflected back and forth between two polished mirrors.

1134 A dream vanishes when a person wakes up. Then he can experience his individual unity with no sense of duality.

1135 When a mirror is taken away the image in it disappears. All that a person experiences is himself.

1136 Some may have the opinion that when a person reaches union he can have no experience of it, but one might as well ask how a word can be uttered by words.

1137 Does the sun shine in a village by means of a lamp? Do people set up a canopy to support the heavens?

1138 How can a man who is not a king enjoy sovereignty? How can darkness embrace the sun?

1139 Can anything that isn't space understand the nature of space?

1140 A person who hasn't become united with Me cannot know where I am. Therefore, it cannot be said that he worships Me.

1141 He who becomes one with Me through the path of action delights in Me, just as a young woman enjoys her youth.

1142 Just as waves delight in the embrace of the water, light rejoices in the sun, and space wanders through the heavens,

1143 Similarly, when he is united with Me he worships Me without action, just as gold ornaments do honor to the gold of which they are made.

1144 It can be said that the fragrance of sandalwood offers its worship to the tree and that the moonlight adores the moon with true joy.

1145 Similarly, although the thought of action is inconsistent with nonduality, yet there is a form of devotion in union. This cannot be described in words; it can only be known through experience.

1146 Whatever such a person may say to Me, arising from the merit he has acquired in former lives, I respond to his appeal.

1147 Yet in this, the speaker meets himself and there is no speech. This silence is the best form of praise.

1148 As soon as he speaks he meets Me, for I am the speaker. In this silence he truly worships Me.

1149 Similarly, O Arjuna, whatever he sees with his eyes or perceives with his mind, the very act of seeing it does away with it and only the seer remains.

1150 Just as a person in front of a mirror sees his own face, in the same way, his perception will see himself as the seer in everything he sees.

1151 When the object that is seen disappears and the seer only sees himself, then their separateness ceases as well as the act of seeing.

1152 If a man wakes up and tries to grasp a woman he saw in his dream, they are not man and wife. Only he remains.

1153 When fire is produced by rubbing together two pieces of wood, both pieces are lost in the fire and are no longer two.

1154 If the sun tried to grasp its own reflection in water, the sun would lose its power of being reflected.

1155 Similarly, when a person who is united with Me looks at any object, neither the object nor the act of seeing exists.

1156 When the sun illuminates darkness, then it no longer exists as the illuminator. Similarly, the object no longer has the power of being visible because it has become Me.

1157 The state in which there is neither visibility nor invisibility is the true perception of Me.

1158 O Arjuna, perceiving Me in whatever he sees, a person experiences that vision which is beyond the duality of seer and seen.

1159 Just as space is immovable because it pervades all space, in the same way he is entirely filled with Me, the Self.

1160 In the final deluge water is everywhere, so it stops running in channels. In the same way, he is wholly pervaded by Me, the Self.

1161 Can one foot climb upon another, fire burn fire, water enter water, or a river bathe in itself?

1162 When such a person has become one with Me, he neither comes nor goes. This is his pilgrimage to Me, the One beyond duality.

1163 A wave on the surface of the water cannot cross the land however strongly it may flow;

1164 For whether it subsides or flows on, the movement which impels it lies in the persistent flux of water.

1165 Wherever it may go, O Arjuna, it never loses its oneness with water.

1166 Similarly, when such a person has become wholly united with Me, he will always be My faithful pilgrim, even though he may be assailed by the sense of individuality.

1167 However, if he is compelled to act in some way because of the nature of his body, I meet him through that very action.

1168 The difference between the action and the doer disappears, and seeing Me as the Self, he becomes one with Me.

1169 If one mirror is placed in front of another, that doesn't produce the action of seeing, just as gold overlaid with gold is not really hidden.

1170 Even if one lamp seems to illumine another lamp, it cannot be said to give light to the other. Similarly, if a person who is one with Me performs action, can it be considered action?

1171 When he acts without any sense of being responsible for the action, it is as though he hadn't acted.

1172 Whatever act he performs after union with Me is not action.

1173 O Arjuna, even a carefully performed action is like no action at all. Such a person serves Me with the highest worship.

1174 Whatever he says is praise of Me, wherever he looks he sees Me, and every movement is a step towards Me, the One.

1175 In whatever he does he worships Me, his every thought is the repetition of My name, and whatever his condition may be, he is absorbed in Me.

1176 Just as a gold bracelet is one with gold, similarly, he is united with Me through his devotion.

1177 Cloth is one with its threads, and a clay pot is made of earth. In the same way, My devotee is also one with Me.

1178 Waves are one with water, the fragrance of camphor is inseparable from camphor, and the luster of a jewel is inherent in the jewel.

1179 O Arjuna, through this one-pointed devotion, he recognizes Me as the seer in all things that are seen.

1180 The whole phenomenal creation which is either manifest or unmanifest, which is perceived in the three states of consciousness, and which is limited by name or form—I, the seer, am all of this.

1181 O Arjuna, when a devotee has this realization that I am the seer, he dances with joy as though he were at a wedding.

1182 A rope may be mistaken for a snake, but when it is clearly seen it is recognized as a rope.

1183 There is nothing but gold in an ornament, and this can be shown by melting it down.

1184 Waves consist only of water. When a person realizes this, he isn't deceived by their form.

1185 If a person tries to determine the substance of a dream after he has awakened, he finds that there was nothing apart from himself.

1186 Similarly, one comes to realize that I am the knower who inspires the desire to know all that is or is not.

1187 He will then know that I am beyond birth and age, imperishable and immortal, unimaginable and boundless joy.

1188 I am unchanging, infallible, eternal, the One without a second, the origin of all, both manifest and unmanifest.

1189 I am both the ruler and the ruled, without beginning, deathless, fearless, and the support as well as what is supported.

1190 I am the everlasting Lord, self-existent and eternal. I am all, I pervade all, and I transcend all.

1191 I am the ancient and the new. I am nothingness, yet I am perfection. I am both the particle and the mass. I am all that is.

1192 I am free from activity, without attachment, and beyond grief. I am the pervader and the pervaded. I am the highest Self.

1193 I am beyond sound and hearing and without form or race. I am without variation or dependence. I am the Supreme.

1194 Through one-pointed devotion I am known as the one Self. He who knows this, knows Me.

1195 When a person awakes from sleep, he realizes that only he as an individual remains.

1196 When the sun rises, it is the illuminator and isn't different from what it illumines.

1197 Likewise, when known objects disappear, the knower alone remains. A person should realize this, and when he does,

1198 O Arjuna, the knowledge by which he realizes this nonduality is none other than Myself.

1199 Then he knows that I am the Self, beyond both duality and nonduality, and he enters into the full realization of this.

1200 When a person awakes from sleep he realizes that he is only one, but when he loses this perception, can he know what happens?

1201 When a person sees with his eye that ornaments are made of gold, it is as though they are reduced to gold without being melted down.

1202 When salt is added to water, it mixes with the water and the two merge. When the water dries up, its existence as salt comes to an end.

1203 In the same way, he loses the perception that he and I are one by being absorbed into the supreme joy of union with Me.

1204 When he has no further sense of his own individuality, how can he see Me as different from himself? Then both he and I are merged in union.

1205 When camphor has been burned up, the fire also disappears. Then space, which transcends them both, is all that remains.

1206 When one is subtracted from one, zero is left. Similarly, after being and non-being come to an end, only I remain.

1207 Consequently, such words as the Absolute, the Self, and the Lord lose their meaning; nor is there any place for silence.

1208 Then one should say only that which can be said without speech, and know only that which is beyond both knowing and not knowing.

1209 In this state of union, knowledge is known through knowledge, joy is experienced through joy, and bliss is realized only through bliss.

1210 Profit is gained through profit, light is embraced by light, and wonder is lost in wonder.

1211 Even-mindedness is contained within itself, peace enters into tranquility, and experience delights in experience.

1212 Similarly, by following the beautiful vine of the yoga of action, a person obtains the fruit of complete union with Me.

1213 O Arjuna, I am the jewel of pure Consciousness on the royal crown of this yoga, and in return he becomes My jewel.

1214 He is the space surrounding the pinnacle of liberation on the temple of the yoga of action.

1215 In the forest of this earthly existence, he is the traveler who reaches the city of union with Me by the road of the yoga of action.

1216 He is like the Ganges of devotion flowing swiftly to the ocean of blissful union with Me on the current of the yoga of action.

1217 O Arjuna, such is the greatness of the yoga of action. This is why I constantly expound it to you.

1218 I cannot be reached by any time, place, or object. By My own nature, I am all in all to everyone.

1219 The established way to reach union with Me is through each disciple's relationship with his Guru.

1220 Therefore, it requires no effort to reach Me. This yoga surely leads to Me.

1221 O Arjuna, treasures lie concealed within the earth, fire is latent in wood, and milk is contained in the udder of a cow.

1222 But to obtain these things, one must use the right methods. I must also be reached by certain means.

1223 If anyone should ask why the Lord is explaining the means after having spoken of the result, I will tell you the reason.

1224 The great teaching of the *Gita* fully explains the way to attain liberation. No other scripture does this with authority.

1225 The wind can drive the clouds from the sky and reveal the sun, but it cannot create the sun. A hand can remove moss from the surface of water, but it cannot create the water.

1226 In the same way, other scriptures may remove the ignorance which obstructs the vision of Self-realization; but only I, the pure One, can reveal Myself.

1227 Other philosophies can destroy ignorance, but they have no power to bring about Self-realization.

1228 When their validity is challenged, the authority to which they turn is the *Gita*.

1229 When the eastern sky is illuminated by the rising sun, all the other directions glow with light. Similarly, the *Gita*, the highest of all, gives support to all other scriptures.

1230 This great *Gita* has already explained in detail the methods to reach the Self as if grasping it with the hand.

1231 Thinking with compassion that Arjuna might not be able at first to understand them,

1232 Lord Krishna explains those principles once more, as if they were buds opening, so they can become firmly established in His disciple's mind.

1233 As the explanation is drawing to a close, He again presents the whole meaning of the *Gita* from beginning to end.

1234 Throughout the *Gita*, many principles have been explained as the occasion arose.

1235 But if anyone should be unable to recognize the consistency of these principles laid down in the scriptures with what has gone before,

1236 Then see now how the various doctrines outlined earlier are connected with the basic principles of the *Gita*.

1237 The main theme of the *Gita* is the destruction of ignorance, and its fruit is the attainment of liberation. Knowledge is the means that leads to these two.

1238 This teaching has been explained at length in this book, and now it will be summarized in a few words.

1239 So although this realization had already been attained, Krishna began to explain further the way to reach this goal.

सर्वकर्माण्य् अपि सदा कुर्वाणो मद्व्यपाश्रयः ।
मत्प्रसादाद् अवाप्नोति शाश्वतं पदम् अव्ययम् ॥
sarvakarmāṇy api sadā
kurvāṇo madvyapāśrayaḥ
matprasādād avāpnoti
śāśvataṁ padam avyayam

56. Performing all actions, he whose reliance is always on Me, attains, by My grace, the eternal, imperishable abode.

1240 The Lord continued, O Arjuna, the yogi who faithfully follows the path of action becomes one with Me, entering into My form.

1241 Worshiping Me with the pure flowers of his good actions, he reaches the highest form of devotion through My grace.

1242 When he practices this form of devotion, worshiping Me brings him delight and he joyfully becomes one with Me.

1243 Realizing that I pervade the whole world, he follows Me as the Self which illumines the universe.

1244 Just as salt may set aside its natural limits and dissolve in water, or as the wind may blow here and there and come to rest in the sky,

1245 In the same way, such a yogi finds refuge in Me with his mind, speech, and body. If by chance he should commit some prohibited action,

1246 Good and bad actions don't affect him once he has realized Me, just as great rivers and drain water from the streets are all one when they reach the Ganges.

1247 The purest sandalwood and wood of poor quality can be distinguished only as long as they aren't consumed by fire.

1248 Both pure and impure gold have the same quality as soon as they are touched by the philosopher's stone.

1249 Similarly, actions appear to be good or bad only as long as a person doesn't experience Me, the One, as illuminating all things.

1250 O Arjuna, a person is aware of the difference of day and night only because the sun rises.

1251 Similarly, O Arjuna, the actions of such a yogi no longer exist once he meets Me, and he is enthroned in supreme union with Me.

1252 He reaches that eternal state in which I dwell, beyond the power of time, space, and nature.

1253 O Arjuna, what blessing can equal that which he obtains through the peace of the Self?

चेतसा सर्वकर्माणि मयि संन्यस्य मत्परः ।
बुद्धियोगम् उपाश्रित्य मच्चित्तः सततं भव ॥
cetasā sarvakarmāṇi
mayi saṁnyasya matparaḥ
buddhiyogam upāśritya
maccittaḥ satataṁ bhava

57. Mentally renouncing all actions in Me, devoted to Me as the Supreme, taking refuge in the yoga of discrimination, constantly think of Me.

1254 Therefore, O Arjuna, surrender all your actions to Me.

1255 This renunciation consists of performing your appointed duties and at the same time concentrating your mind on discrimination.

1256 Then, through that discrimination, you will see yourself as separate from activity and existing in My pure Being.

1257 Moreover, you will see that nature, the source of all activity, is far removed from you.

1258 Having perceived this, O Arjuna, you will find that nature doesn't exist apart from you, just as there is no shadow without a form.

1259 When matter is destroyed in this way, renunciation of actions as well as their causes becomes easy.

1260 When the whole world of action has passed away, nothing remains but Me, the one Self.

So fix your mind on Me, like a wife devoted to her husband.

1261 When the mind is continuously fixed on Me, thought abandons all other objects and is devoted to Me.

1262 Therefore, act in such a way that your mind detaches itself from all other objects of contemplation and always concentrates on Me.

मच्चित्तः सर्वदुर्गाणि मत्प्रसादात् तरिष्यसि ।
अथ चेत् त्वम् अहंकारान् न श्रोष्यसि विनङ्क्ष्यसि ॥
maccittaḥ sarvadurgāṇi
matprasādāt tariṣyasi
atha cet tvam ahaṁkārān
na śroṣyasi vinaṅksyasi

58. Fixing your mind on Me, you shall pass over all difficulties, through My grace; but if, through egoism, you will not listen, then you shall perish.

1263 When your mind becomes filled with Me through wholehearted devotion, you may know that My grace is perfect.

1264 Misery and sorrow, which are the result of repeated births and deaths, however, difficult, will be easy to bear.

1265 When the eyes are helped by the light of the sun, darkness has no power.

1266 Similarly, can the terror of earthly existence frighten the person whose ego has been obliterated through My grace?

1267 Therefore, O Arjuna, through My grace you will overcome all the evils of earthly existence.

1268 But if through egotistical pride you don't allow all My teaching to enter your ears and your mind,

1269 While you are living in the body you will suffer self-destruction at every step, and you will know no peace.

यद् अहंकारम् आश्रित्य न योत्स्य इति मन्यसे ।
मिथ्यैष व्यवसायस् ते प्रकृतिस् त्वां नियोक्ष्यति ॥
yad ahaṁkāram āśritya
na yotsya iti manyase
mithyāiṣa vyavasāyas te
prakṛtis tvāṁ niyokṣyati

59. If, filled with egoism, you think, "I shall not fight," your resolve will be in vain; your own material nature will compel you.

1270 If you pay no attention to My words, you will have to endure the terrible state of dying without succumbing to death.

1271 Neglecting the rules of diet invites fever, aversion to light increases darkness, and failure to develop discrimination fosters egoism.

1272 You call your body by the name of Arjuna, you speak of others as your relatives, and assert that fighting is sinful.

1273 O Arjuna, to think in this way and to state that therefore you will not fight,

1274 This firm resolution that you have mentally made will be powerless to withstand your inner nature.

1275 It isn't truth but illusion to say that you are Arjuna, that these are your relatives, and that to kill them would be a sin.

1276 At first you were ready to fight, and for that purpose you took up your weapons. It would be senseless to refuse to fight now.

1277 Therefore, your words are meaningless, and the world would never consider your action proper.

1278 Moreover, any resolution not to fight would be contrary to your nature.

1279 Even if a person is determined to swim towards the west, if he meets a strong easterly current, only his resolution is left.

1280 If rice were to refuse to grow as rice, could it deny its own nature?

1281 Similarly, O Arjuna, you are endowed with a warrior's qualities. If you should refuse to fight, your very nature would compel you to do so.

1282 O Arjuna, virtues such as courage, spirit, and skill were given to you at birth. They are a part of your nature.

स्वभावजेन कौन्तेय निबद्धः स्वेन कर्मणा ।
कर्तुं नेच्छसि यन् मोहात् करिष्यस्य् अवशो ऽपि तत् ॥
svabhāvajena kāunteya
nibaddhaḥ svena karmaṇā
kartuṁ necchasi yan mohāt
kariṣyasy avaśo 'pi tat

60. What you wish not to do, through delusion, you shall do that against your will, Arjuna, bound by your own karma, born of your own material nature.

1283 O Arjuna, you cannot set aside those virtues by refusing to act in accordance with them.

1284 Therefore, O Arjuna, you are bound by these innate qualities. You must follow the path of the warrior.

1285 On the other hand, if you disregard your inherent nature and are firmly resolved not to fight,

1286 Then, just as a man bound hand and foot and thrown into a cart is carried to the ends of the earth even though he doesn't walk,
1287 You may refuse to act, but you will certainly be compelled to do so.
1288 Does a sick man choose sickness, or a poor man poverty?
1289 This destiny is in the power of the invisible God and doesn't go astray. That God is within you.

ईश्वरः सर्वभूतानां हृद्देशेऽर्जुन तिष्ठति ।
भ्रामयन् सर्वभूतानि यन्त्रारूढानि मायया ।।

īśvaraḥ sarvabhūtānāṁ
hṛddeśe 'rjuna tiṣṭhati
bhrāmayan sarvabhūtāni
yantrārūḍhāni māyayā

61. The Lord abides in the hearts of all beings, Arjuna, causing all beings to revolve, by the power of illusion, as if fixed on a machine.

1290 The Supreme Being rises in the hearts of all creatures with His manifold rays of Consciousness, like the sun rising in the sky,
1291 Illuminating the three states of consciousness throughout the three worlds and awakening those earthly travelers who are deluded by identifying the Self with the body.
1292 Those people are like bees, whose feet are the sense organs, drawn by the sun to feed on the lotuses of sense objects, which bloom on the lake of the world.
1293 Let's leave that metaphor. The Supreme Being forever reveals Himself under the cloak of the individuality of all creatures.
1294 From behind the veil of cosmic illusion, He holds the string with which He causes countless numbers of species to dance like shadow pictures on a screen.
1295 He manifests every creature from the creator to the tiniest insect by giving them bodies.
1296 Then every creature enters the body which is appropriate to its own nature and identifies itself with that body.
1297 Just as thread may be sewn with thread, as grass may be tied with grass, or as a child grasps at his own reflection in water,
1298 Similarly, the individual soul, meeting another creature that has a body, regards it as belonging to himself.
1299 In this way the Lord places each person on the vehicle of a body and manipulates him by the reins of the fruits of his actions in past lives.
1300 When He controls each individual by means of these reins, they all become fit for their particular functions.
1301 In short, O Arjuna, He directs all creatures in this world and the next, just as the wind blows grass up in the air.
1302 Just as iron filings are agitated when they come in contact with a magnet, creatures move in the same way, controlled by the power of the Supreme.
1303 O Arjuna, in the presence of the moon, the ocean and other natural objects move in their various ways.
1304 The ocean has its tides, the moonstone exudes water, and lotuses and the chakora bird are relieved of their distress.
1305 Similarly, all creatures, according to their inherent nature, are activated by the Supreme Being, who is also in your heart.
1306 When you stop identifying yourself as Arjuna, He arises within you.
1307 It is certain that He will direct your inner nature and will cause you to fight, even if you refuse to do so.

तम् एव शरणं गच्छ सर्वभावेन भारत ।
तत्प्रसादात् परां शान्तिं स्थानं प्राप्स्यसि शाश्वतम् ।।

tam eva śaraṇaṁ gaccha
sarvabhāvena bhārata
tatprasādāt parāṁ śāntiṁ
sthānaṁ prāpsyasi śāśvatam

62. Fly unto Him alone for refuge with your whole being, Arjuna. From His grace, you shall attain supreme peace and the eternal abode.

1308 He is the Master, and He has appointed nature as His agent. That agent causes the senses to carry out their appropriate functions.
1309 Whether you act or not depends on nature, and nature itself is directed by the One who is in your heart.
1310 So take refuge in Him with your consciousness, your speech, your mind, and your body, just as the waters of the Ganges flow into the great ocean.
1311 Then by His grace you will be wedded to the bride of supreme peace, and will enjoy the bliss of union with Him.
1312 In the place where creation has its beginning, where rest may take rest, and where

all experience has its origin,

1313 You will reign forever in the kingdom of Self-realization, O Arjuna. Krishna, the consort of Lakshmi, spoke in this way.

इति ते ज्ञानम् आख्यातं गुह्याद् गुह्यतरं मया ।
विमृश्यैतद् अशेषेण यथेच्छसि तथा कुरु ॥

iti te jñānam ākhyātaṁ
guhyād guhyataraṁ mayā
vimṛśyāitad aśeṣeṇa
yathecchasi tathā kuru

63. Thus the knowledge that is more secret than all that is secret has been expounded to you by Me. Having reflected on this fully, do as you please.

1314 This teaching is well known as the *Gita*, the essence of all the Vedas. Through it, one may obtain the jewel of the Self.

1315 This is the knowledge which Vedanta praises, thereby bringing it fame in the world.

1316 Compared with it, the intellect and other means of gaining insight are like rays of light shining through a window revealing Me, the true seer of all.

1317 It is called the wisdom of the Self, the hidden treasure of the concealed One. Yet how can I withhold it from you?

1318 Filled with compassion for you, O Arjuna, I have revealed the mystery of this secret treasure.

1319 A devoted mother may gently scold her child. My great love for you is like this, yet I don't rebuke you.

1320 All this is like trying to strain the sky, to remove the peel from nectar, or to cause an ordeal to go through an ordeal.

1321 It is like rubbing a magic lotion on the eye, to which by its own light the smallest atom in the deepest hell is visible.

1322 I, the omniscient One, have contemplated all knowledge and have clearly explained to you what is best in it, O Arjuna.

1323 So meditate on this and, after deciding what you should do, do what seems proper to you.

1324 Hearing these words, Arjuna remained silent. Then Krishna said, Reflect seriously on this.

1325 If a hungry man says shyly to a person serving him food that he is satisfied, not only will he still suffer from hunger but also he will be dishonest.

1326 Similarly, if a person meets an all-knowing Guru, and out of shyness refrains from questioning him about the knowledge of the Self,

1327 He will deceive himself and commit the sin of dishonesty, and thereby miss the opportunity to know the Truth.

1328 However, O Arjuna, I take your silence to mean that you want Me to repeat this teaching once again.

1329 Then Arjuna said, O Lord, You truly know my innermost thoughts. Is there anyone else who has such understanding?

1330 By Your nature, You know everything that can be known. But does one praise the sun by describing it as the sun?

1331 When He heard these words Krishna said, Why do you say this? Do you think you have praised Me too little?

सर्वगुह्यतमं भूयः शृणु मे परमं वचः ।
इष्टो ऽसि मे दृढम् इति ततो वक्ष्यामि ते हितम् ॥

sarvaguhyatamaṁ bhūyaḥ
śṛṇu me paramaṁ vacaḥ
iṣṭo 'si me dṛḍham iti
tato vakṣyāmi te hitam

64. Hear again My supreme word, most secret of all. You are surely loved by Me; therefore, I shall speak for your good.

1332 Now listen once more with complete attention to My clear explanation.

1333 I am not saying this because it should be said, nor should you listen to it because it should be heard. I am telling it to you because of your destiny.

1334 O Arjuna, as soon as a tortoise sees her babies her milk begins to flow. The sky showers rain for the chataka bird.

1335 Even when a person isn't engaged in activity, he may obtain the fruits of his actions. What impossible thing cannot happen when fortune is favorable?

1336 When duality is removed, you can experience the inner meaning of this teaching in nonduality.

1337 O Arjuna, the unaffected love that I feel for you doesn't arise from separateness. You should know that it is oneness in the Self.

1338 A mirror isn't kept clean for its own sake, but so a person can see himself in it.

1339 Similarly, O Arjuna, under the pretext of speaking to you I am actually speaking to Myself, for there is no separation between you and Me.

1340 For this reason I am telling you, who are My Self, this inner mystery. This is how much I

love those devotees who take refuge in Me.
1341 O Arjuna, salt forgets itself as soon as it is placed in water, and it isn't ashamed to merge into the water.
1342 Similarly, if you don't hold back anything from Me, why should I conceal anything from you?
1343 Therefore, listen to My clear explanation of this mystery, which illumines all other secret teaching.

मन्मना भव मद्भक्तो मद्याजी मां नमस्कुरु ।
माम् एवैष्यसि सत्यं ते प्रतिजाने प्रियो ऽसि मे ।।
manmanā bhava madbhakto
madyājī māṁ namaskuru
mām evāiṣyasi satyaṁ te
pratijāne priyo 'si me

65. Fix your mind on Me, worshiping Me, sacrificing to Me, bowing down to Me; in this way you shall come truly to Me, I promise, for you are dear to Me.

1344 O Arjuna, offer all your actions, inner and outer, to Me, the all-pervasive One.
1345 Just as the wind fills the whole sky, similarly, be one with Me in all your actions.
1346 Let your mind be entirely devoted to Me, and let your ears hear only of Me.
1347 Let your eyes rest only on saints who dwell in Me through Self-knowledge, just as a loving wife looks only at her husband.
1348 I am the supreme resting place. Let your voice be occupied in reciting My pure names, so that they may enter your heart.
1349 Let your hands work for Me, your feet move for Me, and in this way let all your actions be done for My sake.
1350 O Arjuna, whether your actions benefit you or others, be My sacrificer performing these sacrifices for Me.
1351 There is no need to teach you all this in detail. Considering yourself a servant, think of all others as being Me, the one to be served.
1352 Giving up hatred toward any creature, be humble before all, as though you were bowing down to Me. In this way you will receive the most support from Me.
1353 Then any idea of a third will disappear from your mind, and you and I will merge into one.
1354 We will be able to enjoy each other in all conditions, and that bliss will increase.
1355 When the third factor which separates us has disappeared, O Arjuna, you will know that we are one; and you will ultimately reach union with Me.
1356 When water dries up, can anything prevent the sun's reflection in it from returning to the sun?
1357 What can prevent the wind from being absorbed into the sky, or waves into the water of the ocean?
1358 Similarly, you and I seem to be separate because we are in bodies, but when the body passes away, you will be one with Me.
1359 Don't question whether this is so, for I assure you that these things are true.
1360 If I swore by you, it would be only like touching My own form, but love knows no shame.
1361 I am He whom the Vedas describe as the One without difference, through whom this whole worldly appearance seems real, and at whose command time is vanquished.
1362 I am the God of Truth, the Father who cares for the welfare of the world. What need do I have of oaths?
1363 O Arjuna, out of affection for you I have given up the signs of My divine nature, but by your love for Me this incomplete nature has been made whole.
1364 It is as if a king were to swear by himself for his own purpose.
1365 Then Arjuna said, O Lord, You shouldn't speak in this strange way, for the mention of Your name is enough to satisfy me.
1366 Even so, You speak, and while speaking You swear an oath. Is there no end to Your humor?
1367 A single ray of sunlight is enough to cause a bed of lotuses to bloom, yet at the same time the sun sheds its light on all.
1368 The longing of the chataka bird is just a pretext for the clouds to send down rain, which refreshes the earth and fills the ocean.
1369 O ocean of grace, I am, therefore, only the pretext by which all people will receive Your generosity.
1370 The Lord replied, You have said enough, There is no need to speak like this. But these are the means through which you have reached Me.
1371 O Arjuna, salt dissolves as soon as it falls into the sea. Is there anything that can prevent it?
1372 Similarly, when you worship Me as all-per-

vasive and see Me in everything, you will lose your sense of individuality and will truly become one with Me.

1373 In this way, I have clearly explained to you the means by which you can pass from the performance of action to the attainment of union with Me.

1374 O Arjuna, first offer all your actions to Me, and you will receive My grace in every way.

1375 Through My grace you will have perfect knowledge of Me, and that will surely lead to your absorption into My Being.

1376 Then, O Arjuna, no distinction will remain between the goal and the means of reaching it, and there will be nothing more to do.

1377 Because you have offered all your actions to Me, today you have received My grace.

1378 Through its power, this battle hasn't been an obstacle in the way of My love for you.

1379 The knowledge of the *Gita* causes ignorance to pass away and with it the visible world, so that I alone am perceived.

1380 I have explained this to you in various ways and with different examples. This knowledge dispels all ignorance which springs from right and wrong action.

सर्वधर्मान् परित्यज्य माम् एकं शरणं व्रज ।
अहं त्वा सर्वपापेभ्यो मोक्षयिष्यामि मा शुचः ।।

sarvadharmān parityajya
mām ekaṁ śaraṇaṁ vraja
ahaṁ tvā sarvapāpebhyo
mokṣayiṣyāmi mā śucaḥ

66. Abandoning all duties, take refuge in Me alone. I shall liberate you from all evils; do not grieve.

1381 Just as desire gives rise to sorrow, as blame causes sin, and as misfortune brings about poverty,

1382 Similarly, ignorance which leads to heaven and hell is the cause of all good and bad actions. Rid yourself entirely of these through knowledge.

1383 Just as the delusion that a rope is a snake is removed if a person grabs hold of it, and as the activities in his dream come to an end when he wakes up,

1384 As the moon no longer seems to be yellow when his jaundice has been cured, and the bitter taste in his mouth disappears,

1385 A mirage also vanishes when daylight ends, and a fire dies out when the fuel is exhausted.

1386 Therefore, cast out that ignorance which is the cause of the illusion of good and evil actions, and give up all religious practices.

1387 When ignorance is dispelled I alone remain, just as when sleep and dreams have passed only oneself is left.

1388 When nothing is left except Me, there can be no diversity of being; and the person who realizes that he and I are one is united with Me.

1389 The knowledge of oneness with Me, with no sense of separation, is the true meaning of taking refuge in Me.

1390 When a pot is destroyed, the space inside it merges with the space outside. In the same way, taking refuge in Me means being united with Me.

1391 A gold bead is made of gold, and a wave consists of water. Similarly, O Arjuna, merge yourself in Me.

1392 However, don't speak of taking refuge in Me in the same way that the great sea fire, having resorted to the floor of the ocean, burns forever.

1393 Get rid of any thought of resorting to Me and retaining your separate individuality. An intelligent person should be ashamed to think like this.

1394 O Arjuna, if a mere human king takes as a consort a simple serving maid, she attains royalty.

1395 So don't listen to false ideas such as when a person attains union with Me, the Lord of the universe, the bond of his individuality isn't loosened.

1396 True devotion is to become one with Me and serve Me. Seek that knowledge by which you can attain this.

1397 When butter has been churned out of milk and put back into it, it will never again merge with the milk.

1398 Even if iron is hung upright it will still rust; but when it is turned into gold with the philosopher's stone, it can no longer rust.

1399 When fire is kindled from two pieces of wood, it cannot be restricted by the wood.

1400 In the same way, if you seek refuge in Me without any sense of difference, right and wrong actions will have no power to affect you.

1401 O Arjuna, can the sun be aware of darkness? Can the illusions of a dream be perceived after waking?

1402 Similarly, when a person has attained union with Me, nothing else can remain except Me.
1403 Therefore, don't concern yourself with good and evil: I Myself am your sin and your merit.
1404 O Arjuna, just as when salt falls into water it becomes water, in the same way I will be your sole refuge.
1405 The sense of duality, the cause of all bondage, is the only sin that remains; and that will disappear when you understand My nature.
1406 O Arjuna, in this way you will be freed from bondage. Let me enlighten you, and I will liberate you.
1407 Don't let your mind be anxious. Knowing Me, O wise Arjuna, take refuge in Me alone.
1408 Lord Krishna, beautiful in form, the eye which sees in all vision, the dwelling place of all the world, said these things.
1409 Then stretching out His right arm, dark-skinned and adorned with bracelets, He embraced His beloved devotee who had come to Him.
1410 That high state of union from which speech, unable to reach it, turns back taking the intellect with it,
1411 And which neither word nor thought can attain, this was the experience into which Krishna drew Arjuna under the pretext of this embrace.
1412 Just as one lamp lights another, in the same way, He drew Arjuna into Himself without removing the difference between them.
1413 Then Arjuna was overwhelmed by such a flood of joy that the Lord, in spite of His strength, was submerged in it.
1414 If one ocean were to flow into another, the mass of water would be doubled and the flood would fill the sky.
1415 So when the two embraced, the joy of their meeting passed all bounds, and the whole universe was filled with the Lord.
1416 In this way, Lord Krishna revealed the *Gita*, the essence of the Vedas and the holiest of all treatises that are regarded as authority.
1417 Now if anyone asks how the *Gita* came to be the origin of the Vedas, I will tell you the accepted reason.
1418 He from whose breath all the Vedas sprang has Himself declared that it is true.
1419 So it is correct to say that the *Gita* is the source of the Vedas. But there is also another reason for saying this.
1420 That which is imperishable, the expansion of which is concealed within itself, is said to be His seed.
1421 The essence of the three sections of the Vedas is contained within the *Gita*, just as the whole tree is contained within its seed.
1422 Therefore, I consider the *Gita* as the seed of the Vedas. This seems clear.
1423 The three parts of the Vedas are set in the *Gita* just as a body is adorned with jewels.
1424 Now listen and I will show you clearly where to find each of the three branches of the Vedas, about work, devotion, and knowledge.
1425 The first chapter is an introduction to the general teaching of the *Gita*, and the second sets forth the meaning of the Sankhya philosophy.
1426 In this chapter, the fundamental truth which by itself can bring about salvation is expressed in short aphorisms.
1427 The third chapter describes the means by which a person can be delivered from the bondage of ignorance and reach the state of liberation.
1428 He should abandon all sense of individuality, avoid all action arising from desire, and carry out faultlessly all his prescribed duties.
1429 The third chapter, which directs that actions should be performed with true faith, is called the chapter concerning action.
1430 Now, in what way can the performance of daily and periodic actions bring about freedom from ignorance?
1431 The Lord explained that when longing arises and bound souls begin to seek liberation, they should perform all actions as an offering to God.
1432 He said that they should carry out with wholehearted devotion all prescribed actions and should direct them to Him.
1433 In the latter part of the fourth chapter, He has explained the place of worship, praise of God, and the practice of the yoga of action.
1434 Then He describes serving God through action as far as the end of the eleventh chapter, in which there is the vision of the Cosmic Form.
1435 In these eight chapters, He explains the worship of deities. I am removing all diffi-

culties and telling you what the Gita says.

1436 The knowledge obtained by divine grace through the traditional teaching of the Guru, and which is awakened in the disciple,

1437 Is developed in the twelfth chapter, in the verses describing freedom from hatred and freedom from pride.

1438 In the chapters from twelve to fifteen, He explains the ripening of the fruit of knowledge.

1439 These four chapters are called the chapters on knowledge, and in the last one He describes the tree with its root growing upwards.

1440 Thus, in the explanation given in these three sections of the *Gita*, the Vedas are found in a beautiful form, adorned with the jewels of its verses.

1441 Here are the Vedas, with their three sections, which proclaim that a person should obtain at all costs the fruit of liberation.

1442 The first sixteen chapters discuss all those forms of ignorance which are in constant conflict with the knowledge which leads to liberation.

1443 The theme of the seventeenth chapter is that a person can overcome all enemies with the scriptures as his companion.

1444 So from the first chapter to the end of the seventeenth, the Lord has explained the teaching of the Vedas, which were born of His breath.

1445 Finally, the eighteenth is the last chapter. The meaning of all the teachings found in the other chapters is condensed in it.

1446 This book, The Song of the Lord, is therefore the ocean of meaning of the Sankhya philosophy, and in its generosity it surpasses the whole teaching of the Vedas.

1447 Although the Vedas are full of knowledge they are miserly, for only the three higher castes may hear them.

1448 The Vedas take no account of women, of the *shudra* caste, and of other beings who suffer the miseries of earthly existence.

1449 But it seems to me that in order to correct this defect, they have taken the form of the *Gita* so that all people may share in this teaching.

1450 The *Gita* enters their minds, it enters their ears when they hear it, and it dwells in their mouths when they repeat it.

1451 By constant association with those who know the *Gita* by heart, by preserving it through books,

1452 And by other such methods, the pure joy of liberation is offered to all as gifts of food to those who gather in the marketplace of worldly life.

1453 Just as the sky is free to all who live in the air, the earth to all who dwell on it, and in space all can enjoy the light of the sun,

1454 Similarly, the *Gita* doesn't take into consideration whether people are of high or low birth. It refreshes the whole world with the gift of heavenly bliss.

1455 Therefore the Vedas, ashamed of their former defect, were reborn in the womb of the *Gita*, and have thereby achieved fame.

1456 In this way the *Gita*, explained by Krishna to Arjuna, is the essence of the Vedas, made available to all.

1457 Just as a cow, out of love for her calf, will supply milk for the entire household, similarly, Arjuna is the means through which salvation has come to the world.

1458 Clouds send down rain through pity for the chataka bird, but at the same time they relieve the entire animate and inanimate creation.

1459 The sun rises everyday for the sake of the sun lotuses which depend on it, but it also delights the sight of all the three worlds.

1460 In the same way, Krishna, by revealing the *Gita* through Arjuna, has removed the great burden of earthly life from the world.

1461 Isn't the *Gita* like a sun which, in the sky of Krishna's mouth, illuminates for the world the jewels of all the scriptures?

1462 Blessed is Arjuna's family, for he has been found worthy to receive that teaching which, revealed in the *Gita*, has provided a refuge for the whole world.

इदं ते नातपस्काय नाभक्ताय कदाचन ।
न चाशुश्रूषवे वाच्यं न च मां यो ऽभ्यसूयति ।।
idaṁ te nātapaskāya
nābhaktāya kadācana
na cāśuśrūṣave vācyaṁ
na ca māṁ yo 'bhyasūyati

67. This shall not be spoken of by you to one who is without austerity, nor to one who is without devotion, nor to one who does not render service, nor to one who does not desire to listen, nor to one who speaks evil of Me.

1463 Enough of this. Then Lord Krishna, the great Guru, restored to Arjuna the sense of separateness.
1464 He asked Arjuna whether his heart was satisfied with this teaching. Arjuna replied that it was, through the Lord's grace.
1465 O Arjuna, a person is fortunate when he finds a treasure, but to be able to enjoy it is rare.
1466 What efforts the gods and demons put forth in churning the great ocean of milk to obtain a cupful of curds.
1467 Their efforts bore fruit when they saw the nectar with their eyes, but they didn't know how to preserve it.
1468 What they were given to bring them immortality brought about their death. This is what happens when a person doesn't know how to preserve what he finds.
1469 King Nahusha became the lord of heaven, but not knowing how to conduct himself there, he was changed into a serpent. Don't you know this?
1470 Having acquired great merit, O Arjuna, you have become worthy to receive the teaching of this king of scriptures, the *Gita*.
1471 Therefore, accept the traditional method of practicing its teachings and follow them faithfully.
1472 Otherwise, if you try to practice them without following the tradition, you will suffer the same fate as the gods who churned the ocean.
1473 O Arjuna, a person may possess a fine healthy cow, but he can drink its milk only if he knows the art of milking.
1474 Similarly, there may be an excellent teacher and the disciple may acquire much knowledge, but it is fruitful only if he applies it according to the tradition.
1475 Therefore, follow diligently the excellent way taught in the scriptures.
1476 O Arjuna, you shouldn't speak of this teaching of the *Gita*, which you have obtained with such earnestness, to a person who doesn't practice austerity.
1477 Even if a person practices austerity but isn't devoted to his Guru, shun him as the Vedas avoid an outcaste.
1478 Never give these teachings to a person who is without devotion to his Guru, just as you wouldn't throw the rice of a sacrificial offering to a crow, however old the rice might be.
1479 A person may practice physical austerities and be devoted to his Guru, but if he has no desire to hear this teaching,
1480 He isn't worthy to listen to it.
1481 A pearl may be very precious, but unless it has been bored, can it be strung on a thread?
1482 The ocean is already deep, and the rain which falls into it serves no purpose.
1483 If delicious food is offered to a man who is satisfied, it is wasted. Shouldn't it be given to one who is hungry?
1484 Though a person may be worthy in every other respect, if he has no desire for this teaching, don't give it to him even by accident.
1485 Can the eye, which is able to see objects, enjoy the pleasure of scent? A sense can only enjoy the thing for which it is designed.
1486 Therefore, O Arjuna, devotion and austerity should be practiced. Nevertheless, where there is reluctance to hear this teaching, it should be withheld.
1487 On the other hand, you may meet someone who practices austerity and devotion and is eager to learn.
1488 Yet, if such a person belittles Me, the ruler of the universe and author of the *Gita*,
1489 And maligns both Me and My devotees, he too is unfit to receive this knowledge.
1490 All the good qualities he possesses are of no more use than a lampstand at night with no lamp on it.
1491 Such a person is like a lovely body, youthful and adorned with jewels, yet lifeless.
1492 He is like a beautiful house of pure gold which is guarded by a serpent.
1493 He is like a tasty dish of food with deadly poison in it, or a friendship that hides deceit in the heart.
1494 So is a person who possesses understanding and practices penance and devotion, but who slanders Me and My worshipers.
1495 Therefore, O Arjuna, though he may have these virtues, don't let him have any contact with this teaching.
1496 What more can I say? Even if he is as powerful as the creator, don't give him the teaching of the *Gita* even to satisfy his curiosity.
1497 O Arjuna, when the beautiful temple of devotion to the Guru stands on the strong foundation of austerity,
1498 With the doorway of desire to hear the *Gita* always open, and the shining pinnacle of

harmless speech crowning it,

य इदं परमं गुह्यं मद्भक्तेष्व् अभिधास्यति ।
भक्तिं मयि परां कृत्वा माम् एवैष्यत्य् असंशयः ॥
ya idaṁ paramaṁ guhyaṁ
madbhakteṣv abhidhāsyati
bhaktiṁ mayi parāṁ kṛtvā
mām evāiṣyaty asaṁśayaḥ

68. He who shall teach this supreme secret to My worshipers, having performed the highest devotion to Me, shall come to Me, without doubt.

1499 In such a temple, built by My devotees, enshrine the *Gita* as the jeweled image. Then you will be like My equal in the world.
1500 The sacred word of one syllable was imprisoned in the womb of three syllables.
1501 It is the seed of the Vedas and expanded with the Vedas. One could say that Gayatri entered into the flowers and fruit of their verses.
1502 Just as a child that has no other refuge is carried at its mother's breast, he who transmits the secret of the *Gita* to My devotees,
1503 And teaches it to them with reverence, that person becomes one with Me after he has left his body.

न च तस्मान् मनुष्येषु कश्चिन् मे प्रियकृत्तमः ।
भविता न च मे तस्माद् अन्यः प्रियतरो भुवि ॥
na ca tasmān manuṣyeṣu
kaścin me priyakṛttamaḥ
bhavitā na ca me tasmād
anyaḥ priyataro bhuvi

69. And no one among men shall do more pleasing service to Me than he, and no other on earth shall be dearer to Me.

1504 Such a person, though separated from Me while living in the body, is as dear to Me as his life and soul are to him.
1505 Among all those who are enlightened, who are devoted to action, or who practice austerity, it is he who is dearest to Me.
1506 O Arjuna, in all the world there is no one equal to the person who proclaims this teaching to My devotees.

अध्येष्यते च य इमं धर्म्यं संवादम् आवयोः ।
ज्ञानयज्ञेन तेनाहम् इष्टः स्याम् इति मे मतिः ॥
adhyeṣyate ca ya imaṁ
dharmyaṁ saṁvādam āvayoḥ
jñānayajñena tenāham
iṣṭaḥ syām iti me matiḥ

70. And he who shall study this sacred dialogue of ours, by him I shall have been worshiped with the wisdom sacrifice; such is My conviction.

1507 Those devotees who love Me as their supreme deity and who explain the *Gita* with steady purpose are like jewels among the company of saintly men.
1508 They tremble like new foliage in the breeze, or like soft hair on the skin, their eyes filled like flowers with tears of joy.
1509 They chant My name in sweet tones like the singing of the cuckoo, or like the season of spring entering a garden.
1510 These devotees are like the chakora bird, whose life is fulfilled when the moon rises in the sky, or like new clouds answering the call of the peacock.
1511 If anyone showers down the poetic jewels of the *Gita* in an assembly of saints, with his whole heart fixed on Me,
1512 Then among all the devotees who have been or will ever be, there is none as dear to Me as he is.
1513 O Arjuna, I hold in My heart the person who serves to the saints this feast of the meaning of the *Gita*.
1514 This dialogue has taken place here between you and Me so that liberation may triumph in the world.
1515 Whoever recites our dialogue, which contains all truth, without changing any word,
1516 Thereby pleases Me, the highest Self, by pouring into the flaming fire of wisdom the oblation of the origin of all ignorance.
1517 O wise Arjuna, that high state which is attained by people who understand the meaning of the *Gita*, can be reached also by those who chant it.
1518 He who recites the *Gita* obtains the same fruit as the person who knows its meaning. For the *Gita*, as for a mother, there is no distinction of learned and unlearned.

श्रद्धावान् अनसूयश्च शृणुयाद् अपि यो नरः ।
सो ऽपि मुक्तः शुभाँल् लोकान् प्राप्नुयात् पुण्यकर्मणाम् ॥
śraddhāvān anasūyaśca
śṛṇuyād api yo naraḥ
so 'pi muktaḥ śubhāṅl lokān
prāpnuyāt puṇyakarmaṇām

71. Even the man who hears it with faith and free from malice, he also, liberated, shall attain the happy worlds of those whose actions are pure.

1519 When a person has given up all of the other paths, but without scorn, and is in a state of purity, placing all his faith in listening to the *Gita*,
1520 All his sins flee as soon as the words of the *Gita* fall upon his ears.
1521 When a fire spreads through a forest, all the creatures in it will escape in every direction.
1522 Just as when the sun rises over the eastern mountains it sweeps the darkness from the sky,
1523 Similarly, when the sound of the words of the *Gita* enters the gateway of the ear, every sin that has ever been known in the world passes away.
1524 Then the vine of that person's birth becomes pure and full of merit. In addition more and more fruits of his actions accrue to him.
1525 For every word of the *Gita* that he hears, he gains as much merit as if he had performed many horse sacrifices.
1526 In this way, hearing it dispels sin and causes righteousness to increase, so that at last he obtains the joy of heavenly bliss.
1527 In order to reach Me, he first arrives in heaven. He enjoys its pleasures as long as he wishes and ultimately comes to Me.
1528 Thus, O Arjuna, both those who hear the *Gita* and those who study it obtain the fruit of the highest joy. I have said enough.

कच्चिद् एतच् छ्रुतं पार्थ त्वयैकाग्रेण चेतसा ।
कच्चिद् अज्ञानसंमोहः प्रणष्टस् ते धनंजय ॥
kaccid etac chrutaṁ pārtha
tvayāikāgreṇa cetasā
kaccid ajñānasaṁmohaḥ
praṇaṣṭas te dhanaṁjaya

72. Has this been heard by you, Arjuna, with a concentrated mind? Have your ignorance and delusion been destroyed?

1529 Now, have you realized why I have given you this explanation of the *Gita*?
1530 O Arjuna, tell Me whether you have understood with full attention the principles of this great teaching.
1531 Have your ears, to which I have conveyed this teaching, transmitted it to your mind in the same way?
1532 Or has it been lost because your attention has wandered, or because you missed its meaning through negligence?
1533 I won't ask you anything else. Just tell Me if you understand the distinction between right and wrong action.
1534 By asking Arjuna this question, Krishna brought him back to the state of duality, after being absorbed in the joy of the Supreme.
1535 Wasn't the omniscient Krishna aware of His own action? So He asked Arjuna this question for this very purpose.
1536 Then, just as the full moon, leaving the Milky Ocean and illuminating the clusters of stars, seems to be separate from it though in reality it is not,
1537 In the same way, when Arjuna forgot that he himself was God and that the whole world was filled with God, the sense of union with Him passed away.
1538 Then, swinging back and forth between these two states, suspended painfully on the threshold of individuality, he stood up, realizing that he was Arjuna.
1539 With trembling hands he smoothed down his hair and wiped away the beads of perspiration from his body.
1540 He steadied his body, which was swaying with the agitation of his breathing, and stood erect, having lost all sense of movement.
1541 He checked the tears of joy that flowed like a flood of nectar from his eyes.
1542 His throat was choked with emotion, and he forced it down into his heart.
1543 He steadied his faltering voice by controlling the *prana* and reestablished the disturbed rhythm of his breathing.

अर्जुन उवाच । *arjuna uvāca*

नष्टो मोहः स्मृतिर् लब्धा त्वत्प्रसादान् मयाच्युत ।
स्थितो ऽस्मि गतसंदेहः करिष्ये वचनं तव ॥
naṣṭo mohaḥ smṛtir labdhā
tvatprasādān mayācyuta
sthito 'smi gatasaṁdehaḥ
kariṣye vacanaṁ tava

Arjuna spoke:
73. My delusion is destroyed and I have gained wisdom through Your grace, Krishna. My doubts are gone. I shall do as You command.

1544 Then Arjuna said, O Lord, You ask whether I am clinging to my delusion. I assure You that it has entirely passed away.
1545 Is there any meaning in asking whether there

is darkness in one's eyes after the sun has risen?

1546 Isn't it enough, O Lord Krishna, that You have become perceptible to our sight?

1547 Moreover, with a love greater than that of a mother, You have fully revealed to me what I couldn't have known by any other means.

1548 In reply to Your question as to whether my delusion has vanished or not, I can say that I have reached my goal by this union with You.

1549 I have attained Self-realization by Your grace, and I no longer allow the roots of my delusion to remain.

1550 Now I know that there is nothing else but You everywhere, in that duality which leads to the concept of action and inaction.

1551 I have no further doubt about this in my mind. I have reached that state which is beyond activity.

1552 I have attained my true Self. All need to perform action is finished. Nothing remains for me but to obey Your commands.

1553 You are that visible form which destroys all other visible things, which though separate swallows up all separateness, which is one and yet dwells eternally in all.

1554 Bondage to You brings liberation from all bonds, desire for You destroys all desires, and in meeting You one is revealed to oneself.

1555 You are my supreme Guru, who comes to the aid of the lonely and for whose sake one must pass over into the realization of union.

1556 When one becomes united with the Supreme, all necessity for good or bad action is eliminated. Then one should worship Him with boundless devotion.

1557 O Lord Krishna, You are my great Guru, whom I must serve in simple devotion. Shouldn't I consider this to be Your blessing of oneness with God?

1558 The door of separation which stood between You and me has been transformed into the happiness of joyful service.

1559 Now, O Lord of all the gods, I will obey Your commands, whatever You may demand of me.

1560 Hearing these words of Arjuna, the Lord began to dance with joy. He said, Arjuna has become the fruit of the tree of the universe, which is I Myself.

1561 Doesn't the ocean overflow its boundaries when it sees the full moon, its offspring, liberated from all deficiency?

1562 Seeing Krishna and Arjuna thus wedded at the altar of this discourse, Sanjaya also was filled with delight.

संजय उवाच । *sañjaya uvāca*

इत्य् अहं वासुदेवस्य पार्थस्य च महात्मनः ।
संवादम् इमम् अश्रौषम् अद्भुतं रोमहर्षणम् ॥

ity ahaṁ vāsudevasya
pārthasya ca mahātmanaḥ
saṁvādam imam aśrāuṣam
adbhutaṁ romaharṣaṇam

Sanjaya spoke:
74. Thus I have heard from Krishna and the great-souled Arjuna, this wondrous dialogue which causes the hair to stand on end.

1563 In his joy he said to Dhritarashtra, How well we have both been protected by Vyasa!

1564 Although you have no physical sight to see the things of this world, the sage has bestowed on you the vision of spiritual knowledge,

1565 And he has shown these things to me, although I am only in charge of the horses of your chariot.

1566 In this terrible battle, whichever side is defeated, that defeat is our own.

1567 How great is Vyasa's favor, that in this great crisis we are able to experience the supreme bliss of God!

1568 Although Sanjaya said this, his words didn't move the king any more than moonbeams would touch a stone.

1569 Seeing him in this condition, Sanjaya couldn't continue; yet in the wildness of his joy, he went on speaking.

1570 He was elated so he told Dhritarashtra of this experience, even though the king was unworthy to hear it.

1571 Sanjaya then said, O King of the Kurus, your brother's son spoke in this way to Krishna, and Arjuna's words were sweet to Him.

1572 O King, the eastern ocean and the western ocean differ only in name. They form only one mass of water.

1573 Similarly, Lord Krishna and Arjuna appear to be different as far as their bodies are concerned, and yet in their dialogue they were not separate.

1574 When two clear mirrors are set up in front of

each other, each one sees the reflection of the other.

1575 In the same way Krishna saw in Himself both Arjuna and Himself, and Arjuna saw in himself both the Lord and himself.

1576 When Krishna looked deep within Himself for His devotee, He found both of them together in one place.

1577 There was nothing else, so what was there to do? Both were dwelling there in oneness.

1578 If the separation were removed, there could be no questions and answers. If they were united, there would be no joy of conversation.

1579 I heard that dialogue between them in which that duality was enveloped by their speaking together.

1580 When two clean mirrors are placed opposite each other, can a person tell which one is reflected in the other?

1581 Or when two lamps are brought together, who can say which of them is serving the other?

1582 Reason would be baffled if a person tried to determine such things. The union of Krishna and Arjuna in this dialogue was as complete as this.

1583 So when I try to consider this conversation between Krishna and Arjuna, my condition is the same.

1584 As soon as Sanjaya said this, he was overcome by emotion and lost all awareness of himself as Sanjaya.

1585 His hair stood on end, and his body contracted. He became rigid, he trembled, and sweated profusely.

1586 In the bliss of that union his eyes filled with tears. Yet they were not tears; his eyes were melting with joy.

1587 He was unable to contain himself. His throat was choked with emotion, and his speech was impeded by deep sighs.

1588 Utterly overcome by emotion, Sanjaya was possessed by the bliss of that conversation.

1589 It is the nature of this bliss to bring peace. Sanjaya then regained the awareness of his own individuality.

व्यासप्रसादाच् छ्रुतवान् एतद् गुह्यम् अहं परम् ।
योगं योगेश्वरात् कृष्णात् साक्षात् कथयतः स्वयम् ।।

vyāsaprasādāc chrutavān
etad guhyam ahaṁ param
yogaṁ yogeśvarāt kṛṣṇāt
sākṣāt kathayataḥ svayam

75. By the grace of Vyasa I have heard this supreme and most secret yoga which Krishna, the Lord of Yoga, has divulged directly, speaking Himself.

1590 When his joy had subsided, Sanjaya said, Through Vyasa's favor I have heard that truth which not even the Upanishads know.

1591 Vyasa has made easy for me this teaching about that yoga to which all paths lead.

1592 Krishna, by assuming a second form in Arjuna, addressed this teaching to Himself.

1593 My ears were found worthy to hear that teaching. How can I adequately praise the power of my Guru for this?

राजन् संस्मृत्य संस्मृत्य संवादम् इमम् अद्भुतम् ।
केशवार्जुनयोः पुण्यं हृष्यामि च मुहुर् मुहुः ।।

rājan saṁsmṛtya saṁsmṛtya
saṁvādam imam adbhutam
keśavārjunayoḥ puṇyaṁ
hṛṣyāmi ca muhur muhuḥ

76. O King, remembering again and again this marvelous and holy dialogue of Krishna and Arjuna, I rejoice again and again.

1594 Speaking in this way, Sanjaya was filled with wonder and lost consciousness. He was like a jewel eclipsed by its own luster.

1595 Just as the lakes in the Himalayas become like crystals when the moon rises and again become water at sunrise,

1596 Similarly, Sanjaya could recall that conversation as long as he retained his physical consciousness, but then again he would lapse into a state of wonder.

तच् च संस्मृत्य संस्मृत्य रूपम् अत्यद्भुतं हरेः ।
विस्मयो मे महान् राजन् हृष्यामि च पुनः पुनः ।।

tac ca saṁsmṛtya saṁsmṛtya
rūpam atyadbhutaṁ hareḥ
vismayo me mahān rājan
hṛṣyāmi ca punaḥ punaḥ

77. And remembering again and again that marvelous form of Krishna, my amazement is great, O King, and I rejoice again and again.

1597 Then Sanjaya stood up and said, O King, how is it that you remain silent even after that vision of the Cosmic Form of Krishna?

1598 How is it possible to miss that vision which can be seen without sight, which is and is not, which is both forgotten and yet remembered?

1599 Beholding this vision, I had no time even to

describe it as a miracle. The flood of emotion carried me away.

1600 The conversation of Krishna and Arjuna was like the confluence of two rivers. Arjuna bathed in it and all his egoism was removed.

1601 In his uncontrollable joy he began to sob without restraint, and choking with emotion he cried out, O Lord Krishna!

1602 The king of the Kauravas was unable to enter into this state, and while he was trying to understand it,

1603 Sanjaya calmed the delight which he was experiencing and subdued his pride.

1604 The king said to him, You are here to pass the time for me, and you have disregarded this. What has happened to you?

1605 You know why Vyasa placed you beside me. Why are you talking in the irrelevant manner?

1606 If a forest dweller is brought to a palace, he will feel ill at ease wherever he goes. For those who live by night, nightfall is their dawn.

1607 A person who cannot understand greatness will consider it out of place, because it is so strange to him.

1608 Again the king said, Tell me who will finally win this battle which has begun.

1609 Considering all things, I think that Duryodhana is superior in valor.

1610 Moreover, his army outnumbers that of the Pandavas. Therefore, it is clear that he will be victorious.

1611 This is how it seems to me, but I don't know your prophecy. Tell me, O Sanjaya, what you think.

यत्र योगेश्वरः कृष्णो यत्र पार्थो धनुर्धरः ।
तत्र श्रीर् विजयो भूतिर् ध्रुवा नीतिर् मतिर् मम ॥
yatra yogeśvaraḥ kṛṣṇo
yatra pārtho dhanurdharaḥ
tatra śrir vijayo bhūtir
dhruvā nītir matir mama

78. Wherever there is Krishna, Lord of Yoga, wherever there is Arjuna, the archer, there will surely be splendor, victory, wealth, and righteousness; this is my conviction.

1612 To this Sanjaya replied, I don't know what will happen to these two armies, but it is clear that where there is life to be lived, there life will continue.

1613 Wherever the moon is, there will be moonlight; wherever Lord Shiva is, there also will be his consort Ambika; where there is a saint, wisdom will be found in him.

1614 A king is always accompanied by an army, kindness attracts friendship, and wherever there is fire there is the power to burn.

1615 Where there is compassion there is righteousness, where there is righteousness there is happiness, and wherever there is happiness the Supreme may be found within it.

1616 The season of spring brings new foliage to trees, wherever there is foliage there are flowers, and where there are flowers bees will gather.

1617 Knowledge is found in every Guru, in knowledge there is perception of the Self, and in perception of the Self there is contentment.

1618 Good fortune brings pleasure, happiness gives rise to joy, and where the sun shines there will be light.

1619 Lakshmi will always be found where Lord Krishna is. In the same way, the Lord brings fulfillment to a man's every purpose.

1620 Don't all the psychic powers obey the person with whom the Mother of the world and Her consort dwell?

1621 In the country of a person whose parents are Krishna and Lakshmi, wouldn't all the trees rival the wish-fulfilling tree?

1622 Wouldn't all the stones in it be wish-fulfilling gems? Wouldn't the earth be turned to gold?

1623 Would it be strange if the rivers flowing through the towns were filled with nectar? Would this be surprising, O King?

1624 Even his casual conversation could be called the language of the Vedas. Then why shouldn't he himself experience the bliss of union with God while still in the body?

1625 Both heaven and final blessedness will be in the hands of a person who has Krishna as his father and Lakshmi as his mother.

1626 If the consort of Lakshmi stands by a person's side, he will be endowed with every blessing. I cannot say anything other than this.

1627 Clouds that are formed from the waters of the ocean are more useful even than the ocean itself. This is also true of Arjuna, compared with Krishna.

1628 It is true that the philosopher's stone is like a Guru in that it transforms iron into gold, but gold is more valuable in promoting the affairs of the world.

1629 If anyone were to say that this belittles the Guru, I would reply that even fire is ignited by the flame of a lamp.
1630 So through the power of the Lord, Arjuna is even more powerful than He is; yet He likes the praise to be given to Arjuna. Such is His glory.
1631 A father likes to be excelled by his son in every quality, and Arjuna fulfilled this desire in Krishna.
1632 Truly, O King, through Krishna's grace Arjuna has attained such a state. The side on which Arjuna fights with firm purpose will surely be victorious.
1633 Do you doubt this? If this weren't true, there would be no meaning in victory.
1634 Therefore wherever Krishna, Lakshmi, and Arjuna are present, there will also be victory and prosperity.
1635 If you have faith in Vyasa's words, believe also that my words are true.
1636 For wherever the consort of Lakshmi is, with the company of His devotees, there will be happiness and blessing.
1637 If these words were untrue, then I wouldn't call myself Vyasa's disciple. With this statement, Sanjaya raised his hand high.
1638 Thus proclaiming in a single verse the whole essence of the *Mahabharata*, Sanjaya offered it to the king of the Kurus.
1639 How great fire is! If it is set to the wick of a lamp, it can produce light in the absence of the sun.
1640 The limitless Vedas are expressed in the one hundred twenty-five thousand verses of the *Mahabharata*, and the essence of all these is expressed in the seven hundred verses of the *Gita*.
1641 Similarly, the substance of these verses is expressed in this last verse of the *Gita*, which is the final statement of Sanjaya , Vyasa's disciple.
1642 A person who puts his whole trust in this one verse has overcome every form of ignorance.
1643 This verse of the *Gita* upholds all the other seven hundred verses. Yet should they be called verses? Aren't they the finest nectar in the heaven of the *Gita*?
1644 Instead these verses seem to me like pillars erected in the assembly hall of the Self.
1645 The *Gita* is like the goddess Bhagavati, whose praises are sung in the seven hundred hymns of the Saptashati scripture. By joyfully slaying Mahisha, the demon of illusion, she brought about his liberation.
1646 For this reason, he who worships the *Gita* with body, mind, and speech, will become lord of the realm of Self-realization.
1647 By means of the *Gita*, Lord Krishna has created the light of these seven hundred suns in the form of verses, in order to dispel the darkness of ignorance.
1648 They are like an arbor of vines loaded with grapes, under whose shade those who are weary of their journey through life may rest.
1649 They are lotuses in the lake of Krishna, on which the blessed saints, as bees, may feast.
1650 Indeed, they are not verses. They seem rather to be poets who praise the greatness of the *Gita*.
1651 All the scriptures have come to dwell in the city of the *Gita*, after the beautiful wall of these seven hundred verses was built.
1652 Isn't the *Gita* like a wife, lovingly spreading out her verses as arms to embrace her Lord, the universal Self?
1653 These verses are bees attracted to the lotuses of the *Gita*, the waves on the ocean of the *Gita*, or the steeds of Krishna yoked to the chariot of the *Gita*.
1654 They are like the confluence of holy rivers flowing into the Ganges of the *Gita*, with Arjuna as the festival of Sinhastha.
1655 Yet these are not so much verses as wish-fulfilling gems, which grant to the mind the vision of the inconceivable Absolute, or a grove of trees granting the experience of the changeless One.
1656 In this way there are seven hundred verses, each one better than the other. Yet how can any one of them be given special praise?
1657 Can it be said that one light is earlier and another later? Is the sun older or younger? Is the ocean of nectar deep or shallow?
1658 Can one judge whether the wish-fulfilling cow is young or full-grown? Such things cannot be done.
1659 No one could say that some verses of the *Gita* are good and others inferior. Can the flowers of the coral tree be differentiated as old and new?
1660 Is it possible to distinguish between the value of one verse and that of another? Here there isn't even a difference between the reader and what is read.

1661 It is well known that in the *Gita*, Lord Krishna is both the speaker and the listener. Any ordinary person understands this.
1662 The person who understands the meaning of the *Gita* derives the same benefit as the one who repeats it. The *Gita* brings about the union between the reader and what he reads.
1663 Now there is nothing left for me to explain. You should know that the *Gita* is the very incarnation of the Lord's speech.
1664 Any other science bears fruit when its meaning is understood, and then it passes away. But this is not so with the *Gita*, for it is truly God.
1665 See how in the form of Arjuna the Lord has bestowed His grace on the world and made the supreme joy available to all!
1666 For the sake of the chakora bird, the moon with all its phases cools the heated worlds.
1667 Similarly, Krishna, being the cow in the form of the *Gita* and taking Arjuna as a calf, has poured forth milk to satisfy the whole world.
1668 For the sake of Gautama, Lord Shiva brought down from the mountains the waters of the Ganges for the benefit of all who suffer from the distress of Kali Yuga.
1669 If you bathe in the *Gita* with your heart or immerse yourself in it by repeating it with your tongue, then you will experience this.
1670 If iron is touched by the philosopher's stone at only one point, all of it is transformed into gold.
1671 Similarly, if a single verse in the glass of the reading of the *Gita* were brought to the lips, by that drink the whole body would be nourished with the essence of God.
1672 Even if a person were to turn away from it and lie on his side, if a verse fell on his ear the result would be the same.
1673 Just as a generous giver refuses no one, the *Gita* gives nothing less than final liberation to one who hears, reads, or understands it.
1674 Therefore, wise men should study only the *Gita*. Of what value are all other scriptures?
1675 Shri Vyasa has made this conversation between Arjuna and Krishna on the open battlefield so simple that a person could hold it in the palm of his hand.
1676 When a mother sits down to feed her child, she lovingly prepares small mouthfuls which it will be able to eat.
1677 An ingenious person makes a fan in order to capture the limitless wind for his use.
1678 In the same way, Shri Vyasa has expressed in the *anushthubha* meter that which cannot be conveyed by words, so that women and those of low caste can understand it.
1679 If raindrops falling from the auspicious *Swati* constellation didn't become pearls, how would women adorn their bodies?
1680 If sound weren't expressed through musical instruments, how could it be heard? Without flowers, how could there be fragrance?
1681 If there were no delicious foods, how could the tongue enjoy the experience of taste? Without a mirror, how could the eyes see themselves?
1682 If the omniscient and blessed Guru hadn't entered life in a visible form, could the disciple approach him in worship?
1683 In the same way, who could have attained oneness with God if that limitless One hadn't entered into these seven hundred verses?
1684 Clouds hold the water drawn from the ocean, but it is the clouds to which people look. Can one grasp that which is boundless?
1685 If these beautiful verses hadn't been written, how could that which is beyond the power of speech become accessible to the ear or the tongue?
1686 Therefore, the gratitude which the world owes to Shri Vyasa is very great, because he has recorded in this composition the sayings of Lord Krishna.
1687 Now, carefully studying Vyasa's words, I have brought that same book to the Marathi people so they can hear it.
1688 Where even the wisdom of Vyasa and others wavered, I, a humble man, have dared to speak of these things in simple words.
1689 Nevertheless, the *Gita* is as simple as Shankar in accepting the garlands of Vyasa's words and not rejecting my poor offering of *durbha* grass.
1690 Herds of elephants go down to the shores of the Milky Ocean to drink, but they are driven back by mosquitoes.
1691 A fledgling can hardly fly up in the sky, yet it rises in the same space as the eagle which soars through the heavens.
1692 Who can walk with the gait of the royal swan, the finest in the world? Should others therefore not even try to walk?

1693 If a great quantity of water can be drawn from a well in a large jar, can't a little be drawn in the palm of the hand?
1694 If a torch is big it can give out much light, but a small wick can also give light according to its size.
1695 The sea reflects the sky in proportion to its expanse, and the reflection in a puddle is the size of the puddle.
1696 In the same way, if great minds like those of Vyasa and others can ponder over the *Gita*, is it out of place if we do so too?
1697 Don't fish share the same ocean with creatures as large as Mount Mandara?
1698 The sun is clearly visible to Aruna, the dawn, which lies close to it. But can't the ant on the surface of the earth also see it?
1699 Therefore, there is no reason to consider it wrong for us ordinary men to make a version of the *Gita* in our own language.
1700 If a child walks in the footsteps of his father, won't he arrive at the same place?
1701 In the same way, unworthy though I am, I follow the path of Vyasa and constantly ask the way of the great commentators. Yet if I don't reach my goal, where else can I go?
1702 He through whose patience the earth doesn't grow weary of supporting the whole creation, and with whose nectar the moon cools the earth,
1703 From whom the sun takes its light with which it removes the shadow of darkness from the earth,
1704 Who gives water to the ocean, sweetness to water, and beauty to sweetness,
1705 From whom the wind receives its strength, the sky its expanse, and knowledge its supremacy,
1706 From whom the Vedas derive their eloquence, by whom joy is made abundant, and who gives form to the universe,
1707 This is my great Guru, Shri Nivrittinath, all powerful and all gracious, who has entered into me and works in me.
1708 Therefore, is it surprising that I should present the *Gita* to the world in Marathi?
1709 The fisherman Eklavya, who set up on a hill a clay image of his Guru, won universal fame.
1710 Other trees near a sandalwood tree absorb its fragrance, and when Vasishtha spread out a piece of his saffron cloth, it vied with the sun in brilliance.
1711 I am endowed with intelligence and my Guru, whose mere glance can raise me to his own stature, is my guide.
1712 If a person already has clear vision and then this is aided by the light of the sun, is there anything that he cannot see?
1713 Therefore, says Jnanadeva, if every breath that I breathe produces this composition, what is there that cannot be accomplished by the Guru's grace?
1714 For this reason, I have been able to bring the *Gita* within the understanding of the common people through the Marathi language.
1715 I have clothed the *Gita* in the garment of Marathi, but if there is no one who can recite it, there will be nothing missing.
1716 If the *Gita* is to be recited, it won't be of less value if this Marathi version is used.
1717 Even if a jewel isn't worn on a beautiful body, it is still beautiful. But what is finer than a jewel worn on a lovely body?
1718 Pearls enhance the beauty of gold, but they are also valued separately for themselves.
1719 Mogra flowers blooming in springtime are no less fragrant when they are made into garlands than when they are growing on the tree.
1720 Similarly, I have composed this version of the *Gita* in the *ovi* meter in such a way that it may be used either as a commentary or it may be enjoyed by itself, without the Sanskrit *Gita*.
1721 These words, filled with the delicate essence of the Supreme, have been threaded together in the *ovi* meter, which is understood equally by the simple and the wise.
1722 Just as a person doesn't have to wait for the sandalwood tree to flower before he enjoys its fragrance,
1723 Similarly, one experiences union with God as soon as one hears these verses. Once people have heard this commentary, won't they become devoted to it?
1724 Through reading it, a person's mind becomes enlightened. When he understands it, he forgets even the sweetness of nectar.
1725 Without difficulty this poem has come to be our refuge, and merely listening to it is more valuable than meditation and deep thought.
1726 Hearing it enables anyone to share in the joy of Self-realization, and all the sense organs are enriched through the ear.
1727 The chakora bird is called wise for enjoying

the moonlight with its whole being, but anyone can enjoy the moonlight.

1728 Similarly, while only those who have insight into the scriptures about the Self are entitled to read them, all people will be delighted with the poetic skill of this composition.

1729 My Guru, Shri Nivrittinath, is so great that this writing is more the glory of his grace than my composition.

1730 I don't know when Lord Shiva communicated this wisdom to Parvati on the shore of the Milky Ocean,

1731 But it was found by Vishnu, who lay concealed within the womb of a fish in the waves of that ocean.

1732 On the Saptashringa mountain, Matsyendranath met the crippled Chaurangi, whose limbs at once became whole.

1733 Matsyendranath then conveyed this secret wisdom to Gorakshanath, who had a great desire to enjoy undisturbed contemplation.

1734 The great Matsyendranath enthroned Gorakshanath on the highest place of contemplation. Gorakshanath was like a lake of lotuses in the form of yoga and valiant in the destruction of sensual desires.

1735 Then Gorakshanath transmitted to Shri Gahininath the glory of the incomparable joy, with all its power, received from Shankara.

1736 When Gahininath saw that Kali was persecuting all creatures, he gave this command to Nivrittinath.

1737 This teaching has come down to us from Shankara, the great Guru, through the tradition of his disciples.

1738 You should take this and go quickly to relieve the distress of all those who are being vanquished by Kali.

1739 Now Shri Nivritti was compassionate by nature, and receiving this command from his Guru, he became like the clouds bursting with rain in the rainy season.

1740 This composition of mine has arisen from showers of peace in the form of the *Gita*, which have fallen on the distressed out of his compassion for them.

1741 Like a chataka bird, I have come to you with my ardent desire, and for that reason I have been successful.

1742 In this way my Guru, Shri Nivrittinath, has passed on to me in the form of this book that wealth of contemplation which he received from the lineage of Gurus.

1743 How could I be worthy to write this commentary? I am uneducated and don't even know how to serve my Master.

1744 Nevertheless, Nivrittinath has brought liberation to the world through me by means of this composition.

1745 Therefore, if I have spoken too much or too little in my role as a priest, please forgive me as a mother would.

1746 I am unacquainted with the use of words, I don't know how to present a subject, nor do I understand how to use figures of speech.

1747 My Guru has spoken through me in the same way that a puppeteer makes a puppet dance by pulling its strings.

1748 Therefore, I don't ask that you forgive my shortcomings, for I have merely written the book which my Guru had already composed.

1749 So in this assembly of saints, if you find some defect which you cannot correct, I will lovingly be angry with you.

1750 If the philosopher's stone touches a piece of iron and the iron isn't changed, who is to blame?

1751 If a stream were to flow into the Ganges and not become one with it, what could be done?

1752 Through my good fortune I have been able to fall at the feet of you saintly people, so what in the world can I lack?

1753 My Master has enabled me to meet you, so all my desires have been fulfilled.

1754 You have been like my mother's home for me, so I have been able to complete the work I set my mind on doing.

1755 It might be possible to turn the earth into gold, or to transform a range of mountains into wish-fulfilling stones.

1756 The seven seas might easily be filled with nectar, or moons might be made from the stars.

1757 It might not be difficult to plant a garden with wish-fulfilling trees. Yet it isn't possible to clarify the secret meaning of the *Gita*.

1758 As mute as I am, I have made it possible for everyone to read it by using the Marathi language.

1759 I have been able to cross over the great ocean of this work. On the opposite shore, those who celebrate this victory are rejoicing.

1760 I have built a temple of the meaning of the *Gita*, with a pinnacle as high as Mount Meru. Within it I worship the image of my Guru.
1761 The *Gita* is like a trusting mother from whom I, her child, have wandered away. Your devotion has reunited mother and child.
1762 Jnanadeva says, O saintly people, whatever I have said with your help cannot be considered worthless.
1763 What more can I say? The completion of this work, which you have brought about, fulfills my aim in life.
1764 The confidence which I placed in you has been rewarded, and great happiness has come to me.
1765 In this composition, you have created a new world for me. When we see it we can laugh at Vishvamitra,
1766 Who, at the instigation of Trishankara, made another creation in order to bring contempt on the creator. That world was perishable, but this one which you have created is not.
1767 Lord Shiva created the Milky Ocean out of love for Upamanyu. However since it contained poison, it won't serve for comparison.
1768 When demons enveloped all creatures in darkness, the sun came to rescue them; yet the sun also brought the burden of heat.
1769 Although the moon sends down its beams to cool the heated world, the moon has blemishes. How can it be used for comparison?
1770 Therefore, this book is incomparable. Through it, you have enabled me to benefit the whole world.
1771 This song of righteousness has been completed with your help. Now all that I have to do is to serve you.
1772 May the Self of the universe be pleased with this sacrifice of words and bestow His grace on me.
1773 May sinners no longer commit evil deeds, may their desire to do good increase, and may all beings live in harmony with one another.
1774 May the darkness of sin disappear, may the world see the rising of the sun of righteousness, and may the desires of all creatures be satisfied.
1775 May everyone keep the company of saints devoted to God, who will shower their blessings on them.
1776 Saints are walking gardens filled with wish-fulfilling trees, and they are living villages of wish-fulfilling gems. Their words are like oceans of nectar.
1777 They are moons without blemish and suns without heat. May these saints be the friends of all people.
1778 May all beings in all the worlds be filled with joy, and may they worship God forever.
1779 May all those for whom this book is their very life be blessed with success in this world and the next.
1780 Then Nivrittinath, the great Master said, this blessing will be granted. This brought great joy to Jnaneshwar.
1781 All this took place in Kali Yuga in the country of the Marathas, on the south bank of the Godavari River,
1782 In the most holy place in all the three worlds, ten miles long, where the god Shri Mahalaya, the life of the world, lives.
1783 There Lord Ramachandra, the king of the universe, ruled with justice. He was the delight of the Yadava race and the abode of all the arts.
1784 There Jnanadeva, descended from the lineage of Shankara and his disciple Nivrittinath, adorned the *Gita* with the Marathi language.
1785 The *Gita* is the conversation between Lord Krishna and Arjuna, and was narrated in the famous Bhishma Parva of the *Mahabharata*.
1786 This conversation contains the essence of the teachings of the Upanishads and is the home of all sciences. It is the lake in which the most advanced ascetics take pleasure.
1787 Jnanadeva, the disciple of Nivritti, says that this eighteenth chapter is the supreme pinnacle of the *Gita*.
1788 Through the wealth of merit in this work, may all creatures be filled with supreme joy forever and ever.

Jnanadeva composed this commentary during the Shaka year 1212, and Sacchittananda was his reverent scribe.

GLOSSARY

A-u-m. The three letters which make up the sacred syllable, Om. In Sanskrit, the vowel "o" is a compound of the vowels "a" and "u." It is used at the beginning of prayers and ceremonies, and is the essence of all mantras. It is the primal sound from which the universe emanates.

Abhaya mudra. The images and statues of deities often show the hands in two positions: the left hand is raised to an upright position as the hand of reassurance, "Do not be afraid," (*abhaya mudra*); and the right hand is extended as the hand of blessing and the giving of boons (*varada mudra*).

Adhibhuta. Nature, pertaining to the elements and matter.

Adhidaiva. The divine, the individual soul dwelling in the body.

Adhiyajna. The supreme sacrifice, offering the senses to the fire of restraint, by which the awareness of unity is attained.

Adhyatma. The Self.

Adityas. The twelve sun gods, representing the sun during the twelve months of the year.

Agastya. A sage who was born in a pitcher. He drank up the ocean because it had offended him.

Airavata. The elephant of Indra, produced by the churning of the Milky Ocean.

Ajamila. A brahmin who married an outcaste and led an impure life. When the agents of the god of death came to take him, the frightened Ajamila cried out, "Narayana," the name of his eldest son. Hearing his name called, Vishnu saved Ajamila from death. Ajamila became a great devotee of Vishnu and attained liberation.

Amaravati. The city of Indra, lord of the gods, known for its splendor.

Anushthubha. A poetic meter consisting of four quarters of eight syllables each.

Ardhanarishwara. The androgynous form of Shiva, in which he is united with Shakti.

Arjuna. The third of the Pandava brothers. During the great war of the *Mahabharata*, Krishna became his charioteer and related the *Bhagavad Gita* to him.

Aryama. Another name of the sun. One of the Adityas.

Ashwattha. The fig tree. The Tree of Life.

Ashwin gods. Twin gods who were physicians of the celestial realms.

Asita. A sage.

Badarayana. Another name of Vyasa, the author of the *Mahabharata.*

Bali. A demon king. Vishnu incarnated as the Dwarf Avatara to restrain him.

Bela tree. A tree sacred to Lord Shiva.

Bhagavatam. The name of one of the eighteen Puranas, especially related to the worship of Vishnu or Krishna.

Bhagirathi. The Ganges, or one of its three great branches. It was brought down to earth from heaven by the power of King Bhagiratha's austerities.

Bhairavas. A group of manifestations of Shiva.

Bharati. The goddess of speech, Saraswati.

Bhasmasura. The name of a demon who was given special powers of destruction as a boon, which he later misused.

Bhavani. The consort of Lord Shiva.

Bhima. The second of the Pandavas and brother of Arjuna. He was known for his immense strength.

Bhishma Parva. The section of the *Mahabharata* in which the story of the warrior Bhishma is recounted.

Bhishma. The old sage who taught and trained

Pandu and Dhritarashtra in the art of warriorship.

Bhrigu. A sage who wanted to test Vishnu to see if he was worthy of worship. Although Bhrigu kicked him in the breast, Vishnu treated him with humility and generosity.

Bindu. A point or dot containing the entire creation.

Boar. One of the incarnations of Vishnu.

Body of nine gates. The physical body is referred to in this way because of its nine orifices.

Brahma. The creator, along with Vishnu, the preserver, and Shiva, the destroyer.

Brihaspati. The priest of the gods.

Brihatsaman. Hymns composed in a particular meter.

Chaidya. A king of the Chedis who was also called Shishupala. Although both he and Kansa were hostile to Krishna, they won His blessings.

Chakora bird. A bird similar to a partridge, supposed to live on moonbeams.

Chakras. Centers of energy in the subtle body. The most important chakras are situated within the *sushumna nadi*, extending from the base of the spine to the crown of the head. They are: *muladhara* (base of the spine), *svadhishthana* (root of the reproductive organ), *manipura* (navel), *anahata* (heart), *vishuddha* (throat), *ajna* (space between the eyebrows), and *sahasrara* (crown of the head). The awakened Kundalini pierces and purifies these centers as it ascends through the *sushumna nadi*.

Chandrika. One of the names of the Devi, or Shakti.

Chitraratha. The king of the *gandharvas*, the heavenly singers.

Churning rod. When the gods and demons churned the Milky Ocean, they used Mount Mandara as the churning rod.

Consciousness, the three states. Waking, dreaming, and deep sleep. The fourth is the transcendental state in which one experiences the Self.

Cosmic illusion. *Maya*, the illusion of duality in unity.

Devaki. The mother of Krishna.

Devala. A sage.

Devas. The gods.

Dhritarashtra. The blind king of the Kurus. His charioteer Sanjaya described to him the battlefield where the Kauravas and the Pandavas were about to fight.

Dhruva. The son of Uttanapada, an ancient king. Through his austerities, he won the favor of Vishnu, who raised him to the heavens as the pole star.

Dissolution. At the end of a world age, there is a general dissolution of the world through fire, flood, and destruction.

Drona. The archery teacher of the Pandavas and Kauravas.

Drupada. The king of Panchala. He had two children, Dhrishtadyumna and Draupadi, who were born of the sacrificial fire. He was an ally of the Pandavas in the great war.

Duryodhana. The eldest son of King Dhritarashtra. Duryodhana seized the kingdom which his father wished to pass on to Yudhishthira, son of Pandu.

Dust of the feet. The deepest form of obeisance is made by touching the feet of the object of worship and then touching one's forehead or heart.

Dvandva. In grammar, one of the classes of compound words.

Eklavya. A tribal boy who wanted to learn archery from Drona. Drona refused on the ground that he could teach only royal princes. By meditating on a clay image of his Guru, Eklavya imbibed Drona's knowledge of archery and won universal fame.

Elephant and the crocodile. The two doorkeepers of Vishnu were transformed by a sage into an elephant and a crocodile, but they were eventually released from this curse.

Feast of light. Divali, the traditional Festival of Lights, which takes place in the month of October.

Fire of yoga. The sacrifice of the individual self is described in the figurative terms of the *yajna*, or fire sacrifice.

Fish. One of the ten incarnations of Vishnu.

Four goals of life. Duty (*dharma*), wealth (*artha*), pleasure (*kama*), and liberation (*moksha*).

Four-faced. One of the epithets of Brahma. He is said to have had five heads, one of which was destroyed.

Four castes. The brahmins or priests, *kshatriyas* or warriors, *vaishyas* or merchants, and *shudras* or menial workers.

Fourfold division of form. The four classes of beings are those born of eggs, those born of warm vapor or sweat (insects), those born of earth (minerals and vegetables), and those born of the womb.

Fourteen worlds. There are fourteen worlds, seven terrestrial and seven celestial.

Gahininatha. The Guru of Nivrittinath, Jnaneshwar's Guru.

Gandharvas. Celestial singers.

Gandiva. The name of Arjuna's bow.

Ganesh. A god whose special feature is the elephant head. Ganesh, also called Ganapati, is especially popular in Maharashtra. He is the son of Lord Shiva and Parvati, and is the remover of obstacles.

Garuda. The mythical bird which is the vehicle of Vishnu.

Gayatri. A sacred verse of the Rig Veda which every brahmin is required to repeat in his morning and evening devotions.

Ghee. Butter clarified by heating, much used in rites and sacrifices.

Gita. The shortened form of the name of the *Bhagavad Gita*, "The Song of the Lord." It is found in the *Mahabharata* and relates the conversation between Krishna and Arjuna.

God of love. Kama, who visited Lord Shiva while he was practicing penance, bringing Him a message to marry the goddess Parvati.

Gokula. The village where Krishna spent His childhood.

Gopis. These were women of the region around Agra and Mathura. They herded cows, and came to welcome Krishna when He visited that area. Through their devotion they attained union with Him.

Gorakshanatha. The Guru of Gahininatha.

Govardhana. A mountain near Gokula.

Hara. One of the names of Shiva.

Hatha yoga. A yogic discipline in which various bodily and mental exercises are practiced to purify the nervous system and bring about the even flow of *prana*, the vital force.

Highest heaven. Of the seven heavens, the highest is Satya Loka, the realm of Truth.

Hiranyaksha. The name of a demon who took the earth under his arm and threw it into the ocean.

Indra. The king of the gods.

Jahnu. An ancient sage who became angry with the Ganges for flowing through his sacrificial pavilion, so he drank up its waters. He later relented and released the river through his ears.

Jalandhara. The name of a particular yogic *bandha*, or lock.

Janmejaya. The last king of the Pandu dynasty, to whom the *Mahabharata* was related.

Jayadratha. The name of a king fighting on the side of the Kauravas.

Jyoti. Light or flame.

Kala. The manifestation of the world.

Kalakuta poison. The deadly poison which was churned out of the Milky Ocean and was drunk by Lord Shiva.

Kalindi. A name of the river Jamuna.

Kalpa. The heavenly tree which grants all wishes.

Kansa. The maternal uncle of Krishna and tyrannical ruler of the Vraja district. He persecuted Krishna, who eventually killed him.

Kapila. A great sage and founder of the Sankhya philosophy.

Karna. Son of Kunti by Surya, the sun, before her marriage to Pandu. He fought on the side of the Kauravas.

Kashyapa. One of the seven great *rishis* or sages.

Kauravas. Descendants of the king Kuru, especially the sons of Dhritarashtra.

Kinnaras. Mythical beings with human bodies and horse heads.

Kripacharya. The archery teacher of the Pandavas and the Kauravas.

Krishna. The eighth Avatara of Vishnu, who related the *Bhagavad Gita* to Arjuna. The word *krishna* is an adjective with the meaning "dark, or blue." Krishna is usually pictured as having a blue complexion.

Kubera. The god of wealth.

Kundalini. The coiled serpent power situated at the base of the spine. When awakened, it rises through the *sushumna nadi* and leads one to the state of Self-realization.

Kunti. The wife of Pandu and mother of Arjuna.

Kurma. A tortoise, an incarnation of Vishnu.

Kuru. An ancient king of northwest India. He was the ancestor of Pandu and Dhritarashtra.

Kusha grass. A species of grass regarded as sacred.

Lakshmi. The consort of Vishnu. The goddess of wealth and beauty.

Lion and the elephant. The lion is traditionally the destroyer of the elephant.

Lion-man. Narasinha, one of the incarnations of Krishna.

Lotus-born. Brahma, the creator, was born of a lotus which grew from Vishnu's navel.

Lunar race. A lineage which claims descent from the moon. Its two great branches are the Yadavas and the Pauravas.

Madana. The god of love.

Mahabharata. The legendary history of the descendants of Bharata. The great epic poem of the Hindus.

Mahadeva. One of the names of Lord Shiva.

Mahisha. A demon in the form of a buffalo, killed by the Devi or Goddess.

Makara. The "half" syllable, *m*, at the end of the sacred syllable *Aum.* It refers in the text to the highest form of spiritual experience to which the yogi can ascend.

Malati. A tree which produces highly fragrant flowers.

Mandara. The mountain which the gods used as a churning rod when they churned the Milky Ocean.

Manu. The father of the human race. Also, the name of the fourteen progenitors of the race.

Marathi. Jnaneshwar's mother tongue, the language of the state of Maharashtra.

Margashirsha. The ninth month of the Hindu year, from mid-November to mid-December.

Marichi. One of the Maruts, or winds. Vedic gods.

Maruti. The monkey god, Hanuman, son of the wind.

Matsyendranatha. The Guru of Gorakshanatha.

Meru. A mountain of gold in the center of the earth.

Maya. The cosmic illusion of duality in unity.

Monkey god. Hanuman, who delivered Shri Lanka from the possession of the demon Ravana.

Mount Kailas. A peak in the Himalayas where Lord Shiva dwells.

Mulabandha. One of the yogic *bandhas* or locks.

Nada. Primordial sound.

Nadis. Channels of the subtle body which carry the vital force. There are three main *nadis*: the *ida nadi* on the left, the *pingala nadi* on the right, and the *sushumna nadi* in the center. They meet at the *muladhara chakra* at the base of the spine and again at the *ajna chakra* in the space between the eyebrows.

Nagas. Serpents, a semi-divine race of beings who reign in the nether regions in great splendor.

Nahusha. A king of the Solar race who became the sovereign of the three worlds, but who was ruined through his lack of humility.

Nanda. The foster father of Krishna.

Narada. The messenger between the gods and men, and one of the seven great *rishis* or sages.

Narayana. One of the names of Vishnu.

Nine feelings. These are the nine emotional tones in poetry: love or passion, humor, pity, anger, heroism, horror, disgust, wonder, and tranquility.

Nirguda. A shrub with thorns.

Om. See Aum.

Ovi. The meter in which the *Jnaneshwari* is written. Each verse consists of four lines. The first three rhyme and the fourth does not.

Pandavas. The descendants of Pandu.

Pandu. The brother of Dhritarashtra and father of the five Pandavas.

Parijata. The "coral" tree, produced from the churning of the Milky Ocean.

Parrot and the pipe. It was a practice to use a revolving pipe to trap parrots. The parrot felt that it was bound to the pipe and clung to it.

Petals of the lotuses. Because of the configuration of the *nadis* which surround it, each *chakra* appears as a lotus with a certain number of petals. The highest center has one thousand.

Pinaka bow. Lord Shiva's weapon.

Prahlada. The son of a demon king. Prahlada was persecuted because he persisted in worshipping Vishnu.

Prakriti. See *Purusha.*

Pratyahara. Withdrawing the mind from sense objects.

Punyajana. A class of demons. Used in the text as a play on words, for *punya* means merit.

Puranas. The ancient stories and legendary history.

Purusha and *Prakriti. Purusha*, the supreme Spirit, is the passive witness of the activity of *Prakriti*, nature, regarded as the wife of *Purusha.*

Putana. A female demon who tried to kill the infant Krishna.

Rahu. The ascending node of the moon, which periodically "swallows" the sun in an eclipse.

Rajasuya sacrifice. A great sacrifice performed by a universal monarch.

Rakshasas. Demons or evil spirits.

Rama. The hero of the great Sanskrit epic, the *Ramayana*, which tells of the capture of Rama's wife Sita by the demon Ravana and her rescue by Rama.

Rambha. A celestial nymph.

Ravana. The demon king who abducted Sita, Rama's wife.

Rudra. A form of Shiva, the destroyer.

Rudras. A group of eleven gods, manifestations of Shiva.

Sadhyas. A class of inferior deities.

Sahadeva. Son of Pandu by his wife Madri. The fifth of the Pandavas.

Sahasrara. This is the highest center to be reached in yoga, the thousand-petaled lotus situated at the crown of the head.

Samadhi. The eighth and highest stage of development in yogic practice, union with the supreme Self.

Sanaka. One of the mind-born sons of Brahma.

Sankhya. One of the six systems of Hindu philosophy. The doctrine of the final emancipation of the soul.

Sannyasi. One who has taken the vows of *sannyasa,* renunciation of sense pleasures and of involvement in worldly life. The last of the four stages of life.

Saptashringa. The name of a mountain with seven peaks.

Satyaki. Krishna's charioteer.

Shambhu. Another name of Lord Shiva, the "abode of ecstasy."

Shankara. A name of Lord Shiva, "auspicious."

Sharada. A name of Saraswati, goddess of speech and learning.

Sharada. One of the six seasons of the Hindu year, approximately from mid-September to mid-November.

Sharnga. The name of Krishna's bow.

Shesha. The mythical serpent which supports the world.

Shishupala. An ancient king who continuously opposed Krishna. But because he constantly thought of Krishna, he was united with Him after death.

Shiva. One of the highest gods, the destroyer.

Shore, the other. Life in this world is thought of as a river to be crossed, and the goal is to reach liberation or salvation at the other shore.

Siddhas. Perfected beings.

Sinhastha. The festival celebrating the entry of the planet Jupiter into the sign of Leo.

Six qualities. The six qualities or virtues in a man's life are glory, heroism, victory, prosperity, wisdom, and renunciation.

Skanda. Karttikeya, a son of Shiva.

Smritis. These are writings which are based on that which is remembered, a body of literature produced by human authors, not revealed.

Solar race. A dynasty of kings who sprang from Ikshvaku, the grandson of the sun. Rama belonged to this lineage.

Soma. The juice of the soma plant which was used in sacrificial offerings. It also means nectar, the drink of the gods.

Sons of Sagar. The sons of Sagar could attain heaven only if their ashes were sprinkled with water of the Ganges, which at that time flowed only in heaven. Finally King Bhagiratha, through his intense austerities, succeeded in bringing the Ganges down to earth and completed his ancestors' funeral rites by sprinkling their ashes with water of the holy river.

Speech, the four levels. These divisions are as follows: *para,* the highest reality in which no individual sound or concept is manifest; *pashyanti,* the first step toward manifestation; *madhyama,* semantic concepts not yet articulated; and *vaikhari,* articulated speech.

Stages of life. The four stages of life are that of the student and celibacy, the life of a householder with a family, retirement as a forest dweller for spiritual practices, and the last stage of complete renunciation, the homeless life of one who is freed from involvement in worldly life.

Sudama. A boyhood friend of Krishna who was so poor in later life that when he went to visit Krishna to ask for help, all he could bring as a gift was a few grains of rice.

Sushumna nadi. The most important conduit of energy in the subtle body. It extends from the base of the spine to the crown of the head and is the pathway of the awakened Kundalini.

Swayambhu. Brahma, "self-existent one."

That. The Absolute, without attributes and beyond time and space.

Thirty-six principles. The thirty-six evolutionary stages of creation.

Three worlds. Earth, heaven, and the nether world.

Three qualities. The three basic properties of nature are referred to as the qualities: purity (*sattva guna*), activity or passion (*rajo guna*), and ignorance or inertia (*tamo guna*).

Three gods. See Trinity.

Tortoise. One of the ten incarnations of Vishnu.

Treta Yuga. The second of the four *yugas,* or ages of the world. The other three are Krita Yuga, Dwapara Yuga, and Kali Yuga.

Trinity. Brahma the creator, Vishnu the preserver, and Shiva the destroyer.

Triple confluence. The subterranean river Saraswati flows into the confluence of the Ganges and the Jamuna at the Prayaga, or Allahabad, making it a sacred place of pilgrimage.

Tripura. The name of a demon presiding over three cities. He was killed by Shiva.

Trishankara. An ancient king who desired to enter heaven in his mortal body.

Twenty-fifth principle. The twenty-four forms of matter evolve as a result of the connection between the soul (the twenty-fifth principle) and matter.

Ucchaishravas. The white horse of Indra, churned out of the Milky Ocean.

Uddiyana. A yogic *bandha* or lock.

Unstruck sound. A mystic sound proceeding from the heart *chakra.*

Upamanyu. The son of a hermit. He once visited another hermitage with his father where he tasted cow's milk. Upon returning to his own hermitage, he asked his mother to make milk pudding for him. Because they were very poor, they had no milk. His mother told him that he could obtain milk only through Lord Shiva's grace. Upamanyu performed austerities to propitiate Lord Shiva, who became pleased with him and offered him the Milky Ocean.

Upanishads. Mystical writings expounding the meaning of the Vedas. They are *shrutis,* or revelation.

Urvashi. A celestial nymph.

Uttanapada. The father of Dhruva. After Dhruva had practiced great austerities, Vishnu raised him to the position of the pole star.

Uttara. The son of the king of Virata, whose cattle were stolen by the Kauravas in battle. Uttara overcame them and stripped them of their clothes.

Vaijayanti. The necklace of Vishnu.

Vaikuntha. The heavenly abode of Vishnu.

Varada mudra. See *abhaya mudra.*

Varuna. The regent of the ocean and of the western quarter. The deity of rain.

Vasishtha. One of the seven great *rishis* or sages.

Vasudeva. The father of Krishna.

Vasuki. The king of the serpents.

Vasus. A class of eight deities, mainly known as attendants of Indra.

Vedanta. One of the six systems of philosophy.

Vedas. The holy books which are the foundation of the Hindu religion. There are four of them: Rig, Yajur, Sama, and Atharva Vedas. These are the *shrutis,* that which is heard or revealed.

Vishnu. One of the Hindu trinity of gods, the preserver.

Vishvamitra. A great sage who was born into the warrior caste, but by his great austerities he was made a brahmin and became one of the seven great *rishis* or sages.

Vivasvat. The sun, personified as one of the gods.

Vrishnis. Descendants of Yadu and ancestors of Krishna.

Vyasa. The sage to whom the authorship of the *Mahabharata* is attributed.

Wax houses. Huts made of flammable material to be set alight as a defense in battle.

Wish-fulfilling cow. Kamadhenu, the mythical cow which fulfills all desires.

Wish-fulfilling gem. A magical gem which is said to fulfill every desire of the one who possesses it.

Women of Vraja. See Gopis.

Women and outcastes. The brahmins were the privileged caste, and they alone were educated for the religious life. The remaining castes—warriors, merchants, and menial workers—along with women and outcastes were traditionally prohibited from religious practice. At the time of Jnaneshwar and the *bhakti* movement, all came to be included in the practice of devotion to Krishna.

Yadavas. The descendants of the king Yadu. Krishna is referred to as the Lord of the Yadavas.

Yakshas. A class of demi-gods who were attendants to Kubera, the god of wealth.

Yama. The god of death.

Yashoda. The foster mother of Krishna.

INDEX